HUSSERL
Shorter Works

HUSSERL
Shorter Works

Edited by
PETER MCCORMICK
and
FREDERICK A. ELLISTON

Copublished by

 UNIVERSITY OF NOTRE DAME PRESS

THE HARVESTER PRESS

Copyright © 1981 by
University of Notre Dame Press
Notre Dame, Indiana 46556

First published in Great Britain in 1981 by
The Harvester Press Limited
Publisher: John Spiers
16 Ship Street, Brighton, Sussex
British ISBN 0-7108-0351-6

Manufactured in the United States of America

Library of Congress Cataloging in Publication Data

Husserl, Edmund, 1859–1938.
   Husserl, shorter works.

   Bibliography: p.
   Includes index.
   1. Philosophy—Collected works. 2. Phenomenology—
Collected works. I. McCormick, Peter. II. Elliston,
Frederick. III. Title.
B3279.H92E5 1981   193   80-53178
ISBN 0-268-01703-4
ISBN 0-268-01077-3 (pbk.)

To
Anne and Laure
Marie Teresa Awn

Contents

Foreword

Husserl's philosophy has doubtless introduced something of a reversal in twentieth-century philosophy. No longer is a start to be made on the basis of a determinative, systematic kind of thinking whereby all phenomena are to find their clarification and elucidation. Rather, each system is questioned as a system. What is the issue here? The issue is an attempt at a new beginning in doing philosophy, a beginning which must first be expressly discovered and then grounded. This is a difficult undertaking, for such a new beginning must put everything that precedes it into question. Doing philosophy requires setting oneself free from the tradition in which one stands. And yet in this matter we know that all thinking remains embedded in a definite tradition, in this case the tradition of the modern period with its discovery of subjectivity as the ground of certainty.

The fact that every certainty becomes questionable, coupled with the search for an unconditioned certainty, creates the tension in which Husserl's searching inquiry is held from the beginning to the end. This is brought out in a passage from the Postscript to *Ideas*:

If a sensitivity to the seriousness of its beginnings is lacking in the philosophical sketches of the tradition, then the first and most important matter is lacking: the original independently won and genuinely philosophical basis, and thereby the basic steadiness or genuine rootedness, which alone makes real philosophy possible. These convictions on the part of the author have consistently been strengthened in the development of his work, in the evidence of results which are grounded on one another step-by-step. If he has had to tone down the ideal of his philosophical striving practically to that of a genuine beginner, then with age he at least has become completely certain about being able to call himself a *real* beginner.[1]

Throughout all his inquiries Husserl remains on the path to a new beginning. The stages of his work can be understood simply as self-radicalizing new beginnings.[2] Whoever would do philosophy in a phenomenological vein should be brought to the point of learning to see. In order to be understood, a state of affairs must be so clearly presented that it is completely evident. Husserl contrasts this kind of evidentness with the deductive procedures of previous ways of doing philosophy. The principle of all principles[3] is givenness in intuition. Still, the difficulty of this truly philosophical seeing and the little it has to do with the immediate apprehension and description for which phenomenology is all too often misconstrued are shown in that ultimately this principle is a matter of the apprehension and description of the *constitution of meaning*. The manifold achievements of the subject must always be newly investigated, articulated, and researched in their fundamental relationships in order to make the character of anonymous accomplishments accessible. In this context we have to understand the many-sided analyses which are dedicated to the transcendental subject, the meaning-constitutive subject.

This term easily induces one to see in Husserl a mere successor of Kant. But in the way he makes the manifold constitutive accomplishments visible Husserl moves decisively beyond Kant. One need only recall here his analyses of the constitution of things, of time, and his opening up of the logical dimension. Kant's Copernican revolution is freshly thought through under the guiding question How is meaning possible? What is presupposed about the constitutive subject that it can bestow meaning, and what are the manifold senses of meaning and the achievements of the formation of meaning which correspond to them?

Only if we keep these guiding themes in sight can we understand how Husserl's countless analyses ranging from the constitution of things to that of the world and from the constitution of logical forms to the constitution of time do not simply come to a chaotic aggregate but to a whole which Husserl, however, was no longer allowed to articulate as a whole. The demand for radicalness had so mastered him that the analyses he already had carried through were recapitulated afresh in new connections and with new connecting ties.

Consequently there is a special difficulty in reading Husserl's texts which should briefly be explained.

Some philosophical texts are conceived in the form of a dialogue. The most significant examples are the Platonic dialogues. But even in Hegel's *Phenomenology of Spirit* we still have an echo of the dialogue principle. What natural consciousness discovers at the beginning of the work and what philosophers present in their explanatory interpretations correspond to the dialogue character. Objections and criticisms of what is presented are also worked into the dialogue. We find the same thing in many texts of Heidegger too; for example, at the beginning of his *On the Essence of Truth*.[4] By means of this kind of presentation readers are to be raised from their own familiar position into the new, unfamiliar position of doing philosophy. They are to dare to leap from their own approach into the new one offered them. In this way the exact distance between both positions is made clearly visible.

The dialogue form of philosophizing can be contrasted with the monologue form. For the writer of monologues it is especially a matter of letting readers participate in his or her inquiry, of letting them discover the difficulties the philosopher has to struggle with, of showing them every step accomplished in which the philosopher makes clear to oneself what he or she is doing. This

monologue style is reflective; it is the attempt in one's procedures to bring oneself over one's own obstacles into clarity. I would like to describe Husserl's way of doing philosophy as an instance of this monologue form.

The monologue approach is not easy for the reader, who is required to grasp and understand the intentionality of the inquiry, what can come into view in accordance with this intentionality, and just how far what is found (or, respectively, what has not yet been discovered) corresponds to the demands of the inquiry, to judge whether the analysis need be carried through anew. The reader is forced to carry out minutely every detour, every circling round the matter at issue, in order to narrow it down and to untwist it. With this approach to the concrete analyses, with this procedure, the reader can, however, easily lose the larger thread which for the philosopher is the central one. In this style of philosophizing, the emphasis falls not on the results but on finding the right approach, on finding the path whereby readers themselves can then be made part of the inquiry. With this we can also understand why methodological questions are so much emphasized, why Husserl treats these questions as a central piece of his philosophy. From the *Logical Investigations* to the *Crisis* by way of the *Ideas, First Philosophy,* and the *Cartesian Meditations* the question of methodical procedures persists under the guiding theme of the *reduction*. The childhood anecdote which Levinas tells about sharpening the penknife, which was not sharp enough until finally there was hardly anything left of the blade, aptly illustrates this situation.[5]

With unbelievable energy and continuity Husserl forced on himself a rhythm of work whose fruits are preserved in Louvain's Husserl Archives. From the abundance of manuscripts in which we can distinguish among research manuscripts, lecture manuscripts, and texts destined for publication, short texts have been chosen and presented in this collection. Why do these texts have a special significance?

In these texts Husserl draws in the reins on his analytical drive.

There are texts here in which is achieved

something like a crystalization of the movement of his thinking. There are also texts in which his monologue approach is thoroughly overcome. These texts make it possible for readers to acquire a genuine glimpse of what the philosopher is after and thus to grasp his position more clearly. This gives the reader the further possibility to read the comprehensive texts with more understanding and even to classify the monologue analyses correctly. The tension between what is attempted and what is attained which keeps all of Husserl's work in suspense is especially visible in these texts. In no way do we find in these texts something like a popularization of his philosophizing, as for example in Fichte's *Sonnenklarer Bericht über das eigentliche Wesen der neuesten Philosophie* (An Attempt to Compel Readers to Understand). But the subtitle also could reasonably be applied to a series of these texts. The shorter texts do not lessen the effort which is required for the larger works, but in a completely decisive way they facilitate the understanding of those works which verge on the monumental.

The editors have provided a service in presenting in this volume a collection of such texts which range over Husserl's working life, from the early texts on the investigation of number right through to the later works from the context of the *Crisis*. Yet the organization is not chronological but thematic.

In Part One the readers are to come to understand what phenomenology is—to let themselves be introduced into phenomenology by Husserl himself. This was the meaning of the Freiburg Inaugural Lecture and also the Encyclopedia Britannica article. Part Two is dedicated to questions of logic, especially Husserl's quarrel with psychologism. Part Three includes one of the most significant Husserl text, the programmatic work "Philosophy as Rigorous Science" in which Husserl was to clarify his position as well as the related controversy with Dilthey. Part Four is dedicated to the themes of space and time. Here the text "On the Origin of Ge-

ometry" from the texts which make up the context of the *Crisis* book has a special significance as well as the time analyses. Part Five introduces the theme of the social world, which then found in Schütz's work a further echo and through him such an international effect, and the theme, late to Husserl, of historicity.

What I particularly appreciate in this volume is not only the expert selection of texts but also their arrangement. Furthermore, I also particularly appreciate that each text is preceded by its own explanatory introduction allowing the reader to situate the text in Husserl's work and helping in the understanding of specific themes.

This volume is visible proof that today in Canada and the United States not only has phenomenology acquired domiciliary rights but also that phenomenology has experienced a fruitful development. I may be permitted here in conclusion to recall philosophers who in this respect were pioneers. Marvin Farber and his founding of the *Journal of Philosophy and Phenomenological Research,* Aron Gurwitsch who had to struggle for a long time in order to naturalize the understanding of phenomenology in the United States and succeeded in establishing a branch of the Husserl Archives in New York, Alfred Schütz through whose work phenomenology was able to fructify sociology and hence open up new areas, and Herbert Spiegelberg who through his work and its effects encompassed phenomenology as a historical movement and made essential contributions to its knowledge in the Anglo-Saxon world. The present volume with its collaborators is the clearest proof that today a new generation is at work. The wish which Husserl expressed at the end of his Postscript to *Ideas* here begins to be fulfilled. It is written there of the author: "Gladly would he hope that successors would take up these beginnings, continually extend them, but also improve on their great imperfections."[6]

Walter Biemel

NOTES

1. E. Husserl, *Ideen zu einer reinen Phänomenologie und phënomenologischen Philosophie*, ed. Marly Biemel, *Husserliana 5* (Nijhoff, 1952), p. 161.

2. See Walter Biemel, "The Decisive Phases in the Development of Husserl's Philosophy," in *The Phenomenology of Husserl*, ed. R.O. Elveton (Chicago, 1970), pp. 148–73.

3. *Ideen I*, section 24.

4. Martin Heidegger, *Wegmarken* (Frankfurt, 1967), p. 177ff.; see English translation: "On the Essence of Truth," trans. John Sallis, in *Martin Heidegger Basic Writings* (New York: Harper & Row, 1977), pp. 113–42.

5. E. Husserl, *Cartesianische Meditationen*, ed. S. Strasser, *Husserliana 1* (Nijhoff, 1950), p. xxix.

6. *Husserliana 5*, p. 161ff.

Preface

As the list of Husserl's collected works and their translations continues to grow, both scholars and students have become increasingly interested in the nature, scope, and limits of Husserlian phenomenology. The often partisan reception of this material, however, and the uneven character of its discussion are disquieting. Central to the still problematic reception of much of Husserl's work, we believe, is the absence of a carefully crafted collection of texts with research tools which would try to capture much of the range and methodological rigor of Husserlian phenomenology.

The collected works of Edmund Husserl now comprise more than twenty volumes in German, and many more are forthcoming. Although each volume expresses one dimension of phenomenology, no single work captures its full breadth. Moreover, although several of Husserl's interpreters and critics have attempted such a comprehensive survey, their work has remained partial and has necessarily lacked the authority of Husserl's own pronouncements.

The aim of this collection, *Husserl: Shorter Works,* is not to provide a perfectly balanced selection of central, comprehensive, and unabridged excerpts from all of Husserl's works, even from only those key works which have been published so far. Rather, we have tried to gather in one place a wide-ranging selection of Husserl's more important articles and briefer reflections taken from across the entire span of his long philosophical activity. These encompass, if not all of his interests, at least a representative discussion of most of his perduring philosophical concerns. With only several exceptions, we have tried moreover to present complete texts rather than to excerpt sections from major works.

This collection, introduced by Walter Biemel, comprises twenty-one items, six of which are translated here for the first time. These texts are organized into five parts, and each part includes its own brief general introduction. Further, in order to situate these texts as carefully as possible within the fuller framework of Husserl's work as a whole, each individual text is introduced separately to facilitate intelligent understanding and sympathetic criticism of the texts themselves.

More specifically, we have designed this collection in such a way as to bring together in one place Husserl's own programmatic statements about the nature of phenomenology (Part One) and applications and relationships of his methodology to logic (Part Two), science (Part Three), space-time (Part Four), and the social and cultural worlds (Part Five). Many of the previously translated materials have been available until now only in obscure journals or in piecemeal form in various anthologies devoted to phenomenology as a whole rather than to Husserl's philosophical work in particular. Finally, a glossary and comprehensive bibliographies both of Husserl's works themselves as well as of works in English, French, and German about Husserl have also been carefully compiled and published here for the first time in order to assist in a different way with the comprehension of these texts.

Thus, our objective has been a careful, thorough, comprehensive, and authoritative collection on the nature of phenomenology, its scope, and applications. *Husserl: Shorter Works* then, especially when read carefully with its earlier companion volume *Husserl: Expositions and Appraisals,* is presented as an essential instrument for an approach to and mastery of the much longer and more comprehensive major works of Husserl.

This book is addressed to those who are beginning their examination of Husserl's work, and tries to provide such readers with clear and concise accounts of the major themes by Husserl himself. By bringing together materials not readily available elsewhere, however, this collection is also addressed to Husserl scholars as well. Finally, the volume's individual introductions, the glossary of technical terms, and comprehensive bibliographies are useful research tools to students of phenomenology at all levels.

December 1980   Peter McCormick
                             Frederick Elliston

The Husserliana

The following Collected Works (the *Husserliana*) of Husserl are based on post-humous writings published, in cooperation with the Husserl archives at the University of Cologne, by the Husserl archives of Louvain under the direction of H. L. Van Breda. English translation editions follow the German original. The dates given for the German works are for the latest editions published by Martinus Nijhoff (The Hague).

In the notes and elsewhere in the introductions and selections of this book are employed the abbreviations or short titles contained within this listing. There will be some variation of reference to these works of Husserl according to the usage of the various contributors.

1. *Cartesianische Meditationen und Pariser Vorträge.* Edited by S. Strasser. 1973. Abbreviated: *Cartesianische Meditationen.*

   [*Cartesian Meditations.* Translated by Dorion Cairns. The Hague: Nijhoff, 1960.
   Abbreviated: *CM.*]

   [*The Paris Lectures.* 2d ed. Translated by P. Koestenbaum. The Hague: Nijhoff, 1967.
   Abbreviated: *PL.*]

2. *Die Idee der Phänomenologie.* Fünf Vorlesungen. Edited by Walter Biemel. 1973.
   Abbreviated: *Idee.*

   [*The Idea of Phenomenology.* Translated by W. P. Alston and G. Nakhnikian. The Hague: Nijhoff, 1966.
   Abbreviated: *Idea.*]

3. *Ideen zu einer reinen Phänomenologie und phänomenologischen Philosophie.* Erstes Buch: Allgemeine Einführung in die reine Phänomenologie. Edited by Walter Biemel. 1950.
   Abbreviated: *Ideen I.*

   [*Ideas: General Introduction to Pure Phenomenology.* Translated by W. R. Boyce Gibson. New York: Macmillan, 1931.
   Abbreviated: *Ideas.*]

4. *Ideen zu einer reinen Phänomenologie und phänomenologischen Philosophie.* Zweites Buch: Phänomenologische Untersuchungen zur Konstitution. Edited by Marly Biemel. 1952.
   Abbreviated: *Ideen II.*

5. *Ideen zu einer reinen Phänomenologie und phänomenologischen Philosophie.* Drittes Buch: Die Phänomenologie und die Fundamente der Wissenschaften. Edited by Marly Biemel. 1971.
   Abbreviated: *Ideen III.*

   [*Phenomenology and the Foundations of the Sciences.* Translated by T. E. Klein and W. E. Pohl. The Hague: Nijhoff, 1980.]

6. *Die Krisis der europäischen Wissenschaften und die transzendentale Phänomenologie.* Eine Einleitung in die phänomenologische Philosophie. Edited by Walter Biemel. 1962.
   Abbreviated: *Krisis.*

   [*The Crisis of European Sciences and Transcendental Phenomenology.* Translated by David Carr. Evanston: Northwestern University Press, 1970. Abbreviated: *Crisis.*]

7. *Erste Philosophie (1923/24).* Erster Teil: Kritische Ideengeschichte. Edited by Rudolf Boehm. 1956.
   Abbreviated: *Erste Philosophie I.*

8. *Erste Philosophie (1923/24).* Zweiter Teil: Theorie der phänomenologischen Reduktion. Edited by Rudolf Boehm. 1959.
   Abbreviated: *Erste Philosophie II.*

9. *Phänomenologische Psychologie.* Vorlesungen Sommersemester 1925. Edited by Walter Biemel. 1968.
   Abbreviated: *Phänomenologische Psychologie* or *PP.*

   [*Phenomenological Psychology.* Lectures, Summer Semester, 1925. Translated by John Scanlon. The Hague: Nijhoff, 1977.]

10. *Zur Phänomenologie des inneren Zeitbewusstseins (1893–1917).* Edited by Rudolf Boehm. 1966.

    [*The Phenomenology of Internal Time-Consciousness.* Edited by Martin Heidegger; translated by J. S. Churchill. Bloomington: Indiana University Press, 1964.]

11. *Analysen zur passiven Synthesis. Aus Vorlesungs- und Forschungsmanuskripten, 1918–1926.* Edited by Margot Fleischer. 1966.
    Abbreviated: *Passive Synthesis.*

12. *Philosophie der Arithmetik.* Mit ergänzenden Texten (1890–1901). Edited by Lothar Eley. 1970.
    Abbreviated: *Arithmetik.*

13. *Zur Phänomenologie der Intersubjektivität.* Texte aus dem Nachlass. Erster Teil. 1905–1920. Edited by Iso Kern. 1973.

14. *Zur Phänomenologie der Intersubjektivität.* Texte aus dem Nachlass. Zweiter Teil. 1921–1928. Edited by Iso Kern. 1973.

15. *Zur Phänomenologie der Intersubjektivität.* Texte aus dem Nachlass. Dritter Teil. 1929–1935. Edited by Iso Kern. 1973.

16. *Ding und Raum.* Vorlesungen 1907. Edited by Ulrich Claesges. 1973.

17. *Formale und transzendentale Logik.* Versuch einer Kritik der logischen Vernunft. Edited by Paul Janssen. 1974.
    Abbreviated: *Logik.*

    [*Formal and Transcendental Logic.* Translated by Dorion Cairns. The Hague: Nijhoff, 1969.
    Abbreviated: *FTL.*]

18. *Logische Untersuchungen.* Erster Band. Prolegomena zur reinen Logik. Edited by Elmar Holenstein. 1975.
    Abbreviated: *LU.*

19. *Logische Untersuchungen.* Zweiter Band. Edited by Ursula Panzer. 1982.

20. [In preparation]

21. *Studien zur Arithmetik und Geometrie.* Edited by Ingeborg Strohmeyer. 1981.

22. *Aufsätze und Rezensionen (1890–1910).* Edited by Bernhard Rang. 1979.

23. *Phantasie, Bildbewusstsein, Erinnerung.* Zur Phänomenologie der anschaulichen Vergegenwärtigungen. Edited by Eduard Marbach. 1980.

****

Logische Untersuchungen. Erster Band. Prolegomena zur reinen Logik. Halle: 1900; rev. ed. 1913.

Logische Untersuchungen. Zweite Band. Untersuchungen zur Phänomenologie und Theorie der Erkenntnis. Halle: 1901; rev. ed. 1922.

[*Logical Investigations,* trans. J. N. Findlay. New York: Humanities Press, 1970. 2 vols. Based on revised Halle editions.
Abbreviated: *LI.*]

PART ONE

Husserl's Introductions to Phenomenology

A useful starting point for a collection of Husserl's shorter works is a series of programmatic texts which Husserl worked out between 1917 and 1929.

Although a number of other materials which provide something of an overview of Husserl's developing philosophical program during this time are extant, even if not as yet all published, the five texts presented here are of particular value as introductions to the basic problems and concepts of phenomenology.

These texts divide conveniently into two unequal groups. The first group, and by far the most important, comprises Husserl's inaugural lecture as Professor of Philosophy at Freiburg im Breisgau, delivered on May 3, 1977; the highly condensed article for the fourteenth edition of the *Encyclopaedia Britannica*, published in 1929 after many vicissitudes; and, from 1929 also, the summary presentation of Husserl's phenomenology which was to preface Boyce Gibson's English translation of the first volume of *Ideas*.

By comparison, the second group of texts comprises much more fragmentary materials than the first. Included here are the syllabus of a series of four lectures which Husserl presented at University College of London in the first half of June 1922 and the syllabus of four lectures which he presented at the Sorbonne in Paris in late February 1929. Some of the condensed discussions found, for example, in the *Encyclopaedia Britannica* article in the first group are usefully seen in a different context in the syllabi, whereas a number of puzzling remarks in the syllabi sometimes are more clearly detailed in the more expansive texts. When taken together, these materials provide a valuable and irreplaceable perspective on Husserl's philosophical activity, a perspective which, unlike other introductions to phenomenology, has a special claim on our attention by reason of its being sketched by Husserl himself.

In dealing with these texts critically, however, we need to recall that Husserl's philosophical program was, despite the evident continuities here, in almost continual transformation from the earliest period of his unsuccessful struggles with the philosophy of mathematics through the major achievement of the *Logical Investigations* of 1900–01 into the struggles with the vexed problems of phenomenology and idealism and on toward the new insights of his later philosophy. The materials presented here must be taken, then, not as in any absolute sense a complete and final

1

formulation of Husserl's understanding of phenomenology, but as a selection only from some of the most important shorter texts. As Husserl himself insisted repeatedly, he was a perpetual beginner. These introductory texts show him at work trying at different times and with mixed success to make one more new beginning.

The question of "a new beginning" in philosophy is complex. For at issue here, as throughout the history of Western philosophy, is a variety of difficult problems. "How does philosophical activity begin?" is just one of these problems. And what makes it difficult is the different forms this problem must assume as inquiry shifts from a purely historical standpoint (When does philosophy begin?) through a genetic preoccupation (What kinds of mental states or events are characteristic of philosophical activity?) to a more systematic standpoint (Does philosophy begin with metaphysical issues or with epistemological ones?). Another version of the question of "a new beginning" is whether philosophical activity *ought* to proceed in one way rather than another.

A further ramification of the question, of course, involves both identifying and criticizing the traditional historical and systematic beginnings of philosophy in Plato while making out a sufficiently detailed case for our requiring a new start. And still other variants of the question can be articulated. In modern philosophy Hegel agitated several of these issues in the preface to his masterpiece *The Phenomenology of Spirit*. And in contemporary philosophy, as this first set of writings thoroughly documents, it is Husserl who finds himself returning again and again to the way "a new beginning," this time a phenomenological beginning, is to be made.

In this first collection of texts we have, then, not only a series of more or less sustained reflections on the nature of phenomenological philosophy but a recurring concern to establish the necessity and the nature of a new beginning in philosophy. Part of the inherent interest of these texts, besides the specific issues they analyze, is precisely their multiplicity and variety. For in fact Husserl never realized his perduring preoccupation with writing the great systematic work that was to provide the final philosophical justification for his changing conceptions of phenomenology. And the texts we have here—especially in their repeated shifts of emphases, revised sequences of topics, and indeed choice of topics themselves—are part of the evidence which stretched across almost forty years of incessant philosophical activity that "a new beginning" was finally to elude Husserl. While this repeated failure to set out the nature of phenomenology once and for all in clearly acceptable and convincing demonstrative fashion was a continual disappointment for him, Husserl provided his readers nonetheless with a number of privileged points of entry into his philosophical activity as a whole. Many of these points can be seen in the texts provided here.

1

Introduction to
"Husserl's Inaugural Lecture at
Freiburg im Breisgau (1917)"

ROBERT WELSH JORDAN

I

The Freiburg inaugural lecture is of special interest for its very brief summary of Husserl's conception of phenomenology, giving an insight into the approach to phenomenology that Husserl then considered most readily comprehensible to a somewhat general audience. Its omissions indicate the aspects that he considered most esoteric. The term 'transcendental' does not occur at all; and the subject of intuiting universals is merely intimated when he tells us that pure phenomenological reflection posits thematically "only what is given by pure reflection, with all its immanent essential moments absolutely as it is given to pure reflection." It may have been omitted mainly out of temporary deference to the neo-Kantian tradition of the professorship to which he had succeeded. His predecessor, Heinrich Rickert (1863–1936), perhaps the most important figure in the southwestern school of neo-Kantianism, had left the post after 20 years to accept another chair of philosophy, at Heidelberg.*

The lecture was held May 3, 1917, on the

*Connections between what the lecture expressly says and these unmentioned notions will be explored briefly in this introduction's second part, which should be read only as an epilogue. It presupposes familiarity with the lecture, which affords by itself a basic introduction to phenomenology.

official occasion of Husserl's inauguration as *ordentlicher Professor,* the highest academic rank, at the Albert Ludwig University in Freiburg. He had already been teaching there since April 1, 1916. The long delay in holding the official celebration of his inauguration was due to tragic reflections of World War I within his family. Wolfgang Husserl, the younger of his sons, had been killed in action at Verdun on March 8, 1916. On the Flanders front during the succeeding year, his elder son, Gerhart, received a second severe wound from which he was blinded in one eye. It must have cost Husserl considerable effort despite all this to begin the lecture as a triumphant announcement. It ends with a still triumphant note of defiance. Received in the summer of 1915, his invitation to the chair at Freiburg had been accepted as long-delayed recognition and the prospect of a new academic beginning. Having served for some 14 years in the lowest academic position, *Privatdozent,* he had through the success of his *Logical Investigations* (1900–01) been granted a position of intermediate rank, *ausserordentlicher Professor*, at the University of Göttingen, where he remained from September 1901 until removing to Freiburg. His further professional tempering during the years at Göttingen was if not tempestuous then certainly turbulent. Relations with many of his colleagues must have been very strained. The faculty of his college rejected a recommendation from the Prussian ministry of education that he be advanced to *ordentlicher Professor* of philosophy. He was appointed over their opposition by the minister, Friedrich Althoff, in 1906. At the same time, he had been experiencing a personal crisis from his own doubts over his philosophical calling,[1] a crisis that seems to have ended only with his *transcendental* revision of what the *Logical Investigations* had presented as the phenomenological approach to philosophy. In the transcendental turn, expressed in his lectures of 1907 on *The Idea of Phenomenology* and *Ding und Raum,* few if any of his closer students followed him, very likely because they had not been able to follow what was being said. That at least is the judgment he expressed in his notebook on March 6, 1908: "It was a new beginning, not—I regret—received and understood by my following [meinen Schülern] the way I had hoped. The difficulties were after all simply too overwhelming and not to be overcome in the first attempt."[2] Besides pride and reconfirmed confidence, Husserl must have felt more than a little relieved on his departure from Göttingen. Then from the front came the news of his sons.

II

In striking contrast to the *Encyclopaedia Britannica* article written a decade later, the inaugural lecture provides no place in a classification of sciences for a phenomenological psychology. Here psychology is conceived strictly as a natural science, and this promotes a disastrous impression that phenomenology itself is strictly a philosophical discipline. To the ears of most empirically oriented psychologists and social scientists, "phenomenology's tremendous significance for any concrete grounding of *psychology*" would portend only dogmatic pronouncements from on high directing empirical research instead of the clarifying conceptual aids Husserl seems actually to have in mind.[3] The *Encyclopaedia* article's distinctions between phenomenologically psychological and phenomenologically transcendental epoches and reductions are lacking at this stage in Husserl's insight into his

method. No distinction is made here between transcendental phenomenology and pure phenomenological psychology. This promotes in turn, for his audience at least, the confounding of eidetic reduction with what he will later call transcendental phenomenological reduction. As he had in *Ideas,* Husserl here speaks simply of "phenomenological reduction." Ths term is introduced relatively late in the lecture, and it clearly refers to a restriction of phenomenology's field of investigation to pure consciousness. Thus restricted, the field of investigation coincides with that delimited earlier in the lecture when characterizing phenomenology as "a science of objective phenomena of every kind." Thus, the subject matter of phenomenology as characterized in the lecture includes but is not restricted to the subject matter of what is called eidetic phenomenological *psychology* in the *Encyclopaedia* article and is perfectly congruent with that of what is there called eidetic transcendental phenomenology. Husserl began to explicate the concept of phenomenologically pure psychology in the early 1920s in his detailed analyses of phenomenological method.[4] Such a psychology would describe mental life and mental processes purely as "phenomena" in the sense outlined in the lecture and could be carried out as an eidetic discipline without presupposing *transcendental* reduction. Its results would be consistent with those of transcendental phenomenology, to which it would serve as a propaedeutic.

The later differentiation of methodological phases makes clear that phenomenological reduction, whether the transcendental or the psychological, is something quite distinct from what Husserl called eidetic reduction. Phenomenological reduction is a restriction of the field to be investigated to phenomena, objects of whatever kind considered exactly insofar as, but only insofar as, they are actually presented to a consciousness or would be presented to a possible consciousness of them. Phenomena are then objects precisely insofar as they are themselves given to consciousness. Eidetic epoche, on the other hand, refers to a restriction of the investigator's interest in the reduced subject matter to just what is possible, impossible, or necessary within the field of phenomena. Through this second restriction, the phenomenologically reduced subject matter undergoes a *further* "eidetic" reduction whereby it is considered not in its actuality but rather as an evidently given mental life or mental process of a definite kind—*i.e.*, a life or mental process that is an instance of a definite universal essence or *eidos*. Clearly imagining or, as Husserl says, phantasying variations of the actual, clearly grasped instance leads to "eidetic intuition" —*i.e.*, to a clearer and more distinct consciousness of the universal of which the actual mental phenomenon as well as each of the imagined variations is an instance. The resulting consciousness of universals as themselves clearly given or presented enables the phenomenologist to make evident judgments concerning the limits of variability for mental phenomena of this kind, judgments about which characteristics must, may, or cannot belong to phenomena that are instances of the intuitively grasped universal. The primary methodological function of the phenomenological reduction, be it psychological or transcendental, is to assure that the investigation takes as its point of departure phenomena that, being given absolutely through immanent experience or *pure* reflection, can be known to be genuine cases of the kind under investigation. Phenomenological reduction then is the means by which phenomenology earnestly tries to ensure that its a priori judgments do not become "a cloak to cover some ideological extravagance" or what Husserl sometimes called "picture book phenomenology." If its judgments are fallible, their fallibility can be intimated by any plausible indications whatsoever; and their falsity can be established even by an imagined counterinstance, provided only that it be *clearly* imagined. They can be *corrected*, however, only by a more thorough application of the procedure outlined.

III

Husserl's later differentiation of these phases in his method helps prevent some misinterpretations that can easily arise. In writings before 1920 that have so far been published, he does not explicitly contrast the purity of "pure reflection" with the purity of phenomenology as an eidetic, a priori, and strictly nonempirical science. As a result, the reader can easily be misled into believing that phenomenological reduction is at the same time eidetic reduction and consequently that pure consciousness is a field of universal and particular *ideas*.[5] Fewer misinterpretations could be further from what Husserl actually has in mind than the one this suggests. Yet he provides only a weak defense against it. In the first place, his preliminary illustrations of "phenomena" mention only *actual* objects, and all actual objects are, in his view, either temporally or spatially individuated. Moreover, the paragraph wherein phenomena and Objects are initially differentiated states clearly that the differentiation is being made exclusively within the class of *individual* objects. Here and throughout the lecture, the phenomena spoken of are individual objects, and individual objects include *all* conscious processes and *all immanent constituents of conscious processes*.

In order to ward off the interpretation that would regard phenomenologically reduced consciousness as a field of universal and particular ideas, it seems that the field of investigation must now be regarded as consisting entirely of *individual* phenomena. This is somewhat closer to what Husserl actually has in mind. But what is wanting indicates the importance of differentiating between the phenomenological reductions and the further eidetic reduction of the phenomenologically reduced field of investigation. As the lecture itself notes, those individual phenomena that are the objects of the phenomenologist's pure or immanent reflective experience are individually his own, flowing conscious processes. By empirical generalization from these, he could hardly hope to form general judgments that could be known to hold for all phenomena of the sort he is investigating. Indeed, it looks as if no phenomenological science will be possible at all if the sphere of phenomena is limited to the actual instances given to pure reflective *perception*. Within the limits imposed by the lecture's format, Husserl is constrained to indicate a possible resolution of this difficulty by pointing to a vague analogy between phenomenology as an eidetic a priori science and "pure mathematics, pure arithmetic, pure geometry, pure kinematics, etc." How vague he thinks the analogy to be is shown by a passage from a manuscript of 1907:

"This transcendental phenomenology is not a priori ontology; it is neither a matter of formal logic and formal mathematics nor of geometry as a priori theory of space nor of a priori chronometry and phoronomy nor of a priori real ontology of any sort of object (thing, change, etc.)."[6]

In the same year, Husserl had stated emphatically what he considered to be the proper way out of the difficulty. The inaugural lecture cautiously mentions only individual phenomena, but it just as artfully avoids restricting the class of phenomena exclusively to individual objects. One of the central theses of *The Idea of Phenomenology* is that the sphere of phenomena, the sphere of objects that, in contrast to Objects, can be given with absolute evidence, is not at all limited to those individual objects that can be given to pure reflective *experience*, and that every *cogitatio* and every genuinely inherent part of any *cogitatio*, abstract parts as well as concrete ones, is an individual phenomenon.[7] In *Ideas*, he also makes it clear that because mental phenomena are individual objects they can have neither universal ideas nor particular ideas (eidetic singularities) as components.[8] Only the givenness of universals that through eidetic reduction and phantasy variation can be grasped and explicated with absolute evidence makes phenomenology possible as an a priori science.[9]

The field of phenomena includes therefore more than just consciousness and its genuinely inherent parts. Universal and particular ideal objects are transcendent as contrasted with the immanent components of the stream of consciousness. *In this sense*, they are just as transcendent as the individual objects of transcendent *experience*; they can be absolutely given. Having no spatial existence, an ideal object, even though it is something "foreign to consciousness," is not given from any spatial perspective, and so has no sides or "adumbrations" given from

my present perspective; as stated in the lecture, "there are no changing . . . views of it as if it might be seen from above or below, from near or far."[10]

In contrast, Objects *as such* are foreign to consciousness in a way that prevents their being given absolutely. When experienced Objectively, an Object is not a phenomenon. The Object is not really a part of the Objective experiencing of it. Experiencing does, however, have its own intentionality as a really intrinsic part. Experiencing just this Object is an intrinsic characteristic of the experience; and, because Objective experiencing *is* a phenomenon, all its constituents, including its intentiveness to just this Object, are given absolutely or adequately. They can be grasped and explicated with absolute evidence by pure reflective consciousness. The Object, precisely as intended — *e.g.,* as believed in, loved, hated, dreaded, willed, used, etc. — by Objective consciousness of it, turns out to be a phenomenon without ceasing to be alien or transcendent to consciousness, without ceasing to be something that is neither an abstract nor a concrete part of consciousness. Its transcendence is in no way affected by pure reflection or phenomenological reduction. So, transcendent Objects of all kinds find their way into the field of investigation of even the "purest" phenomenology, provided only that there can be *some* straightforward, nonreflective consciousness of them. It makes not the slightest difference if they can not be experienced *adequately* by nonreflective consciousness or even if they cannot be experienced by it at all. The world and all its parts to the extent that there can be any awareness of them whatsoever are "phenomena" and can be exhibited as phenomena to pure reflection.

Rather than isolating consciousness from the world, phenomenological reduction reveals consciousness as being in the world. Its fundamental way of being in the world is its intentionality, which is always the individual intentionality of individual mental phenomena. This individual intentionality is never a bare instance of intentionality in general but is always of a specific kind, such as doxic (believing, disbelieving, doubting, etc.), affective (liking, hating, dreading, rejoicing at, etc., whether decidedly or inde- cidedly), or volitional (wanting, wishing, deciding, doing, etc.). Indeed, the entire familiar world of artifacts is constituted, as the inaugural lecture tells us, only through "the participation of emotional and voli- tional consciousness."[11] Because phenome- nology takes pure reflective experience as its point of departure, it is able to investigate

the various ways in which each kind of ob- ject is there for the correlative species of intentionality, making it possible to dis- criminate those ways of being there in which objects of the kind in question "present themselves" to consciousness and, correla- tively, those ways of intending that are ve- ridical or "authentic."

NOTES

1. See Walter Biemel, "Einleitung des Heraus- gebers," in *Idee, Husserliana* 2: viiff.

2. Ibid., p. xi. Accounts of Husserl's relations with his students in Göttingen are given in Helmut Plessner, "Bei Husserl in Göttingen," in *Edmund Hus- serl, 1859–1959* (The Hague: Nijhoff, 1959), pp. 29– 39; and Herbert Spiegelberg, *The Phenomenological Movement*, 2nd ed. (The Hague: Nijhoff, 1965), pp. 168–71.

3. That the *Encyclopaedia* article is not alien to his earlier views is indicated by his more extensive dis- cussion in *Philosophie als strenge Wissenschaft*, pp. 32–48, corresponding to pp. 310–22 in the original publication in *Logos* 1 (1910–11), and to pp. 85–122 of Quentin Lauer's English translation, "Philosophy as Rigorous Science," in *Phenomenology and the Crisis of Philosophy* (New York: Harper Torchbooks, 1965). The latter is reprinted in the present volume, pp. 166–97.

4. See *Erste Philosophie II, Husserliana* 8.

5. Passages such as the following from the inau- gural lecture promote such a confusion: "pure phe- nomenology was not established to be an empirical sci- ence, and what it calls its 'purity' is not just that of pure reflection but is at the same time the entirely different sort of purity we meet in the names of other sciences . . . just as pure analysis does not treat of actual things and their de facto magnitudes but investigates instead the essential laws pertaining to any possible quantity . . . in *precisely* the same way pure phenomenology proposes to investigate *the realm of pure consciousness and its phenomena* not as de facto existents but as pure possibilities with their pure laws." See pages 16–17 below.

6. Translated from the German as quoted in Bie- mel, *Idee, Husserliana* 2: ix–x.

7. *Idee*, pp. 60–61; *Idea*, pp. 48–49. The same passage includes one of his most succinct statements of what is meant by absolute evidence: "Hence phenome- nological reduction does not entail a limitation of the investigation to the sphere of genuine (*reell*) imma- nence, to the sphere of that which is genuinely con- tained within the absolute this of the *cogitatio*. It en- tails no limitation to the sphere of the *cogitatio*. Rather it entails a limitation to the sphere of things that are *purely self-given*, to the sphere of those things which are not merely spoken about, meant, or perceived, but instead to the sphere of those things that are given in just exactly the sense in which they are thought of, and moreover are self-given in the strictest sense—in such a way that nothing which is meant fails to be given. In a word, we are restricted to the sphere of pure evi- dence . . . " (*Idee*, pp. 60–61; *Idea*, pp. 48–49). "We have no lesser evidence of the universal; *universal ob- jects* and *states of affairs* are presented to us, and they are without doubt given in the very same sense, *viz.*, themselves adequately given in the strictest sense" (*Idee*, p. 60; the translation of this passage is my own.).

8. *Ideen I*, pp. 25–27, 30, 139ff. in the marginal pagination, corresponding to that of the earlier edi- tions (Halle an der Saale: Max Niemeyer, 1913, 1922); in the English translation, *Ideas*, see the entries under "*Singularity*" in the "Analytical Index."

9. *Idee*, p. 51; *Idea*, p. 41.

10. See page 13 below.

11. See page 12 below.

FURTHER REFERENCES

Berger, Gaston. *The Cogito in Husserl's Philoso- phy*. Translated by K. McLaughlin. Evanston: Northwestern University Press, 1972.

Brand, Gerd. *Welt, Ich und Zeit. Nach unveröf- fentlichten Manuskripten Edmund Husserls*. The Hague: Nijhoff, 1955.

Kern, Iso. *Husserl und Kant. Eine Untersuchung über Husserls Verhältnis zu Kant und zum Neukantianismus*. The Hague: Nijhoff, 1964.

Kersten, Frederick. "On Understanding Idea and Essence in Husserl and Ingarden." *Analecta Husserliana* 2 (1972): 55–63.

Kockelmans, Joseph J. *Edmund Husserl's Phe- nomenological Psychology, an Historio-Critical Study*. Pittsburgh: Duquesne University Press, 1967.

Kockelmans, Joseph J. "Husserl and Kant on the Pure Ego". In *Husserl: Expositions and Ap-*

praisals, edited by F.A. Elliston and P. McCormick, pp. 269–85. Notre Dame and London: University of Notre Dame Press, 1977.

Kraus, Oskar, "Einleitung (Auch ein Wort zur Krise in der Psychologie)." In Franz Brentano, *Vom sinnlichen und noetischen Bewusstsein [Psychologie III] I. Teil Wahrnehmung, Empfindung, Begriff,* edited by Oskar Kraus. Leipzig: Felix Meiner, 1928.

Levinas, Emmanuel. *The Theory of Intuition in Husserl's Phenomenology.* Translated by André Orianne. Evanston: Northwestern University Press, 1973.

Marbach, Eduard. *Das Problem des Ich in der Phä-nomenologie Husserls.* The Hague: Nijhoff, 1974.

Mohanty, J.N. *Edmund Husserl's Theory of Meaning.* The Hague: Nijhoff, 1964.

Patočka, Jean. "The Husserlian Doctrine of Eidetic Intuition". In *Husserl: Expositions and Appraisals,* edited by F.A. Elliston and P. McCormick, pp. 150–59. Notre Dame and London: University of Notre Dame Press, 1977.

Pietersma, Henry. "Intuition and Horizon in the Philosophy of Edmund Husserl." *Philosophy and Phenomenological Research* 34 (1973–74): 95–101.

1

Husserl's Inaugural Lecture
at Freiburg im Breisgau (1917)*

INTRODUCTION BY H. L. VAN BREDA

TRANSLATED BY ROBERT WELSH JORDAN**

As a tribute to Aron Gurwitsch as a distinguished phenomenologist and promoter of the contemporary phenomenological movement, we dedicate the following exceptionally rich text selected from the thousands of still-unpublished pages treasured in the Husserl Archives. It is the text of Husserl's Inaugural Lecture as Professor ordinarius at the Albert-Ludwigs-Universität in Freiburg im Breisgau and was delivered on May 3, 1917. In keeping with the academic traditions of such an august occasion, the newly appointed holder of the chair developed a far-reaching program of problems he intended to investigate in the following years.

The text of this address speaks for itself. Let me thank Mr. Jordan for translating it.

*Reprinted with permission of the publisher and translator from Lester E. Embree, ed., *Life-World and Consciousness: Essays for Aron Gurwitsch* (Evanston, Illinois: Northwestern University Press, 1972), pp. 3–18. Translated by Robert Welsh Jordan and edited by H. L. Van Breda, this was the lecture's first publication in any form. The German original was first published only recently. See "Die reine Phänomenologie, ihr Forschungsgebiet und ihre Methode," *Tijdschrift voor Philosophie* 38 (1976): 363–78.
**This new introduction to Husserl's inaugural lecture, like the translation of the lecture itself and its original introduction by the late Professor H. L. Van Breda, both of which follow, is dedicated to Professor Aron Gurwitsch, who died on June 25, 1973. Most of the dates and biographical facts below are taken from Professor Van Breda.

By way of introduction, suffice it for me to sketch the historical events that led up to Husserl's appointment at Freiburg.

Having obtained his *venia legendi* in 1889 at the University of Halle an der Saale, Husserl continued to lecture there until 1901 with the lowest rank on the academic staff, Privatdozent. Following the publication of the *Logische Untersuchungen* (1900–1901), he was offered the post of Professor extraordinarius, still a relatively low position, at the University of Göttingen and began lecturing there in September, 1901. In 1906, Friedrich Althoff, the Prussian minister of education, granted him the title of Professor ordinarius, despite opposition from the faculty of philosophy in Göttingen. By this time, more and more students, including many foreigners, were attending his lectures and seminars. This in time was to become the nucleus of the phenomenological school.

In the summer of 1915, some months after the outbreak of World War I, Husserl was officially invited to succeed Heinrich Rickert (1863–1936) at Freiburg im Breisgau. Rickert was a leading figure of the Neo-Kantian school of Baden in southern Germany and had held the chair in Freiburg for more than twenty years. Due to slow progress, sometimes against the open antagonism of established philosophers, the first twenty years of Husserl's career were arduous, and this invitation from the university and the government of Baden was indeed quite attractive to him. He was now convinced that his talents and merits were at long last gaining recognition.

He started lecturing at Freiburg on April 1, 1916. It is well to remember that his youngest son, Wolfgang, had been killed in action during the battle of Verdun on March 8. This tragic incident completely overshadowed his first contacts with his new students and environment. On top of this, his eldest son, Gerhart, was seriously injured for a second time on the Flanders front during Husserl's first year at Freiburg. In such circumstances, Husserl prepared his official Inaugural Lecture. Nowhere in these pages can one detect the slightest allusion to the opposition of colleagues, who repeatedly failed to appreciate the originality and value of his research. Nor is there any hint of recent distressing events in his family life. Reading this lecture, we perceive in all its purity the voice of a genuine philosopher speaking limpidly about "pure" phenomenology.

This editor has read and studied with lively interest the numerous and varied philosophical publications of Aron Gurwitsch for more than thirty years. As a close friend, he is well aware of the often agonizing history of his *Wanderjahre* through most of the European countries and later in New England. Nonetheless, on reading his works, the uninformed reader will never find the remotest hint of this history. Like his master before him, Edmund Husserl, Aron Gurwitsch *incarnates* the genuine *eidos* of the true "lover of wisdom" — what, in other words, every *philosophos* worthy of the name should really be.

Pure Phenomenology, Its Method and Its Field of Investigation

Ladies and gentlemen, honored colleagues, dear comrades!

In all the areas within which the spiritual life of humanity is at work, the historical epoch wherein fate has placed us is an epoch of stupendous happenings. Whatever previous generations cultivated by their toil and struggle into a harmonious whole, in every sphere of culture, whatever enduring style

was deemed established as method and norm, is once more in flux and now seeks new forms whereby reason, as yet unsatisfied, may develop more freely: in politics, in economic life, in technics, in the fine arts, and — by no means least of all — in the sciences. In a few decades of reconstruction, even the mathematical natural sciences, the ancient archetypes of theoretical perfection, have changed habit completely!

Philosophy, too, fits into this picture. In philosophy, the forms whose energies were dissipated in the period following the overthrow of Hegelian philosophy were essentially those of a renaissance. They were forms that reclaimed past philosophies, and their methods as well as some of their essential content originated with great thinkers of the past.

Most recently, the need for an utterly original philosophy has re-emerged, the need of a philosophy that — in contrast to the secondary productivity of renaissance philosophies — seeks by radically clarifying the sense and the motifs of philosophical problems to penetrate to that primal ground on whose basis those problems must find whatever solution is genuinely scientific.

A new fundamental science, pure phenomenology, has developed within philosophy. This is a science of a thoroughly new type and endless scope. It is inferior in methodological rigor to none of the modern sciences. All philosophical disciplines are rooted in pure phenomenology, through whose development, and through it alone, they obtain their proper force. Philosophy is possible as a rigorous science at all only through pure phenomenology. It is of pure phenomenology I wish to speak: the intrinsic nature of its method and its subject matter, a subject matter that is invisible to naturally oriented points of view.

Pure phenomenology claims to be the science of pure phenomena. This concept of the phenomenon, which was developed under various names as early as the eighteenth century without being clarified, is what we shall have to deal with first of all.

We shall begin with the necessary correlation between object, truth, and cognition — using these words in their very broadest senses. To every object there correspond an ideally closed system of truths that are true of it and, on the other hand, an ideal system of possible cognitive processes by virtue of which the object and the truths about it would be given to any cognitive subject. Let us consider these processes. At the lowest cognitive level, they are processes of experiencing, or, to speak more generally, processes of intuiting that grasp the object in the original.

Something similar is obviously true of all types of intuitions and of all other processes of meaning an object even when they have the character of mere re-presentations that (like rememberings or pictorial intuitions or processes of meaning something symbolic) do not have the intrinsic character of being conscious of the intuited's being there "in person" but are conscious of it instead as recalled, as re-presented in the picture or by means of symbolic indications and the like, and even when the actuality valuation of the intuited varies in some, no matter what, manner. Even intuitions in phantasy, therefore, are intrinsically intuitions of objects and carry "object phenomena" with them intrinsically, phenomena that are obviously not characterized as actualities. If higher, theoretical cognition is to begin at all, objects belonging to the sphere in question must be intuited. Natural objects, for example, must be experienced before any theorizing about them can occur. Experiencing is consciousness that intuits something and values it to be actual; experiencing is intrinsically characterized as consciousness of the natural object in question and of it as the original: there is consciousness of the original as being there "in person." The same thing can be expressed by saying that objects would be nothing at all for the cognizing subject if they did not "appear" to him, if he had of them no "phenomenon." Here, therefore, "phenomenon" signifies a certain content that intrinsically inhabits the intuitive consciousness in question and is the substrate for its actuality valuation.

Something similar is still true of the courses followed by manifold intuitions which together make up the unity of one *continuous consciousness* of one and the same object. The manner in which the object is given within each of the single intuitions belonging to this continuous consciousness may vary constantly; for example, the object's sensuous "looks"—the way in which the object always "looks" different at each approach or remove and at every turning, from above or below, from left or right—may be forever new in the transition from one perception to continuously new perceptions. In spite of that, we have, in the way in which such series of perceptions with their changing sensuous images take their courses, intuitive consciousness not of a changing multiplicity but rather of one and the same object that is variously presented. To put it differently, within the pure immanence of such consciousness one unitary "phenomenon" permeates all the manifolds of phenomenal presentation. It is the peculiar characteristic of such states of affairs which makes for the shift in the concept "phenomenon." Rather than just the thoroughgoing *unity* of intuition, the variously changing modes in which the unity is presented, *e.g.,* the continuously changing perspectival looks of a real object, are also called "phenomena."

The extent of this concept is further broadened when we consider the higher cognitive functions: the multiform acts and coherency of referential, combinative, conceiving, theorizing cognition. Every single process of any of these sorts is, again, intrinsically consciousness of the object that is peculiar to it as a thought process of some particular sort or sorts; hence, the object is characterized as member of a combination, as either subject or *relatum* of a relation, etc. The single cognitive processes, on the other hand, combine into the unity of *one* consciousness that constitutes intrinsically a single synthetic objectivity, a single predicative state-of-affairs, for example, or a single theoretical context, an object such as is expressed in sentences like: "The object is related in this or that way," "It is a whole composed of these and those parts," "The relationship B derives from the relationship A," etc.

Consciousness of all synthetically objective formations of these kinds occurs through such multimembered acts that unite to form higher unities of consciousness, and it occurs by means of immanently constituted phenomena that function at the same time as substrates for differing valuations, such as certain truth, probability, possibility, etc.

The concept "phenomenon" carries over, furthermore, to the changing modes of being conscious of something—for example, the clear and the obscure, evident and blind modes—in which one and the same relation or connection, one and the same state-of-affairs, one and the same logical coherency, etc., can be given to consciousness.

In summary, the first and most primitive concept of the phenomenon referred to the limited sphere of those sensuously given realities [*der sinnendinglichen Gegebenheiten*] through which Nature is evinced in perceiving.

The concept was extended, without comment, to include every kind of sensuously meant or objectivated thing. It was then extended to include also the sphere of those synthetic objectivities that are given to consciousness through referential and connective conscious syntheses and to include these objects just the way they are given to consciousness within these syntheses. It thus includes all modes in which things are given to consciousness. And it was seen finally to include the whole realm of consciousness with *all* of the ways of being conscious of something and all the constituents that can be shown immanently to belong to them. That the concept includes *all* ways of being conscious of something means that it includes, as well, every sort of feeling, desiring, and willing with its immanent "comportment" [*Verhalten*].

To understand this broadening of the concept is very easy if one considers that emotional and volitional processes also have intrinsically the character of being conscious of something and that enormous categories of objects, including all cultural objects, all values, all goods, all works, can be experienced, understood, and made objective *as such* only through the participation of emotional and volitional consciousness. No object of the category "work of art" could occur in the objectivational world of any being who was devoid of all aesthetic sensibility, who was, so to speak, aesthetically blind.

Through this exposition of the concept "phenomenon" we obtain a preliminary

conception of a general phenomenology, viz., a science of objective phenomena of every kind, the science of every kind of object, an "object" being taken purely as something having just those determinations with which it presents itself in consciousness and in just those changing modes through which it so presents itself. It would be the task of phenomenology, therefore, to investigate how something perceived, something remembered, something phantasied, something pictorially represented, something symbolized looks as such, *i.e.,* to investigate how it looks by virtue of that bestowal of sense and of characteristics which is carried out intrinsically by the perceiving, the remembering, the phantasying, the pictorial representing, etc., itself. Obviously, phenomenology would investigate in the same way how what is collected looks in the collecting of it; what is disjoined, in the disjoining; what is produced, in the producing; and, similarly, for *every* act of thinking, how it intrinsically "has" phenomenally in it what it thinks; how, in aesthetic valuing, the valued looks as such; in actively shaping something, the shaped as such; etc. What phenomenology wants, in all these investigations, is to establish what admits of being stated with the universal validity of theory. In doing so, however, its investigations will, understandably, have to refer to the intrinsic nature [*das eigene Wesen*] of the perceiving itself, of remembering (or any other way of re-presenting) itself, and of thinking, valuing, willing, and doing themselves—these acts being taken just as they present themselves to immanently intuitive reflection. In Cartesian terms, the investigation will be concerned with the *cogito* in its own right as well as with the *cogitatum qua cogitatum.* As the two are inseparably involved with each other in being, so, understandably, are they in the investigation as well.

If these are the themes of phenomenology, then it can also be called "science of consciousness," if consciousness be taken purely as such.

To characterize this science more exactly, we shall introduce a simple distinction between phenomena and Objects [*Objekten*]*

---

*Following the practice of Dorion Cairns in his

in the pregnant sense of the word. In general logical parlance, any subject whatever of true predications is an object. In this sense, therefore, every phenomenon is also an object. Within this widest concept of object, and specifically within the concept of individual object, *Objects* and *phenomena* stand in contrast with each other. Objects [*Objekte*], all natural Objects, for example, are objects foreign to consciousness. Consciousness does, indeed, objectivate them and posit them as actual, yet the consciousness that experiences them and takes cognizance of them is so singularly astonishing that it bestows upon its own phenomena the sense of being appearances of Objects foreign to consciousness and knows these "extrinsic" Objects through processes that take cognizance of their sense. Those objects that are neither conscious processes nor immanent constituents of conscious processes we therefore call Objects in the pregnant sense of the word.

This places two separate sciences in the sharpest of contrasts: on the one hand, phenomenology, the science of consciousness as it is in itself; on the other, the "Objective" sciences as a totality.

To the objects, which are obviously correlated to each other, of these contrasted sciences there correspond two fundamentally different types of experience and of intuition generally: *immanent* experience and *Objective* experience, also called "external" or transcendent experience. Immanent experience consists in the mere viewing that takes place in reflection by which consciousness and that of which there is consciousness are grasped. For example, a liking or a desiring that I am just now executing enters into my experience by way of a merely retrospec-

tive look and, by means of this look, is given absolutely. What "absolutely" means here we can learn by contrast: we can experience any external thing only insofar as it presents itself to us sensuously through this or that adumbration [*Abschattung*]. A liking has no changing presentations; there are no changing perspectives on or views of it as if it might be seen from above or below, from near or far. It just is nothing foreign to consciousness at all that could present itself to consciousness through the mediation of phenomena different from the liking itself; to like is intrinsically to be conscious.

This is involved with the fact that the existence of what is given to immanent reflection is indubitable while what is experienced through external experience always allows the possibility that it may prove to be an illusory Object in the course of further experiences.

Immanent and transcendent experience are nevertheless connected in a remarkable way: by a change in attitude, we can pass from the one to the other.

In the natural attitude, we experience, among other things, processes in Nature [*Natur*]; we are adverted to them, observe them, describe them, subsume them under concepts [*bestimmen sie*]. While we do so, there occur in our experiencing and theorizing consciousness multiform conscious processes which have constantly changing immanent constituents. The things involved present themselves through continuously flowing aspects; their shapes are perspectivally silhouetted [*schatten sich ab*] in definite ways; the data of the different senses are construed in definite ways, *e.g.*, as unitary colorings of the experienced shapes or as warmth radiating from them; the sensuous qualities construed are referred, by being construed referentially and causally, to real circumstances; etc. The bestowing of each of these senses is carried out in consciousness and by virtue of definite series of flowing conscious processes. A person in the natural attitude, however, knows nothing of this. He executes the acts of experiencing, referring, combining; but, while he is executing them, he is looking not toward them but rather in the direction of the objects he is conscious of.

---

translation of Husserl's *Cartesian Meditations*, the word 'object', spelled with a small letter, has been and will be used throughout to translate *Gegenstand;* spelled with a capital letter, it translates *Objekt.* In the same way, words derived from *Gegenstand* or from *Objekt* will be translated with words derived from 'object', spelled with a small or with a capital letter, respectively. Where 'object' or one of its derivatives is the initial word in a sentence, the German word will be given in brackets. The practice appears to be justified perfectly by the manner in which the text proceeds to differentiate between the senses of *Gegenstand* and *Objekt.*

On the other hand, he can convert his natural attentional focus into the phenomenologically reflective one; he can make the currently flowing consciousness and, thus, the infinitely multiform world of phenomena at large the theme of his fixating observations, descriptions, theoretical investigations — the investigations which, for short, we call "phenomenological."

At this point, however, there arises what, in the present situation of philosophy, can be called the most decisive of questions. Is not what was just described as immanent reflection simply identical with internal, psychological experience? Is not psychology the proper place for the investigation of consciousness and all its phenomena? However much psychology may previously have omitted any systematic investigation of consciousness, however blindly it may have passed over all radical problems concerning the bestowal, carried out in the immanence of consciousness, of objective sense, it still seems clear that such investigations should belong to psychology and should even be fundamental to it.

The ideal of a *pure* phenomenology will be perfected only by answering this question; pure phenomenology is to be separated sharply from psychology at large and, specifically, from the descriptive psychology of the phenomena of consciousness. Only with this separation does the centuries-old conflict over "psychologism" reach its final conclusion. The conflict is over nothing less than the true philosophical method and the foundation of any philosophy as pure and strict science.

To begin with, we put the proposition: pure phenomenology is the science of *pure* consciousness. This means that pure phenomenology draws upon pure reflection exclusively, and pure reflection excludes, as such, every type of external experience and therefore precludes any copositing of objects alien to consciousness. Psychology, on the other hand, is science of psychic Nature and, therefore, of consciousness as Nature or as real event in the spatiotemporal world. Psychology draws upon *psychological* experiencing, which is an apperceiving that links immanent reflection to experience of the ex-

ternal, the extrinsic [*äusserer Erfahrung*]. In psychological experience, moreover, the psychic is given as event within the cohesion of Nature. Specifically, psychology, as the natural science of psychic life, regards conscious processes as the conscious processes of animate beings, *i.e.,* as real causal adjuncts to animate bodies. The psychologist must resort to reflection in order to have conscious processes experientially given. Nevertheless, this reflection does not keep to pure reflection; for, in being taken as belonging really to the animate body in question, reflection is linked to experience of the extrinsic. Psychologically experienced consciousness is therefore no longer pure consciousness; construed Objectively in this way, consciousness itself becomes something transcendent, becomes an event in that spatial world which appears, by virtue of consciousness, to be transcendent.

The fundamental fact is that there is a kind of intuiting which — in contrast to psychological experiencing — remains within pure reflection: pure reflection excludes everything that is given in the natural attitude and excludes therefore all of Nature.

Consciousness is taken purely as it intrinsically is with its own intrinsic constituents, and no being that transcends consciousness is coposited.

What is thematically posited is only what is given, by pure reflection, with all its immanent essential moments absolutely as it is given to pure reflection.

Descartes long ago came close to discovering the purely phenomenological sphere. He did so in his famous and fundamental meditation — that has nevertheless been basically fruitless — which culminates in the much quoted *"ego cogito, ego sum."* The so-called *phenomenological reduction* can be effected by modifying Descartes's method, by carrying it through purely and consequentially while disregarding all Cartesian aims; phenomenological reduction is the method for effecting radical purification of the phenomenological field of consciousness from all obtrusions from Objective actualities and for keeping it pure of them. Consider the following: Nature, the universe of spatiotemporal Objectivity, is given to us constantly; in the natural attitude, it already is the field for our investigations in the natural sciences and for our practical purposes. Yet, nothing prevents us from putting out of action, so to speak, any believing in the actuality of it, even though that believing continues to occur all the while in our mental processes. After all, speaking quite universally, no believing, no conviction, however evident, excludes by its essence the possibility of its being put in a certain way out of action or deprived of its force. What this means we can learn from any case in which we examine one of our convictions, perhaps to defend it against objections or to re-establish it on a new basis. It may be that we have no doubts at all about it. Yet, we obviously alter during the whole course of the examination the way we act in relation to this conviction. Without surrendering our conviction in the least, we still do not take part in it; we deny to ourselves acceptance, as truth, of what the conviction posits simply to be true. While the examination is being carried out, this truth is in question; it remains to be seen; it is to remain undecided.

In our instance, in the case of phenomenologically pure reflection, the aim is not to place in question and to test our believing in actualities foreign to consciousness. Nevertheless, we can carry out a similar putting-out-of-action for that consciousness of actuality by virtue of which the whole of Nature is existence which, for us, is given [*für uns gegebenes Dasein ist*]; and we can do so utterly *ad libitum*. For the sole purposes of attaining to the domain of pure consciousness and keeping it pure, we therefore undertake to accept no beliefs involving Objective experience and, therefore, also undertake to make not the slightest use of any conclusion derived from Objective experience.

The actuality of all of material Nature is therefore kept out of action and that of all corporeality along with it, including the actuality of my body, the body of the cognizing subject.

This makes it clear that, as a consequence, all psychological experience is also put out of action. If we have absolutely forbidden ourselves to treat Nature and the corporeal at all as given actualities, then the possibility of positing any conscious process whatsoever as having a corporeal link or as being an event occurring in Nature lapses of itself.

What is left over, once this radical methodological exclusion of all Objective actualities has been effected? The answer is clear. If we put every experienced actuality out of action, we still have indubitably given every phenomenon of experience. This is true for the whole Objective world as well. We are forbidden to make use of the *actuality* of the Objective world; for us, the Objective world is as if it were placed in brackets. What remains to us is the totality of the phenomena of the world, phenomena which are grasped by reflection as they are absolutely in themselves [*in ihrer absoluten Selbstheit*]. For, all of these constituents of conscious life remain intrinsically what they were; it is through them that the world is constituted.

So far as their own phenomenal content is concerned, they do not suffer in any way when believing in Objective actuality is put out of play. Nor does reflection, insofar as it grasps and views the phenomena in their own being, suffer in any way. Only now, in fact, does reflection become pure and exclusive. Moreover, even the belief in the Objective, the belief characteristic of simple experience and of empirical theory, is not lost to us. Instead, it becomes our theme just as it intrinsically is and in accord with what is implicit in it as its sense and as the substrate for what it posits; we view the belief; we analyze its immanent character; we follow its possible coherencies, especially those of grounding; we study in pure reflection what takes place in transitions to fulfilling insight, what is preserved of the meant sense in such transitions, what the fullness of intuition brings to this sense, what alteration and enrichment so-called evidence contributes, and whatever advances are made by what, in this connection, is called "attaining Objective truth through insight." Following this method of phenomenological reduction (*i.e.,* keeping out of action all believing in the transcendent), every kind of theoretical, valuational, practical consciousness can be made in the same manner a theme of inquiry; and all the Objectivities constituted in it can be investigated. The investigation will take these Objectivities simply as correlates of consciousness and will inquire solely into the What and the How of the phenomena that can be drawn from the conscious processes and coherencies in question. Things in Nature, persons and personal communities, social forms and formations, poetic and plastic formations, every kind of cultural work—all become in this way headings for phenomenological investigations, not as actualities, the way they are treated in the corresponding Objective sciences, but rather with regard to the consciousness that constitutes—through the intermediary of an initially bewildering wealth of structures of consciousness—these objectivities for the conscious subject in question. Consciousness and what it is conscious of is therefore what is left over as field for pure reflection once phenomenological reduction has been effected: the endless multiplicity of manners of being conscious, on the one hand, and, on the other, the infinity of intentional correlates. What keeps us from transgressing this field is the index that, thanks to the method of phenomenological reduction, every Objective belief obtains as soon as it arises for consciousness. The index demands of us: Take no part in this belief; do not fall into the attitude of Objective science; keep to the pure phenomenon! Obviously, the index is universal in the scope in which it suspends acceptance of the Objective sciences themselves, of which psychology is one. The index changes all sciences to science phenomena; and, in this status, they are among its larger themes.

However, as soon as any proposition about things Objective, any one at all, including even the most indubitable truth, is claimed to be a valid truth, the soil of pure phenomenology is abandoned. For then we take our stance upon some Objective soil and carry on psychology or some other Objective science instead of phenomenology.

This radical suspension of Nature stands in conflict, to be sure, with our most deeply rooted habits of experience and thinking. Yet it is precisely for this reason that fully self-conscious phenomenological reduction is needed if consciousness is to be systematically investigated in its pure immanence at all.

• • •

But still other reservations come to mind. Is pure phenomenology genuinely possible as a science, and, if so, then how? Once the suspension is in effect, we are left with pure consciousness. In pure consciousness, however, what we find is an unresting flow of never recurring phenomena, even though they may be indubitably given in reflective experience. Experience by itself is not science. Since the reflecting and cognizing subject has only his flowing phenomena genuinely and since every other cognizing subject—his corporeality and consequently his consciousness [*seinem Erleben*] as well—falls within the scope of the exclusion, how can an empirical science still be possible? Science cannot be solipsistic. It must be valid for every experiencing subject.

We would be in a nasty position indeed if empirical science were the only kind of science possible. Answering the question we have posed thus leads to most profound and as yet unsolved philosophical problems. Be that as it may, pure phenomenology was not established to be an empirical science, and what it calls its 'purity' is not just that of pure reflection but is at the same time the entirely different sort of purity we meet in the names of other sciences.

We often speak in a general, and intelligible, way of pure mathematics, pure arithmetic, pure geometry, pure kinematics, etc. These we contrast, as a priori sciences, to sciences, such as the natural sciences, based on experience and induction. Sciences that are pure in this sense, a priori sciences, are pure of any assertion about empirical actuality. Intrinsically, they purport to be concerned with the ideally possible and the pure laws thereof rather than with actualities. In contrast to them, empirical sciences are sciences of the de facto actual, which is given as such through experience.

Now, just as pure analysis does not treat of actual things and their de facto magnitudes but investigates instead the essential laws pertaining to the essence of any possible quantity, or just as pure geometry is not bound to shapes observed in actual experience but instead inquires into possible shapes and their possible transformations, constructing *ad libitum* in pure geometric phantasy, and establishes their essential laws, in *precisely* the same way pure phenomenology proposes to investigate *the realm of pure consciousness and its phenomena* not as de facto existents but as pure possibilities with their pure laws. And, indeed, when one becomes familiar with the soil of pure reflection, one is compelled to the view that possibilities are subject to ideal laws in the realm of pure consciousness as well. For example, the pure phenomena through which a possible spatial Object presents itself to consciousness have their a priori definite system of necessary formations which is unconditionally binding upon every cognizing consciousness if that consciousness is to be able to intuit spatial reality. [*Raumdinglichkeit*]. Thus, the ideal of a spatial thing prescribes a priori to possible consciousness of such a thing a set rule, a rule that can be followed intuitively and that admits of being conceived, in accord with the typicality of phenomenal forms, in pure concepts. And the same is true of every principal category of objectivities. The expression 'a priori' is therefore not a cloak to cover some ideological extravagance but is just as significant as is the 'purity' of mathematical analysis or geometry.

Obviously, I can here offer no more than this helpful analogy. Without troublesome work, no one can have any concrete, full idea of what pure mathematical research is like or of the profusion of insights that can be obtained from it. The same sort of penetrating work, for which no general characterization can adequately substitute, is required if one is to understand phenomenological science concretely. That the work is worthwhile can readily be seen from the unique position of phenomenology with regard to philosophy on the one hand and psychology on the other. Pure phenomenology's tremendous significance for any concrete grounding of *psychology* is clear from the very beginning. If all consciousness is subject to essential laws in a manner similar to that in which spatial reality is subject to mathematical laws, then these essential laws will be of most fertile significance in investigating facts of the conscious life of human and brute animals.

So far as philosophy is concerned, it is enough to point out that all ratio-theoretical [*vernunft-theoretischen*] problems, the problems involved in the so-called *critique* of theoretical, valuational, and practical reason, are concerned *entirely* with *essential coherencies* prevailing between theoretical, axiological, or practical Objectivity and the consciousness in which it is immanently constituted. It is easy to demonstrate that ratio-theoretical problems can be formulated with scientific rigor and can then be solved in their systematic coherence only on the soil of phenomenologically pure consciousness and within the framework of a pure phenomenology. The critique of reason and all philosophical problems along with it can be put on the course of strict science by a kind of research that draws intuitively upon what is given phenomenologically but not by thinking of the kind that plays out value concepts, a game played with constructions far removed from intuition.

Philosophers, as things now stand, are all too fond of offering criticism from on high instead of studying and understanding things from within. They often behave toward phenomenology as Berkeley—otherwise a brilliant philosopher and psychologist—behaved two centuries ago toward the then newly established infinitesimal calculus. He thought that he could prove, by his logically sharp but superficial criticism, this sort of mathematical analysis to be a completely groundless extravagance, a vacuous game played with empty abstractions. It is utterly beyond doubt that phenomenology, new and most fertile, will overcome all resistance and stupidity and will enjoy enormous development, just as the infinitesimal mathematics that was so alien to its contemporaries did, and just as exact physics, in opposition to the brilliantly obscure natural philosophy of the Renaissance, has done since the time of Galileo.

On the Misfortunes of Edmund Husserl's
Encyclopaedia Britannica Article
"Phenomenology"*

HERBERT SPIEGELBERG

Husserl's article "Phenomenology" for the *Encyclopaedia Britannica* (or rather the semblance of it which survived the translation from his German original into English) appeared in its Fourteenth Edition of 1929, to remain there in subsequent editions until 1955, when it was replaced for some ten years by a new article written by Professor J. N. Findlay.

About the original invitation to Husserl to contribute such an article very little is known today. No correspondence has survived in the Husserl Archives at Louvain or in those of the *Britannica*. One might suspect some connection with Husserl's four lectures at the University of London in 1922.[1] But the interval seems suspiciously long, especially since Husserl does not seem to have started writing until 1927.

The preparation of Husserl's German text went through the probably unmatched number of four surviving drafts. Their history has been traced in some detail by the editor of three of them, Walter Biemel, for volume 9 (1962) of *Husserliana*, where they appeared as supplementary texts to Husserl's lectures on "Phenomenological Psychology" of 1925.[2] The reason for this unusual amount of care was apparently not so much the challenge of the assignment as the

*Reprinted with permission from *Journal of the British Society for Phenomenology* 2 (1971): 74–76.

chance for a joint production with Martin Heidegger, at that time still in Marburg, a hope which, however, completely miscarried, as Husserl himself put it in retrospect in a letter on January 6, 1931, to Alexander Pfänder. For nothing of Heidegger's draft for version II was absorbed in the final text.[3] A detailed study of the four versions would be of considerable interest in itself, but is irrelevant to this occasion, since only one such version seems to have been used by the translator.

Until 1962 only the English text, printed in the *Britannica* itself, was known, which was republished in 1960 in an anthology by Roderick M. Chisholm,[4] where, however, one revealing correction was made based on "information by Professor H. L. Van Breda" in the last sentence: the replacement of 'phenomenalists' (as the addressees of phenomenology) by 'phenomenologists', although the word 'phenomenalist' actually occurs in the original of Christopher V. Salmon's "translation."[5]

Biemel in his preface characterized this translation as "very free." However, I must confess that when I personally began to compare the four versions of the German original with the English text (which had always puzzled me), I found myself unable to decide which one could have possibly served as the model for the eventual product. However, it is more than likely that Salmon worked from the "fourth last version"[6]; at any rate, this is what Biemel assumes.[7] In fact Husserl's remaining original copy states on the outside of the folder: "The bracketings are mere indications for abridgments proposed in order to make it possible to keep within the prescribed narrow space of the English article (Salmon)."

The spatial restriction, of which Husserl seems to have been insufficiently aware in composing his German text, may well have been the major explanation for what happened to the article. About the scope of this restriction we now have at least indirect information through a Freiburg diary kept by W. R. Boyce Gibson, known to readers of Husserl chiefly through his translation of the *Ideas*. For on November 19, when Husserl lent Boyce Gibson the manuscript of the original, he also told him that Salmon had to reduce it from 7,000 (German) to 4,000 (English) words, a telescoping which, considering the ratio of words in German and English, meant cutting the article at least in half.[8] But even this next to impossible assignment is no full explanation for what happened between the German original and the English translation. To trace this in detail would be an interesting task, but not in the present context. However, what must at least be mentioned is the fact that the fifteen sub-headings of the German text dropped out completely in the translation and that even Part III, entitled "Transcendental Phenomenology and Philosophy," disappeared, although Part II ("Transcendental Phenomenology") now shows a single sub-heading toward the end, entitled "Phenomenology, the Universal Science." In Part I ("Phenomenological Psychology") there was also one new sub-heading halfway through, "Phenomenological-psychological and Eidetic Reductions." The text itself contains formulations which cannot be tracked down to the original, among them such amazing statements as that the goal of phenomenological psychology is "comprehending the being of the soul." Perhaps the worst case is the following new sentence: "The 'I' and the 'we', which we apprehend, presuppose a hidden 'I' and 'we' to whom they are 'present'." This sentence is reprinted in italics in *Realism and the Background of Phe-*

nomenology and repeated in the "Editor's Introduction"[9] by Chisholm, who, however, was not responsible for this change. Besides, the "transcendental" is characterized as "that most general, subjectivity, which makes the world and its 'souls' and confirms them." There is no basis in the original for these interpretive substitutions.

A particularly dangerous departure from Husserl's original occurs in Salmon's rendering of his definition of phenomenology at the very beginning of the article, as revealed by a comparison of the new translation with the following start in the *Britannica* version:

Phenomenology denotes a new, descriptive, philosophical method, which, since the concluding years of the last century, has established (1) an a priori psychological discipline, able to provide the only secure basis on which a strong empirical psychology can be built, and (2) a universal philosophy, which can supply an organum for the methodical revision of all the sciences.

I merely want to point out that this "translation" reverses the order of phenomenological philosophy and phenomenological psychology; that it implies that the new a priori psychology has been already "established" since before 1900; that the new method has also established a "universal philosophy," *i.e.,* presumably an all-comprehensive system, and not only "the tool for a rigorously scientific philosophy"; that it supplies also a tool for the "methodical revision of all the sciences," not only "makes possible a methodical reform."

One may sympathize with the plight of the space-pressed would-be translator, especially in the later sections of the text. But one might at least have hoped for some indication that the author of this text was no longer "E.Hu." as the signature under the article still implied, but rather that the reader was confronted with free and at times wild paraphrases of Husserl's own text. However, this may well have been impossible under the editorial rules of the *Britannica*.

Nothing seems to be known about the aftermath of the publication. Whether Husserl himself saw the published article, either in a complete set of the *Britannica* or in a reprint, is no longer ascertainable. All that can now be found in the Husserl Archives is the dedicated personal copy of Salmon's typescript without reading marks.

There are, however, some strange pieces of negative evidence for Husserl's final response. When at the end of his "Author's Preface to the English Edition" of his *Ideas* Husserl suggested additional readings, he failed to list the *Encyclopaedia* article, his only other published text in English, on which he had spent so much time and labour four years before. Only W. R. Boyce Gibson mentioned this article in his own "Translator's Preface" in introducing C. V. Salmon, its translator, as his helper. Nor am I familiar with any other mention of this article in Husserl's later writings, letters (except the one to Pfänder) and conversations, including those with Dorion Cairns (unpublished). Clearly, Husserl did not consider the final result of his effort a success.

Unfortunately he had ample reasons. But now, thanks to the labours of Prof. Richard E. Palmer, Husserl can at last speak to the Anglo-American readers he had in mind without the Procrustean restrictions of space-conscious word counters and paraphrasers. At least in this piece, in contrast to the London lectures, Husserl did refer to the British empiricists as pacemakers for transcendental phenomenology. It remains to be seen whether the unabridged and faithfully rendered article can now speak to the condition of his readers. It is certainly the concisest introduction to phenomenology he ever prepared and the one on which he worked hardest. It is also the first piece he wrote for publication in the Anglo-American world through its most respected reference work.

NOTES

1. See Herbert Spiegelberg, "Husserl in England: Facts and Lessons," pages 54–66 below.

2. See Walter Biemel, "Einleitung des Herausgebers," *Husserliana* 9: xv. See also Biemel, "Husserl's *Encyclopaedia Britannica* Article and Heidegger's Remarks Thereon," in Frederick Elliston and Peter McCormick, eds., *Husserl: Expositions and Appraisals* (Notre Dame, Indiana: University of Notre Dame Press, 1977) pp. 286–303; and Herbert Spiegelberg, *The Phenomenological Movement*, 2nd ed. (The Hague: Nijhoff, 1965), pp. 279–81. For other information see Roman Ingarden, *Briefe an Roman Ingarden*, Phaenomenologica 25 (The Hague: Nijhoff, 1968), pp. 153ff. Ingarden, whom Husserl asked to criticize the third and fourth versions, seems to have made merely technical suggestions.

3. There is now a translation of this version under the title "Martin Heidegger: The Idea of Phenomenology" by John N. Deely and Joseph A. Novak in *The New Scholasticism* 44 (1970): 325–44.

4. Roderick M. Chisholm, ed., *Realism and the Background of Phenomenology* (New York: Free Press, 1960), pp. 118–28.

5. Salmon, M.A. Oxon, Ph.D. Freiburg, died in 1960 and could no longer be contacted about this and related matters. For other information about him and his relation to Husserl, see Herbert Spiegelberg's notes to W. R. Boyce Gibson, "From Husserl to Heidegger: Excerpts from a 1928 Freiburg Diary by W. R. Boyce Gibson," *Journal of the British Society for Phenomenology* 2 (1971): 58–83.

6. *Phänomenologische Psychologie*, pp. 277–301.

7. *Ibid.*, p. 592.

8. Gibson, "From Husserl to Heidegger," p. 71.

9. Chisholm, ed., *Realism*, p. 21.

"Phenomenology," Edmund Husserl's Article for the *Encyclopaedia Britannica** (1927)

REVISED TRANSLATION BY RICHARD E. PALMER**

Introduction

I.   Pure Psychology: Its Field of Experience, Its Method and Its Function

1. Pure natural science and pure psychology.
2. The purely psychical in self-experience and community experience. The universal description of intentional experiences.
3. The self-contained field of the purely psychical. — Phenomenological reduction and true inner experience.
4. Eidetic reduction and phenomenological psychology as an eidetic science.
5. The fundamental function of pure phenomenological psychology for an exact empirical psychology.

II.   Phenomenological Psychology and Transcendental Phenomenology

6. Descartes' transcendental turn and Locke's psychologism.
7. The transcendental problem.
8. The solution by psychologism as a transcendental circle.
9. The transcendental-phenomenological reduction and the semblance of transcendental duplication.
10. Pure psychology as a propaedeutic to transcendental phenomenology.

III.   Transcendental Phenomenology and Philosophy as Universal Science with Absolute Foundations

11. Transcendental phenomenology as ontology.
12. Phenomenology and the crisis in the foundations of the exact sciences.
13. The phenomenological gounding of the factual sciences in relation to empirical phenomenology.
14. Complete phenomenology as all-embracing philosophy.
15. The "ultimate and highest" problems as phenomenological.
16. The phenomenological resolution of all philosophical antitheses.

*Reprinted with permission from *Journal of the British Society for Phenomenology* 2 (1971): 77–90.

**The translator gratefully acknowledges the help he received from Professor Herbert Spiegelberg (Washington University, St. Louis, Missouri) and Professor Gisela Hess (MacMurray College, Jacksonville, Illinois) in the preparation of the original translation for *JBSP*. For the present edition, the translator has revised his earlier effort in accordance with corrections received from various sources. Principally, the translator wishes to thank Herbert Spiegelberg for his continued help, as well as Karl Schuhmann, who forwarded a marked-up copy of the translation, which he had used as the text for a seminar in parallel with the German original. Under the impetus of the criticisms of Professor Schuhmann, the translator has reviewed the entire text and devised many new renderings (not always those suggested by Professor Schuhmann) which he hopes have improved the present translation.

Introduction

The term 'phenomenology' designates two things: a new kind of descriptive method which made a breakthrough in philosophy at the turn of the century, and an a priori science derived from it; a science which is intended to supply the basic instrument (*Organon*) for a rigorously scientific philosophy and, in its consequent application, to make possible a methodical reform of all the sciences. Together with this philosophical phenomenology, but not yet separated from it, however, there also came into being a new psychological discipline parallel to it in method and content: the a priori pure or "phenomenological" psychology, which raises the reformational claim to being the basic methodological foundation on which alone a scientifically rigorous empirical psychology can be established. An outline of this psychological phenomenology, standing nearer to our natural thinking, is well suited to serve as a preliminary step that will lead up to an understanding of philosophical phenomenology.

I. Pure Psychology: Its Field of Experience, Its Method, and Its Function

1. Pure Natural Science and Pure Psychology.

Modern psychology is the science dealing with the "psychical" in the concrete context of spatio-temporal realities, being in some way so to speak what occurs in nature as egoical, with all that inseparably belongs to it as psychic processes like experiencing, thinking, feeling, willing, as capacity, and as *habitus*. Experience presents the psychical as merely a stratum of human and animal being. Accordingly, psychology is seen as a branch of the more concrete science of anthropology, or rather zoology. Animal realities are first of all, at a basic level, physical realities. As such, they belong in the closed nexus of relationships in physical nature, in Nature meant in the primary and most pregnant sense as the universal theme of a pure natural science; that is to say, an objective science of nature which in deliberate one-sidedness excludes all extra-physical predications of reality. The scientific investigation of the bodies of animals fits within this area. By contrast, however, if the psychic aspect of the animal world is to become the topic of investigation, the first thing we have to ask is how far, in parallel with the pure science of nature, a pure psychology is possible. Obviously, purely psychological research can be done to a certain extent. To it we owe the basic concepts of the psychical according to the properties essential and specific to it. These concepts must be incorporated into the others, into the psychophysical foundational concepts of psychology.

It is by no means clear from the very outset, however, how far the idea of a pure psychology—as a psychological discipline sharply separate in itself and as a real parallel to the pure physical science of nature—has a meaning that is legitimate and necessary of realization.

2. The Purely Psychical in Self-experience and Community Experience. The Universal Description of Intentional Experiences.

To establish and unfold this guiding idea, the first thing that is necessary is a clarification of what is peculiar to experience, and especially to the pure experience of the psychical—and specifically the purely psychical that experience reveals, which is to become the theme of a pure psychology. It is natural and appropriate that precedence will be accorded to the most immediate types of experience, which in each case reveal to us our own psychic being.

Focusing our experiencing gaze on our own psychic life necessarily takes place as reflection, as a turning about of a glance which had previously been directed elsewhere. Every experience can be subject to such reflection, as can indeed every manner in which we occupy ourselves with any real or ideal objects—for instance, thinking, or in the modes of feeling and will, valuing and striving. So when we are fully engaged in conscious activity, we focus exclusively on the specific thing, thoughts, values, goals, or means involved, but not on the psychical experience as such, in which these things are known *as* such. Only reflection reveals this to us. Through reflection, instead of grasping simply the matter straight-out—the values, goals, and instrumentalities—we grasp the corresponding subjective experiences in which we become "conscious" of them, in which (in the broadest sense) they "appear." For this reason, they are called "phenomena," and their most general essential character is to exist as the "consciousness-of" or "appearance-of" the specific things, thoughts (judged states of affairs, grounds, conclusions), plans, decisions, hopes, and so forth. This relatedness [of the appearing to the object of appearance] resides in the meaning of all expressions in the vernacular languages which relate to psychic experience —for instance, perception *of* something, recalling *of* something, thinking *of* something, hoping *for* something, fearing something, striving *for* something, deciding on something, and so on. If this realm of what we call "phenomena" proves to be the possible field for a pure psychological discipline related exclusively to phenomena, we can understand the designation of it as *phenomenological psychology*. The terminological expression, deriving from Scholasticism, for designating the basic character of being as consciousness, as consciousness of something, is *intentionality*. In unreflective holding of some object or other in consciousness, we are turned or directed towards it: our *"intentio"* goes out towards it. The phenomenological reversal of our gaze shows that this "being directed" [*Gerichtetsein*] is really an immanent essential feature of the respective experiences involved; they are "intentional" experiences.

An extremely large and variegated number of kinds of special cases fall within the general scope of this concept. Consciousness of something is not an empty holding of something; every phenomenon has its own total form of intention [*intentionale Gesamtform*], but at the same time it has a structure, which in intentional analysis leads always again to components which are themselves also intentional. So for example in starting from a perception of something (for example, a die), phenomenological reflection leads to a multiple and yet synthetically unified intentionality. There are continually varying differences in the modes of appearing of objects, which are caused by the changing of "orientation"—of right and left, nearness and farness, with the consequent differences in perspective involved. There are further differences in appearance between the "actually seen front" and the "unseeable" [*"unanschaulichen"*] and relatively "undetermined" reverse side, which is nevertheless "meant along with it." Observing the flux of modes of appearing and the manner of their "synthesis," one finds that every phase and portion [of the flux] is already in itself "consciousness-of"—but in such a manner that there is formed within the constant emerging of new phases the synthetically unified awareness that this is one and the same object. The intentional structure of any process of perception has its fixed essential type [*seine feste Wesenstypik*], which must necessarily be realized in all its extraordinary complexity just in order for a physical body simply to be perceived as such. If this same thing is intuited in other modes—for example, in the modes of recollection, fantasy or pictorial representation— to some extent the whole intentional content of the perception comes back, but all aspects peculiarly transformed to correspond to that mode. This applies similarly for every other category of psychic process: the judging, valuing, striving consciousness is not an empty having knowledge of the specific judgments, values, goals, and means. Rather, these constitute themselves, with fixed essential forms corresponding to each process, in a flowing intentionality. For psychology, the universal task presents itself: to investigate systematically the elementary intentionalities, and from out of these [unfold] the typical forms of intentional processes, their possible variants, their syntheses to new forms, their structural composition, and from this advance towards a descriptive knowledge of the totality of mental process, towards a comprehensive type of a life of the psyche [*Gesamttypus eines Lebens der Seele*]. Clearly, the consistent carrying out of this task will produce knowledge which will have validity far beyond the psychologist's own particular psychic existence.

Psychic life is accessible to us not only through self-experience but also through experience of others. This novel source of experience offers us not only what matches our self-experience but also what is new, inasmuch as, in terms of consciousness and indeed as experience, it establishes the differences between own and other, as well as the properties peculiar to the life of a community. At just this point there arises the task of also making phenomenologically understandable the mental life of the community, with all the intentionalities that pertain to it.

3. The Self-contained Field of the Purely Psychical.—Phenomenological Reduction and True Inner Experience.

The idea of a phenomenological psychology encompasses the whole range of tasks arising out of the experience of self and the experience of the other founded on it. But it is not yet clear whether phenomenological experience, followed through in exclusiveness and consistency, really provides us with a kind of closed-off field of being, out of which a science can grow which is exclusively focused on it and completely free of everything psychophysical. Here [in fact] difficulties do exist, which have hidden from psychologists the possibility of such a purely phenomenological psychology even after Brentano's discovery of intentionality. They are relevant already to the construction of a really pure self-experience, and therewith of a really pure psychic datum. A particular method of access is required for the pure phenomenological field: the method of "phenomenological reduction." This *method of "phenomenological reduction"* is thus the foundational method of pure psychology and the presupposition of all its specifically theoretical methods. Ultimately the great difficulty rests on the way that already the self-experience of the psychologist is everywhere intertwined with external experience, with that of extra-psychical real things. The experienced "exterior" does not belong to one's intentional interiority, although certainly the experience itself belongs to it as experience—*of* the exterior. Exactly this same thing is true of every kind of awareness directed at something out there in the world. A consistent epoche of the phenomenologist is required, if he wishes to break through to his own consciousness as pure phenomenon or as the totality of his purely mental processes. That is to say, in the accomplishment of phenomenological reflection he must inhibit every co-accomplishment of objective positing produced in unreflective consciousness, and therewith [inhibit] every judgmental drawing-in of the world as it "exists" for him straightforwardly. The specific experience of this house, this body, of a world as such, is and remains, however, according to its own essential content and thus inseparably, experience "*of* this house," this body, this world; this is so for every mode of consciousness which is directed towards an object. It is, after all, quite impossible to describe an intentional experience—even if illusionary, an invalid judgment, or the like —without at the same time describing the object of that consciousness *as* such. The universal epoche of the world as it becomes known in consciousness (the "putting it in brackets") shuts out from the phenomenological field the world as it exists for the subject in simple absoluteness; its place, however, is taken by the world as given in *consciousness* (perceived, remembered, judged, thought, valued, etc.)—the world *as such*, the "world in brackets," or in other words, the world, or rather individual things in the world as absolute, are replaced by the respective meaning of each in *consciousness* [*Bewusstseinssinn*] in its various modes (perceptual meaning, recollected meaning, and so on).

With this, we have clarified and supplemented our initial determination of the phenomenological experience and its sphere of being. In going back from the unities posited in the natural attitude to the manifold of modes of consciousness in which they appear, the unities, as inseparable from these multiplicities—but as "bracketed"—are also to be reckoned among what is purely psychical, and always specifically in the appearance-character in which they present themselves. The method of phenomenological reduction (to the pure "phenomenon," the purely psychical) accordingly consists (1) in the methodical and rigorously consistent epoche of every objective positing in the psychic sphere, both of the individual phenomenon and of the whole psychic field in general;

and (2) in the methodically practiced seizing and describing of the multiple "appearances" as appearances of their objective units and these units as units of component meanings accruing to them each time in their appearances. With this is shown a two-fold direction—the *noetic* and *noematic* of phenomenological description. Phenomenological experience in the methodical form of the phenomenological reduction is the only genuine "inner experience" in the sense meant by any well-grounded science of psychology. In its own nature lies manifest the possibility of being carried out continuously in infinitum with methodical preservation of purity. The reductive method is transferred from self-experience to the experience of others insofar as there can be applied to the envisaged [*vergegen-wärtigten*] mental life of the Other the corresponding bracketing and description according to the subjective "How" of its appearance and what is appearing ("noesis" and "noema"). As a further consequence, the community that is experienced in community experience is reduced not only to the mentally particularized intentional fields but also to the unity of the community life that connects them all together, the community mental life in its phenomenological purity (intersubjective reduction). Thus results the perfect expansion of the genuine psychological concept of "inner experience."

To every mind there belongs not only the unity of its multiple *intentional life-process* [*intentionalen Lebens*] with all its inseparable unities of sense directed towards the "object." There is also, inseparable from this life-process, the experiencing *I-subject* as the identical *I-pole* giving a centre for all specific intentionalities, and as the carrier of all habitualities growing out of this life-process. Likewise, then, the reduced inter-subjectivity, in pure form and concretely grasped, is a community of pure "persons" acting in the intersubjective realm of the pure life of consciousness.

4. Eidetic Reduction and Phenomenological Psychology as an Eidetic Science.

To what extent does the unity of the field of phenomenological experience assure the possibility of a psychology exclusively based on it, thus a pure phenomenological psychology? It does not automatically assure an empirically pure science of *facts* from which everything psychophysical is abstracted. But this situation is quite different with an a priori science. In it, every self-enclosed field of possible experience permits *eo ipso* the all-embracing transition from the factual to the essential form, the *eidos*. So here, too. If the phenomenological actual fact as such becomes irrelevant; if, rather, it serves only as an example and as the foundation for a free but intuitive variation of the factual mind and communities of minds *into* the a priori possible (thinkable) ones; and if now the theoretical eye directs itself to the necessarily enduring invariant in the variation; then there will arise with this systematic way of proceeding a realm of its own, of the "a priori." There emerges therewith the eidetically necessary typical form, the *eidos;* this *eidos* must manifest itself throughout all the potential forms of mental being in particular cases, must be present in all the synthetic combinations and self-enclosed wholes, if it is to be at all "thinkable," that is, intuitively conceivable. Phenomenological psychology in this manner undoubtedly must be established as an "eidetic phenomenology"; it is then exclusively directed toward the invariant essential forms. For instance, the phenomenology of perception of bodies will not be (simply) a report on the factually occurring perceptions or those to be expected; rather it will be the presentation of invariant structural systems without which perception of a body and a synthetically concordant multiplicity of perceptions of one and the same body as such would be unthinkable. If the phenomenological reduction contrived a means of access to the phenomenon of real and also potential inner experience, the method founded in it of "eidetic reduction" provides the means of access to the invariant essential structures of the total sphere of pure mental process.

5. The Fundamental Function of Pure Phenomenological Psychology for an Exact Empirical Psychology.

A phenomenological pure psychology is

absolutely necessary as the foundation for the building up of an "exact" empirical psychology, which since its modern beginnings has been sought according to the model of the exact pure sciences of physical nature. The fundamental meaning of "exactness" in this natural science lies in its being founded on an a priori form-system—each part unfolded in a special theory (pure geometry, a theory of pure time, theory of motion, etc.) —for a Nature conceivable in these terms. It is through the utilization of this a priori form-system for factual nature that the vague, inductive empirical approach attains to a share of eidetic necessity [*Wesensnotwendigkeit*] and empirical natural science itself gains a new sense—that of working out for all vague concepts and rules their indispensable basis of rational concepts and laws. As essentially differentiated as the methods of natural science and psychology may remain, there does exist a necessary common ground: that psychology, like every science, can only draw its "rigour" ("exactness") from the rationality of the essence." The uncovering of the a priori set of types without which "I," "we," "consciousness," "the objectivity of consciousness," and therewith mental being as such would be inconceivable—with all the essentially necessary and essentially possible forms of synthesis which are inseparable from the idea of a whole comprised of individual and communal mental life—produces a prodigious field of exactness that can immediately (without the intervening link of *Limes-Idealisierung**) be carried over into research on the psyche. Admittedly, the phenomenological a priori does not comprise the complete a priori of psychology, inasmuch as the psychophysical relationship as such has its own a priori. It is clear, however, that this a priori will presuppose that of a pure phenomenological psychology, just as on the other side it will presuppose the pure a priori of a physical (and specifically the organic) Nature as such.

The systematic construction of a phenomenological pure psychology demands:

(1) The description of the peculiarities

universally belonging to the essence of intentional mental process, which includes the most general law of synthesis: every connection of consciousness with consciousness gives rise to a consciousness.

(2) The exploration of single forms of intentional mental process which in essential necessity generally must or can present themselves in the mind; in unity with this, also the exploration of the syntheses they are members of for a typology of their essences: both those that are discrete and those continuous with others, both the finitely closed and those continuing into open infinity.

(3) The showing and eidetic description [*Wesensdeskription*] of the total structure [*Gesamtgestalt*] of mental life as such; in other words, a description of the essential character [*Wesensart*] of a universal "stream of consciousness."

(4) The term "I" designates a new direction for investigation (still in abstraction from the social sense of this word) in reference to the essence-forms of "habituality"; in other words, the "I" as subject of lasting beliefs or thought-tendencies—"persuasions" —(convictions about being, value-convictions, volitional decisions, and so on), as the personal subject of habits, of trained knowing, of certain character qualities.

Throughout all this, the "static" description of essences ultimately leads to problems of genesis, and to an all-pervasive genesis that governs the whole life and development of the personal "I" according to eidetic laws [*eidetischen Gesetzen*]. So on top of the first "static phenomenology" will be constructed in higher levels a dynamic or genetic phenomenology. As the first and founding genesis it will deal with that of passivity—genesis in which the "I" does not actively participate. Here lies the new task, an all-embracing eidetic phenomenology of association, a latter-day rehabilitation of David Hume's great discovery, involving an account of the a priori genesis out of which a real spatial world constitutes itself for the mind in habitual acceptance. There follows from this the eidetic theory dealing with the development of personal habituality, in which the purely mental "I" within the invariant structural forms of consciousness exists as personal "I" and is conscious of itself

*By this expression (*Limes-Idealisierung*), Husserl would seem to mean idealisation to exact (mathematical) limits.

in habitual continuing being and as always being transformed. For further investigation, there offers itself an especially interconnected stratum at a higher level: the static and then the genetic phenomenology of reason.

II. Phenomenological Psychology and Transcendental Phenomenology

6. *Descartes' Transcendental Turn and Locke's Psychologism.*

The idea of a purely phenomenological psychology does not have just the function described above, of reforming empirical psychology. For deeply rooted reasons, it can also serve as a preliminary step for laying open the essence of a transcendental phenomenology. Historically, this idea too did not grow out of the peculiar needs of psychology proper. Its history leads us back to John Locke's notable basic work, and the significant development in Berkeley and Hume of the impetus it contained. Already Locke's restriction to the purely subjective was determined by extra-psychological interests: psychology here stood in the service of the transcendental problem awakened through Descartes. In Descartes' *Meditations,* the thought that had become the guiding one for "first philosophy" was that all of "reality," and finally the whole world of what exists and is so *for us,* exists only as the presentational content of our presentations, as meant in the best case and as evidently reliable in our own cognitive life. This is the motivation for all transcendental problems, genuine or false. Descartes' method of doubt was the first method of exhibiting "transcendental subjectivity," and his *ego cogito* led to its first conceptual formulation. In Locke, Descartes' transcendentally pure *mens* is changed into the "human mind," whose systematic exploration through inner experience Locke tackled out of a transcendental-philosophical interest. And so he is the founder of *psychologism—* as a transcendental philosophy founded *through* a psychology of inner experience. The fate of scientific philosophy hangs on the radical overcoming of every trace of psychologism, an overcoming which not only

exposes the fundamental absurdity of psychologism but also does justice to its transcendentally significant kernel of truth. The sources of its continuous historical power are drawn from out of a double sense [an ambiguity] of all the concepts of the subjective, which arises as soon as the transcendental question is broached. The uncovering of this ambiguity involves [us in the need for] at once the sharp separation, and at the time the parallel treatment, of pure phenomenological psychology (as the scientifically rigorous form of a psychology purely of inner experience) and transcendental phenomenology as true transcendental philosophy. At the same time this will justify our advance discussion of psychology as the means of access to true philosophy. We will begin with a clarification of the true transcendental problem, which in the initially obscure unsteadiness of its sense makes one so very prone (and this applies already to Descartes) to shunt it off to a side track.

7. *The Transcendental Problem.*

To the essential sense of the transcendental problem belongs its all-inclusiveness, in which it places in question the world and all the sciences investigating it. It arises within a general reversal of that "natural attitude" in which everyday life as a whole as well as the positive sciences operate. In it [the natural attitude] the world is for us the self-evidently existing universe of realities which are continuously before us in unquestioned givenness. So this is the general field of our practical and theoretical activities. As soon as the theoretical interest abandons this natural attitude and in a general turning around of our regard directs itself to the life of consciousness—*in which* the "world" is for us precisely that, the world which is present *to us*—we find ourselves in a new cognitive attitude [or situation]. Every sense which the world has for us (this we now become aware of), both its general indeterminate sense and its sense determining itself according to the particular realities, is, within the internality of our own perceiving, imagining, thinking, valuing life-process, a conscious sense, and a sense which is formed in subjective genesis. Every acceptance of something as validly existing is effected within us ourselves; and every evidence in experience and theory that establishes it, is operative in us ourselves, habitually and continuously motivating us. This [principle] concerns the world in every determination, even those that are self-evident: that what belongs *in and for itself* to the world, is how it is, whether or not I, or whoever, become by chance aware of it or not. Once the world in this full universality has been related to the subjectivity of consciousness, in whose living consciousness it makes its appearance precisely as "the" world in its varying sense, then its whole mode of being acquires a dimension of unintelligibility, or rather of questionableness. This "making an appearance" [*Auftreten*], this being-for-us of the world as only subjectively having come to acceptance and only subjectively brought and to be brought to well-grounded evident presentation, requires clarification. Because of its empty generality, one's first awakening to the relatedness of the world to consciousness gives no understanding of *how* the varied life of consciousness, barely discerned and sinking back into obscurity, accomplishes such functions: how it, so to say, manages in its immanence that something which manifests itself can present itself *as* something existing in itself, and not only as something meant but as something authenticated in concordant experience. Obviously the problem extends to every kind of "ideal" world and its "being-in-itself" (for example, the world of pure numbers, or of "truths in themselves"). Unintelligibility is felt as a particularly telling affront to *our* very mode of being [as human beings]. For obviously we are the ones (individually and in community) in whose conscious life-process the real world which is present for us as such gains sense and acceptance. As human creatures, however, we ourselves are supposed to belong to the world. When we start with the sense of the world [*weltlichen Sinn*] given with our mundane existing, we are thus again referred back to ourselves and our conscious life-process as that wherein for us this sense is first formed. Is there conceivable here or anywhere another way of elucidating [it] than to interrogate consciousness itself and the "world" that becomes known in it?

For it is precisely as meant by us, and from nowhere else than in us, that it has gained and can gain its sense and validity.

Next we take yet another important step, which will raise the "transcendental" problem (having to do with the being-sense of "transcendent" relative to consciousness) up to the final level. It consists in recognizing that the relativity of consciousness referred to just now applies not just to the brute fact of *our* world but in eidetic necessity to every conceivable world whatever. For if we vary our factual world in free fantasy, carrying it over into random conceivable worlds, we are implicitly varying *ourselves* whose environment the world is: we each change ourselves into a possible subjectivity, whose environment would always have to be the world that was thought of, as a world of its [the subjectivity's] possible experiences, possible theoretical evidences, possible practical life. But obviously this variation leaves untouched the pure ideal worlds of the kind which have their existence in eidetic universality, which are in their essence invariable; it becomes apparent, however, from the possible variability of the subject knowing such identical essences (*Identitäten*), that their cognizability, and thus their intentional relatedness does not simply have to do with our de facto subjectivity. With the eidetic formulation of the problem, the kind of research into consciousness that is demanded is the eidetic.

8. *The Solution by Psychologism as a Transcendental Circle.*

Our distillation of the idea of a phenomenologically pure psychology has demonstrated the possibility of uncovering by consistent phenomenological reduction what belongs to the conscious subject's own essence in eidetic, universal terms, according to all its possible forms. This includes those forms of reason [itself] which establish and authenticate validity, and with this it includes all forms of potentially appearing worlds, both those validated in themselves through concordant experiences and those determined by theoretical truth. Accordingly, the systematic carrying through of this phenomenological psychology seems to comprehend in itself from the outset in foundational (precisely, eidetic) universality the whole of correlation research on being and consciousness; thus it would seem to be the [proper] locus for all transcendental elucidation. On the other hand, we must not overlook the fact that psychology in all its empirical and eidetic disciplines remains a "positive science," a science operating within the natural attitude, in which the simply present world is the thematic ground. What it wishes to explore are the psyches and communities of psyches that are [actually] to be found in the world. Phenomenological reduction serves as psychological only to the end that it gets at the psychical aspect of animal realities in its pure own essential specificity and its pure own specific essential interconnections. Even in eidetic research [then], the psyche retains the sense of being which belongs in the realm of what is present in the world; it is merely related to possible real worlds. Even as eidetic phenomenologist, the psychologist is transcendentally naive: he takes the possible "minds" ("I"-subjects) completely according to the relative sense of the word as those of men and animals considered purely and simply as present in a possible spatial world. If, however, we allow the transcendental interest to be decisive, instead of the natural-worldly, then psychology as a whole receives the stamp of what is transcendentally problematic; and thus it can by no means supply the premises for transcendental philosophy. The subjectivity of consciousness, which, as psychic being, is its theme, cannot be that to which we go back in our questioning into the transcendental.

In order to arrive at an evident clarity at this decisive point, the thematic sense of the transcendental question is to be kept sharply in view, and we must try to judge how, in keeping with it, the regions of the problematical and unproblematical are set apart. The theme of transcendental philosophy is a concrete and systematic elucidation of those multiple intentional relationships, which in conformity with their essences belong to any possible world whatever as the surrounding world of a corresponding possible subjectivity, for which it [the world] would be the one present as practically and theoretically accessible. In regard to all the objects and

structures present in the world for these subjectivities, this accessibility involves the regulations of its possible conscious life, which in their typology will have to be uncovered. [Among] such categories are "lifeless things," as well as men and animals with the internalities of their psychic life. From this starting point the full and complete being-sense of a possible world, in general and in regard to all its constitutive categories, shall be elucidated. Like every meaningful question, this transcendental question presupposes a ground of unquestioned being, in which all means of solution must be contained. This ground is here the [anonymous] subjectivity of that kind of conscious life in which a possible world, of whatever kind, is constituted as present. However, a self-evident basic requirement of any rational method is that this ground presupposed as beyond question is not confused with what the transcendental question, in its universality, puts into question. Hence the realm of this questionability includes the whole realm of the transcendentally naïve and therefore every possible world simply claimed in the natural attitude. Accordingly, all possible sciences, including all their various areas of objects, are transcendentally to be subjected to an epoche. So also psychology, and the entirety of what is considered the psychical in its sense. It would therefore be circular, a transcendental circle, to base the answer to the transcendental question on psychology, be it empirical or eidetic-phenomenological. We face at this point the paradoxical ambiguity: the subjectivity and consciousness to which the transcendental question recurs can thus really not be the subjectivity and consciousness with which psychology deals.

9. The Transcendental-Phenomenological Reduction and the Semblance of Transcendental Duplication.

Are we then supposed to be dual beings — psychological, as human objectivities in the world, the subjects of psychic life, and at the same time transcendental, as the subjects of a transcendental, world-constituting life-process? This duality can be clarified through being demonstrated with self-evidence. The psychic subjectivity, the concretely grasped "I" and "we" of ordinary conversation, is experienced in its pure psychic ownness through the method of phenomenological-psychological reduction. Modified into eidetic form it provides the ground for pure phenomenological psychology. Transcendental subjectivity, which is inquired into in the transcendental problem, and which subjectivity is presupposed in it as an existing basis, is none other than again "I myself" and "we ourselves"; not, however, as found in the natural attitude of everyday or of positive science; i.e., apperceived as components of the objectively present world before us, but rather as subjects of conscious life, in which this world and all that is present—for "us"—"makes" itself through certain apperceptions. As men, mentally as well as bodily present in the world, we are for "ourselves"; we are appearances standing within an extremely variegated intentional life-process, "our" life, in which this being on hand constitutes itself "for us" apperceptively, with its entire sense-content. The (apperceived) I and we on hand presuppose an (apperceiving) I and we, for which they are on hand, which, however, is not itself present again in the same sense. To this transcendental subjectivity we have direct access through a transcendental experience. Just as the psychic experience requires a reductive method for purity, so does the transcendental.

We would like to proceed here by introducing the *transcendental reduction* as built on the psychological reduction—as an additional part of the purification which can be performed on it any time, a purification that is once more by means of a certain epoche. This is merely a consequence of the all-embracing epoche which belongs to the sense of the transcendental question. If the transcendental relativity of every possible world demands an all-embracing bracketing, it also postulates the bracketing of pure psyches and the pure phenomenological psychology related to them. Through this bracketing they are transformed into transcendental phenomena. Thus, while the psychologist, operating within what for him is the naturally accepted world, reduces to

pure psychic subjectivity the subjectivity occurring there (but still within the world), the transcendental phenomenologist, through his absolutely all-embracing epoche, reduces this psychologically pure element to transcendental pure subjectivity, [i.e.,] to that which performs and posits within itself the apperception of the world and therein the objectivating apperception of a "psyche [belonging to] animal realities." For example, my actual current mental processes of pure perception, fantasy, and so forth, are, in the attitude of positivity, psychological givens [or data] of psychological inner experience. They are transmuted into my transcendental mental processes if through a radical epoche I posit as mere phenomena the world, including my own human existence, and now follow up the intentional life-process wherein the entire apperception "of" the world, and in particular the apperception of my mind, my psychologically real perception-processes, and so forth, are formed. The content of these processes, what is included in their own essences, remains in this fully preserved, although it is now visible as the core of an apperception practiced again and again psychologically but not previously considered. For the transcendental philosopher, who through a previous all-inclusive resolve of his will has instituted in himself the firm habituality of the transcendental "bracketing," even this "mundanization" [*Verweltlichung,* treating everything as part of the world] of consciousness which is omnipresent in the natural attitude is inhibited once and for all. Accordingly, the consistent reflection on consciousness yields him time after time transcendentally pure data, and more particularly it is intuitive in the mode of a new kind of experience, *transcendental "inner" experience.* Arisen out of the methodical transcendental epoche, this new kind of "inner" experience opens up the limitless transcendental field of being. This field of being is the parallel to the limitless psychological field, and the method of access [to its data] is the parallel to the purely psychological one, i.e., to the psychological-phenomenological reduction. And again, the transcendental I [or ego] and the transcendental community of egos, conceived in the full concretion of transcendental life are the transcendental parallel to the I and we in the customary and psychological sense, concretely conceived as mind and community of minds, with the psychological life of consciousness that pertains to them. My transcendental ego is thus evidently "different" from the natural ego, but by no means as a second, as one *separated* from it in the natural sense of the word, just as on the contrary it is by no means bound up with it or intertwined with it, in the usual sense of these words. It is just the field of transcendental self-experience (conceived in full concreteness) which in every case can, *through mere alteration of attitude,* be changed into psychological self-experience. In this transition, an identity of the I is necessarily brought about; in transcendental reflection on this transition the psychological Objectivation becomes visible as self-objectivation of the transcendental I, and so it is as if in every moment of the natural attitude the I finds itself with an apperception imposed upon it. If the parallelism of the transcendental and psychological experience-spheres has become comprehensible out of a mere alteration of attitude, as a kind of identity of the complex interpenetration of senses of being, then there also becomes intelligible the consequence that results from it, namely the same parallelism and the interpenetration of transcendental and psychological phenomenology implied in that interpenetration, whose whole theme is pure intersubjectivity, in its dual sense. Only that in this case it has to be taken into account that the purely psychic intersubjectivity, as soon as the it is subjected to the transcendental epoche, also leads to its parallel, that is, to transcendental intersubjectivity. Manifestly this parallelism spells nothing less than theoretical equivalence. Transcendental intersubjectivity is the concretely autonomous absolute existing basis [*Seinsboden*] out of which everything transcendent (and, with it, everything that belongs to the real world) obtains its existential sense as that of something which only in a relative and therewith incomplete sense is an existing thing, namely as being an intentional unity which in truth

exists from out of transcendental bestowal of sense, of harmonious confirmation, and from an habituality of lasting conviction that belongs to it by essential necessity.

10. *Pure Psychology as Propaedeutic to Transcendental Phenomenology.*

Through the elucidation of the essentially dual meaning of the subjectivity of consciousness, and also a clarification of the eidetic science to be directed to it, we begin to understand on very deep grounds the historical insurmountability of psychologism. Its power lies in an *essential transcendental semblance* which [because] undisclosed had to remain effective. Also from the clarification we have gained we begin to understand on the one hand the independence of the idea of a transcendental phenomenology, and the systematic developing of it, from the idea of a phenomenological pure psychology; and yet on the other hand the propaedeutic usefulness of the preliminary project of a pure psychology for an ascent to transcendental phenomenology, a usefulness which has guided our present discussion here. As regards this point [*i.e.,* the independence of the idea of transcendental phenomenology from a phenomenological pure psychology], clearly the phenomenological and eidetic reduction allows of being *immediately* connected to the disclosing of transcendental relativity, and in this way transcendental phenomenology springs directly out of the transcendental intuition. In point of fact, this direct path was the historical path it took. Pure phenomenological psychology as eidetic science in positivity was simply not available. As regards the second point, *i.e.,* the propaedeutic preference of the indirect approach to transcendental phenomenology through pure psychology, [it must be remembered that] the transcendental attitude involves a change of focus from one's entire form of life-style, one which goes so completely beyond all previous experiencing of life, that it must, in virtue of its absolute strangeness, needs be difficult to understand. This is also true of a transcendental science. Phenomenological psychology, although also relatively new, and in its method of intentional analysis completely novel, still has the accessibility which is possessed by all positive sciences. Once this psychology has become clear, at least according to its sharply defined idea, then only the clarification of the true sense of the transcendental-philosophical field of problems and of the transcendental reduction is required in order for it to come into possession of transcendental phenomenology as a mere reversal of its doctrinal content into transcendental terms. The basic difficulties for penetrating into the terrain of the new phenomenology fall into these two stages, namely that of understanding the true method of "inner experience," which already belongs to making possible an "exact" psychology as rational science of facts, and that of understanding the distinctive character of the transcendental methods and questioning. True, simply regarded in itself, an interest in the transcendental is the highest and ultimate scientific interest, and so it is entirely the right thing (it has been so historically and should continue) for transcendental theories to be cultivated in the autonomous, absolute system of transcendental philosophy; and to place before us, through showing the characteristic features of the natural in contrast to the transcendental attitude, the possibility within transcendental philosophy itself of reinterpreting all transcendental phenomenological doctrine [or theory] into doctrine [or theory] in the realm of natural positivity.

III. Transcendental Phenomenology and Philosophy as Universal Science with Absolute Foundations

11. Transcendental Phenomenology as Ontology.

Remarkable consequences arise when one weighs the significance of transcendental phenomenology. In its systematic development, it brings to realization the Leibnizian idea of a universal ontology as the systematic unity of all conceivable a priori sciences, but on a new foundation which overcomes "dogmatism" through the use of the transcendental phenomenological method. Phenomenology as the science of all conceivable

transcendental phenomena and especially the synthetic total structures in which alone they are concretely possible—those of the transcendental single subjects bound to communities of subjects is *eo ipso* the a priori science of all conceivable beings. But [it is the science] then not merely of the Totality of objectively existing beings, and certainly not in an attitude of natural positivity; rather, in the full concretion of being in general which derives its sense of being and its validity from the correlative intentional constitution. This also comprises the being of transcendental subjectivity itself, whose nature it is demonstrably to be constituted transcendentally in and for itself. Accordingly, a phenomenology properly carried through is the truly universal ontology, as over against the only illusory all-embracing ontology in positivity—and precisely for this reason it overcomes the dogmatic one-sidedness and hence unintelligibility of the latter, while at the same time it comprises within itself the truly legitimate content [of an ontology in positivity] as grounded originally in intentional constitution.

12. Phenomenology and the Crisis in the Foundations of the Exact Sciences.

If we consider the how of this inclusion, we find that what is meant is that every a priori is ultimately prescribed in its validity of being precisely *as* a transcendental achievement; *i.e.,* it is together with the essential structures of its constitution, with the kinds and levels of its givenness and confirmation of itself, and with the appertaining habitualities. This implies that in and through the establishment of the a priori the subjective *method* of this establishing is itself made transparent, and that for the a priori disciplines which are founded within phenomenology (for example, as mathematical sciences) there can be no "paradoxes" and no "crises of the foundations." The consequence that arises [from all this] with reference to the a priori sciences that have come into being historically and in transcendental naïveté is that only a radical, phenomenological grounding can transform them into true, methodical, fully self-justifying sciences. But precisely by this they will cease to be positive (dogmatic) sciences and become dependent branches of the one phenomenology as all-encompassing eidetic ontology.

13. The Phenomenological Grounding of the Factual Sciences in Relation to Empirical Phenomenology.

The unending task of presenting the complete universe of the a priori in its transcendental relatedness-back-to-itself [or self-reference], and thus in its self-sufficiency and perfect methodological clarity, is itself a function of the method for realization of an all-embracing and hence fully grounded science of empirical fact. Within [the realm of] positive reality [*Positivität*], genuine (relatively genuine) empirical science demands the methodical establishing-of-a-foundation [*Fundamentierung*] through a corresponding a priori science. If we take the universe of all possible empirical sciences whatever and demand a *radical* grounding that will be free from all "foundation crises," then we are led to the all-embracing a priori of the radical and that is [and must be] *phenomenological* grounding. The genuine form of an all-embracing science of fact is thus the phenomenological [form], and as this it is the universal science of the factual transcendental intersubjectivity, [resting] on the methodical foundation of eidetic phenomenology as knowledge applying to any possible transcendental subjectivity whatever. Hence *the idea of an empirical phenomenology* which follows after the eidetic is understood and justified. It is identical with the complete systematic universe of the positive sciences, provided that we think of them from the beginning as absolutely grounded methodologically through eidetic phenomenology.

14. Complete Phenomenology as All-embracing Philosophy.

Precisely through this is restored the most primordial concept of philosophy—as all-embracing science based on radical self-justification, which is alone [truly] science in the ancient Platonic and again in the Cartesian sense. Phenomenology rigorously and systematically carried out, phenomenology in the broadened sense [which we have ex-plained] above, is identical with this philosophy which encompasses all genuine knowledge. It is divided into eidetic phenomenology (or all-embracing ontology) as *first philosophy*, and as *second philosophy*, [it is] the science of the universe of *facta*, or of the transcendental intersubjectivity that synthetically comprises all *facta*. First philosophy is the universe of methods for the second, and is related back into itself for its methodological grounding.

15. The "Ultimate and Highest" Problems as Phenomenological.

In phenomenology all rational problems have their place, and thus also those that traditionally are in some special sense or other philosophically significant. For out of the absolute sources of transcendental experience, or eidetic intuiting, they first [are able to] obtain their genuine formulation and feasible means for their solution. In its universal relatedness-back-to-itself, phenomenology recognizes its particular function within a possible life of mankind [*Menschheitsleben*] at the transcendental level. It recognizes the absolute norms which are to be picked out intuitively from it [life of mankind], and also its primordial teleo-logical-tendential structure in a directedness towards disclosure of these norms and their conscious practical operation. It recognizes itself as a function of the all-embracing reflective meditation of (transcendental) humanity, [a self-examination] in the service of an all-inclusive praxis of reason; that is, in the service of striving towards the universal ideal of absolute perfection which lies in infinity, [a striving] which becomes free through [the process of] disclosure. Or, in different words it is a striving in the direction of the idea (lying in infinity) of a humanness which in action and throughout would live and move [be, exist] in truth and genuineness. It recognizes its self-reflective function [of self-examination] for the relative realization of the correlative practical idea of a genuine human life [*Menschheitsleben*] in the second sense (whose structural forms of being and whose practical norms it is to investigate), namely as one [that is] consciously and purposively directed towards this absolute idea. In short, the metaphysically teleological, the ethical, and the problems of philosophy of history, no less than, obviously, the problems of judging reason, lie within its boundary, no differently from all significant problems whatever, and all [of them] in their inmost synthetic unity and order as [being] of transcendental spirituality [*Geistigkeit*].

16. The Phenomenological Resolution of All Philosophical Antitheses.

In the systematic work of phenomenology, which progresses from intuitively given [concrete] data to heights of abstraction, the old traditional ambiguous antitheses of the philosophical standpoint are resolved—by themselves and without the arts of an argumentative dialectic, and without weak efforts and compromises: oppositions such as between rationalism (Platonism) and empiricism, relativism and absolutism, subjectivism and objectivism, ontologism and transcendentalism, psychologism and antipsychologism, positivism and metaphysics, or the teleological versus the causal interpretation of the world. Throughout all of these, [one finds] justified motives, but throughout also half-truths or impermissible absolutizing of only relatively and abstractively legitimate one-sidednesses.

Subjectivism can only be overcome by the most all-embracing and consistent subjectivism (the transcendental). In this [latter] form it is at the same time objectivism [of a deeper sort], in that it represents the claims of whatever objectivity is to be demonstrated through concordant experience, but admittedly [this is an objectivism which] also brings out its full and genuine sense, against which [sense] the supposedly realistic objectivism sins by its failure to understand transcendental constitution. *Relativism* can only be overcome through the most all-embracing relativism, that of transcendental phenomenology, which makes intelligible the relativity of all "objective" being [or existence] as transcendentally constituted; but at one with this [it makes intelligible] the most radical relativity, the relatedness of the transcendental subjectivity to itself. But just this [relatedness, subjectivity]

proves its identity to be the only possible sense of [the term] "absolute" being—over against all "objective" being that is relative to it—namely, as the "for-itself"—being of transcendental subjectivity. Likewise: *Empiricism* can only be overcome by the most universal and consistent empiricism, which puts in place of the restricted [term] "experience" of the empiricists the necessarily broadened concept of experience [inclusive] of intuition which offers original data, an intuition which in all its forms (intuition of *eidos*, apodictic self-evidence, phenomenological intuition of essence, etc.) shows the manner and form of its legitimation through phenomenological clarification. Phenomenology as eidetic is, on the other hand, rationalistic: it overcomes restrictive and dogmatic rationalism, however, through the most universal rationalism of inquiry into essences, which is related uniformly to transcendental subjectivity, to the I, consciousness, and conscious objectivity. And it is the same in reference to the other antitheses bound up with them. The tracing back of all being to the transcendental subjectivity and its constitutive intentional functions leaves open, to mention one more thing, no other way of contemplating the world than the *teleological*. And yet phenomenology also acknowledges a kernel of truth in naturalism (or rather sensationism). That is, by revealing associations as intentional phenomena, indeed as a whole basic typology of forms of passive intentional synthesis with transcendental and purely passive genesis based on essential laws, phenomenology shows Humean fictionalism to contain anticipatory discoveries; particularly in his doctrine of the origin of such fictions as thing, persisting existence, causality—anticipatory discoveries all shrouded in absurd theories.

Phenomenological philosophy regards itself in its whole method as a pure outcome of methodical intentions which already animated Greek philosophy from its beginnings; above all, however, [it continues] the still vital intentions which reach, in the two lines of rationalism and empiricism, from Descartes through Kant and German idealism into our confused present day. A pure outcome of methodical intentions means real method which allows the problems to be taken in hand and completed. In the way of true science this path is endless. Accordingly, phenomenology demands that the phenomenologist foreswear the ideal of a philosophic system and yet as a humble worker in community with others, live for a perennial philosophy [*philosophia perennis*].

3

Introduction to
"Author's Preface to the English Edition of *Ideas*"
M. VAN DE PITTE

I

Most of the first draft of Husserl's *Ideen zu einer reinen Phänomenologie und phänomenologischen Philosophie*, Book I, was produced in a very short period—six to eight weeks during the summer of 1912.[1] Husserl was inclined to carry on immediately with the projected continuation (the posthumously published Books II and III) but was obliged instead to concern himself with preparing the material that he had already completed for press. *Ideen I* appeared on schedule in the first issue of the *Jahrbuch für Philosophie und phänomenologische Forschung* (1913), although Husserl was not convinced that it alone constituted a comprehensive and persuasive account of his new philosophical science.

Husserl adopted *Ideen I* as a seminar text in the summer of 1913 and continued to use it for several semesters. Sections of the book were analyzed systematically and in painstaking detail, disclosing not only infelicitous presentations of certain notions but also what some of his distinguished Göttingen students took to be important substantive problems. His students' testimony, and also the marginalia in Husserl's copies of the text, indicate that the crucial first chapter of Part I proved to be extremely problematic. The notion of the "eidetic" (sections 1–9) was inadequately developed, and the important transitional "logical considerations" (10–17) were found to be opaquely subtle.

Almost the whole of Part II, on the "fundamental phenomenological outlook" (27–60), came in for detailed criticism. Particularly troublesome notions in Part III included the "method of clarification" (66, 68, 125), "neutralization" (113–118), "noema" (88–92, 98), and "hyle/morphe" (85). Although seminar discussions apparently did not extend so far as to include Part IV, naturally the difficulties discerned in the earlier sections affected the cogency of the position developed there.[2]

But clearly the most contentious feature of *Ideen I* proved to be Husserl's idealism. Husserl was absolutely convinced that idealism was logically entailed by the goals and methods of phenomenology. His students, however, as well as other philosophers committed to Husserl's concept of a philosophical science, could only regard the idealist element as unnecessary and unfortunate.[3] An additional problem of no less importance came to light later, when Husserl became more deeply involved in the clarification of the idea of a phenomenological psychology. It became quite apparent that in the *Ideen* the distinction between phenomenological psychology and transcendental philosophy had neither been clearly drawn nor consistently maintained. The result was a barely perceptible shifting back and forth between the two viewpoints.[4]

After his move to Freiburg in 1917, Husserl no longer used *Ideen I* as a text but continued writing critical commentary on it, although apparently without any thought toward doing a systematic revision of the whole. The second edition (1922) contained only minor emendations, and the third (1928) was little more than a new impression of the first.

A fresh opportunity to improve the text arose in July of 1928, when the Australian philosopher William Ralph Boyce Gibson wrote to Husserl proposing to do an English translation of it.[5] Husserl agreed to help and to supply a preface and epilogue. It is supposed, on the basis of notes that Husserl made, that the primary function of the preface would be to situate phenomenology within the philosophic tradition.[6] The contributions of the important "precursors"— Locke, Berkeley, Hume, Bolzano, Brentano —would be discussed in some detail. Characteristic misinterpretations, especially those of phenomenology as a subjective idealism and as a psychologism, would be confronted and shown to be groundless. The epilogue, on the other hand, would be entirely positive. It would sketch the course of phenomenology's development since the publication of *Ideen I,* paying particular attention to the possibility of an alternative approach to phenomenology through a psychological science.

After carefully combing *Ideen I* again, to isolate particularly troublesome passages, Husserl decided that a preface and epilogue, however substantial, would be insufficient. The book needed to be extensively reworked, particularly the material on the reduction, the noesis/noema distinction, and the constitutive problematic. This reworking would destroy the bases for the customary misinterpretations and of course eliminate the need for a preface and epilogue.

Husserl set about this task of revision in earnest, but his plans were not carried through. Gibson, after several months of heroic labor on the 1928 edition, was understandably reluctant to wait for a significantly altered text. He was doubtless relieved when he received a letter from Husserl, dated October 23, 1929, in which Husserl confessed that not only was he too exhausted to carry on with the project but that he had also underestimated the consequences for the rest of the text of the limited revisions he had

felt to be absolutely necessary.[7] Included with that letter was the brief preface reprinted here. Its significance lies in the fact that it is the only commentary that Husserl ever published on the *Ideen* and, more importantly, that it contains the most explicit and sustained defense of his idealism.[8]

II

The preface is primarily an overview of the terrain covered by phenomenological philosophy, together with a brief consideration of the two primary objections to the phenomenological program. Husserl begins by characterizing phenomenology as the science of transcendental subjectivity, a discipline that differs from the remainder of philosophy, and from the sciences of natural experience, in precise and nonmysterious ways.[9] Its purpose is, in effect, to map the structure of the possible. Like its analogue, mathematics, it makes use of facts, in this case the facts of natural experience, in order to understand the universals (essences, meanings), which make the facts intelligible.

Ideen I (Ideas), in addition to explaining the nature of the new science, also presents its axioms, which state the basic structures of (transcendental) consciousness. An understanding of the method used to isolate these axioms is crucial to an understanding of phenomenology. If one does not get clear about the function of the phenomenological reduction, particularly, it becomes impossible to distinguish between transcendental (phenomenological) philosophy and phenomenological (descriptive) psychology.[10] Critics who accuse Husserl of psychologism have simply failed, so Husserl contends, to see how the method transforms the data.

The path to the "transcendental consciousness," the basic category of phenomenological philosophy, does of course traverse psychological terrain. It runs from ordinary experience ("me," here, with others, in a public world), to an (introspective) empirical psychology ("my" experience typified, the psychic as distinct from the nonpsychic), to phenomenological psychology (the essential structures of psychic phenomena, of "soul," or "consciousness"), to transcendental phenomenology (the structure and constituting functions of transcendental subjectivity). Because the focus remains on the subject throughout, because transcendental consciousness is taken to be functionally (because we are engaged in a critique of cognition) a priori in relation to the world, phenomenology is an "idealist" position.

To those who reject his philosophy because it is an idealism, Husserl points out that phenomenological idealism is *sui generis* and bears no resemblance to classical idealist positions. To underscore the point, he affirms unequivocally his orthodox metaphysical realism. (The fact that he shares our usual realist assumptions has, of course, no bearing on what he does as a phenomenologist.)

Both the precise nature of his idealism and the nonpsychologistic character of phenomenology are more easily recognized, Husserl argues, when one understands clearly the difference between phenomenological psychology and transcendental philosophy. That distinction is not obvious because the two disciplines are precisely isomorphic. Husserl emphasizes the naturalistic roots of the psychology and the fact that the phenomenological reduction effectively severs the connection between these roots and the a priori philosophy. Furthermore, phenomenology, unlike psychology, takes into account the objects, the meanings intended, in its analyses of intentional experiences. But were it not for the reduction, which so many commentators tend to regard as a dispensible aspect of the method, Phenomenology would indeed be 'merely' psychology, the putative philosophy would indeed be just a peculiarly complicated instance of psychologism.

The conclusion contains the celebrated remarks about Husserl's status as a professional neophyte. He can only hope to rough in the parameters, to sketch the methods, of the newest and the most crucial of the sciences. *Ideas* is only a collection of "fragments," but these fragments establish, for the first time, the possibility of objective science.

III

Husserl attempted to achieve a great deal in short compass in the preface. It is too much to expect that so much material could be summarized lucidly or that standard interpretations could be shown conclusively to be mistaken. He was primarily interested in stimulating enough curiosity to induce others to explore for themselves the new region of inquiry. To do that, one must adopt the transcendental attitude. Reading about it will not suffice. It is in order, however, to ask if Husserl made any significant headway in his efforts to dissolve the principal criticisms of his position, by showing that they are based on misinterpretations of *Ideas*. Specifically, has he said anything new and helpful in the preface about the distinction between phenomenological psychology and transcendental philosophy, enough to persuade us that he really can avoid a transcendental psychologism? Secondly, has he made progress toward establishing that his "transcendental idealism," although logically entailed, is not of a piece with the "absurd" idealism normally contrasted with realism?

At the time that Husserl was writing *Ideas,* he did not have a fully developed theory of phenomenological psychology, although he had obviously worked out the rudimentary notions.[11] In retrospect, he judged that *Ideas* had led up to the exposition of the proper region of philosophical inquiry in a rather abrupt and naive way—proceeding directly from the level of the natural attitude to the transcendental level. An approach mediated by a phenomenological psychology would have been more easily understood, and perhaps more natural as well. But even the mature accounts of phenomenological psychology[12] strike many critics as being virtually indistinguishable from the account of transcendental philosophy given in *Ideas*. Both disciplines are described as 'science of consciousness', and both bear the peculiar marks of a foundational phenomenological science—*i.e.,* they are both a priori, eidetic, intentional, descriptive, intuitive, etc., science. What, then, differentiates them? Is it in fact either of the indices that Husserl mentions in the preface?

The first index—that the philosophical science does, and the psychological science does not, take into account the noematic (the object intended) aspect of the intentional experiences investigated—does not appear sufficient to the task of distinction at hand. It is not in fact possible to describe an intentional experience from *any* standpoint without taking into account the intentional object.[13] (That is, both the phenomenological psychologist and the phenomenological epistemologist must know what is intended in order to distinguish between perceiving, imagining, remembering, etc.) The fact that the psychologist, after his initial identification of the intentional object, then focuses on the noetic aspect of the complex intentional act shows at best that phenomenological psychology is not the whole of transcendental philosophy.

Perhaps the other index—psychology's persisting rootedness in its mundane point of departure—is alone sufficient to account for the generic difference between the two disciplines. But one cannot determine whether this is so by examining the contents of the respective disciplines. The contents are, as the preface asserts, precisely the same, acquiring now a psychological, now a philosophical, intelligibility (*Seinssinn*) as a function of the attitude taken toward it. If the difference is in fact identifiable, it will be by virtue of getting perfectly clear about the determinative *Nuancierung,* the delicate shift in perspective, whereby the transformation takes place.

Such clarification could only issue from a careful examination of phenomenological procedures, in the hands of the psychologist and the philosopher respectively. Specifically, it would be necessary to show how phenomenological-psychological reducing differs from transcendental phenomenological reducing. Those who have tried have usually discovered a resemblance "so striking that one could believe the two to be completely identical."[14] If that is the case, then one is forced once again to seek the difference in the direction that Husserl indicates —in the attitudes of the practitioners of the reduction.

Why have some critics been reluctant to seek the distinction in the quarter indicated? Simply because it is difficult to believe, except on faith, that a subtle difference of perspective (a subjective attitude) is sufficient as a basis for an objective distinction between two sciences. Husserl's claim that it is, that the indiscernibles are nonidentical when one knows the mind of the beholder, cannot, it seems, be supported by argument. Nuances do not lend themselves to explication. Moreover, the location of the basis for the distinction in subjective attitudes, rather than in the bodies of the relevant sciences, actually lends credence to the charge of psychologism that the "nuance" theory was intended to rebut.

In Husserl's final work, the *Crisis,* only lip service is given to the distinction.[15] Phenomenological psychology, only possible within the "transcendental horizon," inevitably transforms itself into transcendental philosophy without, Husserl adds, ceasing to be itself. Either this trans-substantiation cannot be conceptualized or, as is more likely, the distinction is not genuine.

The defense of his idealism, which Husserl undertook in the preface, is, it would seem, more successful than his refutation of psychologism.[16] Unfortunately, very few critics seem to have noted this.

Let us define realism simply, in terms of the commonsense belief that a world of material objects exists independently of anyone's awareness of it. Idealism we will take to be, among other things, the denial of this view. Husserl's phenomenology has been interpreted by some as being a realism and by others as being an idealism.[17] It is indisputable that both interpretations can be strongly supported with textual evidence. It is equally obvious that neither interpretation can be correct, *simpliciter.* To shed some light on what is amiss with the idealist interpretation will, at the same time, disclose the fallacy of the realist perspective.

Perhaps the most common perspective on Husserl's idealism is still that of his Göttingen students: Husserl began philosophizing in fidelity to the realist cause but was misled by the epoche into idealist byways from which it was impossible to return. His reasoning can be accounted for but not condoned. He became "entrapped" within consciousness, unable to make use of the Cartesian expedient for extricating himself. In this version, Husserl is merely tragic. In a related version, in which the idealist turn is neither condoned nor accountable, Husserl appears to be rather more simpleminded than tragic. His idealism is simply a "sad mistake."[18] He simply assumes "without argument that an idealist explication of the sense of the being of the world is the correct one."[19] The mistake is that of transforming phenomenology into an idealist metaphysics while continuing to insist that a necessary condition for phenomenological objectivity is consistent employment of the epoche, which permanently disallows *all* metaphysical assertions, idealist or otherwise.

It is not likely that Husserl would have permitted himself to be caught in such a fatal and elementary muddle. The matter is in fact a muddle only when viewed through metaphysical glasses. When Husserl claims that his idealism is something quite new, and that it has nothing to do with the classical realism-idealism debate, he doubtless has it in mind that, as a result of methodological strictures, his idealism is not a metaphysical position at all. This is not to deny that it superficially resembles one. But in order to be genuinely metaphysical it would have to constitute a response to the central question about "what there is" that animates the realism-idealism debate. Husserl does not address this issue, however. He does not ask questions such as, "What really exists?" "Are there things that exist independently of my awareness of them?" "Are 'things' actually ideas?" Moreover, he actually contests the claim, although it is not consistent for him to do so, that nothing exists except the transcendental ego and its ideas.[20]

'Idealism' designates an epistemological view as well as a metaphysical one. As epistemology, it embodies either of both of these views: "First, that knowledge about existence and non-existence of everything outside the self originates in immediate experience, or 'the given', which is not strictly

shared; and second, that to any given person, the intelligibility of existential claims originates in his own immediate experience."[21] It has been noted that virtually every major philosopher since Descartes has in some way or another espoused this view.[22] Surely Husserl is to be numbered with them.

If we suppose that the idealism in question is epistemological (or methodological), then passages that are ambiguous when looked at metaphysically become perfectly clear. Take a specimen from the preface:

"The result of the phenomenological clarification of the *meaning* of the manner of existence of the real world (and, *eidetically,* of a real world generally) is that only transcendental subjectivity has ontologically the *meaning* of Absolute Being, that it only is non-relative, that is relative only to itself, whereas the real world indeed exists, but in respect of *essence* is relative to transcendental subjectivity, and in such a way that it can have its *meaning* as existing reality only as the intentional meaning-product of transcendental subjectivity [my italics]."

The talk here is clearly about meaning, not being; and as talk about how we view the world, rather than about the way the world is "in itself," it makes considerable sense. If one interprets it metaphysically, it is contradictory—the world does and does not exist independently of consciousness. Because innumerable ambiguities of this sort in Husserl's writings are cleared up when the "epistemological" interpretation is adopted, that interpretation likely represents the fairest reading of Husserl.

The preface did not succeed in laying to rest the vigorous ghost of psychologism or even, it seems, the more ephemeral specter of vitiating idealism. It does, however, present as concise an account of the overall phenomenological project, and of the philosophical élan behind it, as one is likely to find.

NOTES

1. For historical background on *Ideas* and on Husserl's preface see Karl Schuhmann, *Die Dialektik der Phänomenologie,* vol. 2, *Reine Phänomenologie und phänomenologische Philosophie* (The Hague: Nijhoff, 1973). See also "Einleitung des Herausgebers,"

Husserliana 3; and W. R. Boyce Gibson, "From Husserl to Heidegger: Excerpts from a 1928 Freiburg Diary by W. R. Boyce Gibson," *Journal of the British Society for Phenomenology* 2 (1971), pp. 58–81.

2. See Schuhmann, *Dialektik,* pp. 140–46.

3. See ibid., pp. 141–42. See also Roman Ingarden, "Edith Stein on her Activity as an Assistant of Edmund Husserl," *Philosophy and Phenomenological Research* 23 (1962), pp. 155–175. Two celebrated critiques written by students are Theodor Celms, *Der phänomenologische Idealismus Husserls* (Riga: 1928); and Ingarden, *Der Streit um die Existenz der Welt*, 3 vols. (Tübingen, West Germany: Max Niemeyer, 1964–66).

4. See Karl Schuhmann, *Die Fundamentalbetrachtung der Phänomenologie* (The Hague: Nijhoff, 1971), especially pp. xxviii–xxxvii.

5. Gibson's translation eventually appeared in the Muirhead Library of Philosophy series, published by Allen & Unwin (London) in 1931. A new translation, by F. Kersten, is forthcoming from Nijhoff (The Hague).

6. See Schuhmann, *Dialektik*, pp. 164–65. Husserl sketched a similar preface for the *LU*. See "Entwurf einer Vorrede zu den Logischen Untersuchungen," *Tijdschrift voor Philosophie* 1 (1939), pp. 106–133, 319–339. See also Karl Schuhmann, "Forschungsnotizen über Husserls 'Entwurf einer Vorrede zu den Logischen Untersuchungen'," *Tijdschrift voor Philosophie* 4 (1972), pp. 513–524.

7. See Schuhmann, *Dialektik*, p. 167.

8. It appeared also in a slightly expanded and improved version addressed to German readers, "Nachwort zu meinen Ideen . . . ," *Jahrbuch für Philosophie und phänomenologische Forschung* 11 (1930), reprinted in *Husserliana* 5. See Aron Gurwitsch, "Critical Study of Husserl's Nachwort," in *Studies in Phenomenology and Psychology* (Evanston, Illinois: Northwestern University Press, 1966), pp. 107–115.

9. The contrary view is argued in R. Schmitt, "Transcendental Phenomenology: Muddle or Mystery?" *Journal of the British Society for Phenomenology* 2 (1971), pp. 19–27.

10. See "'Phenomenology,' Edmund Husserl's Article for the *Encyclopaedia Britannica*" in the present volume, pp. 21–35. Contemporary phenomenological psychology is presented in relation to its Husserlian roots in C. F. Graumann and A. Metraux, "Die phänomenologische Orientierung in der Psychologie," in *Wissenschaftstheoretische Grundlagen der Psychologie*, ed. K. Schneewind (Munich: Reinhardt, 1977). See also Gurwitsch, "Critical Study of Husserl's Nachwort," (cited in note 8).

11. See J. J. Kockelmans, "Husserl's Original View of Phenomenological Psychology," in his *Phenomenology: The Philosophy of Edmund Husserl and Its Interpretation* (Garden City, N.Y.: Doubleday, 1967), pp. 418–449.

12. These include, in addition to the *Encyclopaedia Britannica* article reprinted in the present volume, pp. 21–35, the *Cartesian Meditations* and *Crisis*.

13. See the *Encyclopaedia* article cited in note 10.

14. Kockelmans, "Husserl's Original View of Phenomenological Psychology," 443–44.

15. *Crisis*, sections 57–59 and Appendix 10.

16. See R. H. Holmes, "Is Transcendental Phenomenology Committed to Idealism?" *The Monist* 59 (1975), pp. 98–114.

17. For a review of the debate and for bibliographical data see Kockelmans, "Husserl's Transcendental Idealism," (cited in note 11), pp. 183–193.

18. According to J. N. Findlay, "Phenomenology and the Meaning of Realism," in *Phenomenology and Philosophic Understanding*, ed. E. Pivčević (New York: Cambridge University Press, 1975), pp. 143–158.

19. W. Morriston, "Intentionality and the Phenomenological Method: A Critique of Husserl's Transcendental Idealism," *Journal of the British Society for Phenomenology* 7 (1976), pp. 33–43. Additional recent discussions of this problem are K. Ameriks, "Husserl's Realism," *Philosophical Review* 86 (1977), pp. 498–519; and G. B. Madison, "Phenomenology and Existentialism: Husserl and the End of Idealism," in *Husserl: Expositions and Appraisals*, ed. F. Elliston and P. McCormick (Notre Dame, Indiana: University of Notre Dame Press, 1977), pp. 238–246.

20. See *Formal and Transcendental Logic*, section 96b, and the *Cartesian Meditations*, sections 42, 62.

21. C. D. Rollins, "Solipsism," in *Encyclopedia of Philosophy* 7, ed. P. A. Edwards (New York: Macmillan, 1967), 490. Most of Rollins' remarks about solipsism fit idealism as well.

22. See ibid.

FURTHER REFERENCES

Idealism

Adorno, Theodor W. "Husserl and the Problem of Idealism." *Journal of Philosophy* 37 (1940): 5–18.

Boehm, Rudolf. "Husserl und der klassische Idealismus." In *Vom Gesichtspunkt der Phänomenologie*, pp. 18–71. The Hague: Nijhoff, 1968.

de Boer, Theodorus. "The Meaning of Husserl's Idealism in the Light of His Development." *Analecta Husserliana* 2 (1972): 322–32.

Ingarden, Roman. *On the Motives Which Led Husserl to Transcendental Idealism*. Translated by A. Hannibalsson. The Hague: Nijhoff, 1975.

Psychology

Drüe, Hermann. *Edmund Husserls System der phänomenologischen Psychologie*. Berlin: Walter de Gruyter, 1963.

Gurwitsch, Aron. "Edmund Husserl's Conception of Phenomenological Psychology." *Review of Metaphysics* 19 (1966): 689–727.

————. "The Phenomenological and Psychological Approaches to Consciousness." In *Studies in Phenomenology and Psychology*, pp. 89–106. Evanston: Northwestern University Press, 1966.

Kockelmans, Joseph J. *Edmund Husserl's Phenomenological Psychology*. Pittsburgh: Duquesne University Press, 1967.

Landgrebe, Ludwig. "Das Problem der phänomenologischen Psychologie bei Husserl." *Akten des 14. Internationalen Kongress für Philosophie* 2 (1968): 151–63.

Author's Preface to the English Edition of *Ideas**

Translated by W. R. Boyce Gibson

May the author of this work, which first appeared in the year 1913, be permitted to contribute to the English Edition certain explanations that may prove of use to the reader, both before and as he reads?

Under the title "A Pure or Transcendental Phenomenology," the work here presented seeks to found a new science—though, indeed, the whole course of philosophical development since *Descartes* has been preparing the way for it—a science covering a new field of experience, exclusively its own, that of "Transcendental Subjectivity." Thus Transcendental Subjectivity does not signify the outcome of any speculative synthesis, but with its transcendental experiences, capacities, doings, is an absolutely independent realm of direct experience, although for reasons of an essential kind it has so far remained inaccessible. Transcendental experience in its theoretical and, at first, descriptive bearing, becomes available only through a radical alteration of that same dispensation under which an experience of the natural world runs its course, a readjustment of viewpoint which, as the method of approach to the sphere of transcendental phenomenology, is called "phenomenological reduction."

In the work before us transcendental phenomenology is not founded as the empirical science of the empirical facts of this field of experience. Whatever facts present themselves serve only as examples similar in their most general aspect to the empirical illustrations used by mathematicians; much, in fact, as the actual intuitable dispositions of numbers on the abacus assist us, in their merely exemplary capacity, to grasp with insight, and in their pure generality the series 2, 3, 4 . . . as such, pure numbers as such, and the propositions of pure mathematics relative to these, the essential generalities of a mathematical kind. In this book, then, we treat of an a priori science ("eidetic," directed upon the universal in its original intuitability), which appropriates, though as pure possibility only, the empirical field of fact of transcendental subjectivity with its factual (*faktischen*) experiences, equating these with pure intuitable possibilities that can be modified at will, and sets out as its a priori the indissoluble essential structures of transcendental subjectivity, which persist in and through all imaginable modifications. Since the reduction to the transcendental and, with it, this further reduction to the *eidos* is the method of approach to the field of work of the new science, it follows (and we stress the point in advance) that the proper starting-point for the systematic unravelling of this science lies in the chapters which treat of the reductions we have indicated. Only from this position can the reader, who follows with inner sympathy the indications proffered step by step, judge whether something characteristically new has really been worked out here—worked out, we say, and not constructed, drawn from real, general

*Reprinted with the permission of the publisher from E. Husserl, *Ideas: General Introduction to Pure Phenomenology,* trans. W. R. Boyce Gibson (London: George Allen & Unwin, 1931), pp. 11–30.

intuition of essential Being, and described accordingly.

Eidetic phenomenology is restricted in this book to the realm of pure eidetic "description," that is to the realm of essential structures of transcendental subjectivity immediately transparent to the mind. For this constitutes in itself already a systematically self-contained infinitude of essential characteristics. Thus no attempt is made to carry out systematically the transcendental knowledge that can be obtained through logical deduction. Here we have one difference (though not the only one) between the whole manner of this new a priori science and that of the mathematical disciplines. These are "deductive" sciences, and that means that in their scientifically theoretical mode of development mediate deductive knowledge plays an incomparably greater part than the immediate axiomatic knowledge upon which all the deductions are based. An infinitude of deductions rests on a very few axioms.

But in the transcendental sphere we have an infinitude of knowledge previous to all deduction, knowledge whose mediated connexions (those of intentional implication) have nothing to do with deduction, and being entirely intuitive prove refractory to every methodically devised scheme of constructive symbolism.

A note of warning may be uttered here against a misunderstanding that has frequently arisen. When, in an anticipatory vein, it is stated right from the start that, according to the author's views (to be established in those further portions of the whole work which are still to be published), all radically scientific philosophy rests on the basis of phenomenology, that in a further sense it is phenomenological philosophy right through, this does not mean to say that philosophy itself is an a priori science throughout. The task which this book was planned to carry out, that of establishing a science of the eidetic essence of a transcendental subjectivity, is as far as it can be from carrying the conviction with it that philosophy itself is entirely a science a priori. A glance at the mathematical sciences, these great logical instruments for corresponding sciences of fact, would already lead us to an-

ticipate the contrary. The science of fact in the strict sense, the genuinely rational science of nature, has first become possible through the independent elaboration of a "pure" mathematics of nature. The science of pure possibilities must everywhere precede the science of real facts, and give it the guidance of its concrete logic. So is it also in the case of transcendental philosophy, even though the dignity of the service rendered here by a system of the transcendental a priori is far more exalted.

The understanding, or at any rate the sure grasp, of the distinction between *transcendental phenomenology* and "*descriptive*," or, as it is often called nowadays, "*phenomenological*" *psychology*, is a problem that as a rule brings great difficulties with it, which indeed are grounded in the very nature of the case. It has led to misunderstandings, to which even thinkers who subscribe to the phenomenological line of thought are subject. Some attempt to clarify the situation should prove useful.

The change of standpoint which in this work bears the name phenomenological reduction (transcendental-phenomenological we now say, to be more definite) is effected by me, as the actually philosophizing subject, from the natural standpoint as a basis, and I experience myself here in the first instance as "I" in the ordinary sense of the term, as this human person living among others in the world. As a psychologist, I take as my theme this I-type of being and life, in its general aspect, the human being as "psychical." Turning inwards in pure reflexion, following exclusively "inner experience" (self-experience and "empathy," to be more precise), and setting aside all the psychophysical questions which relate to man as a corporeal being, I obtain an original and pure descriptive knowledge of the psychical life as it is in itself, the most original information being obtained from myself, because here alone is perception the medium. If, as is often done, descriptions of all sorts, which attach themselves purely and truly to the data of intuition, are referred to as phenomenological, there here grows up, on the pure basis of inner intuition, of the intuition of the soul's own essence, a phenomenological psychology. A right form of method (on this point we shall have something further to say) gives us in point of fact not only scanty, superficially classificatory descriptions, but a great self-supporting science; the latter, however, properly speaking, only when, as is possible also here, one first sets before oneself as goal a science which deals not with the factual data of this inner sphere of intuition, but with the essence, inquiring, that is, after the invariant, essentially characterisic structures of a soul, of a psychical life in general.

If we now perform this transcendental-phenomenological reduction, this transformation of the natural and psychologically inward standpoint whereby it is transcendentalized, the psychological subjectivity loses just that which makes it something real in the world that lies before us; it loses the meaning of the soul as belonging to a body that exists in an objective, spatio-temporal Nature. This transformation of meaning concerns myself, above all, the "I" of the psychological and subsequently transcendental inquirer for the time being. Posited as real (*wirklich*), I am now no longer a human Ego *in* the universal, existentially posited world, but exclusively a subject *for* which this world has being, and purely, indeed *as* that which appears to me, is presented to me, and of which I am conscious in some way or other, so that the real being of the world thereby remains unconsidered, unquestioned, and its validity left out of account. Now if transcendental description passes no judgment whatsoever upon the world, and upon my human Ego as belonging to the world, and if, in this description, the transcendental Ego exists (*ist*) absolutely in and for itself prior to all cosmic being (which first wins in and through it existential validity), it is still at the same time evident that, at every conversion of meaning which concerns the phenomenological-psychological content of the soul as a whole, this very content by simply putting on another existential meaning (*Seinssinn*) becomes transcendental-phenomenological, just as conversely the latter, on reverting to the natural psychological standpoint, becomes once again psychological. Naturally this correspondence must still hold good if, prior to all interest in the development of

psychological science, and of a "descriptive" or "phenomenological psychology" in particular, a transcendental phenomenology is set up under the leading of a philosophical idea, so that through phenomenological reduction the transcendental Ego is directly set up at the focus of reflexion, and made the theme of a transcendental description. We have thus a remarkable thoroughgoing parallelism between a (properly elaborated) phenomenological psychology and a transcendental phenomenology. To each eidetic or empirical determination on the one side there must correspond a parallel feature on the other. And yet this whole content as psychology, considered from the natural standpoint as a positive science, therefore, and related to the world as spread before us, is entirely non-philosophical, whereas "the same" content from the transcendental standpoint, and therefore as transcendental phenomenology, is a philosophical science —indeed, on closer view, *the* basic philosophical science, preparing on descriptive lines the transcendental ground which remains henceforth the exclusive ground for all philosophical knowledge. Here in fact lie the chief difficulties in the way of an understanding, since it must be felt at first as a most unreasonable demand that such a "nuance" springing from a mere change of standpoint should possess such great, and indeed, for all genuine philosophy, such decisive significance. The wholly unique meaning of this "nuance" can be clearly appreciated only when he who philosophizes has reached a radical understanding with himself as to what he proposes to bring under the title "philosophy," and only in so far as he is constrained to look for something differing in principle from positive science: the theoretic control, that is, of something other than the world ostensibly given to us through experience. From such understanding with one's own self, carried out in a really radical and consistent way, there springs up of necessity a motivation which compels the philosophizing Ego to reflect back on that very subjectivity of his, which in all his experience and knowledge of the natural world, both real and possible, is in the last resort the Ego that experiences and knows, and is thus already presupposed in all the natural self-knowledge of the "human Ego who experiences, thinks, and acts naturally in the world." In other words: from this source springs the phenomenological transposition as an absolute requirement, if philosophy generally is to work out its distinctive purposes upon a basis of original experience, and so contrive to begin at all. It can make a beginning, and generally speaking develop all its further philosophical resources, only as a science working from the transcendental-philosophical standpoint. For this very reason the immediate a priori phenomenology (portrayed in this work in its actual functioning as that which directly prepares the transcendental basis) is the "first philosophy" in itself, the philosophy of the Beginning. Only when this motivation (which stands in need of a very minute and comprehensive analysis) has become a vital and compelling insight, does it become clear that the "change in the shading," which at first appears so strange, transforming as it does a pure psychology of the inner life into a self-styled transcendental phenomenology, determines the being and non-being of philosophy—of a philosophy which knows with thorough-going scientific assurance what its own distinctive meaning calls for as the basis and the method of its inquiry. In the light of such self-comprehension, we understand for the first time that deepest and truly radical meaning of "psychologism" (that is, of transcendental psychologism) as the error that perverts the pure meaning of philosophy, proposing as it does to found philosophy on psychology, on the positive science of the life of the soul. This perversion persists unmodified when, in sympathy with our own procedure, the pure psychology of the inner life is set up also as an a priori science; even then it remains a positive science, and can provide a basis for positive science only, never for philosophy.

In the course of many years of brooding over these matters, the author has followed up different lines of inquiry, all equally possible, in the attempt to exhibit in an absolutely transparent and compelling way the nature of such motivation as propels beyond the natural positive realism of life and science, and necessitates the transcendental

transposition, the "phenomenological Reduction." They are the ways of reaching the starting-point of a serious philosophy, and as they must be thought out in conscious reflexion, they themselves belong properly to the Beginning, as is possible, indeed, only within the beginner as he reflects upon himself. For each of these ways the point of departure is, of course, the natural unsophisticated standpoint of positive reality (*Positivität*) which the world of experience has as the basis of its being, and is confessedly "taken for granted" (the nature of such Being never having been questioned). In the work here presented (Second Section, second chapter, §33 f.), the author selected that way of approach, which then appeared to him the most effective. It develops as a course of self-reflexion taking place in the region of the pure psychological intuition of the inner life, or, as we might also say, as a "phenomenological" reflexion in the ordinary psychological sense. It leads eventually to the point that I, who am here reflecting upon myself, become conscious that under a consistent and exclusive focusing of experience upon that which is purely inward, upon what is "phenomenologically" accessible to me, I possess in myself an essential individuality, self-contained, and holding well together in itself, to which all real and objectively possible experience and knowledge belongs, through whose agency the objective world is there for me with all its empirically confirmed facts, in and through which it has for me at any rate trustworthy (even if never scientifically authorized) essential validity. This also includes the more special apperceptions through which I take myself to be a man with body and soul, who lives in the world with other men, lives the life of the world, and so forth. Continuing this self-reflexion, I now also become aware that my own phenomenologically self-contained essence can be posited in an *absolute* sense, as I am the Ego who invests the being of the world which I so constantly speak about with existential validity, as an existence (*Sein*) which wins for me from my own life's pure essence meaning and substantiated validity. I myself as this individual essence, posited absolutely, as the open infinite field of pure phenomenological data and their inseparable unity, am the "transcendental Ego"; the absolute positing means that the world is no longer "given" to me in advance, its validity that of a simple existent, but that henceforth it is exclusively my Ego that is given (given from my new standpoint), given purely as that which has being in itself, in itself experiences a world, confirms the same, and so forth.

Within this view of things there grows up, provided the consequences are fearlessly followed up (and this is not everybody's business), *a transcendental-phenomenological Idealism* in opposition to every form of psychologistic Idealism. The account given in the chapter indicated suffers, as the author confesses, from lack of completeness. Although it is in all real essentials unassailable, it lacks what is certainly important to the foundation of this Idealism, the proper consideration of the problem of transcendental solipsism or of transcendental intersubjectivity, of the essential relationship of the objective world, that is valid for me, to others which are valid for me and with me. The completing developments should have been furnished in a Second Volume which the author had hoped to be able to supply very soon after the first, as a sequel that had been planned at the same time with it.

The objections raised against this Idealism and its alleged Solipsism seriously impeded the reception of the work, as though its essential significance lay in any way in this sketch of its philosophical import: whereas this was no more than a means devised in the interest of the problem of a possible objective knowledge, for winning this necessary insight: that the very meaning of that problem refers us back to the Ego that is in and for itself; and that this Ego, as the presupposition of the knowledge of the world, cannot be and remain presupposed as having the existence of a world, and must therefore, in respect of the world's being, be brought to its pure state through phenomenological reduction, that is, through epoche. I might have been better advised if, without altering the essential connexions of the exposition, I had left open the final decision in favour of transcendental Idealism, and contented myself with making clear that trains of thought of crucial philosophical significance with a trend that is towards Idealism necessarily arise here, and must by all means be thought out; so that to this end one needs in any case to make sure of the ground of transcendental subjectivity.

I must not hesitate, however, to state quite explicitly that in regard to transcendental-phenomenological Idealism, I have nothing whatsoever to take back, that now as ever I hold every form of current philosophical realism to be in principle absurd, as no less every idealism to which in its own arguments that realism stands contrasted, and which in fact it refutes. Given a deeper understanding of my exposition, the solipsistic objection should never have been raised as an objection against phenomenological idealism, but only as an objection to the incompleteness of my exposition. Still, one should not overlook what is the radical essential in all philosophizing to which, in this book, a path will be opened. Over against the thinking, rich in presuppositions, which has as its premises the world, science, and sundry understandings bearing on method, and rooted in the scientific tradition as a whole, a radical form of the autonomy of knowledge is here active, in which every form of datum given in advance, and all Being taken for granted, is set out as invalid, and there is a reversion to that which is already presupposed *implicite* in all presupposing and in all questioning and answering, and herewith of necessity exists already, immediate and persistent. This is the first to be freely and expressly posited, and with a self-evidence which precedes all conceivable instances of self-evidence, and is contained implicitly in them all. Although it is only with the phenomenological reduction which would convert this radicalism into conscious work, that genuine work-performing philosophizing begins, the whole preparatory reflexion has already been carried through, and precisely in this spirit. It is phenomenological, though still unconsciously so. It follows, therefore, that it is a piece of pure self-reflexion revealing original self-evident facts; and, moreover, when it exhibits in these facts (though incompletely) the outlines of Idealism, it is as far as can be from being one of the usual balancings between Idealism and Realism, and cannot be affected by the arguments involved in any of their objections. Such essential connexions of a phenomenological kind, and such motivations in an "idealistic" direction as are in fact revealed, hold firm under all the improvements and completions that may eventually prove necessary, even as the reality of rivers and mountain ranges, which the first explorer has really seen and described, remains standing despite the improvements and additions to which his descriptions are subjected by later explorers. The first preliminary steps towards a fresh formulation of the transcendental problem (to subserve mere purposes of motivation) must then be taken in accord with its phenomenological content, and in accord with what from this point of departure forecasts with objective necessity the true meaning of an objective being that is subjectively knowable. Moreover, transcendental phenomenology is not a theory, devised merely as a reply to the historic problem of Idealism, it is a science founded in itself, and standing absolutely on its own basis; it is indeed the one science that stands absolutely on its own ground. Only in such wise, however, that when consistently carried forward, it leads, as is already apparent in the important concluding portions of the book, to the "constitutive" problems, which take in all the conceivable objects we could ever meet with in experience, briefly the whole real world spread out before us together with all its categories of the object, and likewise all "ideal" worlds, and makes these all intelligible as transcendental correlates. Whence it clearly follows that transcendental phenomenological Idealism is not a special philosophical thesis, a theory among others; that transcendental phenomenology, rather, as concrete science, is, in itself, even when no word is spoken concerning Idealism, universal Idealism worked out as a science. And it proves it through its own meaning as transcendental science in each of its special constitutive domains. But we also need to make clearly explicit the fundamental and essential difference between transcendental-phenomenological Idealism and that form of Idealism which in popular realism is opposed to it as its incompatible opposite. And in the very first place let this be said:

Our phenomenological idealism does not deny the positive existence of the real (*realen*) world and of Nature—in the first place as though it held it to be an illusion. Its sole task and service is to clarify the meaning of this world, the precise sense in which everyone accepts it, and with undeniable right, as really existing (*wirklich seiende*). *That* it exists—given as it is as a universe out there (*daseiendes*) in an experience that is continuous, and held persistently together through a thread of widespread unanimity —that is quite indubitable. It is quite another consideration, although in the light of the discussions in the text of this work one of great philosophical importance, that the continuance of experience in the future under such form of universal agreement is a mere (although reasonable) presumption, and that accordingly the non-existence of the world, although, and whilst it is in point of fact the object of a unanimous experience, always remains *thinkable*. The result of the phenomenological clarification of the meaning of the manner of existence of the real world (and, eidetically, of a real world generally) is that only transcendental subjectivity has ontologically the meaning of Absolute Being, that it only is non-relative, that is relative only to itself; whereas the real world indeed exists, but in respect of essence is relative to transcendental subjectivity, and in such a way that it can have its meaning as existing (*seiende*) reality only as the intentional meaning-product of transcendental subjectivity. But that first attains its full meaning when the phenomenological disclosure of the transcendental Ego is so far advanced that the experience of fellow-subjects implicit in it has won its reduction to transcendental experience; in other words, when the self-interpretation carried out purely on the basis of transcendental experience has led to the knowledge of the real and whole meaning of the transcendental subjectivity, which, for the Ego reflecting at the time means this: "I, the transcendental, absolute I, as I am in my own life of transcendental consciousness; but besides myself, the fellow-subjects who in this life of mine reveal themselves as co-transcendental, within the transcendental society of 'Ourselves,' which simultaneously reveals itself."

It is thus within the intersubjectivity, which in the phenomenological reduction has reached empirical givenness on a transcendental level, and is thus itself transcendental, that the real (*reale*) world is constituted as "objective," as being there for everyone.

The world has this meaning, whether we are aware of it or not. But how could we ever be aware of it prior to the phenomenological reduction which first brings the transcendental subjectivity as our absolute Being into the focus of experience? So long as it was only the psychological subjectivity that was recognized, and one sought to posit it as absolute, and to understand the world as its correlate, the result could only be an absurd Idealism, a psychological Idealism—the very type which the equally absurd realism has as its counterpart. Now by such as have won their way to the genuine transcendental subjectivity it can assuredly be seen that the great idealists of the eighteenth century, Berkeley and Hume on the one side, Leibniz on the other, had, properly speaking, already reached beyond psychological subjectivity in the sense it bears within the natural world. But since the contrast between psychological and transcendental subjectivity remained unexplained, and the all-dominant sensationalism of the school of Locke could not render intelligible the constituting of what is real as a performance giving to subjectivity meaning and true being, the unfruitful and unphilosophical conflict fought out on the field of nature remained in vogue for the times that followed, and there prevailed a perverse interpretation of the meaning which the great idealists had really intended, yet to be sure without making that meaning scientifically clear.

The new publications which the author began to issue in 1929 (the first since the *Ideen*) will contribute far-reaching advances, clarifications, and completions of what, for the rest, had already been begun in the *Logical Investigations* (1900–1901), and then in the *Ideen,* so that the claim to have set going the necessary beginnings of a philosophy, "which can present itself as a science," cannot well be regarded as self-deception. In any case, he who for decades instead of speculating concerning a New Atlantis has really wandered in the trackless wilds of a new continent and undertaken bits of virgin cultivation, will not allow himself to be diverted by the refusals of geographers who judge the reports in the light of their own experiences and habits of thought, and on the strength of this exempt themselves from all the trouble of making a journey into the land proclaimed to be new.

There is still one point that calls for a remark. In the eyes of those who set aside the phenomenological reduction as a philosophically irrelevant eccentricity (whereby, to be sure, they destroy the whole meaning of the work and of my phenomenology), and leave nothing remaining but an a priori psychology, it often happens that this residual psychology is identified as to its main import with Franz Brentano's psychology of intentionality. Great indeed as is the respect and gratitude with which the author remembers this gifted thinker as his teacher, and strongly convinced as he is that his conversion of the scholastic concept of intentionality into a descriptive root-concept of psychology constitutes a great discovery, apart from which phenomenology could not have come into being at all; nonetheless we must distinguish as essentially different the author's pure psychology implicitly contained in this transcendental phenomenology and the psychology of Brentano. This holds good also of his "psychognosis" limited to pure description in the region of inner experience. It is indeed "phenomenological" psychology if, as has often happened at the present time, we are to give the title "phenomenological" to every psychological inquiry conducted purely within the framework of "inner experience," and, grouping all such studies together, to speak further of a phenomenological psychology. For this latter discipline, quite apart from its name, takes us back, naturally, to John Locke and to his school, including John Stuart Mill. One can then say that David Hume's *Treatise* gives the first systematic sketch of a pure phenomenology, which, though under the name of psychology, attempts to supply a philosophical transcendental philosophy. Like his great predecessor, Berkeley, it is as a psychologist that he is regarded and has exercised his influence. Thus, excluding all transcendental questions, it is this whole "phenomenological" school which alone calls here for our consideration. Characteristic of it and of its psychology is the conception set forth in Locke's "white paper" simile of the pure soul as a complex or heap of temporally co-existing and successive data, which run their course under rules partly their own, partly psychophysical. It would thus be the function of descriptive psychology to distinguish and classify the main types of these "sense-data," data of the "inner sense," of inner experience, and likewise the elementary basic forms of the psychical complex; that of explanatory psychology to seek out the rules of genetic formations and transformations, much as in the case of natural science, and on similar lines of method. And quite naturally so, since the pure psychical being or the psychical life is regarded as a nature-resembling flow of events in a quasi-space of consciousness. On grounds of principle, we may say that it obviously makes no difference whether we let the psychic "data" be blown along in a collective whole "atomistically," though in accordance with empirical laws, like heaps of sand, or regard them as parts of wholes which by necessity, whether empirical or a priori, can alone operate as such parts, and principally perhaps within the whole of consciousness fettered as that is to a rigid form of wholeness. In other words, atomistic and Gestalt-psychology alike participate in that intrinsic meaning of psychological "naturalism," as defined in terms of what we have stated above, which, having regard to the expression "inner sense," may also be termed "sensationalism" (*Sensualismus*). Clearly Brentano's psychology of intentionality also remains fettered to this inherited naturalism, though in virtue of its having introduced into psychology as a main concept, descriptive in type and universal in scope, that of Intentionality, it has worked therein as a reforming factor.

The essentially new influence which in transcendentally directed phenomenology becomes active for descriptive psychology, and is now completely changing the whole aspect of this psychology, its whole method, the setting of its concrete aims, is the insight that a concrete description of the sphere of consciousness as a self-contained sphere of intentionality (it is never otherwise concretely given), a concrete description, for instance, of perceptions or recollections, and so forth, also calls, of necessity, for a description of the object as such, referred to in intentional experiences, as such, we say, indicating thereby that they belong inseparably to the current experience itself as its objectively intended or "objective meaning." Furthermore, that one and the same intentional object as such, from the viewpoint of descriptive psychology, is an ideal indicator of a group of ways of being conscious that are proper to it, whose system of typical differences tallies essentially with the typical articulation of the intentional object. It does not suffice to say that every consciousness is a consciousness-of on the lines, perhaps, of Brentano's classification (to which I cannot subscribe) into "presentations," "judgments," "phenomena of love and of hate"; but one must question the different categories of objects in their pure objectivity as objects of possible consciousness, and question back to the essential configurations of possible "manifolds" to be synthetically connected, through which an object of the relevant category can alone be known as the same, that is, as that which can be known through experiences of very differing description, differing and always differing still again, but always restricted to the descriptive types of such ways of consciousness as belong to it essentially and a priori. The reference to the fact that every object is either experienced or thought or sought after as an end, and so forth, is only a first step, and still tells us very little. The task of a phenomenological "constitution" of objects referred to at the close of this book, in a transcendental setting, it is true, finds its place here, only that now it is conceived as projected back upon the natural psychological standpoint.

Unfortunately, the necessary stressing of the difference between transcendental and psychological subjectivity, the repeated declaration that transcendental phenomenology is not in any sense psychology, not even phenomenological psychology has had this effect upon the majority of professional psychologists (who are wont to be very frugal, moreover, in all that concerns philosophy), that they failed to notice at all the radical psychological reform which was involved in the transcendental; they interpreted my utterances as an intimation that as psychologists they were not concerned in any way with phenomenology, or with any part of it. Even the few who noticed here that it was very relevant to psychology, and sought to make it accessible, have not grasped the whole meaning and scope of an intentional and constitutive phenomenology, and have not seen that here for the first time, in contrast with naturalistic psychology from an outer standpoint, a psychology comes to words and deeds, a psychology in which the life of the soul is made intelligible in its most intimate and originally intuitional essence, and that this original intuitional essence lies in a "constituting" of meaning-formations in modes of existential validity, which is perpetually new and incessantly organizing itself afresh—briefly, in the system of intentional actions, whereby existential (*seiende*) objects of the most varied grades right up to the level of an objective world are there for the Ego as occasion demands.

It was, moreover, not without reason that the psychological reform made its first entry as the concealed implication of a transcendental reform. For only a compulsion grounded on the philosophically transcendental problem, an urge towards extreme radicalism in the clearing up of the modes in which knowledge and object stand to each other in the conscious life itself, necessarily led to a universal and concrete phenomenology of consciousness, which received its primary orientation from the intentional object. In the transition to the psychology of the natural standpoint, it is then obvious that an intentional psychology has a quite different meaning from that of the traditions of the school of Locke or of that of Brentano. A. von Meinong also, although, in writings that appeared subsequently to my *Logical Investigations,* his teaching comes here and there into touch with my own, is in no way to be regarded here as an exception: he remains bound to Brentano's leading conceptions, or to psychological sensationalism, as does the entire psychology of the modern tradition and the whole psychology of the present day.

The present work, however, as a philosophical treatise does not include psychological reform among its themes, although it should not be wholly lacking in indications bearing on a genuine intentional psychology. Even as philosophical, moreover, its task is limited. It does not claim to be anything more than an attempt that has been growing through decades of meditation exclusively directed to this one end: to discover a *radical beginning* of a philosophy which, to repeat the Kantian phrase, "will be able to present itself as science." The ideal of a philosopher, to think out sooner or later a logic, an ethic, a metaphysic, and so forth, which he can at all times justify to himself and others with an insight that is absolutely cogent—this ideal the author had early to abandon, and has not resumed it to this day. And for no reason other than the following, seeing that at any rate this insight was and remained for him indubitable, that a philosophy cannot start in a naïve straightforward fashion—not then as do the positive sciences which take their stand on the previously given ground of our experience of a world, presupposed as something that exists as a matter of course. That they do it causes them all to have problems in respect of their foundations, and paradoxes of their own, a condition which a subsequent and belated theory of knowledge first seeks to remedy. For this very reason the positive sciences are unphilosophical, they are not ultimate, absolute sciences. A philosophy with problematic foundations, with paradoxes which arise from the obscurity of the fundamental concepts, is no philosophy, it contradicts its very meaning *as* philosophy. Philosophy can take root only in radical reflexion upon the meaning and possibility of its own scheme. Through such reflexion it must in the very first place and through its own activity take possession of the absolute ground of pure pre-conceptual experience, which is its own proper preserve; then, self-active again, it must create original concepts, adequately adjusted to this ground, and so generally utilize for its advance an absolutely transparent method. There can then be no unclear, problematic concepts, and no paradoxes. The entire absence of this procedure, the overlooking of the immense difficulties attaching to a correct beginning, or the covering up of the same through the haste to have done with them, had this for its consequence, that we had and have many and ever new philosophical "systems" or "directions," but not the *one* philosophy which as Idea underlies all the philosophies that can be imagined. Philosophy, as it moves towards its realization, is not a relatively incomplete science improving as it goes naturally forward. There lies embedded in its meaning as philosophy a radicalism in the matter of foundations, an absolute freedom from all presuppositions, a securing for itself an absolute basis: the totality of presuppositions that can be "taken for granted." But that too must itself be first clarified through corresponding reflexions, and the absolutely binding quality of its requirements laid bare. That these reflexions become more and more interwoven as thought advances, and lead eventually to a whole science, to a science of Beginnings, a "first" philosophy; that all philosophical disciplines, the very foundations of all sciences whatsoever, spring from its matrix—all this must needs have remained implicit since the radicalism was lacking without which philosophy generally could not be, could not even make a start. The true philosophical beginning must have been irretrievably lost in beginning with presuppositions of a positive kind. Lacking as did the traditional schemes of philosophy the enthusiasm of a first beginning, they also lacked what is first and most important: a specifically philosophical groundwork acquired through original self-activity, and therewith that firmness of basis, that genuineness of root, which alone makes real philosophy possible. The author's convictions on such lines have become increasingly self-evident as his work progressed. If he has been obliged, on practical grounds, to lower the ideal of the philosopher to that of a downright beginner, he has at least in his old age reached for himself the complete certainty that he should thus call himself a beginner. He could almost hope, were Methuselah's span of days allotted him, to be still able to become a philosopher. He has always been able to follow up the problems that issue from the Beginning, and primarily from what is first for a descrip-

tive phenomenology, the beginning of the beginning, and to develop it concretely in what to him have been instructive pieces of work. The far horizons of a phenomenological philosophy, the chief structural formations, to speak geographically, have disclosed themselves; the essential groups of problems and the methods of approach on essential lines have been made clear. The author sees the infinite open country of the true philosophy, the "promised land" on which he himself will never set foot. This confidence may wake a smile, but let each see for himself whether it has not some ground in the fragments laid before him as phenomenology in its beginnings. Gladly would he hope that those who come after will take up these first ventures, carry them steadily forward, yes, and improve also their great deficiencies, defects of incompleteness which cannot indeed be avoided in the beginnings of scientific work.

But when all is said, this work of mine can help no one who has already fixed his philosophy and his philosophical method, who has thus never learnt to know the despair of one who has the misfortune to be in love with philosophy, and who at the very outset of his studies, placed amid the chaos of philosophies, with his choice to make, realizes that he has really no choice at all, since no one of these has taken care to free itself from presuppositions, and none has sprung from the radical attitude of autonomous self-responsibility which the meaning of a philosophy demands. He who believes that he can appeal to the "fruitful $\beta\acute{\alpha}\theta o\varsigma$" of experience in the current sense of that term, or to the "assured results" of the exact sciences, or to experimental or physiological psychology, or to a constantly improved logic and mathematics, and so forth, and therein find premises for his philosophy, cannot have much susceptibility for the contents of this book. He is unable to bring to his reading an intensive interest, nor can he hold that the time and effort have been well spent which the sympathetic understanding of such a way of beginning demands. Only he who is himself striving to reach a beginning will herein behave otherwise, since he must say to himself: *tua res agitur.*

Those who are interested in the author's continued work and progress since 1913 may be referred to the recently published writing entitled "Formale und transzendentale Logik, Versuch einer Kritik der logischen Vernunft" (in the *Jahrbuch f. Phänomenologie und phänomenologische Forschung,* Bd. X, 1929). Also to his *Cartesian Meditations,* an extended elaboration of the four lectures which he had the pleasure of giving first in the spring of 1922 at the University of London, and in this last year in an essentially maturer form at the Sorbonne in Paris. They furnish once again, though merely in outline, an Introduction to phenomenological philosophy, but contain an essential supplement in the detailed treatment of the fundamental problem of transcendental intersubjectivity, wherewith the solipsistic objection completely collapses. They will presumably appear simultaneously with this English edition of the *Ideen* in a French rendering in the *Bulletin de la Société de Philosophie.* In the same year a German edition should be appearing, published by Niemeyer of Halle a.d.S, containing as additional matter a second Introduction, in which the clarification of the idea of a personal (on the lines of a mental science) and natural anthropology and psychology, and lastly of a pure intuitional psychology, is undertaken as an initial problem. At a later stage only is it shown how, starting from this discussion, which, like all that has preceded, remains on natural ground, the Copernican reversal to the transcendental standpoint finds its motive. At the same time a series of publications is being started in my *Jahrbuch*: the concrete phenomenological studies which I have drafted as the years went by, to clear up my own mind, and for the safeguarding of the structure of phenomenology.

In conclusion, let me thank my own honoured friend, Professor W. R. Boyce Gibson, for the disinterested labour involved in this translation. It fills me with some hope when so thorough and so earnest a thinker takes so great an interest in my efforts to furnish philosophy with a scientific beginning as to take upon himself the translating of this extensive work, the language of which is so difficult, even for Germans.

4

Husserl in England:
Facts and Lessons*

HERBERT SPIEGELBERG

The following essay, meant to accompany the publication of the syllabus for the four lectures on "Phenomenological Method and Phenomenological Philosophy" which Edmund Husserl delivered at the University of London in June 1922, is chiefly an attempt to salvage an episode in the history of phenomenology which is rapidly becoming inaccessible. Some of its most important parts are in all probability past recovery. The special reason for this attempt is the present revival of interest in phenomenology in England. This remarkable, if not amazing, comeback makes it doubly important to learn some of the facts about its largely-forgotten past record.

As far as I can tell, the living memory of Husserl's London lectures has practically disappeared. In my inquiries since about 1954 I have been unable to find anyone with the exception of Mrs. G. E. Moore who remembered as much as the fact of these lectures. There is no record of them in the files of the University of London except for an entry in the "University of London Gazette" for 7th June, 1922, announcing the forthcoming four lectures;[1] the only references to them I have come across in the literature occurs in C. K. Ogden and I. A. Richards' *The Meaning of Meaning* of 1923,[2] and in a "Survey of Recent Philosophical and Theological Literature" by George Dawes Hicks.[3] The only

other printed evidence is Husserl's own mention of the lectures in his Preface of 1930 to the English edition of W. Boyce Gibson's translation of his *Ideas*[4] where he referred to them as a less mature form of the Paris lectures of 1929, later expanded into the *Cartesian Meditations*.

Is there any explanation for this near-total eclipse? Does it hold any lessons? Before it makes sense to attempt an answer to these questions, the extant facts of the case have to be assembled.

1. The Invitation for the London Lectures

Neither in the Husserl Archives in Louvain nor in those of the University of London is there any record of the invitation to these lectures, apparently the first extended to a German philosopher after World War I. The only *terminus ad quem* I can find is in Husserl's letter to Roman Ingarden of December 24th, 1921:

Denken Sie, die Londoner Universität hat mich officiell eingeladen, dort 4 Vorlesungen zu halten. Ich habe angenommen, wohl Ende April oder Ende Juni. Ich werde bei Prof. Hicks in Cambridge logieren. (Imagine, the University of London has invited me officially to deliver there four lectures. I have accepted, probably for end of April or end of June. I shall stay with Professor Hicks in Cambridge.)[5]

This passage and other circumstantial evidence makes it highly probable that it

*Reprinted with permission from *Journal of the British Society for Phenomenology* 1 (1970): 4–17.

was George Dawes Hicks (1862–1944), professor of philosophy at the University of London, though residing in Cambridge, who was the moving spirit behind this invitation. There are no indications that any other British philosophers familiar with Husserl's work had anything to do with it. Thus Bernard Bosanquet,[6] who at the time had retired to the vicinity of London, and died in 1923, was already failing in health.[7] As far as Bertrand Russell is concerned, much as he was interested in Husserl, at least up to the time of his letter to Husserl in 1920,[8] there is little likelihood that, in his detachment from British universities at the time, he would have taken much interest in such an invitation.

What could have been the basis for Hicks' interest and initiative? Again, no personal documents about Hicks' relations with Husserl prior to the invitation have survived. In fact all of Hicks' papers, which after his death in 1941 were turned over to the University of London, were apparently lost during the war.[9] And the Husserl Archives in Louvain contain nothing but a copy of a three-page typed letter by Husserl to Hicks of March 15th, 1930, referring to a preceding letter by Hicks, presumably on the occasion of Husserl's seventieth birthday in 1929. However, Husserl's library proves Hicks' interest in Husserl in the form of gift copies of several of Hicks' books, one of them being his Leipzig dissertation of 1887 in German, and a whole carton with twelve reprints of articles, some of them dating back to 1910, at least one of them with signs of Husserl's reading in the form of notations.

In the light of Hicks' own philosophy, and in particular his self-confessed "critical realism," one may well wonder about the reasons for his special interest in Husserl. From his book publications it would appear that his primary interest, as that of so many of other British philosophers of the early century, beginning with Bertrand Russell, was in Alexius Meinong. Husserl is quoted only incidentally and only with references to his *Logical Investigations*. This is true even of Hicks' book on *Berkeley* of 1932, of which he sent a copy to Husserl. He certainly could not have been very sympathetic with Husserl's increasing turn toward idealism, which

had not yet been explicit in his pre-war publications.

However, there is some revealing evidence about Hicks' initial appraisal of Husserl in his unique semi-annual "Surveys of Recent Philosophical and Theological Literature," which appeared in the *Hibbert Journal* from 1910 until his death in 1941. Here he mentioned Husserl for the first time in 1911 as a contributor to the first volume of the new journal *Logos* for his "very able and exhaustive treatment of '*Philosophie als strenge Wissenschaft*'."[10] In 1913 the survey begins with a five-page review of the first volume of Husserl's *Jahrbuch*," preceded by the sentence: "Beyond question the most fruitful contributions to philosophical research in recent years have come from Alexius Meinong, in Graz, and Edmund Husserl, in Goettingen." Husserl's initial contribution, the *Ideas,* is called "extremely elaborate and significant" and "a masterly piece of analysis."[11]

Under these circumstances the most plausible explanation for the invitation would seem to be the following: Since the days of his Hibbert scholarship to and doctorate from the University of Leipzig, Hicks was keenly interested in German philosophy. He also seems to have had a unique command of the German language, as evidenced not only by his dissertation but by his German contribution on English philosophy to the 1928 edition of Ueberweg's *Geschichte der Philosophie*, vol. 5. It is therefore not surprising that as soon as possible after the war he took the initiative in restoring academic relations with German philosophy by inviting its outstanding representative. His first choice might have been Meinong. But after his death in 1917 Husserl was the obvious candidate. And the University of London seemed to be particularly suited to take the lead in issuing such an invitation.

Nothing is known about Husserl's preparations for the visit beyond the fact that he wrote out a complete text of the lectures and the syllabus, which, however, especially in its later parts, does not always contain full sentences but merely keywords and phrases. Presumably Husserl was under considerable time pressure, since he was still in full teaching until the end of February. At any rate, there is no evidence that before his departure he briefed himself about the philosophical situation in England. This is perhaps reflected in an episode about which I learned from Martin Heidegger in 1953. When seeing the Husserls off at the Freiburg railway station, Heidegger, in answer to some briefing Husserl had given him about his plans, asked somewhat jokingly: *"Und wie, Herr Geheimrat, steht es mit der Geschichte?* (And what about history?)" Whereupon Husserl replied, looking him straight in the eye: *"Die habe ich vergessen.* (That is what I have forgotten.)" In reading the text of the London lectures one may indeed wonder about the scarcity of historical references, especially in the Syllabus, and, most significant, the omission of the names of any British philosophers.

2. The Visit

The exact length of the stay of the Husserls in England can no longer be ascertained. But in view of the fact that Husserl had to interrupt his Freiburg semester for the lectures, it is not likely that they stayed for more than two weeks. Husserl's letter to Dawes Hicks of 1930 makes it likely that the Husserls carried out the plan, mentioned in the letter to Ingarden of December, 1921, of accepting Hicks' hospitality at 9, Cranmer Road, Cambridge, about which he reminisces later as follows:

Mit niemand habe ich über die Grundgedanken dieser Schrift (i.e., the *Méditations Cartésiennes* which he had sent to Hicks) *so anregende Gespräche gepflogen wie mit Ihnen—an den unvergessenen schönen Abenden am fireplace in Ihrem Studierzimmer.* (With no one did I engage in such stimulating conversations about the fundamental ideas of this text [*i.e.,* the *Cartesian Meditations*] as with you—on those unforgotten nice evenings in front of the fireplace in your study.)

Probably Husserl conducted most of his philosophical conversations in Cambridge with Hicks. For in the letter, declining a second invitation by Hicks, he mentioned that *"die vielen interessanten Persönlichkeiten, die ich da (i.e.,* in Oxford) *träfe, blieben*

mir bei meiner Unfähigkeit, mich englisch zu verständigen doch unzugänglich." (The many interesting personalities which I would meet there (*i.e.,* in Oxford on the occasion of the International Congress of Philosophy of 1930) would remain inaccessible to me in view of my inability to communicate in English.) Apparently, Mrs. Husserl was much more at home in English.

Presumably Husserl commuted by train from Cambridge to London for the four afternoon lectures on June 6th, 8th, 9th and 12th, accompanied by Hicks. For the last lecture they were joined by G. E. Moore, who was to chair it. According to Dorothy Moore (Mrs. G. E. Moore), "my husband had some talk with him,"[12] but, as she told me later in conversation, she did not know of what nature. Nor did she remember any pronounced reaction of G. E. Moore to the lectures. Similar conversations could have taken place with James Ward, the chairman of the second lecture, who had once studied under Lotze in Goettingen and might have been particularly sympathetic to Husserl's idealistic leanings, as expressed in the lectures.[13] There is no reference to the third chairman, Wildon Carr, of King's College, London, chiefly known as an expositor of Bergson and Croce, whose idealism may have provided some points of contact.

About the actual delivery of the London lectures in University College, Gower Street, there is again only indirect information. C. K. Ogden and I. A. Richards, or more specifically, Ogden, since Professor Richards told me he was not present, mentions a "large English audience." It is more than unlikely that there was any subsequent discussion. However, on the last day (June 12th), Husserl also took part in a session of the Aristotelian Society under Dawes Hicks' chairmanship, and, according to the *Proceedings* of 1921–22, led off the discussion of a paper by T. M. Greenwood on "Geometry and Reality."[14]

Husserl's daughter, Mrs. Elly Rosenberg, remembers hearing from her parents about an official reception at the German Embassy in London, one of them attended by Viscount Haldane, the statesman philosopher, a Germanophile in politics and follower of Hegel in philosophy. According to the "Acta

Authentica" in the Husserl Archives in Louvain, Husserl was also asked to speak subsequently at Oxford, an invitation which he declined.

On the whole, Husserl seems to have been well pleased with the visit itself and especially with his election as a Corresponding Member of the Aristotelian Society soon after his return to Freiburg.[15]

Thus the immediate echo to the lectures, as it came back to Husserl, was clearly positive and encouraging. Hicks himself referred to the lectures specifically in his first Survey for 1922 in the *Hibbert Journal,* expressing the hope for an early publication in English.[16] One might even suspect that the request for an article on phenomenology for the 1929 edition of the *Encyclopaedia Britannica* was an after-effect of the London lectures. But in this case, too, no correspondence about the background of this ill-fated[17] piece has survived, either at the Husserl Archives or in the files of the *Encyclopaedia Britannica.*

However, Husserl's letter to Hicks in 1930 clearly shows that Husserl was aware of the fact that the immediate effect of the London lectures did not last. In particular, he was clearly disappointed, if not hurt, by the fact that the preparatory committee for the International Congress of Philosophy in Oxford in 1930, in contrast to the preceding congress at Harvard in 1926, had ignored him, let alone invited him for a major lecture.

In fact, there had been negative reactions from the very start. The most conspicuous one can be found in Ogden and Richards' *The Meaning of Meaning,* which expressed presumably the views of British analytical philosophy of the time. Here Husserl, introduced as a representative of the "Terminological" method of attack on the problem of meaning, figures in Appendix D as the first of six "Moderns" illustrating "strange and conflicting . . . languages which the most distinguished thinkers have thought fit to adopt in their attempts to deal with Signs, Symbols, Thoughts and Things."[18] The authors begin their documentation with a reference to the London lectures, quoting five sentences from the "explanatory Syllabus in which he (Husserl), or his official translator, endeavoured to indicate both his method and his vocabulary," after which they switch

to an account of Husserl's earlier work by Joseph Geyser, whom they call a "disciple": in the case of this highly critical neo-scholastic certainly a highly misleading label. There is actually no connection between this account and the sentences from the London lectures, which, in themselves and quoted out of context, can hardly make sense to any readers. In any case, the great influence of Ogden and Richards' work is likely to have scared away the British public not only from the London lectures but from Husserl's phenomenology in general.

But even more telling than this attempt at ridicule was probably the complete oblivion of the London lectures. Thus in the discussions of phenomenology which continued in the 1930s, for instance in the symposium of the Aristotelian Society of 1932, the London lectures were never mentioned. Nor were they in the first review of Philosophy in Germany by Helen Knight in the *Journal of Philosophical Studies* of 1927, where Husserl's *Logical Investigations* and the *Ideen* provided the first exhibit of German philosophy since the beginning of the century.

How far did the lectures meet Hicks' own expectations beyond the fact that he called them "remarkable" in his Survey? Again, there is no explicit information, especially since none of his letters to Husserl have been preserved. Husserl had sent Hicks copies of his *Formale und Transzendentale Logik* and of the French *Méditations Cartésiennes,* with personal dedications, which can still be found in the Library of the University of London, to which Hicks bequeathed all his books. But Hicks' own works after the London lectures, of which he sent Husserl at least the one on Berkeley, mention Husserl only incidentally in connection with the familiar topics of universals and of intentionality. But there seems to be no further reference to the London lectures. Brentano and Meinong continue to be his major continental authorities.

One must, of course, realise that Hicks' own philosophical development took in a sense exactly the opposite course from Husserl's. In fact he entitled his contribution to Muirhead's *Contemporary British Philosophy* (vol. 2, 1925) "From Idealism to Realism." Coming from the position of German Idealism, which he had studied not only in Oxford but during his five years in Leipzig with Wundt and Heinze, devoted to Kantian philosophy, he had in 1917 reached the position of "Critical Realism,"[19] which he tried to develop further in such later books as *Critical Realism* (1937). Thus one can well imagine that Husserl's progressive turn toward idealism in the London lectures, even though the term does not occur in the Syllabus, as it did in the actual lectures, did not appeal to Hicks particularly. Perhaps this was one of the topics discussed between the two in front of the fireplace at 9, Cranmer Road. All the same, the personal relations between the two remained unaffected by Hicks' possible philosophical disappointment as can be gathered from Hicks' second invitation to Husserl in 1929, which he declined in his letter of 1930.

But signs of Hicks' reservations toward, if not disenchantment with, Husserl's later work can be culled from Hicks' later references to Husserl in his *Hibbert* surveys after 1922. Thus in his survey of 1927, on the occasion of commenting on Marvin Farber's *Phenomenology as a Method and as a Philosophical Discipline,* Hicks voiced doubts about the possibility of presenting Husserl's ideas in English.[20] In 1929 Hicks also reviewed briefly Heidegger's edition of "some extremely valuable lectures of Husserl delivered in Goettingen many years ago on the *Phänomenologie des inneren Zeitbewusstseins,*" published in the Husserl *Jahrbuch* of 1928.[21] In 1931 he discussed W. R. Boyce Gibson's translation of Husserl's *Ideen I,* "indeed a formidable task": "It is to be hoped that, as a result of his labours, the leading conceptions of a mode of thought, now so influential in Germany, will become better known than they are at present to students of philosophy in this country. Of the value and interest of the mode of thought in question there can be no doubt."[22] There is, however, no reference to either the *Formale und Transzendentale Logik* of 1929 or the *Méditations Cartésiennes* (1931), both personal gifts from Husserl to Hicks, in the following surveys. But in the survey for 1936,[23] when discussing the new international *Phi-*

losophia, Hicks singled out Husserl's first instalment of the *Krisis* as "beyond question the most important contribution to the volume." The 1938 survey[24] begins with a two-page obituary of Husserl, including major events of his biography, but strangely omitting reference to the London lectures.

What should also not go unmentioned is that in December, 1940, Hicks "co-operated" actively in the founding of the International Phenomenological Society and, at the time of his death, was a member of the Advisory Committee,[25] as the only British philosopher to have served in this capacity. To this extent his interest in a wider phenomenology remained undiminished.

What then was Husserl's own retrospective appraisal of the London lectures? According to Rudolf Boehm[26] he apparently thought for a short while of publication, but then enlarged them into a "system of philosophy in the sense of phenomenology and in the form of 'meditations on first philosophy'." But this was only the beginning of further transformations which led to the Paris lectures and the *Cartesian Meditations.* Even in his letter of 1930 to Hicks, Husserl stated that he had found it necessary to execute concretely (*konkrete Durchführung*) the fundamental ideas of the London lectures, that he had deepened them in the Paris lectures, and that he was to enlarge them further in the German edition of the *Cartesian Meditations.*

Perhaps even more revealing was what Husserl told Dorion Cairns in a conversation on August 28th, 1931. Here, in response to one of Cairns' remarks about the problem of the right beginning in phenomenology, Husserl commented on the fact that this point had made him dubious about his own attempts of giving introductions. A first attempt, destined not only to introduce other people to phenomenology but also to provide himself with guide lines, had been the series of lectures he had given in London. A later attempt had been the Paris lectures, and a still later one the German text of the *Cartesian Meditations.* So Husserl admitted that in London he was actually pursuing a double purpose, namely to introduce phenomenology to his (British) audience and at the same time to provide guidance for himself. How far were the two purposes compatible?

Also, on September 1st he confessed that "for years he had been under the illusion that it would be a comparatively simple matter to write a 'popular' introduction, but that in reality all his attempts throughout the last ten years, attempts which had resulted in the London and Paris lectures and the French *Méditations,* had been without satisfactory results."

Husserl's dissatisfaction with his own achievement is, of course, nothing new. And in many ways it does him credit. But in this particular case it has special significance. For it poses the question not only of an introduction to phenomenology in general, but of the proper introduction for a British audience.

3. The Syllabus of the London Lectures in British Perspective

What kind of a response might one expect from a typical English listener to Husserl's cycle? In order to answer this question one must try to put oneself into the place of a listener generally interested in German philosophy, but not yet briefed about any of its recent developments.

From this perspective one might assume that the title, with its promise of an introduction to a new method and to a philosophy based on it, had aroused his interest, together with the fact that the announcement listed such leading British philosophers as James Ward and G. E. Moore from Cambridge University, in addition to Wildon Carr and Dawes Hicks from the University of London as chairmen of the four lectures. Even the topics announced for each one of the four lectures, beginning with "The Aims of Phenomenological Philosophy" may well have sounded attractive. Also, for those not sufficiently sure of their command of German there was the reassuring promise of an English syllabus as a listening guide. In fact, one may well suspect that for a good part of the audience this syllabus provided the major basis for understanding what went on during the German reading. It might,

therefore, be well to reflect first independently on how this syllabus must have struck the typical listener. In trying to reconstruct his reaction I am referring to the text of the syllabus as published in this issue.

The very first sentences must have startled the audience. What are "the fundamental considerations" to which Husserl here refers and from which the phenomenological method is supposed to have arisen? And what is the point of an unspecified "radical change of the attitude of natural experience and knowledge" which it promises? This is supposed to "open out" a "peculiar realm of given entities" of which Descartes' "ego cogito" is mentioned as the prime example. Is this Cartesianism all over? However, presently this new realm is identified with "transcendental phenomenological subjectivity as immediate phenomenological self-experience," an experience which is not supposed to be psychological experience. Why 'transcendental' a term at once associated in England with Kantian philosophy? Why 'subjectivity'? And what does 'phenomenological' mean in this context? Next, the reader is told that this makes possible an a priori science extracted purely from concrete phenomenological intuition. All these claims must have struck the unprepared audience as extremely puzzling and certainly thus far as mere assertions.

The second paragraph can only have added to this puzzlement by speaking of the transformation of the originally "egological" phenomenology into a "transcendental sociological phenomenology"—incidentally a term which Husserl never seems to have used elsewhere. Equally strange must have sounded the next claim, namely that a systematically consistent development of phenomenology would lead necessarily to an all-comprehensive logic concerned with the correlates "knowing-act," "knowledge-significance," and "knowledge-objectivity." What weird conception of logic does this imply? And what does it mean that this transcendental phenomenology realises the idea of a "first philosophy"? Is this anything like Aristotle's metaphysics or Descartes'? Supposedly it contains in itself "the systematically-arranged totality of all possible a priori sciences, the principles of construction for the a priori forms of all the sciences of realities for all possible worlds." Since when is it to be taken for granted that all sciences have such a priori principles?

In a second section of the first lecture we are supposed to learn about the Cartesian way to the ego cogito and the method of phenomenological reduction. It begins with mere key phrases hinting at the connection of this approach with the Platonic Tradition in philosophy. They are followed by such claims as: "The necessary form of the philosophical beginning" is a "meditation on the 'I'," and "The ultimate basis of all philosophy must be . . . a basis of 'apodictic experience'." Whatever this apodicticity may mean, can this make sense for an English listener?

In the syllabus for the second lecture on "The Realm of Phenomenological Experience" we may expect to enter the realm of phenomenological philosophy proper, as distinguished from its method. It should present us with the field covered by a phenomenological philosophy. Here the syllabus, even with its fragmentary phrases interrupted by a few full sentences, can convey a little more about concrete topics for the new science clustered around the ego cogito. Perception, recollection, *Einfühlung*, etc., are listed among many related topics. In a second section the question of the possibility of an egological science is raised and the necessity of "reduction" to the "absolutely given" postulated, resulting in transcendental phenomenology as the mother of all a priori sciences. Here the reader may at least hope that the variety and novelty of some of these topics will be elucidated by the actual lecture.

The syllabus for the third lecture promises to throw light on what transcendental phenomenology can establish about the possibility of knowledge, science, and the objective world. It is this lecture which announces Husserl's peculiar brand of idealism and his monadology. First difficulties are hinted at, but not explained. The phenomenology of a puzzling "primordial" consciousness of time seems to offer a solution. The systematic divisions of phenomenology are sketched as subdivisions of intentional-

ity. All this remains programmatic. It can hardly mean much to the uninitiated. Questions of traditional epistemology are mentioned, leading to the thesis that they are all transcendental phenomenological questions. The thesis is followed immediately by the startling claim that it is I who assign the significance of opinion, knowledge, proof, etc. This general phenomenology is to be developed into constitutive phenomenologies of our knowledge of nature, etc. But what 'constitutive' means in this context does not become clear.

Next, we are told that subjectivity or "monadologism" is the necessary consequence of the phenomenological attitude, and that any objectivity is what it is only through "intentional meaning." Subjectivity is even called the only genuine "substance." All other being is merely an "ideal pole." Clearly these claims come closest to the actual assertion of an ego-centered idealism. But where is its demonstration? In the following sections we are told that this does not mean solipsism, and that the *alter ego* is guaranteed by *Einfühlung* into the other's body, which suddenly appears. This position is now called "phenomenological monadology."

The promise of the last lecture is that of a concrete logic and of a concrete aim (in contrast to the "general aim" of the first lecture?) for a phenomenological philosophy. Supposedly this lecture talks only about logic, but, as it turns out, it also deals with all the other sciences. After being told again about the claims of transcendental phenomenology as absolutely justified, we learn that such disciplines as mathematics are naively dogmatic. These sciences are said to be contained in phenomenology. This, we are told, is the realisation of the original and genuine idea of logic in the Platonic sense. "Historical logic," too, is called dogmatic. The exploration of its necessary requirements is claimed to lead to transcendental phenomenology.

Next, transcendental monadism is said to make "essence requirements" of the individual monads and of the condition of compossible monads, now called a "metaphysical inquiry." Here we have clearly arrived in the Leibnizian world. The topics of teleology, the world, its history and the problem of

God are added. But the bases for these abrupt claims remain unexplained. From here we are referred back to the world of non-apriori facts. These in turn are supposed to lead to the knowledge of possibilities as their presupposition. The ideal goal for the future is an absolute theory of monads. And a single universal science on a single universal foundation is to take the place of independent sciences, which is none other than transcendental phenomenology.

How many English readers will have followed Husserl to this climax? There is, of course, a good chance that those who could keep up with Husserl's German delivery of the lectures were able to make better sense of the syllabus than by simply reading it. And here one would like to know whether and how far the actual lectures followed the text of the syllabus and of his typed text, how far Husserl simplified or complicated it, how far he improvised, etc. The following section will make at least a preliminary study of the relation between the syllabus and the typed text of the lectures.

4. The German Text of the Lectures

Thus far the text of the lectures has not yet been published. My subsequent observations are based on a first examination of the transcript of the text, as typed out by Ludwig Landgrebe, Husserl's assistant at the time. On the basis of this examination I have come to the definite conclusion that Husserl had composed the syllabus before writing out the lectures and that he used it as an outline in preparing them. Specific evidence for this conclusion can be found at the very start,[27] where Husserl refers his listeners to the succinct theses of the syllabus in their hands as something which he does not want to duplicate in the lecture, hence in a sense as the basic aid for the understanding of the lecture itself. Later, in the third lecture,[28] Husserl refers to a thesis to be found in the syllabus as something which he has now demonstrated in the lecture, namely, that all questions of philosophy are either transcendental-phenomenological or non-sensical.

In contrast to the syllabus in its often peremptory and sketchy style, the lectures develop a continuous argument. Thus in the first two lectures Husserl makes a painstaking case for the new transcendental approach, supported by suggestive examples which, as far as I can tell, do not occur in other texts. In many regards these first two lectures strike me as much more persuasive than the first *Cartesian Meditations*.

On the whole the text of the lectures follows the order of topics outlined in the syllabus. But there are also significant departures. One interesting case at the very beginning of the first lecture is that Husserl does not resume the strange expression 'transcendental sociological (*transzendental-soziologische*) phenomenology' (a phrase picked up in Ogden and Richards' ridiculing quotations) for a phenomenology which is to take the place of a merely 'egological phenomenology' something which he later will call intersubjective phenomenology.

Also, while in the syllabus Husserl stopped short of calling his own position 'idealism' the lectures themselves contain the term 'transcendental idealism' as a new alternative to 'transcendental philosophy'[29] in which Husserl sees an unclear pre-stage (*Vorstufe*) of its authentic form. Then, at the beginning of the last lecture, Husserl designates this position in retrospect as 'phenomenological idealism',[30] as contrasted to traditional transcendental idealism.[31] In view of the fact pointed out by Rudolf Boehm that Husserl did not use this term in any of his publications prior to the *Formale und Transzendentale Logik* of 1929, this may well have been the first occasion when he launched this phrase in public. The fact that this happened in London under the very chairmanship of G. E. Moore, whose "Refutation of Idealism" had marked the turn from British idealism to realism, represented a strange historical irony, which made Husserl's message appear even more anachronistic in twentieth century England.

Another significant feature of the lectures is Husserl's outspoken plan of a scientific metaphysics based on phenomenology, capable of revealing the meaning of the world through a "phenomenological monadology."

Even the full text of the lectures does not contain a single reference to British philosophers. Plato and Descartes are named as the chief inspirers (of the new approach). Leibniz, Spinoza and Kant are mentioned near the end. On one occasion[32] in referring to the recent revolution in mathematics and physics, Husserl introduces the names of Einstein, Brouwer and Weyl, but not those of Russell and Whitehead, of whom Husserl was demonstrably aware. Clearly these lectures did not make any attempt to play up to his British audience. One cannot help wondering how these omissions affected his listeners, and in particular the initiator of the lectures, G. Dawes Hicks.

How far in planning and developing this series did Husserl think of his prospective listeners as a British audience? The answer seems clear enough. Actually the omission of all references to British philosophy is not only unfortunate but strange indeed considering the fact that Husserl was not only familiar with British philosophy from Locke to Mill, but recommended the British empiricist philosophers as one of the best, if not *the* best, approach to transcendental phenomenology,[33] calling for instance Hume "almost the first phenomenologist."[34] Besides, his *Britannica* article uses the "phenomenological psychology" of Locke and the British empiricists as stepping stones for showing the need for transcendental phenomenology.

The truth, as it now emerges, seems to be that Husserl did not think of these lectures as an introduction for a British public. In fact, as it turns out, he soon forgot about his audience completely and thought of the text chiefly as a guide for himself, a new way out of the mazes of his own thought.

Perhaps the clearest confirmation of this interpretation can be found in a postcard which Husserl wrote less than three months after the lectures on September 1st, 1922, to one of his former Goettingen students, the later Socialist Prussian Minister of Education, Adolf Grimme:

Dieses Jahr war eine Zeit groser Besinnungen. Ich durchdachte noch ein letztes Mal die principiellen Grundgedanken und Grundlinien der Phänomenologie. Demgemäss wählte ich auch das Thema fuer meine Londoner Vorträge (Phänomenologische Methode und phänomenologische Philosophie), die schön ausfielen, aber

ziemlich schwierig waren. (This year was a time of great meditations. For a last time I thought through the basic principles and guide lines of phenomenology. Accordingly I chose the theme for my London conferences (Phenomenological Method and Phenomenological Philosophy) which turned out beautifully, but were rather difficult.)

"Demgemäss" (accordingly): so Husserl's own problems were the decisive factor in the choice of his approach to the London assignment; "Ziemlich schwierig" (rather difficult): so he knew in retrospect how he had taxed his audience, not only in the Syllabus, but in the lectures themselves. Let us remember that Husserl presupposed on the part of his audience:

1. the recognition of the need of a radical change of the "natural attitude";
2. the acceptance of Descartes' cogito, including the ego as a safe basis for all philosophy;
3. a clear idea of what is meant by the term 'transcendental' apart from what it may mean to those familiar with Kantian philosophy;
4. the acceptance of "subjectivity," as a legitimate basis of philosophy;
5. some idea of what is meant by egology and what it could possibly include;
6. an understanding of his new idea of logic, which is clearly no longer the pure logic of his *Logical Investigations*;
7. the distinction between knowing-act, knowledge-significance and knowledge-objectivity, a distinction never explored in the text.

5. Some Lessons

Considerable caution must be exercised in any attempt to draw lessons from the mitigated failure of Husserl's first presentation of phenomenology to the English world: too little is known about the background of the lectures for indulging in fault-finding and hindsight about "might-have-beens." But even so, on the basis of the preceding analysis of what one could now imagine as the probable reaction of the original British audience curious to find out about and sympathetic to renewed cultural and philosophical relations with German philosophy, it makes some sense to reflect on the London episode, if only in the interest of doing a better job in the situation of today, which is in many ways so much more favourable—ultimately still as a result of Husserl's pioneering.

The first lesson from the London lectures one might be tempted to draw is simply: How *not* to do it. But that would be grossly unfair. There was nothing wrong in the idea of the lecture cycle. The title could hardly have been framed better to arouse intelligent interest. Even the subtitles for the four lectures, though not always clearly related to the general title, made fairly clear sense. The real problems began with the syllabus, in itself a good idea, possibly suggested by Hicks, since the whole device of a syllabus is practically unknown on the Continent. What, then, can be learned from this first exposure of a British public to phenomenology or rather phenomenology to British reactions?

First of all, I want to make it plain that, after studying the main texts I would consider it not only superfluous but fatuous and pedantic to spell out in detail what Husserl could have done differently in his lectures. After all, it is now perfectly clear that Husserl was not so much interested in helping a specifically British audience, but in working out a general introduction into his evolving "system" of transcendental phenomenology, something he had not yet tried before on this scale. As far as the lectures are concerned, all I would like to suggest is that some of the damage of the first attempt to import phenomenology into the English-speaking world could still be repaired by the belated publication of some of the authentic texts in responsible translations. What I have in mind is specifically:

1. the full text of the London lectures from the German original.
2. the complete text of the original text of the *Encyclopaedia Britannica* article.

In the case of both texts, the printing of the German original and the translation on facing pages may be particularly valuable and feasible. But what should be even more helpful is the publication of David Carr's translation of Husserl's last work, incomplete though it remained, the *Krisis der europäischen Wissenschaften und die trans-*

zendentale Philosophie. In fact Husserl himself in his last conversation with Alfred Schutz "repeatedly designated this series of essays as the summary and crowning achievement of his life work."[35] It is, therefore, not surprising that in one of his last letters to Dorion Cairns (August 20th, 1936) he put the importance of an early translation of this work even ahead of that of *Formal and Transcendental Logic* and *Cartesian Meditations,* on which Cairns was working at the time.

However, there is now new and definite reason for us who believe that phenomenology, and Husserl's phenomenology in particular, have something to offer to the Anglo-American world, to reflect on how to present them more effectively and how to avoid some of the mistakes of the pioneer days. What I intend to offer here is not a specific list of recommendations and recipes but guidelines together with one basic query.

As to such guidelines all one really needs is to put oneself in the position of readers and/or listeners having been exposed to nothing except the mystifying and all but attractive label 'phenomenology', and approaching it with the suspicion that all there is behind it is another Germanic system à la Hegel. Further, one ought to be aware that this public has been exposed to two generations of analytic philosophy, and that the only Continental philosophers that have made sense to it thus far are logical positivists and Ludwig Wittgenstein. Besides, this new analytic way of doing philosophy with its prolific production has been largely self-sufficient to the extent that there is no longer any need for continental imports, and that such imports have often been considered as a necessary nuisance, necessary only for the sake of cultural politics rather than in order to learn anything from it. What this calls for is a patient attempt to take account of this situation and to discover possible points of contact and openings where a philosophy such as phenomenology can offer real help. It also calls for a return to the common roots of both traditions, especially those which are still alive in the guest country. In the case of Anglo-American philosophy this was and is definitely no longer German idealism. Instead, the obvious common background is the tradition of British empiricism from Locke to Mill, in which Husserl had grown up philosophically. At times an attempt to begin such introductory work at the level of one's audience may involve simplifications which, in the eyes of purists, may look like betrayals. I believe that this risk, much as one has to be on one's guard against it, is worth taking. For I have every confidence that, once the ice of distrust is broken, the pure doctrine, insofar as it is sound, will prevail on its own strength.

But in order to meet these requirements, an even more basic adjustment of attitude is required: we have to realise more fully than before that we have no right to assume that others owe us the extraordinary effort it takes to study a philosophy like phenomenology in its present state on our own and Husserl's terms. Among the flood of competing philosophies of our day, national and international, it is by no means obvious that phenomenology has any special claims. To assume this means not only self-righteous arrogance but a type of provincialism. We may as well admit that, had it not been for the accident of our birth and history, we probably would not have arrived at this philosophy, at least not as early as we did. This calls for a special effort and for a genuine sensitivity for the difficulties and needs of one's audience. What I am pleading for is the attitude of epistemic humility without relativism, which never presupposes that one is right, and even less that one has a right to be right. If one is right, and thinks one can demonstrate it, one has to earn this right by patiently and empathically considering and understanding the case for alternative positions, which through no merit of our own we happen not to occupy.

POSTSCRIPT

The possibility of conversations between Husserl and James Ward during Husserl's Cambridge visit mentioned on p. 56 above can now be considered an established fact. Thanks to Dr. Karl Schuhmann of the Husserl Archives in Louvain, to whom I am indebted for much additional information and help, I learned about a diary by W. R. Boyce Gibson, kept during his Freiburg visit in 1928. A copy of this diary has just been turned over to the Archives by his son, A. Boyce Gibson, from which he has kindly allowed me to quote. The most important passage occurs in an entry of June 15th, 1928, based clearly on Husserl's information "over the punchbowl"; presumably at a reception in his home:

Husserl had a fine time at Cambridge at Hicks' house, and had greatly enjoyed the evening chats by the fire, leather arm-chairs and smoke. He had met Ward there and, by accident, Stout, who was examining at Cambridge.

Another entry (October 19th) states:

Husserl met Broad and Stout at Cambridge. They were external examiners there. Couldn't get on with Stout, as Stout couldn't speak German. Had to do everything through an interpreter.

Took to Moore. Moore admired the *Logical Investigations*, but couldn't swallow *Ideen*.

Even allowing for the indirectness of this information and the time lag between 1922 and 1928, the names of the British philosophers in this account can hardly be questioned.

As to James Ward, the Husserl library, now in Louvain, contains a copy of his *Naturalism and Agnosticism* with Husserl's entry "Geschenk des Verfassers, Cambridge, Juni, 1922." His *Psychological Principles,* likewise there, show a pencil note "Geschenk von G. Dawes Hicks, Cambridge, 1922, Juni."

The contact with Stout could have been particularly meaningful in view of Stout's interest in Brentano, of which Husserl was aware, but also in Meinong and Husserl himself. Husserl owned Stout's *Analytical Psychology* of 1896, but only in a second hand copy. His inability to communicate with Stout could have been intensified by Stout's being "terribly deaf."[36] This has just been confirmed by a long letter for which I am indebted to his son, A. K. Stout. He also supplied ample correspondential evidence for Stout's continued high regard for Husserl such as sending one of his students to Husserl in 1933 for special tutoring.

In the case of C. D. Broad the Husserl library has two interesting items: his *Perception, Physics and Reality* (1914) with a personal dedication, and, perhaps even more revealing, Part II (only) of W. E. Johnson's *Logic* (1922) with the inscription "To Prof. Husserl with kind regards from C.D.B." Could it be that this gift was related to the striking parallel between Johnson's conception of "intuitive induction" in Chapter VIII and Husserl's *Wesensschau* ("ideating abstraction")? A letter card by C. D. Broad of April 27th, 1937, also in the Husserl Archives, acknowledges the receipt of a reprint of Husserl's "Die Krisis der europæischen Wissenschaften" (*Philosophia* I), "which I have been reading with much interest."

The information about G. E. Moore's admiration for the *Logical Investigations* and rejection of the *Ideen,* is at best puzzling. Personally I find it hard to reconcile it with the fact that, when in 1937 I had several contacts with Moore while attending his Cambridge lectures and had introduced myself as a student of phenomenology, Moore never responded to this cue. Nor did Broad. And, unfortunately, no one referred me to the still living crown witness of the story of this article, G. Dawes Hicks.

NOTES

1. Letter of May 30, 1968, by J. T. Richnell, B.A., F.L.A., Goldsmith Librarian of the University of London Library.

2. C. K. Ogden and I. A. Richards, *The Meaning of Meaning,* 10th ed. (London: Kegan Paul, 1956), p. 269.

3. George Dawes Hicks, "Survey of Recent Philosophical and Theological Literature," *Hibbert Journal* 22 (1922): 182; see below note 15.

4. *Ideas,* p. 30; see page 53 above.

5. Edmund Husserl, *Briefe an Roman Ingarden* (The Hague: Nijhoff, 1968), p. 24.

6. See Herbert Spiegelberg, *The Phenomenological Movement* (The Hague: Nijhoff, 1969), p. 624.

7. Helen Bosanquet, *Bernard Bosanquet* (London: Macmillan, 1924), p. 145.

8. Recent evidence from the Bertrand Russell Archives at MacMaster University in the form of his letters to his brother Frank of June 3, 10, and July 1, 1918, show that he had promised G. F. Stout a review of the *Logical Investigations* for *Mind,* which never materialized; this explains *Mind*'s apparent neglect of this work.

9. Letter of August 26, 1968, from the librarian, Miss J. L. Randall-Cutler.

10. Hicks, "Survey," *Hibbert Journal* 10 (1911): 476.

11. Ibid. 12 (1913): 198ff.

12. Personal letter of April 5, 1968.

13. For a late confirmation of this possibility see the Postscript to this introduction, page 64.

14. T. M. Greenwood, "Geometry and Reality," in *Proceedings of the Aristotelian Society* (1921–22): 228.

15. Letter of December 14, 1922: "In England fand ich wärmste Aufnahme, nachträglich hat mich die Arist. Soc. z. Corresp. Mitglied gemacht." (In England I found a very warm reception; subsequently the Aristotelian Society has made me a corresponding member.) Edmund Husserl, *Briefe an Roman Ingarden,* p. 25.

16. "Last June Professor Edmund Husserl delivered, on the invitation of the University of London, at University College a remarkable series of lectures on 'Phänomenologische Methode und Phänomenologische Philosophie'; and these lectures will, it is hoped, be published in English at no distant date" (*Hibbert Journal* 22 [1922]: 182).

17. I call it "ill-fated" in view of the fact that the fourth and last version of Husserl's German draft, now published in *Phänomenologische Psychologie* (pp. 277–301), was not only telescoped by the translator but also paraphrased to such an extent that the original is hardly recognizable and at times distorted.

18. Ogden and Richards, *The Meaning of Meaning,* p. 269.

19. See, *e.g.,* W. G. DeBurgh, "George Dawes Hicks," in *Proceedings of the British Academy* 17 (1941): 415.

20. "It is far from being an easy task, for Husserl and his followers have introduced a whole galaxy of new technical terms, for many of which it is well-nigh hopeless to look for English equivalents" (*Hibbert Journal* 27 [1929]: 166).

21. *Jahrbuch* 9 (1928): 368–449; reviewed by Hicks in *Hibbert Journal* 28 (1928): 165.

22. *Hibbert Journal* 30 (1931): 167.

23. Hicks, "Survey," ibid. 35 (1936): 451.

24. Ibid. 37 (1938): 156.

25. See the obituary by John Wild in *Philosophy and Phenomenological Research* 2 (1942): 266–67.

26. *Erste Philosophie I,* p. xxii. See also Husserl, *Briefe an Roman Ingarden,* p. 26.

27. M 11 3b, p. 2 of the German typescript.

28. Ibid., p. 64.

29. Ibid., p. 74.

30. Ibid., p. 68.

31. *Vom Gesichtspunkt der Phänomenologie* (The Hague: Nijhoff, 1969), p. 26.

32. Ibid., p. 96.

33. See my "Perspektivenwandel" in *Edmund Husserl 1859–1959*, p. 58.

34. About Husserl's strong sympathy for and interest in English and American philosohy see also the diary note by Ralph Barton Perry quoted in Karl Schuhmann, *Husserl-Chronik. Denk- und Lebensweg Edmund Husserls*, Husserliana Dokumente 1 (The Hague: Nijhoff, 1977), p. 363.

35. *Collected Papers* 1 (The Hague: Nijhoff, 1962), p. 119.

36. See C. D. Broad, "Notes. Professor G. F. Stout (1860–1944)," *Mind* 54 (1945): 285.

Syllabus of a Course of Four Lectures on "Phenomenological Method and Phenomenological Philosophy"*

TRANSLATED BY G. DAWES HICKS

INTRODUCTION BY HERBERT SPIEGELBERG

REMARKS ON THE TEXT OF HUSSERL'S SYLLABUS

The following text, the earliest Husserl wrote for English readers, is published here for the first time. Previously only five sentences (the last sentences of the first, the two first of the second paragraph and the penultimate two-sentence paragraph) have been printed in Appendix D of *The Meaning of Meaning*.[1] For permission to publish the text in its entirety in this journal I wish to thank Professor Gerhart Husserl and Professor H. L. Van Breda, the director of the Husserl Archives in Louvain.

A few remarks are in order to give today's reader the optimum chance for understanding this text. The syllabus is mentioned first in the Announcement of Husserl's four lectures delivered in German "to advanced students of the University and to others interested in the subject" in the final sentence as follows: "A Syllabus in English of the Lectures will be obtainable in the Lecture Room."[2] Apparently, copies of this text no longer exist in England, nor are they at the Husserl Archives. After looking for them in vain last summer in London, I was finally handed one in Munich by Dr. Eberhard

Avé-Lallemant, who had come across it among the papers of the late Hedwig Conrad-Martius in Starnberg. Since the same carton contained papers left with the Conrads by Alexander Koyré at a visit with them in Bergzabern in August 1922, chances are that he had obtained the copy from Husserl himself when he stayed with the Husserls for three weeks during the summer following the London lectures in the Black Forest.[3] Incidentally, Koyré later played an important part in connection with the preparation of Husserl's Paris lectures in 1929 and with the translation of his subsequent *Cartesian Meditations* in 1931.

The text of the Syllabus is clearly a translation from a German original. Of this original all that has survived is Husserl's shorthand version.[4] Mr. Eduard Marbach, to whom I am greatly indebted for a transcription and for other judicious help, comments on this MS as follows:

The shorthand text of this syllabus is written in ink and shows many cuts and reformulations, underlinings and subdivisions in blue, red and black pencil, and some additions and stylistic changes in pencil. A transcription of this shorthand text must have preceded the translation, but it is not extant in the Husserl Archives in Lou-

*Reprinted with permission from *Journal of the British Society for Phenomenology* 1 (1970): 18–23.

vain. Presumably Husserl had revised this transcription once more *before* the translation, which can be gathered from minor deviations, mostly small additions or omissions, in the English text (translated from the German).

The translation itself was mimeographed on seven and one half pages legal size (12" x 8") singlespaced sheets. This format and even more such features as the typing of the Umlauts of German words added in parentheses after some words indicate that the typing was done in England. At the beginning of the text the translator has inserted auxiliary verbs into Husserl's incomplete telegram-style sentences; later he seems to have abandoned these editorial changes.

In the present reproduction of the Syllabus only obvious spelling mistakes have been corrected. No attempt will be made here to relate the Syllabus to the unpublished text of the actual London lectures.[5]

This German text typed out by Husserl's research assistant at the time, Ludwig Landgrebe, actually mentions the Syllabus as a separate document. Thus Husserl pointed out that he did not want to repeat the main theses of the Syllabus. It therefore represents in Husserl's eyes an independent text. Also, chances are that for a major part of the audience it was more accessible than Husserl's German presentation.

Notes

1. Ogden and Richards, *The Meaning of Meaning,* p. 269f.
2. For a reproduction of a copy of the Announcement, whose original can be found at the Husserl Archives, see Herbert Spiegelberg, *The Phenomenological Movement,* 3rd ed. (The Hague: Nijhoff, 1968), Table 8 (opposite p. 155).
3. See Edmund Husserl, *Briefe an Roman Ingarden* (The Hague: Nijhoff, 1968), p. 24.
4. M 113b, 2b–11b of the German typescript.
5. M 11 3 a, b of the German typescript.

LECTURE I

Introductory: The Aim of Phenomenological Philosophy.

The phenomenological method is a procedure that has arisen from fundamental considerations and through which a radical change of the attitude of natural experience and knowledge is rendered possible. A peculiar realm of given entities, concretely and intuitively perceived, is thereby opened out. *The ego cogito.* This transcendental phenomenological subjectivity, as immediate givenness of phenomenological self-experience, is not the "soul," the givenness of psychological experience. There has been made possible, and is now on foot, a new a priori science extracted purely from concrete phenomenological intuition *(Anschauung),* the science, namely, of transcendental phenomenology, which inquires into the totality of ideal possibilities that fall within the framework of phenomenological subjectivity, according to their typical forms and laws of being.

In the proper line of its explication lies the development of the originally "egological" (referred to the ego of the philosophising subject for the time being) phenomenology into a transcendental sociological phenomenology having reference to a manifest multiplicity of conscious subjects communicating with one another. A systematically consistent development of phenomenology leads necessarily to an all-comprehensive logic concerned with the correlates: knowing-act, knowledge-significance, and knowledge-objectivity. The unfolding in special directions of this wide-reaching logic leads by an inner necessity to the systematically arranged totality of all possible a priori sciences. Accordingly there is realised in transcendental phenomenology the necessary idea of a "first philosophy." It makes possible sciences of fact as "philosophies" ("second philosophies"), as sciences, namely, which in their methical working out are completely and "absolutely" justified as being derived from absolutely clear and ultimate principles. Ideally speaking, phenomenology is the in itself absolutely clear science of these sources; it contains in itself the theoretical system of the absolutely explicated principles of all possible sciences, the principles of construction for the a priori forms of all the sciences of realities for all possible worlds, and consequently these forms themselves.

On the basis of phenomenology the original ideal of philosophy evinces itself as a practical ideal; the ideal, namely, of a system to be constructed of all sciences as of absolutely strict and certain theories the rationality of which in all its stages rests on a priori insight. At the back of the system, as an inner unified totality, of such philosophical sciences there cannot be still further possible a "metaphysic," and beside these sciences there can be no special sciences (transcendental and philosophically naive) that rest upon themselves. Accordingly, the source of all that is philosophical, of all that is in the highest sense, scientific, lies in phenomenology. Its systematic development is the greatest of all the scientific problems of our time.

2

The Cartesian way to the *ego cogito* and the method of phenomenological reduction.

Historical connexion with Plato, the creator of the idea of philosophy as a universal system of absolutely justifiable knowledge and the pioneer of the idea of a preliminary rational science of method. Ancient philosophy and scepticism. Descartes' revival of the Platonic intentions. What was lost of the Platonic *Ethos:* philosophy as fulfilment and correlate of an ethical demand, the cognitive-ethical demand of radical intellectual conscientiousness. The cognitive-ethical resolve through which the philosopher becomes first of all in his own estimation a philosopher. The necessary consequences; the Cartesian "revolution" and the search for an absolutely unquestionable beginning. The

transformation of the Cartesian way to such beginning (*i.e.,* to the *ego cogito*) in its main outlines, through which it becomes the phenomenological introductory method.

a. *General preliminary considerations.* The necessary form of the philosophical beginning as meditation on the "I." The question as to the meaning of "absolutely justified" knowledge. Unquestionableness as norm of such knowledge and its fundamental significance. Evidence and adequate evidence. The source of all absolute justification must lie in adequate evidence. Apodictic character of this evidence. Mediate and immediate adequacy. The beginning we are in search of must be immediately and apodictically evident. Thus the ultimate basis of all philosophy must be a basis of experience (always accessible for him who philosophises) but a basis of apodictic experience.

b. The historical way pursued by Descartes to the *ego cogito* by means of the methodical negation of the sensuous world. The justification of this way in its fundamental re-interpretation. The "I am," the "I think" of naturally naive evidence, is not the *ego cogito* grasped in virtue of this method in apodictic experiential evidence. The method is needed in order to subordinate the naive attitude in experience and knowledge generally, in order to render possible the new phenomenological attitude and to make the *ego cogito* capable of being experienced as a field of view unique and complete in itself. This "transcendental phenomenological subjectivity" is not the Cartesian *mens* as pure soul; phenomenological experience of self is not psychologically "inner" experience.

LECTURE II

The Realm of phenomenological Experience and the possibility of a phenomenological science. Transcendental Phenomenology as science of essence in respect of transcendental subjectivity.

1

What is to be our mode of setting out theoretically with the *ego cogito?* A Carte-

sian metaphysic? A speculative philosophy of the ego? We must remember the demand for adequate apodictic evidence as principle of the "beginning." In view of the wholly unfamiliar character of the phenomenological field, it is necessary at the outset to explore it as inquirers, to become acquainted with it in tentative observations and to describe it. The necessary guarantee of confining oneself to phenomenological territory and of the purity of phenomenological description by the rule of phenomenological bracketing or putting between quotation marks (*Einklammerung*). That rule prohibits any naively natural assertion and the use of any objective judgments whatsoever; it permits only reflective judgments upon such judgments as my "phenomena," upon my belief and that which is thereby believed *as such*, and likewise judgments upon any kind of "I feel or immediately experience" (*Ich erlebe*), and upon all that is immanent therein.

Adequate descriptions according to the threefold title: *ego, cogito, cogitatum.* By way of example, analyses along the parallel lines, *cogito, cogitatum*, whereby manifold modifications of intentionality emerge.

Perception as immediate presentness. Recollection as immediate pastness. Modes of mediate presentness and pastness through gesture, picture, sign and expression. *Einfühlung* and expression of a mental life in a body. Modes of intuitiveness and non-intuitiveness, of determinateness and indeterminateness, of knownness and strangeness. Modes of attention. A fragment of phenomenological analysis in the case of a perceived spatial thing: the multiplicity of its perspective ways of appearing, form-perspective, colour-perspective, etc. Manifoldness of the modes of orientation. The absolute "here," the manifold "there," near and far, the far horizon. Discrimination of the body, etc. Continuous perception and synthetic unity in continuity. The continuously one and the same object of perception. Discrete synthesis and the identical One.

The ideality of the object in the multiplicity of vital experiences (*Erlebnisse*) which are consciousness of it: it is involved in them not as an active part but as "intentional pole." The object *as* in a certain sense what is meant or intended: even the sensuous form is not an actual part of the vital experiences. "Intentional form" as contrasted with "actual" moments of vital experience.

Modalities of belief and the intentional modes of being (being, possible being, probable being, doubtful being, etc.). Presumptive intention as directly aimed and

confirmation of the intention. Presumptive being and being in the character "it is really so." Opposite case of annulling. Character of non-being. Realisation of the intentio in the transition into a self-giving (*selbstgebende*) intuition or "evident justification"; intentional character of "true being." Analogous modalities of feeling and willing. Endless multiplicity of such modalities.

Possible descriptions in reference to the *ego* as "centre" of the attending, convinced, acting intentionality, as also "centre" of affective states. All such occurrences establish the fact of the phenomenologically constituted I or *ego*. But they only indefinitely constitute the actually lived stream of life of "the natural *ego*." Bifurcation of the *ego* in the transition into the phenomenological focus or attitude; it becomes an "impartial spectator" of what belongs to itself. Phenomenological reflexion of a higher level: phenomenological experience and thought as subject-matter of reflexion. All descriptions result in "pure intuition," in adequate experiential evidence. No naturalistic prejudices, no *tabula rasa* interpretations.

2

The question as to the possibility of an egological science. A further consideration: the phenomenological subjectivity is experienced as extending beyond the range of the actually present, as stretching forward into an endless past and future. Possibility of doubt in respect of my recollected past, as also in respect to the future stream of experiences. Necessity of a fresh elimination for the reduction to the absolutely given. The impossibility of "objectively" fixed or scientific expressions for the sphere of the merely present: accordingly a science of facts in respect of the *ego cogito* cannot in the philosophical "beginning" be attained.

Radical removal of an empiricist prejudice: extension of the notion of "Experience." Adequate self-comprehension (adequate "experience") is also possible of pure possibilities; further, in respect to pure possibilities, of "species" of a single one of a species, of particular and universal possible relations, of essential necessities and impossibilities. Independence of all such a priori statements of experience in the ordinary sense—that is to say, of the trustworthiness of perception, recollection, etc. Indubious possibility of intuitive and adequate apprehension of such a priori certainties in the sphere of the transcendental *ego*. To the philosophising *ego* the totality (*universum*) of its egological possibilities according to its essence and essential laws is accessible in the framework of adequate and apodictic evidence. The phenomenological "bracketing" (*Einklammer-* *ung*) of all transcendental natural possibilities for the purpose of reduction to the sphere of purely egological possibilities. An essential theory, operative within the boundaries of absolute evidence, of my possible egological certainties (for possible *ego*, possible consciousness, possible intentional forms) *can and must be the first of all philosophies*— the first in possible and absolute proof. And this science is transcendental phenomenology, the mother of all a priori sciences.

LECTURE III

Transcendental phenomenology, and the problems of possible knowledge, possible science, possible objectivities and worlds.

1

Difficulties of a systematic structure of phenomenology.

Transcendental subjectivity in the form of phenomenological time as the field of inquiry of descriptive phenomenology. A wider range of problems of a still higher stage of reflexion. Phenomenology of the primordial consciousness of time.

Sketch of the systematic divisions of descriptive phenomenology.

Elimination of the relatively poor hyletical phenomenology (sense-data in the sensuous fields). The endless realm of the phenomenology of intentionality. (a) The correlative problems in reference to *ego*, consciousness and intentional objectivity prior to all question of justification, truth and reality. (b) Higher stage: Phenomenology of reason. Its specialisation into rational theoretical disciplines in accordance with a priori distinguishable regions of intentional objectivity.

2

Realisation of these merely indicated differences by consideration *of the meaning of the traditional Epistemology and its relation to phenomenology.*

The problems of "right," of "validity," of knowledge and its relation to objectivities, to things *per se*, to ideas, inherently valid, truths, theories, to ideals inherently valid and norms, worths, etc. The problems of the possibility of transcendent knowledge and of the possible meaning of a world which is knowable by the objective sciences. The subjectivity of all that is accomplished by knowledge, *e.g.*, in the passive bringing together of sensuous appearances, in the active production of notions, propositions, theories; the objects of knowledge in itself as merely immanent substrata of experience and theory; legitimate evidences, felt necessities of thought as subjective characteristics in knowledge. How then can what is purely subjective acquire "transcendent" objective significance, or what meaning can such objective significance have? The struggle with sceptical negativism and agnosticism.

Thesis to be maintained: All rationally framed questions proposed to knowledge as the work of reason are either transcendental phenomenological questions or confused and absurd questions.

It is I, and I indeed as *the absolute ego*, that effectuates in my diversified *cogito* that assignment of significance through which *everything* that can have any meaning for me wins such meaning: the meaning of mere opinion, genuine knowledge, legitimate proof, empirical or a priori evidence, etc.; but also of normal or delusive appearance, asserted truth and falsity, existence and nonexistence, etc.; and again of an intended and true object, of that which is in itself over against the act of knowing, more specifically of thing, nature, social world, culture, etc. Only transcendental phenomenology comprises and comprehends in its adequately evident method the absolutely unique being of the knowing consciousness and all the correlations included within it, in all their stages and forms. Only in its focus are the problems of knowledge (and all imaginable problems) capable of being formulated in adequate clearnesss and of being apodictically solved.

General epistemology merges into general phenomenology and in a complete treatment would be covered by the latter. But concrete theories of knowledge (constitutive phenomenologies) are necessary, *e.g.*, a concrete phenomenology of the knowledge of nature, a systematic analysis of the strata and stages of the experiencing subject and its intentional correlata (visual thing, a thing of touch, a sensuous thing of many parts, an actually causal thing, etc.) The "Idea" of a complete experience and insight into the complete working of a possible harmonious experience generally; its correlate the Idea of a "real" object of experience. The necessity of parallel constitutive disciplines for every region of objectivities.

3

Transcendental phenomenological subjectivity or monadologism as necessary consequence of the transcendental phenomenological attitude. The knowledge that any objectivity is only what it is through intentional meaning or significance shows that there is only one possibility for an absolute and concrete being: the being of a concretely full transcendental subjectivity. *It* is the only genuine "Substance." The *ego* is what it is from its own fundamental meaning. The *ego* is in so far as it constitutes itself for itself as being. All other being is merely being relative to the *ego* and is encompassed within the regulated intentionality of subjectivity. It is only as "Ideal Pole," be it as a temporally individualised idea (empirical reality), be it as supra-temporal species, etc.

4

Problem of the *alter ego* (Phenomenology of *Einfühlung*). Transcendental egology does not signify solipsism. The *ego* that comes to expression in the body of another person is determined from the peculiar meaning of the experience of *Einfühlung* and its possible vindication not as relative to an *ego* but as itself an *ego*. Thereby egological phenomenology acquires at the same time intersubjective validity. In further working out of the point of view, every actual or supra-temporal object acquires relativity to the totality of the *alter egos* and to "everybody." Phenomenological monadology.

LECTURE IV

The concrete idea of logic as a theory of scientific knowledge and the system of all ontological inquiries. The concrete aim of phenomenological philosophy.

1

A reverting to the line of thought in the first lecture and to the treatment of the problem of making a "philosophy" possible. In phenomenology, there is not only obtained a first and absolutely legitimate science, but as a radical theory of knowledge it contains the absolutely warranted principles for the justification of all possible kinds of knowledge. The ideal that leads to the philosophical "beginning," the ideal of absolute justification, of adequate evidence, is confirmed in *the* sense that any ultimate justification of knowledge is only possible in the form of an adequate essential knowledge of knowledge, that is to say as transcendental phenomenology. The true significance of the method of phenomenological "bracketing" (*Einklammerung*) does not lie absolutely in the rejection of all transcendent knowledge and objects of knowledge but in the rejection of all naively dogmatic knowledge in favour of the knowledge that is alone in the long run justified from the phenomenological point of view of essence.

The logically legitimate function of the historically transmitted disciplines, *e.g.*, of the recently constituted mathematical syllogistic, of the disciplines of pure mathematics, of geometry, of the pure theory of time, of motion, pure mechanics, etc. (We speak of "formal" and "material ontologies" as a priori sciences of objects generally, or of objects of a special region of being.) What these sciences as naively dogmatic have been able to achieve is insufficient. Bracketing (*Einklammerung*) and phenomenological critique of these sciences. Constitutive phenomenology must in itself rest upon the fundamental notions and axioms of the logic of propositions and in like manner upon all ontological fundamental notions and axioms. But it obtains them in their ultimately primitive clearness and legitimacy. Thus the phenomenology of the knowledge of nature and of nature itself (as its intentional correlate) acquires the ultimately purified fundamental notions and propositions for material thing, space and spatial form, physical property, physical causality, etc., which supply critical norms for all legitimate judgments of nature. A systematically developed phenomenology needs no preceding sciences, ideally it contains within itself the totality of all imaginable a priori sciences, and indeed as absolutely established "philosophical" sciences. It is, therefore, the universal a priori philosophy.

Precisely on this account it realises (thought of as developed) the original and genuine idea of logic. For originally (in the Platonic dialectic) logic was to be the science or rendering clear the significance, result and legitimacy of possible knowledge and was thereby to make possible genuine wisdom and a universal philosophy. Necessarily it turned its gaze to all the correlative sides, to the side of the "I" striving after truth and of the knowing consciousness (evidence, proof), to the side of the meaning of knowledge (notion, proposition, truth), and to the side of the object. The dogmatic character of the historical logic, the confused boundaries associated therewith, its clinging to mere generalities; its predominant psychologism. A dogmatic logic can be no pro-

paedeutic of genuine science, no theory of the principles of method, no absolute theory of norms. Consideration of the necessary requirements of the idea of a logic as a theory of science (*Wissenschaftslehre*) lead inevitably to transcendental phenomenology (for the historical development see my *Logical Investigations*). The logical outcome leads beyond a universal phenomenological "logic" to the totality of the a priori sciences, an objectively directed and constitutive phenomenology. It leads also to an a priori deduction of the system of all the categories of being and thereby to that of the system of the a priori sciences. In like manner it leads to other problems of a universal systematic (*e.g.*, the necessary constituents of the idea of a world of individuals).

The transcendental monadism, which necessarily results from the retrospective reference to absolute subjectivity, carries with it a peculiar a priori character over against the constituted objectivities, that of the essence-requirements of the individual monads and of the conditions of possibility for a universe of "compossible" monads. To this "metaphysical" inquiry there thus belongs the essence-necessity of the "harmonious accord" of the monads through their relation to an objective world mutually constituted in them, the problems of teleology, of the meaning of the world and of the world's history, the problem of God.

Transition from the a priori to the *factum*. The philosophy of reality. I, my life, my world, the multiplicity of other *egos*, as *factum*, as a single possibility in the universal system of a priori possibilities. An ultimately established knowledge of possibilities. A perfectly strict empirical science presupposes for its possibility an absolutely valid universal logic, and that is transcendental phenomenology. The naively dogmatic sciences of fact and their phenomenological critique. Their transformation into correlate sciences and therewith into scientific phenomenologies of matters of fact. The ideal of the future is essentially that of phenomenologically based ("philosophical") sciences, in unitary relation to an absolute theory of monads. Phenomenology as "first philosophy" and as method of all "secondary" philosophies. Thus phenomenology is the realisation of the way to a universal philosophy in the old sense. There cannot be independent sciences side by side and as one amongst them philosophy, but only a single universal science on a single absolute foundation.

Introduction to
Husserl's Syllabus for the Paris Lectures on
"Introduction to
Transcendental Phenomenology"*

HERBERT SPIEGELBERG

1. The Case for an English Translation of the German Syllabus

At first sight there may seem to be little point in an English translation of Husserl's German syllabus of his four lectures at the Sorbonne on February 23 and 25, 1929, considering the fact that the text of the actual lectures as reconstructed by Stephan Strasser has been translated and introduced by Peter Koestenbaum in 1961.[1] Was not the syllabus meant only for the specific occasion and has no longer any permanent value? Clearly the situation is different in the case of the University of London lectures of June 7, 8, 9 and 12, 1922, whose main text is not yet published, much as it deserves to be, so that the recently recovered syllabus in the translation which was distributed to the audience is the only available substitute.[2]

Nevertheless, the original German text of the Sorbonne syllabus, published in *Husserliana,* is significant enough to warrant an English translation for the following reasons in inverse order of importance:

(1) Now that the editor's introduction to

both the *Paris Lectures* and the *Cartesian Meditations* has been translated, the syllabus is the only part of this volume, except for the excerpts from Ingarden's comments, still missing in English.

(2) The syllabus was the first authentic Husserl text put into the hands of the French public, though only in the printed form of a French "Sommaire," added to the German *Inhaltsverzeichnis* in *Husserliana* 1. Since Husserl delivered the actual lectures in German, the syllabus was presumably much more accessible to most of the audience.

(3) The reconstructed text of the Paris lectures may not be identical with what Husserl actually said to his audience, much as it was based on his manuscript. All we know his audience received exactly as we know it now was the French summary.

(4) However, a close comparison of the *Sommaire* with the German original reveals that it was an increasingly free translation, especially toward the end, where whole sentences are missing. This was hardly the text Husserl wanted his audience to have. Certainly for an English reader it is no adequate substitute for the German syllabus.

(5) In the syllabus at the end of the first lecture, there is a distinction between the epoche and the "now following" turn of the glance (*Blickwendung*), which seems to be

*Reprinted with permission of the publisher and translator from *Journal of the British Society for Phenomenology* 7 (1976): 18–23, with revisions to the introduction.

the equivalent of the phenomenological reduction.[3] This becomes even clearer at the end of the paragraph, where Husserl puts the two methods of the transcendental-phenomenological epoche and that of the transcendental-phenomenological reduction to the transcendental ego side by side as replacements for the Cartesian method. There is nothing equally explicit in the Paris lectures, where Husserl merely says that by means of the phenomenological epoche the natural human I is reduced (*reduziert sich*) to the transcendental ego.[4] In the *Cartesian Meditations* Husserl even says that the transcendental epoche "insofar as it leads back" is *called* the transcendental-phenomenological reduction, making the difference apparently merely a matter of names, although it is clear that even here "leading back" is something different from mere abstaining.[5] I have discussed the significance of this distinction elsewhere.[6]

2. Textual Problems and Their Significance

The present translation is based merely on the text and incidental information as given in *Husserliana* I. It is therefore possible that by going back to the original manuscripts some of the questions I shall now raise may still be answered. The most important one concerns the chronological relation between the syllabus and the two manuscripts[7] that Husserl had prepared for the Paris lectures, from which Strasser reconstructed his text. This question could also throw light on the role and the relative significance of the two texts.

According to Strasser Husserl did not begin his preparations for the lectures until January 25.[8] Now, since the syllabus had to be translated and printed in French, it would seem likely that it had to be sent to Paris well in advance of the lectures on February 23 and 25. So the syllabus was hardly the last thing Husserl worked on. The fact that the syllabus was divided up only for the first two lectures, whereas the third and fourth of these lectures are not yet separated, suggests that when Husserl sent off the German syllabus he had not yet completed his lectures. Also only the first lecture

was given a special title. In this respect the Paris syllabus differs strikingly from its London predecessor, where, to be sure, Husserl did not give "double lectures" on only two days but offered separate lectures on four different days. However, even in other regards the London syllabus, with all its linguistic and other defects, emerges as a much more detailed and impressive piece. To be sure, Husserl himself was apparently no longer aware of this difference when he put into the margin of the first page of the Paris syllabus the remark (in German): "probably for the table of contents of the London lectures? Or of the Paris ones?"[9]

However, the style of the two syllabuses is pretty much the same. Next to complete sentences there are merely key words or sentence fragments, which could not have meant much to readers who could not follow the actual lecture. In fact, whole paragraphs consist only of sequences of seeming subtitles to be spelled out in the lecture.

Under these circumstances the relative importance of the Paris syllabus and of Strasser's text of the lectures for the genesis of the *Cartesian Meditations* is hard to assess. What has to be realized is that according to Strasser's textual apparatus (*Textkritischer Anhang*)[10] he had to reconstitute the text of the lectures from two manuscripts, the *Urtext* apparently still containing most of the original pages and a second shorthand manuscript entitled "Development for the Printing" (*Ausarbeitung für den Druck*), to which numerous pages had been transferred. Strasser returned those which "probably" (*vermutlich*) belonged to the *Urtext,* but he does not describe the criteria for the solution of the resulting problems of identification, which were clearly not easy to solve. In any case the present text remains a reconstruction not authenticated by Husserl himself, as was the text of the syllabus. On the other hand most of the lecture texts may be later than the syllabus and hence closer to the actual lectures of February 23 and 25. Also the lecture text is considerably richer than the syllabus. Yet the syllabus contains significant differences in the formulation, such as the distinction between epoche and reduction which first attracted my attention. Certainly both texts are worth studying as stages of Husserl's developing thought.

The most helpful and reliable informa-tion about the genesis and background of the Paris lectures can now be found in Karl Schuhmann's indispensable *Husserl-Chronik*.[11]

NOTES

1. *The Paris Lectures*.
2. Reprinted in this volume, pages 67–74.
3. *Cartesianische Meditationen*, p. 189.
4. Ibid., p. 10, l. 36–p. 11, l. 3 (*PL*, p. 10).
5. Ibid., p. 61 (p. 21).
6. Herbert Spiegelberg, "Is the Reduction Necessary for Phenomenology?" *Journal of the British Society for Phenomenology* 4 (1973):6.
7. *Cartesianische Meditationen*, p. 221.
8. Ibid., p. xxiii; translated by Thomas Attig in *Journal of the British Society for Phenomenology* 7 (1976): 12–17.
9. Ibid., p. 245, where the editor reports that on page 187, line 28, of the original manuscript there is a note in the margin: "Probably for the table of contents of the London lectures? Or of the Paris ones?"
10. Ibid., pp. 221–22.
11. (The Hague: Nijhoff, 1977), pp. 341–44.

5

Syllabus for the Paris Lectures on "Introduction to Transcendental Phenomenology"

TRANSLATED BY HERBERT SPIEGELBERG

SURVEY

First Lecture

The Cartesian Meditations and their Critical Transformation into a Meditative Disclosure of the Transcendental Ego

1. Introductory

An introduction to transcendental phenomenology connects quite naturally with Descartes' *Meditations,* whose critical transformation has influenced its origin. Descartes' postulate of a universal science on absolute grounds; after the overturn of traditional science its reconstruction on absolute foundations. The subjective turn of this postulate and its model character. The idea of the true philosopher in the making, its necessary start with meditations of the Cartesian type as to how the first and absolutely certain foundation can be found. The result: the meditating person must keep out the existence of the world as questionable and thus "win" his pure ego as absolute and unique. From this start the way of the construction of the knowledge of the world and of all objective sciences purely under the direction of the principles innate in the ego.

Perennial value and historical significance of these fundamental meditative considerations. The positive sciences have pushed them aside, but philosophically they were the source of the completely new developmental sense of modern philosophy in the direction of a transcendental philosophy, whose last most radical form is phenomenology. The decline and hopeless fragmentation of philosophy since the middle of the nineteenth century calls for a newer beginning and new Cartesian meditations. Phenomenology as their conscious resumption and purest result.

2. The Cartesian Meditations in Critical Transformation

I, as radically starting philosopher, invalidating for me all pre-existing sciences. Even the idea of universal science on absolute grounds is not yet settled regarding its possibility and attainability, although it directs our meditating. Interpretation of its sense through empathy into the intention of scientific work: scientific statements through self-evidence [by way of] appeal to the things (*Sachen*), the states of affairs "themselves"—[*i.e.*] those that are directly or indirectly founded. Not [merely] incidental self-evidences and true statements of everyday life but scientific truths which are valid once and for all and for everybody. The incipient philosopher [for whom] the sciences are being overturned does not own anything like this, yet [he does own] the self-evidences of life. He begins with the principle of judging from pure self-evidence

78

and the critical analysis of the self-evidences themselves with regard to their perfection [and] their scope, an analysis carried out by self-evidences of a higher type in turn. From this basis he poses the question whether self-evidences primary in themselves which precede all others can be demonstrated and can at the same time be designated as "apodictic," as valid once for all.

Life and the positive sciences refer to the obviously existing world. [But] asks the meditating person, is the existence of the world the certainty primary in itself and apodictic? Descartes' first, but superficial, critique of sense experience: that it lacks apodicticity; and by this means his great step to include this experience universally into the overturn and then to show that the *ego cogito* remains unaffected by the possible non-existence of the world.

3. *Critical Delimitation of the Cartesian Procedure*

All positive sciences presuppose the validity of the belief in [the existence of] the world that is implied in all experience of the world. This universal self-evidence is in need of criticism, hence is to be deprived of its validity claim. But this abstention from the belief in the existence of the world deprives the meditator of the world as the ground of being (*Seinsboden*) for sciences, relating to it as a point of reference, but not of all ground of being and all self-evidence in general. Rather, behind the being of the world, the being of the experiencer and of his entire meditating and otherwise absolute life reveals itself as the ultimate existential presupposition [of being], even for the validity of experience and the invalidity of the world and its questioning. With the universal epoche as universal abstention from the natural practice of experiential belief and the now following turn of the glance to the experiencing life in which the world has in me its sense and being (plain reality), transcendental subjectivity makes its appearance as the meditating ego, which finds itself as the absolute and ultimate presupposition for everything that is at all and that now no longer finds itself as man in the world but as the ego in whom just as the world in general

this man receives his sense of being. As this ego and only as such am I apodictically certain for myself and am ultimate presupposition of being to whom everything that is meaningful for me is relative. What remains out of the question, and must remain so, is every misinterpretation as if this ego were a last remaining little piece of the world which strangely is given apodictically, and the plan to prove again as an addition the [existence of the] balance of the world in order to rebuild subsequently on the old ground of mundane science. [But] meditation must move on toward a comprehensive self-reflection of the pure ego in order to clarify the meaningful problems it includes as their ground of being and knowing generally. Thus it is that from the Cartesian method the method of transcendental phenomenological epoche and of transcendental phenomenological reduction—the one leading to the transcendental ego—has arisen.

Second Lecture

Introduction

What can I, the meditator, undertake philosophically with the transcendental *ego cogito?* Preview of its utilization, not as foundational axiom, but as a foundational sphere of experience and being. The idea of a new type of foundation, the transcendental, as compared with the objective one, a novel transcendental type of experiental knowledge and science from purely egological self-reflection—the first egological phenomenology.

Execution

Step by step opening up of the field of transcendental self-experience by phenomenological reflection. Psychological and transcendental self-reflection as parallels. Psychological reflection on the basis of a real world claims objective validity; transcendental experience claims merely egological validity. First fundamental statements: the *cogito* as consciousness *of something* (intentional experience), the *cogitatum qua cogitatum* an inseparable descriptive part within the *cogito*. Continuing self-reflection as coherent self-experience and radical revelation and pure description of typical modes of the intentional experiences and of their meant (appearing, thought about, valued, etc.) objectivities exactly as we are conscious of them. In addition to these two dimensions of description a third one, that of the ego of the *cogitationes* themselves, enters.[1] [The world, despite the epoche with regard to all side-takings as a major theme of phenomenological descriptions: the world as *phenomenon*. Contrasting of natural and phenomenological consideration of the world. The phenomenologically meditating ego as transcendental spectator of its own being and life in the condition of being immersed (*Hingegebenheit*) in the world. I, as a naturally oriented I, am also and am always a transcendental I, but know of it only through the performance of the phenomenological reduction. Only through this transcendental attitude do I see that everything natural exists for me merely as a *cogitatum* of changing *cogitationes,* and only this is what I hold to be valid in my judging. Thus in general I must describe objects (real as well as ideal) only in correlation with their ways of being conscious.].

A piece of phenomenology of thing-perception as example of phenomenological description combined with the sharing of the correlative belonging together of what appears and the modes in which it appears. Unity and variety—the unity of an object as synthesis of identifying congruence (*Deckung*) of appearances of the same thing. The synthesis as the fundamental fact of the sphere of consciousness, as combination of consciousness and consciousness into a new consciousness of founded intentionality. The universal unity of conscious life in the ego a unity of consciousness in which the ego becomes conscious for itself as unity.

The ego in the potential state of possible consciousness. The intentional horizons in each *cogito* and their disclosure. Explication of the intentional implications as the main task of intentional analysis. Fundamental difference of phenomenological analysis and analysis in the usual sense. In phenomenology always an interweaving of part analysis (*reell*) with intentional analysis— Conscious life as Heraclitean flux and the

possibility of phenomenological descriptions as descriptions of the types of consciousness. Transition to the phenomenology of reason, of its actualities and potentialities.

Third and Fourth Lectures

Reason and unreason, fulfilment and disappointment of the intentions as structural forms of transcendental subjectivity. Being and possible experience—possible self-evidence. Possibility as subjective accessibility related to presumptive horizons. The constitutive questions as questions for the system of fully verifying experience which are predelineated in transcendental subjectivity as possibilities for each kind of object with their specific types. Each object meant indicates presumptively its system. The essential relatedness of the ego to a manifold of meant objects thus designates an essential structure of its entire and possible intentionality. The constitutive problems comprise the whole transcendental subjectivity, for even the being-for-itself of the ego is a constitutive problem. The self-constitution of the I in a specific sense as personal I. I as pole of specific acts, the side-taking acts, and as pole of "affections" [states of being affected]. Contrast of polarization in the object and polarization in the subject. But the ego is not a mere pole of fleeting acts, each (act of) side-taking establishes in the ego a lasting *conviction.*

Advance to the eidetic method; all transcendental phenomenological problems are problems of essence, transcendental phenomenology a science of the innate a priori of transcendental subjectivity.

Transition to the phenomenology of genesis. Phenomenology of association as essential law-likeness of passive genesis. Active genesis. By means of the genesis the lasting intentional achievements come into being, among them the constitution of lasting worlds for the ego, of the real and ideal world of numbers, of the theoretical con struct [*Gebilde*].

The theory of the transcendental constitution of being and the traditional epistemology. Explication of the usual problem of transcendence as problem of natural human knowledge and as related to intentionality as a psychological fact. How can a spectacle in the immanent psychic interior and the experiences of self-evidence arising in it have objective significance? Critical demonstration of the absurdity of this formulation of the problem. Every genuine transcendental problem is a phenomenological one. The transcendental subjectivity in its universality has no meaningful outside. The task is not to infer transcendent being, but to understand it as an occurrence in transcendental subjectivity by disclosure of its constitution. Phenomenological idealism as a radically novel idealism is in contrast with that of Berkeley-Hume but also with the Kantian.

The objection of transcendental solipsism. The constitutive problem of the *alter ego* (empathy), of intersubjectivity, of nature and world as an identical world for everyman. The method of the solution: the methodical stratification of the sphere of consciousness given to the subject by abstracting from all its contents that presuppose the *alter ego*. Construction of the ego proper, the concrete I-myself as foundation for the analogizing empathy. Everything originally perceivable and experienceable is a determination of the I-myself. The other ego and the secondary experience of empathy is not directly perceivable but indirectly experienceable through indication, which has its way of concordant confirmation. In my originally experiencing mind the other mo-

nads (Leibniz) are mirrored. The disclosure of the constitution yields it as transcendental and thus enlarges the phenomenological reduction to transcendental subjectivity as a transcendental community of monads (*Monadengemeinschaft*). This is the transcendental ground for the constitution of the objective world, as the world which exists identically for all men of the community and for the intersubjective validity of the ideal objectivities.

The Cartesian problem of a universal science on absolute foundations and its solution in phenomenology. Naïveté of prescientific life, naïveté of the positive sciences. This naïveté as a lack of a deepest foundation from the disclosure of the transcendental achievements. Radically founded theory of science. Its step[s]: the solipsistically restricted egology; this ontology as a aprioristic foundation for the most radical foundation of a universal science of facts, a philosophy of factual being. The genuine metaphysical problems as those of the highest level within a phenomenology. Contrasting the Cartesian with the phenomenological realization of the idea of a philosophy. The phenomenological philosophy as the most universal and most radical development of the idea of self-knowledge which is not only the primal source of all genuine knowledge but also comprises all genuine knowledge within itself.

NOTE

1. The critical apparatus (Cartesianische Meditationen, p. 242) mentions that in his manuscript Husserl had surrounded the subsequent lines by brackets.

PART TWO

Husserl on Logic and Psychologism

In the light of both Hume's and Mill's repeated and sustained criticisms of the nature of both inductive and deductive reasoning, a series of questions about the nature of logical laws continues to command the attention of many philosophers today. Some of these questions might usefully be summarized in such terms as the following: Are logical laws inductive generalizations, or a priori insights into reality, or descriptions of mental operations, or verbal conventions, or still something else altogether different?

One of the most fundamental and pervasive themes in Husserl's phenomenology is the critical preoccupation with these and related questions about the status of logical laws. These issues are the background of the materials presented in Part Two of this collection.

Although each of the four texts published here can profitably be approached with this general theme in mind, nevertheless it is useful to insist on a distinction between the first text on the concept of number and the remaining three texts on the problems of logical psychologism. For the first text is a case of a variety of errors which Husserl is at pains to identify, analyze, and finally overcome in the subsequent articles. Husserl, in other words, came to reject most of the assumptions that control his extended essay on the concept of number. What the other, shorter articles indicate, however—although without demonstrating—is that this revision in Husserl's early philosophical position came about not only because of the criticisms which his work here on number and elsewhere on the philosophy of arithmetic provoked from Frege and others but also, and perhaps primarily, because of Husserl's own efforts to formulate the problem of logical psychologism with more perspicacity and rigor.

Taken as a whole, then, these materials provide a detailed instance of Husserl at work on the task of trying to overcome some of the most important difficulties involved in his starting point. The early work presented here is later developed in still further detail in his major works, the *Logical Investigations* (1900–1901) and *Formal and Transcendental Logic* (1929), and is still prominent in his posthumous work, *Experience and Judgement* (1948).

The question remains open for many of Husserl's contemporary readers whether Husserl ever satisfactorily resolved the complex issues of logical psychologism and the particular status of logical laws[1] which he himself raised at the outset of his philosophical career.

One convenient way of summarizing this difficult topic is to isolate a series of different formulations of logical psychologism in the positions Husserl presents from Mill, Lipps, Wundt, Sigwart, and others. We can then reduce these various formulations to two basic theses, each with a corollary, one being a stronger version than the other. This, in fact, is the strategy worked out in a recent important paper on psychologism. Here is a slightly amended version of the results.

> *Strong logical psychologism*: Psychological investigations of actual human thought processes are the necessary and sufficient conditions of logical investigations. [Corollary: The analysis of logical laws is equivalent to the analysis of particular human thought processes.][2]

This strong formulation is easily weakened to accommodate more nuanced views by omitting the phrase "and sufficient" in the thesis statement and substituting "consists partly" for "is equivalent to" in the corollary statement. An example of this thesis is to be found in Husserl's discussion of Mill. Mill subscribes to logical psychologism when he interprets the principle of contradiction as consisting of the view that no two contradictory statements can be *judged* to be true at the same time. The nonpsychologistic formulation would be: no two contradictory statements can be true at the same time. On the first view, logical contradictories are two statements, both of which it is impossible to believe to be true at the same time; on the second, logical contradictories are two statements, both of which cannot be true at the same time.

Two basic arguments are usually used to support logical psychologism in the versions that Husserl discusses. The first calls attention to the fact that logic must deal with mental activities just because it deals with judging, inferring, proving, and so on. The second reminds us that nothing, not even logical laws, can be dealt with independently of thinking. Nothing, the claim is, can be an object without at the same time already being dependent on mind. The first argument is properly psychologistic, whereas the second is more generally idealistic. Of the two, the general argument is more powerful, as we would expect.

The point at issue here is whether indeed there are objects or simply things we take to be objects. More basically, the issue is one of truth. Are there truths or are there no more than what we take to be truths? This is the formulation which Frege settles for in his preface to *The Basic Laws of Arithmetic* (1893): "All I have to say to this is," he writes there, "being true is different from being taken to be true, whether by one or many or everybody, and in no case is to be reduced to it. There is no contradiction in some things being true which everybody takes to be false. I understand by 'laws of logic' not psychological laws of takings to be true but laws of truth."[3]

Once the errors in the first volume of *The Philosophy of Arithmetic* (1891) were grasped, this position becomes Husserl's as well. But both Frege and Husserl are aware that such a position cannot itself be defended with the help of the laws of logic. In short, whether a law of logic is acknowledged to be true or not comes down to nothing more than opinion. This explains both the force of the strong psychologistic position and its continued recurrence especially in Husserl's thought. Although Frege remained with this view, by the time of the first edition of the *Logical Investigations* in 1900–01 Husserl came to believe that the psychologistic position could be refuted. Whether his arguments were sufficient to refute as well the strong or idealistic position that troubled Frege so deeply still remains controversial.

NOTES

1. See, among other accounts, S. Barker's description of the problem in his *The Elements of Logic,* 3rd ed. (New York, 1980), pp. 299–307, and S. Haack, *Philosophy of Logics* (Cambridge, 1978).

2. M. Sukale, *Comparative Studies in Phenomenology* (The Hague, 1976), p. 24.

3. Cited by Sukale, *Comparative Studies, p. 25.*

Introduction to "On the Concept of Number"
DALLAS WILLARD

Husserl took his doctorate in mathematics, with a minor in philosophy. Hence, it is not surprising that his first published writing, which follows below, was in the philosophy of mathematics. And since it was widely agreed among mathematicians of that time that the logically basic concept for mathematics is that of number, Husserl assumed that "it is with the analysis of the concept of number that any Philosophy of Mathematics must begin." Just such an analysis is the goal of the following essay. Its contents were worked into form during the academic year 1886–87. But, according to its author, the first part of *Philosophie der Arithmetik,* published in 1891, repeats this essay "almost word-for-word" (nahezu wörtlich).[1] Indeed, this early essay sets forth the basic elements in a view of number which Husserl adhered to for the remainder of his life, and does so by using much the same method of analysis which he also retained, with elaborations and name changes, to the end of his career.

The essay presents special difficulties for the contemporary reader, because it attempts conceptual analysis in a manner now totally out of use. So it may be helpful to divide it explicitly into the following parts: (I) The "Introduction" states the goal of the essay and describes the philosophical significance of that goal. With no elucidation, the method to be followed is here referred to as "psychological" analysis. (II) Section 1 makes a preliminary identification of the concept to be analyzed by giving some historical references and then by specifying the extension

which belongs to the concept of *a number of things* or *a totality.* This extension is said to consist of "sets or groups of determinately given things," for example, the sheets of paper in a box or the vehicles passing a certain spot in an hour's time. Beyond this, section 1 indicates that the concept must be analyzed by studying its "origin"—namely, by studying the process of abstraction through which it and its parts are derived. Moreover, because a "number" of things is one sort of whole, this section also contains a discussion of the general manner in which abstraction proceeds toward the concept of *any* sort of whole. The point is made that abstraction must, in such cases, single out the combining relation which makes up the particular sort of whole in question, binding its parts together. (See the last five paragraphs of section 1.) (III) With section 2, then, the analysis proper of the concept begins. Husserl discusses various theories as to what must be the essential nature of that combining relation which shows up within a "number" of things. These theories, listed in the last sentence of the first paragraph of section 3, are all rejected for reasons given. (IV) Section 3 advances Husserl's own view of the combining relation (the "collective combination") which is present wherever we have a "number" of things, and the intuition of which provides an essential part of the *origin* of the concept of number. This view is summarized in the penultimate paragraph of section 3, and again in the penultimate paragraph of section 4. (V) Finally, section 4 states the *content* of the concept of number, thus completing the concept's analysis.

With this overview in mind, we turn to consider the method of conceptual analysis here used by Husserl. For purposes of understanding this essay, we may say that a concept is *a repeatable and shareable thought,* and that *to analyze* a certain concept is to discern what is of necessity thought *of* or meant—the partial intentions essentially involved—whenever that concept is deployed. Now Husserl's assumption is that concepts cannot be analyzed directly. That is, one cannot (at least in the philosophically most interesting cases) simply focus one's reflexive attention upon the concept or thought in question and thereby discern the partial intentions which go into its makeup. Following Carl Stumpf, his colleague in Halle at the time, Husserl supposed that we best discern the *content* of a concept by examining the concept's origin: by tracing the "idea," as it were, to the partial "ideas" and, finally, to the "impressions" from whence it developed. As Stumpf had remarked in his *Über den Psychologischen Ursprung der Raumvorstellung* (1883), a book which greatly influenced Husserl:

the question "Whence arises a representation?" is of course (though this is not always done) to be clearly distinguished from the other question, "What is its knowledge content, once we have it?" However, these two questions are methodologically related, insofar as the question about the origin of a representation leads us to the separate parts of which it is composed, and therefore yields a more precise grasp of its content. (p. v; see also pp. 3–4)

And so Husserl, guided by the supposed methodological imperative, describes the following essay as dealing with the "specific question . . . about the content and origin of the concept of number" and as aiming at "the exhibition of the origin and content of the concepts *multiplicity* and *number.*" By far the greater part of the essay is, in fact, devoted to discussions of the *origin* of the concept: the appropriate means, following Stumpf, of analyzing its *content.* Only four pages at the very end are given to a statement of the concept's content, and much of that really turns out to be a discussion of the "origin" of the concept *something.* Husserl

simply assumed that the content of a concept is obvious, once the concept's origin is made clear.

Now the "origin" which Husserl seeks is ultimately the *abstractive source* of the concept, especially of its parts. In general he assumes that a concept applies to an object in virtue of the fact that certain qualities or relations which the concept primarily intends or connotes are *in* the object. To "have" a concept, on the other hand, is at least to have a capacity to think of those qualities, and to think of things *as having* those qualities. It is Husserl's view that one comes to have a concept by fixing the mind intuitively upon the relevant qualities or relations in relevant objects as they are given to *intuition* [*Anschauung*]. The objects given are the ultimate "origin" or source of concepts which apply to them. Hence the concept is derived through apprehension of "the things themselves." Once the relevant extension is determined for a given concept, the full investigation of the concept's origin requires only a clear indication of what it is *in* those objects which one focuses upon in coming to "have" the concept.

In the case of the concept of number, as well as the concepts of determinate numbers, the most common objects to which application is made are sets or groups of determinately given things, such as pencils on a desk or strokes of a clock. But it is clear that merely to be intuitively aware of the members of a group is not to intuit them *as a* "number" of things, or as a totality in the sense here in question. To intuit them as a "number" of things, one must perform a characteristic, complex act which we might describe as the intuitive enumeration of the objects in the group. In such an act I serially consider certain objects from among those presented to me, with that distinct type of emphatic, purposive, and ordered noticing which is essential to (but not limited to) the explicit counting of objects. Husserl's claim is that when I do consider them thus, a new and distinctive type of whole is present to me in intuition: the totality or multiplicity —a concrete unity of *x* number of objects. Such a unified "totality" appears to me with clear, nonspatial boundaries within my total field of consciousness—boundaries defined by the range of the characteristic, noticing acts in question. The wholes (totalities) thus bounded are not intuitively given in any type of mental act other than the sort of articulated considering just described. They are, in the language of that day, "objects of a higher order," and hence are only graspable in acts of thought which essentially rest upon subordinate acts, those in the ordered noticing mentioned.[2]

Now we must carefully consider this point about the intuitability of totalities. In the givenness of "a number of things" we have one instance of what Husserl was later to call "categorial intuition" in the sixth chapter of "Investigation VI" of the *Logical Investigations* (1901).[3] It is perhaps the one point where we cannot misunderstand what he is saying if we are to understand his view of number. At the opening of section 2 in the following essay he states that "the shortest answer to the question about what kind of unification is present in the totality lies in a direct reference to the phenomena. And here we are genuinely dealing with ultimate facts." They are ultimate in the sense that if we do not *see* them, we cannot come to grasp them correctly, because the unification in a mere "number" of things is unanalyzable and indefinable. So let us try to *look,* by living reflectively through a concrete case. If I attempt to count the trees in a certain area of a park, I must do something more than just be conscious of them, or even see them—whether as spatially clumped together or taken individually. I must rather, as I view them, think in a characteristic manner: *There is that one and that one and that one and. . . .* Now as I go through these acts in which the things enumerated are "separately and specifically noticed," as Husserl says, there arises for me a division of the trees into those "already" enumerated and those not or "not yet" enumerated. His view is that this division is a fact intuitively given to me. If this division does not *present itself to me* with some force and clarity, I simply cannot number the trees. But in that it does arise for me, the trees already enumerated appear somehow united or "together," and in their unification with each other they stand "apart from" the remaining trees—of which I nonetheless may be quite conscious.

It is *this* "together" which is the ultimate phenomenal fact of number, and to which Husserl gives the name 'collective combination'. Once we have *seen* it, all that remains is to show (as Husserl does in section 2) why this "together" is not the same as certain other relations which have been offered as its substitute, and to see (section 3) what can be given by way of a description of the essence of this peculiar "together" relation as it presents itself to us. This will then complete Husserl's account of the origin of the most important element in the concept of number.

We may represent Husserl's account schematically as follows:

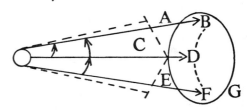

Here A through G are objects in a given field of consciousness. The unbroken lines to B, D, and F are those characteristic acts of noticing which are involved in enumerating. The small arrows crossing between the unbroken lines are awarenesses of earlier such acts built into subsequent such acts, ordering them into a *progression.* The diffuse arrow formed from broken lines is the founded consciousness of the higher order object, the totality BDF. The dotted lines connecting B to D to F are the "collective combinations" in virtue of which these three elements form a *number* of things, excluding the other objects in the field of consciousness. Please note that the totality as thus represented by the closed curved line, like the relations which it contains, is not a *part* of the complex act in which it is grasped.

Husserl now makes a fateful choice of terminology. He decides to call the collective combination a 'psychical' relation. Having refuted various theories concerning the precise nature of the unifying relations in the totality, he turns to a positive account in section 3 (see fourth paragraph). Since he assumes that the collective combination can have *any* type of object for its terms—anything is countable—it cannot be marked out in terms of a restricted class of terms.

Thus, one has to find something in the collective combinations themselves which can characterize them. They do, in fact, Husserl believes, possess "noteworthy peculiarities which very essentially distinguish them in their phenomenal existence from all of the remaining kinds of relations" (paragraph four). Thus we can "classify relations in terms of their particular phenomenal character" (paragraph six). As to what the precise character of the collective combination is, he takes his clue from Brentano's distinction between the psychical (mental) and the physical. The psychical relation of intentionality comprises its object term in a peculiar, indefinable manner, marked by the term 'intentional inexistence'. This manner stands out clearly when compared with how, for example, similarity grasps its terms. This apparent difference is regarded by Husserl as the difference between, respectively, a "psychical" relation and a physical relation. But how is this difference to be spelled out further?

Upon closer examination (see under arabic number 2 in section 3), psychical relations turn out to have three essential phenomenal features which can be stated. *First,* they admit of an unlimited variety in the types of terms which they take. Anything at all can be (i) an object of consciousness, (ii) collectively combined into a "number" of things, or (iii) stand in the "relation of 'distinctness' in the widest of senses, . . . in the case of which two contents are brought into relation merely by means of an evident, negative judgment." These are the three cases of "psychical" relations which Husserl mentions here. *Second,* in order to be aware of things *as* psychically related, we must be aware—in some prepredicative and possibly nonthetical manner, no doubt—of a prior act (or acts) of consciousness in relation to those things. To be aware of X *as* an object of consciousness, I must be (marginally) aware of my simple consciousness of X; to be aware of it *as* one of a "number" of things, I must be aware of a prior emphatic and ordered noticing of it and of the others in the "number"; and to be aware of two things *as* different, I must, Husserl thinks, be aware of a prior act of judging them to be different. And *finally,* Husserl was, following

Brentano, a critical realist at this stage of his career. This meant that every nonmental object was intended on the basis of an apperceptive grasp of something actually present in (a part or constituent of) consciousness. But then there is a problem with the "psychical" relations, for Husserl finds that there corresponds to them no sense content (sensum or image) in the mind itself. And this is the *third* and final feature of psychical relations: one which leads Husserl to remark that we "could also quite appropriately call physical relations 'content relations'." Now in the absence of such a literal *mental content,* the prior *mental acts* reflected upon in grasping a psychical relation function structurally as sense contents do in grasping physical relations: as, that is, a kind of apperceptive support of the intention directed upon the psychical relation.

These three features give the psychical relation only a very weak connection with its terms: "the relation does not immediately reside in the phenomena themselves, but, so to speak, is external to them." Yet, Husserl says, "a certain unity is present in the totality, and is perceivable with *Evidenz.*"

The above completes Husserl's account of the abstractive basis of that *relational* concept which is an essential part of the concept of a "number" of things, or of a mere totality or multiplicity. However, there is one more essential part of that concept, and Husserl discusses it briefly, almost as an afterthought. How are the elements related by the collective combination in a "number" of things to be referred to in the concept of number or totality? Since these elements must be utterly without restriction as to kind, there can "enter into the general concept of the multiplicity no peculiarities of content. However, . . . parts must be somehow thought of in it," since it is a whole (third paragraph of section 4). Husserl's solution is to say that in the concept of number things are referred to as mere "somethings." "The concept of *something* owes its origination to reflection upon the psychical act of representing, as the content [object] of which just any determinate object may be given" (fourth paragraph of section 4). That is, it derives from the psychical relation (i), mentioned above. The feature of being a "something" also has, as will have been suggested by the above discussion of psychical relations, no corresponding "partial content," such as a sensum or image. And, like the collective combination, the character of "something" "belongs to the content of any concrete object only in . . . [an] external and non-literal fashion" (loc. cit.).

The concept of number contains, then, two subconcepts. Husserl thought, following Bolzano, that the collective combination was designated in common language by the conjunction 'and'. To grasp a "number" of things is simply to grasp certain objects under the phenomenal character of a mere "something" and as united by the phenomenal relation of a mere "and." Thus, the concept of a multiplicity or totality is just *something and something and something, etc.* A particular number such as four merely suppresses the "etc." at a certain point. Thus *a* number is a property of similar groups which are seen or conceived of as mere "somethings" joined by a mere "and."

Now it must be stressed that his account of the totality, and of number, is very close to, if not identical with, one given much earlier by Bolzano. We know from Husserl's autobiographical writings[4] that between 1884 and 1886 he heard Brentano lecture on "the descriptive psychology of the continua, with detailed consideration of Bolzano's *Paradoxien des Unendlichen*." And we find the essence, and much of the form, of Husserl's analysis of the content of the concept of the totality in subsection 3 of Bolzano's book. It is clear from this book, as well as the *Wissenschaftslehre,* that the use to which Husserl puts the "and" and the "something" is substantially the same as Bolzano's—especially in relation to the analysis of number.

But some will say with Werner Illemann[5] that, unlike Bolzano, the word 'totality' is "used by Husserl as a designation for a psychical fact." Now it must be admitted that there is much to justify this interpretation. Not the least is Husserl's decision to use the term 'psychical' as a designation for the general *type* of relation within which the collective combination is found as one case. This was a very unfortunate use of terminology, but if one looks closely at the following essay, one sees that by "psychical" Husserl

does not mean "part of a mind" or even "intentional." Rather he means "having a certain character which is most well-known as showing up in the intentional (psychical) nexus." But the collective combination is not itself an intentional relation. It interrelates the members of a totality, but these members do not thereby cognize, do not refer to, each other. Nor are the only things collectively combinable mental acts or contents—as Husserl explicitly says. Those who read Husserl were, however, to find it practically impossible to transfer the term 'psychical' from its ordinary sense, designating the mental, to the more general sense proposed by him.

This was, of course, made all the more difficult by Husserl's use of the term 'content' to refer both to the *object*—either real or merely intentional—of a representation and to a *constituent,* or part, of a representation. He seems not to have been aware of the problems. In his (1903) review of Palágyi he admitted that for some time he did not know *what* to make of Bolzano's "objective" concepts and propositions.[6] By 1894, in his "Psychological Studies in the Elements of Logic" (subsection 3 of part 1),[7] he had become aware of the difficulties, and said, "I think that it is a good principle to avoid such equivocal names as 'representation', so far as this is possible." In chapter six of "Investigation V" of the *Logical Investigations* (1901) he singled out thirteen equivocations associated with the term '*Vorstellung*'. And in a note from September 25, 1906, he wrote concerning his *Philosophie der Arithmetik* (1891): "How immature—how naive and almost child-like—this work seems to me. Well, it was not without reason that my conscience punished me at its publication. It in fact came, in essentials, from 1886–1887. I was a mere beginner, without correct appreciation of philosophical problems, without proper training of my philosophical faculties."[8] He went on to say, in particular, that he had at that time no idea of how to bring together the world of the purely logical and the world of the act of consciousness. And it is precisely this inability which shows up in the obscure and equivocal talk of representations and their contents in the following essay, and thus creates the main problem of its interpretation.

It is nonetheless true to say, with Marvin Farber, "that Husserl means to name something objective when he speaks of totalities or pluralities."[9] By examining the act of enumeration through which a totality is rendered present, it is clear that no relation which is a constituent of that act is a mere "and." Hence, no mere intuition of the mental act as such would present a totality or allow us to get the concept thereof. The intended objective character of this "totality" is well brought out a few years later in the *Philosophie der Arithmetik*, where Husserl places the concepts expressed by 'and' and 'something' (along with, of course, *multiplicity* and *number*) altogether beyond such qualitative distinctions as that between the mental and the physical. These concepts, he says, are the "most general and empty of content of all concepts" and "can with full right be designated as form-concepts or categories."[10] It seems to me that the following essay provides good evidence that even in this earliest of Husserl's publications a nonsubjectivist analysis of number was intended and carried out.[11]

NOTES

1. See *Philosophie der Arithmetik, Husserliana* 12 (1970), p. 8.

2. Ibid., p. 74, lines 20–30. This passage does not occur in the essay "On the Concept of Number."

3. The wording "categorial intuition" is perhaps new with "Investigation VI," but the viewpoint is present from 1887 on. In the essay below Husserl says, for example: "In the totality there is a lack of any intuitive unification, as that sort of unification so clearly manifests itself in the metaphysical or continuous whole. And this is so, although a certain unity *is* present in the totality, and is perceivable with Evidenz." And see the talk of form-concepts, or *categories*, in *Philosophie der Arithmetik*, pp. 84–85.

4. Page 157 of his "Erinnerungen an Franz Brentano" in Oskar Kraus, *Franz Brentano* (Munich, 1919).

See the English translation "Recollections of Franz Brentano" in this volume, p. 344.

5. *Husserl's Vor-phaenomenologische Philosophie* (Leipzig, 1932), p. 13.

6. See page (154) below.

7. See translation by Dallas Willard, *The Personalist* 58 (1977): 302; see also page (129) below.

8. *Philosophy and Phenomenological Research* 16 (March 1956): 294.

9. *The Foundations of Phenomenology* (New York: Paine-Whiteman Publishers, 1962), p. 26.

10. *Philosophie der Arithmetik*, p. 84.

11. For further discussion see my "Concerning Husserl's View of Number," *Southwestern Journal of Philosophy*, vol. 5, no. 3 (1974): 97–109; also chapter 2 of my *Studies in Husserl's Early Philosophy*, forthcoming.

FURTHER REFERENCES

Farber, Marvin. *The Foundation of Phenomenology: Edmund Husserl and the Quest for a Rigorous Science of Philosophy.* 2d ed. New York: Paine-Whitman, 1962, pp. 15–43.

Willard, Dallas. "Husserl on a Logic That Failed." *Philosophical Review* 89 (1980): 46–64.

6

On the Concept of Number: Psychological Analyses*

Translated by Dallas Willard

Introduction

From Antiquity—in fact, for millennia—men have repeatedly attempted the analysis of the concepts upon which mathematics is based, of the elementary truths from which it is built up, and of the methods owing to which it has always stood as the model of rigorously scientific deduction. And this endeavor has not been exclusively one of mathematicians. Rather, it has mainly been metaphysicians and logicians who, out of the plentitude of problems present here, have taken up now this matter, now that, depending upon the peculiar interest moving them, and have made it into the object of special investigation. In fact, these are not problems which are either solely or mainly the concern of the mathematicians. A fleeting glance at the history of philosophy teaches one how views with reference to the theoretical character of mathematics have influenced in an essential and often decisive manner the formation of significant, philosophical *Weltanschauungen*. In mutual opposition, the most diverse of philosophical schools have each thought that they could invoke the testimony of mathematics: the Rationalists as well as the Empiricists, the Phenomenalists as well as the Realists. Even Skeptics did not shun this battefield.

*Reprinted with permission of the publisher and translator from *Philosophia Mathematica* 9 (1972): 44–52 and 10 (1973): 37–87. Revised and corrected.

Especially since Kant, the issues of the philosophy of mathematics have moved ever more forceably into the foreground. As for Kant himself, investigations into the nature of mathematical knowledge form the foundations of his theory of knowledge.

During the most recent times in Germany it has been, in the main, the widespread Neo-Kantianism which, in an effort to secure anew the basic principles of the Kantian critique of reason and to support them against the Empiricism imported from England, has focussed its primary attention upon these questions. Not without influence in this connection were the discussions carried on in England—for many years and with great brilliance—between Whewell and Hamilton (and his students), on the one hand, as representatives of Kantian views, and the thinkers of the Empiricist School, on the other hand, led by J. Stuart Mill.

But beyond the narrowly confined circle of questions to which these epistemological controversies originally had reference, there yet lay a number of considerably more difficult questions, which at first were dealt with only by professional mathematicians, but later were drawn to more general attention and presented new matter for philosophical reflection. The interests which brought mathematicians into such manifold contact with philosophy had their origins in the state of their own science:

It is well known what great progress mathematics has made during the course of the last one-hundred years. A series of new and very far-reaching instruments of investigation has been found, and an almost boundless profusion of important pieces of knowledge has been won. It has been an exhilaratingly creative period—where the great ideas of a Newton and a Leibniz were yet to be worked out, and ever new domains of knowledge were still to be impregnated by those ideas. It is easy to understand, in such a case, how reflections concerning the logical nature of all of the puzzling, auxiliary concepts, to the introduction and subsequent application of which mathematicians have seen themselves forced, would have to be postponed in favor of the quest for results, for discoveries, and for the utilization of all those admirable tools. Only later— when the main or most proximate consequences of the new principles were drawn, and when errors which arose in consequence of obscurity about the nature of the auxiliary means used, and about the limits of reliability of the operations involved, became more and more numerous—only then there arose the need, which constantly became more vivid and was finally inescapable, for: (i) logically clarifying, surveying and securing what had been attained, (ii) an exact analysis of the primitive and of the derived concepts, (iii) logical insight into the interdependency of the various mathematical disciplines, which at some points are only loosely connected, but at other points again are inextricably intertwined, and, finally, (iv) a rigorously deductive development of the whole of mathematics out of the smallest possible number of self-evident principles.

Since the beginning of this century the number of works giving such logical analyses of mathematics has increased immeasurably. One promises us a complete and consistent system of mathematics. Others promise an elucidation of the relationship of general arithmetic to geometry. Others again attempt to clarify those obscure auxiliary concepts (seemingly laden with contradiction, but still indispensable for analysis) such as imaginary and irrational numbers, such as integrals and differentials, such as the continuous, and so on. Others again—and their number is legion—deal with the axioms of geometry: especially, Euclid's eleventh axiom. They attempt to prove it, to refute alleged proofs of it, or finally, by means of fictive constructions of geometries *without* that axiom, to show its dispensability and merely inductive certainty, in opposition to assertions of its a priori necessity.

Of course the philosophy of our times has had to take a lively interest in this literature which arose within mathematics; and not merely with regard to the needs of *metaphysics,* but also with regard to the needs of *logic.* In fact, ever since modern logic came, in contrast to the older logic, to understand its true task to be that of a practical discipline (that of a *Kunstlehre* of judging correctly), and came to seek, as *one* of its principal goals, a general theory of the methods of a science,[a] it has found many urgent reasons for giving special attention to questions about the character of mathematical methods, and about the logical nature of the primitive concepts and principles of those methods. In the context of metaphysical and logical works, therefore, discussions of such mathematical questions are considerably expanded, while, in addition, a large number of philosophical treatises on special topics deal now with this, now with that question from the fringe area between philosophy and mathematics.

Modern psychology also is not wholly a stranger to this domain; even if it does come in only to subject to separate investigation a few questions which either have always been treated in confusion with metaphysical and logical questions, or have as of yet not been clearly raised at all—viz., the questions about the phenomenal (*phänomenalen*) character and the psychological origin of the representations of space, time, number, continuity, etc.[b] But that the results of such investigations must also be of significance for metaphysics and logic is perfectly clear to everyone.

After so many attempts, undertaken from different approaches and in different epochs, one should expect that, at least with regard to the main ones among the problems in question, resolution and general agreement would have been attained. Nonetheless, the centuries have passed away and the questions remain. In fact, to the old ones some new ones have been added. Will our time be more fortunate in this respect? There are many indications that in this, as in other respects, it may be permitted to our age to resolve old puzzles. Certainly the conviction that it will be so is justified to us by the great steps of progress made in the period just passed by scientific psychology and logic. The tools now lie ready for the framing of final judgments. But certainly one also must seek out these tools: One will never succeed in charming away material difficulties by means of verbal or formalistic tricks.

In the light of the way things have gone in the past, many have come to the opinion that the issues debated in the philosophy of mathematics are nothing more than a hopeless knot of superfluous subtleties, which it is not worthwhile to unravel. Sidestepping these issues, science calmly pushes onward, all unconcerned. However, this view is in fact false. Even were we to disregard the fact that the solutions of those subtleties constitute an essential interest of philosophy, yet the merest allusion to the many portentous errors which have been committed within mathematics itself—because of false views of the concept of the differential and other concepts—also teaches how far such a view goes wrong.

Now as to the reasons for this lack of a completely satisfactory solution, excluding all doubt, to such important problems, they lie, as a more exact critique would prove, partly in crippling metaphysical prejudices, and partly in deficiencies of method.

In the latter respect, failure to interrelate the studies which have been made has, in particular, been a hindrance to progress. The intimate, systematic connexity within the range of problems under discussion would have necessitated a sequence of treatment which followed the order in the nature of the subject matter. In actual fact, however, what was followed were special interests dominant from time to time. People thus sought to understand by itself that which could be understood only in its dependency upon other things. An excellent example of this is offered by the well-known Riemann-Helmholtz theory of space. The method which that theory holds to be superbly suited to the solution of the questions of principle connected with the axioms of geometry, and which it also uses to that

end, is the method of analysis through algebraic calculation. Helmholtz repeatedly extolled, as the special advantage of analytic geometry, its characteristic of calculating with concepts of pure magnitudes and of needing no intuition in its proofs.[1] In this way it obviates—in contrast with the purely intuitive procedure of Euclidean geometry— "the danger of taking customary facts of intuition for conceptual necessities."[2]

However, grave doubt immediately arises on this point. Does not even the analytic method in geometry presuppose certain facts of intuition? Obviously it does. How, otherwise, could one come by these general rules, according to which every geometrical form can be algebraically defined by means of an equation, and according to which, then, from every algebraic relation a geometrical relation can be derived? For does not the well-known, fundamental expedient of analytic geometry, which first makes possible the transposition just mentioned—namely, the univocally characterizing statement of any spatial point by means of the vectorial numbers of its distances from three fixed "co-ordinate axes"—rest upon the peculiar properties of our representation of space? And could those properties be abstracted from anything other than intuition? What, therefore, are the facts of intuition upon which, in the last analysis, the possibility of applying general arithmetic to geometry is based?

But these and so many other questions were not even raised up to now, not to speak of being answered. It is obvious that, so long as the relation of arithmetic to geometry is not completely cleared up, no attempt to answer questions of principle in geometry by numerical analysis offers us a sure guarantee that we are not being led in a circle— as, in my opinion, actually occurs with the Riemann-Helmholtz theory.

A definitive removal of the real and imaginary difficulties in the problems which constitute the fringe area between mathematics and philosophy is to be expected only when, in sequence conforming to the natural order in the subject matter, first the concepts and relations which are in themselves simpler and logically earlier, and then, subsequently, the more complicated and more derivative ones—and these taken, indeed, in the order of their degree of derivativeness —are subjected to analysis. But the very first term of this natural sequence is *the concept of number*.

In a sense this point also appears to be generally acknowledged. Today there is a general persuasion that a rigorous and thoroughgoing development of higher analysis (the totality of *arithmetica universalis* in Newton's sense), excluding all auxiliary concepts borrowed from geometry, would have to emanate from elementary arithmetic alone, in which analysis is grounded. But this elementary arithmetic has, as a matter of fact, its sole foundation in the concept of number; or, more precisely put, it has it in that never-ending series of concepts which mathematicians call "positive whole numbers." All of the more complicated and more artificial forms which likewise are called numbers—the fractional and irrational, and negative and complex numbers—have their origin and basis in the elementary number concepts and in their interrelations. With these latter elementary concepts also the former (and, in fact, the whole of mathematics) would fall away. Therefore, it is with the analysis of the concept of number that any philosophy of mathematics must begin.

This analysis is the goal which the present treatise sets for itself. The means which it employs to this end belong to psychology, and they must do so if such an investigation is to attain solid results. Certainly one might ask right off: What, after all, does number have to do with psychology? We must compare this question with others: What have space, time, color, intensity, etc. to do with psychology? Is not space the object of the geometer, color the object of the physicist, and so on? And yet what an extensive psychological literature—still growing day by day—has been occasioned by these concepts!

In regard to the concept of number, to be sure, this is not so. But the lack here is very improper. In truth, not only is psychology indispensable for the analysis of the concept of number, but rather this analysis even *belongs within* psychology. As to the first part of this claim, it must be proven in this work itself. In reference to the second part, note that, in general, analysis of elementary con-

cepts, or those which present us with only a *few* levels of complication—and, indeed, the number concepts *are* of this sort—may nowadays be counted among the more essential tasks of psychology. For how otherwise could it attain insight into the internal structure of that fantastically interwoven tissue of thoughts which constitutes the substance of our thought-life? The understanding of the first and most simple modes of composition of representations is the key to the understanding of those higher levels of complication with which our consciousness constantly operates as with seamless and fixed formations.

The preceding remarks may serve to justify exclusive engagement with such a specific question as that about the content and origin of the concept of number. They should suffice to characterize summarily the significance of that question for philosophy, on the one hand, and for mathematics, on the other hand; and should, at the same time, indicate the more profound reasons which have led the author into the investigations which follow.

Chapter 1.ᶜ The Analysis of the Concept of Number as to Its Origin and Content

Section 1. The Formation of the Concept of Multiplicity (Vielheit) *out of That of the Collective Combination.*

Common consciousness finds two sorts of numbers: *cardinal numbers* and *ordinal numbers.* The former are usually intended when simply "numerals" or "numbers" are spoken of. Already in ordinary discourse a special emphasis appears to be laid upon the intimate relationship between the two sorts of number concepts by the likeness in their denominations: the spoken and written signs for cardinal numbers go over by slight modifications into the signs for the corresponding ordinal numbers (1,2,3,4, . . . ; 1st, 2nd, 3rd, 4th . . .). As cardinal numbers refer to *sets*, so ordinal numbers refer to *series.* But series are ordered sets; and so one may perhaps a priori suppose that the concepts of ordinal numbers proceed merely by a certain delimitation out of those of the cardinal numbers. However, noted investigators, such as *W.R. Hamilton, H. Grassman, Helmholtz,* and *L. Kronecker,* among others, have held that the natural starting point is the series. In this way they hope to show the superiority of the ordinal numbers (or related concepts) in respect to generality. The question as to whether the one or the other of these views—or perhaps a third view which completely rejects all logical subordination of the one class of concepts to the other—is worthy of preference, must be dealt with later. In now beginning with the analysis of the concept of the cardinal number, we do not aim to prejudge the issues in favor of any of these views. In the light of the reference of the two sorts of numbers to the representation of sets, in the one case, and to the representation of series, in the other case —as is already impressed upon us by superficial consideration of the matter—the loose characterization of the one as "set-numbers," and of the other as "series numbers," appears to be quite adequate.

Now to mention *all* of the authors who ground the concept of number upon that of the set would hardly be possible. Already in *Euclid* we find the definition (in the preamble to Book VII of his *Elements*):

An unit is that by virtue of which each of the things that exists is called one. A number is a multitude composed of units.[3]

As on other points, so also here, Euclid was *the* authority for a long time. *Hobbes* declares: "Number is 1 and 1, or 1, 1 and 1, and so on, which is the same as saying, number is unity."[4]

In his chief work, on the human understanding, *Locke* gives extensive descriptions of the psychological process involved in enumerating, but without ever putting his view on the content of the concept of number into the form of a definition. In the context of his discussions, however, numbers are characterized as representations composed out of units (as "complex ideas," or "collective ideas"); more precisely, as "ideas for several collections of units, distinguished one from another."[5]

In a letter to *Thomasius, Leibniz* gives a definition which reads almost the same as Hobbes: "Numerum definio unum, et unum etc. seu unitates."[6] In the *New Essays,*

Book II, Ch. 16,[7] the (whole) number is defined as a multiplicity (multitude) of units. When compared to the earlier statement, there is obviously no difference here worth noting; only there the word 'multiplicity' is avoided—but the use of the plural means the same thing.

These outstanding examples will perhaps suffice.

So the most common definition reads: The number is a multiplicity of units. Instead of 'multiplicity', the terms 'plurality', 'totality', 'aggregate', 'collection', 'set', etc. are also used; clear expressions, which are equivalent or very closely interrelated, although they are not without distinguishable nuances.[8]

But there certainly is very little accomplished with this definition. What is "multiplicity"? And what is "unity"? Most controversies revolve around precisely these questions. Also, "multiplicity" appears to signify almost the same thing as "number." In fact, the name 'number' is used in a more extended sense—namely, where it is not supposed to designate a *determinate* number— in which it becomes completely equivalent with "multiplicity." Because of all this, many authors have supposed that they had to leave this definition (if one wants to call it that) aside. However, it is precisely "number" which here is used in an *extended* sense. And, in any case, this much is clear: The concrete phenomena (*Phänomena*) to which determinate, numerical assertions are applied are concrete multiplicities, *i.e.,* sets or groups of determinately given things; and, hence, they are precisely *the same* phenomena which also fall under the general concept of multiplicity. Precisely herein resides the necessity of setting out from these phenomena, and of considering how it is from them that the more indeterminate and universal concept which underlies that sequence of names, 'multiplicity', 'plurality', 'set', etc., as well as the determinate number concepts, are to be abstracted.

The first question which we have to answer is the question about the *origin* of the concepts in question.

The concrete phenomena which form the basis for the abstraction of these concepts are, as just noted, totalities of determinate objects. But we also add that these totalities are completely arbitrary and optional. In the formation of concrete totalities there is in fact no limitation whatever upon what particular contents are to be included. Any object of representation, whether physical or psychical, abstract or concrete, whether given in sensation or in imagination, and so on, can be united into a totality with any, and with arbitrarily many, other objects. *E.g.,* a few particular trees; the sun, moon, earth, and Mars; a feeling, an angel, the moon and Italy; and so on.[9] In these examples we can, in each case, speak of a totality, of a plurality, or of a determinate number. The nature of the particular contents makes no difference at all.

But, if this be true, exactly *how* does one succeed in getting from concrete totalities to the general concept of plurality, of totality, or of number? What abstraction process is supposed to yield the concept? What is it that one retains, in abstraction, as the content of the concept? And what is that *away from which* abstraction is made?

We assume that concepts originate through a comparison of the specific representations which fall under them. Disregarding the attributes which differ, one holds to the ones which are common; and these latter are the ones which then constitute the general concept. Let us now attempt to follow this guideline in the case at hand.

It is obvious that a comparison of the particular contents which we find before us in given totalities would not straightaway yield to us the concept of multiplicity, of totality, of number. And, even if it did happen, it would be absurd to *expect* it. Those particular contents are, in fact, not the basis of the abstraction. Rather, the basis is the concrete totalities *as wholes* in which the particular contents are caught up together. But even comparison of the totalities appears not to offer the desired result. The totalities, one might say, consist *merely* of the particular contents. How, then, are the *wholes* to exhibit some common attribute, when the *parts* constituting them may be utterly heterogeneous?

However, this specious difficulty is easily resolved. It is misleading to say that the to-

talities consist merely of the particular contents. However easy it is to overlook it, there still is present in them something more than the particular contents: a "something more" which can be noticed, and which is necessarily present in all cases where we speak of "totalities." This is the *combination (Verbindung)* of the particular elements into the whole. And it is here as it is in the case of many other classes of relations: There can be the greatest of differences between the related contents, and yet there be identity of kind with respect to the combining relations. Hence, similarities, gradations (*Steigerungen*), and mediating continuities are found in wholly heterogeneous domains; and they can occur between sensible as well as between psychical phenomena. It is, therefore, quite possible for two wholes, *as wholes,* to be similar, although the parts constituting the one are completely heterogeneous to those constituting the other.

Those combinations which, always the same in kind, are present in all cases where we speak of multiplicities are, then, the bases for the formation of the general concept of multiplicity.

As to the sort of abstraction process which yields our concept, we can best characterize it by referring to the way in which concepts of other composites (wholes) originate. If we consider, for example, the cohesion of the points on a line, of the moments of a span of time, of the color nuances of a continuous series of colors, of the tonal qualities in a "tone progression," and so on, then we acquire the concept of combination-by-continuity and, from this concept, the concept of the continuum. This latter concept is not contained as a particular, distinguishable, partial content in the representation of any concretely given continuum. What we note in the concrete case is, on one hand, the points or extended parts, and, on the other hand, the peculiar combinations involved. These latter, then, are always identically present where we speak of continua, however different may be the absolute contents which they connect (places, times, colors, tones, etc.). Now in reflection upon this characteristic sort of combination of contents there arises the concept of the continuum, as a *whole* the parts of which are united precisely in the manner of continuous combination.

Or, to take another example, consider the quite peculiar way in which, in the case of any arbitrary visual object, spatial extension and color (and color, in turn, and intensity) reciprocally penetrate and connect with each other. With reference to *this* manner of combination—which, following F. Brentano, we shall call "metaphysical"—we, again, can form the concept of a corresponding type of whole, the parts of which are united in just such a manner.

We can say quite generally: Wherever we are presented with a particular class of wholes, the concept of that class can be originated *only* through reflexion upon a well-distinguished manner of combining parts, a manner which is identical in each whole of the class in question.

How, then, does the matter stand in the case with which we are concerned? We can also say that a totality forms a whole. The representation of a totality of given objects is a *unity* in which representations of single objects are contained as partial representations. Certainly the combination of parts as found in any arbitrarily selected totality must be called loose and external, when compared to other cases of combination. So much so, in fact, that one would almost hesitate to speak here of any combination at all. But, however that may be, there *is* a peculiar unification there; and it would, as such, also have to have been noticed, since otherwise the concept of totality, and that of multiplicity, never could have originated. So, if our view is correct, the concept of the multiplicity originates by means of reflexion upon the peculiar and, in its peculiarity, quite noticeable manner of unification of contents, as it shows up in every concrete totality (concrete multiplicity). And it arises in a way analogous to that of the concepts of other sorts of wholes, all of which are come by through reflection upon the modes of combination peculiar to those wholes. From here on, we shall use the name 'collective combination' (*kollective Verbindung*) to designate that sort of combination which is characteristic of the totality.

Now before we proceed with the development of our subject, it will be good to deflect an apparent objection. We could be charged as follows: If the multiplicity is defined as a whole the parts of which are united by collective combinations, then this definition is circular. For in speaking of "parts" we certainly represent a multiplicity; and, since the parts are not individually determinate, we have a general representation of this multiplicity. Consequently, we are explaining multiplicity by means of itself.

Nonetheless—and however much plausibility this objection may have—we cannot concede its cogency. First, note that what is in question here is not a *definition* of the concept of multiplicity, but rather a *psychological characterization* of the phenomena upon which the abstraction of that concept rests. All which can serve to this purpose we must therefore regard as welcome. Now the plural term, 'parts', certainly involves (disregarding its necessary correlation with the concept of the whole) the general representation of a multiplicity; but *that* term does not express what peculiarly characterizes this multiplicity *as* multiplicity. By adding that the parts are collectively combined, we make reference to the point upon which our special interest reposes, and in virtue of which the multiplicity is characterized precisely *as* a multiplicity, in contrast to other sorts of wholes.

Section 2. Critical Exposition of Certain Theories

The shortest answer to the question about what kind of unification (Einigung) is present in the totality lies in a direct reference to the phenomena. And here we are genuinely dealing with ultimate facts. By saying that, however, we do not avoid the task of considering this kind of combination more carefully, and of bringing into relief its characteristic differences from other kinds: —especially since false characterizations of it, and confusions of it with other species of relations, have been a common enough occurrence. In order to accomplish this task we shall try out a series of possible theories, ones which have only in part actually been formulated. Each theory characterizes the collective unification in a different way and, in relation thereto, seeks also to explain in a different way the origin of the concepts *multiplicity* and *number*.

I

The combination of representations to make up a totality, someone could say, still scarcely deserves the name of a 'combination'. What is then present when we speak of a totality of certain objects? Nothing further than the co-presence of those objects in our consciousness. The unity in representations of the totality consists, thus, only in their belonging to the consciousness which encompasses them. Still, this 'belonging' is a fact which can be attended to; and with reflection upon it there originate, then, those concepts the analysis of which is here in question.

Now this view is obviously wrong. An immense number of phenomena constitute, in each moment, the total state of our consciousness. But it is the role of a special interest to lift *certain* representations out of that plenum and collectively unite them. And this occurs without the disappearance of all of the remaining representations from consciousness. Were this view correct, then in each moment there would be only a single totality, consisting of the whole of the present partial contents of our total consciousness. But at any time, and in any way we choose, we can form various totalities, can expand one already formed by the addition of new contents, and can narrow others down by taking contents away (without necessarily excluding these contents from consciousness). In short, we are conscious of a spontaneity which would be inconceivable on this view.

But this view contains, in its general and indeterminate form, a further absurdity. In fact, do not continua, with their infinite sets of points, belong to the material (*Bestande*) of our consciousness? Who has ever actually represented them in the manner of a totality? It is important to stress that a totality can have as elements only contents of which we are conscious in the manner of things separately and specifically noticed (*als für sich bemerkter*). All contents which are present only as things incidentally noticed, and which either cannot be separately noticed at all (like the points of continua), or merely

are not, for the moment, separately noticed: — these cannot yield elements out of which a totality is constituted.

All of this will perhaps be quickly conceded; and the representative of the view just criticized might forthwith restrict his assertion in such a way that by the "encompassing consciousness" which unites representations into a multiplicity is to be understood a special act of consciousness, and not consciousness in the widest sense, where it takes in the whole of our psychic phenomena. So it would be, accordingly, a question of unity in an encompassing act of noticing, or of a unity of interest, and so on. We intend to come back later to consider more closely the theory as thus corrected.

II

Let us now turn to consideration of a new theory, which argues as follows:

If a totality of contents is present to us, what else are we to notice but that every content is there *simultaneously* with each other one? Temporal co-existence of contents is indispensable for the representation of their multiplicity. Now, indeed, there is required in any composite act of thought the co-existence of its parts. But whereas in other cases there are present, *in addition to* simultaneity, distinctive relations or combinations which unify the parts, it is precisely the distinguishing feature of the representation of the totality that it contains *nothing more* than the simultaneous contents. Hence, multiplicity *in abstracto* signifies nothing other than the simultaneous givenness of certain contents.

This view, as is easily seen, comes under precisely the same objections as does the previous view, and under many others besides. It would be superfluous to repeat the former objections; and, of the latter, it is sufficient to emphasize the fact that to represent contents simultaneously is still not to represent contents *as simultaneous*. For example, in order for the representation of a melody to come about, the single tones which compose it must be brought into relation with one another. But every relation requires the simultaneous presence of the related contents in one act of consciousness. Thus, the tones of the melody must also be simultaneously represented. But they are not at all to be represented *as* simultaneous. Quite to the contrary, they appear to us as situated in a certain temporal succession. It is not otherwise in the case where we represent a multiplicity of objects. That we must simultaneously represent the objects is certain. But that we do not represent them as simultaneous, and that, rather, special acts of reflection are required in order to notice the simultaneity in the representing of the objects: this is directly proven by a reference to inner experience.

III

A third view is likewise based upon time as an insuppressible psychological factor. In direct contrast with the foregoing, it argues as follows:

In virtue of the discursive character of our thinking, it is true in general that several contents which are different from each other cannot be thought at the same time. Our consciousness can be employed about only *one* object in each moment. All mental activity of a relational or higher sort becomes possible only in that the objects with which it has to do are given *in temporal succession.* So, then, each complex thought-structure, each whole composed of certain parts, is something which has come about gradually out of simple factors. In such cases we always have to do with step-by-step processes and operations which, proceeding through time, intertwine and extend themselves more and more. In particular, therefore, each collection (*Kollection*) presupposes a collecting (*Kolligiren*); and each number presupposes an enumeration. And herewith there is necessarily given a temporal disposition of the collected objects or of the enumerated unities. But yet more. The totality is the loosest of ways of combining parts into a whole. Indeed, we speak of a totality or multiplicity there where contents are united by *no further connexions* than those in the insuppressible form of intuition, time—where contents, therefore, are presented in consciousness *merely* as ordered in the temporal sequence of their entrance into it. Accordingly, it also follows that *multiplicity in abstracto* is nothing more than *succession*; succession of *any sort of* contents separately and

specifically noticed. However, the number concepts represent determinate forms of multiplicity or succession *in abstracto*.

Now in order not to dissipate attention through fruitless, individual critiques, I have here chosen—instead of criticizing in sequence the authors which have represented such theories or similar ones—rather to state *the* view which more or less clearly underlies all of those theories, as plainly and as fully as is possible, and to exercise my critique upon *that* view. And the view which must be combatted here is in fact based upon crude psychological and logical errors.

First, it appeals to the psychological fact of the narrowness of consciousness. However, it exaggerates and falsely interprets this narrowness. It is true that the number of distinct contents to which we can turn our attention in any one moment is very restricted. In fact, at the highest concentration of interest, the number shrinks to one. But it is false that we can *never be conscious* of more than *one* content in one and the same moment. Indeed, just the fact that there is thought which relates and connects—as well as, in general, all of the more complicated mental and emotional activities to which this very theory appeals—teaches with evidence the utter absurdity of this viewpoint. If in every instant only one content is present to our consciousness, how should we be able to notice even the simplest of relations. If we represent the one term of the relation, then the other either is not yet in our consciousness, or it is no longer there. We certainly cannot connect a content of which we are not conscious—and which, therefore, *is not at all* for us—with the single content which, supposedly, is present to us and is really given. Hence, reference to the temporal succession of the representations which are to be related can contribute nothing at all to an explanation of the possibility of relational thinking.

. But, then, does not experience teach (so, perhaps, our adversary replies) that we really can always have only *one* present representation, and that it is very well possible to bring it into relation with past representations? In that a representation is past, it in no wise ceases therefore to be.

However, it is easily seen that such an answer would rest upon misinterpretations of experience. One must not confuse temporally present representations with representations of what is temporally present, and past representations with representations of what is past. Not every present representation, as we must emphasize here once again, is a representation of what is present. Precisely all representations which are directed upon the past constitute an exception; for they all are, in truth, present representations. If I recall a song which I heard yesterday, for example, then the memory representation involved is, yet, a temporally present representation; only it is referred by us to the past. Now, of course, there is no problem in the fact that we are able to bring representations with present contents into relation with representations with past contents. In doing this these representations are all, in fact, simultaneously present in our consciousness. They are *in toto* representations which are temporally present. On the other hand, we can relationally unite past representations neither with each other, nor with present representation; for, as past, they cannot be brought back, and are gone forever.

The alleged fact of experience which our adversary has in view reduces, therefore, to the claim that, whenever we represent a plurality of contents, there is always one alone which is a temporally present content, whereas all of the others exhibit greater or smaller temporal differences. Naturally, then, each total representation composed out of distinct (separately and specifically noticed) parts has to be originated through *successive* acts of noticing and relating the individual, partial contents, while the total representation itself, as something finished and completed, contains all of the parts at the same time—only each furnished with a different temporal determination.

Now it is indeed certain that, already with a very modest number of contents, a comprehensive noticing of them is only possible by apprehending and retaining them successively or in small groups. But, on the other hand, experience does seem to teach with sufficient clarity that we are able to survey two, three, or four contents of a very simple kind with one glance, as it were, and

to unite them collectively in one representation, without being conscious of any sort of serial progress from one content to another. (Consider, for example, a small group of sharp dots standing very close to each other upon a sheet of paper.)

However that may be, we can acknowledge it as a fact that for the formation of representations of sets and numbers (and most clearly with the former) temporal succession is an indispensable psychological requirement. One is, therefore, quite justified in designating sets and numbers as results of processes, and, insofar as our will is thereby engaged, as results of activities, of "*operations,*" of colligating or of enumerating.

But this also is *all* to which we can agree. Only this one thing, and no more, is proven: that succession in time forms an insuppressible, *psychological precondition* for the formation of by far the main part of number concepts and of concrete multiplicities, as well as of all of the more complicated concepts in general. These have a temporalized mode of becoming, and thereby each constituent of the completed whole receives a different temporal determination in our representation. But does that also prove that temporal order enters into the *content* of these concepts, or that it perhaps is the special relationship which characterizes the plurality as such, in contrast to concepts of other composites? In fact, people are often satisfied with such paltry arguments, without taking thought that time forms, in precisely the same manner, the basis for *all* thinking of higher order (*höhere Denken*), and that, for example, one could with equal right infer that the relation of premises to conclusion is identical with their temporal succession. However, such obvious absurdities are already avoided by the very formulation which we gave the time-theory for our purposes. That formulation asserts solely that the case of the totality (or of the plurality) is distinguished from cases of wholes composed in other ways by the fact that in it *mere* succession of partial contents is present, while with the other wholes there is yet *beyond that* some *other* sort of combination.

So the argument is not simply that, because enumerating requires a temporal succession of representations, number is the comprehensive form of the successive *in abstracto*. Rather, the theory in question also invokes the factual distinction between the totality (or collective whole) and all other sorts of wholes. Thus, it appeals to the testimony of inner experience.

However, it does not rightly do so. Again and again an error has been committed by the one party, and censured by the other, with respect to this point: To perceive temporally successive contents is still not necessarily to perceive those contents as temporally successive. The clock sounds off with its uniform tick-tock. I hear the particular ticks, but it need not occur to me to attend to their temporal sequence. But even if I do notice how one tick sounds *after* the other, that still does not involve a lifting out of a number of ticks and a uniting of them, by a comprehensive noticing, to form a totality. Or take another example: Our eyes roam about in various directions, fixing now upon this, now upon that object, and providing manifold representations succeeding one another in a corresponding order. But a *special* interest is necessary if the temporal sequence involved here is to be separately and specifically noticed. And in order to single out to themselves some or all of the objects noticed, to relate them to each other, and to unite them into a totality, here again are required special interests and special acts of noticing directed upon just those contents picked out and no others. But even if the temporal sequence in which objects are colligated were always attended to, it still would remain incapable of grounding by itself alone the unity of the collective whole. And since we cannot even concede that temporal succession enters into the representation of each concrete totality merely as an invariable constituent which is always attended to, then it is clear that even less can it in any way enter into the corresponding *general concept* (*i.e.*, that of multiplicity or number). Herbart is completely justified in saying that "number has . . . no more in common with time than do a hundred other sorts of representations which also can be produced only gradually."[10]

Were it merely a question of describing the phenomenon (*Phänomen*) that is present when we represent a multiplicity, then certainly we would have to make mention of the temporal modifications which the separate contents have undergone, although those modifications were not by themselves given any special notice. But disregarding the fact that the same holds true of every composite whole, we have, in general, to distinguish between the phenomenon as such, on the one hand, and that for which it serves, or which it signifies for us, on the other hand. Accordingly, we must also distinguish between the psychological description of a phenomenon and the statement of its signification. The phenomenon is the foundation of the signification, but is not identical with it.

If a totality of objects, *a, b, c . . . f*, is in our representation, then, in light of the successional process through which the whole representation arises, perhaps only *f* will be given at the last as a sense representation, the remaining contents being then given merely as phantasy representations which are modified temporally and also in other aspects of their content. If, conversely, we pass from *f* to *a* then the phenomenon is obviously a different one. But the logical signification suppresses all such distinctions. The modified contents serve as signs, as deputies (*Vertreter*), of the unmodified ones which were. In forming the representation of the totality we do not attend to the fact that the contents are changed as the colligation progresses. We *intend* actually to fix upon them and to unite them; and, consequently, the logical content of that representation is not, perhaps, *f*, just-passed *e*, earlier-passed *d*, and so on up to *a*, which is the most strongly modified. Rather, its logical content is nothing other than (*a, b, c, d, e, f*). The representation takes in every single one of the contents, irregardless of the temporal differences and of the temporal order grounded in those differences.

Thus we see that time only plays the role of a psychological *precondition* of our concepts, and that it does so in a two-fold manner: 1) Most—in fact, almost all—of our representations of multiplicities are results of *processes*, are wholes originated gradually out of elements. Insofar as this is so, each element bears in itself a different temporal determination. 2) It is essential that the partial representations which are united in the representation of the multiplicity ultimately be present in our consciousness *simultaneously*. But we have decided that neither the simultaneity nor the successiveness in time thus required enters in any way into the *content* of the representation of multiplicity; and so, likewise, with that of the representation of number.

As is well known, already in Aristotle time and number appear to be brought into intimate connection through his definition: "Time is the number of movement in respect to earlier and later." However, it is only since Kant that it has become more generally common to stress the temporal "form of intuition" as the foundation of the number concept. To be sure, this happens much more as a consequence of the authority of his name than as a consequence of the weight of his arguments. We do not find in Kant a serious attempt at a logical or psychological analysis of the concept of number. Unity, multiplicity and totality are the categories of quantity in his metaphysics. Number is the transcendental schema of quantity. Kant fully states his view as follows, in the *Critique of Pure Reason:* "But the pure schema of magnitude (*quantitatis*), as a concept of the understanding, is *number,* which is a representation that comprehends the successive addition of one thing to another thing (of the same kind). Thus, number is nothing other than the unity of the synthesis of the manifold of a homogenous intuition in general, a synthesis which comes about through the fact that I engender time itself in the apprehension which goes on in the intuition."[11]

This passage is obscure and, also, will not exactly agree with the elucidations which Kant gives of the function of the schema. These elucidations themselves certainly are not exactly uniform. Thus he says: "We wish to call . . . the formal and pure condition of sensibility, to which the concept of the understanding is restricted in its use, the *schema* of this concept of the understanding."[12] On the other hand we read, a few lines later: "The representation . . . of a general procedure of the imagination in giving a concept its model (*Bild*) I call the schema of this concept."

Were we to carry this last definition over to the schema of quantity, then we would have to say that number is the representation of a general procedure of the imagination in giving to the concept of quantity its model. However, by this "procedure" can only be meant the process of enumerating. But is it not clear that "number" and "representation of enumerating" are not the same? Further, it is not very easy to see how, starting out from the category of quantity, we are a priori to attain, by means of the representation of time (as the common schema of all the categories), to the particular, determinate number concepts. Still less intelligible is the necessity which determines us to ascribe to a concrete multiplicity a certain number which is always the same: precisely that number of which we say that it belongs to the concrete multiplicity. The theory of the schematism of the pure concepts of understanding appears here, as elsewhere, to fail in the realization of the purpose for which it was especially created.

We can omit enumeration of *all* those investigators who, following Kant, based the concept of number upon the representation of time. Let us mention here only two famous names. Sir William Rowan Hamilton flatly called algebra "the science of pure time," as well as "the science of order in progression."[13] In Germany, H. von Helmholtz, in a philosophical treatise which recently appeared,[14] has published a detailed investigation into the foundations of arithmetic, and into the justification of the application of arithmetic to physical magnitudes. Herein he represents this same Kantian point of view. When we come later to certain other developments (concerning the analysis of the concept of the ordinal number)[d] we will find occasion to deal with this treatise thoroughly.

Finally, it should be noted that, in general, most of these investigators who take the representation of the *series* as basic for the development of the number concepts and the axioms of arithmetic have been essentially influenced by the time-theory.

IV

Whereas Kant put number into an intimate relation with the representation of time, F.A. Lange thought that everything which could be done with the representation of time could be derived with far greater simplicity and certainty from the *representation of space*. In the *Logische Studien*[15] he says: "Baumann has already shown that number has far greater unison with the representation of space than with that of time. . . . The oldest phrasings of the words for numbers always designate, so far as we can discern their meaning, spatial objects with determinate properties which correspond to the number in question. Thus, for example, rectangularity (*Viereckiges*) corresponds to the number four (*vier*). From this we also see that number did not originally arise through systematic addition of one to one, and so on; but rather that each number, from the smaller ones to those based upon the system arising later, is formed through a special act of synthesis of intuitions; so that it is only later, then, that the relations of numbers to one another, the possibility of adding, and so on, are recognized." "The algebraic axioms rest, like the geometric axioms, upon spatial intuitions."[16]

"It is peculiar to the representation of space that within the great all-inclusive synthesis of the manifold there can be segregated, with ease and certainty, smaller units of the most various kinds. Space is, therefore, the archtype, not only of continuous, but also of discrete magnitudes, to the latter of which number belongs; whereas we scarcely can think of time otherwise than as a continuum. To the properties of space belong, further, not only the relations which obtain between the lines and surfaces of geometrical figures; but, rather, there no less belong there the relations of *order* and *position* of discrete magnitudes. If such discrete magnitudes are considered as homogeneous with each other, and if they are united by a new act of synthesis, *then* number arises as sum."

Consider yet one more passage, from the *Geschichte des Materialismus:* "We originally receive each number concept in the form of a sensuously determinate image of a group of objects, whether they are fingers, or the buttons and spheres of an abacus."[17]

Now our critique will certainly not have to look very far for a handle. The last quotation is especially offensive; for the well-known *general* concept of number appears here as an *individual* phenomenon, as the sensuously determinate image of a group of spatial things. However, we may very well have here only an imprecise mode of expression. The view probably is that number is something noticeable in such groups (and, indeed, after the manner of a partial phenomenon), something which must be lifted out of them by abstraction. The influence of J. St. Mill stands out clearly here. For Mill, number is a "*physical* fact," "a visible and feelable phenomenon." It is for him a sensible property on a level with color and weight, etc.[18] But whereas Mill explicitly declines to state wherein really consists numerical difference (whether because he held this to be too difficult, or, in the light of the elementary nature of the phenomena, held it to be superfluous), Lange, by contrast, believes that he can detect its source in the nature and properties of the *representation of space*. If we look at the passages quoted above we find that, in fact, spatial localization of the things enumerated is always emphasized. The spatial relations of order and position of discrete magnitudes considered as homogeneous with each other and united by an act of synthesis—*this* would be the content of the representation of number.

But one immediately wants to raise the question: *Where* are the four cardinal virtues, the two premises of an inference, and so on, located? What spatial order and position serves as the basis for numerical designation in the case of any arbitrary psychical phenomena? This objection certainly would not alarm Lange. He simply reduces all logical thinking to spatial intuition. For him everything that is psychical is located. We do not wish here to involve ourselves in criticism of this intrinsically obscure and utterly untenable view. We stress only a few points which especially concern our problem.

It is clear that, even if we were to concede Lange's premiss, no more would be proven in reference to the representation of space than was earlier admitted in reference to the representation of time. The representation of space would be an insuppressable psychological precondition of the concept of number—and this to no greater extent, and in no other way, than it is for all other concepts. If spatial determination did also belong to all contents which we unite in thought, yet it would always remain two different things (i) to represent spatially dispersed contents and (ii) to represent contents in terms of their spatial relations. Now what *does* actually happen when we collectively unite or enumerate certain spatial things? Do we then attend to the relations of order and position? Does the selective interest within which we form the representation of number turn to those relations? Certainly not. There are a great many positions and orders, but the number remains unchanged. Two apples remain two apples whether we set them together or apart, whether we shift them to the right or to the left, up or down. Number has exactly nothing whatsoever to do with relations of spatial position. It *may* be, nevertheless, that relations of order and position are co-represented in the phenomenon (implicitly) when there is a representation of a multiplicity of spatial objects. It is still certain that they do *not* constitute the objects of selective interest in enumeration. Not as separately and specifically noticed, but only as partial representations which are implicitly co-thought, are they then given in the phenomenon. The fact that the oldest phrasings of the words for numbers refer to objects in space with determinate properties which correspond to the numbers "is still no serious counter-instance" to this claim, and has such obvious explanations that we can dispense with discussion of it.

But Lange stresses, not merely the spatiality of the numbered; rather, he also speaks of the *acts* of synthesis through which discrete magnitudes are united to form number. For our present investigation, which mainly has to do with a more precise characterization of the collective combination, it would be of interest to learn how Lange conceived of this synthesis of singulars into the multiplicity. But if we attentively go through the frequent discussions, in relation to the concept of synthesis, which are in the *Logische Studien,* a serious confusion shows up. It will have already struck the reader of the above quotations that Lange, while he speaks once of acts of synthesis, yet another time calls the representation of space a synthesis.

Already in Kant the word 'synthesis' (combination) is used in a double sense: first, in the sense of the unity of the parts of a whole, whether these parts are properties of a thing, parts of an extension, units in a number, and so on; second, in the sense of the mental activity (actus) of combining (*Verbinden*). The two significations are intimately related in Kant because, on his view, every whole, of whatever kind it may be, is one which originated from parts by means of the spontaneous activity of the mind. "Synthesis" therefore signifies simultaneously, for him, combining *and* the result of combination. That we suppose ourselves to observe combinations in the phenomena themselves, and to extract them therefrom by means of abstraction: that is only an illusion. It is we ourselves who have contributed the combinations, and, indeed, by means of the "pure concepts of the understanding," the categories.

Lange mounts a polemic against the Kantian concept of synthesis; but, certainly, not where it deserved censure. Rather, in his polemic we find only progress in obscurity and confusion. In opposition to Kant, his view is that synthesis is something noticeable in the content of the representation. Synthesis in this sense would signify representation of a relation (*Relationsvorstellung*), and indeed — since, according to Lange, space is "the intuitional form of the ego with its variable content" — all synthesis would ultimately turn out to be *spatial* combination and relation. But synthesis also is supposed by him to be a *process,* occurring wholly in the unconscious, through which *we as subjects* first originate. And, finally, Lange speaks of special (and apparently conscious) acts of synthesis which, for example, yield numbers.

Now, with this multivocal use of the same name, fundamental obscurities are connected. Space is repeatedly designated as the archtype of all synthesis—in fact, as the true, objective counterpart of our transcendental ego. The properties of space are supposed to form the norm of all of the functions of our understanding,[19] and so on. Throughout there is presupposed the erroneous view that a psychic act and its content stand to one another in the relation of pictorial resemblance. Not the least part of the source of this absurdity resides, perhaps, in the equivocation of the word 'synthesis', in consequence of which it at one time signifies the relational content, and at another time signifies the act of relating.

But Lange certainly was also influenced by *Baumann* on this point, whose work[20] he quotes. On the one hand, Baumann calls number the result of an activity, of a mental "sketching"(*Entwerfens*). But, on the other hand, he says that we find "number again in the external world." According to him, external experience bears the mathematical in itself, independently of our mind; but, over against this we are said to form in ourselves "purely mental" mathematical representations. In this way the applicability of mathematics to the external world is supposed to be grounded. With respect to the relations of space and number Baumann observes — and this passage is one quoted by Lange — "It [number] is together with space and everywhere present in it. It is therefore that geometry also is brought to arithmetical expression."[21]

It is not here our task to criticize in its full extent Baumann's theory, according to which, to a certain extent, the mathematical outside of us is known by the mathematical inside of us. (A suspicious similarity with the ancient Empedoclean theory, that "like is known by like," leaps to the eye.) So far as his theory concerns number — and this alone concerns us, dealing with the influence which it exercised on Lange's theories — it is obviously incorrect. It is based upon an erroneous view of that abstraction process which supplies us with the number concepts. Neither are they "purely mental" creations of an "inner intuition," nor can one speak of a new discovery of the same concepts in the external world, or of their being together with space and in space.

Certainly it is true that the formation of numbers, as also of multiplicities *in concreto,* is no matter of a passive acceptance, or a mere noticing which throws a content into relief. If anywhere at all, here are present spontaneous activities which attach to the contents. Depending upon will and interest, we can unite discrete contents, and

again take away from, or newly add to, the contents just united. A unifying interest directed upon the total content, plus — with and in it, in that reciprocal interpenetration which is peculiar to psychic acts — a simultaneous act of noticing: these throw the contents into relief. And the intentional object of this act of noticing is precisely the representation of the multiplicity or the totality of those contents unified. In this manner the contents are simultaneously and together present. They are a unit; and it is with reflection upon this unification of separate contents by the psychic acts mentioned that the general concepts of multiplicity and (determinate) number arise.

If, now, this is the truth of the matter, then it is clear that designation of numbers as purely mental creations of an inner intuition involves an exaggeration of, and a departure from, the true state of affairs. Numbers are mental creations insofar as they are results of activities which bear upon concrete contents. But what these activities create are not new, absolute contents which could then be found again somewhere in space or in the "external world." Rather, they are peculiar, relational concepts, which can only be produced again and again, but which absolutely cannot be simply *found* somewhere already completed.

Also, *how* are all of the conceivable numbers which we can count off by arbitrarily combining spatial contents to be contained in space? That which is intuitively present, which we can find before us in space and can notice, certainly does not consist of numbers in and for themselves, but consists, rather, only of spatial objects and of their spatial relations. But with that no number is yet given. But if a number is given, it is not, and cannot be, identical with the spatial syntheses which enclose the number of spatial objects (or the concrete totality) as a spatially unifying bond. The adjacency of objects in space is still not that collective unification in our representation which is essential to number. This unification is first brought about *by us* through that unified emphasis which is in the psychical act of interest and of noticing. It was by misunderstanding this that Lange managed to explain the intuition of space as the "archtype" of all synthesis, and, hence, as the archtype of the synthesis of discrete magnitudes, of numbers, as well. This error was aided and abetted by Baumann's theory of the "rediscovery" of number in space. However we now wish to discontinue this critique of the views of Lange and Baumann, especially since they offer no positive suggestions for our further developments.

V

Much more scientific and plausible than all of the theories of the origination of the concepts of multiplicity and number which have been criticized up to this point is the theory to the development of which we now wish to turn. But in order to make completely clear whether or not it does what it promises to do, I shall endeavor to give it as full (*konsequente*) a development as is at all possible, and I shall decline directly to tie my critique down to any one of the forms in which this theory has actually been represented by this or that outstanding author. The following line of argument may be easily admitted:

A totality can be spoken of only where objects which *differ* from each other are present. Were all of the objects identical, then we would in fact have no totality, no multiplicity, of objects, but just one object alone. But these differences must also be *noticed*. Otherwise the different objects would form for our apprehension only one unanalyzed whole, and we would again have no possible way of coming to the representation of a multiplicity. Hence, representations of differences essentially belong within the representation of any totality. In that we, further, distinguish each single object within the totality from the others in it, along with the representation of *difference* there also is necessarily given the representation of the *identity* of each object with itself. In the representation of a concrete multiplicity each single object is, therefore, thought of; and it is thought of both as an object which is different from all of the others, and as an object which is identical with itself.

Given this, the origination of the general concept of multiplicity also, it seems, lies in the clear. In fact, what common thing could

be present in all cases where we speak of multiplicity other than these representations of *difference* and *identity*. All of which fits the fact that, as is well known, in the abstraction of the *general* concept of multiplicity absolutely nothing depends upon the peculiarities of the individual contents. Thus, setting out from any one *concrete* multiplicity, we get the determinate *general concept* of multiplicity under which it falls, *i.e.,* its *number,* by relating each content to each other one as different—but this completely in abstraction from the peculiar character of the concretely given contents—and by considering each content merely as something which is identical with itself. In this way there originates the concept of multiplicity as, to a certain extent, the *empty form of difference.* But now the concept of *unity* is also easy to explain. In numbering, *i.e.,* in carrying out the abstraction of numbers, we bring each thing to be counted under the concept of unity. We consider it merely as *one.* That means just this: We consider each thing merely as something which is identical with itself and different from everything else. As distinguishing and identifying are reciprocally conditioning functions which are inseparable from each other, so the general concepts of multiplicity and unity, which are formed through reflection upon those functions, are also correlative concepts, mutually interdependent.

We especially find ideas of these and similar kinds in the logical works of W. Stanley Jevons[22] and Christoph Sigwart.[23] Thus we read in Jevons: "Number is but another name for diversity. Exact identity is unity, and with difference arises plurality." And, "Plurality arises when and only when we detect difference."[24] Here, as one sees, "number" is taken in the broader sense noted above, where it is synonymous with "plurality." With respect to the kind of abstraction which is here present this same author remarks: "There will now be little difficulty in forming a clear notion of the nature of numerical abstraction. It consists in abstracting the character of the difference from which plurality arises, retaining merely the fact. . . . Abstract number, then, is the *empty form of difference*; the abstract number *three* asserts the existence of marks without specifying their kind."[25] "Three sounds differ from three colors, or three riders from three horses; but they agree in respect of the variety of marks by which they can be discriminated. The symbols 1 + 1 + 1 are thus the empty marks asserting the existence of discrimination."[26]

But these statements suffer—presupposing the correctness of their basis—from essential indetermination; and, indeed, this is made most apparent when we inquire about the origination and content of the singular, numerical representations, 2, 3, 4, . . . They, indeed, are all "empty forms of difference." What differentiates three from two, four from three, and so on? Are we to give the dubious answer: With the number two we notice *one* relation of difference, with three, *two*, with four, *three* such relations, and so on? The information which the last of the passages quoted gives us is obviously very meager. That phrase, "variety of marks," either signifies the same thing again as "number," or it signifies the same as "form of difference." But what characterizes these "forms" psychologically in contrast to each other, so that they can be grasped by their peculiar determinations, clearly distinguished from each other and, accordingly, also denominated by distinct names?

Let us try to go deeper here. For the sake of simplicity we will consider only a totality of three objects A, B, C. Into the representation of this totality there must enter, according to the view in question, these relations of difference: $\widehat{AB}$, $\widehat{BC}$, $\widehat{CA}$ (where the ties indicate the relations). They are given together in our consciousness, and they supposedly effect the unification of the objects into the collective whole. Now one may replace *A, B,* and *C* with contents of any kind whatsoever, but these differences always remain as determinate anyway. They thus constitute the "form" of difference which is characteristic of the number three.

However, certain objections to this present themselves: If these relations of difference are together in our representation, then, in case the basic viewpoint of the theory is correct, each of the differences represented (*Unterschiedsvorstellungen*) must also be perceived as self-identical and as dif-

ferent from each other. For were $\widehat{AB}$ and $\widehat{BC}$, for example, not recognized as different, then they would just blend together as undifferentiated; and then, as one immediately sees, their terms also could not show up in the representation of the totality as distinct from each other. So the sum total of the differences of differences in our representation must be

$$\widehat{AB} \quad \widehat{BC} \qquad \widehat{BC} \quad \widehat{CA} \qquad \widehat{CA} \quad \widehat{AB}$$

But the same would also be true in respect to them. And so on indefinitely. Hence, in order to get hold of the "form of difference" we would fall into a pretty *regressus in infinitum*.

But there still might be a way of avoiding this consequence. One could say: If we proceed, in our distinguishing, from *A* to *B*, and from *B* to *C*, then a new distinction of *C* from *A* is no longer required. That is to say, in relating the two differences $\widehat{AB}$ and $\widehat{BC}$ (which are connected by the one term *B*) to one another in a higher act of differentiation, the possibility of *C* and *A* blending into one is *eo ipso* excluded. So the true schematication would be:

$$\widehat{A \quad B} \quad C$$

Then, whatever *A, B* and *C* may signify, this schematic figure refers us to a process which is everywhere the same. If we therefore abstract from the peculiarities of the particular contents, retaining each only as *somehow* determinate, then we have here the desired form which is common to all multiplicities with three contents, and in virtue of which we also ascribe the number three to such multiplicities.

In such a way one could bring forth all of the forms of difference which are to form the basis of the numerical denominations. Thus, for example, the schema of the simplest number, two, would be: $\widehat{AB}$.[e] In fact, as one could say, what is represented in all cases where a duo lies before us but this?— One object is there, and yet an object *different* from it is there; and the general idea of this fact forms the content of the number concept *two*. If a concrete totality of two contents is given to us, and if we assign to it the number two, then this means that we direct our attention merely upon the fact that one content, and still one *other* content, is present. Our attention does not come to rest upon the peculiarity of the difference, but rather upon the mere fact of it.

The schematic form for the number four would be

$$A \quad B \quad C \quad D$$

And one now easily grasps the rule for how the forms are further complicated. In all cases, the distinctions are ones which bound one another (*i. e.,* have a term in common), making it possible for all of them ultimately to be grasped together in a single act, by means of higher-order acts of distinguishing.

These schemata would perhaps best be regarded as models of those mental processes which occur in the representation of any totality of two, three, four or more contents. And in reflection upon those mental processes, the well characterized differences between which would have to be immanently noted (*innerlich bemerket*), the number concepts would arise.

The extremely rapid increase of complication in these forms would also explain why we attain to authentic (*eigentliche*) representations[f] only with the very first numbers, whereas we can conceive of larger numbers only symbolically, or to a certain extent only indirectly.

Further, one easily sees that the independence of number from the *order* of the enumerated objects follows, on this theory, directly from the nature of the concept of number.

Finally, one could also invoke linguistic usage to support this theory. For example, the same thing is usually meant when it is said that *A* and *B* are different as is meant in saying that *A* and *B* are two things. And so on. So it appears that we have here a well-grounded theory with a claim upon our assent.

However, even if we accept all of the essential supplements which alone would shape Jevon's assertions into a theory (these

assertions being of little use in their indeterminate state), the psychological foundation of the theory yet remains, it seems to me, untenable. But before going deeper into this matter, I must reject as misleading the invocation of linguistic usage. More closely considered, usage says much more against this view than it says for it. Only when given a certain emphasis does the statement, "These are *two* things," have the same signification as the statement, "This thing is different from that thing." It is that emphasis, namely, which is given when one wishes to ward off a threatened confusion of things with each other.

Now let us turn to a critique of the psychological foundations of this theory.

It is true that we can speak of a totality only where there are contents present which are different from each other. But the assertion here connected to this truth is false; viz. that these differences must be represented *as such*, and that otherwise there would be in our representation only an undifferentiated unity, and no multiplicity. It is important to keep these things distinct: to notice two different contents, and to notice two contents *as different from one another*. In the former case there is, presupposing the simultaneous, unified grasping of the contents, a representation of a totality; in the second case there is a representation of a difference. There where a totality is given, our apprehension primarily goes merely upon absolute contents (namely, those which compose the totality). By contrast, where a representation of a difference is given (or a complex of such representations), our apprehension goes upon *relations* between contents. This much alone is correct: Where a plurality of objects is perceived, we are *always justified,* on the basis of the particular contents, in making evident judgments to the effect that every one of the contents is different from each other one. But it is not true that we *must* make these judgments.

With regard to the concepts of *distinguishing* and *distinction*, certain obscurities generally prevail which have their origin in equivocations, and which certainly may have contributed not a little to the errors which I have touched upon here:

(1) "Distinction" or "difference" signifies

the result of a comparison. A comparison can yield either of two results: that the contents considered are the same, or that they are different, *i.e., not* the same. Thus, difference here signifies something negative, the mere absence of an identity. In this sense one speaks of comparing and distinguishing as correlative, intimately connected *activities*. In fact, in *any* case where we have an arbitrary act of comparison, two sorts of results may occur: an affirmative judgment which acknowledges identity is made, or, on the other hand, a negative judgment which rejects identity is made. To this affirming of identity there refers, then, the term 'comparing', while the term 'distinguishing' refers to the denial of identity, whenever these terms are used in the sense of the phrase, "comparing and distinguishing."

In the case where comparison of contents in a certain respect leads to the result, *non-identity*, it can, nonetheless, happen that at least a similarity, "gradation" (*"Steigerung"*), or such like is noticed. These are well-characterized classes of relations, in the case of which, quite as in the case of identity, the representation of the relation evinces (*reprasentiert*) a real (*reellen*), positive content of the representation in question. Now these relations, too, are called relations of difference; and, in particular, the names "distinction" and "difference" are customary for *intervals* in continua (distinction of place, distinction of time, distinction of pitch in tones, etc.). But now this narrower signification of those terms led again, on the other hand, to cases of *mere* non-identity (since such cases, too, do imply distinctions) being thought of as if they were content-relations; *i.e.,* as if in their case too the relation lay in the positive content of the representation; whereas, in fact, nothing further than an evident negative judgment which denies the presence of one such a content-relation (*viz.,* the specific relation of identity) is given.

From the *practical* viewpoint, it may still be useful to classify all of the results to which comparison can lead under the two headings, "Identity" and "Difference." It must not, however, be overlooked that under the latter heading there stand together classes of relations which, as to their phe-

nomenal character, are foreign to each other, while, moreover, a part of them are closely related to the identity relations which have been brought under the other main heading. But from the *psychological, scientific* point of view, the relations of similarity, identity, metaphysical combination,[g] etc. — in short, all relations which have the character of phenomena for representations in the narrower sense (hence, not the character of *merely* represented psychical phenomena[h]) — belong in one class, that of content-relations. But difference, in the broadest sense, does not belong in that class; for it is *not* a positive content of representation which is immediately inspectable at the same time as the terms are. Rather, it is a negative judgment made, or represented as made, upon the basis of those terms.

(2) But the term 'distinguishing' is used in yet another signification, which is connected with analysis. According to this signification, the "distinguished" is that which has been thrown into relief and especially noticed through analysis; and "to distinguish" means the same as "to segregate" or "to analyze."

By investigating the conditions which favor analysis, it is found that a plurality of partial contents are the more easily and certainly segregated the greater, in number and degree (or disparity), are their distinctions amongst themselves and over against the environs. Now these reflections about analysis consisted of comparisons and distinctions of contents that were *already analyzed*; and thus they commonly misled people into believing that the activity of distinguishing (in the sense of analyzing) is also such a *judgmental* activity of distinguishing (in the sense of distinguishing compared contents by their predicates). Then one reasoned: to be able to receive into consciousness several contents as *segregated* — *i.e.,* as analyzed and separately and specifically noticed — they must be thought of as *distinguished* from each other — *i.e.,* as compared and specifically characterized in terms of their distinctions. But this is false. In fact, it is obviously absurd. The *judgmental* activity of distinguishing evidently presupposes pre-prepared contents which are segregated and separately and specifically noticed. Hence, these contents cannot have *first* become noticeable through their being predicatively distinguished from one another.

Now it is this error which the theory we are contesting commits by arguing: "The differences between objects of a multiplicity must have been noticed *as such*. Otherwise, in our representation we would never get beyond an unanalyzed unity, and there would be no talk of any multiplicity. Hence, representations of differences must be explicitly contained in the representation of the multiplicity."

It is true that, if the contents were not different from each other, then there would be no multiplicity. Further, it is true that the distinctions must not be too small. Otherwise just no analysis at all would occur. But it is not true that every content first becomes a distinct content, *i.e.,* one which is separately and specifically noticed, by means of apprehension of its distinctions from other contents; whereas it *is* surely evident that every representation of such a distinction presupposes, as its terms, contents which are *already* separately and specifically noticed and, in *that* sense, are distinguished. In order for a concrete representation of a totality to originate, all that is necessary is that each of the contents comprised therein should be a content which is noticed separately and specifically, and thus is segregated. However, there is no unconditioned necessity that the distinctions of the contents be attended to, even though this frequently will occur—and does so as a rule, where the distinctions are intervals.

Precisely the same thing which has been stated above of the representation of mere distinction holds true also of the representation of *identity*. Here also we have to do with results of reflection upon content which are subsequently slipped into the content as something supposed to have been originally given with and in it. According to Sigwart, identifying and distinguishing must be the functions which supply the concept of unity. "For what is posited as identical and is distinguished from another thing, is, *eo ipso*, like this other thing, posited as one."[27] However, distinction and identification are judgment activities which pursue a

wholly different end than the one here ascribed to them. "*A* is identical with itself, *i.e.*, *A* is not non-*A*, is not *B*, *C* . . . , but rather is just *A*." Such a line of reflection has the aim of staving off confusions of the content *A* with other contents. This intent is realized by seeking out and throwing into relief the points of distinctions of *A* from *B*, *C*, and so on. But while *this* process develops, *A*, *B*, *C*, etc., are *already* present to consciousness as contents which are distinct from one another. The task of this process absolutely is not to articulate *for the first time* what originally is a self-identical unity, but rather is only this: for the ulterior purposes of thought, to segregate similar things from each other, and to obviate, thus, all future confusion by the use of characterizing earmarks supplied by distinctions expressed in judgments. It is here in this process in nowise a question of "constant activities which are repeated in every act of thought," in which "self-consciousness, identically the same in all acts, is realized." Nor is it a question of "factors which constitute the unity of our self-consciousness." (loc. cit.)

So I believe I have shown that representations of identity and of distinction do not explicitly belong among the contents of the representation of multiplicity. Thus they also could not have constituted the basis for the abstraction of this concept. Likewise for the number concepts.

Section 3. Establishment of the Psychological Nature of the Collective Combination

Now let us review our reflections up to now and their results. We undertook to exhibit the origin (*Ursprung*) of the concepts *multiplicity* and *number*. For this purpose it was requisite to get a precise view of the concrete phenomena from which they are abstracted. These phenomena come to light as concrete totalities or sets. However, special difficulties appear to obstruct the transition from these to the general concepts sought. We distinguished and discussed a series of views—rejecting them all, however. Our attention especially rested upon the sort of synthesis which unites the objects of a multiplicity into a whole; for in the false characterization of that synthesis lies the source of the main errors. Our results were, briefly, the following: Whenever we represent a totality we are conscious of the contents as separately and specifically noticed. But, in order to characterize the unification of the contents, we may have recourse neither to appertainance to one consciousness, nor to the relations of simultaneity, temporal succession, spatial combination, or, finally, difference. Now what possibilities remain?

We have not yet investigated all classes of relations. Is collective combination to find its place among those which yet remain? For obvious reasons, however, we are here exempted from a detailed examination of the various particular species of relations. Since we know that the most heterogeneous of contents, whether physical or psychical, can be united in the collective manner, all relations with a range of applicability restricted by the nature of peculiar contents are jettisoned a priori. Thus it is with similarity, gradation, continuous combination, etc. In fact, it appears that none whatever of the familiar sorts of relations can satisfy the set requirements, after temporal relations and relations of mere distinction are excluded. Possibly relations of resemblance still could be brought in here; for, however much two contents may deviate from each other, it will always be possible to state a respect in which they are similar to one another. In fact it is often thought (indeed, as a rule it is) that with regard to the origination of the number concepts recourse to similarity relations must be had. We must take this up later on. Here it is sufficient to point out that, as to concrete totalities, the similarities which it is possible to discover cannot constitute the relations which unite the elements of a totality. The clock and the pen—this is a totality. But in thinking of it I do not need antecedently to bring the two contents under the concepts *colored, extended,* etc.

So there is nothing left to do but to claim for the collective combination a new class of relations, quite different from all others. Accordingly, we must also say: The representation of totality presents us with a whole of a special kind, the parts of which are united by certain relations exclusively char-acteristic of it—precisely those called by us "collective combinations."

Inasmuch as it is now established that we have here to do with a new and original class of relations, we wish to turn to a closer characterization of them, in contrast to other relations. There in fact do belong to them noteworthy peculiarities which very essentially distinguish them in their phenomenal existence from all of the remaining kinds of relations. Since I am not in a position to base my remarks upon a generally acknowledged theory of relations, I think I must fit in here some general observations concerning this very dark chapter of descriptive psychology.

First, it will be useful to come to agreement on the term 'relation'. What is the element common to all cases where we speak of a 'relation', in virtue of which precisely this name is used? To this question J. St. Mill gives us—in a note to his father's book on psychology—an intelligible answer, which, in my opinion, is adequate: "Objects, whether physical or psychical, are in relation to one another in virtue of one complex state of consciousness into which they both enter: even for that case where the complex state consists of nothing more than thinking of the two together. And they are related to one another in as many different ways—or, in other words, they stand in as many distinct relations to one another—as there are specifically different states of consciousness of which *both* are parts."[28]

For purposes of a classification of relations, one might at first use as a guide-line the character of the phenomena which they interrelate (*i.e.,* of the "terms"). However, such a classification would be superficial. In the most diverse of domains we find relations which have one and the same character. Thus, identity, similarity, etc., occur both in the domain of "physical phenomena" and in that of "psychical phenomena."[29] But one can also (and here is the more penetrating principle of division) classify relations in terms of their particular phenomenal (*phänomenalen*) character. From this vantage point, relations fall into two main classes:

1. Relations which possess the character

of "physical phenomena," in the sense defined by Brentano.

Every relation rests upon "terms." It is a complex phenomenon which comprises—in a certain way which cannot be more closely described—partial phenomena. But in nowise does every relation comprise these its terms intentionally,[30] i.e., in that specifically determinate manner in which a "psychical phenomenon" (an act of noticing, of willing, etc.) comprises its content (what is noticed, willed, etc.). Compare, for example, the way in which the representation called the similarity of two contents includes these contents themselves, with any case of "intentional inexistence," and it will have to be acknowledged that we have here two wholly different kinds of inclusion. Precisely because of this, similarity must not be designated as a "psychical," but rather as a "physical" phenomenon. The same is true of other important relations as well, e.g., identity, gradation, continuous combination (i.e., the combination of the parts of a continuum), "metaphysical" combination (i.e., the combination of properties in individual objects, as in the case of color and spatial extension), logical inclusion (as color is included in red), and so on. Each of these relations present us with a peculiar "physical" phenomenon (in the signification assumed here for this term); and with regard to that "physical" character, each belongs in the same main class.

I would, in addition, expressly point out that it makes no difference here whether the terms, i.e., the contents, which are interrelated are themselves physical phenomena, or are some sort of psychical phenomena (represented psychical states). Such identities, similarities, etc., as we perceive to hold between psychical acts or states (judgments, acts of will, and so on) are also physical phenomena. In these cases they only show up on the occasion of psychical phenomena, and are grounded in them.

Relations of this class could most briefly be designated by the name, 'physical relations.' But one would have to guard against the misunderstanding that we here have to do with relations of (or "between") physical contents, whereas, as was just emphasized, it is not a matter of this at all.

2. On the other hand there stands a second main class of relations, which is characterized by the fact that here the relational phenomenon is "psychical." If a unified psychical act is directed upon several contents, then, with regard to it, the contents are combined or are related to each other. Were we to realize such an act, then, of course, we would seek in vain, among the contents of the representation which it includes, for a relation or combination (unless in addition a physical relation were there). The contents are, in this case, unified precisely by the act alone; and the unification, therefore, can only be noticed by means of a special reflection upon the act. Any arbitrary act of representation, judgment, or emotion and will, which is directed upon a plurality of contents, can do as an example. Of any of these psychic acts we can say, in agreement with Mill's definition: It sets the contents into relation with each other. To be specific, there belongs here the relation of "distinctness" in the widest of senses, which has already been discussed, and in the case of which two contents are brought into relation merely by means of an evident, negative judgment.

The characteristic distinction between the two classes of relations can also be marked by saying that physical relations belong among the respective contents of representation in the same sense as do their terms, but that this is not so with psychical relations. In reference to this, one could also quite appropriately call physical relations "content relations."

After this digression into the theory of relations, we turn back now, once again, to those particular relations upon the characterization of which we have set our aim; and we put the question: Are the relations which unify the objects of the totality, and which we called "collective combinations," content relations, in the sense just now made precise —as, for example, metaphysical and continuous combinations are? Or must we perhaps assign them to the class of psychical relations? More exactly expressed: Are collective combinations intuitively contained in, and separately noticeable among, the contents of the representation of the totality as partial contents—as are, say, metaphysical combinations in the metaphysical whole? Or is no trace of a combination to be noticed *in* the representation contents themselves, but rather only in the psychical act which unifies the parts in its embrace? In order to decide this question let us, to begin with, compare the totality with something which is *given* whole *to* a representation (*einem Vorstellungsganzen*).

In order to note the uniting relations in such a whole, analysis is necessary. If, for example, we are dealing with the representational whole which we call "a rose," we get at its various parts successively, by means of analysis: the leaves, the stem, etc. (the physical parts); then the colors, their intensities, the odor, etc. (the properties). Each part is thrown into relief by a distinct act of noticing, and is steadily held *together with* those parts already segregated. As the next issue of the analysis there results, as we see, a totality: namely, the totality of the separately and specifically noticed parts of the whole. But then by means of a simultaneous reflection upon this whole in which the parts are unified there also stands forth the combining relations, as separate, specifically determinate phenomena of representation. In our example we have the continuous combinations within the leaves; or the combinations of the properties, like redness and spatial extension, which combinations are characterized quite differently again from the continuous. In such a way, therefore, *these* combining relations present themselves as, so to speak, a certain "more," in contrast to the mere totality, which appears merely to seize upon its parts, but not really to *unite* them. What, then, distinguishes a case of physical combination from a case of collective combination? Obviously it is this: that in the first case a unification is intuitively noticeable *in* or *among* the contents of representation, while this is not so in the latter case. In the totality there is a lack of any intuitive unification, *as* that sort of unification so clearly manifests itself in the metaphysical or continuous whole. And this is so even though a certain unity *is* present in the totality, and is perceivable with evidence (*Evidenz*).

This same thing is also shown by a com-parison of the collective combination with the relations of identity, similarity, grada-tion, etc. (which, within the class of content relations, constitute, like the combining relations, a group of relations that are psychologically well characterized). Although they do not "combine" the contents upon which, as terms, they are based, yet they constitute perceptible phenomena *for* representation; and in contrast with them, again, the collective combination appears almost as a case of unrelatedness. And so one also speaks of "disjoined" or "unrelated" contents when it is a matter of emphasizing the absence of any content relation whatever, or of content relations upon which the current governing interest is directed. In such cases the contents are just simply thought of "together," *i.e.,* as a totality. But on nowise are they *really* disjoined or unrelated. To the contrary, they are joined by means of the psychical act grasping them together. It is only *within* the content of that act that all perceptible unification is lacking.[31]

The following circumstance also shows that between the collective combination and all of the elementary content relations which are known to us there is an essential distinction, which can make sense only upon the assumption that the former really is not to be counted among the content relations. Every relation rests upon terms and, in a certain manner, is dependent upon them. But whereas, with all content relations, the variability of terms which is admissible without a change in the species of relation is limited, with the collective combination, any term can be varied completely without restriction and arbitrarily, while the relation yet remains. The same also holds true of the relation of distinctness in that widest sense discussed above. Not every content can be conceived of as similar to, continuously joined to, etc., every other content. But each *can* be conceived of as different from, and also as collectively united with, every other. These two latter cases are, precisely, cases where the relation does not immediately reside in the phenomena themselves, but, so to speak, is external to them.

So testimony from many sources—and, above all, from inner experience itself—tells us that we must decide in favor of the second view mentioned above, according to which collective unification is not intuitively given *in* the representation content, but has its existence only in certain psychical acts which unifyingly embrace the contents. And obviously these acts can only be those elementary acts which are capable of enclosing any and all contents, be they ever so disparate. So, then, an attentive inspection of the phenomena teaches the following:

A totality originates in that a unified interest—and, simultaneously with and in it, a unified noticing—throws into relief and encompasses various contents by themselves. Hence, the collective combination also can only be observed by means of reflection upon that psychical act through which the totality comes about. And this also is positively confirmed by inner experience. Wherein, for example, consists the combination when I think of a number of such disparate things as redness and the moon? Obviously only in this: that I think of them "together," think of them in *one* act.

Collective combination plays a highly important role in our mental life as a whole. Every complex phenomenon which presupposes parts that are separately and specifically noticed, every higher mental and emotional activity, requires, in order to be able to occur at all, collective combinations of partial phenomena. There could never even be a representation of one of the more simple relations (*e.g.,* identity, similarity, etc.) if a unified interest and, simultaneously, an act of noticing did not throw into relief together, and unifiedly seize upon, the terms of the relation. This psychical relation called "collective combination" is, thus, an indispensable psychological precondition of every other relation and combination whatsoever.

The abstraction which provides the general concept of the collective combination requires, then, no further special discussion. In any case, in virtue of its elementary nature this concept found its expression in language very early. A mere collective combination is expressed in language by the occurrence of the conjunction "and" between the names of particular things mentioned.

Section 4. The Analysis of the Concept of Number as to its Origin and Content

Since we have established the "psychological" nature of the collective combination, we can bring to completion the solution of our problem, which was the exhibition of the origin and content of the concepts *multiplicity* and *number*.

We stated[i] that the abstraction which yields the concept of multiplicity or totality requires reflection upon the collective mode of combination, similarly as, for example, abstraction of the concept *metaphysical whole* requires reflection upon the metaphysical mode of combination. In order to render such abstraction possible, all that is necessary is that the combining relations between the elements of the totality always be perceptible as what they are in essence, well distinguished from all other relations; and it is in this respect unimportant whether these combining relations are given among the contents of the representation itself, or merely in the psychical act which represents the totality. Now we have decided in favor of the latter. In reflection upon that elementary act of emphatic interest and noticing which has for its content the totality representation, we attain to the abstract representation of the collective combination; and, by means of this abstract representation, we form the general concept of the multiplicity as a whole the parts of which are united merely in the collective mode. However it is better to avoid the terms 'whole' and 'part'. They involuntarily evoke the thought of a more intimate unification of contents, such as is not present here at all. Hence we prefer to say that a representation which is occupied with contents merely as "collectively" united, this all thought *in abstracto*:—such is the concept of multiplicity.

But with this we still have only a paraphrase. What is the actual conceptual content when we think the concept *multiplicity*? The contents which can be colligated to form totalities are, as we know, utterly without restriction. There can also, therefore, enter into the general concept of the multiplicity no sort of peculiarities of content.

However, since this concept is a relational concept, parts must somehow be thought of in it. And, without any difficulty, this also is what takes place in a suitable manner. The particular contents are thought of, not as determinate, but rather as totally indeterminate, as *some sort of* content: each one as *something or other,* as *some one* thing. If, now, we dispense with the scientific term, 'collective combination', and hold ourselves merely to the little word 'and', which designates or indicates the same thing in a completely clear and intelligible manner, then we can quite simply say without any circumlocution: totality or multiplicity *in abstracto* is nothing other than "something or other," and "something or other," and "something or other," etc.; or, more briefly, one thing, and one thing, and one thing, etc. Thus we see that the concept of the multiplicity contains, besides the concept of collective combination, only the concept *something*. Now this most general of all concepts is, as to its origin and content, easily analyzed.

'Something' is a name which is proper for any conceivable content. Any real or conceptual being is a "something." But we also can give this name to a judgment, an act of will, a concept, an impossibility, a contradiction, and so on. Of course the concept *something* is not to be obtained by any conceivable *comparison* of contents which takes in all objects, both physical and psychical. Such a comparison would simply remain without a result. In fact, "something" is no partial content. That wherein all objects— actual and possible, real and unreal, physical and psychical, etc.—agree, is this alone: They either are contents of representations, or are represented in our consciousness by means of contents of representations. Obviously the concept *something* owes its origination to reflection upon the psychical act of representing, as the content of which just any determinate object may be given. Hence, the "something" belongs to the content of any concrete object only in that external and non-literal fashion common to any sort of relative or negative attribute (such as, for example, with similar-to-B, non-C, etc.). In fact, it itself must be designated as a relative determination. Of course the concept *something* never can be thought

unless some sort of a content is present, on the basis of which that reflection mentioned above is carried out. Yet for this purpose any content is as well suited as another: even the mere name 'something'.

Let us turn back, now, to the concept of the multiplicity. We elucidated it as: something and something and something, etc.; or one thing and one thing, etc. This "etc." indicates an indetermination which is essential to the concept. It does not, of course, mean that we must continue on *ad infinitum.* Rather it means only that no determination of our continuation is met with. *De facto,* to be sure, in thinking out "multiplicity" a boundary is speedily found. But it is always with the consciousness that it is an arbitrary one, which is of no significance at all. This gives us the concept of *multiplicity in the widest of senses.*

By suppression of that indetermination just noted there arises out of this general concept the determinate multiplicity concepts, or *numbers.* The more general concept of multiplicity encompasses all concepts of the same sort as *one and one, one and one and one, one and one and one and one,* etc., as its special cases. These special cases are, in their determinate delimitation from each other, well distinguished; and accordingly they would receive separate names: "two," "three," "four," etc. Each concrete totality falls under one—and, indeed, a determinate one—of these concepts. To each such totality there "belongs a certain number." It is easy to characterize the abstraction which must be exercised upon a concretely given multiplicity in order to attain to the number concept under which it falls. One considers each of the particular objects merely insofar as it is a "something" or "one," herewith fixing the collective combination; and, in this manner, there is obtained the corresponding general form of multiplicity, one and one and . . . and one, with which a number name is associated. In this process there is total abstraction *from* the specific characters of the particular objects. But this neither means nor implies that the concrete objects have to disappear from our consciousness. To "abstract" from something merely means to pay no special attention to it. Thus, also in our case at hand, no special interest is directed upon the peculiarities of content in the separate individuals; while those peculiarities, nonetheless, do constitute the precondition of the acts of reflection which yield the "units" of the respective number, and are the ground of the distinctness of those units.

Let us look once more, then, at the psychological foundation of the number concepts. *Two things constitute (konstituiert), on our view, the concept of number: 1) the concept of "collective unification" (Einigung) and 2) the concept of "something." The abstraction of the former concept becomes possible in virtue of the fact that, in all cases where discrete contents are thought together, i.e., in a totality, there is present one and the same, constantly uniform act of collecting interest and noticing, which act separates each of the particular contents off to itself (as separately and specifically noticed), and simultaneously holds it together in a union with the others. It is with reference to this unifying act that we win the abstract representation of collective combination. As to the subsumption of any content under the concept of "something," that requires reflection upon the act in which that content is represented.*

The two psychological constituents of the concept of number obviously are not independent of each other. We cannot conceive of a collective unification without united contents; and, if we wish to represent them *in abstracto,* then they must be thought of as "something or other." But if this is so, what, then, constitutes the distinction between the concepts *collective unification* and *multiplicity?* The answer is obvious. In the first case, interest rests exclusively upon the *combination* of the arbitrarily conceived contents; but in the latter, it rests upon the totality of those contents *as a whole, i.e.,* upon *the elements* attended to *in* this their unification. So both concepts are equally essential to the concept of the multiplicity—the concept of "something," and that of "collective unification." It is clear that the concept *something* is related to a concrete content in exactly the same way as the concept *number* is related to a totality of concretely given contents. However, the concept *something* is the more primitive one. Without it there would be no number. The elementary fact which originally manifests itself in it, and essentially conditions it, is that which makes possible the concept of the collective unification.[32]

NOTES

1. Cf. "Über die tatsachlichen Grundlagen der Geometrie," *Wissenschaftliche Abhandlungen,* II:611.

2. Cf. "Über den Ursprung der geometrischen Axiome," *Vorträge und Reden,* II:16.

3. "Μονάς ἐστι, χαϑ᾽ ἥν ἕχαστον τῶν ὄντων ἓν λέγεται. Ἀριϑμὸς δὲ τὸ ἐχ μονάϑων συγχείμενον πλῆϑος." [T.L. Heath, *The Thirteen Books of Euclid's Elements* (tr.), (1926), I:277 (D.W. [Translator]).]

4. *De Corpore,* chap. VII, sect. 7; cf. Baumann, *Die Lehren von Raum, Zeit und Mathematik,* I:274.

5. *Essay on the Human Understanding,* bk. II, chap. 16. sect. 5 [Husserl erroneously cited "bk. II, chap. 4, sect. 5," retained in the 1970-edition (D.W.).]

6. God. Guil. Leibnitii, *Opera philosophica,* ed. J.E. Erdmann (Berlin, 1840), p. 53 ["I define number as one and one and one, etc., or as unities," L. E. Loemker, tr.-ed., *G.W. Leibniz, Philosophical Papers and Letters* (Chicago, 1956), I:157 (D.W.).]

7. *Opera philosophica,* p. 243.

8. For the present we omit to exclude these nuances by using only one of these names. However, for reasons which will appear later, the words 'totality' (*Inbegriff*) and 'multiplicity' are preferred.

9. Probably there is little need to recall that, where we are dealing with objectively real things, these still must be represented in our consciousness by means of representations. The represented totality is related, in such cases, to the intended totality of real things as the representation of a single real thing also is related to that thing itself.

10. *Psychologie als Wissenschaft* (1825), I:162.

11. *Werke,* Hartenstein edition, III:144.

12. Ibid., p. 142.

13. Cf. Hankel, *Complexe Zahlensysteme,* p. 17.

14. In *Philosophische Aufsätze zu Zeller's Jubiläum,* I, "Über Zählen und Messen."

15. Ibid., p. 140.

16. Ibid., p. 141.

17. Vol. II, p. 26.

18. *Logik,* Gomperz translation, I:237.

19. Lange, *Logische Studien,* pp. 148–49.

20. J.J. Baumann, *Die Lehren von Raum,* II:668f., 670, 675.

21. Ibid., p. 670.

22. *The Principle of Science,* 2nd. ed. (London, 1883).

23. *Logik,* vol. II (Tübingen, 1878).

24. Jevons, *The Principle of Science,* p. 156.

25. Ibid., p. 158.

26. Ibid., p. 159.

27. Sigwart, *Logik*, II:37.

28. James Mill, *Analysis of the Phenomena of the Human Mind*, ed. J. St. Mill, (London, 1879), II:7ff. Cf. Meinong, *Hume-Studien*, II, "Zur Relationstheorie" (Vienna, 1882), p. 40. (Here I have translated Husserl's translation of Mill's words—D.W.)

29. In regard to the significations of the terms 'physical' and 'psychical' phenomenon, and the fundamental distinction underlying them, which also is indispensable for the following reflections, cf. F. Brentano: *Psychologie vom empirischen Standpunkte*, vol. I, bk, 2, ch. 1. [See the Brentano selections in R.M. Chisholm, *Realism and the Background of Phenomenology* (Glencoe, 1960), pp. 39ff.—D.W.]

30. Ibid., p. 115.

31. Therefore Mill is right in expressly stressing that objects already stand in relation to each other even if we only think of them together. Precisely with respect to the psychical act which thinks of them together, they constitute parts of a psychical whole; and they also can, at any time, be recognized as joined by means of reflection upon that whole. This whole constitutes their "relation." And only if one were to restrict this term to what we have called "content relations" could there, of course, be no more talk of relation in the case of a psychical combination. On one hand, this certainly is a terminological matter. But, on the other hand, there is *de facto* so much in common between the content relation and the psychic relation, as to their main moment, that I fail to see why a common term should not be justified here.

32. These pages contain the first chapter of a book which will shortly be published by C.E.M. Pfeffer (R. Stricker) of Halle.

TRANSLATOR'S NOTES

a. A "Kunstlehre" in Husserl's sense is a theory (Lehre) of a technique or art (Kunst). It is a teaching about how to do something correctly. In the case of what is commonly taught as logic, Husserl supposed is best regarded as a practical theory about how to arrive at *knowledge,* as distinct from mere opinion or conjecture. He parallels logic to "technologies" (his term) such as surveying and mechanical and chemical engineering, each of which utilizes a strictly theoretical body of knowledge—*e.g.,* mathematics, physics, chemistry—to attain some goal. See *Logical Investigations,* vol. I, subsect. 13, for this parallel.

Chapters 2 to 3 of this volume explain in detail the sense in which Husserl regarded logic as a "Kunstlehre," and how he regarded the relation between "Kunstlehren" and the norms and strictly theoretical segments of knowledge that they presuppose.

b. The term 'psychology' caused Husserl so much grief that he eventually abandoned it as a means of expressing what he was doing. However, even in this earliest of his published efforts he is doing *essentially* the same sort of thing as he is engaged in during the remainder of his philosophical life.

All methodological subtleties aside, in this essay he advances an eidetic and noematic analysis of a certain, fundamental *type* of experience, that of assigning a number to groups of objects, or at least of seeing that there are "a number" of objects in a group. Specifically, he details the *sorts* of things *necessarily* represented or intended in this *type* of experience. The later contortions and re-interpretations staged, with little or no effect upon his critics, in the effort to dodge charges of "psychologism" do not alter the fact that his fundamental enterprise never essentially changed.

Concerning an important phase of Husserl's supposed "removal" from psychologism see Dallas Willard, "The Paradox of Logical Psychologism: Husserl's Way Out," *American Philosophical Quarterly* 9 (1972): 94–100.

c. It seems that, at the time this essay was printed, Husserl intended it to be the first chapter in his projected book on the philosophy of arithmetic. See note 32 above. When, approximately four years later, in 1891, his *Philosophie der Arithmetik* did appear, the present essay had been largely modified, to form its first four chapters.

His views on fundamental points were, however, unmodified; and crucial statements, such as that near the end of subsection three, concerning the origination of totality, are repeated word for word. This statement on the totality appears again on p. 79 of the 1891 edition, and on p. 74 of the 1970 edition of *Philosophie der Arithmetik.* See also the third from the last paragraph of the "Preface" to that book, on the sameness of wording in it and the "Habilitationsschrift."

d. The analysis here referred to is not carried out in this essay.

e. One must not be confused by the fact that there is only *one* relation of difference involved in the schematic form for the number *two,* or that there are *six* such relations in the schema for the number *four,* given below. The theory which Husserl is explaining here holds only that for every number there is, founded in the concrete totalities to which it applies, a distinct and determinate set of relations, relations of relations, relations of relations of relations, and so on, which is *its* peculiar "form of difference." The set for the number five would contain ten such relations, for six it would contain fifteen, and so on.

f. A genuine (or *eigentliche*) representation is one for which every element intended is actually given in perception or intuition. It is very like a Cartesian clear and distinct idea. Or, see the distinctions between kinds of ideas developed by Leibniz in his paper: "Reflections on Knowledge, Truth and Ideas" (*Leibniz Selections,* ed. P.P. Wiener (New York, 1951); cf. also L. Loemker as in note 6 above).

Husserl's point here is that we cannot, for example, directly *see* that there are 105,073 grains of wheat in a basket, as we *can* see that there are 3 apples on the table. In the latter case we may have an "eigentliche" representation, but not in the former. For a further development of his theory of "eigentliche" representations, and for an acknowledgement of his debt here to

Brentano, see the opening paragraphs of chap. 11 of *Philosophie der Arithmetik*.

g. On the meaning of "metaphysical combination," recall the reference to Brentano on p. 98 above. "Metaphysical" does not have, in Husserl's language, the inclusive sense in which it is often used, but is restricted to what has, by some other philosophers, been called "cosmology"; namely, to the theory of the first principles of substances, or individuals causally bound into the texture of temporal world process.

h. What is meant here is probably the sort of thing described in the second sentence of the fifth paragraph below.

i. The back-reference here is to the fourth paragraph from the end of subsection 1 above.

Introduction to
"Psychological Studies for Elementary Logic"
RICHARD HUDSON

The "Psychologische Studien zur elementaren Logik" first appeared in the *Philosophische Monatshefte* in 1894. This text belongs to Husserl's earliest period, coming only three years after his first philosophical publication (the *Philosophie der Arithmetik*) and six years before the publication of the *Logical Investigations*.

This early period is usually overlooked. There are very few works devoted to it, and it is not often discussed in any detail in the various books which attempt to give a view of the whole of Husserl's career. In fact, as Th. de Boer, one of the few authors to go into the specifics of this period, notes: "The works on Husserl mostly begin with his main work—the *Logical Investigations*."[1] Only in recent years has attention begun to be focused on these earlier writings: de Boer's long book (*The Development of Husserl's Thought* was published in English by Nijhoff in 1978), Jacques English's translation of the early writings into French; *Aufsätze und Rezensionen* (*Husserliana* 21, ed. Bernhard Rang) containing the early writings; and a few other translations and articles.[2]

There are probably two basic reasons why commentators have ignored Husserl's writings of this period. One is that they were relatively inaccessible, hidden away in various German philosophical journals. The main reason, however, is probably that they were thought not particularly important and not worth the time required to study them.

That these writings were felt to be unimportant was due to the general view that Husserl's earliest period was marked by a mistake, the mistake of logical psychologism, which Husserl recognized and rejected in a slashing attack in the *Logical Investigations*. Since Husserl himself rejected psychologism it was felt that his early psychologistic writings could safely be forgotten.

However, although Husserl did severely attack the position of logical psychologism in the *Logical Investigations* (quoting Goethe that one is the most severe on mistakes that one has made oneself),[3] he did not reject his early work. In later years he often complained that the *Philosophie der Arithmetik* was not studied, and he used several parts of the early works in the *Logical Investigations*, taking over whole sentences and paragraphs with little or no changes. Thus various parts of the "Psychological Studies" are reproduced in the *Logical Investigations*, particularly in the third investigation, and also in the fifth and the second.[4]

Still, the importance of the "Psychological Studies" for us today is probably primarily historical—to understand the debates in logic at the end of the nineteenth century, and to understand the development of Husserl's thought. De Boer sees the beginnings of many later themes in the early work, especially in the way Husserl took over various concepts from his teacher, Franz Brentano. According to de Boer: "In order to understand the development of Husserl's thought, it is necessary to study all of his works. Of exceptional importance in this regard are the often neglected first works: the *Philosophie der Arithmetik* and a series of articles on logic and psychology."[5] Of these articles, probably the most important is the "Psychological Studies."

The problems which interested Husserl at the time of the "Psychological Studies" were problems in the foundations of mathematics and logic, which led him to problems in epistemology in general.[6] Only ten years before the "Psychological Studies" he had completed his doctorate in mathematics, but under Brentano's influence, he decided to devote himself to philosophy instead.[7] He felt, as did many others at that time, that the problems of the foundations of mathematics and logic could be solved by psychological analyses. Mathematics and logic, it was felt, dealt with thinking, and thus with man's psyche. The study of the psyche was psychology; the study of the foundations of these sciences was properly a matter of psychology. Such things as the law of contradiction was, then, a law which expressed how the mind worked, and its study was a study of the actual workings of the minds of real people.

Among the most serious problems which occupied Husserl in attempting to establish the foundations of mathematical thought was how, if Brentano was right and all knowledge starts with intuition, conceptual thought manages to start with given particulars and yet arrive at universal statements. Another problem was how conceptual thought manages to give universal a priori statements, which by their very nature deal with things which have no existence in intuition, and yet which seem to accord so well with whatever intuitive test we design for their verification.

These two problems are the background for the two special studies Husserl attempts in the "Psychological Studies." The first study deals with the distinction of abstract and concrete contents; the second, with the distinction of intuitions and representations.[8]

Husserl's aim in the first study is, as he says in an article of 1897, to show that the concepts of abstract and concrete contents can be reduced to Stumpf's distinction between dependent and independent contents.[9] His more general aim is to show how conceptual thought operates in arriving at a priori truths (as in mathematics). According to de Boer the problems being dealt with here later led Husserl on to the theory of the *Wesensschau* (intuition of essences), *i.e.*, to the theory of how we can arrive at essential knowledge through examining particulars.[10]

The first of the three sections of this study deals with the distinction of dependent and independent contents. Husserl says that an independent content is such that we can alter or suppress all other contents given with it without altering it itself. For dependent contents this is not the case. There is always at least one other content given with them which we cannot alter or suppress without changing them.

Husserl claims we can determine whether a particular content is dependent or not by operating a kind of thought experiment. If we find that in phantasy we can vary all the contents given with—to use his example—a horse's head, then we can say the head is an independent content. However if we find that we cannot do this, then the content would be dependent. Husserl's example here is the case of the intensity and the quality of a tone, where changing one changes the other.

Husserl stresses that our statements based on this kind of experiment are not just factually true, but necessarily true. In the case of the horse's head, for example, that there is no absurdity in saying we can vary the other contents is seen by him as sufficient evidence to show the head is an independent content. Husserl is claiming here, then, that we can arrive at essential and necessary knowledge through the examination of particular cases by the mind.

The other ways which exist for determining whether contents are dependent are, Husserl feels, inferior since they are incapable of supplying evidence.

The second section of this first study links the distinction of dependent and independent contents to that of abstract and concrete contents. Obviously dependent contents must be parts of some whole, so Husserl looks at different relations of parts and wholes. He says that "abstract parts" of a whole are dependent, while the concrete "pieces" are independent.[11]

Husserl notes that although the distinctions he is dealing with come from intuition, and most of the examples (the horse's head, tones, etc.) are intuitive examples, these distinctions are extended beyond intuition. Thus all concepts are called abstract, while the objects they refer to are called concrete. Husserl objects to this use. The problem is that although many concepts refer to objects which can be intuited, many others do not. The latter is the case for the concepts which interest Husserl most, *i.e.*, mathematical concepts. Numbers cannot be seen, and true geometric figures cannot be intuited either. Other concepts also share this lack of corresponding adequate intuitions—sometimes because of the limitations of our minds (*e.g.*, we cannot clearly imagine groups of more than about twelve similar objects; if there are more than twelve, we simply imagine "many"), and sometimes because there are no intuitions due to the nature of the concepts, as with mathematical concepts, or as in the cases of the famous incompatible concepts (round squares and the like).

In the final section of the first study Husserl makes some critical comments, mainly about a theory of abstraction which he rejects. According to this theory, abstracting is a special mental activity which brings things into relief. Husserl feels this does not distinguish abstract from concrete contents, since to notice even concrete things, such as a box, we have to bring them into relief. There is, he says, no difference as far as he can see between the consciousness of the concrete and that of the abstract.

The second study is entitled "On Intuitions and Representations." In the 1897 article Husserl calls this study "a piece of pure descriptive psychology."[12] Husserl describes here two different "modes of consciousness." The first, intuition, is such that it actually contains its object as an immanent content. The second, representation, does not. Rather it uses an immanent content to point to, aim at, or intend some other content which is not immanent.

Of the two functions, representations are clearly the more interesting for Husserl. He says that they give rise to "astonishment"[13] and that it is most important they be investigated.

They are interesting mainly because all mathematical and logical concepts are representations. The question Husserl is interested in here is how representations operate and what distinguishes them from intuitions. His more basic aim is to understand how mathematical thought works and more generally, how conceptual thought is possible.

Husserl dealt with the same sort of questions in the *Philosophie der Arithmetik*. There he talked of "inauthentic presentations" instead of "representations." (Although the two terms are not totally identical, they aim at the same problem.) Mathematical concepts were inadequate or inauthentic presentations because they do not actually present their objects to consciousness (*i.e.*, bring their objects into consciousness as immanent contents) as authentic presentations do. Instead, mathematics operates with symbols. It uses symbols to point to or intend objects which by their very nature cannot be presented authentically. For Husserl we have an authentic presentation of what we intuit, for example, we have an authentic presentation of the moon when we are actually looking at it, because we have a presentation of it as an immanent content in consciousness. The moon itself is of course not in consciousness—as Frege notes it would weigh rather heavily on our minds if it were[14]—but the presentation of the moon is there. What interests Husserl in the *Philosophie der Arithmetik* is that all mathematical concepts are such that they can never be authentically present in consciousness but must always be symbolized or substituted for by some other content which itself *is* present to consciousness. The question he asks is how such inauthentic presentations operate and, since it seems that mathematical knowledge is the most secure knowledge man possesses, how is it that they operate so well.

In the "Psychological Studies" Husserl uses the term 'representation' to extend the range of the concept of inauthentic presentation. While all mathematical concepts and all basic concepts of logic are representations, other contents are representations as well. He refers to all words as representations, and he says that the intuition of one side of a thing can function as a representation of the whole thing. It is clear that there are many different kinds of representations for Husserl, some of which are more symbolic and more inauthentic than the others. In fact, unlike the inauthentic presentations of the *Philosophie der Arithmetik,* some of the representations can be "fulfilled," *e.g.* we can sometimes intuit what is represented —as when we see what we were only talking about.

Husserl divides the second study into seven sections. In these sections he attempts to replace the term 'presentation' by two other concepts: intuition and representation.

The first section looks at various examples aimed at arriving at the meaning of the term 'intuition'.

The second section gives the definitions of 'intuition' and 'representation' and of various related concepts.

An intuition contains its object as an immanent content. A representation does not, but merely uses an immanent content to intend its object. Intuitions are not necessarily related to representations, but representations always refer to some intuition not yet actual.

When the content intended by a representation becomes an immanent content of consciousness, Husserl says we can talk of the fulfillment of the representation. There are different levels of fulfillment. Although some fulfillments may themselves serve as representations of yet other contents not present to consciousness, the ultimate fulfillment is always purely an intuition. As in the *Philosophie der Arithmetik* such an ultimate fulfillment is denied to certain representations—for example, mathematical ones—since there is no intuition corresponding to them.

The third and fourth sections deal with various difficulties and attempt to determine what belongs to the content of an intuition.

One difficulty quickly disposed of is the inauthenticity of saying that the content of an intuition is immanent to consciousness. If we hear a melody we actually hear only one note at a time, not the whole melody.

Similarly if we see a thing, we see one side of it at a time but not the whole thing. Despite this, we tend to say we intuit the melody and the thing. Husserl claims that to resolve this difficulty all we need to do is say that intuition is not necessarily momentary, but that it can take place in a process in which the various contents of the melody and of the thing are actually intuited.

A more important difficulty concerns what exactly is intuited. Husserl says that only what we pay attention to is intuited— backgrounds and the like are unintuited. This stipulation is partly aimed at section 5, the central section of this study, where the distinction of intuition and representation is made.

In the 1897 discussion of the "Psychological Studies," Husserl notes that the main thesis of this study is in section 5—namely, that "the distinction between intuition and representation is not a distinction in their contents but rather only a difference in their 'mode of consciousness.'"[15] Husserl establishes this thesis by examining some linguistic examples.

The main example is that of the arabesque. The arabesque can be seen as a mere design which may be pleasing to the eye. In this case it is intuited. However it may also be seen and understood as a word by someone who can read Arabic. It now represents what the word means. This latter, since it is not actually present, is not intuited. The arabesque is no longer intuited either, since according to section 4 we intuit only what we pay attention to. Instead of paying attention to the arabesque we are occupied with what it represents. Thus the arabesque is now a representation since it is a content in consciousness which intends another content not presently in consciousness.

For Husserl the difference between the two situations cannot lie in the immanent contents, since in both cases what is immanent is the arabesque. Thus the difference must lie elsewhere. For Husserl the new psychic situation which results when the word is understood means that we are dealing with a new "mode of consciousness." Somehow consciousness does not passively receive the arabesque as its content, but it actively goes beyond the immediate content to yet another. De Boer sees here the first indication of Husserl's later concept of the meaning-conferring activity, and ultimately of the concept of constitution.[16]

Husserl notes that although the two functions of intuition and representation are different modes of consciousness, they work closely together. The one passes over into the other and the two are very often intertwined. Despite these close relationships, however, Husserl insists that the distinction can and must be made. He attacks, in the sixth section, the ambiguity which results from calling them both "presentations." He claims that this failure to clearly distinguish the two gives rise to serious errors in psychology and epistemology.

The final section gives some indication of Husserl's general aims in the article. He notes the importance of the investigation of these two functions for psychology, logic, and epistemology. He stresses the need for showing how conceptual thought can operate with such seemingly inadequate presentations as the representations. He finally notes some problems, such as that of the presentation of space, which might be cleared up if his distinctions were made. Unfortunately, he says, the necessary descriptions are missing.

The "Psychological Studies," then, deals with two special problems—the distinctions of concrete and abstract contents, and of intuitions and representations. Husserl comes to these problems because his interest in establishing the foundations of mathematics and logic leads him to more general problems in epistemology.

In the "Psychological Studies" the two distinctions being made are traced back to consciousness. In both cases we are dealing with contents immanent to consciousness, and all talk of existing things is rejected as "unpsychological."[17] The difference of abstract and concrete contents is that in the one case we can alter in phantasy all simultaneously given contents and in the other case we cannot. This distinction is however already somewhat of a move away from the psychologistic school since Husserl says he cannot note any difference in the mode of consciousness of the abstract from that of the concrete. The distinction of intuition and representation is more clearly an example of Husserl's logical psychologism. This distinction does not consist in a difference in the contents of the respective acts, since the contents can be the same in both cases. Instead, it is a matter of different modes of consciousness.

Although the "Psychological Studies" belongs to Husserl's period of logical psychologism, the descriptive analyses are such that they can be taken over, in some cases word for word, in the analyses of descriptive psychology in the *Logical Investigations*. In the later work the themes and problems of the early work are continued and further developed. Husserl, of course, also expands the scope of his philosophic activity in later years, moving from the early concern with mathematics and logic to more general concerns such as the life-world and history. However, although he at times calls his early work immature, he never rejects it.

NOTES

1. Th. de Boer, *De Ontwikkelingsgang in het Denken van Husserl* (Assen: Van Gorcum, 1966), p. 577. An English translation of de Boer's book (*The Development of Husserl's Thought*, translated by Theodore Platinga [The Hague: Nijhoff, 1978]) has appeared as number 76 of the Phaenomenologica series.

2. As noted above (note 1) de Boer's book was published in Dutch in 1966 and in English in 1978. The French translation of the early articles is entitled *Articles sur la logique*, trans., notes, comments, and index by Jacques English (Paris: P.U.F., 1975). Among the translations relevant to this period is that of Gottlob Frege's classic 1894 "Review of Dr. E. Husserl's *Philoso-*

phy of Arithmetic," translated by E. W. Kluge in *Mind* 81 (1972): 321–37, reprinted in *Husserl: Expositions and Appraisals*, ed. with introductions by Frederick A. Elliston and Peter McCormick (Notre Dame and London: University of Notre Dame Press, 1977), pp. 314–21. One of the most active scholars in English on this period is Dallas Willard. His article "The Paradox of Logical Psychologism: Husserl's Way Out" can be found in the same volume as Frege's review just mentioned (pp. 10–17). In late 1977 he published a translation of the "Psychological Studies" and announced his intention to translate three of the other early articles. See *The Personalist* 58 (1977): 295–96 for Willard's introduction; pp. 297–320 for Husserl's "Psychological Studies in the Elements of Logic."

3. *Logische Untersuchungen* [or *LU*], p. 7; *Logical Investigations* [or *LI*], p.00.

4. See "Edmund Husserl—Persönliche Aufzeichnungen," ed. Walter Biemel, *Philosophy and Phenomenological Research* 16 (1956): 293–302. See particularly p. 295, where in the note dated September 25, 1906, Husserl says of the "Psychological Studies" that this article "is a first draft for the *Logical Investigations,* particularly for investigations III and V."

5. De Boer, *De Ontwikkelingsgang,* p. 577.

6. See the "Preface" to the first edition of the *Logische Untersuchungen.* See also section 7 of the second study of the "Psychological Studies."

7. See "Recollections of Franz Brentano" in this volume, pages 342–48.

8. The word translated as 'representation' in this text is *'Repräsentation'*. Husserl makes a sharp distinction in the "Psychological Studies" between this term and the word *'Vorstellung'*, which is usually translated as "representation" but which I have translated here as "presentation." In making this rather unusual translation, I am merely following the use of Findlay in *Logical Investigations.* Farber, too, in his discussion in *The Foundation of Phenomenology* (Albany: SUNY Press, 1967) translates these terms in this way. English's excellent translation into French of the "Psychological Studies" attempts to make the distinction by using a hyphen (représentation vs. re-présentation). Although this makes the distinction clear, it is not a very satisfactory procedure. Willard uses 'representation' and 'representative' for *'Vorstellung'* and *'Repräsentation'*. This avoids the strange use of 'presentation' for 'Vorstellung' but leads to great difficulties in translating the verbs and adjectives connected with the two terms in question. Since the "Psychological Studies" is one of the texts leading to the *Logical Investigations,* it is probably best to adhere to the use of the translator of that work, even if it is not totally satisfactory.

9. Edmund Husserl, "Bericht über deutsche Schriften zur Logik aus dem Jahre 1894," *Archiv für systematische Philosophie* 3 (1897): 224.

10. See de Boer, *De Ontwikkelingsgang,* pp. 30–31, 65–66, 114, 119, 296–97.

11. The distinction Husserl is making here is between *'Teile'*, which is translated as 'parts', and *'Stücke'*, which is translated as 'pieces'. Husserl uses the corresponding verbs *'teilen'* and *'zerstücken'* to refer to the processes of dividing into 'parts' or 'pieces'. Unfortunately good English equivalents are not available, so, roughly following Cairns (Dorion Cairns, *Guide for Translating Husserl* [The Hague: Nijhoff, 1973]) and the advice of the Husserl Archives at Louvain, I have used 'partition' for *'teilen'* and 'divide into pieces' for *'zerstücken.'*

12. Husserl, "Bericht," p. 225.

13. See the "Psychological Studies," p. 140 below.

14. See Frege's "Review of Husserl's *Philosophy of Arithmetic*," in Elliston and McCormick, *Husserl,* p. 316.

15. Husserl, "Bericht," p. 225.

16. De Boer, *De Ontwikkelingsgang,* pp. 578, 22, 582, 40–41.

17. See, for example, the "Psychological Studies," p. 129 below.

Psychological Studies for Elementary Logic*

TRANSLATED BY R. HUDSON AND P. MCCORMICK

I. On the Distinction Between Abstract and Concrete

1. Independent and Dependent Contents

Total consciousness is at any one time a unity in which each feature is connected with every other one. Considerable differences, however, are to be found in the manner, in the relative stability, and in the mediacy or immediacy of the connection. The division of contents here between *independent*[1] ("separable," "presentable by itself") and *dependent* ("inseparable," "not presentable by itself") is related to such distinctions. Certain complex contents are noticed separately with somewhat greater ease; they impose themselves, as it were, upon our attention as natural units. Moreover, in contrast to the observable contents combined with them, they show a characteristic independence which we do not find in members of other kinds of connections. This is the way the intuitive content of perceptible things presents itself when compared with the less complex but likewise intuitive contents which we call their intrinsic traits (color, form, and the like). Just what this independence consists in is not easy to say. One might perhaps try to characterize this independence in the following way: objective things affect each other and thus condition

dependency relations between the perceived appearances and thus also between their intuited contents. We also know in many cases that the alteration of one appearance (or of one intuition) will bring about a corresponding alteration in the coordinated appearance. But it does not lie in the nature of the intuited contents themselves that they are in these relations of dependence. We find nothing in them which makes the necessity of the connection evident; the connection itself does not concern the contents as such but the objective things only. In fact, by means of phantasy we can think of the causal connections as totally suppressed without finding the intuitive content of the perception altered. The contents which are to be considered here exhibit just such a separability from what is conjoined but to a much greater extent, not merely with regard to what is causally joined but also with regard to *all* contents which can be simultaneously noticed and with which the contents are connected in whatever way. The exception, of course, is the case of the contents' own parts where one would not really speak of "joining." These contents it seems remain what they are, whether the contents connected with them are presented as disappearing or as changing in any way whatsoever. I can in phantasy retain by itself the head of a horse and, while the head remains intuitively unaltered, make disappear or alter as I wish the remaining parts of the horse as well as the entire intuitive context.[2] We can say more precisely that there are either no modifications at all, or they are too slight

*© 1977 P. McCormick and R. Hudson. Translated and printed with the permission of Professor Elmar Bund, executor of Husserl's estate. Originally published as "Psychologische Studien zur elementaren Logik," *Philosophia Mathematica* 30 (1894): 159–91.

to be noticed, or (and this may correspond most of all to the psychic state of affairs) they are overlooked as insignificant. In any case, eventual corresponding alterations of the connected contents which do not escape us in the requisite attention to what is actually experienced [*das wirklich Erlebte*] appear to us as merely *factual*; there is nothing in the contents which would require a functional dependence of their alterations as an *evident necessity*.

We have started here from the phenomena which first present themselves to reflection—that is, from appearing things. We indicated the characteristic features of independence in their intuitive content. But we also find such features in non-things, for example, in auditory appearances when we think of them as free from any relationship to objects, such as in tones or in figures of tones which are intuitively self contained. Odors and tastes have a similar independence under the same conditions. Intuitions connected with the sense of touch make the possibility of such freedom from objects rarer and more difficult.

With regard to these matters *dependent* contents behave quite differently.

The intensity of a tone is not something indifferent to the quality; it is not, so to speak, something external to the quality. The same is true conversely. We cannot maintain the intensity by itself as what it is and alter or entirely suppress the quality as we wish. An alteration of the quality necessarily conditions an alteration in the character of the intensity, even if a moment (which we call "degree") of each remains unaltered. Intensity is precisely nothing by itself; rather it is only something with and in the quality. If we think of the quality as entirely suppressed, then the intensity is also suppressed, and this is not a mere fact, but rather an evident necessity. The same occurs in the case of the converse. An alteration of the intensity means unavoidably a certain alteration of the quality, even if its species remains untouched. What we are considering is not a sum in which one member can be varied while the other remains identically (instead of as here merely specifically) the same. The two contents interpenetrate; they exist in one another and not outside one an-

other. Once more, nullifying the intensity conditions a complete annihilation of the quality, and this is not just factual, but rather an evident necessity. We sense a gradual approach of the intensity towards zero as being also a gradual reduction of the qualitative impression. In this case moreover the accompanying alteration of the quality which we claimed above is particularly clear.[3]

Another example is extension in relation to quality, shape in relation to both. Further examples are offered in infinite abundance by the quasi-qualitative moments of intuitions (von Ehrenfels's form qualities for which Meinong has proposed the name "founded" contents[4]), the quasi-quantitative moment in the domain of tones, etc.

These observations would lead to the following definitions of the concepts:

A content, in regard to which we have the evidence that the alteration or suppression of at least one of the contents given with it (but not comprised in it) must alter or suppress the contents itself, we call "*dependent*"; a content for which this is not the case we call "*independent*." For the latter, the thought that the suppression of all simultaneous contents leaves it untouched does not contain any absurdity. With contents of the first kind, one could also say, we have the evidence that they, as they are, are only conceivable as parts of more inclusive wholes, while with contents of the second kind this evidence is lacking.

There is another way in which one can try to give an account of the characteristic traits for the distinction between independent and dependent contents. We cannot notice or even attend to a figure or color by itself without at first having noticed the shaped or colored object. Occasionally a "striking" color or form seems to impose itself on us immediately. When we reflect however on what has happened, we find that here too the chances are that at first it is the whole object that strikes us, but that it does so precisely by virtue of that particularity upon which our interest settles without stopping. Noticing one content for example is occasionally the foundation for noticing another which closely belongs to it. This could suggest the following definition: a content which is noticeable without necessarily presupposing a prior noticing of any other content is independent; in the opposite case, it is dependent. Such a definition, however, would be inferior to the previous one, insofar as the evidence for the state of affairs which grounds it is lacking. Nonetheless this definition is at least of some interest.

We must now mention those contents which occupy a kind of middle position, insofar as they give the impression of being dependent because of their inner connection with other contents, although in the strict sense there is no such dependence. It is the association of ideas which often creates excessively strong bonds of this kind. This is how things stand with the unification of the qualities belonging to the different senses in the presentation of an intuited thing. Whoever is able to see from birth believes he sees the thing with all its qualities, and they all appear to him thus as equally inseparable. This illusion is difficult to overcome even in reflection, especially when a nonvisual quality is firmly associated with a state of the visual image which presents the main intuitional kernal. Usually the (specifically determined) tactile roughness fuses with certain characteristic visual unevennesses, and since the latter are actually seen and are dependent, the illusion arises that the character of roughness—this associative complex—is seen and is dependent. If we wanted to also call these contents "dependent," we would have to drop the feature of necessarily evident functional dependence of the conjoined contents. We would thereby add to the *strict* concept of dependence a *loose* concept, or add to the narrow concept a *wider* one.

Up to now we have considered independence as an absolute, as a characteristic independence from *all* connected contents. Dependence has been considered as its contradictory opposite, as the corresponding dependence on at least one of these contents. If, however, we limit our theoretical interest to a particular association of contents, then, provided that these contents possess the traits of independence in their relation to each other, we can surely talk of *relative independence* as opposed to the *absolute independence* defined up to now.

The physical parts of a blackboard are absolutely independent; those of the *surface* of the blackboard however are only relatively independent, namely, in relation to the remaining parts of the surface. It is noteworthy that even when a content is inseparable from another, this other can be separable from it. A line which with another line founds a configuration is an independent content, but the configuration itself in relation to the line is dependent. For if, for example, the quality of the line were suppressed in thought, then, although this quality adds nothing positive to it, the configuration would also be modified. A presented content is independent vis-à-vis a connected judgment; the judgment however is dependent vis-à-vis what is presented.

2. Abstract and Concrete Contents

We begin now with any unitary content and consider its parts in relation to the distinctions of dependency already discussed. By the term 'disjunct parts', we mean as is usual such parts which have no identical parts (not even themselves) in common. Now there are two possibilities: either a part under consideration is independent in relation to all the disjunct parts of the whole which correspond to it, or it is not. In the first case we speak of *"pieces,"* in the latter of *"abstract* parts" of this whole. If a whole is decomposed into a multitude of disjunct pieces, then we say it is *"divided into pieces."* We have not stated whether the whole itself, whose partition we are speaking of here, is or is not only an abstract part of another whole. Actually both cases occur: abstract parts can be divided into pieces; pieces or absolutely independent contents can be abstractly partitioned. If an abstractum permits of a division into pieces such that the pieces are abstracta of the same lowest genus as that which is determined by the unpartitioned whole, then we call it a *"physical whole"* and its pieces *"physical parts."* Examples are the partition of an extension into extensions, of a tone formation into tone formations and so on.

Parts can be *immediate* or *mediate* parts of a given whole. Mediate parts are parts of parts. Only exceptionally are parts of parts also immediate parts of the whole; for example, when parts of physical parts are both related to the same lowest genus. In the case of a visual intuition, by contrast, extension and color are immediate abstracta, while quality and brightness of the color, volume and form of the extension are mediate abstracta. As mentioned above, noticing the mediate abstractum presupposes noticing the immediate abstractum. The complex content of which an immediate part is an abstractum is called the "*direct concretum*" of this part; the term 'indirect concretum' does not, after this definition, need to be explained. A concretum which is not itself abstract we call an "*absolute concretum.*" Since every absolutely independent content possesses abstract parts, each one can also be considered and designated as an "absolute concretum." Both concepts therefore have the same extension. This also accounts for why the independent content which yields the foundation for the abstractions constructed coordinately and hierarchically is also called in relation to all attained abstracta "the (absolute) concretum." "Relative concreta" is what we call all concreta which are not absolute. Where the word 'concretum' is used alone, as a rule the absolute concretum is meant.

Besides the authentic uses of the terms 'abstract' and 'concrete' discussed so far, inauthentic uses must also be taken into consideration. The relation based upon intuition is extended to cases where there is no intuition. Every concept is called "abstract"; every object of a concept "concrete." That no adequate intuitions, if indeed any intuitions, correspond to most concepts in actual thought, that many conceptual contents because of the weakness of our mental powers, or because of evident incompatibilities can never be intuited as abstracta of the appropriate concreta—this does not hinder us. The basis of this extension is clear: if the conceptual contents and the objects were actually given, then the corresponding relations would also be known intuitively. And since, as a rule, we have no explicit knowledge of the imperfection involved in representative presenting, the extension is not even noticed.

A partial content which by means of its relation to the whole serves or is called to serve as a determination of the whole is called its "trait." There are abstract and concrete traits, even concrete traits in the absolute sense (for example, the landmark of a city).

3. Critical Remarks

The difference between concrete and abstract presentations is occasionally drawn by saying that the former can be presented by themselves whereas the latter can only be noticed by themselves. Berkeley's own interpretation from his polemic against Locke might go as follows: concrete presentations are presentations of things or parts of things. Their characteristic is that they can be presented separately from the things or parts that are bound up with them, for example, a head or a nose by itself, separated from the man to whom they were originally presented as belonging. Such objects or parts could even exist separately from everything that is bound up with them. Abstract presentations (but naturally not those which Berkeley so zealously attacks under this name) are presentations of properties. They cannot be presented separately from what bears them nor can they exist without their bearers; they can only be noticed by themselves. Höfler and Meinong in their *Logik* add further the evidence for this incapacity to exist separately.

All these and similar definitions seem to me to suffer from the handicap of operating with vague and misleading expressions such as 'to present by itself', 'to present separately', without sharply fixing the limits of their meanings and without clearly distinguishing their characteristic traits. Insofar as these definitions are correct, clearly they can not mean anything other than what we tried above to make precise. I must object also to Berkeley's recourse to existing things as unpsychological. I have furthermore for good reasons avoided speaking of abstract and concrete *presentations*. I think it is a good principle to avoid wherever possible such an equivocal term as 'presentation'. The objection has been made that 'abstract' and 'concrete' are terms which could be applied only to presentations, not however to presented things.[5] To the things, certainly not; but why not to the contents? The things are of course not the actual contents of our presentations, but rather objective unities and thus presumed, merely intended contents.

The basis for the distinction between abstract and concrete is often, if not primarily, sought in the mode of presenting—or, more precisely, in the mode of the psychic activity through which the one and the other come to particular notice. The positive feature of the distinction is on the side of the "abstract presentations" since their contents are not merely presented but, more, they are set off from the concretum through a particular psychic activity of abstracting. I have tried in vain to find the slightest difference between the consciousness of the abstract and the consciousness of the concrete. To abstract, it is said, is to pay attention to something by itself. But do we not require just this "abstracting" in order to segregate an absolute concretum from its more inclusive background and to make it an object of particular occupation? If I look at this box, I pay attention to it in particular, and only by my doing so does it come to me in a particular consciousness and become an object of an intuition. Should it then be called an "abstractum?" No one would claim this. It might well be pointed out that the box stands out from its background and thus can be noticed without our exclusively paying attention to it, while its form or color only manages to stand out through exclusive attention, as we ourselves stressed above. But this does not ground the proposed distinction since the concretum can also be noticed by itself, and wherever it is an object of psychic occupation it must be noticed by itself. Thus it is not acceptable to define a concrete presentation as one which is not abstracted. And it is not acceptable either to define it as a presentation on which (or on whose content) no kind of abstraction has been performed, since the abstractions which I carry out on an independent content, for example, on the intuited box, far from allowing this content to appear as abstract, stamp it with the stamp of the concrete.[6]

II. On Intuitions and Representations

1. Introductory Analysis of Examples

In order to reach a suitable demarcation of the concepts of intuition and representation, it would be well initially to pursue some considerations suited to illustrating the range of the actual use of the word 'intuition' and the appreciable nuances of its meaning.

The original sense of 'intuition' is "seeing," that is, the perceiving of visual objects. Thus one occasionally hears statements like: "I want to see this house, that picture," etc. An extension of this use, grounded in the preponderance of visual presentations in all external perception, is the identification of intuition with *external* perception. And, following on this identification is the identification of intuition with perception in general. Thus, for example, Wundt uses the two terms as synonyms.[7] In order to serve certain psychological interests, Meinong would define 'intuition' as the perceptual presentation which grounds an actual or possible perceptual judgment.[8] Thus even hallucinations, and not only the deceptive ones but also the unmasked ones, are drawn into the concept of intuition.

If we try to adhere to the concept delineated in this way, the psychologists remind us that perception would not be understood in the ordinary sense. Not everything which we believe to perceive in non-reflective observation is, they claim, actually perceived. This comes out clearly in certain comparative judgments in whose matter equalities or inequalities are "presented," while the corresponding substrate in the actually present content of the perceptual presentation is lacking. We believe we see the equality of the sides of a perceived die, although those actually seen are unequal. The perceptual judgment does not raise the factual content of the perceptual presentation into objective consciousness, but rather has in this content, or more precisely in certain of its moments, its occasioning cause. It is inconvenient however to deny the name of 'perceptual presentation' [*Wahrnehmungsvorstellung*] to the perceptual presentation which is naturally given as such, since in fact there is here an acceptance as true [*Fürwahrnehmen*] of what is presented, even if inauthentically, in the presentation.* Furthermore in normal cases this acceptance is immediate. (The mediacy in the procurement of the material of a judgment, the transition from the sign to what is signified—even if it were *actually* performed—does not for all that make the judgment mediate.) In this connection one feels forced to distinguish the intuitive content of the perceptual presentation from its intended, full content.⁹ The idea behind this distinction is clear: the perceptual presentation, one says, was considered by natural consciousness to be an intuition because in the presentation natural consciousness thought it possessed as an immanent object what the presentation rather merely intended and thus "presented" in an entirely different sense. I have an intuition of our theater when I see it. I believe then to have an actual presentation of what the expression 'our theater' means at any given time, and what, when I do not see it, can only be designated, determined or replaced by a surrogate, through a conceptual or pictoral presentation. Natural consciousness believes it grasps in a single glance, in a simple intuitive act, the objective thing itself—this unitary manifold—both what it is and as what it is intended as. We know that this is a mere illusion. Only a small part of what we here presume to intuit is actually intuited. Only a few features of the factual content are so present in this act, as they are intended in the presentation of the thing which it mediates, and as they actually coexist in the "thing itself." The full content of the presentation of the thing only becomes intuited in a continual flow of content in which there are certain psychic acts. These accompany the series of obtrusive partial intuitions, identify those which through intimation of each other are related and, pro-

ceeding within a single continual act, work out the objective unity. In thus contesting the status of most perceptual presentations as full and authentic intuitions, we are only conforming to the real intention of the term, which holds true even in the false presumptions mentioned above, and which could be perhaps expressed as follows: intuition is not a "presentation" in that inauthentic sense of a mere substitute through pieces, images, signs, and the like, nor a mere determination through traits—by means of which the presented would not really be set down before us. Rather it is a presentation in a more authentic sense, namely, a presentation which actually sets its object down before us, so that it itself is the substratum of the psychic activity. Consequently it is also clear that ordinary perception, although it is not an intuition *of the thing,* may however be designated as intuition once again from another viewpoint, that is, from another direction of interest. If a particular interest, for example, a psychological interest, is aimed at the momentarily present content, at the partial aspect as it is, then we have *with relation to this content* an intuition.

We are far from having exhausted the range of the actual use of our term. Not merely perceptual presentations but also *phantasy presentations* in the broadest sense of the term are called "intuitions." We find nothing unusual in someone saying he still has an intuition of the Borghese gladiator, instead of saying he has a lively memory presentation of it. We hear often enough of artistic intuition, of the mythical intuition of a people, etc. Nevertheless several psychologists will object even here for the same reasons as above. The psychologist will want to claim that in this example we have an intuition of the Borghese gladiator only in an inauthentic sense. We have a presentation which, by virtue of a similarity of content which may extend quite far, serves as a surrogate for the not present and merely intended intuition, but is not the intuition itself. Our presentation has thus once again an intention which reaches out beyond the immanent content of the act. And only if its fulfillment became a part, only if the in-

---

*Husserl is here playing on two German words: '*Wahrnehmung*' ('perception') and '*Fürwahrnehmen*' ('to take as true' or, as I have translated it, 'to accept as true'). Brentano had denied that perception should be called a truth-taking (*wahr-nehmung*). He claimed it should be called a false-taking (*falsch-nehmung*) since it does not really deliver its object to us.

tended content became an immanent one, would we be completely justified in speaking of intuition.[10] And we would be justified if an intention directed to this *hic et nunc* given content actually found its fulfillment in the content as it is, if thus a particular, for example, psychological, interest referred to the immanent content of the phantasy presentation itself. Naturally in phantasies which present external objects, another inauthenticity besides the one just mentioned has to be considered, namely, the inauthenticity which we have become acquainted with in the corresponding perceptual presentations. Even in phantasy the thing is, as a rule, replaced by inadequate representatives through a one-sided more or less fragmentary "aspect."

In the broad domain of *conceptual* presentation, we find even more prominent examples of the contrast between the intuitive and the nonintuitive, examples whose correct appreciation does not require any critical deliberations. We are often able to intuit what we conceptually present. But also we often cannot. In the latter case the fault at times is based on factual incapacity and at times on evident impossibility. All conceptual presentations which include evident incompatibilities are necessarily nonintuitive. Examples are the famous round squares, wooden irons, etc. They are not for this reason meaningless; they are presentations precisely in the sense that any representation is. They have an entirely determinate and perfectly understandable intention, but they are directed towards something impossible.

A doubt might intrude here. The first intention of a conceptual presentation is frequently directed to a corresponding phantasy presentation, and if this latter makes its appearance, then generally we say we had the intended intuition. We will continue to hold that this way of speaking is correct even though one might point out that the phantasy presentations themselves have the character of those inauthentic presentations which we are calling in this article "representations." We shall soon (see section 5) find the opportunity to do away with this doubt. We only want to mention here that we do not deny intuitive character to the phantasy presentations in every sense or in every case.

One should realize though that when the presentations here in question are called "intuitions," they come under the particular conditions which govern the correct application of the term.

A justified use of the term 'intuition' is possible not only in the case of concrete contents, which we have primarily dealt with up to now, but also in the case of *abstract* contents. The person blind from birth, we say, has no intuition of red. For him red is "what sighted people call red." He has only this inauthentic presentation of red; he cannot present red itself as an immanent object, as an abstractum in a concretum, like the sighted person who can and who, insofar as he does represent red as an immanent object, has the intuition of red.

Several scholars do not want to admit the extension of the concept "intuition" to presentations of abstract contents. They object that the expression 'intuition of red' refers directly and authentically not to the abstractum but to what is red, to the red object. Here however we lack a basis which would justify preference of the object over the abstractum. What characterizes the two in relation to each other is accorded by the concepts of the absolutely concrete and abstract; what characterizes them outside of their reciprocal relation is accorded by the concepts of independence and dependence. Neither pair of concepts contains what is meant with 'intuitiveness' and 'nonintuitiveness'. It is only the first pair that seems to, and then only because the concept of abstract presentation, as the discussions in section 5 (below) will show, is equivocal. The name of 'abstract presentations' is not given just to the presentations of dependent partial contents, that is, abstracta in the sense above described (I, section 2) which includes the objective unity and, in regard to presentation, the authenticity. Rather the name is also conferred on those unities, mediated merely through "relational thinking," of partial contents A, B, C . . ., which (if they are not themselves represented through the mere words) are extracted from various concreta and are brought together into thoroughly inauthentic presentations, presentations which we linguistically express in the forms: 'Something that possesses the traits

A, B, C . . .' or 'an A which is at the same time B and C,' and the like. Abstract presentations in the latter sense are certainly classical cases of the nonintuitional (and we obviously take them as such only because they merely aim at their objects instead of actually presenting them). This does not hold however of abstract presentations in the former sense, with which they should not be thrown together indiscriminately.

Even in abstract moments it happens that something supposedly intuited is substituted for what is actually intuited. This is what happens, for example, in the case of geometrical intuition. The geometrical figures and relations are in general not intuitable, if those who shy away from attributing corresponding phantasms to ideal characteristics which cannot be produced by spatial perceptions are right. The goals of idealizing, that is conceptual, processes are *eo ipso* nonintuitive. By virtue of certain analogies (which when measured by the ideal of definition are infinitely rough) the actually intuited figures and relations "place before us" ["*stellen uns vor*"] the actually intended geometric figures and relations; in actual geometric thought they even serve as surrogates for them. Whoever is clear on this point will instantly reject talk of an intuition of geometric abstracta as inauthentic. The drawn figure is naturally when viewed in itself an intuition; not so the geometric figure with which the former is not identical and which it merely represents.

Let us take now as the last example presenting in the sense of designating. If not as a rule, at least occasionally we do hear someone say of a sign that it stands for [*vorstellt*]* what it designates. The mathematician says sometimes: "the sign 'a' stands for [*vorstellt*] some number, it stands for [*vorstellt*] the root of this equation" instead of saying "it designates it." Hardly anyone would be inclined to call this "standing for" [*Vorstellen*]

*In this paragraph it becomes impossible to hold to the translation of 'present' for '*Vorstellen*'; there is simply no way of avoiding the use of some other term. Since 'represent' has been reserved for '*repräsentieren*', the best compromise available is 'stand for'. To make clear to the reader that 'stand for' is translating '*Vorstellen*' here, the German word shall be placed in brackets each time it is so translated.

an "intuiting," obviously for reasons analogous to those discussed above. For Kant of course even the conventional sign of the arithmetician, like the drawing of the geometrician, was a construction in intuition; he called the former "characteristic construction" and the latter, "ostensible construction." Actually in neither case do we construct what is designated. At most in the latter case because of a certain analogy between sensual and geometric figures there is at first the illusion of a construction. The construction would be an actual one if the intuited figures were exactly like the geometrical ones, and thus actual representatives of the geometric concepts as they are defined. For surely this is the meaning of all construction: to present as an intuition what is thought only inauthentically and actually grasped only through conceptual determinations, and thus to make the concept "intuitive." It is however entirely inadmissible to regard the writing of an arithmetic sign as a construction. The sign and what is designated have here totally different contents and are connected only associatively. Thus the sign does not make the thought intuitive but only points to the thought. In the case of arithmetic, moreover, what is designated is almost always something that cannot be made intuitive.

2. *Provisional Delimitation of the Concepts*

This series of observations yields a distinction of those "presentations" which are intuitions and those which are not. Certain psychic experiences which are generally called "presentations" have the peculiar property of not containing their "objects" in themselves as immanent contents (that is, contents present in consciousness), rather they *merely intend* them in a certain way which still remains to be characterized more precisely. For the time being the following definition, which is obviously suitable but deliberately too complicated, will suffice, namely that 'merely intend' means here: by means of some contents given in consciousness to aim at other contents which are not given, to mean them, to point to them with understanding, consciously to use the former as representatives for the others, and to do so without there being a conceptual knowledge of the relation which obtains between the presentation and the intended object. We will call such presentations "representations." Contrasted with these are other psychic experiences also called "presentations" in the vocabulary of many psychologists. These "presentations" do not merely intend their "objects" but *actually contain* them as immanent contents in themselves. Presentations in this sense we will call "*intuitions.*"

We need to eliminate another ambiguity here which is connected with our explication of this term as well as with its customary usage. "Intuition" can mean on the one hand the mental experience in which the ultimate goal of a representation is reached: an immanent object of the act appears to us as being at the same time what is intended in the representation. "Intuition" on the other hand can also mean only that in "presenting" we are primarily turned to the object as something immanent and not, as occurs so frequently, merely intending the object. This is the case regardless of whether *in this* act or simultaneously with it there is a consciousness or an indication of a relationship back to a corresponding representation. A correlation between the concepts "intuition" and "representation", as obviously exists in the first interpretation, could even exist in the second. Given this latter interpretation, then, every representation whether immediate or mediate points to a corresponding, but not itself actual, intuition. By contrast, not every intuition refers back to a particular representation correlated with it. Nevertheless, the clear intention of the term 'intuition' is to relate a presentation of the type encompassed by the term to some representation, which may be either determined or undetermined. Examples would be when we say "A is intuited and not merely presented," or "a representation passes over into its corresponding intuition," and the like. In order to remain in agreement with the, if I am not mistaken, prevailing use of the word, we have decided to define the word 'intuition' according to the *second* concept. In fact hardly anyone would object to the statement that the child has an intuition of the first sensual content it turned towards. Here

representations cannot be involved since they have not yet been formed at all. Moreover, it may serve us as a welcome confirmation that our definitions agree essentially with certain ones which Kant gives. For example, Kant opposes intuitions as immediate presentations to the conceptual and pictoral presentations as mediate.

As to the first concept which will occupy us a great deal in the following investigation, we can easily outline it with the help of a complex expression. If a representation passes over into its correlate phenomenon, for example, into an intuition immediately intended by the representation, then the immediate psychic experience that what is intuited is also what is intended shall be designated as the consciousness of the *fulfilled intention*. In this case then we say of the intuition that it is borne upon a consciousness of a fulfilled intention; of the representation we say more simply that it has found its *fulfillment*. The latter term we want to use in general as the designation of the immediate or mediate correlate of a representation. It is normal that representations aim merely mediately at intuitions, however immediately at other representations. Thus, for example, the arithmetical concept a^n directly represents only the concept of a product of n factors of a. If this presentation, which itself is a representative presentation, appears, then the consciousness of fulfilled intention occurs. But the intention continues on in the new phenomenon, and thus already in this simple example a whole series of representations mediates between the original representation and the intuition (which here is denied to us). With reference to such cases, we want to call the correlate phenomenon which directly adjoins the representation its "*first fulfillment.*" The ultimate fulfillment of any representation is the intuition which corresponds to it. This is a *pure* intuition—a term which tries to express that a content is not afflicted with any representative function, in opposition to which we speak of an "*impure*" or "*substitute*" intuition when a representing content by virtue of its equality or similarity of content with the represented content serves us for a while as an equivalent, provisional substitute for the former, so that we are turned towards it (as is to be discussed in section 5) in the way which is characteristic for pure intuition. An impure intuition is called *"incomplete"* if the immanent content of the representation consists of one part of what it represents. The terms *'immediate'* and *'mediate'* representations are in view of the above example of a^n obvious.

3. *The Immanent Content of Momentary and Continuous Intuition*

The provisional definition of the concepts "intuition" and "representation" which we obtained above still leaves something to be desired. First of all the use of the term 'immanent content' with regard to intuition may arouse opposition. The content of the intuition is claimed to be immanent to it. But surely this can mean nothing but that the content is a content of the intuiting consciousness. Do we not come here into an intolerable conflict with the ordinary way the term is generally used? In attempting to follow the natural intention of the term as much as possible, have we not stretched it too far until it is unusable? We say quite reasonably of a melody we are listening to that we intuit it. But the melody is surely not an immanent content. While the melody is playing, the immanent contents of our hearing differ from moment to moment, but in none of them do we grasp the melody itself. Similarly we commonly say that we have an intuition of visual things. We allowed that this way of talking is inauthentic for the cases where we must be satisfied with a one-sided view of the thing. But are we then not even to be permitted to speak of intuition with complete validity when we regard the thing (presupposing the normal conditions of perception) from all sides, viewing all visible parts and traits? Even in this case, however, the thing does not become an immanent object. We intuit from moment to moment different aspects of the thing, but in no moment do we intuit the thing itself. And then—and this is here a further difficulty—how should we intuit the thing itself, that is, what is objectively real, in which, according to the interpretation of the common man, all aspects, all intuitible parts and traits coexist?

Referring, for now, to the last example, the difficulties can be resolved in the following way. First we must differentiate between the phenomenal and the transcendent thing. Naturally no intuition corresponds to the concept of an objective unity of such-and-such composed parts and traits which coexist independently of our consciousness, for this would be a contradiction. But this concept has no place in the realm of natural thought either. It is the product of a reflection on the thing-presentation of common life, a reflection which remains far removed from most men, as it does for all animals, their whole life long. For natural thought such a sequence of connected contents, which are accompanied and encompassed by certain psychic acts and which we experience under normal perceptual conditions when we "observe the thing from all sides," is the thing itself. And this sequence of contents alone is meant whenever there is talk of a thing, a house, a tree, and the like. If this flow of contents occurs, then the thing-representations aiming at it find their *ultimate* fulfillment; there is nothing left to intend. We could also express our view in this way: talk of an intuition always involves a relation to some representation or other. The question whether intuition of things is possible leads back to the question about what the intention of the corresponding representations is. If we take "thing" in the sense of a transcendent unity, then there is *eo ipso* no question of intuition. But if we take the word in the sense of the representations of natural consciousness, like the sense connected with, for example, the words 'house', 'tree', and the like, then the ultimate fulfillment of these words lies in a continuous flow of intuited contents—a flow which is encompassed by and thus is immanent to a unitary act, which continually endures through all successive manifolds of content.

The related difficulty, however, whether one can say of such a flow of contents that it is intuited, still has to be settled since, after all, flow of contents and immanent object appear to be incompatible concepts. Here, I think, it is only a matter of how we decide to use our terms. Why should we insist on understanding as "immanent content of an act" merely the immanent content of it in some moment of its existence? We stipulate here that this expression also applies to the immanent flow of contents or the immanent continuum of contents during its total continual existence. Depending then on the direction of our interest, we can, without any incompatibility, mean at times the one and at times the other. Accordingly, one will speak sometimes of continual and sometimes of momentary intuitions. In any case, limiting the concept of intuition to momentary acts would impair all too much the normal and useful employment of this concept. In a way similar to our momentary intuiting, we of course intuit even melodies and generally all phenomenal temporal units (in which the temporal relations themselves belong to the immanent content).

4. The Immanent Content of Intuition as the Content of a Circumscribing Act

Much more important difficulties lie in another direction. The immanent object is "intuited," the merely intended object of a certain "presenting" act is "represented." But what kind of acts are these? Do our definitions mean that both are performed in essentially the same psychic function which is called "presenting," so that the distinction— which cannot be based on the intended content since this "content" is nonexistent—lies in the respective immanent content of the two acts or in conjoined thoughts and the like?

Let us put aside the representation for the moment and ask first whether intuition is a psychic function which enters into relation with *all* contents of consciousness, as is usually claimed of "presentation." Does there then correspond to each content of consciousness an act which intuits it? When we, for example, have an intuition of a shape, is the inseparably connected color then a content of this *same* intuition? After all, we have simultaneously a certain consciousness of it. The same holds good for the background insofar as it is present in no matter how undetermined a delimitation, and also for those objects which are particularly contrastive and which force a simultaneous notice. Should we perhaps say all of that is also intuited, although not in the same act

which intuits the shape? Does *one* intuiting act perhaps relate to the content of total consciousness at any one time, and inside of that act does a particular intuition then direct itself to a partial content?

Disregarding all other difficulties, I think that these interpretations are far from the true meaning of the term 'intuition'. Only what is noticed for itself can be designated as being intuited. If I glance at the knife which lies before me, then only the knife is intuited and not simultaneously the unattended to background which in no way forces itself upon us to become an object. It is only with what is actually brought into relief that I am particularly occupied, it is only to it that I have attended, it is only it that I "intuit." But noticing something by itself, this peculiar bringing into relief[11] of a part against the more inclusive whole, obviously does not suffice. Often several partial contents are isolated for themselves; they bring themselves into relief against the common background, and yet we have only attended to one and we only intuit the one. This knife, together with the inkwell, the pen-wiper and pencil which are beside it, form a group of objects each of which is noticed for itself. Now it can happen that, turned towards this group as a whole, I intuit it as a whole; whereby this orientation distributes itself more or less equally among the members and alternatingly favors this one or that. It can also happen that an exclusive orientation towards a particular member takes place, that it endows this member with a characteristically exclusive preference and so stamps it as something intuited, while nevertheless the whole group remains noticed. While we are listening to a melody, various noises indifferent human voices, the rumble of coaches and the like may force us to take incidental notice but not to even momentarily assume a particular orientation. We have heard but not intuited the noise.

Intuition is thus a particular occupation with or a peculiar orientation towards a content noticed for itself. It is a delimited and delimiting act. The same cannot be said with regards to consciousness of the background and of the remaining contents which, although noticed for themselves, are excluded from the boundary of the act's content. This cannot be said at least if we rest on the statements of inner experience only and not on psychological constructions. We become conscious of contents of the second kind incidentally through circumscribing acts in that these acts when viewed more precisely have, besides their included content (their *main content* we might say) also an excluded content, a *secondary content.*[12] When one speaks only of the "content" or when one speaks of the "immanent content," only the first is meant.

5. With Regard to its Immanent Content, the Representation Is Not an Intuition, but Rather a New Mode of Consciousness

We want now to bring into our considerations the correlate function, that is, the representation, and to consider the question suggested above as to whether, whatever meaning the word 'presentation' may have in our definitions, one might perhaps not also conclude that the same mode of consciousness is given in the two functions. Obviously not every psychic act, in view of its content (or at least its main content), can be designated as intuition. No one would call aesthetic dissatisfaction with a painting an intuition of the painting; the dissatisfaction is based upon an intuition but it is not itself an intuition. Similarly, it is unacceptable to call a representation an "intuition" because of its immanent content. In fact to do so would be to deny every essential distinction between intuitions and representations. If the term 'representation' means nothing more nor less than that a certain act besides the contents which it does intuit does not intuit some other contents, then surely the distinction is merely incidental. The situation is actually quite different. A sharp descriptive distinction regarding the mode of consciousness (of the "state of mind" [*Zumutesein*], of psychic sympathy) separates representations from intuitions. This can best be seen when cases which are as pure as possible are contrasted — those cases where (so far as this is possible in developed consciousness) the same content is first the basis of a mere intuition and then the basis of a representation. Consider for example certain figures or arabesques which first affect us purely aesthetically, and then suddenly we understand that they might be symbols or word-signs. Let us fix our attention upon the new state of affairs, before, as often happens only after a long time, it comes to explicit logical consciousness through thoughts and words, thus before even a one-word judgment like "a sign!" or "a symbol!" has been made. Or let us take the case of someone listening attentively to a word which is totally foreign to him and hearing it as a mere complex of sounds without even suspecting that it is a word. And again take the case that someone hears a familiar word in the middle of a conversation and understands it without the contents of its meaning accompanying it at all. What makes the difference between simply accepting a concretum A as it is or interpreting it as a representative some other A? Moreover we could also very well use cases which are less pure (even those cited above are not wholly pure): such as when we compare our orientation to a melody we are singing with the consciousness of an understood word or sentence, where once again the contents of their meaning does not accompany them; or when we compare the observation of an arabesque with the totally different kind of observation of an arithmetic sign in its living function. In these examples which could be added to as we like, there is obviously not a mere difference of content. It is also clear that an increase in content could justify talk of more comprehensive contents only but not of intuited contents in contrast to representing ones. Someone may hold that the distinction lies in accompanying "thoughts." But without insisting on the fact that the thoughts would have to be attributed to the unnoticed "background of consciousness," which in this regard is no more or less patient and effective than the "unconsciousness," I would like to point out here that there are no thoughts without representation. In the example of the sign which is understood despite the absence of the contents of its meaning, one may not say: To the sign belongs the meaning presentation, that the sign requires it, and, that, by virtue of accompanying thoughts, we know this no matter how obscure or fleeting our knowledge may be. For since we cannot actually present what is lacking as such, it must be represented somehow in these thoughts. Then, however, the difficulty is merely postponed. What constitutes and in what do we notice the representing function of the thoughts at issue? There would have to be a mediation by new thoughts, new representations, and so on *in infinitum*. Some persist in saying that the meaning contents are not unconscious, but only unnoticed, and they perhaps tend as well generally to look for the distinction between intuition and representation in some unnoticed contents. But even if unnoticed contents of whatever sort should exist in one case and not in another, surely they *are* not for all that the differences of the *noticed* contents; at best they condition these contents. Exactly the same objection of course applies to those who pay attention exclusively to the distinction between inborn and acquired psychic dispositions, or to the distinctions among the states which provoke them, or even to the distinctions among the corresponding physiological processes. If the witness of inner experience is clear anywhere, then it is here. And it yields the conviction that in the two cases there is a different mode of reception of the content into consciousness, a different mode of psychical occupation with or in the content.

In the examples considered above it may be that the representation is based upon an immediately preceding intuition. But the representation itself is not therefore an intuition, any more than an aesthetic feeling is an intuition just because it is based upon intuition. In the moment when the arabesque becomes a sign and thus acquires the character of a representing content, the psychic situation has totally changed. To be sure, we see the sign; but we have not aimed at it, nor do we intuit it. Similarly, when we hear words without thinking, perhaps because we are captivated by a particular timbre of the voice or by the strangeness of the pronunciation and are thus diverted from understanding, the words we hear are only intuited. If however the words exert their natural effect, then, although heard, they are not intuited. At most one could ask whether in the moment of orientation to the word content as it

appears there does not take place an intuition, which however instantly is transformed into a representation.

One additional remark. If in these examples it is doubtful whether intuition and representation do not occur in the most intimate connection with one another, the one introducing the other or vice versa where both are not completely intermingled, then this is not doubtful in other examples like those discussed at the beginning of our observations. When we "intuit" a thing, usually when precisely viewed, a mixture of both sorts of activities takes place. What is actually seen serves as a means to understand the whole thing which is merely represented. But on the other hand we are also intuitively turned toward what is actually seen, and thus the two functions are conjoined. Phantasy presentations have a representative function in regard to the perceptual intuitions which correspond to them. But this does not keep us from being able to be intuitively turned toward them, as indeed we often enough are. When the geometer operates with intuition whether in respect to perceived or phantasized figures, then both functions again come into play. The same is true of any conceptual thinking which begins with intuition or is accompanied by intuitions or returns to intuitions, for example, "a flower like this (intuited) one standing before me." There are quite certainly many different ways that a representation can fasten onto an intuition or can ground itself on an intuition. But this fact does not contradict at all the above thesis that the immanent content of a representation as such is not intuited.

The alternating use of the terms on the basis of the same phenomena is also based upon this state of affairs (as already touched on in section 1 above). The intermingling of the two functions does not imply, of course, that every designation of a complex phenomenon as intuition or representation becomes vague or even erroneous. If the whole has a decisively representative character such that the intermingled intuitions are *mere* presuppositions or foundations of the representation (mere means of representation), then it can be designated only as a representation. Similarly in the opposite case the whole can be designated only as an intuition, as when we say in the process of a psychological analysis that we had an intuition of a representation. The designation does become vague in cases where both functions preserve an equally justified independence; the one is not consumed in providing the basis for the other. It can even happen here that the founding function determines the character of the whole, so that, as was pointed out earlier (p. 00), what is undoubtedly a representation forces us to designate it as an intuition. We spoke in this regard of "impure" or "substitute" intuitions. In them the intuitional character prevails in that the representing contents, because of their identity or similarity with the represented contents, become the basis or a primary intuitive orientation (and thus are not mere means of representation). Their representative character withdraws entirely and may even temporarily be transformed into the mere phase of "stimulated" disposition.[13]

6. Supplementary Remarks

However much they may be in need of completion, the preceding observations have awakened or strengthened the conviction that in intuition and representation we have to do with characteristically different states of consciousness. But we have not yet found the answer to the question as to *what kind* of states of consciousness they are. We do not even know yet whether simple or composite phenomena are given in them and thus not even how they relate to otherwise known phenomena—if they are not reducible to such phenomena. It has become clear that their designation as "presentations" does not mean anything for descriptive analysis. I would hope that one will not here have misunderstood our definitions as claiming to have, by means of this designation, contributed even the smallest amount to the analysis of the phenomena themselves. This is what we have had to be on guard against in the whole way we used the term 'presentation.' The term was unavoidable and, despite its equivocations, it served to give a provisional comprehensible delimi-

tation of the groups of phenomena to be examined, that is, of the concepts with respect to their extension. But the term did not intend and was not able to arouse a clearly determined, descriptively well-founded concept. For this purpose the term is far too equivocal, and the concepts it involves have been far too little examined. We want to point out here further that calling both intuitions and representations "presentations" leads to at least one equivocation, the one which is the most often overlooked. For if the two are specifically different modes of consciousness, then at least one of them is not a presentation whatever may be the specifically determined phenomenon we do name in this way. If however presentation is understood as a generic character in which both species participate—and I am not arguing against such a view—then the term is surely not equivocally used by someone who understands it in this way. Nonetheless such a use does lead to an equivocation, a very dangerous one it seems to me. It easily leads to understanding the generic term as a specific term, then to holding that the modes of consciousness are specifically and not merely generically alike, and finally to seeking the distinction between the two in content only. But overlooking and falsely interpreting, and thus not doing sufficient justice to the distinction between intuitional and representing consciousness, have led to grave errors in epistemology and psychology. For this reason I have avoided resorting here to terms which are composed from the term 'presentation.' The distinction itself, although insufficiently examined, has been known for a long time. It did not totally escape the Scholastics. Terms like 'inadequate', 'inauthentic', 'indirect presentations' refer to representations whereas corresponding opposite terms refer to intuitions. But what one had in view was only partly the distinction between intuited and nonintuited concepts or between intuitable and nonintuitable concepts. Some of what was meant but taken much too broadly was the distinction which, when transposed to the contents, can be designated as the opposition between the authentic contents of consciousness and those which are merely intentional.

7. *Appendix. On the Psychological and Logical Meaning of the Two Functions and the Importance of Their Investigation*

The investigation of the psychic functions discussed here, especially of the extremely remarkable "representation," is of fundamental significance, it seems to me, for the whole of psychology and in particular for the psychology of knowledge and logic. For psychology, since for a series of acts of the highest importance (I mention only desiring and willing), it is essential to have presentations in the sense of representations as foundations or presuppositions, while this is not the case with other acts. For logic, since concepts, judgments, and all other logical activities themselves belong to the group of functions just characterized. I believe I can claim in particular that no theory of judgment not founded on a deep study of the descriptive and genetic relations of intuitions and representations manages to do justice to the facts.

I have just called representation an extremely remarkable function. Actually it gives rise in various ways to astonishment. It is already in and for itself highly remarkable that a psychic act can point beyond its immanent content to something else which is in no way present to consciousness. And yet it seems that we are conscious of it in a certain way. For, and this is again highly remarkable, while we are engaged with the representing contents, we believe that we are occupied with the represented objects themselves. In the flux of conceptual thought, in most cases the optical and acoustical flow of words solely, or almost solely,[14] represent. The contents of the meaning either do not enter at all or enter only rudimentarily into consciousness. And occasionally completely different contents which are distantly related to them (as when with the mention of London merely the outline of England emerges in a shadowy way) substitute for them. But even where conceptual thought withdraws, where in the commerce of everyday life linguistic representations are aimed at the intuitables of the external surroundings, things are not much better. How wretchedly the sum of substituting intuitions presents itself to the unprejudiced observer. In places

they are totally lacking, and where they occur they are as a rule faded, defective, often ungraspably fleeting and inadequate even in the typical features for the intended intuitions. But all that does not disturb us. It seems to us as though the basis of the sequence of words is the meant object itself. The state of affairs at issue here lies so far from the usual directions of research that even the best psychologists and logicians have disregarded it. And yet great and unresolved riddles are here; we are touching on the most obscure parts of epistemology. What I have in mind is not the psychological clarification of this oversight and of the entire state of affairs, although this would be basic for all which is to follow. Rather it is the possibility of knowledge at all. Scientific knowledge—the kind of knowledge which first comes to one's mind here—rests entirely on the possibility of abandoning oneself to the greatest extent to a merely symbolic or otherwise extremely inadequate thinking or in being permitted (with certain precautions) to prefer it deliberately to a more adequate thinking. But then how is understanding possible, how does one arrive in such a fashion even at only empirically adequate results? Mathematics is considered to be a model of exact science. But the arguments of its representatives, which have dragged on through the centuries and have not even yet been resolved about the meaning of its elementary concepts and the foundation of the soundness of its method, are in a peculiar conflict with the supposedly thorough evidence of its procedures. In various periods of his life the great mathematician Cauchy defended totally different theories of imaginary numbers.[15] Which of them actually guided his evident procedures? One cannot object that two different things are involved here, insight and reflecting on such insight reasonably. For in these theories it is not a matter at all of mere reflection but a matter of certain and actually very complicated chains of conclusions which must necessarily mediate scientific thought if such thought is to be at all reasonable. Theories change but the procedure remains the same. The evidence produced by such a procedure —there is no doubt about this at all—is mere illusion. But how then can results be arrived at which agree to such an amazing degree with subsequent "tests" or with experience and thus condition a corresponding measure of practical confidence? Since analogous difficulties hold for all the sciences (and also for ordinary thought), should we return to the viewpoint of Humean scepticism and extend it further than its great originator did, to mathematics and to all "a priori" sciences as well? We turn in vain to the old and to the new logic for resolution of such doubts; logic here leaves us entirely in the lurch. Logic, the "theory of science", must concede if it is to be honest that all science is a mystery to it. This is where we are today, despite the efforts which a series of truly significant men have expended on logic in recent decades. I do not want to deny in any way now that one can considerably advance the logical understanding of the soundness of symbolic thinking (first of all naturally of mathematical thinking) without a more deeply penetrating insight into the essence of those elementary processes of intuition and representation which mediate this understanding throughout.[16] But without this insight a full and really satisfactory understanding of this and of all other logical processes will not be obtained.

I have already pointed out above that this insight is also of fundamental significance for the rest of psychology. I want to raise here however another important problem, which we can make no serious step in solving without this insight. I refer to the often studied problem of the origin of the presentation of space. If I am correct, then the

masterful investigations[17] devoted to it have merely led to the insight that certain theories which at first sight are very appealing are definitely false. No one has yet managed to prove a theory, and the reason is simply that none of the supposed theories gets beyond generalities, none of them has viewed sharply enough the tasks which actually have to be solved, namely the tasks of explaining the actual psychological and logical state of affairs in its *determinate particularity*. The concept of space is the concept of a manifold constituted in a determinate way. But what kind of manifold? And definable through which logical traits? Space, as it exists psychologically and from which the concept of space derives (in what way?), is a complex of phenomena and dispositions characterized by definite traits. But which traits? Where are the descriptions? Who has undertaken to fix these determinate psychological and logical states of affairs in order to explain them later in their particularity as these determinate states of affairs?[18] Just as soon as this is seriously touched on however, one runs up against the intuitive and representative functions, which here work together throughout and without whose understanding one gropes helplessly in the dark.

These indications will in any case suffice to indicate the importance of the suggested problems. I do not presume that I can overcome the extremely important difficulties which stand in the way of their solution. I hope however in subsequent articles to be able to clarify some of the points involved or at least provide some stimulation for others.

NOTES

1. See Stumpf, *Über den psychologischen Ursprung der Raumvorstellung*, p. 109.

2. Actually this naturally does not happen. If we suppress the context through a total alteration in phantasy, then of course some context or other can always return (as, for example, with visual objects). However this context can always be so formed that, through an exclusive attention to the content given, it completely retreats. It is overlooked as if it were in fact not there at all.

3. See Stumpf, *Über den psychologischen Ursprung*, pp. 112f. For futher detail on this point see subsection 5 of this work, to which here as elsewhere I owe much.

4. See von Ehrenfels, "Über Gestaltqualitäten," in *Vierteljahrsschrift für wissenschaftliche Philosophie*, XIII; my *Philosophie der Arithmetik*, vol. 1, ch. 12; Meinong, "Zur Psychologie der Relationen und Complexionen," *Zeitschrift für Psychologie* 2: 253.

5. A. Meinong, "Phantasievorstellung und Phantasie," *Zeitschrift für Philosophie und philosophische Kritik* 95 (1889): 202.

6. See as opposed to this Meinong's "Humestudien I," in *Sitzungsber. d. Wiener Ak. d. Wiss.* (1887), p. 200; see also the *Logik* of Meinong and Höfler, p. 23, and in relation to this whole article see also pp. 21f. of the same valuable work.

7. *Physiol. Psyc.*, vol. 2, 4th ed., p. 1

8. Meinong, "Phantasievorstellung und Phantasie," p. 202.

9. Quite often the misleading expression is heard that the "genuinely perceived" should be distinguished from the "merely presented" which is added to it in thought. A distinction is easily slipped in here which should not be mixed up with the distinction validly drawn above—namely, between what in the perceptual presentation is conditioned through peripheral stimuli and what is conditioned through central stimuli, or in other words between what in the perceptual presentation originates from the arousal of innate and what from acquired dispositions.

10. Perhaps the above exposition includes the motive which has led various researchers (like Meinong, "Zur Psychologie") to speak, in the case of presentations of imagination, more readily of "intuitive *presentations*" than simply of "intuitions." This would also accord better with the prevalent way of talking.

11. It does not matter here whether it is a question of a mere bringing into relief in a literal sense or rather of parallel changes in content, of the part as well as the whole.

12. William James would most probably speak here of a "fringe," of a "psychic overtone," of a "suffusion." See his *Principles of Psychology*, vol. 1, ch. 9, pp. 258f.

13. Concerning this concept see the instructive treatment by B. Erdmann, "Z. Theorie d. Apperception," *Vierteljahrsschrift für wissenschaftliche Philosophie* 10: 343.

14. See James, *Principles of Psychology*, vol. 1, ch. 9, pp. 270f.; B. Erdmann, *Logik* 1: 229f.

15. See Cauchy, *Cours d'analyse algébrique*, as well as his *Exercises d'analyses et des physiques mathématiques*, part IV.

16. Moving in this direction are investigations concerning the algorithmetic methods which I began a few years ago, which however have only been published in small parts and in regard to special problems. See my *Philosophie der Arithmetik*, vol 1 (1891), ch. 12 and 13, *e.g.*, pp. 268–86, 299f. The cases analyzed there could serve as typical however only for certain classes of symbolic processes. For a general theory of algorithms quite different points come into question.

17. On the psychological side one thinks here naturally of Lotze's and Stumpf's admirable works, as well as of the ingenious and stimulating writings of Th. Lipps.

18. It is really astounding what one calls a "theory" here. If three series of gradable feelings or sensations (whose participation in the perception of space is made probable) are brought together in any way at all and if one gets used to their fusion, then the problem is solved. But what is then explained? As good as nothing. Three series of sensations—three coordinates—this is the connection. As if the concepts "threefold graduated homogenous manifold" and "threefold Euclidian manifold" were identical concepts (which is demonstrably false). And as if, even if this were true, the question of the origin of the presentation of space were now solved instead of just being grasped.

Husserl's Critique of Psychologism
THOMAS SHEEHAN

On May 2, 1900, nineteen days before completing his preface to the first volume of *Logical Investigations,* Edmund Husserl delivered a lecture to the *Philosophische Gesellschaft* of the University of Halle with the title, "Über psychologische Begründung der Logik" ("On the Psychological Grounding of Logic"). A summary of that lecture, which Husserl recorded in the protocol book of the society, was discovered and copied out in 1931 by Professor Hans Reiner, now of Freiburg, and published in 1959.[1] Reiner writes in his "Editor's Epilogue": "The entry in the protocol book, as I clearly remember, was entirely in Husserl's own hand" with the orthography, emphases, and abbreviations that Husserl used at that time. The whereabouts of the protocol book with the autograph is not now known, although Reiner surmises that it may be lost, since in 1943 all documents were moved out of the Philosophical Seminar because of air-raid precautions.

The following text constitutes Husserl's earliest summary of the contents and intention of his "Prolegomena to Pure Logic" and provides insight into what he saw as the major points of that work. Because it is somewhat self-explanatory, my remarks seek only to elucidate the context of Husserl's critique of psychologism, and to locate the present text in relation to the central chapters of the "Prolegomena."

The significance of Husserl's critique of psychologism is basically understandable only in terms of the final goal of the *Logical Investigations,* and that goal in fact lies beyond the two published volumes. The *Investigations* as we have them consist of epistemological clarifications of principles and essential concepts, in the service of laying the theoretical groundwork of a new discipline, pure logic—what Husserl would later call the "logic of the absolute science."[2] As the ultimate idea of the unity of theory, pure logic is a *Wissenschaftslehre*—the doctrine of the conditions of the possibility of science as such—insofar as it is the scientific system of all the a priori laws constituting the idea of theory as such.[3] In the last chapter of the "Prolegomena" (paragraphs 62–66) Husserl merely sketched the idea of such an a priori discipline and the tasks to be assigned to it as a theory of manifolds, that is, a science of the "essential types of possible theories or fields of theory"[4] (paragraphs 67–70). However, the full epistemological criticism and clarification of pure logic, the elucidation of its essential concepts and principles and of its relation to and manner of regulating other sciences, is not given within the two volumes but remains the goal to which the investigations lead.[5]

The six investigations of volume two, therefore, remain a propaedeutic to pure logic, an "epistemological or phenomenological groundwork of pure logic,"[6] a "new grounding of pure logic and epistemology,"[7] insofar as they only lay bare "the 'sources' from which the basic concepts and ideal laws of *pure* logic 'flow' and back to which they must once more be traced."[8] The second volume remains an *Erkenntnistheorie,* an epistemology or theory of cognition in the service of a yet-to-be-written *Wissenschaftslehre,* or doctrine of the theory of all science.[9] The investigations have as their preliminary aim the phenomenological clarification of the essences of thought and experience (where phenomenology is "a pure theory of the essences of experience"[10]), specifically of the "thought-unities and knowledge-unities that arise in logical acts."[11] That aim is fulfilled in the phenomenological clarification of intentionality in the Fifth Investigation and of identity-synthesis in the Sixth Investigation. By securing and clarifying the essence of the field of consciousness as such in terms of intentionality, volume two constitutes the elements of a basic and critical theory of knowledge that answers the question, "What must the psychical *as such* (*i.e.,* essentially) be in order that an empirical natural science of it be possible?"[12]

Against this background it becomes clear why the "Prolegomena" attempts a refutation of psychologism, that is, the grounding of logic in empirical psychology. The "Prolegomena" is in no way animated by a polemic against empirical psychology. Rather, the hidden reasons for the attack on psychologism in the first volume of *Logical Investigations* lie in Husserl's conception of the essence of the psyche in the second volume. The goal of volume two is not, as it was in Brentano's "Classification of Psychic Phenomena" in *Psychologie vom empirischen Standpunkt,* to show *that* intentionality lies at the base of all psychic relations, but rather to clarify the *essence* of intentionality as such, that is, to determine the ideal structure of real psychical acts and in so doing to actually achieve what psychologism clumsily and inadequately attempts. Husserl criticizes psychologism not because it drags psychology into a field where it does not belong but rather because it introduces a psychology whose bases have not been worked out in their essence, hence a psychology that finally is not a unified and closed theory of the psychical at all. Thus it is the positive phenomenological clarification of intentionality as the essence of the psychical in volume two that requires the negative critique of psychologism in volume one.

Finally, a word on the location of the present text in relation to the chapters of the "Prolegomena." The whole of the first volume of *Logical Investigations* can be divided into three parts: I. The Need to Ground Logic, as a Normative Practical Discipline, in a Theoretical Discipline (chapters 1 and 2); II. Refutation of Two Attempts to Ground Logic and Epistemology in Empirical Disciplines (chapters 3 through 10); and III. The Idea of Pure Logic (chapter 11). The second part in turn has the following complex articulation:

A. The Grounding of Logic and Epistemology in Psychology (ch. 3–8)
   Introduction: The State of the Question (ch. 3)
   1. The Contradictory Consequences of Psychologism (ch. 4–7)
      a. Empiricistic Consequences (ch. 4–6)
         i. Three Empiricist Consequences Refuted (ch. 4)
         ii. Psychological Interpretations of Basic Laws of Logic (ch. 5–6)
            a'. The Law of Contradiction (ch. 5)
            b'. The Laws of Syllogism (ch. 6)
      b. Sceptical Relativism as a Consequence (ch. 7)
   2. Direct Analysis of the Prejudices of Psychologism (ch. 8)
B. The Grounding of Logic and Epistemology in Biology (ch. 9)
Conclusion: End of the Critical Treatment (ch. 10)

In the text which follows, the first paragraph corresponds roughly to part one (chapters 1 and 2) above, whereas the second and third paragraphs of the text correspond to the introduction to the critique of psychologism (chapter 3). The fifth paragraph of the text proposes the division which above is called A.1 and A.2, and the sixth paragraph of the text takes up A.2 (chapter 8). The seventh, or last, paragraph of the text corresponds to part three (chapter 11) on the idea of pure logic.

In the translation of Husserl I have followed Dorion Cairns' *Guide* except in a few places where Professor J. N. Findlay's translation seemed more adequate. I gratefully acknowledge the assistance of the staff of the Husserl Archives, Leuven, in correcting errors in a previous draft.

NOTES

1. Edmund Husserl, "Über psychologische Begründung der Logik," ed. Hans Reiner, *Zeitschrift für philosophische Forschung* 13 (1959): 346–48.

2. *Formal and Transcendental Logic*, trans. Dorion Cairns (The Hague: Nijhoff, 1969), p. 291.

3. Cf. E. Husserl, "Selbstanzeige" in *Vierteljahrsschrift für wissenschaftliche Philosophie* 24 (1900): 512. English translation: *Introduction to the Logical Investigations*, trans. P. J. Bossert and C. H. Peters (The Hague: Nijhoff, 1975), p. 4.

4. *LU* I, 249 (241). References to the *Logische Untersuchungen* (*LU*) are to the pagination in the first edition (1900/1901) and then, in parentheses, to *Logical Investigations*, trans. J. N. Findlay (London: Routledge & Kegan Paul, 1970).

5. Cf. *LU* I, 228 (225); I, 243 (236).

6. *LU* II, 4 (250).

7. *LU* I, vii (43).

8. *LU* II, 4 (249).

9. On the relation of Fichte's *Wissenschaftslehre* to Husserl see Jean Hyppolite, "L'idée fichtéenne de la doctrine de la science et le projet husserlien," in *Husserl et la pensée moderne*, ed. H. L. Van Breda and J. Taminiaux (The Hague: Nijhoff, 1959), pp. 173–82.

10. This is Husserl's designation of phenomenology in the 1913 revision of *LU* (Findlay, p. 213, n.).

11. E. Husserl, "Selbstanzeige" (of *LU* II), *Vierteljahrsschrift für wissenschaftliche Philosophie* 25 (1901): 260. (*Introduction to the Logical Investigations*, p. 5.) In the foreword to his edition of Husserl's lectures on time-consciousness, Heidegger notes that *LU* II dealt only with "the 'higher' acts of cognition," whereas the time lectures were to investigate the underlying acts of perception, imagination, memory, consciousness of time, etc. E. Husserl, *The Phenomenology of Internal Time-Consciousness*, ed. Martin Heidegger, trans. James S. Churchill (Bloomington: Indiana University Press, 1964), p. 15.

12. For this and the following see Martin Heidegger, *Logik: Die Frage nach der Wahrheit*, ed. Walter Biemel (Frankfurt: Klostermann, 1976), paragraphs 6–10, pp. 31ff.; English translation: *Logic: The Question of Truth*, trans. Thomas Sheehan (Bloomington: Indiana University Press, forthcoming).

FURTHER REFERENCES

Bachelard, S. *A Study of Husserl's Formal and Transcendental Logic*. Translated by L.E. Embree, pp. 92–113. Evanston: Northwestern University Press, 1968.

Eley, L. "Life-World Constitution of Propositional Logic and Elementary Predicate Logic." *Analecta Husserliana* 2 (1972): 333–53.

Gotesky, Rubin. "Husserl's Conception of Logic as *Kunstlehre* in the *Logische Untersuchungen*." *The Philosophical Review* 40 (1938): 375–89.

Heidegger, Martin. *Prolegomena zur Geschichte des Zeitbegriffs*. Collected Works, vol. 20. Edited by Petra Jaeger, pp. 13–182. Frankfurt: Klostermann, 1979.

Husserl, Edmund. "A Reply to a Critic of My Refutation of Logical Psychologism." *The Personalist* 52 (1972): 5–13 (see pages 152–58 below).

————. "Psychological Studies in the Elements of Logic." *The Personalist* 58 (1977): 297–320 (see pages 126–42 above).

————. "A Review of Volume I of Ernst Schröder's *Vorlesungen über die Alegbra der Logik*." *The Personalist* 59 (1978): 115–43.

————. "The Deductive Calculus and Intensional Logic." *The Personalist* 60 (1979): 7–25.

————. "Remarks on A. Voigt's 'Elementary Logic' in Relation to My Statements on the Logic of the Logical Calculus." *The Personalist* 60 (1979): 26–35.

Mohanty, J.N., ed. *Readings on Edmund Husserl's "Logical Investigations."* The Hague: Nijhoff, 1977.

Schuhmann, Karl. *Husserl-Chronik: Denk- und Lebensweg Edmund Husserls*. The Hague: Nijhoff, 1977.

Sokolowski, Robert. "The Structure and Content of Husserl's *Logical Investigations*." *Inquiry* 14 (1971): 318–47.

On the Psychological Grounding of Logic* (May 2, 1900, Halle)

TRANSLATED BY THOMAS SHEEHAN

Today it is the custom to define logic as a practical discipline, in fact most appropriately as a methodology of scientific knowledge, a technology of science. But every technology presupposes some theoretical knowledge by means of which the technology grounds its own rules; thus the technology points back to certain theoretical disciplines in which its "theoretical foundations" lie. Consequently we can raise the question in relation to logic — in the legitimate sense of this definition of logic — as to what are the theoretical disciplines in which its theoretical foundations lie, above all its essential theoretical foundations.

Psychologism is characterized by the thesis that the theoretical foundations of logic lie in psychology. For it is unquestionable, so the argument goes, that the rules of knowledge as a psychological function are to be grounded only through the psychology of knowledge. Thus logic is related to psychology as analogously the art of surveying is related to geometry, the mechanics of building to physics, and so forth.

If we concede the unquestionableness, if not of this argument, then in any case of the proposition that a technique of knowing would have to be dependent on a psychology of knowledge, this, however, in no way proves that all the foundations of logic, es-

*Reprinted with the permission of the publisher and translator from *Zeitschrift für philosophische Forschung* 13 (1959): 346–48.

pecially the most essential theoretical ones, lie in psychology. The possibility remains open that perhaps yet another discipline contributes to the grounding of logic, indeed in a far more significant way insofar as out of it spring the so-called logical norms taken in a strict sense, norms, moreover, whose a priori character appears incompatible with origin from an empirical discipline. And here would be the place for the historically controverted "formal" or "pure" logic which Kant and Herbart must have had in mind when they emphatically denied the dependence of logic on every other discipline and above all on psychology, and declared it to be a theoretical and demonstrative science in its own right.

Thus indeed the true state of affairs is marked out. *Pure* logic is related to logic in the sense of the art of cognition just defined, as geometry is to the art of surveying, as pure arithmetic is to accounting — and thus the position that psychologism assigns to psychology is the very position that logical objectivism assigns to *pure* logic. But this discipline by its nature would have to be broadened into a universal mathesis comprising all of pure arithmetic and a theory of manifolds.

Two ways can be taken to overcome psychologism. One can (1) follow out the contradictory consequences in which psychologism, as an absurd relativism or anthropology and scepticism, gets entangled. (2) One can, through direct analysis of the prejudices that mislead psychologism, demonstrate the unsoundness of its position.

The lecture favors the second way. The supposed unquestionableness of the proposition, "Rules of knowledge must be grounded in the psychology of knowledge" dissolves under closer consideration of the purely logical principles and theorems (principle of contradiction, syllogistic formulae). The state of affairs is similar to the case of the propositions of formal arithmetic, *e.g.,* $(a + b) \bullet (a - b) = a^2 - b^2$. Such propositions are empty of every psychological content and, considered in themselves, are of a purely theoretical nature; they acquire an ought-content only through a turn to the practical, if they are taken as rules for a practice. In connection with that, the essential distinction is stressed between the purely logical rules and the technical-logical rules; the former are a priori and valid for every intelligent being, the latter are rules for a specifically human technique of thinking suited to the peculiarity of the human constitution (without human eyes, no coloration process, no microscopic methods, etc.).

The lecture then refers to the clarification of the idea of a pure logic that must be detached from any intention of regulating acts of knowledge. This pure logic serves as the basis for the preordination of those laws that are logical in the strict sense (the principle of contradiction, syllogistic principles) and that are to be the rules of scientific thinking. To the idea of science in an objective respect (namely, according to its content in systematic theories) there belongs obviously certain constitutive concepts—for example, truth, proposition, object, property, ground, consequence, and so on. And it is obvious that truths that are grounded a priori in the content (sense) of these propositions—thus, truths which can not be abrogated without all discussion of truth, proof, theory and ultimately science itself becoming an *absurdity* —designate the limits within which all rational thinking must move. Of course, to become acquainted with these limits must be the first task of every art of cognition. At the same time these propositions, developed as to a comprehensive mathesis, ground the most important deductive methods—this could be pursued more closely.

Introduction to "A Reply to a Critic"

DALLAS WILLARD

The following selection originated through a request, by the editor of the *Zeitschrift für Psychologie und Physiologie der Sinnesorgane,* that Husserl review Melchior Palágyi's *Der Streit der Psychologisten und Formalisten in der modernen Logik* (1902). This was a book which attempted to criticize both positions mentioned in its title, and to develop a third position as an alternative. In the course of this attempt, the author took Husserl (along with Bolzano) as representative of the Formalist position. That was in itself a considerable mistake, but it at least led to a response by Husserl which is especially valuable because it reacts to a *typical* difficulty met by those trying to understand his philosophy of logic. The difficulty in question led some to accuse him of irredeemable "Platonism" and "Formalism," and others to say that he never escaped from Psychologism. It was the difficulty involved in understanding precisely *how* the ideal entities called "propositions" and "concepts," which both Bolzano and Husserl held to constitute the subject matter of pure logic, are to be related to concrete acts of thinking and speaking.

Palágyi charged Husserl and Bolzano with being "Formalists"; but the dispute over formalism in logic is not easy to specify, since it involves points in the philosophy of mind which are among the most difficult in all of philosophy. (The dispute had been running long before Palágyi wrote his book, and continued afterward.) Nevertheless, those who *charge* others with being Formalists usually have one rather simple point in mind. They take the Formalist to define the subject matter of logic in such a manner that logic is (or seems to be) of *no possible use* in appraising and directing concrete processes of thinking and speaking by individual persons. For the Formalist, symbols, concepts, and propositions are, in so far as the logician is interested in them, things with no essential dependence upon concrete mental and linguistic events—which events, in consequence, are of no interest to the logician as such. Still, the aim of logic is, at least among other things, to enable us to appraise particular mental and linguistic sequences for logical coherence and consistency. This seems to the anti-Formalist to be an intolerable inconsistency of practice if not of theory.

In a later flare-up of the altercation over Formalism,[1] the anti-Formalist F. C. S. Schiller asks C. A. Mace (a Formalist) to "divulge what is the 'minimum of reference to the fact that people think' which is permissible in Formal Logic? Does he [Mace] really believe that if there was *no* thinking there would still be logic?" (p. 208). Mace replies: "'The minimum of reference' is, in my opinion, no reference whatever." And: "Do I really believe that even if there were *no* thinking there would still be logic? I certainly do believe that under such circumstances there would still be *the facts with which Formal Logic is concerned*" (p. 208; Mace's italics). It was, of course, Schiller's view that "there can be no meaning without some one to mean it, and (for all social purposes) without others to understand it, and so, that self-subsistent, autonomous meanings are a myth" (p. 54). When logicians "omit and conceal the personal context in which all meanings arise" (p. 54), they create "an excellent word-game, as stimulating as cross-word puzzles and easier than mathematics" (p. 56). But, the point is, such "games" are of little use in the serious work of rational critique of actual thinking and speaking.

Now these are exactly Palágyi's concerns about Husserl's view. For Husserl also supposes, in Mace's words, that if no thinking ever occured, there "would still be the facts with which Formal Logic is concerned."[2] Therefore Palágyi takes him to have fallen into an "unfruitful and sterile formalism," and to have "split the blanket between Logic and Psychology" in such a way that they cannot be put back into a relation which will allow the principles of logic to be applied to the sorts of concrete mental events studied by psychology. He sees Husserl allowing "Logic to degenerate . . . into Mathematics."

How does Husserl respond to this? And first, what does he take a concept, proposition or "truth" to be? To begin with there is, for example, a characteristic *difference* between thinking of Carter and thinking of Reagan—or in language, between referring to Carter and referring to Reagan. Of five people in a room, two might at any instant think of Carter and three of Reagan. There would, thus, be "something" true of the two which is not true of the three, and conversely. These "somethings" are, for Husserl, intentional qualities, universals, or, as he usually calls them, "species." Now these intentional qualities are concepts, such that to think of Carter is (whatever else may also be involved) precisely to instance the quality *of-Carter.* And when expressed in language they are *significations (Bedeutungen).* Of significations Husserl states: "We know what 'signification' is just as directly as we know what color and tone are. It cannot be further defined: it is a descriptive ultimate. So often as we understand an expression, it signifies something to us; we realize its sense. And this understanding, this signifying, this realizing of a sense, is not the hearing of some word-sounds or the having of some image simultaneously with that hearing. And just as well as distinctions between

sounds are evidently given to us, so well are differences between significations also given."[3]

Now *propositions*—"truths," "falsehoods"—are only complexes ultimately composed of simple intentional species or concepts and their unifying forms. It is the totality of all concepts and propositions, understood as universals, or "ideal" (not real) entities, which constitutes the domain of investigation of *pure* logic. Husserl holds that "*an sich* there exists no necessary connection between the ideal units which, in fact, function as significations and the signs to which they are bound; *i.e.,* by means of which they are actualized in the mental life of human beings. We, thus, also cannot maintain that all ideal units of this kind are significations of expressions. . . . As numbers . . . do not arise and pass away with acts of counting, and as, therefore, the infinite number-series presents an objectively fixed totality of general objects which is sharply delimited by an ideal law, and which no one can augment or diminish, so the matter also stands with the ideal, pure-logical units, the concepts, propositions, and truths—in short, the significations dealt with in logic. They form an ideally closed totality of general objects to which being thought and expressed is accidental. There are, thus, innumerable significations which, in the common, relative sense of the word, are merely possible significations, . . ."[4]

All this looks like so much grist for Palágyi's mill! But not quite. For Husserl, by locating concepts and propositions ontologically as *qualities of* mental and linguistic acts, has availed himself of a familiar ontological schema, and paved the way for a plausible solution to the problem raised by the anti-Formalists. As he points out in the following review,[5] Palágyi "misinterpreted the *contrast* between ideal and real as a *lack of relation*." But, he continues, "since ideal significations are instanced in acts of signifying, each pure law of logic expresses a universal connection which *eo ipso* can be referred to the ideal extensions of the respective signification species, and thus to possible acts of thought in the realm of the real." Hence, as in the case of Aristotle's prime mover in relation to the world which it moves, we may say that, while ideal significations are indifferent to real processes of thought and talk, those real processes *are not* indifferent to the relationships which hold within the domain of ideal significations. If, for example, we look into that domain and see that no proposition of the form $(x) ((Fx \lor Gx) > Hx)$ can be true and the corresponding proposition of the form $(x) (Gx > Hx)$ false, then we know that *any* concrete event of inferring or asserting the latter on the basis of the former is a valid inference or argument. And if we further know that, say, *this* event here and now before us is such an event, we then know that *it,* the completely concrete process, is valid, and could not be otherwise—and we know this solely on the basis of our nonempirical ("pure") knowledge of the ideal significations present in that concrete process. Thus, though *only* thus, does pure logic "govern" concrete events. The charge of "Formalism" is disarmed.

It is important to stress that the concept or proposition, as Husserl understood it around 1900, is present in the particular act of thought *as its quality*—a part of its very nature or essence—and *not* as its intentional *object,* standing over against it and quite exterior to it, in the manner of the Fregean *thought.* Husserl states in the First Logical Investigation that "in the actual experience of signification there corresponds to the unitary signification an individual aspect, as a singular instance of that [significational] species: in the same way as in the red object the red-moment corresponds to the specific difference red. If we actualize the act and, as it were, live in it, *then we naturally mind the act's object and not its signification.* When, for example, we make an assertion, we judge about the fact concerned, and not about the signification of the indicative sentence, not about the judgment in the logical sense. This latter becomes an object for us only in a reflective act of thought, in which we do not merely look back upon the realized assertion, but rather carry out the required abstraction (or, better said, ideation)."[6] It is, I suspect, failure to understand that the signification is not essentially an intentional *object* which lends weight to the conviction of the anti-Formalist that the

analysis of such ideal entities can be of no use in analyzing the flow of thought and speech itself. Husserl's view, to the contrary, shows *why it is* of such use.

Now it must, I believe, be admitted that volume one of the *Logical Investigations,* to which Palágyi mainly referred, is not at all clear on the above matters. Examination of the main relevant passages in this volume, the "Prolegomena to Pure Logic," sections 39, 46, 51, 59, and 66, will show that Husserl definitely does treat "truths" as species, and does speak of them being "lived through." He insists upon the necessity of a logic which is the theory of the technique (a "*Kunstlehre*") of scientific knowings, and states that *such* a logic "in a large measure has to do with psychic experiences."[7] He even states that, in connection with such a logic, "terms such as 'representation', 'concept', 'judgment', 'inference', 'proof', 'theory', 'necessity', 'truth', and the like, . . . are class names for psychical experiences and dispositional structures." But there nonetheless remains a lack of clarity in stating *precisely how* the "species," which the concept or proposition is, is "in" the particular act of thinking or speaking. And it is the clearer treatment of "in" as the *in* of the *exemplification* of the universal by the instance which makes the following selection so useful in clearing up Husserl's views in the philosophy of logic.

It should, finally, be noted that what follows, as well as the account in *Logical Investigations,* volume two, was not Husserl's final account of how the proposition is "in" the act of thought. In *Ideas,*[8] and elsewhere in his later writings, he makes the proposition of the logician into something (a noema) which is "had" *by the essence (a noesis) of* the act of judgment "and is necessarily one with it." Thus, the proposition moves into that superrefined subdomain of ideal being which Husserl calls the *nichtreelle* or *irreelle.*[9] It is difficult to know precisely what to make of this new complication to which Husserl felt himself forced by examination of the phenomena. But it is clear that the noema is neither "in" the noesis nor in the act of judgment, simply by the relation of exemplification; though it seems that Husserl still holds the noesis itself to be the property or species of the mental or linguistic act. The doctrine of the middle and later Husserl places the proposition at such an ontological distance from actual thinking and speaking that a recent (and in general, plausible), interpretation[10] identifies it, as noema, with the Fregean *Sinn* or *Gedanke*—the precise relationship of which to concrete mental events has *never yet* been made clear. Palágyi's criticism *may* have been more appropriate to the later Husserl than they were to the Husserl of whom he spoke.

NOTES

1. C. A. Mace, "Formalism" *Mind* 41 (1932): 208–211, and F. C. S. Schiller, "The Value of Formal Logic," *Mind* 41 (1932): 53–71.
2. *Logical Investigations*, "Investigation I," sections 31 and 35.
3. Ibid., "Investigation II," section 31, paragraph 2.
4. Ibid., "Investigation I," section 35.
5. "A Reply to a Critic," third paragraph from the end (p. 156 infra).
6. *Logical Investigations*, "Investigation I," section 34.
7. Ibid., "Prolegomena to Pure Logic," last paragraph of section 46.
8. *Ideas*, section 94; see also *Formal and Transcendental Logic*, sections 48–57.

9. *Ideas*, section 97. The terms '*nichtreelle*' and '*irreelle*' cannot be translated. The main contrast involved in their definition is the contrast between temporalized entities and events (the actual) and nontemporalized entities (the ideal, universal). But not all ideal entities are *ir-* or *nichtreelle*. Only noematic ones are. Numbers and geometrical forms, as well as colors and flavors, are not, though they also are neither *real* nor *reel*. Most of the major problems in interpreting Husserl have to do with the nature and bearings of the *ir-* or *nichtreelle*.
10. David W. Smith and Ronald McIntyre, "Intentionality via Intensions," *Journal of Philosophy* 68 (1971): 541–61.

FURTHER REFERENCES

Deubel, Werner. "Melchior Palágyi zum Gedächtnis." *Zeitschrift für philosophische Forschung* 4 (1949–50): 283–87.

Gibson, W.R. Boyce. "The Philosophy of Melchior Palágyi." *Journal of Philosophical Studies* (later: *Philosophy*) 3 (1928): 15–28 and 158–72.

Mohanty, Jitendranath N. "Husserl's Thesis of the Ideality of Meanings." In *Readings on Edmund Husserl's Logical Investigations*, edited by J.N. Mohanty, pp. 76–93. The Hague: Nijhoff, 1977.

Natorp. "On the Question of Logical Method in Relation to Edmund Husserl's Prolegomena to Pure Logic." In *Readings on Edmund Husserl's Logical Investigations*, edited by J.N. Mohanty, pp. 55–66. The Hague: Nijhoff, 1977.

"Palágyi, Menyhert." In *Encyclopedia of Philosophy*, vol. 6, edited by Paul Edwards, p. 18. New York: Macmillan, 1967.

Willard, Dallas. "The Paradox of Logical Psychologism: Husserl's Way Out." *American Philosophical Quarterly*, vol. 9, no. 1 (1972): 94–100; reprinted in *Husserl: Expositions and Appraisals*, edited by Frederick Elliston and Peter McCormick, pp. 10–17 (Notre Dame: University of Notre Dame Press, 1977).

A Reply to a Critic of My Refutation of Logical Psychologism*

TRANSLATED BY DALLAS WILLARD

One does not need to read very far in this work to see that its content deviates fundamentally from its title. Namely, it does not really give a general treatment of the quarrel between the psychologistic and the formalistic logicians. Rather, it deals only with *my* quarrel with Psychologism in my *Logical Investigations,* which appeared in 1900. It is the author's intent to oppose the "formalistic tendency in modern logic" (p. 5), the "precipitous, retrograde movement which writes on its banner the warcry—'Away from psychology!'" He will oppose the "formalistic danger" of an "unfruitful and sterile formalism" (p. 1). Thus he puts his task, quite generally, in his "Introduction." But then, as we proceed, we immediately hear also that Bolzano is to be regarded as "the true originator of modern formalism in logic"; and we are reminded that Husserl is, so far, the only modern logician who has linked his positions to Bolzano's *Wissenschaftslehre* in essential points. Then we further notice that the author mentions no other formalists.

*This is a translation of Husserl's review of *Der Streit der Psychologisten und Formalisten in der modernen Logik,* by Melchior Palágyi, published in Leipzig by Engelmann in 1902. The review appeared in *Zeitschrift für Psychologie und Physiologie der Sinnesorgane* 31 (1903): 287–94. It is especially valuable because it reponds to *typical* criticisms which followed Husserl throughout his career, and is one of the very few times when Husserl explicitly undertook to meet his critics. All footnotes have been added by the translator. Reprinted with permission of the publisher and translator from the *Personalist* 53 (1972): 5–13.

Rather, his attacks—some in particular chapters, and some in the form of sorties interspersed throughout the text—relate solely and only to Husserl. So we must, so far as this work is concerned, form the equation: Modern Formalists = Husserl. If, now, the malice in the tone preferred by the author does not suffice to keep me from complying with the kind invitation of the editor of this journal to review this work, it is in order that I might fulfill the obligation, which every serious worker has, not to let his work fall victim to attacks that would distort it.

My logical investigations place themselves against the dominant current of logical and epistemological persuasion:—at least as an irksome impediment. It is indeed conceivable how a work which, like the one before us, energetically guarantees to have done away with the impediment, or proven it to amount to nothing, can calculate on easy laurels of victory; and how it might easily transmute present inclination into agreement with itself, and thereby mislead many readers into orienting themselves about my point of view according to the author's statements, instead of according to my writings. But I must keep this from happening. In his very orientation toward my views Mr. Palágyi employs a peculiar, though certainly quite convenient, method. He is satisfied with a cursory reading of a few chapters or paragraphs of volume one of my *Logical Investigations.* All of the rest is, for him, non-existent. Of volume two, which appeared fully three-quarters of a year before his work, he says not a word, regardless of the relevant points it might bring to bear on the discussion. The astounding thoroughness of the author, together with an equally astounding incapacity to grasp the plain sense of any sort of conceptual distinction, brings it about that he —and this is to be taken quite literally—also is unable to report on even *one* of my or Bolzano's theories without twisting it into something which is unbelievable.

This is immediately revealed by his general characterization of my position. He repeatedly ascribes to me the tendency "to allow Logic to sink, where possible, into Mathematics" (p. 9), the "struggle" to "tear Logic loose" (p. 43) from Psychology and to "split the blanket between Logic and Psychology" (p. 37), and so on. *Of course* he is silent about the distinction—one which is decisive for the simple understanding of the sense of my tenents, and which has been justified in detail—which I make between "Logic" in that most inclusive sense which it has as a practical discipline, and "pure Logic," as the theoretical system of purely formal (categorial) truths. He also does not mention that I abundantly approve of a logic which has that tendency toward being a methodology exhibited in the logics of Mill, Sigwart, and Wundt. Nor does he remark that I in no wise contest the founding of logic, in *this* common sense, upon empirical psychology, but even require that such a founding be extensively provided. He does not mention that "pure" or "formal Logic" is for me only a title introduced to aid in understanding historical traditions and tendencies; one joined to a certain class of propositions which are called 'logical' in the fullest sense, and of which I sought to show the following:—that they belong to a distinct discipline which is a priori and independent of all psychology, and that this discipline, through a natural extension, also takes in formal mathematics (its theories being a priori, and foreign to psychology in the same sense), and is ultimately identical with *mathesis universalis* in the generalized sense coined by Leibniz. Whoever takes his directions from the author must assume that I intend to reject Logic—in the common sense of "Logic"—and aim to reduce it to

mathematics—"mathematics" in the common sense; or that I intend, in any case, to reduce it to a 'class logic' (eine 'Umfangslogik') in the style of the Boolean school. That I laid bare the follies of extensional (quantifizierenden) logic over twelve years ago in a very detailed critique (see the *Göttingische Gelehrte Anzeiger* for 1891) might be unknown to Mr. Palágyi. But he cannot be ignorant of the distinctions just stressed, the neglect of which can only have the effect of transforming the sense of my views into nonsense.

Mr. Palágyi is also quiet about my distinction between the mere technique which is associated with theories of formal logic, (and which can be consigned to the mathematicians), and, on the other hand, the sphere of genuinely philosophical tasks, *viz.,* elucidation (*Aufklärung*) of the primitive concepts and propositions of pure logic through comprehensive, descriptive-psychological (or "phenomenological") analyses. He is silent on how—as is to be seen from volume two of my *Logical Investigations* —I have worked at these philosophical tasks, and especially at the descriptive phenomenology of the experience of thought, at lengths scarcely ever gone to before. My work shows that my struggle against Psychologism is in no wise a struggle against the psychological grounding of Logic as methodology, nor against the descriptive-psychological elucidation (*Aufklärung*) of the origin (*Ursprungs*) of the logical concepts. Rather, it is only a struggle against an *epistemological* position, though certainly one which has had a very harmful influence upon the way in which *Logic* is done.—So *that* struggle is what Mr. Palágyi, manifesting an exemplary reliability, characterizes as "splitting the blanket" between Logic and Psychology.

If, now, we go in sequence through the four polemical sections of the work which follow the *Introduction,* we find that the first bears the title, "Facts and Truths." All of my arguments against Psychologism rest —so the author says—on the proposition *that truth is no fact. I.e.,* the proposition that the act of judging correctly is indeed a temporal process, but truth is not. Now, out of this mere distinction of reason (*begrif-*

flichen Unterscheidung) between the act and the content of the judgment—thus, that distinction in virtue of which we speak, for example, of *the* proposition, 2 × 2 = 4, whoever may express *it,* one and the same thing—there arises, under the hands of the author, a real distinction between two allegedly connected moments (*Momente*): "*Husserl* supposes that, after *subtraction* of the judgment content, he can retain as *remainder* a psychic act" (p. 14, cf. p. 47 among others). And now the critique is worthy of the interpretation:—Not a psychic act, but rather a "mechanical process," is what is left over after "subtraction" of the judgment content; and so my view wavers, "in an unceasing equivocation, between the physical and the psychical" (p. 15). After this searching probe there probably is no need to go into the other twists through which Palágyi seeks to support his darling objection to the effect that I confuse psychology and physics (science of fact). Having previously decided to read all sorts of absurdities out of my statements, he no longer comes to them in order genuinely to read them according to their sense and interconnection.

In the next two sections of his work Palágyi concerns himself with plugging up the source of "modern Formalism." These sections are directed against Bolzano's theories about concepts (*Vorstellungen*), propositions (*Sätze*) and truths (*Wahrheiten*) 'in themselves.' Here I must first mention the suggestive manner in which Palágyi conceives of my relations with Bolzano. In a series of hints which would be insignificant taken separately, but which are efficacious when taken in sequence, he gives the reader no less a notion than that I have exploited Bolzano in a dishonest manner and have kept silent about my dependence upon him. Suppressing judgment on the author's procedure I note, for the benefit of the uninformed, that not only—as the author once mentions (p. 16)—have I "remembered" Bolzano and "named" him one of the greatest of logicians. Rather—in an 'appendix' to chapter 10 of *Logical Investigations,* vol. 1, an appendix specifically devoted to this purpose—I have pointed out the significance of the *Wissenschaftslehre* as one of the foundation works of logic, and have stressed

the necessity of building upon this work and studying it with the greatest care. This I have done in such a detailed manner, and with such emphasis, as has never before occurred, either in earlier times or contemporary. And, not satisfied with that, I expressly designated Bolzano as the one (along with Lotze) by whom I have been "decisively influenced." These words I quote from *Logische Untersuchungen,* vol. 1, p. 226 (1st ed.).

As to my concept of "ideal" significations, and "ideal" contents of representations and judgments, to speak specifically, they originally derive, not from Bolzano at all, but rather—as the term "ideal" alone indicates—from Lotze. In particular, Lotze's reflections about the interpretation of Plato's theory of forms had a profound effect on me. Only by thinking out these ideas of Lotze—and in my opinion he failed to get completely clear on them—did I find the key to the curious conceptions of Bolzano, which in all their phenomenological naivity were at first unintelligible, and to the treasures of his *Wissenschaftslehre.*

If, like all earlier readers of Bolzano, his "propositions in themselves" ("*Sätze an sich*") previously appeared to me as mythical entities, suspended between being and non-being, it then became clear to me, with one stroke, that here we basically have a quite obvious conception which traditional logic did not adequately appreciate. I saw that under "proposition in itself" is to be understood, then, what is designated in ordinary discourse, which always objectifies the ideal, as the "sense" ('*Sinn*') of a statement. It is that which is explained as one and the same where, for example, different persons are said to have asserted the same thing. Or, again, it is what, in science, is simply called a theorem, *e.g.,* the theorem about the sum of the angles in a triangle, which no one would think of taking to be someone's experience of judging. And it further became clear to me that this identical sense could be nothing other than the universal, the species, which belongs to a certain *moment* present in all actual assertions with the same sense, and which makes possible the identification just mentioned, even where the descriptive content of the individual experiences (*Erlebnisse*) of asserting varies considerably in other respects. The proposition thus relates to those acts of judgment to which it belongs as their identical meaning (*Meinung*) in the same way, for example, as the species *redness* relates to individuals of "the same" red color. Now with this view of things as a basis, Bolzano's theory, that propositions are objects which nonetheless have no "existence," comes to have the following quite intelligible signification:— They have the "ideal" being (*Sein*) or validity (*Gelten*) of objects which are universals ("*allgemeiner Gegenstände*")—and, thus, that being which is established, for example, in the "existence proofs" of mathematics. But they do not have the real being of things, or of dependent, thing-like *moments* —of temporal particulars in general. Bolzano himself did not give the faintest intimation that these phenomenological relationships between signification, signification moment, and full act of signifying* had been noticed by him. And this notwithstanding the fact that he treats the psychology of knowledge in great detail in vol. III of his *Wissenschaftslehre*. Indeed, everything indicates just the contrary—that his conception of the *Satz an sich* wound up unclarified, in spite of all his efforts to avoid it.

Now as to Mr. Palágyi, he has adopted my view, or that from it which was immediately intelligible to him, without qualification. He interprets Bolzano's concepts through my ideas and expressions, but does it as if he drew directly upon Bolzano, and also as if the corresponding statements by me were only just borrowings—underhanded borrowings, moreover—from Bolzano. He adopts my theory of the identical, ideal sense (*Sinn*), without mentioning it in his *ever* so friendly statements. But this *sense* he makes out to be an identical, ideal *moment* of experience. Then the distinction, stressed by me, between the species and particular,

between the sense as the *Idea* (*Idee*) which becomes an object for us through species-abstraction (*spezifizierende Abstraktion*) and the sense *moment* (*Sinnesmoment*) of descriptive psychology:—*this* distinction Palágyi overlooks or does not understand. Then, since I make a distinction of reason between the identical signification and the signifying act (in the sense in which, say, the quality-species (*Qualitätsspezies*) *redness* is distinct from a red thing), he has the concrete, psychic experience of judging consisting of *two moments*—of the supra-temporal (!) sense-moment and the act. After this distortion he objects to Bolzano and to me that we would tear the sense-*moment* away from the act. As if *his* sense-moment (which, inconsistently with its being a *moment,* he characterizes as ideal and supra-temporal) were identical with Bolzano's "proposition in itself," or with the sense as species! Obviously the author could have spared himself the effort of emphasis—hauled out with ceaseless repetition—upon the indissolubility of the sense *moment* from the act, by which he thinks to refute us so decisively, through mere quotations from my *Logical Investigations*.

Of the same nature and value are the other objections which Palágyi advances in these sections. Thus, for example, the reference to propositions of a kind with "I am now thinking" (25ff.), which include in their objective content a reference to the one judging—in a word, the 'occasional' propositions* already treated in detail in vol. II of my *Logical Investigations*—is of no use whatsoever in somehow calling into question that "independence" which is characteristic of the species *vis-à-vis* the singular case, and thus of the proposition *vis-à-vis* the fortuitous act of judging. It is of no use, that is, unless—deceived by the ambiguity of the phrase "content of judgment"—one follows Palágyi in confusing *proposition* (*Satz*) with *fact* (*Sachverhalt*). Again, the "intrinsic contradiction in Bolzano's philosophy," which with no little pathos is brought forth in subsection #4, is in truth a contradiction between what Bolzano is supposed, according

---

*"Bedeutung, Bedeutungsmoment und vollem Akt des Bedeutens." There is no more fundamental analysis in Husserl than that of the concrete individual, whose essence is to be temporally located, into quality, quality phase or moment, and whole individual. See the opening paragraph and section 19 of "Investigation II," and also the second sentence of "Investigation V." Also, the first chapter of "Investigation III" and section 3 of "Investigation IV."

*cf. Hans Reichenbach's notion of "token reflexive" terms, in *Elements of Symbolic Logic*, §50.

to Palágyi, to have maintained, and what he really did maintain. One is immediately convinced of this by comparison of Palágyi's remarks with the passage concerned (*Wissenschaftslehre*, vol. I, sub-section 25). While, according to the clear sense of his repeated statements, Bolzano taught that to the "truth in itself" (i.e. the truth in that quite common sense in which we designate, not an act of judging, but rather a *proposition* [*Satz*] as a truth) being thought or, more precisely, being judged or known is *non-essential,* the author has him teaching that being *un*thought of or *un*known is *essential* to it. Bolzano's careless use of the ambiguous expression "proposition thought" ("gedachten Satz") offers the author a handhold for ascribing, here and further on, a series of crude inconsistencies to this exceptionally clear thinker. Of the duties of a fair interpretation, or of a careful reading which compares passage with passage, Mr. Palágyi is ignorant. And so, throughout two long sections, one must patiently endure such utterly untenable statements: statements which, of course, are supposed equally to uproot the whole of Bolzano's philosophy and my *Logical Investigations*—as if they did not go their own peculiar ways.

In section IV Palágyi again turns himself directly and exclusively against my *Logical Investigations,* and especially against my distinction between laws of the real and laws of the ideal, which I bring to bear upon logic. The basic error of Psychologism consists, according to my view, in its obliteration of this fundamental distinction between pure and empirical generality, and in its misinterpretation of the *pure* laws of logic as *empirical* laws of psychology. Of course our author finds obvious absurdity in this view: So our actual course of thinking is supposed to be governed by two sorts of laws, is it? And by laws which belong to two worlds separated by an "infinite abyss"? But it is simply impossible to see how extratemporal laws of the ideal could come to have some sort of causal efficacy. Such an estrangement of the real and the ideal means the utter impossibility of any knowledge at all (pp. 41f.). Or so says Mr. Palágyi.

Unfortunately, the author has read too

selectively. Otherwise he would have stayed on guard against misinterpreting the *contrast* between ideal and real as *lack of relation.* Since the ideal significations are instanced (*sich . . . vereinzeln*) in acts of signifying, each pure law of logic (*rein logisches Gesetz*[*]) expresses a universal connection which *eo ipso* can be referred to the ideal extensions of the respective signification species, and thus to possible acts of thought in the realm of the real. Thus, as I have sufficiently explained, there can be derived from *any* ideal law whatsoever (*e.g.,* any arithmetical law) universal truths about ideally possible or impossible connections of psychic fact. The character of these ideal laws, as truths of reason (*vérités du raison*), is transmitted to such derivations and is not affected by them. All of the forceful expressions with which the author embellishes his criticisms cannot change the fact that he is passing judgment upon matters which he has not sufficiently studied.

It is hardly worthwhile to enter into his further objections, which often evince a striking lack of intelligence. Thus, a contradiction of my contrast between real and ideal law is supposed to proceed from the fact that I myself allow law contents to function as thought motives in judging. Through this function, Palágyi supposes, the ideal law in fact attains the significance of a real law of our thinking (p. 45). Thus, according to this way of reasoning, the law of gravitation, where it guides the thinking of the engineer, and likewise any law that guides us in practice, would attain the significance of a law of thought.

And what is one supposed to say to the objection that, through my separation of the laws of pure logic, as laws of the ideal, from laws of psychology, as laws of the real, these latter laws "appear to fall into the same category as the laws of mechanics, and that then one at least no longer knows wherein

---

[*]"Purely logical law" does not get at what Husserl intends, since a law may be a rule or law of logic without being one of *pure* logic, or a *non-empirical* law of logic. See chapters 2 and 3 of *Logical Investigations,* vol. 1, on this point. Hence, here and elsewhere the phrase, 'rein logische Gesetz', has been translated as above.

the psychic could be distinguished from the physical" (p. 43)? Likewise for the objection that the truth is simply one, so that the separation of truths into two classes, separated by an "unbridgeable abyss," is impossible (p. 52)? Likewise to the misconstruction, related to these objections, that—as it would not be possible for me to do otherwise—I base that distinction of laws just referred to upon a distinction between modes of human knowledge (namely, knowledge through "induction" and through "insight"); and that I thus perpetually confuse two sorts of laws with two ways of knowing one law (p. 53)? I need not say that I do hold the distinction between the two kinds of laws to be grounded *solely* in the essence of their signification (*in ihrem bedeutungsmässigen Wesen*), but that with that essence there is connected a phenomenological distinction in the mode of knowledge of the states of affairs (*Sachverhalte*), of the one and the other sort, corresponding to laws. In the context of the critiques in the "Prolegomena,"* the phrase "law of the real" does not signify just any arbitrary universal proposition referring to the real, but rather a universal fact (*allgemeine Tatsache*); or at least a proposition which, in the manner of our assertions of natural laws, is weighted with factual content. So my point here essentially comes down to the distinction between factual truths and purely conceptual truths (*i.e.*, ideal laws, or laws in the most narrow and rigorous sense of the word). Were the world so made that all of the spheres in it were red, then, arriving at an inductive belief that this is so, we would speak of a "natural law" to that effect. However, in itself it would be no (genuine) law, no proposition grounded in the conceptual essence "sphere" and "red"; rather, it would be a universal fact (*allgemeine Tatsache*). It is precisely this objective distinction, which is fundamental for both logic and epistemology, between what Hume called "relations of ideas" and "matters of fact" that our author surely rejects as invalid. But the inadequacy of his polemic against this great thinker works an immediate embarrassment, since he does

*I.e., volume one of Logical Investigations.

not once grasp the sense of the distinction in question. Palágyi objects, against Hume's well-known statements, that even facts come under the principle of contradiction. For, he says, the opposite of a fact is *never* possible. The fact can never be undone. As if Hume doubted *that*! Is it really so difficult to understand that Hume's referral of the principle of contradiction to his "relations of ideas" is intended to mean no more than that truths about relations of ideas are rooted precisely in the ideas (*Ideen*) alone (*i.e.*, merely in the relevant concepts), and therefore cannot be denied without contradiction; whereas negations of factual truths are indeed false, but not self-contradictory?

After this fruitful search into the innumerable absurdities which he imputed to his adversaries, in the concluding section of his book the author explains his own views about the relationship between Logic and Psychology. On page 72 he distinguishes knowing (*Wissen*) as a general or abstract (!) psychic function—to the character of which it belongs to stand in the most intimate of relations to the remaining psychic functions —from sensing, feeling or willing as "concrete" (!) psychic functions, or as "isolated psychic functions" ("*psychische Sonderfunktionen*"), which lack the capability of relating to other psychic functions or to themselves. The investigation of the former function falls to Logic. The investigation of the latter functions falls to Psychology. In other words, what we have here is a division of what everyone calls psychology into "Logic" and "Psychology":—namely, into the psychology of knowing and the psychology of the remaining psychic functions. The author is thus so naive as to suppose he can settle, through a slight displacement of terminology, such a weighty epistemological question as that about the relationship between Logic and Psychology. A formula with the ring of profundity to it is supplied to the author, for the expression of his views, by the new terminological distinction between "unreflected" and "reflected" consciousness (*e.g.*, the seeing of the red and acquaintance (*Wissen*) with this seeing), and by the—not precisely unheard of— introjection of the notion of the furtherance of knowledge into the concept of Logic. Then it is said (p. 81) that Logic "reflects on the reflected consciousness, and endeavours to raise our knowing processes to a higher power by investigating the laws of our re-flected consciousness. Psychology, on the other hand, will try to carry reflection raised to a higher power by Logic over into the investigation of unreflected consciousness."

PART THREE

Husserl on Science and Phenomenology

From the very beginnings of philosophy among the Pre-Socratic thinkers to our own day philosophers have continually returned to the difficult questions of whether and how philosophical reflection is to be distinguished from scientific reflection. Is philosophy a science, a protoscience, or not a science at all? These have been some of the quite general forms which a great variety of particular questions about the relation between philosophy and science has assumed.

As a doctoral student in mathematics in Berlin and then afterwards as a student of Brentano and a careful reader of Bolzano, Husserl was preoccupied with these kinds of issues from the very start of his professional career as a philosopher. And in his first mature work, the *Logical Investigations,* he analyzed several of these problematic issues. Although he was to return to these questions on a number of occasions throughout his long career, most notably perhaps in *The Crisis of European Sciences and Transcendental Phenomenology,* the much earlier extended essay "Philosophy as Rigorous Science," which is reprinted here in its entirety together with the Husserl-Dilthey correspondence, remains the most important short statement of his views in 1911, only two years before the publication of the first volume of the *Ideen.*

A closer analysis of the major themes in "Philosophy as Rigorous Science" can be found in summary form in the introduction to Husserl's texts which follows immediately as well as in the extensive secondary literature which Husserl's essay has occasioned. However, we need note here briefly that Husserl's reflections on science arise in part from his earlier reflections on the problems of psychologism. Moreover, these reflections carry over into the questions about historicism which will exercise him at great length in the *Crisis* and which are already sketched in part in the Dilthey-Husserl correspondence included here also. This 1911 text is thus continuous with a major theme in Husserl's phenomenology as a whole.

One of the most consequential elements in this essay, were one to look for an initial question that could provide an entry into the richness of Husserl's work here, is the claim that phenomenology is to be understood as a scientific philosophy in the sense that no presuppositions must remain unexamined. It is important to point out that Husserl does not claim phenomenology is without any presuppositions at all, a claim which his own repeated investigations into logical and epistemological issues had sufficiently disproved. Rather, the emphasis here is above all on the absence of *unexamined* presuppositions and the consequent affinity Husserl proposes between phenomenology and science.

Husserl spends some time at the outset of his essay before turning to his major theses, "naturalist philosophy" and "historicism and Weltanschauung philosophy," with the inability of traditional philosophy to substantiate its own claims to be scientific. This inability, however, Husserl is careful to put into a rather special perspective. For what is at issue on his reading of this traditional claim is, not whether the scientific character of philosophy can be improved, but whether philosophy can yet be characterized as scientific at all. "I do not say that philosophy is an imperfect science," he writes; "I say simply that it is not yet a science at all, that as science it has not yet begun." In short, previous philosophy for Husserl is unscientific.

But what for Husserl would count as a scientific philosophy? As his philosophical views continue to develop, Husserl changes his mind about the correct answer to this question. Here, however, his initial answer is plain enough: to be scientific, philosophy must be systematic. "System," of course, is a slippery concept in the history of philosophy, and Husserl is quick to dissociate himself from any of the classical German idealist interpretations of that notion in order to emphasize the foundational, indeed Cartesian, interpretation of system where the order of reasons is essential to the content of the doctrines themselves. The central element of systematic philosophy for Husserl is thus what he thinks makes his own attempts at revolution in philosophy a critique of reason, a part of the series of revolutions which include Plato, Descartes, and Kant and excludes Hegel. And it is this critique of reason, which much of his still unpublished later work demonstrates, that finally is to assume the form of a phenomenology of reason.

Whether the ideal of phenomenology as a science of all possible sciences, a science which remains without unexamined presuppositions, is finally coherent is one of the cardinal questions a careful and critical reading of this essay leaves with us. And this question continues to exercise Husserl's critics in part because of the difficulty in getting from Husserl a clear, accurate, and, above all, sufficiently differentiated understanding of what science itself is. Husserl himself was aware of the need for such a straightforward account as his extended discussion of this topic in the "Prolegomena" to the *Logical Investigations* shows. And his much more influential discussion here, although written some years later, still incorporates the results of those earlier analyses. Still, despite its many stimulating details, Husserl's "Philosophy as Rigorous Science" does not seem to unfold from a sufficiently thoughtful account of just what science is. The result is, on one level, the penetrating criticism of a series of competing philosophical views and, on the other, a kind of "promissory note" which must be cashed in much later in such texts as the *Crisis*.

10

Husserl on Philosophy as Rigorous Science
PETER McCORMICK

One of the many insistent questions which keeps recurring in critical discussion of phenomenology in general and Husserl's philosophy in particular is whether claims advanced by phenomenologists can be criticized at all.[1] If, for example, the cardinal point on which a particular phenomenological analysis is supposed to turn is nothing more nor less daunting than the phenomenologists' intuition[2] of essences, then many contemporary nonphenomenological philosophers are sorely tempted to give up the pretense of any kind of philosophical appraisal of phenomenological claims at all.[3] However, a close reading of the relevant secondary literature shows that at least one central issue this kind of question touches on is not yet widely discussed. The issue basically is whether there is indeed a characteristic kind of argument, at least sometimes present in Husserl's work, which could reasonably be described as a species of its own, as a phenomenological argument.[4] If so, then the question arises whether there is at least one necessary assumption such a characteristic argument makes that effectively excludes the possibility of criticism.

There are of course many controversies in the extensive work which we owe to Husserl, notably the struggle against psychologism from the time of *The Concept of Number* (1887) to its culmination in the Prolegomena in the first edition of the *Logical Investigations*.[5] In these introductory remarks, however, I want to look closely at only one of those less prominent cases where Husserl is involved in philosophical argument,

namely, in exchanges with Dilthey which are part of the essential background of his major text "Philosophy as Rigorous Science."[6] By stressing those exchanges here I want to show briefly that although no distinctive phenomenological kind of argument is included here (unlike the Husserl-Heidegger controversy), nevertheless the Husserl-Dilthey correspondence[7] focuses critical attention on a central and neglected theme in the seminal text in rigorous science.

Husserl provides a brief sketch of his later view of Dilthey in *Phänomenologische Psychologie*.[8] The passage is centrally important for Husserl's intellectual background and should be cited at length:

It was Dilthey himself who first initiated our relationship, for, unfortunately, under the influence of Eddinghaus' brilliant rebuttal,[9] I had thought it unnecessary to read Dilthey's great work. . . . In my inner struggle to fundamentally overcome positivism, I had to repel the strong inclination toward positivism which had been prominent in Dilthey's previous work, the *Einleitung in die Geisteswissenschaften*.[10] At first I was quite surprised to hear Dilthey personally say that phenomenology, and especially the descriptive analysis of the specifically phenomenological second part of the *Logische Untersuchungen*, was essentially in harmony with his *Ideen*,[11] and that one would have to view them as a starting point for an actual realization, using a matured method, of the psychology that he thought was ideal. Dilthey always conceded that this concurrence between our investigations, despite our fundamentally different points of departure, was of the greatest importance and in his old age he reviewed, with a truly useful enthusiasm, his once-abandoned investigations on the theory of the human sciences.[12]

This sketch, it must be recalled, was written rather late in Husserl's development. Already in his article on "Philosophy as Rigorous Science" in the first volume of the journal *Logos* (1911) Husserl had criticized Dilthey's position somewhat generally.[13] The result was a brief and enlightening exchange of letters in which Dilthey clarified his position and Husserl responded in kind. In order then to situate this exchange, we need to look briefly at Husserl's comments in the *Logos* article.

Husserl's aim in the *Logos* article is to show how phenomenology can finally make of philosophy a rigorous science. In order to achieve this ideal, phenomenology must overcome both naturalism (and this is the sense of the reference which Husserl makes in the 1925 text cited above to positivism) and historicism. The first tendency for Husserl is the error of reducing all phenomena to physical states, whereas the second is the error of reducing all phenomena to particulars. Phenomenology is proposed as a philosophical enquiry into the invariant (and therefore nonhistoricist) features of pure (and therefore nonphysical) consciousness.[14]

Husserl sees Dilthey as a representative of the historicist error. He objects to the skeptical consequences of Dilthey's historicism. In particular, Husserl focuses on Dilthey's work *Weltanschauung, Philosophie und Religion in Darstellungen* (Berlin, 1911) and characteristically cites several passages from the beginning of this work. One of the central sentences reads as follows: "Thus the formation of a historical consciousness destroys more thoroughly than does surveying the disagreement of [philosophical] systems a belief in the universal validity of any of the philosophers that have undertaken to express in a compelling manner the coherence of the world by an ensemble of concepts."[15] The problem with this opinion, from Husserl's standpoint, is that it leads to what he calls "extreme skeptical subjectivism." The issue is sharpened, Husserl thinks, just as soon as we consider the consequences of historicism in logic. Thus a consistent historicism, Husserl thinks, results in the following: "The ideas of truth, theory, and science would then, like all ideas, lose their absolute validity. That an idea has validity would mean that it is a factual construction of spirit which is held as valid and which in its contingent validity determines thought. There would be no qualified validity, or validity in itself" (p. 325). For Husserl logical laws are universally valid and hence ahistorical.[16] Consequently the historicist position in general and Dilthey's position in particular are unacceptable to him.

So much for the background to the controversy.[17]

Shortly after the appearance of Husserl's article Dilthey wrote to Husserl at some length on June 29, 1911, thereby initiating the correspondence.[18] Dilthey expressed surprise that Husserl had characterized his position as an instance of historicism. For, Dilthey continued, he had always been concerned with working out a "universally valid science" whose aim it was to fix the formulations of the human sciences. Moreover, Dilthey agreed "that there is, in general, a universally valid theory of knowledge." The major claim that separated his view from Husserl's, Dilthey wrote, concerned the capacities of metaphysics "to conclusively explain the world's coherence by using an interconnection of concepts." Dilthey thinks this an impossible task for metaphysics. Given such views, Dilthey rejects Husserl's conflation of his view with historicism and consequently Husserl's charge that his view leads to skepticism.[19]

Dilthey also objects to Husserl's basing his account on "a few sentences" from the introduction to Dilthey's book, a practice which, as we have seen above, Husserl himself had condemned eight years earlier in Palágyi's reading of his own *Logical Investigations*. And again just like Husserl's practice with Palágyi, Dilthey refers Husserl to other places in his work which support his denial that skepticism is the logical outcome of his *Weltanschauung* philosophy. An even stronger claim which Dilthey makes but which he does not take the space to support is that Husserl's own "argumentation (pp. 324–28) does not prove that the outcome of my statements (*Typen*, p. 6) leads to skepticism."[20] Finally, just to mark the extent of

Husserl's misinterpretation, Dilthey cites a series of conclusions to Husserl's own arguments which he fully accepts. These conclusions, tellingly, entail a rejection of the historicist charge Husserl first brought against Dilthey.

Husserl's reply is dated July 5/6, 1911. The text, however, is incomplete, since the entire first page is missing.[21]

Husserl thinks that after Dilthey's letter "there are no serious differences between us." He claims that "all objective validity . . . refers to ideal and thus to absolute principle," which he calls an a priori. The task of phenomenology is the clarification of this a priori. Moreover, this task includes the clarification of objective validity because, Husserl writes, "all objective validity a posteriori has its principles in the a priori."[22] Husserl elaborates by specifying certain areas of phenomenology such as that of nature or that of religion. Thus in the case of nature the task of phenomenology "is to submit the consciousness that is constitutive of nature to an essential investigation with regard to all of its structures and correlations so that all the principles underlying being (in the sense of nature) a priori are finally clarified, and all the problems which in this sphere concern the correlations between being and consciousness can be resolved." Husserl proceeds then to elaborate some of his strictures about metaphysics.

The basic agreement between the two, Husserl thinks, comes from the shared conviction about the impossibility of metaphysics. Thus Husserl writes:

When you speak of an analysis that pertains to the human sciences (an analysis by which you lead up to the demonstration of the impossibility of metaphysics), this coincides to a great extent with what I—who am only limited and guided by certain methodological viewpoints—consider to be phenomenological analysis. And naturally the impossibility of metaphysics—namely in that especially false ontological sense—can only be evidenced by such analyses pertaining to the human sciences.[23]

Dilthey replied to Husserl in a letter of July 10, 1911, and enumerated three areas of agreement: "The effort needed to reach a universally valid foundation for the real sci-

ences," the opposition to "constructive metaphysics," and the repetition of the assumption that "an in-itself lies behind the reality that is given to us." Whatever differences still remained could perhaps be a consequence, Dilthey politely wrote, of his not yet understanding some of Husserl's explanations.[24]

Husserl's offer to write a clarificatory note in *Logos* was accepted, but when Dilthey died on October 1, 1911, the note by Husserl was never published.

So much for the Husserl-Dilthey correspondence.

Now, what if anything does this show us of a distinctively phenomenological kind of argumentation?

I fear very little.

If we scrutinize the background of this controversy in the *Logos* article and its details in the correspondence once again, we nowhere find evidence of any distinctive Husserlian style of kind of argument. Indeed, what we do find is self-referential inconsistency, namely, Husserl's practice of a type of overly selective and unsympathetic criticism which he himself had fulminated against in the Palágyi case.[25] The exchange between Dilthey and Husserl, largely thanks to Dilthey's own clarity and understanding, does dissipate a number of nebulous criticisms. The result is that Husserl is able to see for the first time that his agreements with Dilthey are far more extensive than his disagreements. One central issue, the nature of metaphysics, stands out as calling for more analysis and discussion on the part of both. But precisely here, where we would expect Husserl if anywhere to deploy whatever characteristic approaches he may be recommending in his phenomenological philosophy, no further clarification is offered. Husserl claims that metaphysics is impossible, and he adds suggestively, metaphysics "in that especially false ontological sense." But this suggestion is not pursued.

At least one basic assumption in many but not all areas of Husserl's work makes criticism of that work impossible without question-begging. That assumption is the doctrine of the reduction.[26] Although Husserl himself subjects this doctrine to many reformulations and criticism of his own, nonetheless, to the degree that some identifiable version of that doctrine is operative in a particular philosophical analysis, such an analysis precludes the usual kinds of criticism.

In the light of the *Logos* article and the Husserl-Dilthey exchanges here cited I want to suggest now a further complication for the task of criticizing constructively Husserl's many provocative remarks in "Philosophy as Rigorous Science." To the degree that Husserl's claims for phenomenology necessarily involve the peculiar ontological sense of a metaphysical basis, then these claims are ultimately dependent for their justification on sorting out the kinds of problems Dilthey brings to Husserl's attention. Thus such a fundamental claim as the view that phenomenology is "presuppositionless" (*vorauslosig*) requires for its appraisal not only particular scrutiny in the light of Husserl's doctrines of the reduction but, much more interestingly, general scrutiny in the light of Husserl's insufficiently examined use of the term 'metaphysics'.

NOTES

1. See for example the articles in the section "Comparisons and Contrasts" in F. Elliston and P. McCormick, eds., *Husserl: Expositions and Appraisals* (Notre Dame, 1977), pp. 247–365. This collection is hereafter cited as *Husserl*.

2. On intuition see E. Levinas, *The Theory of Intuition in Husserl's Phenomenology*, tr. A. Orianne (Evanston, 1973); H. Pieterma, "Intuition and Horizon in the Philosophy of Husserl," *Phenomenology and Philosophical Research* 34 (1973–74): 95–101; S. Strasser, "Intuition and Dialektik in der Philosophie Edmund Husserls," in *Edmund Husserl 1859–1959* (The Hague, 1959), pp. 148–53.

3. On essences see D.M. Lewin, "Husserlian Essences Reconsidered," in *Explorations in Phenomenology*, ed. D. Carr and E.S. Casey (The Hague, 1973), pp. 169–83.

4. Similar concerns are to be found, for example, in R. Schmitt, "Husserl's Transcendental-Phenomenological Reduction," *Phenomenology and Philosophical Research* 20 (1959–60): 238–45.

5. See the critical edition of the Prolegomena to the *Logical Investigations*, ed. E. Holenstein, in *Husserliana* 18 (The Hague, 1975).

6. The other texts are Husserl's exchanges with Palágyi and those with Heidegger. For the first see Husserl's "Reply to a Critic" in part two of this collection, and for the second see *Husserliana* 9, ed. W. Biemel (The Hague, 1962), 237–302, and Biemel's commentary in his "Husserl's Encyclopaedia Britannica Article and Heidegger's Remarks Thereon," trans. P. McCormick and F. Elliston, in *Husserl*, pp. 286–304.

7. For the text see *Revista de Filosofia de la Universidad de Costa Rica* 1 (1957): 101–24. The text is edited by W. Biemel. The English translation of Biemel's introduction and Husserl's texts are reprinted below.

8. Ed. W. Biemel, *Husserliana* 9 (The Hague, 1962). See also the editor's introduction, xvi–xxi.

9. In the *Zeitschrift für Psychologie und Physiologie der Sinnesorgane* (1895)—Biemel's note.

10. Ed. B. Groethuysen, *Gesammelte Schriften* I, 4th ed. (Stuttgart, 1959).

11. *Ideen über eine beschreibende und zergliedernde Psychologie* (1894)—Biemel's note.

12. *Husserliana* 9: 34; *Phenomenological Psychology*, pp. 24–25.

13. "Philosophie als strenge Wissenschaft," *Logos* 1 (1910–11): 289–341, tr. Q. Lauer; reprinted below. For detailed analysis and a useful specialized bibliography see the edition by R. Berlinger (Frankfurt, 1965).

14. Husserl of course changes his conception of phenomenology later in the development of his work. For an overview of this development see W. Biemel, "The Decisive Phases in the Development of Husserl's Philosophy," in *The Phenomenology of Edmund Husserl*, ed. R.O. Elveton (Chicago, 1970), pp. 148–73.

15. Husserl, in *Logos*, p. 325. All further references to this work appear in the text.

16. See L. Eley, "Life-World Constitution of Propositional Logic and Elementary Predicate Logic," *Analecta Husserliana* 2 (1972): 333–53.

17. Despite Husserl's position here on logic he was also interested in the philosophy of history but from a perspective different than Dilthey's. See D. Carr, *Phenomenology and the Problems of History* (Evanston, 1974); L. Landgrebe, *Phänomenologie und Geschichte* (Darmstadt, 1967); F. Kaufmann, "The Phenomenological Approach to History," *Philosophy and Phenomenological Research* 2 (1941–42): 159–72.

18. Citations from the correspondence are all taken from the English translation printed below.

19. The best general work on Dilthey in English is R.A. Makkreel, *Dilthey: Philosopher of the Human Sciences* (Princeton, 1975), which gives the background of Dilthey's remarks here together with full bibliographical information.

20. Dilthey's reference here is to the pagination of the *Logos* article.

21. For more detail see Biemel's "Introduction" to "The Dilthey-Husserl Correspondence," pp. 198–202 below.

22. But see R. Ingarden, "A Priori Knowledge in Kant versus A Priori Knowledge in Husserl," *Dialectics and Humanism* 1 (1973): 5–18.

23. The Kantian background here is centrally important. See I. Kern, *Husserl und Kant* (The Hague, 1964); P. Ricoeur, "Kant und Husserl," *Philosophy Today* 10 (1966): 145–68; and K. Hartmann, "Husserl

and Kant," *Kantstudien* 3 (1967): 370–75.

24. See also T. Seebohm, *Die Bedingungen der Möglichkeit der Transzendentalphilosophie. Edmund Husserls transzendental-phänomenologischer Ansatz* (Bonn, 1962).

25. On self-referential inconsistency see R. Rorty, "Recent Metaphilosophy," *Review of Metaphysics* 15 (1961): 299–319.

26. See E. Fink, "Reflexionen zu Husserls phänomenologischer Reduktion," *Tydschrift voor Filosofi* 33 (1971): 540–58; R. Boehm, "Basic Reflections on Husserl's Phenomenological Reduction," *International Philosophical Quarterly* 5 (1965): 183–202; and especially H.L. van Breda, "A Note on Reduction and Authenticity according to Husserl," trans. F. Elliston and P. McCormick, in *Husserl*, pp. 124–25.

FURTHER REFERENCES

Berlinger, R. "Inhaltsanalyze und Nachwort." In Husserl, *Philosophie als strenge Wissenschaft,* by E. Husserl, edited by R. Berlinger, pp. 75–101. Frankfurt, 1965.

Diemer, A. "Die Phänomenologie und die Idee der Philosophie als strenge Wissenschaft." *Zeitschrift für philosophische Forschung* 13 (1959): 243–62.

Gutting, G. "Husserl and Scientific Realism." *Philosophy and Phenomenological Research* 39 (1978): 42–56.

Hippolyte, J. "The Fichtean Idea of the Science of Knowledge and the Husserlian Profect. *Auslegung* 1 and 2 (1973–75): 77–84.

Husserl, E. *Die Idee der Phänomenologie,* edited by W. Biemel. The Hague, 1950.

Lauer, Q. Introduction to *Phenomenology and the Crisis of Philosophy,* by E. Husserl, translated by Q. Lauer, pp. 1–68. New York, 1965.

Seidler, M.J. "Philosophy as Rigorous Science: An Introduction to Husserlian Phenomenology." *Philosophy Today* 21 (1977): 306–26.

Sokolowski, R. "Exact Science and the World in Which We Live." In *Lebenswelt und Wissenschaft in der Philosophie Edmund Husserls,* edited by E. Ströker, pp. 92–107. Frankfurt, 1979.

Ströker, E. "Edmund Husserl's Phenomenology as Foundation of Natural Science." *Analecta Husserliana* 2 (1972): 245–57.

10

Philosophy as Rigorous Science*

TRANSLATED BY QUENTIN LAUER

From its earliest beginnings philosophy has claimed to be rigorous science. What is more, it has claimed to be the science that satisfies the loftiest theoretical needs and renders possible from an ethico-religious point of view a life regulated by pure rational norms. This claim has been pressed with sometimes more, sometimes less energy, but it has never been completely abandoned, not even during those times when interest in and capacity for pure theory were in danger of atrophying, or when religious forces restricted freedom of theoretical investigation.

During no period of its development has philosophy been capable of living up to this claim of being rigorous science; not even in its most recent period, when—despite the multiplicity and contradictory character of its philosophical orientations—it has followed from the Renaissance up to the present an essentially unitary line of development. It is, in fact, the dominant characteristic of modern philosophy that, rather than surrender itself naïvely to the philosophical impulse, it will by means of critical reflection and by ever more profound methodological investigation constitute itself as rigorous science. But the only mature fruit of these efforts has been to secure first the foundation and then the independence of rigorous nat-

ural and humanistic sciences along with new purely mathematical disciplines. Philosophy itself, in the particular sense that only now has become distinguished, lacked as much as ever the character of rigorous science. The very meaning of the distinction remained without scientifically secure determination. The question of philosophy's relation to the natural and humanistic sciences—whether the specifically philosophical element of its work, essentially related as it is to nature and the human spirit, demands fundamentally new attitudes, that in turn involve fundamentally peculiar goals and methods; whether as a result the philosophical takes us, as it were, into a new dimension, or whether it performs its function on the same level as the empirical sciences of nature and of the human spirit—all this is to this day disputed. It shows that even the proper sense of philosophical problems has not been made scientifically clear.

Thus philosophy, according to its historical purpose the loftiest and most rigorous of all sciences, representing as it does humanity's imperishable demand for pure and absolute knowledge (and what is inseparably one with that, its demand for pure and absolute valuing and willing), is incapable of assuming the form of rigorous science. Philosophy, whose vocation is to teach us how to carry on the eternal work of humanity, is utterly incapable of teaching in an objectively valid manner. Kant was fond of saying that one could not learn philosophy, but only to philosophize. What is that but an admission of philosophy's unscientific char-

*Edmund Husserl, "Philosophy as Rigorous Science," in *Phenomenology and the Crisis of Philosophy,* translated by Quentin Lauer (New York: Harper & Row, 1965), pp. 71–147. Reprinted by permission of Harper & Row, Publishers, Inc. English translation copyright © 1965 by Quentin Lauer.

acter? As far as science, real science, extends, so far can one teach and learn, and this everywhere in the same sense. Certainly scientific learning is nowhere a passive acceptance of matter alien to the mind. In all cases it is based on self-activity, on an inner reproduction, in their relationships as grounds and consequences, of the rational insights gained by creative spirits. One cannot learn philosophy, because here there are no such insights objectively grasped and grounded, or to put it in another way, because here the problems, methods, and theories have not been clearly defined conceptually, their sense has not been fully clarified.

I do not say that philosophy is an imperfect science; I say simply that it is not yet a science at all, that as science it has not yet begun. As a criterion for this, take any portion —however small—of theoretical content that has been objectively grounded. All sciences are imperfect, even the much-admired exact sciences. On the one hand they are incomplete, because the limitless horizon of open problems, which will never let the drive toward knowledge rest, lies before them; and on the other hand they have a variety of defects in their already developed doctrinal content, there remain evidences here and there of a lack of clarity or perfection in the systematic ordering of proofs and theories. Nevertheless they do have a doctrinal content that is constantly growing and branching out in new directions. No reasonable person will doubt the objective truth or the objectively grounded probability of the wonderful theories of mathematics and the natural sciences. Here there is, by and large, no room for private "opinions," "notions," or "points of view." To the extent that there are such in particular instances, the science in question is not established as such but is in the process of becoming a science and is in general so judged.[1]

The imperfection of philosophy is of an entirely different sort from that of the other sciences as just described. It does not have at its disposal a merely incomplete and, in particular instances, imperfect doctrinal system; it simply has none whatever. Each and every question is herein controverted, every position is a matter of individual conviction,

of the interpretation given by a school, of a "point of view."

It may well be that the proposals presented in the world-renowned scientific works of philosophy in ancient and modern times are based on serious, even colossal intellectual activity. More than that, it may in large measure be work done in advance for the future establishment of scientifically strict doctrinal systems; but for the moment, nothing in them is recognizable as a basis for philosophical science, nor is there any prospect of cutting out, as it were, with the critical scissors here and there a fragment of philosophical doctrine.

This conviction must once more be expressed boldly and honestly, and precisely in this place, in the first issue of *Logos*, whose aim is to testify to a significant revolution in philosophy and to prepare the ground for the future philosophical "system." For with this blunt emphasis on the unscientific character of all previous philosophy, the question immediately arises whether philosophy is to continue envisioning the goal of being a rigorous science, whether it can or must want to be so. What is this new revolution supposed to mean to us? Some sort of departure from the idea of a rigorous science? And what meaning should be given to the "system" for which we yearn, which is supposed to gleam as an ideal before us in the lowlands where we are doing our investigative work? Is it to be a philosophical "system" in the traditional sense, like a Minerva springing forth complete and full-panoplied from the head of some creative genius, only in later times to be kept along with other such Minervas in the silent museum of history? Or is it to be a philosophical system of doctrine that, after the gigantic preparatory work of generations, really begins from the ground up with a foundation free of doubt and rises up like any skillful construction, wherein stone is set upon stone, each as solid as the other, in accord with directive insights? On this question minds must part company and paths must diverge.

The revolutions decisive for the progress of philosophy are those in which the claim of former philosophies to be scientific are discredited by a critique of their pretended scientific procedure. Then at the helm is the fully conscious will to establish philosophy in a radically new fashion in the sense of rigorous science, determining the order in which tasks are undertaken. First of all, thought concentrates all its energy on decisively clarifying, by means of systematic examination, the conditions of strict science that in former philosophies were naïvely overlooked or misunderstood, in order thereafter to attempt to construct anew a structure of philosophical docrine. Such a fully conscious will for rigorous science dominated the Socratic-Platonic revolution of philosophy and also, at the beginning of the modern era, the scientific reactions against Scholasticism, especially the Cartesian revolution. Its impulse carries over to the great philosophies of the seventeenth and eighteenth centuries; it renews itself with most radical vigor in Kant's critique of reason and still dominates Fichte's philosophizing. Again and again research is directed toward true beginnings, decisive formulation of problems, and correct methods.

Only with romantic philosophy does a change occur. However much Hegel insists on the absolute validity of his method and his doctrine, still his system lacks a critique of reason, which is the foremost prerequisite for being scientific in philosophy. In this connection it is clear that this philosophy, like romantic philosophy in general, acted in the years that followed either to weaken or to adulterate the impulse toward the constitution of rigorous philosophical science.

Concerning the latter tendency to adulterate, it is well known that with the progress of the exact sciences Hegelianism gave rise to reactions, as a result of which the naturalism of the eighteenth century gained an overwhelming impetus; and with its scepticism, which invalidated all absolute ideality and objectivity, it has largely determined the *Weltanschauung* and philosophy of the last decades.

On the other hand, as a tendency to weaken the impulse toward philosophic science Hegelian philosophy produced aftereffects by its doctrine on the relative justification of every philosophy for its own time —a doctrine, it is true, that in Hegel's system, pretending to absolute validity, had an

entirely different sense from the historic one attributed to it by those generations that had lost along with their belief in Hegelian philosophy any belief whatever in an absolute philosophy. As a result of the transformation of Hegel's metaphysical philosophy of history into a sceptical historicism, the establishment of the new *Weltanschauung* philosophy has now been essentially determined. This latter seems in our day to be spreading rapidly, and what is more, warring as it does for the most part against naturalism and, when the occasion offers, even against historicism, it has not the least desire to be sceptical. To the extent, however, that it does not show itself, at least in its whole intention and procedure, any longer dominated by that radical will to scientific doctrine that constituted the great progress of modern philosophy up to Kant's time, what I said regarding a weakening of philosophy's scientific impulse referred particularly to it.

The following arguments are based on the conviction that the highest interests of human culture demand the development of a rigorously scientific philosophy; consequently, if a philosophical revolution in our times is to be justified, it must without fail be animated by the purpose of laying a new foundation for philosophy in the sense of strict science. This purpose is by no means foreign to the present age. It is fully alive precisely in the naturalism that dominates the age. From the start, naturalism sets out with a firm determination to realize the ideal of a rigorously scientific reform of philosophy. It even believes at all times, both in its earlier and in its modern forms, that it has already realized this idea. But all this takes place, when we look at it from the standpoint of principle, in a form that from the ground up is replete with erroneous theory; and from a practical point of view this means a growing danger for our culture. It is important today to engage in a radical criticism of naturalistic philosophy. In particular, there is need of a positive criticism of principles and methods as opposed to a purely negative criticism based on consequences. Only such a criticism is calculated to preserve intact confidence in the possibility of a scientific philosophy, a confidence threatened by the absurd consequences of a naturalism built on strict empirical science. The arguments contained in the first part of this study are calculated to afford just such a criticism.

However, with regard to the remarkable revolution in our times, it is in fact—and in that it is justified—anti-naturalistic in its orientation. Still under the influence of historicism, it seems to desire a departure from the lines of scientific philosophy and a turn toward mere *Weltanschauung* philosophy. The second part of this study is devoted to an exposé, based on principles, of the differences between these two philosophies and to an evaluation of their respective justifications.

Naturalistic Philosophy

Naturalism is a phenomenon consequent upon the discovery of nature, which is to say, nature considered as a unity of spatio-temporal being subject to exact laws of nature. With the gradual realization of this idea in constantly new natural sciences that guarantee strict knowledge regarding many matters, naturalism proceeds to expand more and more. In a very similar fashion historicism developed later, consequent upon the "discovery of history," constantly guaranteeing new humanistic sciences. In accord with each one's dominant habit of interpretation, the natural scientist has the tendency to look upon everything as nature, and the humanistic scientist sees everything as "spirit," as a historical creation; by the same token, both are inclined to falsify the sense of what cannot be seen in their way. Thus the naturalist, to consider him in particular, sees only nature, and primarily physical nature. Whatever is is either itself physical, belonging to the unified totality of physical nature, or it is in fact psychical, but then merely as a variable dependent on the physical, at best a secondary "parallel accompaniment." Whatever is belongs to psychophysical nature, which is to say that it is univocally determined by rigid laws. From our point of view, there is no essential alteration in this interpretation, when in the positivistic sense (whether it be a positivism that bases itself on a naturalistically interpreted Kant or one that renews and consistently develops

Hume) physical nature is sensualistically broken up into complexes of sensations, into colors, sounds, pressures, etc., and in the same way the so-called "psychical" is broken up into complementary complexes of the same or of still other "sensations."

Characteristic of all forms of extreme and consistent naturalism, from popular naturalism to the most recent forms of sensation-monism and energism, is on one hand the naturalizing of consciousness, including all intentionally immanent data of consciousness, and on the other the naturalizing of ideas and consequently of all absolute ideals and norms.

From the latter point of view, without realizing it, naturalism refutes itself. It we take an exemplary index of all ideality, formal logic, then the formal-logical principles, the so-called "laws of thought," are interpreted by naturalism as natural laws of thinking. That this brings with it the sort of absurdity that characterizes every theory of scepticism in the fullest sense has elsewhere been demonstrated in detail.[2] One can submit naturalistic axiology and practical philosophy (including ethics) as well as naturalistic practice to a radical criticism of the same sort. For theoretical absurdities are inevitably followed by absurdities (evident inconsistencies) in actual theoretical, axiological, and ethical ways of acting. The naturalist is, one can safely say, idealist and objectivist in the way he acts. He is dominated by the purpose of making scientifically known (*i.e.*, in a way that compels any rational individual) whatever is genuine truth, the genuinely beautiful and good; he wants to know how to determine what is its universal essence and the method by which it [namely, that which is genuinely true, or genuinely beautiful, or genuinely good] is to be obtained in the particular case. He believes that through natural science and through a philosophy based on the same science the goal has for the most part been attained, and with all the enthusiasm that such a consciousness gives, he has installed himself as teacher and practical reformer in regard to the true, the good, and the beautiful, from the standpoint of natural science. He is, however, an idealist who sets up and (so he thinks) justifies theories, which deny precisely what he presupposes in his idealistic way of acting, whether it be in constructing theories or in justifying and recommending values or practical norms as the most beautiful and the best. He is, after all, going on presuppositions, to the extent that he theorizes at all, to the extent that he objectively sets up values to which value judgments are to correspond, and likewise in setting up any practical rules according to which each one is to be guided in his willing and in his conduct. The naturalist teaches, preaches, moralizes, reforms. (Häckel and Ostwald are good examples.) But he denies what every sermon, every demand, if it is to have a meaning, presupposes. The only thing is, he does not preach in express terms that the only rational thing to do is to deny reason, as well theoretical as axiological and practical reason. He would, in fact, banish that sort of thing far from him. The absurdity is not in his case evident, but remains hidden from him because he naturalizes reason.

From this point of view the controversy has been factually decided, even if the flood of positivism and pragmatism, which latter exceeds the former in its relativism, mounts still higher. It is manifest, of course, by this very circumstance how slight is the practically effective force of arguments based on consequences. Prejudices blind, and one who sees only empirical facts and grants intrinsic validity only to empirical science will not be particularly disturbed by absurd consequences that cannot be proved empirically to contradict facts of nature. This sort of argument he will put aside as "Scholasticism." What is more, arguments drawn from consequences lead easily to an undesired result in the other direction, that is, for those who are inclined to credit them with demonstrative force.

Since naturalism, which wanted to establish philosophy both on a basis of strict science and as a strict science, appears completely discredited, now the aim of its method seems to be discredited too, and all the more so because among non-naturalists, too, there is a widespread tendency to look upon positive science as the only strict science and to recognize as scientific philosophy only one that is based on this sort of science. That, however, is also only preju-

dice, and it would be a fundamental error to want for that reason to deviate from the line of strict science. Precisely in the energy with which naturalism seeks to realize the principle of scientific rigor in all the spheres of nature and spirit, in theory and practice, and in the energy with which it strives to solve the philosophical problems of being and value—thinking it is proceeding in the manner of "exact natural science"—lies its merit and the major part of its strength in our era. There is, perhaps, in all modern life no more powerfully, more irresistibly progressing idea than that of science. Nothing will hinder its victorious advance. In fact, with regard to its legitimate aims, it is all-embracing. Looked upon in its ideal perfection, it would be reason itself, which could have no other authority equal or superior to itself. There belong in the domain of strict science all the theoretical, axiological, and practical ideals that naturalism, by giving them a new empirical meaning, at the same time falsifies.

Still, general convictions carry little weight when one cannot give them a foundation; hopes for a science signify little if one is incapable of envisioning a path to its goals. If, then, the idea of a philosophy as a rigorous science of the aforesaid problems and of all problems essentially related to them is not to remain without force, we must have before our eyes clear possibilities of realizing it. Through a clarification of the problems and through penetration into their pure sense, the methods adequate to these problems, because demanded by their very essence, must impose themselves on us. That is what has to be accomplished, so that at one and the same time we may acquire a vital and active confidence in science and an actual beginning of it. For this purpose the otherwise useful and indispensable refutation of naturalism based on its consequences accomplishes very little for us.

It is altogether different when we engage in the necessary positive and hence principiant criticism of its foundation, methods and accomplishments. Because criticism distinguishes and clarifies, because it compels us to pursue the proper sense of the philosophical motivations that are usually so vaguely and equivocally formulated as problems, it is calculated to call up representations of better ends and means and to promote our plan in a positive manner. With this end in view we comment more in detail on that characteristic of the controverted philosophy that was particularly highlighted above, *i.e.*, the naturalizing of consciousness. The more profound connections with the above-mentioned sceptical consequences will of their own accord come forward in what follows, and by the same token the extent to which our second objection regarding the naturalizing of ideas is intended and is to be given a foundation will be made clear.

Obviously we are not directing our critical analysis toward the more popular reflections of philosophizing natural scientists. Rather we are concerned with the learned philosophy that presents itself in a really scientific dress. Above all, however, we are concerned with a method and a discipline whereby this philosophy believes that it has definitely attained the rank of an exact science. So sure is it of this that it looks down disdainfully on all other modes of philosophizing. They stand in relation to its exactly scientific philosophizing as the muddy natural philosophy of the Renaissance to the youthful exact mechanics of a Galileo, or like alchemy in relation to the exact chemistry of a Lavoisier. If we ask about exact though as yet scarcely developed philosophy, the analogue of exact mechanics, we are shown psychophysical and, above all, experimental psychology, to which, of course, no one can deny the rank of strict science. This, they tell us, is the long-sought scientific psychology, that has at last become a fact. Logic and epistemology, aesthetics, ethics, and pedagogy have finally obtained their scientific foundation through it; they are in fact already on the way toward being transformed into experimental disciplines. In addition, strict psychology is obviously the foundation for all humanistic sciences and not less even for metaphysics. With regard to this last, of course, it is not the preferential foundation, since to the same extent physical natural science also has a share in supplying a foundation for this general theory of reality.

In answer to this, these are our objections. First of all, it should be seen clearly, and a brief consideration would show, that psychology in general, as a factual science, is not calculated to lay the foundations of those philosophical disciplines that have to do with the pure principles for the establishing of norms, of pure logic, pure axiology, and practical discipline. We can spare ourselves a more detailed exposition: it would evidently bring us back to the already discussed sceptical absurdities. With regard to the theory of knowledge, however, which we do distinguish from pure logic, in the sense of pure *mathesis universalis* (having as such nothing to do with knowing), much can be said against epistemological psychologism and physicism, whereof something should be indicated here.

All natural science is naïve in regard to its point of departure. The nature that it will investigate is for it simply there. Of course, things there are, as things at rest, in motion, changing in unlimited space, and temporal things in unlimited time. We perceive them, we describe them by means of simple empirical judgments. It is the aim of natural science to know these unquestioned data in an objectively valid, strictly scientific manner. The same is true in regard to nature in the broader, psychophysical sense, or in regard to the sciences that investigate it—in particular, therefore, in regard to psychology. The psychical does not constitute a world for itself: it is given as an ego or as the experience of an ego (by the way, in a very different sense), and this sort of thing reveals itself empirically as bound to certain physical things called bodies. This, too, is a self-evident pre-datum.

It is the task of psychology to explore this psychic element scientifically within the psychophysical nexus of nature (the nexus in which, without question, it occurs), to determine it in an objectively valid way, to discover the laws according to which it develops and changes, comes into being and disappears. Every psychological determination is by that very fact psychophysical, which is to say in the broadest sense (which we retain from now on), that it has a never-failing physical connotation. Even where psychology —the empirical science—concerns itself with determination of bare events of consciousness and not with dependences that are psychophysical in the usual and narrower sense, those events are thought of, nevertheless, as belonging to nature, that is, as belonging to human or brute consciousnesses that for their part have an unquestioned and coapprehended connection with human and brute organisms. To eliminate the relation to nature would deprive the psychical of its character as an objectively and temporally determinable fact of nature, in short, of its character as a psychological fact. Then let us hold fast to this: every psychological judgment involves the existential positing of physical nature, whether expressly or not.

As a result, the following is clear: should there be decisive arguments to prove that physical natural science cannot be philosophy in the specific sense of the word, can never in any way serve as a foundation for philosophy, and can achieve a philosophical value for the purposes of metaphysics only on the basis of a prior philosophy, then all such arguments must be equally applicable to psychology.

Now, there is by no means a lack of such arguments. It is sufficient merely to recall the "naïveté" with which, according to what was said above, natural science accepts nature as given, a naïveté that in natural science is, so to speak, immortal and repeats itself afresh, for example, at every place in its procedure where natural science has recourse to pure and simple experience—and ultimately every method of experiential science leads back precisely to experience. It is true, of course, that natural science is, in its own way, very critical. Isolated experience, even when it is accumulated, is still worth little to it. It is in the methodical disposition and connection of experiences, in the interplay of experience and thought, which has its rigid logical laws, that valid experience is distinguished from invalid, that each experience is accorded its level of validity, and that objectively valid knowledge as such, knowledge of nature, is worked out. Still, no matter how satisfactory this kind of critique of experience may be, as long as we remain within natural science and think according to its point of view, a completely different critique of experience is still possible and indispensable, a critique that places in question all experience as such and the

sort of thinking proper to empirical science.

How can experience as consciousness give or contact an object? How can experiences be mutually legitimated or corrected by means of each other, and not merely replace each other or confirm each other subjectively? How can the play of a consciousness whose logic is empirical make objectively valid statements, valid for things that are in and for themselves? Why are the playing rules, so to speak, of consciousness not irrelevant for things? How is natural science to be comprehensible in absolutely every case, to the extent that it pretends at every step to posit and to know a nature that is in itself—in itself in opposition to the subjective flow of consciousness? All these questions become riddles as soon as reflection on them becomes serious. It is well known that theory of knowledge is the discipline that wants to answer such questions, and also that up to the present, despite all the thoughtfulness employed by the greatest scholars in regard to those questions, this discipline has not answered in a manner scientifically clear, unanimous, and decisive.

It requires only a rigorous consistency in maintaining the level of this problematic (a consistency missing, it is true, in all theories of knowledge up to the present) to see clearly the absurdity of a theory of knowledge based on natural science, and thus, too, of any psychological theory of knowledge. If certain riddles are, generally speaking, inherent in principle to natural science, then it is self-evident that the solution of these riddles according to premises and conclusions in principle transcends natural science. To expect from natural science itself the solution of any one of the problems inherent in it as such—thus inhering through and through, from beginning to end—or even merely to suppose that it could contribute to the solution of such a problem any premises whatsoever, is to be involved in a vicious circle.

It also becomes clear that just as every scientific, so every prescientific application of nature must in principle remain excluded in a theory of knowledge that is to retain its univocal sense. So, too, must all expressions that imply thetic existential positings of things in the framework of space, time, causality, etc. This obviously applies also to all existential positings with regard to the empirical being of the investigator, of his psychical faculties, and the like.

Further: if knowledge theory will nevertheless investigate the problems of the relationship between consciousness and being, it can have before its eyes only being as the correlate of consciousness, as something "intended" after the manner of consciousness: as perceived, remembered, expected, represented pictorially, imagined, identified, distinguished, believed, opined, evaluated, etc. It is clear, then, that the investigation must be directed toward a scientific essential knowledge of consciousness, toward that which consciousness itself "is" according to its essence in all its distinguishable forms. At the same time, however, the investigation must be directed toward what consciousness "means," as well as toward the different ways in which—in accord with the essence of the aforementioned forms—it intends the objective, now clearly, now obscurely, now by presenting or by presentifying, now symbolically or pictorially, now simply, now mediated in thought, now in this or that mode of attention, and so in countless other forms, and how ultimately it "demonstrates" the objective as that which is "validly," "really."

Every type of object that is to be the object of a rational proposition, of a prescientific and then of a scientific cognition, must manifest itself in knowledge, thus in consciousness itself, and it must permit being brought to givenness, in accord with the sense of all knowledge. All types of consciousness, in the way they are, so to speak, teleologically ordered under the title of knowledge and, even more, in the way they are grouped according to the various object categories—considered as the groups of cognitive functions that especially correspond to these categories—must permit being studied in their essential connection and in their relation back to the forms of the consciousness of givenness belonging to them. The sense of the question concerning legitimacy, which is to be put to all cognitive acts, must admit of being understood, the essence of grounded legitimation and that of ideal groundableness or validity must admit

of being fully clarified, in this manner—and with respect to all levels of cognition, including the highest, that of scientific cognition.

What it means, that objectivity is, and manifests itself cognitively as so being, must precisely become evident purely from consciousness itself, and thereby it must become completely understandable. And for that is required a study of consciousness in its entirety, since according to all its forms it enters into possible cognitive functions. To the extent, however, that every consciousness is "consciousness-of," the essential study of consciousness includes also that of consciousness-meaning and consciousness-objectivity as such. To study any kind of objectivity whatever according to its general essence (a study that can pursue interests far removed from those of knowledge theory and the investigation of consciousness) means to concern oneself with objectivity's modes of givenness and to exhaust its essential content in the processes of "clarification" proper to it. Even if the orientation is not that which is directed toward the kinds of consciousness and an essential investigation of them, still the method of clarification is such that even here reflection on the modes of being intended and of being given cannot be avoided. In any case, however, the clarification of all fundamental kinds of objectivities is for its part indispensable for the essential analysis of consciousness, and as a result is included in it, but primarily in an epistemological analysis, that finds its task precisely in the investigation of correlations. Consequently we include all such studies, even though relatively they are to be distinguished, under the title "phenomenological."

With this we meet a science of whose extraordinary extent our contemporaries have as yet no concept; a science, it is true, of consciousness that is still not psychology; a phenomenology of consciousness as opposed to a natural science about consciousness. But since there will be no question here of an accidental equivocation, it is to be expected beforehand that phenomenology and psychology must stand in close relationship to each other, since both are concerned with consciousness, even though in a different way, according to a different "orientation." This we may express by saying that psychology is concerned with "empirical consciousness," with consciousness from the empirical point of view, as an empirical being in the ensemble of nature, whereas phenomenology is concerned with "pure" consciousness, *i.e.,* consciousness from the phenomenological point of view.

If this is correct, the result would then be —without taking away from the truth that psychology is not nor can be any more philosophy than the physical science of nature can—that for essential reasons psychology must be more closely related to philosophy (*i.e.,* through the medium of phenomenology) and must in its destiny remain most intimately bound up with philosophy. Finally, it would be possible to foresee that any psychologistic theory of knowledge must owe its existence to the fact that, missing the proper sense of the epistemological problematic, it is a victim of a presumably facile confusion between pure and empirical consciousness. To put the same in another way: it "naturalizes" pure consciousness. This is in fact my interpretation, and it will be illustrated somewhat more clearly in what follows.

It is true that what has just been said by way of general indication, and particularly what was said of the close affinity between psychology and philosophy, applies very little to modern exact psychology, which is as foreign to philosophy as it can possibly be. No matter how much this psychology may consider itself on the strength of the experimental method the sole scientific psychology and look down on "armchair psychology," I am obliged to declare its opinion that it is the psychology, psychological science in the full sense, a serious error heavy with consequences. The ubiquitous fundamental trait of this psychology is to set aside any direct and pure analysis of consciousness (*i.e.,* the systematic realization of "analysis" and "description" of the data that present themselves in the different possible directions of immanent seeing) in favor of indirect fixations of all psychological or psychologically relevant facts, having a sense that is at least superficially understandable without such an analysis of consciousness, at best an outwardly understandable sense. In determining experimentally its psychophysical regularities, it gets along in fact with crude

class concepts such as perception, imaginative intuition, enunciation, calculation and miscalculation, measure, recognition, expectation, retention, forgetting, etc. And of course, on the other hand, the treasury of such concepts with which it operates limits the questions it can ask and the answers it can obtain.

One can very well say that experimental psychology is related to originary psychology in the way social statistics is related to originary social science. A statistics of this sort gathers valuable facts and discovers in them valuable regularities, but of a very mediate kind. Only an originary social science can arrive at an explicit understanding and a real clarification of them; that is, a social science that brings social phenomena to direct givenness and investigates them according to their essence. In like manner, experimental psychology is a method of determining psychophysical facts and norms, which may be valuable but which without a systematic science of consciousness that explores the psychic in respect of what is immanent in it lack every possibility of becoming understood more deeply or utilized in an ultimately valid scientific manner.

Exact psychology is not aware that herein lies a serious defect in its procedure, especially as it becomes alarmed at the method of introspection and expends its energy in trying to overcome the defects of the experimental method by the experimental method itself. It seeks to overcome the defects of a method that, as can be shown, has no competence in regard to what is to be accomplished here. The compulsion of facts, however, which are precisely psychical, proves too strong for analyses of consciousness not to be made from time to time. But as a rule these are of a phenomenological naïveté that stands in remarkable contrast to the indubitable seriousness with which this psychology strives for—and in some spheres (when its aims are modest) achieves— exactness. This latter is true wherever experimental determinations are concerned with subjective sensible appearances, the description and characterization of which is to be accomplished precisely as it is with "objective" appearances, *i.e.,* without any introduction of concepts and elucidations that go over into the proper sphere of consciousness. Something is also achieved where the determinations are related to roughly circumscribed classes of the properly psychical, to the extent that these determinations from the very beginning present themselves sufficiently without more profound analysis of consciousness, so long as one foregoes the pursuit of the properly psychological sense of the determinations.

The reason for the lack of anything radically psychological in the occasional analysis, however, lies in the fact that only in a pure and systematic phenomenology do the sense and method of the work to be accomplished here come to the fore. The same is true in regard to the extraordinary wealth of consciousness-differences, which for the methodologically inexperienced flow into each other without differentiation. In this way modern exact psychology, by the very fact that it considers itself as already methodically perfect and strictly scientific, is actually unscientific wherever it will pursue the sense of the psychical element that enters into psychophysical regularities, *i.e.*, wherever it will penetrate to a real psychological understanding. On the other hand, it is equally unscientific in all those cases where the deficiencies of unclarified representations of the psychical lead to obscure posing of problems and consequently to mere apparent results. The experimental method is indispensable particularly where there is question of fixing intersubjective connections of facts. Still, it presupposes what no experiment can accomplish, the analysis of consciousness itself.

Rare psychologists like Stumpf, Lipps, and others of their kind, have recognized this defect of experimental psychology and have been able to appreciate Brentano's truly epoch-making impulse. In accord with it they have made an effort to continue a thorough analytical and descriptive investigation of intentional experiences begun by him, but are either denied full recognition by the experimental fanatics or, if they were experimentally active, are appreciated only from this point of view. Again and again they are attacked as scholastics. It will be quite a source of wonder to future generations that the first modern attempts to investigate the immanent seriously and in the only possible manner, which is that of an immanent analysis, or as we now say with better insight, by means of an essential analysis, could be treated as scholastic and thus brushed aside. The only reason for this is that the natural point of departure for such investigations is the ordinary terminology designating the psychical. Only after we have made their meanings our own do we look into the phenomena to which such designations are first of all vaguely and equivocally related. Of course, even scholastic ontologism is guided by language (by which I am not saying that all scholastic research was ontologistic), but it loses itself by deriving analytical judgments from word meanings, in the belief that it has thereby gained knowledge of facts. Is the phenomenological analyst to be branded scholastic, too, because he derives no judgments at all from word concepts but rather looks into the phenomena that language occasions by means of the words in question, or because he penetrates to the phenomena constituted by the fully intuitional realization of experimental concepts, etc.?

There is food for thought in the fact that everything psychical (to the extent that it is taken in that full concretion wherein it must be, both for psychology and for phenomenology, the first object of investigation), has the character of a more or less complex "consciousness-of"; in the fact that this "consciousness-of" has a confusing fullness of forms; that all expressions that at the beginning of the investigation could help toward making clearly understandable and toward describing objectively are fluid and ambiguous, and that as a result the first beginning can obviously only be to uncover the crudest equivocations that immediately become evident. A definitive fixation of scientific language presupposes the complete analysis of phenomena—a goal that lies in the dim distance—and so long as this has not been accomplished, the progress of the investigation, too, looked at from the outside, moves to a great extent in the form of demonstrating new ambiguities, distinguishable now for the first time, ambiguities in the very concepts that presumably were already fixed in the preceding investigations. That is obviously inevitable, because it is rooted in the nature of things. It is on this basis that one should judge the depth of understanding manifested in the disdainful way the professional guardians of the exactness and scientific character of psychology speak of "merely verbal," merely "grammatical," and "scholastic" analysis.

In the epoch of vigorous reaction against Scholasticism the war cry was: "Away with empty word analyses! We must question things themselves. Back to experience, to seeing, which alone can give to our words sense and rational justification." Very much to the point! But what, then, are things? And what sort of experience is it to which we must return in psychology? Are they perhaps the statements we get from subjects in answer to our questions? And is the interpretation of their statements the "experience" of the psychical? The experimentalists themselves will say that that is merely a secondary experience, that the primary lies in the subject himself, and that with the experimenting and interpreting psychologists it must be in their own former self-perceptions, that for good reasons are not and must not be introspections. The experimentalists are not a little proud of the fact that they, as critics par excellence of introspection and of — as they call it — armchair psychology based exclusively on introspection, have so developed the experimental method that it uses direct experience only in the form of "chance, unexpected, not intentionally introduced experience,"[3] and that it has completely eliminated the ill-reputed introspection. Though in one direction, despite strong exaggerations, there is in this something unquestionably good, still, on the other hand, there is a fundamental error of this psychology that should be brought out. It places analysis realized in empathetic understanding of others' experience and, likewise, analysis on the basis of one's own mental processes that were unobserved at the time, on the same level with an analysis of experience (even though indirect) proper to physical science, believing that in this way it is an experimental science of the psychical in fundamentally the same sense as physical science is an experimental science of the physical. It overlooks the specific character of certain analyses of consciousness that must have previously taken place, so that from naïve experiences (whether observational or non-observational, whether taking place in the framework of actual presence to consciousness or in that of memory or empathy) they can become experiences in a scientific sense.

Let us try to make this clear.

The psychologists think that they owe all their psychological knowledge to experience, thus to those naïve recollections or to empathetic penetration into recollections, which by virtue of the methodical art of the experiment are to become foundations for empirical conclusions. Nevertheless the description of the naïve empirical data, along with the immanent analysis and conceptional grasp that go hand in hand with this description, is affected by virtue of a fund of concepts whose scientific value is decisive for all further methodical steps. These remain — as is evidenced by a bit of reflection — by the very nature of experimental questioning and method, constantly untouched in the further procedure, and they enter into the final result, which means into the empirical judgment, with its claim to be scientific. On the other hand, their scientific value cannot be there from the beginning, nor can it stem from the experiences of the subject or of the psychologist himself, no matter how many of them are heaped up; it can in fact be obtained logically from no empirical determinations whatever. And here is the place for phenomenological analysis of essence, which, however strange and unsympathetic it may sound to the naturalistic psychologist, can in no way be an empirical analysis.

Beginning with Locke and continuing down to our own day there is a confusion between the conviction drawn from the history of the development of empirical consciousness (which therefore already presupposes psychology) that every conceptional representation "stems" from former experiences, and the entirely different conviction that every concept derives from experience the justification of its possible use, for example in descriptive judgments. Now that means here that only in considering what actual perceptions or recollections afford can legitimizing grounds be found for the concept's validity, its correspondence to an essence (or correspondence to no essence), and consequently for its valid applicability in the given single case. In description we employ the words perception, recollection, imaginative representation, enunciation, etc. What a wealth of immanent components does a single such word indicate, components that we, "grasping" what is described, impose on it without having found them in it analytically. Is it sufficient to use these words in the popular sense, in the vague, completely chaotic sense they have taken on, we know not how, in the "history" of consciousness? And even if we were to know it, what good is this history to do us, how is that to change the fact that vague concepts are simply vague and, by virtue of this character proper to them, obviously unscientific? So long as we have no better, we may use them in the confidence that with them enough crude distinctions for the practical aims of life have been attained. But does a psychology that leaves the concepts that determine its objects without scientific fixation, without methodical elaboration, have a claim to "exactness"? No more, obviously, than would a physics that would be satisfied with the everyday concepts of heavy, warm, mass, etc. Modern psychology no longer wants to be a science of the "soul" but rather of "psychical phenomena." If that is what it wants, then it must be able to describe and determine these phenomena with conceptual rigor. It must have acquired the necessary rigorous concepts by methodical work. Where is this methodical work accomplished in "exact" psychology? We seek for it in vain throughout its vast literature.

The question as to how natural, "confused" experience can become scientific experience, as to how one can arrive at the determination of objectively valid empirical judgments, is the cardinal methodological question of every empirical science. It does not have to be put and answered in the abstract, and in any case it does not have to be answered purely philosophically. Historically it finds an answer in practice, in that the genial pioneers of empirical science grasp intuitively and in the concrete the sense of the necessary empirical method and, by pursuing it faithfully in an accessible sphere of experience, realize a fragment of objectively valid empirical determination, thus getting the science started. The motive for their procedure they owe not to any revelation but to penetrating the sense of the experiences themselves, or the sense of the "being" in them. For, although already "given," in "vague" experience it is given only "confusedly." Consequently the question imposes itself: how are things really? How are they to be determined with objective validity? How, that is, by what better "experiences" and how are they to be improved— by what method? With regard to the knowledge of external nature, the decisive step from naïve to scientific experience, from vague everyday concepts to scientific concepts in full clarity, was, as is known, first realized by Galileo. With regard to knowledge of the psychical, the sphere of consciousness, we have, it is true, "experimentally exact" psychology, which considers itself the fully justified "opposite number" of exact natural science—and yet, though it is scarcely aware of it, this science is still from the most important point of view pre-Galilean.

It can well seem strange that it is not aware of this. We do understand that prior to science naïve nature study lacked no natural experience, which is to say, nothing that could not in the ensemble of natural experience itself be expressed in naturally naïve empirical concepts. In its naïveté it was not aware that things have a "nature" which can be determined by means of certain exact concepts in an empirically logical procedure. But psychology, with its institutes and apparatus of precision, with its keenly thought-out methods, justly feels that it is beyond the stage of the naïve empirical study of the soul belonging to former times. In addition, it has not failed to make careful, constantly renewed reflections on method. How could that which is in principle the most essential escape it? How could psychology fail to see that in its purely psychological concepts, with which it now cannot at all dispense, it necessarily gives a content that is not simply taken from what is actually given in experience but is applied to the latter? How fail to see that in so far as it approaches the sense of the psychical, it effects analyses of these conceptual contents and recognizes valid corresponding phenomenological connections, which it applies to experience but which in relation to experience are a priori? How could it miss the fact that the experimental method, to the extent that it will realize really psychological knowledge, cannot justify its own presuppositions, and that its procedure is radically distinct from that of physics precisely in so far as this latter excludes in principle the phenomenal in order to look for the nature that presents itself in the phenomenal, whereas psychology wanted precisely to be a science of phenomena themselves?

The phenomenal had to elude psychology because of its naturalistic point of view as well as its zeal to imitate the natural sciences and to see experimental procedures as the main point. In its laborious, frequently very keen considerations on the possibilities of psychophysical experiment, in proposing empirical arrangements of experiments, in constructing the finest apparatus, in discovering possible sources of error, etc., it has still neglected to pursue the question more profoundly, *i.e.,* how, by what method, can those concepts that enter essentially into psychological judgments be brought from the state of confusion to that of clarity and objective validity. It has neglected to consider to what extent the psychical, rather than being the presentation of a nature, has an essence proper to itself to be rigorously and in full adequation investigated prior to any psychophysics. It has not considered what lies in the "sense" of psychological experience and what "demands" being (in the sense of the psychical) of itself makes on method.

What has constantly confused empirical psychology since its beginnings in the eighteenth century is thus the deceptive image of a scientific method modeled on that of the physicochemical method. There is a sure conviction that the method of all empirical sciences, considered in its universal principles, is one and the same, thus that it is the same in psychology as in the science of physical nature. If metaphysics suffered so long a time from a false imitation—whether of the geometrical or of the physical method—the same procedure is now being repeated in psychology. It is not without significance that the fathers of experimentally exact psychology were physiologists and physicists. The true method follows the nature of the things to be investigated and not our prejudices and preconceptions. From the vague subjectivity of things in their naïvely sensible appearance natural science laboriously brings out objective things with exact objective characteristics. Thus, they tell themselves, psychology must bring that which is psychologically vague in naïve interpretation to objectively valid determination. The objective method accomplishes this, and it is evident that this is the same as the experimental method brilliantly guaranteed in natural science by countless successes.

Nevertheless, questions such as how the data of experience came to be objectively determined and what sense "objectivity" and "determination of objectivity" have in each case, what function experimental method can in each case take over—these all depend on the proper sense of the data, *i.e.,* on the sense given to them according to its essence by the empirical consciousness in question (as an intention of precisely this and no other being). To follow the model of the natural sciences almost inevitably means to reify consciousness—something that from the very beginning leads us into absurdity, whence stems the constantly renewed tendency toward the absurd problematizing and the false orientations of the investigation. Let us examine that more closely.

Only the spatiotemporal world of bodies is nature in the significant sense of that word. All other individual being, *i.e.,* the psychical, is nature in a secondary sense, a fact that determines basically essential differences between the methods of natural science and psychology. In principle, only corporeal being can be experienced in a number of direct experiences, *i.e.,* perceptions, as individually identical. Hence, only this being can, if the perceptions are thought of as distributed among various "subjects," be experienced by many subjects as individually identical and be described as intersubjectively the same. The same realities (things, procedures, etc.) are present to the eyes of all and can be determined by all of us according to their "nature." Their "nature," however, denotes: presenting themselves in experience according to diversely varying "subjective appearances."

Nevertheless, they stand there as temporal unities of enduring or changing properties, and they stand there as incorporated in the totality of one corporeal world that binds them all together, with its one space and its one time. They are what they are only in this unity; only in the causal relation to or connection with each other do they retain their individual identity (substance), and this they retain as that which carries "real properties." All physically real properties are causal. Every corporeal being is subject to laws of possible changes, and these laws concern the identical, the thing, not by itself but in the unified, actual, and possible totality of the one nature. Each physical thing has its nature (as the totality of what it, the identical, is) by virtue of being the union point of causalities within the one all-nature. Real properties (real after the manner of things, corporeal) are a title for the possibilities of transformation of something identical, possibilities preindicated according to the laws of causality. And thus this identical, with regard to what it is, is determinable only by recourse to these laws. Realities, however, are given as unities of immediate experience, as unities of diverse sensible appearances. Stabilities, changes, and relationships of change (all of which can be grasped sensibly) direct cognition everywhere, and function for it like a "vague" medium in which the true, objective, physically exact nature presents itself, a medium through which thought (as empirically scientific thought) determines and constructs what is true.[4]

All that is not something one attributes to the things of experience and to the experience of things. Rather it is something belonging inseparably to the essences of things in such a way that every intuitive and consistent investigation of what a thing in truth is (a thing which as experienced always appears as something, a being, determined and at the same time determinable, and which nevertheless, as appearances and their circumstances vary, is constantly appearing as a different being) necessarily leads to causal connections and terminates in the determination of corresponding objective properties subject to law. Natural science, then, simply follows consistently the sense of what the thing so to speak pretends to be as experienced, and calls this—vaguely enough—"elimination of secondary qualities," "elimination of the merely subjective in the appearance," while "retaining what is left, the primary qualities." And that is more than an obscure expression; it is a bad theory regarding a good procedure.

Let us now turn to the "world" of the "psychical," and let us confine ourselves to "psychical phenomena," which the new psychology looks upon as its field of objects—i.e., in beginning we leave out of consideration problems relative to the soul and to the ego. We ask, then, whether in every perception of the psychical, just as in the sense of every physical experience and of every perception of the real, there is included "nature"-objectivity? We soon see that the relationships in the sphere of the psychical are totally different from those in the physical sphere. The psychical is divided (to speak metaphorically and not metaphysically) into monads that have no windows and are in communication only through empathy. Psychical being, being as "phenomenon," is in principle not a unity that could be experienced in several separate perceptions as individually identical, not even in perceptions of the same subject. In the psychical sphere there is, in other words, no distinction between appearance and being, and if nature is a being that appears in appearances, still appearances themselves (which the psychologist certainly looks upon as psychical) do not constitute a being which itself appears by means of appearances lying behind it—as every reflection on the perception of any appearance whatever makes evident. It is then clear: there is, properly speaking, only one nature, the one that appears in the appearances of things. Everything that in the broadest sense of psychology we call a psychical phenomenon, when looked at in and for itself, is precisely phenomenon and not nature.

A phenomenon, then, is no "substantial" unity; it has no "real properties," it knows no real parts, no real changes, and no causality; all these words are here understood in the sense proper to natural science. To attribute a nature to phenomena, to investigate their real component parts, their causal connections—that is pure absurdity, no better than if one wanted to ask about the causal properties, connections, etc. of numbers. It is the absurdity of naturalizing something whose essence excludes the kind of being that nature has. A thing is what it is, and it remains in its identity forever: nature is eternal. Whatever in the way of real properties or modifications of properties belongs in truth to a thing (to the thing of nature, not to the sensible thing of practical life, the thing "as it appears sensibly") can be determined with objective validity and confirmed or corrected in constantly new experiences. On the other hand, something psychical, a "phenomenon," comes and goes; it retains no enduring, identical being that would be objectively determinable as such in the sense of natural science, e.g., as objectively divisible into components, "analysable" in the proper sense.

What psychical being "is," experience cannot say in the same sense that it can with regard to the physical. The psychical is simply not experienced as something that appears; it is "vital experience" and vital experience seen in reflection; it appears as itself through itself, in an absolute flow, as now and already "fading away," clearly recognizable as constantly sinking back into a "having been." The psychical can also be a "recalled," and thus in a certain modified way an "experienced"; and in the "recalled" lies a "having been perceived." It can also be a "repeatedly recalled," in recollections that are united in an act of consciousness which in turn is conscious of the recollections themselves as recalled or as still retained. In this connection, and in this alone, can the a priori psychical, in so far as it is the identical of such "repetitions," be "experienced" and identified as being. Everything psychical which is thus an "experienced" is, then, as we can say with equal evidence, ordered in an overall connection, in a "monadic" unity of consciousness, a unity that in itself has nothing at all to do with nature, with space and time or substantiality and causality, but has its thoroughly peculiar "forms." It is a flow of phenomena, unlimited at both ends, traversed by an intentional line that is, as it were, the index of the all-pervading unity. It is the line of an immanent "time" without beginning or end, a time that no chronometers measure.

Looking back over the flow of phenomena in an immanent view, we go from phenomenon to phenomenon (each a unity grasped in the flow and even in the flowing) and never to anything but phenomena. Only when immanent seeing and the experience of things come to synthesis, do viewed phenomenon and experienced thing enter into relation to each other. Through the medium of thing-experience empathy appears at the same time as a sort of mediate seeing of the psychical, characterized in itself as a reception into a second monadic connection.

Now, to what extent is something like rational investigation and valid statement possible in this sphere? To what extent, too, are only such statements possible which we have just now given as most crude descriptions (passing over in silence entire dimensions)? It goes without saying that research will be meaningful here precisely when it directs itself purely to the sense of the experiences, which are given as experiences of the "psychical," and when thereby it accepts and tries to determine the "psychical" exactly as it demands, as it were, to be accepted and determined, when it is seen—above all where one admits no absurd naturalizings. One must, it was said, take phenomena as they give themselves, i.e., as this flowing "having consciousness," intending, appearing, as this foreground and background "having consciousness," a "having consciousness" as present or prepresent, as imagined or symbolic or copied, as intuitive or represented emptily, etc. Thus, too, we must take phenomena as they turn this way or that, transforming themselves, according as the point of view or mode of attention changes in one way or another. All that bears the title "consciousness-of" and that "has" a "meaning," "intends" something "objective," which latter—whether from one standpoint or other it is to be called "fiction" or "reality"—permits being described as something "immanently objective," "intended as such," and intended in one or another mode of intending.

That one can here investigate and make

statements, and do so on the basis of evidence, adapting oneself to the sense of this sphere of "experience," is absolutely evident. Admittedly, it is fidelity to the demands indicated above that constitutes the difficulty. On the single-mindedness and purity of the "phenomenological" attitude depends entirely the consistency or absurdity of the investigations that are here to be carried out. We do not easily overcome the inborn habit of living and thinking according to the naturalistic attitude, and thus of naturalistically adulterating the psychical. Furthermore, overcoming this habit depends to a great extent on the insight that in fact a "purely immanent" investigation of the psychical (using the term in its widest sense, which means the phenomenal as such) is possible, the kind of research that has just been generally characterized and that stands in contrast to any psychophysical investigation of the same, the latter being a kind of investigation we have not yet taken into consideration and which, of course, has its justification.

If the immanently psychical is not nature in itself but the respondent of nature, what are we seeking for in it as its "being"? If it is not determinable in "objective" identity as the substantial unity of real properties that must be grasped over and over again and be determined and confirmed in accordance with science and experience, if it is not to be withdrawn from the eternal flux, if it is incapable of becoming the object of an intersubjective evaluation—then what is there in it that we can seize upon, determine, and fix as an objective unity? This, however, is understood as meaning that we remain in the pure phenomenological sphere and leave out of account relationships to nature and to the body experienced as a thing. The answer, then, is that if phenomena have no nature, they still have an essence, which can be grasped and adequately determined in an immediate seeing. All the statements that describe the phenomena in direct concepts do so, to the degree that they are valid, by means of concepts of essence, that is, by conceptual significations of words that must permit of being redeemed in an essential intuition.

It is necessary to be accurate in our understanding of this ultimate foundation of all psychological method. The spell of the naturalistic point of view, to which all of us at the outset are subject and which makes us incapable of prescinding from nature and hence, too, of making the psychical an object of intuitive investigation from the pure rather than from the psychophysical point of view, has here blocked the road to a great science unparalleled in its fecundity, a science which is on the one hand the fundamental condition for a completely scientific psychology and on the other the field for the genuine critique of reason. The spell of inborn naturalism also consists in the fact that it makes it so difficult for all of us to see "essences," or "ideas"—or rather, since in fact we do, so to speak, constantly see them, for us to let them have the peculiar value which is theirs instead of absurdly naturalizing them. Intuiting essences conceals no more difficulties or "mystical" secrets than does perception. When we bring "color" to full intuitive clarity, to givenness for ourselves, then the datum is an "essence"; and when we likewise in pure intuition—looking, say, at one perception after another—bring to givenness for ourselves what "perception" is, perception in itself (this identical character of any number of flowing singular perceptions), then we have intuitively grasped the essence of perception. As far as intuition— i.e., having an intuitive consciousness— extends, so far extends the possibility of a corresponding "ideation" (as I called it in *Logical Investigations*, or of "seeing essence." To the extent that the intuition is a pure one that involves no transient connotations, to the same extent is the intuited essence an adequately intuited one, an absolutely given one. Thus the field dominated by pure intuition includes the entire sphere that the psychologist reserves to himself as the sphere of "psychical phenomena," provided that he takes them merely by themselves, in pure immanence. That the "essences" grasped in essential intuition permit, at least to a very great extent, of being fixed in definitive concepts and thereby afford possibilities of definitive and in their own way absolutely valid objective statements, is evident to anyone free of prejudice. The ultimate differences of color, its finest nuances, may defy fixation, but "color" as distinguished from "sound" provides a sure difference, than which there is in the world no surer. And such absolutely distinguishable—better, fixable—essences are not only those whose very "content" is of the senses, appearances ("apparitions," phantoms, and the like), but also the essences of whatever is psychical in the pregnant sense, of all ego "acts" or ego states, which correspond to well-known headings such as perception, imagination, recollection, judgment, emotion, will—with all their countless particular forms. Herein remain excluded the ultimate "nuances," which belong to the indeterminable element of the "flow," although at the same time the describable typology of the flowing has its "ideas" which, when intuitively grasped and fixed, render possible absolute knowledge. Every psychological heading such as perception or will designates a most extensive area of "consciousness analyses," *i.e.,* of investigations into essences. There is question here of a field that in extent can be compared only with natural science—however extraordinary this may sound.

Now, it is of decisive significance to know that essential intuition is in no way "experience" in the sense of perception, recollection, and equivalent acts; further, that it is in no way an empirical generalization whose sense it is to posit existentially at the same time the individual being of empirical details. Intuition grasps essence as essential being, and in no way posits being-there. In accord with this, knowledge of essence is by no means matter-of-fact knowledge, including not the slightest shade of affirmation regarding an individual (*e.g.,* natural) being-there. The foundation, or better, the point of departure for an essential intuition (*e.g.,* of the essence of perception, recollection, judgment, etc.) can be a perception of a perception, of a recollection, of a judgment, etc., but it can also be a mere—but mere—imagination, so long as it is clear, even though obviously as such not an experience, that is, grasps no being-there. The grasp of essence is thereby in no way touched; as "grasp of essence" it is intuitive, and that is precisely an intuition of a different kind from experience. Obviously essences can

also be vaguely represented, let us say represented in symbol and falsely posited; then they are merely conjectural essences, involving contradiction, as is shown by the transition to an intuition of their inconsistency. It is possible, however, that their vague position will be shown to be valid by a return to the intuition of the essence in its givenness.

Every judgment which achieves in definitive, adequately constructed concepts an adequate experience of what is contained in essences, experiencing how essences of a certain genus or particularity are connected with others—how, for example, "intuition" and "empty intention," "imagination" and "perception," "concept" and "intuition" unite with each other; how they are on the basis of such and such essential components necessarily "unifiable," corresponding to each other (let us say) as "intention" and "fulfillment," or on the contrary cannot be united, founding as they do a "consciousness of deception," etc.—every judgment of this kind is an absolute, generally valid cognition, and as such it is a kind of essential judgment that it would be absurd to want to justify, confirm, or refute by experience. It fixes a "relation of idea," an a priori in the authentic sense that Hume, it is true, had before his eyes but which necessarily escaped him because of his positivistic confusion of essence and "idea"—as the opposite of "impression." Still, even his scepticism did not dare to be consistent here and to destroy itself on such a knowledge—to the extent that it sees it. Had his sensualism not blinded him to the whole sphere of intentionality, of "consciousness-of," had he grasped it in an investigation of essence, he would not have become the great sceptic, but instead the founder of a truly "positive" theory of reason. All the problems that move him so passionately in the *Treatise* and drive him from confusion to confusion, problems that because of his attitude he can in no wise formulate suitably and purely—all these problems belong entirely to the area dominated by phenomenology. Without exception they are to be solved by pursuing the essential connections of the forms of consciousness as well as of the intentionalities correlatively and essentially belonging to them, solved in a generally intuitive understanding that leaves no meaningful question open. Thus are solved the vast problems of the identity of the object in face of the various impressions or perceptions there are of it. As a matter of fact, how various perceptions or appearances come to the point of "bringing to appearance" one and the same object so that it can be "the same" for them and for the consciousness of unity or identity that unifies their variety, is a question that can be put clearly and answered only by phenomenological essential investigation (which, of course, our manner of formulating the problem has already preindicated). The desire to answer this question empirically on the basis of natural science means that the question has been misunderstood, has been misinterpreted in such a way as to make it an absurd question. That a perception, like any experience whatever, is precisely perception of this object oriented, colored, formed in precisely these ways is a matter of the perception's essence, whatever the situation may be with regard to the "existence" of the object. Again, that this perception is inserted in a continuity of perception, but not in an arbitrary one, in one wherein constantly "the same object presents itself in a constantly different orientation, etc.," that, too, is purely a matter of its essence. In short, here lie the great fields of "consciousness analysis," fields which, up to the present, are in the literature uncultivated, wherein the title consciousness (just as above the title psychical), whether it fits expressly or not, would have to be stretched so wide that it would have to designate everything immanent, and thus everything intended in consciousness, as so intended, and that in every sense. When freed from the false naturalism that absurdly misconstrues them, the problems of origin, for centuries so much discussed, are phenomenological problems. In like manner, the problems regarding the origin of "space representation," regarding representations of time, thing, number, "representations" of cause and effect, etc., are phenomenological problems. Only when these pure problems, meaningfully determined, are formulated and solved do the empirical problems regarding the occurrence of such representations as events of human consciousness acquire a sense that

can be scientifically grasped and comprehended with a view to their solution.

The whole thing, however, depends on one's seeing and making entirely one's own the truth that just as immediately as one can hear a sound, so one can intuit an "essence" — the essence "sound," the essence "appearance of thing," the essence "apparition," the essence "pictorial representation," the essence "judgment" or "will," etc. — and in the intuition one can make an essential judgment. On the other hand, however, it depends on one's protecting himself from the Humean confusion and accordingly not confounding phenomenological intuition with "introspection," with interior experience — in short, with acts that posit not essences but individual details corresponding to them.[5]

Pure phenomenology as science, so long as it is pure and makes no use of the existential positing of nature, can only be essence investigation, and not at all an investigation of being-there; all "introspection" and every judgment based on such "experience" falls outside its framework. The particular can in its immanence be posited only as this — this disappearing perception, recollection, etc. — and if need be, can be brought under the strict essential concepts resulting from essential analysis. For the individual is not essence, it is true, but it "has" an essence, which can be said of it with evident validity. To fix this essence as an individual, however, to give it a position in a "world" of individual being-there, is something that such a mere subsumption under essential concepts cannot accomplish. For phenomenology, the singular is eternally the *apeiron*. Phenomenology can recognize with objective validity only essences and essential relations, and thereby it can accomplish and decisively accomplish whatever is necessary for a correct understanding of all empirical cognition and of all cognition whatsoever: the clarification of the "origin" of all formal-logical and natural-logical principles (and whatever other guiding "principles" there may be) and of all the problems involved in correlating "being" (being of nature, being of value, etc.) and consciousness, problems intimately connected with the aforementioned principles.[6]

Let us now turn to the psychophysical attitude. Therein the "psychical," with the entire essence proper to it, receives an orientation to a body and to the unity of physical nature. What is grasped in immanent perception and interpreted as essentially so qualified, enters into relation to the sensibly perceived and consequently to nature. Only through this orientation does it gain an indirect natural objectivity, mediately a position in space and in nature's time (the kind we measure by clocks). To a certain but not more precisely determined extent, the experiential "dependence" on the physical provides a means of determining intersubjectively the psychical as individual being and at the same time of investigating psychophysical relationships to a progressively more thorough extent. That is the domain of "psychology as natural science," which according to the literal sense is psychophysical psychology, which is hence, obviously in contrast to phenomenology, an empirical science.

Not without misgivings, it is true, does one consider psychology, the science of the "psychical," merely as a science of "psychical phenomena" and of their connections with the body. But in fact psychology is everywhere accompanied by those inborn and inevitable objectivations whose correlates are the empirical unities man and beast, and, on the other hand, soul, personality, or character, *i.e.,* disposition of personality. Still, for our purposes it is not necessary to pursue the essential analysis of these unity constructions nor the problem of how they by themselves determine the task of psychology. After all, it immediately becomes sufficiently clear that these unities are of a kind that is in principle different from the realities of nature, realities that according to their essence are such as to be given through adumbrating appearances, whereas this in no way applies to the unities in question. Only the basic substrate "human body," and not man himself, is a unity of real appearance; and above all, personality, character, etc. are not such unities. With all such unities we are evidently referred back to the immanent vital unity of the respective "consciousness flow" and to morphological peculiarities that distinguish the various immanent unities of this sort. Consequently, all psychological knowledge, too, even where it is re-

lated primarily to human individualities, characters, and dispositions, finds itself referred back to those unities of consciousness, and thereby to the study of the phenomena themselves and of their implications.

There is no need now, especially after all the explanations already given, of further refinements to enable us to see most clearly and for the most profound reasons what has already been presented above: that all psychological knowledge in the ordinary sense presupposes essential knowledge of the psychical, and that the hope of investigating the essence of recollection, judgment, will, etc. by means of casual inner perceptions or experiences, in order thereby to acquire the strict concepts that alone can give scientific value to the designation of the psychical in psychophysical statements and to these statements themselves—that such a hope would be the height of absurdity.

It is the fundamental error of modern psychology, preventing it from being psychology in the true, fully scientific sense, that it has not recognized and developed this phenomenological method. Because of historical prejudices it allowed itself to be held back from using the predispositions to such a method that are contained in every clarifying analysis of concepts. Linked to this is the fact that the majority of psychologists have not understood the already present beginnings of phenomenology, that often, in fact, they have even considered essential investigation carried out from a purely intuitive standpoint to be metaphysical abstraction of the scholastic variety. What has been grasped from an intuitive point of view, however, can be understood and verified only from an intuitive point of view.

After the foregoing explanations it is clear, and it will, as I have good reason to hope, soon be more generally recognized, that a really adequate empirical science of the psychical in its relations to nature can be realized only when psychology is constructed on the base of a systematic phenomenology. It will be, when the essential forms of consciousness and of its immanent correlates, investigated and fixed in systematic connection on a basis of pure intuition, provide the norms for determining the scientific sense and content proper to the concepts of any phenomena whatever, and hence proper to the concepts whereby the empirical psychologist expresses the psychical itself in his psychophysical judgments. Only a really radical and systematic phenomenology, not carried on incidentally and in isolated reflections but in exclusive dedication to the extremely complex and confused problems of consciousness, and carried on with a completely free spirit blinded by no naturalistic prejudices, can give us an understanding of the "psychical" — in the sphere of social as well as of individual consciousness. Only then will the gigantic experimental work of our times, the plenitude of empirical facts and in some cases very interesting laws that have been gathered, bear their rightful fruit as the result of a critical evaluation and psychological interpretation. Then, too, will we again be able to admit—what we can in no way admit with regard to present-day psychology— that psychology stands in close, even the closest, relation to philosophy. Then, too, the paradox of antipsychologism, according to which a theory of knowledge is not a psychological theory, will cease to scandalize, in so far as every real theory of knowledge must necessarily be based on phenomenology, which thus constitutes the common foundation for every philosophy and psychology. Finally, there will no longer be the possibility of that kind of specious philosophical literature that flowers so luxuriantly today and, with its claim to the most serious scientific character, offers us its theories of knowledge, logical theories, ethics, philosophies of nature, pedagogical theories, all based on a "foundation" of natural science and, above all, of "experimental psychology."[7] In fact, faced with this literature, one can only be amazed at the decline of the sense for the extremely profound problems and difficulties to which the greatest spirits of humanity have devoted their lives. Unfortunately one must also be amazed at the decline of the sense for genuine thoroughness, which thoroughness still demands from us so much respect within experimental psychology itself—despite the basic defects that (according to our interpretation) cling to it. I am thoroughly convinced that the historical judgment of this literature will

one day be much more severe than that of the much-decried popular philosophy of the eighteenth century.[8]

We now leave the controversial area of psychological naturalism. We may perhaps say that psychologism, which had been progressing since the time of Locke, was only a muddy form in which the only legitimate philosophical tendency had to work through to a phenomenological foundation of philosophy. In addition, in so far as phenomenological investigation is essence investigation and is thus a priori in the authentic sense, it takes into full account all the justified motives of apriorism. In any case, it is hoped that our criticism will have made it clear that to recognize naturalism as a fundamentally erroneous philosophy still does not mean giving up the idea of a rigorously scientific philosophy, a "philosophy from the ground up." The critical separation of the psychological and phenomenological methods shows that the latter is the true way to a scientific theory of reason and, by the same token, to an adequate psychology.

In accord with our plan, we now turn to a critique of historicism and to a discussion of *Weltanschauung* philosophy.

Historicism and Weltanschauung Philosophy

Historicism takes its position in the factual sphere of the empirical life of the spirit. To the extent that it posits this latter absolutely, without exactly naturalizing it (the specific sense of nature in particular lies far from historical thinking and in any event does not influence it by determining it in general), there arises a relativism that has a close affinity to naturalistic psychologism and runs into similar sceptical difficulties. Here we are interested only in what is characteristic of historical scepticism, and we want to familiarize ourselves more thoroughly with it.

Every spiritual formation—taking the term in its widest possible sense, which can include every kind of social unity, ultimately the unity of the individual itself and also every kind of cultural formation—has its intimate structure, its typology, its marvelous wealth of external and internal forms which in the stream of spirit-life itself grow and transform themselves, and in the very manner of the transformation again cause to come forward differences in structure and type. In the visible outer world the structure and typology of organic development afford us exact analogies. Therein there are no enduring species and no construction of the same out of enduring organic elements. Whatever seems to be enduring is but a stream of development. If by interior intuition we enter vitally into the unity of spirit-life, we can get a feeling for the motivations at play therein and consequently "understand" the essence and development of the spiritual structure in question, in its dependence on a spiritually motivated unity and development. In this manner everything historical becomes for us "understandable," "explicable," in the "being" peculiar to it, which is precisely "spiritual being," a unity of interiorly self-questioning moments of a sense and at the same time a unity of intelligible structuration and development according to inner motivation. Thus in this manner also art, religion, morals, etc. can be intuitively investigated, and likewise the *Weltanschauung* that stands so close to them and at the same time is expressed in them. It is this *Weltanschauung* that, when it takes on the forms of science and after the manner of science lays claim to objective validity, is customarily called metaphysics, or even philosophy. With a view to such a philosophy there arises the enormous task of thoroughly investigating its morphological structure and typology as well as its developmental connections and of making historically understandable the spiritual motivations that determine its essence, by reliving them from within. That there are significant and in fact wonderful things to be accomplished from this point of view is shown by W. Dilthey's writings, especially the most recently published study on the types of *Weltanschauung.*[9]

Up to this point we have obviously been speaking of historical science, not of historicism. We shall grasp most easily the motives that impel toward the latter if in a few sentences we follow Dilthey's presentation. We read as follows: "Among the reasons that constantly give new nourishment to scepticism, one of the most effective is the anar-chy of philosophical systems" (p. 3). "Much deeper, however, than the sceptical conclusions based on the contradictoriness of human opinions go the doubts that have attached themselves to the progressive development of historical consciousness" (p. 4). "The theory of development (as a theory of evolution based on natural science, bound up with a knowledge of cultural structures based on developmental history) is necessarily linked to the knowledge of the relativity proper to the historical life form. In face of the view that embraces the earth and all past events, the absolute validity of any particular form of life-interpretation, of religion, and of philosophy disappears. Thus the formation of a historical consciousness destroys more thoroughly than does surveying the disagreement of systems a belief in the universal validity of any of the philosophies that have undertaken to express in a compelling manner the coherence of the world by an ensemble of concepts" (p. 6).

The factual truth of what is said here is obviously indubitable. The question is, however, whether it can be justified when taken as universal in principle. Of course, *Weltanschauung* and *Weltanschauung* philosophy are cultural formations that come and go in the stream of human development, with the consequences that their spiritual content is definitely motivated in the given historical relationships. But the same is true of the strict sciences. Do they for that reason lack objective validity? A thoroughly extreme historicist will perhaps answer in the affirmative. In doing so he will point to changes in scientific views—how what is today accepted as a proved theory is recognized tomorrow as worthless, how some call certain things laws that others call mere hypotheses and still others vague guesses, etc. Does that mean that in view of this constant change in scientific views we would actually have no right to speak of sciences as objectively valid unities instead of merely as cultural formations? It is easy to see that historicism, if consistently carried through, carries over into extreme sceptical subjectivism. The ideas of truth, theory, and science would then, like all ideas, lose their absolute validity. That an idea has validity would mean that it is a factual construction of spirit which is held as valid and which in its contingent validity determines thought. There would be no unqualified validity, or validity-in-itself, which is what it is even if no one has achieved it and though no historical humanity will ever achieve it. Thus too there would then be no validity to the principle of contradiction nor to any logic, which latter is nevertheless still in full vigor in our time. The result, perhaps, will be that the logical principles of noncontradiction will be transformed into their opposites. And to go even further, all the propositions we have just enunciated and even the possibilities that we have weighed and claimed as constantly valid would in themselves have no validity, etc. It is not necessary to go further here and to repeat discussions already given in another place.[10] We shall certainly have said enough to obtain recognition that no matter what great difficulties the relation between a sort of fluid worth and objective validity, between science as a cultural phenomenon and science as a valid systematic theory, may offer an understanding concerned with clarifying them, the distinction and opposition must be recognized. If, however, we have admitted science as a valid idea, what reason would we still have not to consider similar differences between the historically worthwhile and the historically valid as at least an open possibility—whether or not we can understand this idea in the light of a critique of reason? The science of history, or simply empirical humanistic science in general, can of itself decide nothing, either in a positive or in a negative sense, as to whether a distinction is to be made between art as a cultural formation and valid art, between historical and valid law, and finally between historical and valid philosophy. It cannot decide whether or not there exists, to speak Platonically, between one and the other the relation between the idea and the dim form in which it appears. And even if spiritual formations can in truth be considered and judged from the standpoint of such contraries of validity, still the scientific decision regarding validity itself and regarding its ideal normative principles is in no way the affair of empirical science. Certainly the mathematician too will not turn to historical science to be taught about the truth of mathematical theories. It will not occur to him to relate the historical development of mathematical representations with the question of truth. How, then, is it to be the historian's task to decide as to the truth of given philosophical systems and, above all, as to the very possibility of a philosophical science that is valid in itself? And what would he have to add that could make the philosopher uncertain with regard to his idea, *i.e.*, that of a true philosophy? Whoever denies a determined system, and even more, whoever denies the ideal possibility of a philosophical system as such, must advance reasons. Historical facts of development, even the most general facts concerning the manner of development proper to systems as such, may be reasons, good reasons. Still, historical reasons can produce only historical consequences. The desire either to prove or to refute ideas on the basis of facts is nonsense—according to the quotation Kant used: *ex pumice aquam.*[11]

Consequently, just as historical science can advance nothing relevant against the possibility of absolute validities in general, so it can advance nothing in particular against the possibility of an absolute (*i.e.*, scientific) metaphysics or any other philosophy. It can as historical science in no way prove even the affirmation that up to the present there has been no scientific philosophy; it can do so only from other sources of knowledge, and they are clearly philosophical sources. For it is clear that philosophical criticism, too, in so far as it is really to lay claim to validity, is philosophy and that its sense implies the ideal possibility of a systematic philosophy as a strict science. The unconditional affirmation that any scientific philosophy is a chimaera, based on the argument that the alleged efforts of millennia make probable the intrinsic impossibility of such a philosophy, is erroneous not merely because to draw a conclusion regarding an unlimited future from a few millennia of higher culture would not be a good induction, but erroneous as an absolute absurdity, like $2 \times 2 = 5$. And this is for the indicated reason: if there is something there whose objective validity philosophical criticism can refute, then there is also an area within which something can be grounded as objectively valid. If problems have demonstrably been posed "awry," then it must be possible to rectify this and pose straight problems. If criticism proves that philosophy in its historical growth has operated with confused concepts, has been guilty of mixed concepts and specious conclusions, then if one does not wish to fall into nonsense, that very fact makes it undeniable that, ideally speaking, the concepts are capable of being pointed, clarified, distinguished, that in the given area correct conclusions can be drawn. Any correct, profoundly penetrating criticism itself provides means for advancing and ideally points to correct goals, thereby indicating an objectively valid science. To this would obviously be added that the historical untenableness of a spiritual formation as a fact has nothing to do with its untenableness from the standpoint of validity. And this applies both to all that has been discussed so far and to all spheres whatever where validity is claimed.

What may still lead the historicist astray is the circumstance that by entering vitally into a historically reconstructed spiritual formation, into the intention or signification that is dominant in it as well as into the ensembles of motivations that belong to it, we not only can understand its intrinsic sense but also can judge its relative worth. If by a sort of assumption we make use of the premises a past philosopher had at his disposition, then we can eventually recognize and even marvel at the relative "consistency" of his philosophy. From another point of view, we can excuse the inconsistencies along with shifts and transformations of problems that were inevitable at that stage of the problematic and of the analysis of signification. We can esteem as a great accomplishment the successful solution of a scientific problem that would today belong to a class of problems easily mastered by a high-school student. And the same holds true in all fields. In this regard we obviously still maintain that the principles of even such relative evaluations lie in the ideal sphere, which the evaluating historian who will understand more than mere developments can only presuppose and not—as historian—justify. The norm for the mathematical lies in mathematics, for the logical in logic, for the ethical

in ethics, etc. He would have to seek reasons and methods of verification in these disciplines if he also wanted to be really scientific in his evaluation. If from this standpoint there are no strictly developed sciences, then he evaluates on his own responsibility—let us say, as an ethical or as a religious man, but in any case not as a scientific historian.

If, then, I look upon historicism as an epistemological mistake that because of its consequences must be just as unceremoniously rejected as was naturalism, I should still like to emphasize expressly that I fully recognize the extraordinary value of history in the broadest sense for the philosopher. For him the discovery of the common spirit is just as significant as the discovery of nature. In fact, a deeper penetration into the general life of the spirit offers the philosopher a more original and hence more fundamental research material than does penetration into nature. For the realm of phenomenology, as a theory of essence, extends immediately from the individual spirit over the whole area of the general spirit; and if Dilthey has established in such an impressive way that psychophysical psychology is not the one that can serve as the "foundation for the humanistic sciences," I would say that it is the phenomenological theory of essence alone that is capable of providing a foundation for a philosophy of the spirit.

We pass now to evaluating the sense and justification of *Weltanschauung* philosophy, in order thereafter to compare it with philosophy as a rigorous science. Modern *Weltanschauung* philosophy is, as has already been indicated, a child of historical scepticism. Normally the latter stops short of the positive sciences, to which, with the inconsistency characteristic of every kind of scepticism, it accords real validity. Accordingly, *Weltanschauung* philosophy presupposes all the particular sciences as treasuries of objective truth, and insofar as it has as its goal to satisfy as far as possible our need for thoroughgoing and unifying, all-embracing and all-penetrating knowledge, it looks on all particular sciences as its basis. In view of this, by the way, it calls itself scientific philosophy precisely because it builds on solid sciences. Nevertheless since, properly understood, the scientific character of a discipline contains the scientific character not only of its foundation but also of the aim-providing problems as of its methods, as also a certain logical harmony between the guiding problems on the one hand and, on the other, precisely such foundations and methods, then the designation "scientific philosophy" still says little. And in fact this title is not generally understood as being completely serious. The majority of *Weltanschauung* philosophers feel quite sure that their philosophy with its claim to scientific rigor does not have a very good case, and quite a few of them admit openly and honestly at least the inferior scientific rank of its results. Still, they esteem very highly the worth of this sort of philosophy, which wants precisely to be rather *Weltanschauung* than science of the world, and they esteem it all the more highly the more, precisely under the influence of historicism, they look sceptically at the orientation toward strict philosophical world science. Their motives, that at the same time more exactly determined the sense of *Weltanschauung* philosophy, are approximately the following:

Every great philosophy is not only a historical fact, but in the development of humanity's life of the spirit it has a great, even unique teleological function, that of being the highest elevation of the life experience, education, and wisdom of its time. Let us linger awhile over the clarification of these concepts.

Experience as a personal habitus is the residue of acts belonging to a natural experimental attitude, acts that have occurred during the course of life. This habitus is essentially conditioned by the manner in which the personality, as this particular individuality, lets itself be motivated by acts of its own experience, and not less by the manner in which it lets experiences transmitted by others work on it by agreeing with it or rejecting it. With regard to cognitive acts included under the heading of experience, they can be cognitions of natural existence of every kind, either simple perceptions or other acts of immediately intuitive cognition, or the acts of thought based on these at different levels of logical elaboration and confirmation. But that does not go far enough. We also have experiences of art works and or-

other beauty values, and no less of ethical values, whether on the basis of our own ethical conduct or of looking into that of others; and likewise of real goods, practical utilities, technical applications. In short, we have not only theoretical but also axiological and practical experiences. Analysis shows that these latter refer back to vital experiences of evaluating and willing as their intuitive foundation. On such experiences too are constructed experiential cognitions of a higher, logical dignity. In accord with this, the man of many-sided experience, or as we also say, the "cultivated man," has not only experience of the world but also religious, aesthetic, ethical, political, practicotechnical, and other kinds of experience, or "culture." Nevertheless, we use this admitted cliché "culture," insofar as we have its contrary "unculture," only for the relatively superior forms of the described habitus. With regard to particularly high levels of value, there is the old-fashioned word 'wisdom' (wisdom of the world, wisdom of world and life), and most of all, the now-beloved expressions 'world view' and 'life view', or simply *Weltanschauung.*

We shall have to look upon wisdom, or *Weltanschauung,* in this sense as an essential component of that still more valuable human habitus that comes before us in the idea of perfect virtue and designates habitual ability with regard to all the orientations of human attitudes, whether cognitional, evaluational, or volitional. For evidently hand in hand with this ability goes the well-developed capacity to judge rationally regarding the objectivities proper to these attitudes, regarding the world about us, regarding values, real goods, deeds, etc., or the capacity to justify expressly one's attitudes. That, however, presupposes wisdom and belongs to its higher forms.

Wisdom, or *Weltanschauung,* in this determined sense, which includes a variety of types and grades of value, is—and this needs no further explanation—no mere accomplishment of the isolated personality (this latter would moreover be an abstraction); rather it belongs to the cultural community and to the time, and with regard to its most pronounced forms there is a good sense in which one can speak not only of the culture and *Weltanschauung* of a determined individual but also of that of the time. This is particularly true of the forms we are now to treat.

To grasp in thought the wisdom that in a great philosophical personality is vital, interiorly most rich, but for this personality itself still vague and unconceptualized, is to open out the possibilities of logical elaboration; on higher levels it permits the application of the logical methodology developed in the strict sciences. It is evident that the collective content of these sciences, which in fact confront the individual as valid demands of the collective spirit, belongs on this level to the substructure of a full-valued culture, or *Weltanschauung*. Insofar, then, as the vital and hence most persuasive cultural motives of the time are not only conceptually grasped but also logically unfolded and otherwise elaborated in thought, insofar as the results thus obtained are brought, in interplay with additional intuitions and insights, to scientific unification and consistent completion, there develops an extraordinary extension and elevation of the originally unconceptualized wisdom. There develops a *Weltanschauung* philosophy, which in the great systems gives relatively the most perfect answer to the riddles of life and the world, which is to say, it affords as well as possible a solution and satisfactory explanation to the theoretical, axiological, and practical inconsistencies of life that experience, wisdom, mere world and life view, can only imperfectly overcome. The spirit-life of humanity, with its plenitude of new connections, new spiritual struggles, new experiences, evaluations, and orientations, progresses constantly; with the broadened horizon of life into which all the new spiritual formations enter, culture, wisdom, and *Weltanschauung* change, philosophy changes, mounting to higher and ever higher peaks.

Insofar as the value of *Weltanschauung* philosophy (and thereby also the value of striving toward such a philosophy) is primarily conditioned by the value of wisdom and the striving for wisdom, it is hardly necessary to consider in particular the goal it sets itself. If one makes the concept of wisdom as wide as we have made it, then it certainly ex-

presses an essential component in the ideal of that perfect ability achievable in accord with the measure proper to the respective phase in humanity's life, in other words, a relatively perfect adumbration of the idea of humanity. It is clear, then, how each one should strive to be as universally able a personality as possible, able in all the fundamental orientations of life, which for their part correspond to the fundamental types of possible attitudes. It is clear, too, how each should strive to be in each of these orientations as "experienced," as "wise," and hence also as much a "lover of wisdom" as possible. According to this idea, every man who strives is necessarily a "philosopher," in the most original sense of the word.

From the natural reflections on the best ways to achieve the lofty goal of humanity and consequently at the same time the lofty goal of perfect wisdom, there has grown up, as is known, a technique—that of the virtuous or able man. If it is as usual defined as the art of correct conduct, it obviously comes to the same thing. For consistently able conduct, which is certainly meant, leads back to the able, practical character, and this presupposes habitual perfection from the intellectual and axiological point of view. Again, conscious striving for perfection presupposes striving for universal wisdom. In regard to content, this discipline directs the one striving to the various groups of values, those present in the sciences, the arts, religion, etc. that every individual in his conduct has to recognize as intersubjective and unifying validities; and one of the highest of these values is the idea of this wisdom and perfect ability itself. Of course, this theory of ethical conduct, whether considered more as popular or as scientific, enters into the framework of a *Weltanschauung* philosophy that for its part, with all its fields, in the way it has developed in the collective consciousness of its time and comes persuasively before the individual as an objective validity, must become a most significant cultural force, a point of radiation for the most worthwhile personalities of the time.

Now that we have seen to it that full justice has been accorded to the high value of *Weltanschauung* philosophy, it might seem that nothing should keep us from unconditionally recommending the striving toward such a philosophy.

Still, perhaps it can be shown that in regard to the idea of philosophy, other values —and from certain points of view, higher ones—must be satisfied, which is to say, those of a philosophical science. The following should be taken into account. Our consideration takes place from the standpoint of the high scientific culture of our time, which is a time for mighty forces of objectified strict sciences. For modern consciousness the ideas of culture, or *Weltanschauung,* and science—understood as practical ideas—have been sharply separated, and from now on they remain separated for all eternity. We may bemoan it, but we must accept it as a progressively effective fact that is to determine correspondingly our practical attitude. The historical philosophies were certainly *Weltanschauung* philosophies, insofar as the wisdom drive ruled their creators; but they were just as much scientific philosophies, insofar as the goal of scientific philosophy was also alive in them. The two goals were either not at all or not sharply distinguished. In the practical striving they flowed together; they lay, too, infinitely far away, no matter what lofty experiences the aspirant may have had in their regard. Since the constitution of a supratemporal universality of strict sciences, that situation has fundamentally changed. Generations upon generations work enthusiastically on the mighty structure of science and add to it their modest building blocks, always conscious that the structure is endless, by no means ever to be finished. *Weltanschauung,* too, is an "idea," but of a goal lying in the finite, in principle to be realized in an individual life by way of constant approach, just like morality, which would certainly lose its sense if it were the idea of an eternal that would be in principle transfinite. The "idea" of *Weltanschauung* is consequently a different one for each time, a fact that can be seen without difficulty from the preceding analysis of its concept. The "idea" of science, on the contrary, is a supratemporal one, and here that means limited by no relatedness to the spirit of one time. Now, along with these differences go essential differences of practical orientations. After all, our life goals are in general of two kinds, some temporal, others eternal, some serving our own perfection and that of our contemporaries, others the perfection of posterity, too, down to the most remote generations. Science is a title standing for absolute, timeless values. Every such value, once discovered, belongs thereafter to the treasure trove of all succeeding humanity and obviously determines likewise the material content of the idea of culture, wisdom, *Weltanschauung,* as well as of *Weltanschauung* philosophy.

Thus *Weltanschauung* philosophy and scientific philosophy are sharply distinguished as two ideas, related in a certain manner to each other but not to be confused. Herein it is also to be observed that the former is not, so to speak, the imperfect temporal realization of the latter. For if our interpretation is correct, then up to the present there has been no realization at all of that idea, *i.e.,* no philosophy actually in existence is a rigorous science; there is no "system of doctrines," even an incomplete one, objectively set forth in the unified spirit of the research community of our time. On the other hand, there were already *Weltanschauung* philosophies thousands of years ago. Nevertheless, it can be said that the realization of these ideas (presupposing realizations of both) would approach each other asymptotically in the infinite and coincide, should we want to represent to ourselves the infinite of science metaphorically as an "infinitely distant point." The concept of philosophy would thereby have to be taken in a correspondingly broad sense, so broad that along with the specifically philosophical sciences it would embrace all particular sciences, after they had been turned into philosophies by a rationally critical explanation and evaluation.

If we take the two distinct ideas as contents of life goals, then accordingly, in opposition to the aspiration proper to *Weltanschauung,* an entirely different research aspiration is possible. This latter, though fully conscious that science can in no wise be the complete creation of the individual, still devotes its fullest energies to promoting, in cooperation with men of like mind, the breakthrough and gradual progress of a scientific philosophy. The big problem at present is, apart from clearly distinguishing them, to make a relative evaluation of these goals and thereby of their practical unifiability.

Let it be admitted from the beginning that on the basis of the individuals who philosophize no definitive practical decision for the one or the other kind of philosophizing can be given. Some are pre-eminently theoretical men inclined by nature to seek their vocation in strictly scientific research, provided the field that attracts them offers prospects for such research. Herein it may well be that the interest, even passionate interest, in this field comes from temperamental needs, let us say from needs rooted in a *Weltanschauung*. On the other hand, the situation is different for aesthetic and practical natures (for artists, theologians, jurists, etc.). They see their vocation in the realization of aesthetic or practical ideals, thus of ideals belonging to a nontheoretical sphere. In this class we likewise put theological, juristic, and in the broadest sense technical scholars and writers, to the extent that by their writings they do not seek to promote pure theory but primarily to influence practice. In the actuality of life, of course, the separation is not entirely sharp; precisely at a time when practical motives are making such a powerful upsurge, even a theoretical nature will be capable of giving in to the force of such motives more thoroughly than its theoretical vocation would permit. Here, however, particularly for the philosophy of our time, lies a great danger.

We must ask, however, not only from the standpoint of the individual but also from that of humanity and of history (insofar, that is, as we take history into account), what it means for the development of culture, for the possibility of a constantly progressive realization of humanity as an eternal idea—not of the individual man—that the question be decided predominantly in the one or the other sense. In other words, whether the tendency toward one type of philosophy entirely dominates the time and brings it about that the opposite tendency— say, the one toward scientific philosophy— dies out. That, too, is a practical question. For the influences we exert upon history,

and with them our ethical responsibilities, extend to the utmost reaches of the ethical ideal called for by the idea of human development.

How the decision in question would present itself to a theoretical nature, if there already existed indubitable beginnings of a philosophical doctrine, is clear. Let us take a look at other sciences. All "wisdom" or wisdom doctrine whose origin is mathematical or in the realm of the natural sciences has, to the extent that the corresponding theoretical doctrine has been given an objectively valid foundation, forfeited its rights. Science has spoken; from now on, it is for wisdom to learn. The striving toward wisdom in the realm of natural science was not, so to speak, unjustified before the existence of strict science; it is not retroactively discredited for its own time. In the urgency of life that in practice necessitates adopting a position, man could not wait until—say, after thousands of years—science would be there, even supposing that he already knew the idea of strict science at all.

Now, on the other hand, every science, however exact, offers only a partially developed system of doctrine surrounded by a limitless horizon of what has not yet become science. What, then, is to be considered the correct goal for this horizon? Further development of strict doctrine, or *Anschauung,* "wisdom"? The theoretical man, the investigator of nature, will not hesitate in answering. Where science can speak, even though only centuries from now, he will disdainfully reject vague *Anschauungen.* He would hold it a sin against science to "recommend" projects of nature—*Anschauungen.* In this he certainly represents a right of future humanity. The strict sciences owe their greatness, the continuity and full force of their progressive development, in very large measure precisely to the radicalism of such a mentality. Of course, every exact scholar constructs for himself *Anschauungen;* by his views, his guesses, his opinions, he looks beyond what has been firmly established, but only with methodical intent, in order to plan new fragments of strict doctrine. This attitude does not preclude, as the investigator of nature himself knows quite well, that experience in the prescientific sense—though in connection with scientific insights—plays an important role within the technique proper to natural science. Technical tasks want to be done, the house, the machine is to be built; there can be no waiting until natural science can give exact information on all that concerns them. The technician, therefore, as a practical man, decides otherwise than the theoretician of natural science. From the latter he takes doctrine, from life he takes "experience."

The situation is not quite the same in regard to scientific philosophy, precisely because as yet not even a beginning of scientifically rigorous doctrine has been developed, and the philosophy handed down historically as well as that conceived in a living development, each representing itself as such a doctrine, are at most scientific half-fabrications, or indistinguished mixtures of *Weltanschauung* and theoretical knowledge. On the other hand, here too we unfortunately cannot wait. Philosophical necessity as a need for *Weltanschauung* forces us. This need becomes constantly greater the wider the circle of positive sciences is extended. The extraordinary fullness of scientifically "explained" facts that they bestow on us cannot help us, since in principle, along with all the sciences, they bring in a dimension of riddles whose solutions become for us a vital question. The natural sciences have not in a single instance unraveled for us actual reality, the reality in which we live, move, and are. The general belief that it is their function to accomplish this and that they are merely not yet far enough advanced, the opinion that they can accomplish this—in principle—has revealed itself to those with more profound insight as a superstition. The necessary separation between natural science and philosophy—in principle, a differently oriented science, though in some fields essentially related to natural science—is in process of being established and clarified. As Lotze puts it, "To calculate the course of the world does not mean to understand it." In this direction, however, we are no better off with the humanistic sciences. To "understand" humanity's spirit-life is certainly a great and beautiful thing. But unfortunately even this

understanding cannot help us, and it must not be confused with the philosophical understanding that is to unravel for us the riddles of the world and of life.

The spiritual need of our time has, in fact, become unbearable. Would that it were only theoretical lack of clarity regarding the sense of the "reality" investigated in the natural and humanistic sciences that disturbed our peace—*e.g.,* to what extent is being in the ultimate sense understood in them, what is to be looked on as such "absolute" being, and whether this sort of thing is knowable at all. Far more than this, it is the most radical vital need that afflicts us, a need that leaves no point of our lives untouched. All life is taking a position, and all taking of position is subject to a must—that of doing justice to validity and invalidity according to alleged norms of absolute validation. So long as these norms were not attacked, were threatened and ridiculed by no scepticism, there was only one vital question: how best to satisfy these norms in practice. But how is it now, when any and every norm is controverted or empirically falsified and robbed of its ideal validity? Naturalists and historicists fight about *Weltanschauung,* and yet both are at work on different sides to misinterpret ideas as facts and to transform all reality, all life, into an incomprehensible, idealess confusion of "facts." The superstition of the fact is common to them all.

It is certain that we cannot wait. We have to take a position, we must bestir ourselves to harmonize the disharmonies in our attitude to reality—to the reality of life, which has significance for us and in which we should have significance—into a rational, even though unscientific, "world-and-life-view." And if the *Weltanschauung* philosopher helps us greatly in this, should we not thank him?

No matter how much truth there is in what has just been asserted, no matter how little we should like to miss the exaltation and consolation old and new philosophies offer us, still it must be insisted that we remain aware of the responsibility we have in regard to humanity. For the sake of time we must not sacrifice eternity; in order to alleviate our need, we have no right to bequeath to our posterity need upon need as an eventually ineradicable evil. The need here has its source in science. But only science can definitively overcome the need that has its source in science. If the sceptical criticism of naturalists and historicists dissolves genuine objective validity in all fields of obligation into nonsense, if unclear and disagreeing, even though naturally developed, reflective concepts and consequently equivocal and erroneous problems impede the understanding of actuality and the possibility of a rational attitude toward it, if a special but (for a large class of sciences) required methodical attitude becomes a matter of routine so that it is incapable of being transformed into other attitudes, and if depressing absurdities in the interpretation of the world are connected with such prejudices, then there is only one remedy for these and all similar evils: a scientific critique and in addition a radical science, rising from below, based on sure foundations, and progressing according to the most rigorous methods—the philosophical science for which we speak here. *Weltanschauungen* can engage in controversy; only science can decide, and its decision bears the stamp of eternity.

And so whatever be the direction the new transformation of philosophy may take, without question it must not give up its will to be rigorous science. Rather as theoretical science it must oppose itself to the practical aspiration toward *Weltanschauung* and quite consciously separate itself from this aspiration. For here all attempts at reconciliation must likewise be rejected. The proponents of the new *Weltanschauung* philosophy will perhaps object that to follow this philosophy need not mean letting go the idea of rigorous science. The right kind of *Weltanschauung* philosopher, they will say, will not only be scientific in laying his foundations, *i.e.,* using all the data of the rigorous particular sciences as solid building blocks, but he will also put into practice scientific method and will willingly seize upon every possibility of advancing philosophical problems in a rigorously scientific manner. But in contrast to the metaphysical irresolution and scepticism of the age just past, he will courageously pursue even the loftiest meta-

physical problems in order to achieve the goal of a *Weltanschauung* that, according to the situation of the time, harmoniously satisfies both intellect and feeling.

To the extent that this is intended as a reconciliation calculated to erase the line of demarcation between *Weltanschauung* philosophy and scientific philosophy, we must throw up our defense against it. It can only lead to a softening and weakening of the scientific impulse and to promoting a specious scientific literature destitute of intellectual honesty. There are no compromises here, no more here than in any other science. We could no longer hope for theoretical results if the *Weltanschauung* impulse were to become predominant and were to deceive even theoretical natures by its scientific forms. When over thousands of years the greatest scientific spirits, passionately dominated by the will to science, have achieved not a single fragment of pure doctrine in philosophy and have accomplished all the great things they have accomplished (even though imperfectly matured) only as a result of this will to science, the *Weltanschauung* philosophers will certainly not be able to think that they can merely by the way promote and definitively establish philosophical science. These men who set the goal in the finite, who want to have their system and want it soon enough to be able to live by it, are in no way called to this task. Here there is only one thing to do: *Weltanschauung* philosophy itself must in all honesty relinquish the claim to be a science, and thereby at the same time cease confusing minds and impeding the progress of scientific philosophy—which, after all, is certainly contrary to its intentions.

Let its ideal goal remain *Weltanschauung,* which above all is essentially not science. It must not allow itself to be led into error here by that scientific fanaticism only too widespread in our time that discredits all that is not to be demonstrated with "scientific exactitude" as "unscientific." Science is one value among other equally justified values. That in particular the value of *Weltanschauung* stands with utmost firmness on its own foundation, that it is to be judged as the habitus and accomplishment of the individual personality whereas science is to be judged as the collective accomplishment of generations of scholars, we have made quite clear above. And just as both have their distinct sources of value, so they also have their distinct functions, their distinct manners of working and teaching. Thus *Weltanschauung* philosophy teaches the way wisdom does: personality directs itself to personality. As a teacher in the style of such a philosophy, then, he alone may direct himself to a wider public who is called thereto because of a particularly significant character and characteristic wisdom—or he may be called as the servant of lofty practical interests, religious, ethical, legal, etc. Science, however, is impersonal. Its collaborator requires not wisdom but theoretical talent. What he contributes increases a treasure of eternal validities that must prove a blessing to humanity. And as we saw above, this is true to an extraordinarily high degree of philosophical science.

Only when the decisive separation of the one philosophy from the other has become a fact in the consciousness of the time is it proper to think of philosophy's adopting the form and language of genuine science and of its recognizing as an imperfection one of its much-praised and even imitated qualities, profundity. Profundity is a mark of the chaos that genuine science wants to transform into a cosmos, into a simple, completely clear, lucid order. Genuine science, so far as its real doctrine extends, knows no profundity. Every bit of completed science is a whole composed of "thought steps" each of which is immediately understood, and so not at all profound. Profundity is an affair of wisdom; conceptual distinctness and clarity is an affair of rigorous theory. To recast the conjectures of profundity into unequivocal rational forms—that is the essential process in constituting anew the rigorous sciences. The exact sciences, too, had their long periods of profundity, and just as they did in the struggles of the Renaissance, so too, in the present-day struggles, I dare to hope, will philosophy fight through from the level of profundity to that of scientific clarity. For that, however, it needs only a correct assurance regarding its goal and a great will directed with full consciousness toward this goal and a putting forth of all available sci-

entific energies. Our age is called an age of decadence. I cannot consider this complaint justified. You will scarcely find in history an age in which such a sum of working forces was set in motion and worked with such success. Perhaps we do not always approve the goals; we may also complain that in more tranquil epochs, when life passed more peacefully, flowers of the spirit's life grew whose like we cannot find or hope for in our age. And too, sometimes that which is so constantly desired in our age may repel the aesthetic sense, which finds so much more appeal in the naïve beauty of that which grows freely, just as extraordinary values are present in the sphere of the will only so long as great wills find the correct goals. It would mean doing our age a great injustice, however, if one wanted to impute to it the desire for what is inferior. He who is capable of awakening faith in, of inspiring understanding of and enthusiasm for the greatness of a goal, will easily find the forces that are applied to this goal. I mean, our age is according to its vocation a great age—only it suffers from the scepticism that has disintegrated the old, unclarified ideals. And for that very reason it suffers from the too negligible development and force of philosophy, which has not yet progressed enough, is not scientific enough to overcome sceptical negativism (which calls itself positivism) by means of true positivism. Our age wants to believe only in "realities." Now, its strongest reality is science, and thus what our age most needs is philosophical science.

If, however, in specifying the sense of our age we apply ourselves to this great goal, we must also make clear to ourselves that we can achieve it in only one way, which is to say, if with the radicalism belonging to the essence of genuine philosophical science we accept nothing given in advance, allow nothing traditional to pass as a beginning, nor ourselves to be dazzled by any names however great, but rather seek to attain the beginnings in a free dedication to the problems themselves and to the demands stemming from them.

Of course, we need history too. Not, it is true, as the historian does, in order to lose ourselves in the developmental relations in which the great philosophies have grown up, but in order to let the philosophies themselves, in accord with their spiritual content, work on us as an inspiration. In fact, out of these historical philosophies there flows to us philosophical life—if we understand how to peer into them, to penetrate to the soul of their words and theories —philosophical life with all the wealth and strength of living motivations. But it is not through philosophies that we become philosophers. Remaining immersed in the historical, forcing oneself to work therein in historico-critical activity, and wanting to attain philosophical science by means of eclectic elaboration or anachronistic renaissance —all that leads to nothing but hopeless efforts. The impulse to research must proceed not from philosophies but from things and from the problems connected with them. Philosophy, however, is essentially a science of true beginnings, or origins, of *rizōmata panton*. The science concerned with what is radical must from every point of view be radical itself in its procedure. Above all it must not rest until it has attained its own absolutely clear beginnings, *i.e.,* its absolutely clear problems, the methods preindicated in the proper sense of these problems, and the most basic field of work wherein things are given with absolute clarity. But one must in no instance abandon one's radical lack of prejudice, prematurely identifying, so to speak, such "things" with empirical "facts." To do this is to stand like a blind man before ideas, which are, after all, to such a great extent absolutely given in immediate intuition. We are too subject to the prejudices that still come from the Renaissance. To one truly without prejudice it is immaterial whether a certainty comes to us from Kant or Thomas Aquinas, from Darwin or Aristotle, from Helmholtz or Paracelsus. What is needed is not the insistence that one see with his own eyes; rather it is that he not explain away under the pressure of prejudice what has been seen. Because in the most impressive of the modern sciences, the mathematico-physical, that which is exteriorly the largest part of their work, results from indirect methods, we are only too inclined to overestimate indirect methods and to misunderstand the value of direct comprehensions. However, to the extent that philosophy goes back to ultimate origins, it belongs precisely to its very essence that its scienific work move in spheres of direct intuition. Thus the greatest step our age has to make is to recognize that with the philosophical intuition in the correct sense, the phenomenological grasp of essences, a limitless field of work opens out, a science that without all indirectly symbolical and mathematical methods, without the apparatus of premises and conclusions, still attains a plenitude of the most rigorous and, for all further philosophy, decisive cognitions.

NOTES

1. Obviously I am not thinking here of the philosophico-mathematical and scientific-philosophical controversies that, when closely examined, do involve not merely isolated points in the subject matter but the very "sense" of the entire scientific accomplishment of the disciplines in question. These controversies can and must remain distinct from the disciplines themselves, and in this way they are, in fact, a matter of indifference to the majority of those who pursue these disciplines. Perhaps the word 'philosophy', in connection with the titles of all sciences, signifies a genus of investigation that in a certain sense gives to them all a new dimension and thereby a final perfection. At the same time, however, the word 'dimension' indicates something else: rigorous science is still rigorous science, doctrinal content remains doctrinal content, even when the transition to this new dimension has not been achieved.

2. Cf. my *Logical Investigations*, vol. I (1900). [Nos. 25–29.—Tr.]

3. Cf. in this connection Wundt, *Logic*, II (2nd ed.), 170.

4. It should be noted that this medium of phenomenality, wherein the observation and thought of natural science constantly moves, is not treated as a scientific theme by the latter. It is the new sciences, psychology (to which belongs a good portion of physiology) and phenomenology, that are concerned with this theme.

5. The *Logische Untersuchungen*, which in their fragments of a systematic phenomenology for the first time employ essence analysis in the sense here characterized, have again and again been misunderstood as attempts to rehabilitate the method of introspection. Admittedly, part of the blame for this lies in the defective characterization of the method in the Introduction

to the first investigation of the second volume, the designation of phenomenology as descriptive psychology. The necessary clarifications have already been brought out in my third "Bericht über deutsche Schriften zur Logik in den Jahren 1895–99," *Archiv für systematische Philosophie* 9 (1903): 397–400. [In *Ideen II*, pp. 313–14, Husserl explained in detail why phenomenology cannot be a "descriptive psychology." Even a "pure" psychology is only a preliminary step toward a transcendental phenomenology. — Tr.]

6. The definiteness with which I express myself in an epoch when phenomenology is at best a title for specializations, for quite useful detail work in the sphere of introspection, rather than the systematic fundamental science of philosophy, the port of entry to a genuine metaphysics of nature, of spirit, of ideas, has its background throughout in the unceasing investigations of many years, upon whose progressive results my philosophical lectures in Göttingen since 1901 have been built. In view of the intimate functional connection of all phenomenological levels and consequently of the investigations related to them, and in view of the extraordinary difficulty the development of the pure methodology itself brings with it, I did not consider it advantageous to publish isolated results that are still problematical. In the not too distant future I hope to be able to present the wider public with researches in phenomenology and in phenomenological critique of reason that have in the meantime been confirmed on all sides and have turned into comprehensive systematic unities.

7. Not the least considerable reason for the progress of this sort of literature is the fact that the opinion according to which psychology—and obviously "exact" psychology—is the foundation of scientific philosophy has become a firm axiom at least among the groups of natural scientists in the philosophical faculties. These groups, succumbing to the pressure of the natural scientists, are very zealous in their efforts to give one chair of philosophy after another to scholars who in their own fields are perhaps outstanding but who have no more inner sympathy for philosophy than, let us say, chemists or physicists.

8. By chance, as I write this article, there has come into my hands the excellent study by Dr. M. Geiger (Munich), "On the Essence and Meaning of Empathy," *Bericht über den IV. Kongress für experimentelle Psy-*

chologie in Innsbruck (Leipzig, 1911). In a very instructive manner the author strives to distinguish the genuine psychological problems that in previous efforts at a description and theory of empathy have partly come clearly to light and have partly been obscurely confused with each other, and he discusses what has been attempted and accomplished with a view to their solution. As can be seen in the account of the discussion (p. 66), his efforts were not well received by the gathering. Amid loud applause Miss Martin says: "When I came here, I expected to hear something about experiments in the field of empathy. But what have I actually heard? Nothing but old—very old—theories. Not a word about experiments in this field. *This is not philosophical society.* It seemed to me that it is high time for anyone who wants to introduce such theories here to show whether they have been confirmed by experiments. In the field of aesthetics such experiments have been made, *e.g.,* Stratton's experiments on the aesthetic significance of ocular movements. There are also my own investigations on this theory of inner perception." Further, Marbe "sees the significance of the theory regarding empathy in the impulse it gives to experimental investigations, such as have, in fact, already been conducted in this field. The method employed by the proponents of the empathy theory is in many ways related to the experimentally psychological method in the way the method of the pre-Socratics is related to that of modern natural science." To these facts I have nothing to add.

9. Cf. W. Dilthey *et al., Weltanschauung, Philosophie und Religion in Darstellungen* (Berlin: Reichel and Co., 1911).

10. In the first volume of my *Logical Investigations.*

11. Dilthey too (op. cit.) rejects historic scepticism. I do not understand, however, how he thinks that from his so instructive analysis of the structure and typology of *Weltanschauungen* he has obtained decisive arguments against scepticism. For as has been explained in the text, a humanistic science that is at the same time empirical can argue neither for nor against anything laying claim to objective validity. The question changes —and that seems to be the inner movement of his thought—when the empirical point of view, directed as it is toward empirical understanding, is replaced by the phenomenological essential point of view.

Introduction to
The Dilthey-Husserl Correspondence
WALTER BIEMEL
TRANSLATED BY JEFFNER ALLEN*

The period from 1900 to 1910 may be considered as the time in which phenomenology matured. With his *Logical Investigations* (1900–01), Husserl laid the foundation for phenomenology, found his own way, and broke with his previous investigations, which were still caught in psychologism. The decisive step, after the *Logical Investigations,* was taken by extending phenomenological analyses from the purely logical domain to all objectivity in general. Thus, in the "Zeitvorlesungen" (1904–05), Husserl first thematically investigated the constitution of time. How important these investigations must have appeared to Husserl himself may already be gathered from the fact that he had Heidegger edit them in 1928, even

*Translator's note: "Der Briefwechsel Dilthey-Husserl" first appeared in the *Revista de Filosofía de la Universidad de Costa Rica* (San José) 1 (1957): 101–24 (introduction and notes in Spanish text only; correspondence in German and Spanish text). The entire German text of the article appears in *Man and World* 1 (1968): 428–46.

I would like to thank the following for granting permission to publish this translation: Professors Elmar Bund, executor of Husserl's estate; Walter Biemel; Rafael Herra, editor of the *Revista de Filosofía de la Universidad de Costa Rica;* and Joseph J. Kockelmans, co-editor of *Man and World.* I would also like to thank Professors Keith Hoeller and Joseph J. Kockelmans for their many helpful comments and suggestions on the translation. In addition, I am grateful to the Husserl Archives for their help with this project.

though he had formerly taken a very critical view toward his earlier works.[1]

The next decisive step took place in Husserl's "Dingvorlesung," a four-hour lecture course that was given in 1907. (The five introductory lectures to the course have been published as *The Idea of Phenomenology, Husserliana* 2.) The significance of the "Dingvorlesung," to which Husserl also expressly refers in his personal notes from this period,[2] is twofold: here Husserl explains, for the first time in a lecture, the idea of the reduction which—although it was certainly to be more fully developed—was to remain decisive until the end of his life. In the reduction, he discovered the methodological way to uncover the essence of intentional consciousness and thereby changed his viewpoint. No longer accepting the naive straight-forward attitude which focuses on what is immediately given, he rather upheld the validity of our reflection on consciousness and its functions, through which the objects are presented *as* objects. By bracketing the world, it is certainly not annihilated; rather, it is merely disregarded and gazed upon, which makes it possible for it to be presented. The other factor that this lecture distinguishes in the development of phenomenology is that here Husserl seeks, for the first time, to comprehend the constitution of the thing, that is, of a spatially extended object in consciousness. As Husserl already explained in a letter to Hocking in 1902, by "constitution" one should certainly not understand something like a creating and producing, but rather the becoming-present of the object. From his personal notes from this period, it is evident that Husserl wrestled with these questions and underwent a crisis in which he sought more clearly to comprehend his goal.[3]

During this period, Husserl made the acquaintance of Dilthey, concerning which, unfortunately, little has been known until now. In his *Phänomenologische Psychologie: Vorlesungen, Sommersemester, 1925* (*Husserliana* 9: 34) (*Phenomenological Psychology*, p. 24), Husserl says:

Dilthey himself initiated this relationship; for, unfortunately, under the influence of Ebbinghaus' brilliant rebuttal,[4] I had thought it unnecessary to read Dilthey's great work, especially since, in those years, I was not at all receptive to the significance of Dilthey's writings. In my inner struggle for a fundamental overcoming of positivism, I had to repel the strong tendency toward positivism, which had been prominent in Dilthey's previous work, the *Einleitung in die Geisteswissenschaften.* At first I was quite surprised to hear personally from Dilthey that phenomenology, and especially the descriptive analyses of the specifically phenomenological second part of the *Logical Investigations,* were essentially in harmony with his *Ideen*[5] and were to be viewed as a first foundation for an actual realization, using a matured method, of the psychology that he thought was ideal. Dilthey always conceded that this concurrence between our investigations, despite our fundamentally different points of departure, was of the greatest importance and, in his old age, he renewed, with a truly youthful enthusiasm, his once abandoned investigations on the theory of the human sciences. The result was the last and most beautiful of his writings on this subject, although, unfortunately, he passed away while preparing it: "Der Aufbau der geschichtlichen Welt" (1910), in the *Abhandlungen der Berliner Akademie.*

Although Husserl, in his lecture course during the summer of 1925, clearly sets forth Dilthey's significance for the transformation of psychology and the human sciences, his article, "Philosophy as Rigorous Science,"[6] published in the journal *Logos,* nevertheless contains a critique of Dilthey or, at least, statements that could be understood as such. Consequently, this article was the occasion for the following correspondence, which seems important to us, not so much as a personal exchange of views, but rather as a discussion between both thinkers, in which their respective conceptions of the essence of philosophy come to light.

We shall briefly set forth the major points of the *Logos* article:

Husserl's guiding thought is that philosophy, since its beginning, has claimed to be rigorous science, but has been unable to fulfill this claim. Phenomenology must finally bring philosophy to the point where it becomes rigorous science. In order to reach this goal, to clearly set forth the special character of the phenomenological method of research, and, above all, to explain its necessity, Husserl distinguishes it from two tendencies which, from his point of view, were dominant around the turn of the century: naturalism on the one hand, and *Weltanschauung* philosophy on the other. The latter is determined, according to Husserl's interpretation, "as a result of the transformation of Hegel's metaphysical philosophy of history into a sceptical historicism" (p. 293; see p. 168 above). The *Logos* article may be viewed as phenomenology's manifesto, as it is often characterized by the overstatements typical of a manifesto. For a manifesto is supposed to make apparent to everyone its author's inherent right to his own philosophy; consequently, it must emphasize not what the author shares with other people, but rather what distinguishes him from them.

Husserl wages a war on two fronts: against naturalism on the one side, and against historicism on the other. What does "naturalist" mean in Husserl's language? "The naturalist . . . sees nothing but nature and, above all, physical nature. Everything that is is either itself physical, belonging to the unified totality of physical nature, or it is indeed psychical, in which case it is simply a variable that is dependent on the physical. . . . All being belongs to psychophysical nature, which is unequivocally determined according to fixed laws" (p. 294; see p. 169 above). And, to continue, "What characterizes all forms of extreme and consistent naturalism, from popular materialism to the most recent forms of sensation-monism and energetism, is on the one hand, the *natural-*

ization of consciousness, including all intentionally immanent data of consciousness and, on the other hand, the *naturalization of ideas,* and consequently, of all absolute ideals and norms" (p. 294f.; see p. 169 above). Husserl then points out how the naturalist contradicts, in his behavior and in his theorizing, precisely the conception which he himself requires. "He is . . . an idealist who sets up and supposedly establishes theories which deny precisely what he presupposes in his idealistic behavior, whether it be in constructing theories or in establishing and recommending values or practical norms as the most beautiful and the best. Namely, he makes presuppositions insofar as he theorizes at all, insofar as he objectively sets up values to which value judgments are to correspond . . . " (p. 295; see pp. 169–70 above).

After this refutation of principles, Husserl enters into a detailed discussion of the naturalization of consciousness, such as it occurs in experimental psychology. He next shows how the difficulties and enigmas immanent in natural science cannot be resolved by it, since this would signify its placing itself in question, which it is incapable of doing; this would signify its jumping over its own shadow.

To the natural science of consciousness Husserl opposes the new science, the phenomenology of consciousness, which has nothing to do with empirical consciousness, but only with *pure* consciousness. This science of consciousness makes apparent those close relationships which exist between psychology, when it is correctly understood, and philosophy. Husserl remains loyal to this idea until the end of his life. For in the *Crisis* he will still refer to the approach from psychology as a way into transcendental phenomenology. At the close of his critique of the concept of naturalistic consciousness, Husserl develops, in his *Logos* article, his phenomenological interpretation and conception of consciousness and that which it contains in itself, from his basic concept of phenomenon to his decisive method of the seeing of essences. "The critical separation of the psychological and phenomenological methods shows that the latter is the true way to a scientific theory of reason and, likewise,

to an adequate psychology" (p. 322; see p. 185 above).

But what are Husserl's objections to historicism and to *Weltanschauung* philosophy? Husserl maintains that such a philosophical orientation tries to comprehend what is typically spiritual in its structure, and seeks to understand the development of its own forms.

With regard to such philosophies, there thus arises the great task of thoroughly examining their morphological structure and typology, as well as their developmental connections, and of making historically understandable the spiritual motivations that determine their essence, by reliving them from within. That there are significant and, in fact, admirable things to be accomplished from this point of view is shown by W. Dilthey's writings, especially by his most recently published essay on the types of *Weltanschauung* (p. 323f.; see p. 186 above).

Thus if Husserl attacks Dilthey, he does so because he thinks that the seed for a relativism lies precisely in these structural-morphological analyses. He cites from Dilthey's essay on the types of *Weltanschauung* a passage to which he repeatedly refers in the correspondence:

The theory of evolution . . . is necessarily associated with the recognition of the relativity of the historical form of life. The absolute validity of any one particular form of conception of life, religion or philosophy, vanishes before the view that encompasses the earth and all past times. Thus the development of the historical consciousness destroys—even more completely than does our survey of the conflict between systems—our belief in the universal validity of any one of the philosophies which have undertaken to conclusively express the world's coherency by using an interconnection of concepts (p. 6).

Husserl rebels against this interpretation. He will indeed grant that there is a coming and going of cultural formations—among which he also includes the *Weltanschauungen*—but not that there is such for what he calls rigorous science. Husserl opposes factual truth to fundamental truth. The former is relative, for it is bound up with the historical periods in which it is accepted and considered to be true and correct; in contrast, fundamental truth must not be bound up with anything factual, not even with any factual-historical development. It is true whether or not it is thought and consequently carried out. According to Husserl, historicism tends to dissolve every truth into factual truth and, accordingly, to deny a universally valid truth.

The ideas of truth, theory, and science would then, [that is, if the historicistic standpoint were correct] like all ideas, lose their absolute validity. That an idea has validity would mean that it is a factual formation of the spirit which is held to be valid and which, in this factual validity, determines thinking. There would not be any absolute validity, or validity "in itself," which is what it is even if no one has achieved it and though no historical mankind will ever achieve it (p. 325; see pp. 186–87 above).

With reference to this objection, the difference between Dilthey and Husserl's starting points must be considered. Husserl proceeds from the validity of logical formations which, in his opinion, are ahistorical; in contrast, Dilthey's point of departure arises from works of art and spiritual formations, which can only be conceived of as having arisen historically, as belonging to a specific epoch by virtue of a particular style—namely, as manifestations of life through which life itself is understood.

Since Husserl does not have a historical view—at least, not in this period—he also believes that the diversity of systems may simply be explained by pointing out what, in the previous systems, was "distorted": whether the system operated with confused concepts, whether those concepts had brought about conceptual confusion, or whether false conclusions had caused some confusion. On the other hand, Dilthey has to reject this view, for it originates in a misunderstanding of what is properly historical.

Basically, the opposition between Dilthey and Husserl's conceptions of the essence of philosophy lies in their different attitudes toward history. While for Dilthey, history is essentially the place in which the spirit develops, in which it actualizes its self-understanding, for Husserl, in this period, history is rather the place in which the idea only obscurely comes to appearance, and therefore must be purified through the seeing of essences, which abstracts from everything that is historically factual. However, here we are not attempting to comment extensively on, or even to bridge over, this opposition—which also appears, in another manner, in their different conceptions of metaphysics; rather, the fruitful conversation between the two philosophers who have undoubtedly been decisive for the philosophy of our century can speak from the correspondence itself. For in spite of everything that separates them, they nevertheless have in common the desire to save the essence of philosophy from the domination of the sciences. Certainly, the title of Husserl's *Logos* article is confusing if we do not consider what "science" means here and what the type of "rigor" is that is required of philosophy—a rigor through which the sciences are surpassed in such a way that they shall only receive their genuine foundation by means of philosophy.

In conclusion, we would like to express our most cordial thanks to Professor Gerhart Husserl, as well as to Professor Fr. H. L. Van Breda, Director of the Husserl Archives, for having granted permission for the publication of this unknown correspondence, by means of which we are immediately placed within the great events of philosophy at the beginning of our century.

EDITOR'S NOTES

1. The entire collection of the manuscripts on time was first made accessible by Rudolf Boehm in *Zur Phänomenologie des inneren Zeitbewusstseins (1893–1917)* (*Husserliana* 10), (The Hague: Nijhoff, 1966).
2. Edmund Husserl, "Persönliche Aufzeichnungen," *Philosophy and Phenomenological Research*, vol. 16, no. 3 (March 1956).
3. See also Walter Biemel's article, "Die entschei-

denden Phasen der Entfaltung von Husserl's Philosophie," *Zeitschrift für Philosophische Forschung*, vol. 13, no. 2; English translation: "The Decisive Phases in the Development of Husserl's Philosophy" in *The Phenomenology of Husserl: Selected Critical Readings*, ed. R. O. Elveton (Chicago: Quadrangle Books, 1970). And concerning the problematic of the reduction see in particular *Erste Philosophie* II (*Husserliana* 8).
4. Hermann Ebbinghaus' rebuttal appeared in

the *Zeitschrift für Psychologie und Physiologie der Sin-nesorgane* (October 1895).

5. *Ideen über eine beschreibende und zergliedernde Psychologie,* 1894.

6. In *Logos,* vol. 1, no. 3 (Tübingen: Mohr [Siebeck], 1910–11). At the time when this was written, Husserl noted the following: "Sketched out during the beginning or middle of the Christmas holidays, 1910–1911, worked out from January to February, 1911, and printed around the beginning of March." Husserl's copy, on which these remarks are found, is in the possession of the Husserl Archives, Louvain. *Philosophie als Strenge Wissenschaft,* has recently been edited by Wilhelm Szilasi (Frankfurt: Vittorio Klostermann, 1965). See translation "Philosophy as Rigorous Science" on pp. 166–97 above.

11

The Dilthey-Husserl Correspondence

EDITED BY WALTER BIEMEL

TRANSLATED BY JEFFNER ALLEN

Letter from Wilhelm Dilthey
to Edmund Husserl

June 29, 1911

Dear Colleague,

I do not want my brief essay on Niebuhr, which arose from a recent lecture at the Academy, to appear without finally giving you my opinion on your article in *Logos*.

Frankly, it was difficult for me to form an immediate opinion, for your characterization of my standpoint as historicism, whose legitimate consequence would be scepticism, could not but surprise me. A great part of my life's work has been dedicated to formulating a universally valid science which should provide the human sciences with a firm foundation and a unified internal coherency. This was the original conception of my life's task, as it was presented in the first volume of the *Geisteswissenschaften*.[1] We agree that there is, in general, a universally valid theory of knowledge. We also agree that the way into such a theory can only be carved out through investigations that clarify the sense of the terms which, first of all, are needed for such a theory and, moreover, are necessary for all areas of philosophy. But then our ways part with respect to any further development of the structure of philosophy. It seems impossible to me that there could be a metaphysics which would attempt to conclusively express

the world's coherency by using an interconnection of concepts ("Typen," p. 6).[2]

This standpoint can hardly be characterized as historicism, if I correctly understand your definition of this word (p. 323; see p. 186 above).[3] And if, according to the general use of the term, the sceptic denies the possibility of knowledge in general, I cannot possibly be considered as a sceptic or as having any relation whatsoever to scepticism. I merely adhere to the movement which, since the second half of the eighteenth century, has continued to negate metaphysics, as understood in the sense given above.

Moreover, in keeping with my relation to this movement, it does not seem fair to form, from a few sentences in the "Introduction" to my "Typen," an interpretation of my standpoint, according to which scepticism would be its intentional or unintentional consequence. After all, in the statement concerning the relativity of our *Weltanschauungen,* I only sought to bring to light the significance of the problem of their truth content in order to arouse the reader's interest.

I am not blameless in this misunderstanding. The article in my book on the *Weltanschauung* was partly a condensation, and partly an expansion, of a manuscript on the theory of the *Weltanschauung,* from which I gave a lecture at the Academy many years ago. Due to the limited time allotted me, I had to limit myself precisely to the first half of the lecture, and I was rather happy to be able to retain the second half in order to further reflect upon it. Since I found it unnecessary at that time to mention this in the collection of my individual articles, there could easily arise the view that seems to lie at the basis of my position (*Logos*, p. 326, note; see p. 187 above),[4] as though the published text already contained the foundation for relativism and for the higher view that is to overcome it. Then, simultaneously with the publication of the text, I agreed with the publisher that, in the near future, I would separately edit the entire "Weltanschauungslehre."

But the meaning of those sentences is clarified in the brief outline of my theory of the *Weltanschauung,* which is set forth according to its position in the whole of philosophy, as is shown in my treatise on the essence of philosophy (*Kultur der Gegenwart, Systematische Philosophie,* p. 37ff.).[5] And I have also made reference to this treatise in my "Typen" (p. 28). From this treatise, it is quite clear that my standpoint does not lead to scepticism; it excludes your interpretation of my statements, for there, in order to prove the impossibility of a universally valid metaphysics, I refer to "the arguments developed since Voltaire, Hume and Kant."[6] I did not arrive at this conclusion (pp. 60–61)[7] from the previous failure of metaphysics, but rather from the general relation between its tasks and our means of solution. In the treatise, I also made use of the outcome of my analysis of value and purpose. There both the conflict between systems and the previous failure of metaphysics appear only as the historical facts which have brought philosophical thinking to the dissolution of metaphysics, and not as the proof for its impossibility. That is to be sought in the very essence of metaphysics itself.[8] And the statement (p. 6)[9] that forms the basis for its arguments totally agrees with this interpretation. Its cursory nature is explained by its preparatory character. There I define the metaphysical systems about which I spoke there, by saying "that they have undertaken to conclusively express the world's coherency by using an interconnection of concepts." I subordinate such systems, which contain a religious or metaphysical *Weltanschauung,* to the historical "forms of life," to which con-

stitutions and religions also belong. Such forms have a special relation to life, one that is different from that of the universally valid sciences: a relation which, in the lecture at the Academy, is explained by the position of establishing values and goal-setting in the *Weltanschauung.* Finally, I maintain that these forms of life—when one adds to them our understanding of the development of spirit—prove to be relative. In consequence, these references to the cursory "Introduction" point to a systematic investigation that is historically grounded, that makes use of the entire interconnection of my philosophical thoughts, and that should also bring to a higher conception the solution to the problem that relativism poses for us (see my treatise, "Das Wesen der Philosophie," p. 61).[10]

According to this, I am neither an intuitionist, nor a historicist, nor a sceptic, and I myself even suggest that your article's argumentation (pp. 324–328) does not prove that the consequence of the quoted statements ("Typen," p. 6) leads to scepticism.

From this you conclude (pp. 324–25; see pp. 186–87 above) that not only the *Weltanschauung,* but also rigorous science, is historically conditioned and subject to changes; that one must totally separate historical relativity from validity: for if that historical relativity of the sciences were to annul their validity, the very idea of knowledge itself would lose its validity, so that even the statement that such an idea does not have any validity could not even be maintained. I am in complete agreement with this. Likewise, I maintain, of course, that every statement concerning the domain of the *Weltanschauung* (for example, a religious one) may be examined with regard to its validity just as thoroughly as a scientific one. It is precisely on matters such as these that the work of clarification focuses. Likewise, I subscribe to what you then say from p. 325 (the mathematician, etc.), until the end of the paragraph.[11] For all of that is really contained within the standpoint of my laying of my own foundation.

But when (from p. 325: "But if we have," etc.)[12] you then deduce, from the universal validity of the idea of knowledge, the possibility of supposing that there is a "valid religion or art," and where you find it possible that between such a valid religion and historical religion there is the relation of the idea and its murky form of appearance, there I certainly believe that the method—which, in the context of the foundation of my philosophical thoughts that I have set forth, utilizes the historical analysis of the *Weltanschauung*, religion, art, metaphysics, development of the human spirit, etc.—can show the impossibility of such concepts and can solve the question of the truth content of the *Weltanschauung*.

And what if it could not solve this problem? Then it would follow that even the question of the possibility of a metaphysics, in the sense that I have defined, would have to remain open until a decision could be reached. But how is it possible that, on the basis of such an insight into the temporarily undecided state of the question, someone like yourself (p. 326; see p. 187 above) could draw the conclusion that a scepticism is contained in my standpoint?

Nor do I understand your line of reasoning (from p. 326 to p. 327; see pp. 187–88 above).[13] I, too, really do not consider the instance against metaphysics, on the basis of its previous failure, to be decisive. And, moreover, what should really demonstrate the impossibility of metaphysics is not historical empiricism, but rather the "formation of our historical consciousness," an ongoing systematic investigation that takes place by a human-scientific analysis. . . . I will stop with this, since I only wanted to clarify my standpoint. As I already mentioned earlier, I hope to be able to deliver the other half of the "Weltanschauungslehre" in the foreseeable future. It amplifies considerably what I have said in my treatise on philosophy.

And so you see that we are really not as far apart from each other as you suppose: we are allies in some highly debated issues. And, provided that I live that long, among the older colleagues you will not have any more unbiased reader for your new work than I. It is better to rejoice in such collaboration than to submit our friendly relationship to such strong tests as your polemic in *Logos*.

Faithfully yours,
Wilhelm Dilthey

Edmund Husserl's Reply to Dilthey's Letter of June 29

(The letter is dated July 5/6, 1911. The copy that was in the possession of Husserl's daughter is preserved in the Husserl Archives, Louvain. Unfortunately, the first page of the letter is missing and the text begins in the middle of a sentence.)

. . . as I think I have gathered from your friendly lines, [I have] also grasped the essentials of your real point of view.

Thank you, most honorable privy councillor, for all of your apt comments, which are esteemed and valued by me as decisive and penetrating expressions of your spirit. But you must absolutely convince yourself that the presupposition from which you proceed is incorrect: namely, your belief that my arguments were directed against you. Also, I will immediately publish a note in *Logos* in order to avoid any further misunderstandings.[14]

Now I would like to refer to your attempt to point out, on the basis of the all too few suggestions in my article, the boundaries within which our philosophical views agree and in which they differ.

All things considered, I would much prefer not to acknowledge these boundaries, and it truly seems to me that there are no serious differences whatsoever between us. I think a lengthy conversation would lead to our complete agreement. All objective validity, including even that of religion, art, etc., refers to ideal, and thus to absolute ("absolute" in a certain sense) principles, to an a priori which, as such, is thus in no way limited by anthropological-historical facticities. The sense of the corresponding mode of objective validity reaches just as far as this a priori, whose total clarification from the ontological and specifically phenomenological viewpoint constitutes our great task. But this in no way excludes certain sorts of relativity. Thus, the entire sphere of corporeal nature is—a priori—a sphere of relativities. Corporeal being is being in a connection of infinite relativities. But insofar as it is "being," and consequently, the correlate of empirical validity, it stands under ideal laws, and these laws delimit the sense of this being (*i.e.*, the sense of the truth of the natural sciences), as something that is relative in principle and, nevertheless, identical in its relationships. All objective validity in what is a posteriori has its principles in the a priori. Analogously, a religion may be "true religion," and its "truth" a "merely relative" one—namely, with reference to a "mankind" that lives in relation to a "nature," that is found in a certain stage of development, etc. In this case, truth depends on the content of your presuppositions, which must be grasped ideally—(the *idea* of a determinate "mankind" with certain specific characteristics, the *idea* of a "nature" having a certain character, the *idea* of individual or social motivations that are to be characterized in a specific manner, etc.). If we were to think of the presuppositions as being altered in their essential content, then either another religion, or no religion at all, would be the "true" one. Thus, the truth of a religion would be something relative and yet, like all truth, an ideal, namely, referring to relations which, by means of their essential content, determine principles a priori as the conditions for the possibility of *such* truth at all.

The task of a phenomenological theory of nature is to submit the consciousness that is constitutive of nature to an eidetic investigation with regard to all of its structures and correlations, to the extent that all the principles under which being (in the sense of nature) is a priori, are finally clarified, and all the problems which, in this sphere, concern the correlations between being and consciousness can be resolved. In *exactly the same manner*, the task of a theory of religion (phenomenology of religion), with reference to possible religion as such, would be to examine the consciousness that is constitutive of religion in a suitable manner. (That is, "possible" religion understood in a way similar to Kant's "possible nature," whose essence is explained by pure natural science.) So the phenomenological theory of religion requires, or rather, *is* for the most part, exactly what *you* demand again and again: a return to the *inner life*, to the "life forms" which first come to be genuinely understood in the reliving [*Nacherleben*] of our inner motivations. Such reliving and understanding is the concrete intuitive consciousness from which we should and can bring forth religion as an ideal unity, from which we respectively clarify and show by well-founded proofs the differences between supposedly and actually valid religion and the corresponding essential relations. Historical facticity thereby serves as an example when we are directed toward what is *purely* ideal. However, if we judge the historical fact itself with respect to its validity, we will find: *this* factual religious behavior is the correct one because, *as such,* on ideal grounds, a religious behavior, when its motivational content is of a *certain character* and is related to valid "presuppositions" of a *certain character,* is valid, is justified.

I do not think that the convictions that guide me here, and the goals which I specifically assign to a phenomenological philosophy of culture, really diverge from what is required by you, most honorable privy councillor, nor do I think that any fundamental differences really separate us. But it also seems to me that what you attack as metaphysics is not the same as what I accept and promote under the same name.[15]

July 5/6

Every science of existence [*Daseinswissenschaft*], for example, the science of physical nature, or science of the human spirit, etc., turns *eo ipso* into metaphysics (according to my concept), insofar as it is related to the phenomenological doctrine of essences and undergoes, from its origins, a final clarification of sense, and thus a final determination of its truth content. The truth which is thus expounded, for example, the truth in natural science, regardless of how limited and relative it may be from another point of view, is ultimately a component of "metaphysical" truth, and its knowledge is metaphysical knowledge, namely, ultimate knowledge of existence [*Dasein*]. The idea that a metaphysics in this sense is necessary in principle—vis-à-vis the natural and human sciences which have arisen from the great labor of modern times—has its origin in the fact that a stratification is rooted in the essence of knowledge and that, connected with it, there is a two-fold epistemic attitude: on the one hand, the attitude can be purely directed toward being, which is consciously intended and which is thereby thought and given in appearance; but on the other hand, the attitude can be directed to the enigmatic essential relations between being and consciousness. All natural knowledge of existence, all knowledge within the first attitude, leaves open an area of problems on whose solution depends the ultimate definitive determination of the sense of being and the ultimate evaluation of the truth that has already been reached in the "natural" (first) attitude. I believe I can see that there can be no other meaningful problems behind the ultimate ones, namely, the "constitution" of being in consciousness, along with the related problems of being; that, therefore, no other science can lie behind the phenomenologically expanded and founded (universal) science of existence (which, in its work, includes *all* the natural sciences of existence); or rather, that it is nonsense to speak of a *fundamentally* unknowable being that still lies beyond these ultimates. This excludes every Kantian "metaphysics" of the thing-in-itself, as well as every ontological metaphysics that is extracted from a system of pure concepts that forms a science of existence, à la Spinoza. — In all of this, don't we really mean the same thing? When you speak of an analysis that pertains to the human sciences (an analysis by which you might lead up to the proof of the impossibility of metaphysics), this coincides, to a great extent, with what I — limited and formed only by certain methodological viewpoints — consider to be phenomenological analysis. And naturally, the impossibility of a metaphysic — namely, in that especially false ontological sense — can only be evidenced by such "analyses pertaining to the human sciences."

What we are seeking and investigating — although we arise from different studies, are determined by different historical motives, and have gone through different developments — fits together and belongs together: elementary phenomenological analysis and phenomenological analysis as a whole, along with the morphology and types of the great cultural structures which you have uncovered.[16]

• • •

Wilhelm Dilthey's Reply to Husserl's Letter of July 5/6

July 10, 1911

Dear Friend,

Thank you very much for your pleasant and detailed letter, and for clearing up my misunderstanding. You may, above all, be assured that your cordial remarks will never lead me to falsely evaluate the relation between my life's work and your fresh endeavor. I admire your genius for philosophical analysis. From your comments, I am happy to surmise that my work has been of some use to you. I am glad that you feel as do I — I who belonged to a time in which some courage was needed to wage a common war, from various sides, against the domination of the natural sciences over philosophy — that we agree in regard to the effort needed to reach a universally valid foundation for the sciences of the real, in opposition to constructive metaphysics, and against every assumption that an in-itself lies behind the reality that is given to us. Our difference, as I indicated in my previous letter, may remain in force until I receive from you more detailed publications which, I only hope, will not arrive too late for me. I have recently been actively occupied time and again with the explanations in your letter; but, dear friend, you do not know, and it is natural that you do not know, how difficult it is, even after your explanations, to penetrate into a world of such very different thoughts.

I gratefully accept your intention to write a note in the next issue of *Logos,* in order to rectify the misunderstanding that your arguments concerning historicism might be directed against me. For the misunderstanding is not merely my own; it is shared by various noteworthy parties. Perhaps my work on the structure of the human sciences will give you access [to my ideas] in a natural and unobtrusive way inasmuch as my orientation towards a universally valid foundation for the human sciences and towards a presentation of the objectivity of historical knowledge so clearly stands out in it.

I have received with genuine interest the news concerning your present situation.[17] When consulted by Tübingen, I immediately gave them your name and, of course, since at first I only vaguely knew of your desire to go there, I gave your name along with that of other possible candidates. As soon as I heard further of your intention to leave, I explained to Tübingen that they had only one choice, that of doing whatever might be necessary in order to get you. However, this prospect disappeared several weeks ago. Un-fortunately, the Kaiser-Wilhelm-Gesellschaft is limited, at least for now, to the natural sciences. But certainly . . . another prospect will soon open up which will allow you to leave a situation which has suddenly become so unpleasant for you.

Faithfully yours,
Wilhelm Dilthey

EDITOR'S NOTES

1. *Einleitung in die Geisteswissenschaften: Versuch einer Grundlegung für das Studium der Gesellschaft und der Geschichte,* 1883 (Stuttgart: Teubner, 1959).

2. "Die Typen der Weltanschauung," in *Weltanschauung,* selected texts (Berlin, 1911).

3. He refers to the following definition, which Husserl gives to historicism: "Historicism takes its position in the factual sphere of the empirical life of the spirit and, since it posits such a life absolutely, without exactly naturalizing it . . . there arises a relativism that has a close affinity to psychologism and that is entangled in similar sceptical difficulties" (p. 323; see p. 185 above).

4. Dilthey refers to the following note in the *Logos* article: "Elsewhere Dilthey also rejects historical scepticism; but I do not understand how he thinks that he has gained any decisive ground *against* scepticism by means of his very instructive analysis of the structure and typology of *Weltanschauungen.* For as has been pointed out in the text, a human science that is nevertheless empirical cannot argue either *for* or against something that lays claim to objective validity. The matter changes—and that seems to be the inner movement of his thought—when the empirical attitude, which gives rise to an empirical understanding, is replaced by the phenomenological, eidetic point of view" (p. 326; see p. 197, n. 11 above).

5. *Kultur der Gegenwart,* part 1, section 6, *Systematische Philosophie* (Berlin and Leipzig: Teubner, 1907). Dilthey's first contribution is found here: "Das Wesen der Philosophie." This treatise is divided into two parts:

A. The Historical Procedure for Determining the Essence of Philosophy.

B. The Essence of Philosophy Understood from Its Position in the Spiritual World.

Part B has the following subdivisions:

I. Classification of the Function of Philosophy in Relation to Psychic Life, Society and History.

II. Theory of the *Weltanschauung.* Religion and Poetry in Their Relations to Philosophy.

III. The Philosophical *Weltanschauung.* The Attempt to Raise the *Weltanschauung* to Universal Validity.

IV. Philosophy and Science.

V. The Concept of the Essence of Philosophy. A Survey of Its History and Its Systematic Ideas.

In his letter Dilthey refers to p. 37ff., where section 2, "Theory of the *Weltanschauung* . . . ," begins.

6. He is quoting "Das Wesen der Philosophie," p. 60. In context the quote reads: "Metaphysics must rise above the reflections of the understanding in order to find its own object and its own method. The attempts to achieve this in the sphere of metaphysics have been examined, and their insufficiency has been shown. We shall not repeat here the arguments developed since Voltaire, Hume and Kant, and which explain the constant change of metaphysical systems and their inability to satisfy the demands of science."

7. The decisive passage reads: "Knowledge of reality according to causal relationships, experience of value, significance and meaning, and behavior guided by the will . . . these are the various modes of behavior which are united in our psychic structure. . . . The subject comports itself towards objects in these various ways; one cannot go back behind this fact to a reason for it. Thus, the categories of being, cause, value, and purpose, in keeping with their origin from these modes of behavior, can neither be reduced to one another nor to a higher principle. We can only comprehend the world under one of the fundamental categories. We can never perceive, as it were, more than one side of our relation to it—never our whole relation, such as it would be determined by the interconnection of these categories. This is the first reason for the impossibility of metaphysics: If metaphysics wants to be successful, it must either always use sophisms to bring these categories into an internal coherency, or it must distort the contents of our actual behavior. A further limit of conceptual thinking appears within each of these modes of behavior. We cannot think back to any final cause as something unconditioned in the conditioned relationship of events: For the ordering of a multiplicity, whose elements are uniformly related to one another, remains an enigma, and neither change nor plurality can be conceived of as arising from the immutable One . . ." ("Das Wesen der Philosophie," pp. 60–61).

8. In addition, the following passage may be cited: "Philosophy is incapable of grasping the world in its essence by means of a metaphysical system and of demonstrating the universal validity of this knowledge; but just as in every serious poem there opens up an aspect of life such as has never been seen before, as in its ever new works poetry discloses to us the various sides of life, as we do not possess in any work of art the

total view of life and nevertheless all of us, through works of art, approximate this total view: so in the typical *Weltanschauungen* of philosophy, one world confronts us as it appears when a powerful philosophical personality makes one of the modes of behavior toward the world dominant over the others, and its categories dominant over the other categories. Thus, of the enormous work of the metaphysical spirit, there remains the historical consciousness, which repeats this work in itself, and thereby experiences in it the unfathomable depths of the world. The final word of the spirit, which has passed through all *Weltanschauungen,* is not the relativity of each *Weltanschauung,* but rather the sovereignty of the spirit over against every single one of them and, at the same time, the positive consciousness of how in the various modes of the spirit's behavior there is for us the one reality of the world, and the permanent types of *Weltanschauung* are the expression of the many faces of the world" ("Das Wesen der Philosophie," pp. 61–62).

9. This is a reference to "Die Typen der Weltanschauung," which Husserl cited.

10. He is referring to "Das Wesen der Philosophie," see note 11.

11. The text to which Dilthey is referring reads: "Certainly the mathematician will not turn to history in order to be taught about the truth of mathematical theories; it will not occur to him to relate the theoretical development of mathematical representations and propositions to the question of truth. Accordingly, how shall it be the historian's task to decide as to the truth of given philosophical systems and, especially, as to the possibility of a philosophical science that is valid in itself? And what would he really have to add that could make the philosopher uncertain with respect to his belief in his idea, the idea of a *true* philosophy? Whoever denies a specific system, and even more, whoever denies the ideal possibility of a philosophical system as such, must advance reasons. Historical facts of development, even the most general facts concerning the manner of development proper to systems as such, may be reasons, good reasons. However, historical reasons can only produce historical consequences. The desire either to prove or to refute ideas on the basis of facts is nonsense—as Kant said: *ex pumice aquam*" (*Logos,* p. 325f.; see p. 187 above).

12. The passage in the *Logos* article, to which Dilthey alludes, reads: "But if we have admitted science as a valid idea, what reason would we still have not to consider similar differences between what is historically worthwhile and what is historically valid as at least an open possibility—whether or not we can understand this idea in the light of a "critique of reason"? History, empirical human science in general, can of itself decide nothing, either in a positive or a negative sense, as to whether a distinction is to be made between religion as a cultural formation and religion as an idea, namely as valid religion, between art as a cultural formation and valid art, between historical and valid law, and finally, between historical and valid philosophy; it cannot decide whether or not there exists between one and the other, to speak Platonically, the relation between the idea and its murky form of appearance" (p. 325; see p. 187 above).

13. The passage to which Dilthey is referring reads: "Accordingly, just as history cannot advance anything relevant against the possibility of absolute validity in general, it cannot advance anything in particular against the possibility of an absolute (that is, scientific) metaphysics, or any other philosophy. As history, it can in no way prove even the assertion that *as yet* there has not been any scientific philosophy; it can only prove this on the basis of other sources of knowledge, and they are clearly philosophical sources. For it is clear that even philosophical criticism, insofar as it is actually to lay claim to validity, is philosophy and its sense implies the ideal possibility of a systematic philosophy as rigorous science. The *unconditional* assertion that every scientific philosophy is a chimera, based on the argument that the alleged efforts of millennia make probable the intrinsic impossibility of such a philosophy, is therefore erroneous not only because to draw a conclusion regarding an unlimited future from a few millennia of higher culture would not be a good induction, but rather would be erroneous as an absolute absurdity, like 2 × 2 = 5. And this may be said to be the case for the following reason: If there is something whose objective validity can be refuted by philosophical criticism, then there is also a field within which something can be established as objectively valid. If problems have been demonstrably posed "incorrectly," then it must be possible to rectify this and accurately pose them. If criticism shows that philosophy, which has developed historically, has operated with confused concepts, and has used mixed concepts and false conclusions, then, if one does not wish to fall into nonsense, that very fact makes it undeniable that, ideally speaking, the concepts can be illustrated, clarified, and distinguished, and that accurate conclusions can be drawn in any given field. Every correct, deeply penetrating criticism itself already provides the means for progressing and ideally points to correct goals and ways and, in so doing, to an objectively valid science. Naturally, to all of this it must be added that the historical untenability of a spiritual formation as a matter of fact has absolutely nothing to do with its untenability in the sense of validity; and this applies to everything that has been discussed so far, and to all spheres whatsoever where validity is claimed" (p. 326f.; see pp. 187–88 above).

14. Since Dilthey died on October 1, 1911, Husserl did not go ahead with his planned publication of the "note."

15. At this place there is a greater break in the copy; at the beginning of the continuation there is the date, July 5/6. Husserl notes, in regard to this matter: "I do not know why the copy has a gap here or why the date is in this place."

16. At this place, the copy ends. Husserl noted this in the copy preserved in the Archives.

17. This news must have been found in the part of the letter which was not preserved. In fact, that is probably why Husserl did not keep this part of the letter.

PART FOUR

Husserl on Space and Time

One of the several persistent difficulties many contemporary philosophers have in dealing sympathetically with Husserl's phenomenology is developing a close critical knowledge of nonprogrammatic texts such as the materials presented in Part One and Part Three of this collection. The difficulty when left at the general level comes to the query whether there is anything more to Husserl's work than talk about what phenomenology may or may not be, anything more, in short, than a too-lengthy series of "introductions to phenomenology" which only rarely get beyond the programmatic into the practice of philosophical reflection itself.

Much of Husserl's finest analytic work, of course, is available in the two volumes of the *Logical Investigations*. But in a shorter compass, without going into the as-yet unpublished material which provides compendious examples of Husserl actually doing phenomenology instead of just talking about it, not a great deal is available. This section hence tries to meet the need for examples of detailed work in phenomenology by providing two sets of texts, the first on space and the second, and more important, on time.

The materials on space are of two kinds. To begin with, an extended example of Husserl's so-called "meditations," or daily reflections, is provided, his "Foundational Investigations of the Phenomenological Origins of the Spatiality of Nature," together with a lengthy and comprehensive introduction which attempts to indicate clearly the major areas of philosophic interest in what is necessarily a fragmentary text. A second example of this first kind of tenuous, probing, and incomplete texts is "The World of the Living Present." A second kind, a more finished piece, is offered in which Husserl discusses in a much more synthetic way several aspects of his later reflections on geometry.

The materials on time, on the other hand, are somewhat more homogeneous. A selection from Husserl's lectures on internal time-consciousness is provided first as an example of the earlier material on this central theme in Husserl's philosophy, and then an important section on perceptual problems with time is selected from the much later materials gathered together in Husserl's posthumous work *Experience and Judgment*. The major texts from the intervening decades are not as yet published although several volumes on time-consciousness are in preparation by the editors of the *Husserliana* series. The two texts here stand roughly at the beginning and at the end of those protracted reflections.

Some philosophers who know Husserl's work thoroughly believe that Husserl presented not just a program for philosophy but also, in the materials on space and especially in those on time, one of the finest examples of his own philosophical practice. The materials here are only a short sample of that extensive work.

It is important, however, for the proper understanding of these materials on space and time not to overlook their dependence, in great measure although not completely, on Husserl's continuing reflections on both logic and science.

As for logic, we need to recall that, in *Formal and Transcendental Logic* above all, Husserl proposed a multiple inquiry into the philosophy of logic. Beginning with a pure logical grammar which would separate the meaningful from the meaningless in possible assertions or propositions, Husserl moved on to a pure logic of noncontradiction which deals with the distinction between analytic consistency and analytic contradiction in possible assertions or propositions. And he arrived at a pure logic of truth which is concerned with formal law as governing only the use of the predicates "true" and "false" in actual assertions or judgments. In order to deal with the question of a pure form for all deductive theories, however, Husserl added finally a theory of forms of all the various possible forms of theories, what he called a *Mannigfaltigkeitslehre*. At such a level Husserl tried to keep open several options. For the inquirer is to retain the choice, Husserl thinks, of adopting a formal attitude, or of turning to ontologies in considering logical objectivities, or of adopting the phenomenological inquiry into how consciousness presents such objectivities.

Two questions, then, which these texts on space and time open up for us are just how and to what degree the extended development of Husserl's analyses of space and time represent different options in the further reflection on his philosophy of logic. And, of course, similar questions arise as to Husserl's further reflections on his philosophy of science and his philosophy of mathematics.

When taken together, despite the very important differences which this set of materials exhibits, the texts detail for us nevertheless an impressive series of philosophical investigations which here and there can be set alongside some of the magisterial sections in both the *Logical Investigations* and the later volumes of *Ideen*.

12

Introduction[1]

FRED KERSTEN

Under the title of "Foundational Investigations of the Phenomenological Origin of the Spatiality of Nature," part of an unfinished manuscript by Edmund Husserl was published as a supplement to *Essays in Memory of Edmund Husserl*, edited by Marvin Farber in 1940.[2] In this same year the rest of the manuscript was edited and published by Alfred Schutz in the first volume of *Philosophy and Phenomenological Research* under the title of "Notizen zur Raumkonstitution" ("Notes on Space Constitution").[3] Presumably it was Alfred Schutz who edited the supplement in the Farber volume, and one may likewise presume that his "Editor's Preface" in *Philosophy and Phenomenological Research* also applies to the manuscript translated there.

This manuscript is a good example of Husserl's daily work, his *"Meditationen"* as he called them, which, as Dorion Cairns reported, Husserl would only interrupt when the desire came over him to write a book.[4] When that happened, he would shove aside his daily work and write like "someone in a trance . . . he would write a page and put it to one side on his desk, another page and put it to the side on his desk, without numbering any of these pages. He would just throw them aside and leave to himself or his assistant the later task of going through them to find the order of the pages for the book he had finished. . . . His daily work, however, which was thus interrupted, consisted in daily meditations. . . . And he said once: 'When I go back to what I have written in an earlier meditation, I always go

back to that which is most obscure to me and I wrestle with that problem. I never go on and leave a problem unsolved and that is why I shall never write a philosophy. My work is not that of building but of digging, of digging in that which is most obscure and of uncovering problems that have not been seen or if seen have not been solved'."[5] Husserl's "meditations" are, accordingly, basic to an understanding of his phenomenology. And in 1939 Cairns had already called attention to the fact that, "according to those in a position to know, the bulk of Husserl's philosophy lies not in his published works but in his literary remains,"[6] in the mountain of manuscripts making up his daily "meditations."

While many of those manuscripts have since been published,[7] the task of understanding and appreciating them nonetheless remains a difficult one. The manuscript translated here is no exception not only because of the often tentative, unfinished nature of the "digging into that which is most obscure," but also because Husserl himself published very little of an extended and systematic nature on space constitution. As a result, there are relatively few public expressions of his views about space against which his "meditations" can be adequately measured in order to formulate his considered opinion. Indeed, almost all of Husserl's discussions of space constitution must be drawn from his daily "meditations."[8]

How then should one initially approach such a "meditation"?

In his "Editor's Preface" to the "Notes on

Space Constitution," Alfred Schutz observes that, on the one hand, such manuscripts "reflect the ecstasy of discovery, the freshness and the originality of a first look into realms as yet unknown, the rapture of the creative spirit . . . the superabundance of ideas, and the adventure of catching the thought in transition. On the other hand, the thought is not yet organized; the problems are intermingled . . . the language is aphoristic and obscure with odds and ends of meaning substituted for detailed cross-references. *These manuscripts of Husserl should not be considered as papers, not even as rough drafts of future literary works, but rather as a philosophical diary, a scrapbook of his thought."*[9] For better or worse, it is in this "scrapbook of thought" that we must look for Husserl's views about space constitution. And therein lies the danger, for as Schutz also notes, many passages of the manuscript "could provoke enormous misunderstandings of Husserl's general conception of philosophy among those who are beginners in phenomenological research or especially among those who never studied Husserl's chief works." In particular Schutz observes that one of the "most serious misinterpretations of Husserl's attempt at an analysis of space . . . would be the supposition that this philosopher ever had the intention of substituting constructions of a primitive speculation for the accomplishments of modern science and mathematics, which he knew as thoroughly as anyone."[10]

But Schutz also perceives a significant positive side to this fragment of Husserl's work in progress when he characterizes it with Beethoven's words, *"quasi una fantasia,"* and asks: "But where is the friend of music who would not be delighted to have a true record of an improvisation of Beethoven, played by him, offhand, in the seclusion of his workshop?" In the case of Husserl, at least, we are more fortunate in having such an "improvisation, played by him, offhand," in the seclusion of his study. To be sure, in an English translation not all of the "improvisation" can be expressed; not everything "offhand" can be left as it is. Occasionally, one's own "cadenzas" must be added along with key signatures and transitions. Nevertheless, within the strictures of a translation

every attempt has been made to preserve the original character of Husserl's daily "meditation" on space.

Space was not only an important philosophical problem in its own right on which Husserl ceaselessly worked during his lifetime, but its phenomenological investigation was paradigmatic, for instance, for formulating the investigations into the "origin" of the constituting of "internal time" within the framework of the transcendental phenomenological reduction;[11] and it was fundamental for developing the investigation into the transcendental phenomenology of reason at the end of the first volume of the *Ideen.*[12] The substance of the large number of manuscripts on space constitution can be seen now in their posthumous publication in *Husserliana,*[13] many of which were reviewed by Ulrich Claesges in his *Edmund Husserls Theorie der Raumkonstitution* (1964).[14] It is curious, however, that Claesges does not refer to the manuscript translated here, nor to its continuation in *Philosophy and Phenomenological Research.* In addition, his book is confined for the most part to discussion of daily "meditations" and lectures written before and shortly after the First World War. Husserl's views on space in the 1920s were developed by his Freiburg student Oskar Becker in a doctoral dissertation published in 1923.[15]

Becker's study was, and still is, valuable not only because it worked out Husserl's views about space constitution in terms of the transcendental reduction, but also because it went a long way toward carrying out the critique of scientific cognition of space in physics and mathematics up to that time by disclosing the various "prescientific" substrata of importance for constituting the spatiotemporal form of the real, objective world of concern to physics and mathematics. Concluding that the spatiotemporal forms of those substrata are neither "Euclidean" nor "non-Euclidean," that is, that they of necessity entail no specific systemforms of Euclidean geometry (below, pp. 228–29), Becker's discussion is concerned more particularly with examining the various substrata of *visual* "prespace" and of "schematic" (or "phantom") quasi-space—

the former proving to be a two-dimensional manifold founding the three-dimensional manifold of the latter.[16] This result, and the "transcendental deduction" adduced to demonstrate it (which can only be described as a phenomenological *tour de force*), still does not encompass Husserl's later position when writing the manuscript translated here.

The reason for this is that by 1934 Husserl had already enlarged and deepened not only the transcendental setting within which he located the problems relating to the constituting of the spatial aspect of the real, objective world. In addition he had refashioned and radicalized his critique of scientific cognition. That is to say, by 1929 Husserl had already prepared much of what would later (1931) be published as *Méditations cartésiennes,* in which he introduced a transcendental monadology whose space-time has its "origin" in "primordial 'Nature'," and in which the "genetic problems of birth and death" as well as the "psychological origin" of the "idea of space" are grasped in their proper sense "by means of a change of the natural into the transcendental attitude . . . open to a 'Copernican conversion'" so that they have a place "within a transcendental 'metaphysics'."[17] Moreover, in 1929 Husserl published his *Formale und transzendentale Logik* in which he sought to achieve the "*original grounding of all the sciences,* and of the formal ontologies . . . exercising in their behalf the function of a theory of science, the normative function," which "*gives all of them unity,* as branches of a constituted production from the one transcendental subjectivity,"[18] so that there is only "one philosophy, one actual and genuine science" which comprises a "formal ontology" in the sense of the "form," "allness of realities, with the allness-'forms', space and time. . . ."[19] And, finally, almost a year to the day after writing the manuscript translated here Husserl would begin his last work, *Die Krisis der europäischen Wissenschaften,* in which a historical form of modern science, which makes a certain idea of space go bail for the "allness of reality," is subjected to a critique that explicates the space-time of the "life-world" as the "source" of science in the "Galilean style."[20]

If we thus try to anchor the "Foundational Investigations into the Origin of the Spatiality of Nature" within the context of the whole of Husserl's thought, we can see that it both presupposes the advances in his thought begun in 1929 and looks forward to his last work. While it would be impossible here to trace all of the innovations, differences, and perhaps even regressions of Husserl's thought which our manuscript represents, it clearly goes beyond the systematic picture reported by Claesges and developed by Becker under Husserl's supervision. The task that now remains in this Introduction is to show the significance of Husserl's manuscript for his later view of space constitution in the light of his thought after 1929.

In a note on the envelope containing the manuscript of "Foundational Investigations," Husserl refers to Nature as Nature in the "first sense," that is, as Nature conceived by the natural sciences, "posited as infinite" in acts of scientific thinking. He contrasts this sense of Nature with another and *second* sense of Nature as the "original ark, earth." Investigating this second sense of Nature in the part of the manuscript translated here, Husserl concludes that its transcendental phenomenological investigation as much supports the "Copernican" as it does the "non-Copernican" interpretation of Nature in the first sense (below, pp. 228–29). This assertion presupposes that the investigation leading to this conclusion has been set into a certain framework which may be formulated as follows:

All *de facto* natural sciences assume as a matter of course that the spatiotemporal Nature encountered in prescientific life exists (below, pp. 223–24). Thus a foundational investigation into Nature as determined (or interpreted) and further determinable by "Copernican" or "non-Copernican" scientific thinking therefore involves an investigation of Nature encountered in daily life as a "product" of prescientific thinking and experiencing—Nature in the sense of the "original ark, earth." In other words, the task of a foundational investigation is to recover a sense which Nature has regardless of the sense or senses it acquires or can acquire from "Copernican" or "non-Copernican" scientific thinking.[21] This is the case, more particularly, with respect to the *spatial form* of Nature in the second sense. Thus a foundational investigation into space as determined and further determinable by "Copernican" or "non-Copernican" scientific thinking also involves an inquiry into space purely as "product" of prescientific thinking and experiencing.[22] It is this latter investigation that is the subject matter of the manuscript translated here (as well as its continuation in *Philosophy and Phenomenological Research*).

Husserl also states that his investigation is to be a "transcendental" one and, at the end of the manuscript (below, p. 231), he sharply distinguishes it from a (phenomenological) psychological investigation which, while referring back to the transcendental one, cannot be immediately "converted" into a transcendental investigation.[23] That is to say, in the psychological phenomenological attitude my own mental living (or "Ego") is in fact presented as having a sense which it can only have as a consequence of its basic characteristic of experiencing the "original ark, earth," and things in, on, and over it; in this attitude, my mental living is found as going on in that of which it apperceives itself as a nonself-sufficient component. But that also signifies that my mental living is that *for* which Nature and things are and must be so that my mental living can necessarily and "correctly apperceive itself as a component of Nature" (below, p. 230). My mental living, then, is not only in and part of Nature, but also and equally of Nature— no matter how it has been or is interpreted by natural scientific thinking. When, now, I make explicit this "status" of my mental living as that for which Nature is, as an actual living awareness or consciousness of Nature, then I have adopted the *transcendental* phenomenological attitude. My theme in this further and transcendental attitude is the sense that my mental living is presented as having: "believing in itself as a process in Nature, perhaps even if nothing else in Nature exists" (below, p. 231). Equivalently stated: I refrain from accepting the sense, "original ark, earth," of which my mental living apperceives itself as a nonself-sufficient component. *But this refraining, in consequence of which is disclosed the transcendental "status" of my own mental living, as*

that for which the world is, is still not a refraining from believing in or accepting the transcendental "status" of my mental living as actual.

Precisely because these two refrainings are *not equivalent* it is impossible to proceed from, or, as Husserl says, "convert" the psychological attitude into the transcendental one.

This nonequivalence of the two refrainings is presupposed by Husserl in casting his "meditation" into the framework of the transcendental phenomenological attitude to investigate Nature, the "original ark, earth," regardless of how it has been or is interpreted or determined and posited as infinite in acts of scientific thinking. And this case not only determines the meaning that must be attached to his statements; it determines as well the specific nature of the problem he sets himself to resolve, namely the constitution of *"space" as a transcendentally "reduced" phenomenon.*

At the beginning of the manuscript Husserl notes that "confirmation of the new 'idea of world', in the derivative sense" of world—that is, "world" as "product" of prescientific thinking and experiencing "has its first support and core in my perceptual field" in which my own percipient organism is the central body among other bodies in the field and in which they are presented as at rest or in motion relative to Here (below, p. 224). "Of necessity," Husserl continues, "a motion is relative when experienced with respect to a 'basis-body' experienced as at rest" and which is identified as "my corporeal animate organism." My own percipient organism, copresented as at rest or in motion, however, is "relatively at rest and relatively in motion with reference to the earth-basis which is not experienced as body." That signifies: I have exercised the transcendental epoche whereby I refrain, first, from positing the perceptually and apperceptually constituted "earth" on which I and all other sorts of animate organisms find ourselves as having a locus in the real space of the real, objective world; and, second, correlatively from positing my sensory-perceptual fields constituted in "apperceptive transfers"[24] as having a locus in the real space of the real, objective world where the fields are located as on the surface of or inside this real physical thing, my percipient organism.

This correlative refraining, however, in no way implies that "earth" on the one hand and my sensory-perceptual fields on the other hand are therefore not transcendent to my experiencing. That is to say, it does not entail refraining from positing "earth" and perceptual fields as having their *own inherent spatial* (and temporal) *spreadoutness*.[25] So "reduced," and copresented with motion and rest from Here (below, pp. 225–26), the "earth" as "earth-basis" and my own animate percipient organism are constituted as "anomalies"[26] and not as bodies among other bodies in an infinite homogeneous space where any body can take the place of any other body: "earth" and "organism" are presented each with its own peculiar spreadoutness, with its own "place" that cannot be exchanged for any other "place"—there is no conceivable course of experience in which the Here of my own organism would be There.[27] To be sure, "space" is presented as that which surrounds the "earth," as a system of "possible terminations of motions of bodies (below, p. 225). While all bodies on the earth have their own particular loci in that system of places, the "earth" itself does not.

A good deal of the phenomenological clarification of the "space" peculiar to the "original ark, earth" hinges on the clarification of the "space" peculiar to the percipient organism. In turn, the "space" of the organism requires a clarification, ultimately, of the role played by the various kinaesthetic systems in space perception.[28] Here we can only indicate a small—but crucial—dimension of Husserl's analysis.

It is a phenomenological "truism" that one's percipient organism is always coperceived in the perceiving of something else. The perspectival appearances through which things are perceived are functionally dependent on coperceived states of motion and rest of one's own organism or its parts oriented in one way or another, under these or those aspects. The perspectival, one-sided appearances through which I see and touch the table vary in functional correlation with the motion of my organism when, for instance, I walk around the table or when I

turn my head from side to side, squinting my eyes. In turn, these coperceived states of the organism are themselves presented as dependent on various sensed kinaesthesias flowing in one manner or another. If there is flow in one manner, *e.g.,* locomotive kinaesthesia, then the organism is coperceived as in motion; if in another manner, then the organism is coperceived as at rest. Universally, Husserl seeks to establish the correlation not only between coperceived states of the organism and the various systems of kinaesthesias (*e.g.,* locomotor and cephalic kinaesthesias), but also between perspectival appearances of the organism dependent on actualization of those kinaesthesias, on the one hand, and, on the other hand, perspectival appearances of things other than the organism. Thus any account of the perceived world and its spatial aspect requires an account of the perceived or coperceived organism.[29] The various kinaesthesias are presented as subject to the will, hence kinaesthetic changes are presented as *immediately* actualizable (or nonactualizable); the correlative changes in appearances are presented as *mediately* actualizable (or nonactualizable). By virtue of actualizing this rather than that course of locomotive kinaesthesias, changes in appearance of the table are (mediately) effected such that the table appears here rather than there, the organism correlatively appears as in motion rather than as at rest.

Husserl's many studies of this quite complex perceptual situation concern the various functions, correlations, and dependencies of kinaesthesias at different levels of constituting the real, objective world.[30] And in each case that he studies Husserl seeks the limiting case of the functions, correlations, and dependencies by means of what he calls "setting kinaesthesias at zero"[31]—the perceptual situation where the patterns of kinaesthetic flows are "held still" or are "at zero" ("*Null- oder Stillkinaesthese*"), and where appearances of things persist just as they are such as when we jump on or off moving vehicles, or are carried by a vehicle of some sort. We can illustrate this with a brief example. Suppose that I "set at zero" *oculomotor* kinaesthesias. This means that I institute actually or in phantasy a course of kinaesthetic flows accompanied by the perceiving of my eyes as not moving in their sockets relative to my torso and not moving as they would if a course of kinaesthetic flows were going on accompanied by perceiving my organism as moved by, *e.g.*, my legs relative to my torso. At the same time, I disregard thematically (or "abstract from," Husserl says) the possibility of a "nonzeroed" course of "zeroed" kinaesthesias and every sort of change in appearances functionally dependent on a "nonzeroed" course of "zeroed" kinaesthesias along with every sort of change in appearances functionally dependent on "nonzeroed" kinaesthesias.[32]

The *purpose*, now, of so "setting at zero" oculomotoric kinaesthesias is to uncover the visual correlate belonging to the "zeroed" kinaesthesias and the inherent "spatial" spreadoutness of that correlate. There is, then, according to Husserl, to be discriminated an intrinsic spreadoutness in which "things" are "at rest" or in "motion" relative to the distinct "parts" of the visual spread on the one hand, and, on the other hand, an "experiencing" of an enduring spreadoutness whose "parts" may differ qualitatively but in which nothing can be "at rest" or "in motion."[33] Without developing Husserl's account further, and granting for the moment its extension to all cases of perceptual experience without exception, we can note that such limiting cases reveal an "intuition of space" more fundamental constitutively than that correlated with the coperceived rest and motion of the percipient animate organism. We shall return in a moment to the consequences of this account for Husserl's later view of space constitution. At this point in our discussion we can turn to the nature of the task Husserl has set himself in the manuscript translated here.

The phenomenological task of the "foundational investigations into the origin of the spatiality of Nature" is not only to make thematic the way of constitution of the correlative "anomalies" earth and animate organism in their own intrinsic "spatiality," *but also,* and of equal importance, *to demonstrate how, at higher levels of constitution, they acquire the "appearance"*[34] *of a body among other bodies, a "place" among other places and, in addition, how the constitu-*

tion of those "anomalies" plays a necessary and not accidental role in determining the spatiality (and temporality) *of Nature in the sense posited in acts of scientific thinking.* Nature in this first sense "presupposes" a "primordial constitution" of earth as basis and of animate organism which enters into the "secondarily constituted" Nature — Nature in the first sense — such that the latter is necessarily presented as a "horizon of being" which is "accessible from the primordial and discoverable in a particular order."[35]

The "origin of the spatiality of Nature" is to be found, then, in the basic features of the constitutive substrata of "earth as basis," as "original ark," and of "animate organism." And this is itself a radical departure from the prevailing "Copernican" conception of the world, because if what Husserl asserts is indeed the case, then the "origin" of spatiality lies not only in founding and more primitive layers of the constitution of Nature, but also in a constitutive level presupposed by motion and rest of bodies in space. In other words, the "origin" of the "perception of space" does not consist of the "perception of motion," but is rather constitutively presupposed by the latter. As a consequence, one "need not perpetrate the absurdity . . . of presupposing tacitly beforehand the naturalistic . . . conception of the world and . . . of then seeing human history . . . anthropologically and psychologically . . . as an obviously accidental event on the earth which might just as well have occurred on Venus or Mars" (below, p. 230). This conclusion brings us back to our discussion of Husserl's notion of kinaesthesias and motion and rest of the animate organism.

The results of Husserl's daily "meditations" on space in his later manuscripts may be restated in terms of those views about space in later modern philosophy and psychology with which he takes issue. Basically, he takes issue with the Kantian position which holds that only if space (and time) attach to things in relation to our sensibility can it be explained how it is possible to know a priori that whatever is presented to us must have the spatiotemporal determinations which are prescribed by natural scientific thinking. In other words, only if physical things give rise to "sensations" can their spatiotemporal properties appear as necessary and subject to the laws of geometry and kinematics. Two assumptions are at work in this view: first, that the propositions of geometry and kinematics will be true of intuited spatiotemporal properties of things; and, second, that space is that in which things are, and hence is basically—in the words of John Stuart Mill—"room for movement, which its German name, *Raum,* distinctly confirms." As a result, the propositions of geometry, which traditionally have been understood as rendering the intelligibility of space, are reducible to those of kinematics.

Thus fundamental to what we may call in shorthand terms the "Kantian" conception of space—and by extension, fundamental to the "Copernican" view formulated by Husserl —is the notion that the "sensation of motion" is basic to the "perception of space."[36] In terms of the transcendental phenomenological investigation of the origin of the spatiality of Nature, this signifies that indispensable to the constituting of the spatial aspect of Nature are the constitutively primitive substrata of the functional correlations between immediately actualizable kinaesthetic flows and mediately actualizable changes in the sensory-perceptual fields, and the founded correlations between changes in somatic states and the perspectival appearances "through" which perceived things are presented. *However, as shown by the analysis of kinaesthesias "set at zero," they are indispensable only because of a still more fundamental and primitively intrinsic "spatiality" or "spreadoutness" of what is neither in motion nor at rest and upon which the perception of the earth as earth-basis is built up.*[37] "But if this is the case, need we say with Galileo: *par si muove?*

And not on the contrary: it does not move? It is certainly not so that it moves in space, although it could move, but rather as we tried to show above: the earth is the ark which makes possible in the first place the sense of all motion and all rest as mode of motion. But its rest is not a mode of motion" (below, p. 230).

Thus if geometry and kinematics define space by rendering it intelligible, and if, as on the "Copernican" view, space defines the reality of Nature (hence it is Nature in the *first* sense), then it follows that geometry and kinematics define reality. It is this "Copernican" idea which Husserl challenges by seeking to show (below, p. 229) that what is taken for granted in scientific naïvety—even if it may seem amusing and may contradict all modern scientific thinking about what is real (below, p. 229)—does not find confirmation in a "foundational investigation into the origin of the spatiality of Nature." The definition of reality, hence the correct sense of a universal physical science of Nature, is found rather in "constituting subjectivity"[38] apperceiving itself as on the "original ark, earth" and as that for which the "original ark, earth" is in the first place.

There is much more to say by way of clarifying the originality and novelty of Husserl's later account of space constitution expressed in the manuscript translated here. Like so many other daily "meditations" of Husserl, this one also pushes toward the frontiers of phenomenology, perhaps even overreaching them. But by overreaching the frontiers, this "meditation," this *"quasi una fantasia,"* can only give rise to the many more and still unrecognized frontiers that "constitute" the ongoing course of the development of phenomenological philosophy.

NOTES

1. I wish to acknowledge here my indebtedness to Dr. Frederick Elliston both for his invitation to translate Husserl's manuscript and for his invaluable and thorough help in rendering Husserl's difficult text into English.

2. (Cambridge: Harvard University Press, 1940), pp. 307–25.

3. Edmund Husserl, "Notizen zur Raumkonstitution," ed. Alfred Schutz, *Philosophy and Phenomenological Research* 1 (1940): 23–27, 217–26.

4. Dorion Cairns, "My Own Life," in *Phenomenology: Continuation and Criticism. Essays in Memory of Dorion Cairns,* ed. F. Kersten and R. Zaner (The Hague: Nijhoff, 1973), p. 10.

5. Ibid.

6. Dorion Cairns, "Some Results of Husserl's In-

vestigations," *Journal of Philosophy* 36 (April 27, 1939): 236.

7. Edmund Husserl, *Gesammelte Werke (Husserliana)*, (The Hague: Nijhoff, 1950ff.)

8. Systematic attempts to do this are few; chief among them are Ulrich Claesges, *Edmund Husserls Theorie der Raumkonstitution* (The Hague: Nijhoff, 1964), perhaps the most thorough account to date; and Noel Mouloud, "Le principe spatial d'individuation: Fondement phénoménologique et signification géométrique," *Revue de Métaphysique et de Morale* 1 (January–March 1956): 53–73; and 3A (July–December 1956): 259–82. In my doctoral dissertation, "Husserl's Investigations Toward A Phenomenology of Space" (1964), I sought to develop Husserl's later view of space constitution, but without being able to consult the inedita.

9. Husserl, "Notizen zur Raumkonstitution," p. 21. Husserl usually wrote these "meditations" after his morning walk; in the afternoon at his desk he would write "what he had considered during the morning walk . . . a continued meditation, his pen in hand . . . The manuscripts so produced, therefore, contain the most important meditations of a passionate thinker as well as repetitions of ideas which the author himself had presented in a better and clearer manner elsewhere," *loc. cit.*

10. Ibid., p. 22. Alfred Schutz promised a study of the manuscript translated here and its continuation "in an early issue" of *PPR*, but so far as I know nothing exists of that study.

11. Edmund Husserl, "Vorlesungen zur Phänomenologie des inneren Zeitbewusstseins," ed. Martin Heidegger, *Jahrbuch für Philosophie und phänomenologische Forschung* 9 (1928): section 1.

12. Edmund Husserl, "Ideen zu einer reinen Phänomenologie und phänomenologischen Philosophie," I, *Jahrbuch für Philosophie und phänomenologische Forschung* 1 (1913): part 4, chapter 4.

13. Especially important are volume 16, *Ding und Raum. Vorlesungen 1907*, ed. Ulrich Glaesges (The Hague: Nijhoff, 1973) and volume 9, *Phänomenologische Psychologie. Vorlesungen Sommersemester 1925*, ed. Walter Biemel (The Hague: Nijhoff, 1962), sections 22ff.

14. See Claesges, *Edmund Husserls Theorie der Raumkonstitution*, p. 146 for a list of the manuscripts reviewed.

15. Oskar Becker, "Beiträge zur phänomenologischen Begründung der Geometrie und ihrer physikalischen Anwendungen," *Jahrbuch für Philosophie und phänomenologische Forschung* 6 (1923).

16. A similar account had already been worked out by Heinrich Hofmann in a dissertation under Husserl at Göttingen, "Untersuchungen über den Empfindungsbegriff," *Archiv für die gesamte Psychologie* 26 (1913): 52ff.

17. Edmund Husserl, *Méditations cartésiennes*, trans. Gabrielle Peiffer and Emmanuel Levinas (Paris: Colin, 1931); English translation: Edmund Husserl, *Cartesian Meditations*, trans. Dorion Cairns (The Hague: Nijhoff, 1960), pp. 139ff.

18. Edmund Husserl, "Formale und transzendentale Logik," *Jahrbuch für Philosophie und phänome-nologische Forschung* 10 (1929); English translation: Edmund Husserl, *Formal and Transcendental Logic*, trans. Dorion Cairns (The Hague: Nijhoff, 1969), section 103, p. 272.

19. Ibid., p. 271.

20. Indeed, the manuscript translated here bears many resemblances to others written in preparation for *Krisis*. See Edmund Husserl, *Die Krisis der europäischen Wissenschaften und die transzendentale Phänomenologie*, ed. Walter Biemel (The Hague: Nijhoff, 1954), pp. xiiif., and the first three supplements, pp. 349ff.

21. For this "philosophical epoche" see Husserl, *Ideen I*, section 18. In a marginal note, probably dating from the 1920s, Husserl notes that this "philosophical epoche" should not be confused with the phenomenological reduction; see the *Husserliana* edition of *Ideen I*, ed. Walter Biemel (The Hague: Nijhoff, 1950), p. 40, n. 1.

22. For the meaning of "thinking" and "experiencing" here see F. Kersten, "The Life-World Revisited," *Research in Phenomenology* 1 (1971): 54f.

23. See the parallel passage in *Cartesian Meditations*, section 61, pp. 144f.

24. See below, p. 224, and *Cartesian Meditations*, section 50.

25. In this manner the doctrine of so-called "hyletic data" is rejected precisely because "reducing" the fields of perception does not entail regarding them as not having their own inherent extension or spreadout-ness, as not being transcendent to the experiencing of them. Correlatively, there is no need to appeal to "animating intentions" required to yield "adumbrations" of extension and transcendence. It is just this which distinguishes Husserl's earlier and later views of "space perception."

26. Cf. below, p. 231. See also the discussion by Claesges, *Edmund Husserls Theorie der Raumkonstitution* p. 103ff., of similar ideas in manuscripts of Husserl dating from 1931.

27. See the parallel passage in *Cartesian Meditations*, section 55, p. 123.

28. For an outline of the systematic presentation of the role of the various kinaesthetic systems in space perception, see the manuscript of Husserl prepared by Edith Stein printed in *Ding und Raum*, pp. 322–36.

29. Cf. *Cartesian Meditations*, pp. 116f.

30. For a schematic presentation of these various levels of constitution see ibid., p. 145.

31. See Husserl, "Notizen zur Raumkonstitution," pp. 28f.; *Ding und Raum*, pp. 309ff.; and below, pp. 230f. The example of "setting at zero" oculomotor kinaesthesias is based on *Ding und Raum*, p. 328, and "Notizen zur Raumkonstitution," pp. 221, 224f.

32. Cf. *Ding und Raum*, pp. 309f., 329f., 371f.

33. See "Notizen zur Raumkonstitution," pp. 34f. and 35, note 7; and below, p. 224.

34. See below, pp. 227–28; and *Cartesian Meditations*, section 49, p. 107; section 58, pp. 133f.

35. *Cartesian Meditations*, p. 134.

36. To be sure, according to this view, the changes and nonchanges in the sensory-perceptual fields, the "sensations," are aspatial in contrast to the bodies, any bodies, in space posited as infinite in ("Copernican")

scientific thinking—a characteristic nineteenth-century assumption found, for instance, in Helmholtz, Lotze, and Bain and challenged only by the "nativism" of Hering and James.

37. This is what Husserl calls the "first level in itself," p. 000, of space constitution, regardless of the next higher level.

38. Below, p. 000. What Husserl means by this may be interpreted in the following way: If we use the terms "space" and "spatial" to include not only space as part of the spatiotemporal form of the real, objective Nature, but also what we called the "intrinsic spread-outness" at various constitutive levels, then this signifies that "constituting subjectivity," transcendental mental life, is not only temporal and intentive to spatiotemporal Nature; it is also aware of itself as temporal and apperceives itself as within the spatiotemporality of Nature (namely, as an "animate organism") at various levels of constitution. But one and the same "con-stituting subjectivity" constitutes itself as intrinsically temporal, as a "product" of the structure of "retentions" and "protentions" comprising the "consciousness of internal time"—a structure identical at each level of constitution (see *Cartesian Meditations*, p. 114). Thus at each level of constitution, "constituting subjectivity" is, we may say, spatiotemporalized with the identical structure of the "consciousness of internal time." If that is the case, Husserl asks, "do I not find then that my transcendental life and my psychic, my worldly life have, in each and every respect, a like content? How can it be understood that the 'ego' has constituted in himself the whole of what belongs to his own peculiar essence as, at the same time, 'his psyche,' psychophysically objectivated in connection with 'his' bodily organism and as thus woven into the spatial Nature constituted in him qua ego?" (*Formal and Transcendental Logic*, section 96)

FURTHER REFERENCES

Becker, Oskar. "Beiträge zur phänomenologischen Begründung der Geometrie und ihrer physikalischen Anwendungen." *Jahrbuch für Philosophie und phänomenologische Forschung* 6 (1923): 385–560.

Claesges, Ulrich. *Edmund Husserls Theorie der Raumkonstitution*. The Hague: Nijhoff, 1964.

Husserl, Edmund. *Ding und Raum. Vorlesungen 1907*, edited by Ulrich Claesges. The Hague: Nijhoff, 1973.

Husserl, Edmund. "Notizen zur Raumkonstitution," edited by Alfred Schutz. *Philosophy and Phenomenological Research* 1 (1940): 23–27, 217–26.

Husserl, Edmund. *Phänomenologische Psychologie. Vorlesungen Sommersemester 1925*, edited by Walter Biemel. The Hague: Nijhoff, 1962.

Mouloud, Noel. "Le principe spatial d'individuation: Fondement phénoménologique et signification géométrique." *Revue de Métaphysique et de Morale* 1 (January–March 1956): 53–73 and 3A (July–December 1956):259–82.

Ströker, Elisabeth. *Philosophische Untersuchungen zum Raum*. Frankfurt am Main: Klostermann, 1965.

Foundational Investigations of the Phenomenological Origin of the Spatiality of Nature*[1]

TRANSLATED BY FRED KERSTEN

Regardless of their many repetitions and corrections, the following pages are, in any case, foundational for a phenomenological *theory of the origin of spatiality, corporeality, Nature in the sense of the natural sciences,* and therefore for a *transcendental theory of natural scientific cognition.* Doubtless it remains open whether it might still be necessary to supplement them.

Distinction: the world in the openness of the surrounding world[2]—posited as infinite in acts of thinking. The sense of this infinity —"world existing in the ideality of infinity." What is the sense of this existence, of the existing infinite world? The openness is not given as perfectly conceived, as made objective, but as a horizon already implicitly formed. Territorial openness—knowing that I have finally arrived at the borders of Germany, then arriving at the French, Danish, etc. territories. I have not paced off and become acquainted with what lies in the horizon, but I know that others have become acquainted with a piece further on, then again others yet another piece—objectivation[3] of a synthesis of actual experiential fields which mediately produces the idea[4] of Germany, Germany within the boundaries of Europe,

and gives rise to an idea of Europe itself, etc.—ultimately of the earth. The idea of the earth comes about as a synthetic unity in a manner analogous to the way in which the experiential fields of a single person are unified in continuous and combined experience. Except that, analogously, I appropriate to myself the reports of others, their descriptions and ascertainments, and frame all-inclusive ideas. Explicitly the following distinctions must be drawn:

1. Making intuited the horizons of the ready-made "idea of the world," just as it is framed in apperceptive transfers, conceptual anticipations and projects;

2. the way the idea of the world is further constituted on the basis of an already-made idea of the world, *e.g.,* the surrounding world of the Negroes, or the Greeks, in contrast to the modern Copernican world of the natural sciences.

We Copernicans, we moderns say:

The earth is not the "whole of Nature"; it is one of the stars in the infinite world-space. The earth is a globe-shaped body, certainly not perceivable in its wholeness all at once and by one person; rather it is perceived in a primordial synthesis as a unity of mutually connected single experiences. Yet, it is a body! Although for us it is the experiential basis for all bodies in the experiential genesis of our idea of the world. This "basis" is not experienced at first as body but be-

*Translated and printed with permission of the publisher from M. Farber, ed., *Philosophical Essays in Memory of Edmund Husserl* (Cambridge: Harvard University Press, 1940), pp. 305–25.

comes a basis-body at higher levels of constitution of the world by virtue of experience, and that nullifies its original basis-form. It becomes the total-body: the vehicle of all bodies that, until now, could be fully (normally) experienced with empirical sufficiency on all sides as they are experienced provided that the stars are not to be regarded as bodies. But now the earth is a huge block on which smaller bodies exist and on the basis of which they also always have become, and could have become, for us by division into pieces or by separating them off from the whole.

If the earth gains constitutive acceptance[5] as body—and, on the other hand, the stars are apprehended as appearing in distance-appearances, only not as perfectly accessible bodies—then that includes the objectivations[6] of rest and motion which must be attributed to them. Motion occurs on or in the earth, away from it or off it. In conformity with its original idea, the earth does not move and does not rest; only in relation to it are motion and rest given as having their sense of motion and rest. But, subsequently, the earth "moves" or is at rest—and quite like the stars "move" or are at rest, and the earth as one star among the others. How do motion and rest acquire their rightful sense of being in the extended or refashioned "world view"? How do they acquire their evidence, the intuition that verifies their givenness as in motion or at rest?[7] It is certainly not apperceptive transfer but, as always, the rightful sense of motion and rest must be capable of being shown.[8]

Universally, the working out of the world view, the intuition of single bodies, the intuition of space, the intuition of time, the intuition of the causality of Nature: all these belong together.

Bodies moving in the original intuitional function of the earth as "basis," or bodies understood in originality,[9] actual or possible mobility and changeability. Bodies thrown into the air, or somehow or other in the process of moving, I know not to where—in relation to the earth as earth-basis. Bodies moveable in earth-space have a horizon of possible motion and if motion ends, experience nevertheless indicates in advance the possibility of further motion, perhaps si-

multaneously with the possibility of new causes of motion by a possible push, etc. Bodies exist actually in open possibilities which are realized in their actuality, in their motion, change (nonchange as a possible form of change). Bodies are in actual and possible motion and <there is> the possibility of always open possibility in actuality, in continuation, in change of direction, etc. Bodies are also "among" actual and possible bodies, and correlatively are actually or possibly experienced in their actual motions, changes, etc., in their actual "circumstances." Possibilities which, in advance, are a priori open; and, as existing possibilities, they can be intuitively presented, they have their intuitional demonstration. They have these as modes which belong to the being of bodies and the plurality of bodies.

The unity of a "world view" must confirm the world-possibility in all further fashioning of world-apperception—as *the* possibility and the universum of open possibilities which make up a fundamental composition of the world's actuality. The core of actual experience is ontically what is experienced of the world from this or that side; and it possibly already obtains as known actuality on the basis of the experiential synthesis in harmony. The core becomes as an experiential core of the world, a core of what is predesignated by the world and as an open range of possibilities: and this signifies a range of harmonious possibilities to be iteratively[10] continued. The world is constituted progressively and is finally—with respect to Nature as its abstractable component—constituted according to horizons in which something existent is constituted as actual in being-possibilities predesignated at any time; the world is predesignated and is subsequently conceptualized and expressed in judgments by ontology; the world-form is "taken into consideration" along with its being-possibilities. And all relatively determined, inductive predesignation moves within the world-form —induction which, in every case, is determined through expectation and in the course of actual experience, my own and communicative experience, as a consequence of actuality is shown to be confirmed or disconfirmed.

Inductively predesignated actual experience in the frame of actual possibilities harmoniously-synthetically penetrates the horizon and seizes upon a piece of the actually intuitive and, as confirmed being, world-field being offered; bodies at rest or in motion, in nonchangeableness or changeableness are furnished for me and perhaps for us in an actual communalization. But what results there is an aspect in which everything is still not decided, what, in view of the still horizoned possibilities, still determines sense for the fully constituted world. Obtaining here: rest is given as something decisive and absolute, and likewise motion: that is to say, they are so given at the first level in itself of constitution of the earth as basis.

But rest and motion cease to be absolute as soon as the earth becomes a world-body in the open plurality of surrounding bodies. Motion and rest necessarily become relative. And if this claim can be disputed, this dispute can only happen because the modern apperception of the world as world of infinite Copernican horizons has not become for us a world-apperception confirmed by virtue of a world view actually accomplished. ("Apperception" of the world, any apperception whatever, is acceptive consciousness with the sense of being, World, inclusive of levels of constitution.) Apperceptive transfer has taken place such that it remains but a reference for a confirmative intuition rather than actually being constructed at the end as demonstration.

How is a body properly determined in itself, and therefore to be thought as determinable; and how are its place, its temporal locus, its duration and figure as thus qualified identifiable and recognizable in it? All demonstration and all confirmation of the world-apperception progressively becomes fashioned and is progressively fashioned—as advancing apperceptive transfers in which "*the*" self-same world is furnished with sense at higher levels on the basis of already constituted Objectivity[11] and world; and the fully constituted world in its own peculiar firm style is further constituted—: all demonstration, I say, has its subjective departure-point and ultimate anchorage in the Ego who does the demonstrating.[12] The confirmation of the new "idea of the world," in the derivative sense of "world," has its

first support and core in my perceptual field and the oriented exhibiting of the segment of the world about my animate organism as the central body among the others—all of which are given with their own essential contents at rest or in motion, in change or nonchange. Already a certain relativity of rest and motion is fashioned here. Of necessity a motion is relative when experienced with respect to a "basis-body" experienced as at rest and in unity with my corporeal animate organism. The latter itself can be in motion moving itself, but can come to rest at any time and then be experienced as at rest. However the relative basis-body is, naturally, relatively at rest and relatively in motion with reference to the earth-basis which is not experienced as body—not actually, originally experienced. Consider the relative "basis-body": I can be in a moving vehicle which is then my basis-body; I can also be borne by a railway car, in which case my basis-body is first of all the body carrying me while moving, and for this, again, the basis-body is the railway car, etc. The vehicle is experienced as at rest. But when I look out the window I say that the railway car moves even though I see that the countryside is in motion. I know that I have climbed into the vehicle; I have seen such vehicles in motion with people in it. I know that they, like me, when I climb in, see the countryside in motion. I know the reversal of the ways of experiencing the rest and motion of the toy wagon from which I have so often jumped on and off. But all this is nonetheless directly related to the basis of all relative basis-bodies, to the earth-basis: in apperception I have implied all mediacies[13] and can return to them in harmonious confirmation.

Now, when I "conceive" the earth as a moved body I use a basis to which all experience of bodies, and hence all experience of continuing to be at rest and in motion, is related. I do so in order to be able to conceive, indeed, to conceive the earth at all, as a body in the original sense, *i.e.*, to acquire a possible intuition of the earth in which its possibility as being a body can be directly evident. What is to be emphasized here is that I can always go farther on my earth-basis and, in a certain way, always experience its "corporeal" being more fully. Its horizon consists of the fact that I go about on the earth-basis, and going from it and to everything on it I can always experience more. Similarly with other people who bodily go about on it and, in common with me, experience it with everything on and above it, and can come to an agreement about it. Piece by piece I become acquainted with the earth and also experience the division into pieces which are true bodies having, as pieces so divided, their being in rest and motion—relative to the earth now functioning again as a resting earth-basis. I say possibly, the "resting earth"—but the "earth" as the unitary earth-basis cannot be at rest and therefore cannot be experienced as a body. It cannot be experienced as "a" body which not only has its extension and its qualitiedness but also its "place" in space, and which can possibly exchange its place and be at rest or in motion. As long as I do not have a presentation of a new basis, as a basis, from which the earth can have sense in interconnected and returning locomotion as a self-contained body in motion and at rest, and as long as an exchange of bases is not presented such that both bases become bodies, to that extent just the earth itself is the basis and not a body. The earth does not move—perhaps I may even say that it is at rest. But that can only mean that each earth-piece, which I or someone else separates off or is broken off by itself and which is at rest or in motion, is a body. The earth as a whole whose parts—if conceived by themselves as they can be as separated off, as separable—are bodies; but as a "whole" the earth is not a body. Here a whole "consisting" of corporeal parts is still not for that reason a body.

Now, what about the possibility of new basis "bodies"? What about new "earths" as relational foundations for the experience of bodies with the expected possibility that, as a consequence, the earth could become a normal body just like any other basis-body? It could have been said immediately that it is senseless to speak beforehand of an empty world-space in the sense we speak of an empty, infinite "astronomical" world, as a space in which the earth is in the same way that bodies are in the space which surrounds the earth. We have a surrounding space as a system of places—*i.e.*, as a system of possible terminations of motions of bodies. In that system all earthly bodies certainly have their particular "loci," but not the earth itself. The situation becomes different when the exchange of bases is "conceivable."

Objection: Is not the difficulty of the constitution of the earth as a body hopelessly exaggerated? The earth is after all a whole of implied parts, each of which is implied in the possibility of division into real parts,[14] and a body: each has its place—and thus the earth has an inner space as a system of places or (even when not conceived mathematically) a continuum of places when referred back to a complete divisibility. Thus for the same reason every formerly divisible body has its place with respect to its parts. However the inner and outer space of the earth form a single space. Or is there something left over? Any part of the earth could move. The earth has its inner motions. Similarly, any ordinary body is not only divisible but also has its deformations and its continual inner motions, while as a whole it can in its own way preserve or change its locus in space. Thus the earth has deformation and continual inner motion, etc. But how can it move as a "whole," how is that conceivable? It is not as though it were firmly forged—the "basis" is lacking for that. Is motion, hence corporeality, meaningful for it? Is its place in the totality of space actually a "place" for it? On the other hand, is the totality of space not precisely the system of places of all bodies which, accordingly, are divided into implied parts of the earth (as separated and moveable) and free outer bodies? What are these as curiosities of "intuition of space," or of space at this level?

But now we still have to consider outer bodies—the free bodies which are not implied pieces of the earth—and animate organisms, "my animate organism" and "other animate organisms."[15] These are perceived as bodies in space, always in their place, and unperceived yet perceivable (or experienceable in a modified way) as what is continually enduring, in a motion-rest that is spread out over this duration (also inner motions and inner rest).

Consider my animate organism. In primordial experience it has no motion away and no rest, only inner motion and inner rest unlike the outer bodies. In "I go," in any "I move myself" kinaesthetically whatever, not all bodies "move themselves" and the whole earth-basis under me does not move. For it pertains to a bodily rest that the aspects of the body flow "movingly" or do not flow kinaesthetically according to whether or not I hold still, etc. I have no motion away; I stand still or go, thus I have my animate organism as a center and resting and moved bodies around me and a basis without mobility. My animate organism has extension, etc., but no change and nonchange of place in the sense of the way whereby an outer body is presented as in motion receding or approaching, or not in motion as near, far away. But the basis on which my animate organism goes or does not go is also not experienced as a body, as *wholly* to be moving away or not moving away. Animate organisms of others are bodies at rest and in motion (always: in the sense of approaching or receding from me). But they are animate organisms in the form of "I move," whereby the ego is an "alter ego" for which my animate organism is a body, and for which all outer bodies which are not animate organisms for it, are the same outer bodies that I have. But every animate organism as well, which for me is the animate organism of someone else, is for all other egos (with the exception of their own animate organism) identically the same body and the same animate organism of the same ego. Likewise for every ego my animate organism is the same body and at the same time the same animate organism for the same ego (which for them is an alter ego) that I myself am for myself.

For all the earth is the same earth—on it, in it, over it, the same bodies hold sway. "On it," etc., the same organismal subjects,[16] subjects of animate organisms, which, in an altered sense, are the bodies for all. For all of us, however, the earth is the basis and not a body in the complete sense. Let us now assume that I am a bird and can fly—or assume that I watch the birds which also belong to the earth. To understand them is to put oneself in their place as flying. The bird sits on the branch or on the ground, then leaps into the air and flies upwards: the bird is like me in experiencing and doing when it

is on the earth, and experiences just as I do the basis, experiences different bodies, also other birds, animate organisms of others, and organismal egos, etc. But the bird flies upward—that is like locomotion under kinaesthesia whereby all courses of appearance, otherwise perceived as rest and motion of bodies, undergo variation and in ways similar to locomotion. Different only in so far as, for the bird, holding its flight still and being "borne by the wind" (which, however, does not have to signify an apprehension of something bodily) is a <possibly> experienced combination with the "I am moving" and which results in "apparent motion." The same result is obtained, but in a different way, in a "change of location in flight" and holding still once more. The latter terminates as "falling."[17] As a result, the bird no longer flies but sits on the tree or on the earth and then possibly leaps up, etc. The bird leaves the earth on which it has nonflight experiences like us, flies upward and again returns. Returning, the bird again has manners of appearance of rest and motion like me as one who is earth-bound. Flying and returning the bird has other manners of appearance motivated by other kinaesthesias (by its particular kinaesthesias of flying), but analogously modified. Yet these have the meaning of rest and motion in the modification because the kinaesthesias of flying and locomotion form a single kinaesthetic system for the bird. We who understand the bird understand precisely this extension of its kinaesthesias, etc. What rests has its appearance-system always to be produced again as nonlocomotion, nonflying, etc.

Let us consider leaping upon and away from a moving body. The reversal of courses of appearance yields rest and motion in the old way not only for me but for everyone. Thus I necessarily understand everyone. Indeed, I understand their leaping away as leaping away. I understand bodies entering my visual field, entering, *e.g.*, "from empty space" as falling into view, precisely as entering. "How" do I do that? Moving on the earth they are moving for me such that I vary and can possibly accompany kinaesthesias and in such a way that changes in appearance of rest are preserved—the same rest which would signify rest for me were I kinaesthetically still. I can do that in the case of bodies which do not move in extraterrestrial space; I could do it if I were to fly. But I can throw stones into the air and see them come back down as the same. The throwing can be more or less weak; obviously, the appearances are therefore analogous to motions based on the earth so that they become experienced as motions. Just as bodies become moved as rolling balls upon impact, so bodies thrown, etc. I would also mention the experience of the motion of falling, in the case of falling from a body above the earth, from the roof of the house or a tower.

My organismal flight-vessel is based upon a moved body (the vehicle). "I can fly so high that the earth seems like a globe." The earth can also be so small that I could traverse it from all sides and indirectly arrive at the idea of a globe. I therefore discover that it is a large globe-body. But the question is whether and how I would arrive at corporeality in the sense that the earth is "astronomically" just one body among others among which are the celestial bodies. No more than one can say how, when I imagine at will the bird on high and now mean that it can, accordingly, experience the earth as a body like any other. Why not? The bird, or the flying-machine, moves for us humans on earth, for the bird itself and the people on the flying-machine in so far as the bird experiences the earth as root-"body," as basis-"body." But cannot the flying-machine function as "basis"? Can I conceive basis and body moved in contrast to the basis as being exchanged or exchanged for the primitive place of my motion? What would that be in terms of a change in apperception and what would its demonstration be? Must I not conceptually transfer to the flying-machine what the earth as my basis, as the basis of my animate organism, universally presents in constitutive acceptance (with respect to form)?

Is that like the way in which I still presuppose my primordial animate organism and everything belonging to it in understanding someone else's animate organism? But here, in a comprehensible way, I necessarily take others as existing. The difficulty is repeated in the case of the stars. In order to be able to "experience" them as bodies in indirect apprehending, I must already be a human be-ing for myself on the earth as my root-basis. Perhaps one might say that the difficulties would not arise if I and if we were able to fly and have two earths as basis-bodies, being able to arrive at the one from the other by flight. Precisely in this way the one body would be the basis for the other. But what do two earths mean? Two pieces of one earth with a humanity. Together, they would become one basis and, at the same time, each would be a body for the other. Surrounding them would be a common space in which each, as body, possibly would have a moveable place, but motion would always be relative to the other body and nonrelative to the synthetic basis of their being together. The places of all bodies would have this relativity. However, one would always still have to ask, motion and rest with respect to which of the two basis-bodies?[18]

Only "the" earth-basis can be constituted originaliter with the surrounding space of bodies. This constitution already presupposes that my animate organism and known others are constituted along with open horizons of others. These horizons are divided into spaces within spaces which surround the earth as an open near-far field of bodies. As a result bodies are given as having the sense of being earthly bodies and space is given as having the sense of being earth-space. The totality of the We, of human beings or "animate beings," is in this sense earthly—and immediately has no contrary in the nonearthly. This sense is rooted and has its orientation-center in me and in a narrower We living with one another. But it is also possible for the earth-basis to be extended, possibly such that I learn to understand that in space my first earth-bases are large vessels of flight traveling in it for a long time: I am born on one of them and my family lives on one of them. It was my being-basis until I learned that we are vessels on the larger earth, etc. Thus a plurality of basis-places, of home-places, is unified into a basis-place. However, more about this later in necessary supplementations.[19]

But if the earth is constituted with animate organisms and corporeality, then the "sky" is also necessarily constituted as the field of what is outermost, yet which can be spatially experienced for me and all of us—

with respect to the earth-basis. Or an open horizon of reachable distance is constituted; extending from any spatial point reachable for me, there is an outermost horizon or limit (global horizon) in which what can still be experienced as a distant physical thing finally disappears by moving away from me. Conversely, I can naturally phantasy to myself that "points" becoming visible are distant bodies coming closer and now approach until they reach the earth-basis, etc. But now I can also phantasy to myself that they are home-places.

But consider this. Each of us always has his "historicity"[20] with respect to his ego made at home in it. If I am born on a vessel, then I have a piece of my development on the vessel and that, however, would not be characterized as a ship for me in relation to the earth—as long as no unity with the vessel would be produced. It would itself be my "earth," my primitive home. But my parents are not then primitively[21] made at home on the vessel; they still have the old home, another primitive home. In the interchange of home-places (if home-place has the ordinary sense of territory peculiar to individual or family in each case) there remains, universally stated, the fact that each ego has a primitive home—and every primitive people with their primitive territory has a primitive home. But every people and their historicity and every cosmopolitan people (cosmopolis) are themselves ultimately made at home, naturally, on the "earth." All developments, all relative histories have to that extent a single primitive history of which they are episodes. In that connection it is indeed possible that this primitive history would be a togetherness of people living and evolving completely separated, except that they all exist for one another in open, undetermined horizons of earth-space.

We may now consider the stars after having made clear the possibility of flying arks (which can also be a name for primitive home-places). These are exhibited in "experience" (that is, in historicity in which world, and in the world corporeal Nature, space belonging to Nature and space-time, humanity and the animate universe, are constituted) as mere "air ships," "space ships" of the earth. They depart from it and then

return inhabited and guided by human beings who have made their home on the earth-basis as their ark in accord with their last generational and, for "they themselves," historical origin. We therefore now consider "stars"—first of all, as points of light, specks of light. In the course of experience in the process of being fashioned, they are apperceived as distant bodies, but without the possibility of normal experiential confirmation; they enter into that confirmation in the first sense, in the narrower sense of a direct demonstrative showing.[22] We deal with "celestial bodies" just as we deal with bodies that are for each of us (but possibly for others) accidentally, factually inaccessible for a while in the present. With respect to them, we draw experiential inferences, make our empirical observations of place, observations of their inductively inferred motions, etc., as though they were bodies like any others. All of that is relative to the earth-basis ark and "earthly globe" and to us, earthly human beings, and Objectivity is related to the All of humanity. What about the earth-ark itself? It is not itself already a body, not a star among other stars. Only when we think of our stars as secondary arks with their possible humanities, etc., phantasy ourselves as transplanted there among these humanities, possibly flying there, is it otherwise. Then it is like children born on ships, but yet modified. The stars are indeed hypothetical bodies in a specific sense of As-if, and so too the hypothesis that they are home-places in an attainable sense of a particular kind.

Making celestial distance homogeneous even by iteration generates phenomenological questions.[23] What is the eidetic possibility there, and the pregiven possibility with the earthly world, as coconstitutive of its being, by its essential kind of being? With the hypothetical interpretation of visible stars as distant bodies, and by the eidetic form of the limit of what can be experienced of distance there is already given the open infinity of the earthly world as endowed with an infinity of possibly existing distant bodies. We understand the homogeneity without further ado such that the earth itself is a body on which by chance we wander around. With the problems now being considered we confront properly the great problem of the correct sense of a universal, purely physical science of "Nature"—of an astronomical-physical science operating in "astronomical" infinity in the sense of our modern physics (in the broadest sense, astrophysics), and the problem of an inner infinity, the infinity of the continuum and the way to atomize or quantify—atomic physics—in the open endlessness or infinity. In these sciences of the infinity of the totality of Nature, the mode of observation is usually the one in which animate organisms are only accidentally particularized bodies which can therefore also conceivably be completely ignored so that a Nature without organisms, without brutes and humans is possible. One almost means, and occasionally even also seriously means that it is mere facticity, a factuality determined by the laws of Nature that hold in the world, if animate organisms with psychical lives are (causally) combined with certain bodies or body-types of physical structure; accordingly, it would be conceivable that the animate organisms, that precisely bodies of such a character, are just mere bodies. As one also believes can be proved with respect to the earth, there was once no "life" on it, long space-times were needed until highly complicated substances were fashioned and subsequently animate life emerged on the earth. And that also takes for granted that the earth is only one of the accidental world-bodies, one among others, and that it would be well-nigh amusing to want to believe after Copernicus that the earth is the midpoint of the world "merely because by accident we live on it," favored even by its "rest" in relation to which everything moveable moves. It would seem that in our natural scientific naïvety (not in so far as natural science is treated theoretically, but in so far as it naively believes it has acquired absolute truth about the world in its theories, even at levels of relative completeness), we have already broken through what has been previously taken for granted. Perhaps phenomenology has supported Copernican astrophysics—but also anti-Copernicanism according to which God had fixed the earth at a place in space. Perhaps at the level of phenomenology, notwithstanding the calculations and mathematical theories

of Copernicus, subsequent astrophysics and thus the totality of physics preserve a legitimacy within its boundaries. Quite different is the question if a pure physical biology (which, however, accordingly should be biology) can retain its sense and legitimacy.

Therefore let us reflect: How should we acquire the right to accept the earth as a body, as a star among stars? At first the earth is given only as possibly another star. But let us start with another possibility. The scientific investigator will agree that it is a mere fact that we see the stars at all. He will say: Could it not just as well be that the stars, even the sun, are so far away that they would not be there for us? Indeed, in fog they are invisible. Thus it could have been in all historical times—we lived therefore in a generational historicity and could have had our earthly world, our earth and earth-spaces, flying and floating bodies there, etc., everything as before, only without visible stars that could be experienced by us. Perhaps we would have had an atomic physics or a microphysics, but not an astrophysics or a macrophysics. But we would have to consider to what extent the former would have been changed. We would have had our telescopes, our microscopes, our ever more precise instruments of measurement. We would have had our Newton and law of gravitation. We would have been able to discover that bodies exert gravitation on one another, that accordingly bodies could have been regarded at the same time as divisible, as wholes of component bodies which therefore exert their gravitation as self-sufficient bodies and operate according to the laws of mechanics, yield results, etc. We would have discovered that the earth is a "globe" divisible into bodies, that as total unity of corporeal parts it exerts, as totality, a gravitation in relation to all bodies detached from it, bodies that are visible and invisible in earth-space. We would know that these are bodies in earth-space which we can perceive only by telescopes and always better telescopes as always again lying beyond what is usually visible for us. We can then tell ourselves that, finally, naturally, bodies of any size whatever still could not and could never be inaccessibly far from our senses. Without seeing them or having direct cognizance of them, even if distant-bodies are to be equated by hypothesis with the ordinary bodies, we can make inductions and, on the basis of gravitational effects, etc., reckon the existence of such "stars." The earth, finally, would be a body conceived in physics like any other and would even have stars around it. As a matter of fact we already have stars in view and scientifically find them in relations to the earth calculable by physics and find the earth as equivalent to what in physics is a body among bodies. Thus we do not even touch upon physics.

But everything comes to this: we must not forget the pregivenness and constitution belonging to the apodictic Ego or to me, to us, as the source of all actual and possible sense of being, of all possible broadening which can be further constructed in the already constituted world developing historically. One need not perpetrate the absurdity, absurdity in fact, of presupposing tacitly beforehand the naturalistic or prevailing conception of the world. We must not perpetrate the absurdity of then seeing human history, the history of the species anthropologically and psychologically within the evolution of the individual and people, the cultivation of science and the interpretation of the world as an obviously accidental event on the earth which might just as well have occurred on Venus or Mars. This holds too for the earth and we humans, I with my animate organism and I in my generation, my people, etc. This whole historicality belongs inseparably to the Ego, and is in essence not repeatable, but everything relates back to this historicity of transcendental constitution as appertinent core and as an ever-widening core—everything newly discovered as world-possibility is connected with the sense of being already established. Following implicitly from this, one might therefore think that the earth can no more lose its sense as "primitive home-place," as ark of the world, than my animate organism can lose its wholly unique sense of being as originary animate organism from which every animate organism derives a part of its sense of being and as we human beings in our sense of being precede the brutes, etc. As a consequence, however, nothing of that constitutive dignity or order of values can be changed if animate organism and body are conceived as necessarily equivalent (made homogeneous), or if corporeal animate organism is conceived as a body like any other, if humanity is conceived as a brute-species among brute-species, and therefore finally if the earth is conceived as a world-body among world-bodies.[24] I could just as well think of myself as transplanted to the moon. Why should I not think of the moon as something like an earth, as therefore something like a dwelling place of living beings? Indeed, I can very well think of myself as a bird flying off from the earth to a body that lies far away, or as a pilot of an airplane that flies off and lands there. Certainly, I can conceive of human beings and brutes already being there. But I ask, perhaps, "how have they come there?" —just as similarly in the case of a new island where cuniform writing is found, I ask: How did the people in question come there? All brutes, all living beings, all beings whatever, only have being-sense by virtue of my constitutive genesis and this has "earthly" precedence. Indeed, a fragment of the earth (like an ice floe) may have become detached, and that was made possible by a particular historicality. But that does not mean that the moon or Venus could not just as well be conceived as primitive places in an original separation and that it is only a fact that the earth is just for me and our earthly humanity. There is only one humanity and one earth—all fragments belong to it which are or have been detached from it. But if this is the case, need we say with Galileo: *par si muove?* And not on the contrary: it does not move? It is certainly not so that it moves in space, although it could move, but rather as we tried to show above: the earth is the ark which makes possible in the first place the sense of all motion and all rest as mode of motion. But its rest is not a mode of motion.

But now one may find that it is wrong to rather extravagantly contradict all natural-scientific knowledge of actuality and real possibility. It is possible that entropy will put an end to all life on earth, or that celestial bodies will crash into the earth, etc. But even if one found in our attempts the most unbelievable philosophical hybris—: we would not back down from the consequences for the clarification of necessities pertaining to all bestowal of sense for what exists and for the world. We do not back down even when confronting the problems of death in the new way phenomenology conceives them. In the present, I as something present am progressively dying, others die for me when I do not find a present connection with them. But unity by recollection permeates my life—I still live, although in being other, and continue to live the life that lies behind me and where its sense of being behind me lies in reiteration and the ability to reiterate. Thus the We lives in the reiterableness and itself continually lives in the form of reiterableness of history while the individual "dies." That is, the individual can no longer be "remembered" empathically by others, but "lives" only in historical memory whereby the memory-subject can be substituted for the individual who "dies."[25]

What belongs to constitution is, and is alone, absolute and final necessity. Only on that basis is everything conceivable concerning the constituted world to be determined. What sense could the collapsing masses have in space, in one space constructed a priori as

absolutely homogeneous, if the constituting life were eliminated? Indeed, does that elimination itself not have sense, if any at all, as elimination of and in the constituting subjectivity? The ego lives and precedes all actual and possible beings, and anything existent whether in a real or irreal sense. Constituted world-time, more particularly, conceals in itself psychological time, and the psychological refers back to the transcendental. But it does not do so in such a way that one can simply convert the objectively psychical into the transcendental and above all such that one converts each manner in which, under any abstractly and relatively justified point of view, one harmoniously presupposes the homogeneous world and, more precisely, Nature and the psychical psychophysically attached to it. In practice one can operate very well with that presupposition (e.g., by fashioning and utilizing science for human praxis). But not even that allows for conversion into the transcendental or for making valid over against phenomenology the paradoxes which arise.[26]

NOTES

1. *Unsigned "Note of Editor" in Farber volume:* This manuscript was written between May 7 and May 9, 1934. Its very informality and incompleteness give a vivid impression of Husserl at work. The following descriptive comment was written on the envelope: "*Overthrow of the Copernican theory* in the usual interpretation of a world view. The original ark, earth, does not move. Foundational investigations of the phenomenological origin of *corporeality of the spatiality pertaining to Nature* in the first sense of the natural sciences. Of necessity all are initial investigations." The publication of the manuscript has been duly authorized. (All other notes are those of translator.)

2. *Umwelt*

3. *Vorstellung*

4. *Vorstellung*

5. That is to say, if the earth is posited as body in natural-scientific thinking.

6. In other words, to objectivate something physical posited as body is of necessity to objectivate it as in motion or as at rest. Husserl has in mind the notion peculiar to science in the "Copernican style" that the mathematization of Nature comprises all change and variation which, by hypothesis, are referred to spatiotemporal events. In turn, all spatiotemporal events are understood in terms of motion (and rest as a mode of motion).

7. As Husserl will try to show in what follows,

there is no "motivation" in prescientific thinking and experiencing for the natural-scientific conception of Nature and earth as body. In the next paragraphs, as well as at the end of this manuscript, Husserl suggests a view that he will work out again in the *Crisis of European Sciences*, Section 9: the view, namely, that the "Copernican" world view is a progressive historical process made up of a sequence of verifications and confirmations of a hypothetical interpretation of Nature. By this means what is available in the course of actual experience, fragmentary and finite even in its "communalization," inductively predesignates the construction of the surrounding world "posited as infinite in scientific thinking." According to this view, then, perceiving of the world presented in prescientific thinking and experiencing is *eo ipso* apperceiving of the self-same world presented in scientific thinking; this "transfer" by way of apperception is so interpreted that it is regarded as referring to a step in the sequence of inductive verifications that progressively fashion the "Copernican" world view. Thus the prescientific world in which we live and pursue our goals, and which remains a *prescientific* world no matter how interpreted scientifically, is taken to be a product of a method of verification of a specific hypothesis. Is there any confirmation, any "motive," in the prescientific world for this "new 'idea of the world'"? See below, note 12.

8. Even if the "apperceptive transfer" is not "motivated" by the regularities and uniformities of prescientific thinking and experiencing, the problem still remains for phenomenology to show the "rightful" sense of motion and rest as constructed by scientific thinking, *i.e.*, to show the validation of scientific thinking in the domain of the prescientific.

9. That is to say, the most original or "evident" way in which bodies are presented as "they, themselves" in scientific thinking; see note 6, above.

10. *iterativ*: as used here, the term refers to formal logic as a function of the theory of science, to the "possible determination by any arbitrarily selectable objects whatever" (namely, bodies defined as "matter in motion") which aids scientific cognition having a material content (namely, physics or astrophysics); see *Formal and Transcendental Logic*, section 83.

11. *Objektivität*: This term, and the term '*Objekt*', are often used to designate the noematic correlates of acts and processes of consciousness at different levels of constitution; see, for instance, *Cartesian Meditations*, section 20, pp. 47f.; *Formal and Transcendental Logic*, section 96, a, pp. 239f. The distinction between "*Gegenständlichkeit*" and "*Objektivität*," "*Gegenstand*" and "*Objekt*," is an important one in both early and late writings of Husserl. For the importance of the distinction see Aron Gurwitsch, "The Kantian and Husserlian Conceptions of Consciousness," in *Studies in Phenomenology and Psychology* (Evanston: Northwestern University Press, 1966), pp. 149ff.

12. The ultimate demonstrative showing or exhibiting of the validity of scientific thinking is rooted in the prescientific domain of experience. This is an important idea for Husserl and is tied up with the "attempt to start a consistent transcendental philosophy" in such a way that the illusion of a "transcendental solipsism" will be overcome in working out the "whole many-leveled problem of the constitution of the Objective world" (*Formal and Transcendental Logic*, section 96, b, p. 241). The solution to the enigma of solipsism lies, Husserl says, "firstly, in the systematic unravelling of the constitutional problems implicit in the fact of consciousness which is the world always existing for *me*, always having and confirming its sense by *my* experience; and, secondly, in progressively advancing exhibitions that follow the hierarchical sequence of problems. The purpose of these exhibitions [namely, demonstrative showings], however, is none other, and can be none other, than actually to disclose, as matters included in that very fact of consciousness, the actualities and potentialities (or habitualities) of life, in which the sense, world, has been, and is continually being, built up immanently" (ibid., pp. 241f.).

13. That is to say, all *founding* levels of constitution are "implied" in the apperceiving of something as at rest or in motion; for instance, the visual parallax is "corrected" on the basis of more primitive visual experiences (the "mediacies").

14. *reellen Abteilung*. For Husserl's theory of "wholes" and "parts" see *Logical Investigations*, translated by J. N. Findlay (London: Routledge & Kegan Paul, 1970), 2:436ff., 484ff. Here Husserl considers what he calls "nonself-sufficient 'moments'" in the *Logical Investigations*.

15. For the notion of "animate organism" see especially *Formal and Transcendental Logic*, section 96a, pp. 240f.: "In the nexus of this first Nature, as holding sway in that body (within this Nature) which is called my bodily organism, as exercising psychophysical functions in that body in a unique manner, my psychic Ego makes his appearance, 'animating' it as the unique animated body, according to original experience." This "first Nature or world, this first, not yet intersubjective, Objectivity, is constituted in my ego as . . . *my own*," and yet must "contain the *motivational foundation* for the constitution of those *transcendencies* that are *genuine*, that go beyond it, and originate first of all as 'others' (other psychophysical beings and other transcendental egos), the transcendencies that . . . make possible the constitution of an Objective world in the everyday sense. . . ."

16. *leiblichen Subjekte*

17. The German text reads: "Nur insofern anders, als das Stillhalten und vom 'Winde getragen sein' (was aber keine körperliche Auffassung zu bedeuten hat) eine Erfahrungskombination mit dem 'ich bewege' ist und immer noch die 'Scheinbewegung' ergibt, bei einer 'Änderung der Flügellage' und beim Stillhalten dabei abermals, aber in anderer Weise. Letztere endet als 'Fallen', damit dass der Vogel nicht mehr fliegt, sondern auf dem Baum oder der Erde sitzt und dabei ev. springt, etc."

18. The German text reads: "Die Orte aller Körper hätten diese Relativität, welche für Bewegung und Ruhe die Fraglichkeit ergeben würde: in bezug auf welchen der beiden Bodenkörper?"

19. It is not clear what supplementations Husserl has in mind here; in the continuation of this manuscript in *Philosophy and Phenomenological Research* Husserl does not return to this theme.

20. "*Historizität*": Husserl also uses the terms "*relativen Historien*," "*Urhistorie*," and "*Geschichtlichkeit*." "*Historizität*" ("historicity") as he uses the term here refers to the "genetic" process of transcendental constitution (see below, p. 230); "*relativen Historien*" ("relative histories") refers to the history of a people (e.g., the history of the Athenian people, the American people), each of which is an "episode" in "world history." These terms seem to be more or less synonymous with the terms (p. 230) "*Menschengeschichte*" and "*Speziesgeschichte*" ("human history" and "history of the species")—that is to say, "history" in the ordinary sense of "history." At the core, Husserl says, of "historicity" or transcendental constitution is "*Geschichtlichkeit*" ("historicality") which may be interpreted as the transcendentally reduced phenomenon of human history in the ordinary sense. This interpretation is consistent with the main thrust of Husserl's thought in the manuscript, but he offers little basis for its clarification. For a good review of Husserl's ideas in this connection, see René Toulemont, *L'Essence de la Société selon Husserl* (Paris: Presses Universitaires de France, 1962), pp. 133ff.; cf. also F. Kersten, "Phenomenology, History and Myth," in *Phenomenology and Social Reality. Essays in Memory of Alfred Schutz*, ed. Maurice Natanson (The Hague: Nijhoff, 1970), pp. 235–41.

21. "Primitive," that is to say, in both a generational and a constitutional sense.

22. See above, note 12; and also *Formal and Transcendental Logic*, section 94, pp. 233f.

23. *Homogenisierung*: That is to say, the idea in "Copernican" natural-scientific thinking that all events in Nature are enacted in one space-time—an idea that raises questions of legitimacy whether arrived at by abstraction and formalization of "apperceptive transfers" (see above, notes 6 and 7)—which therefore allows of infinite iteration of distances as the same no matter what objects are involved—or by regarding motion as a "state" of a body, in which case motion is not so much repetition of change but rather retention of a given "state"; hence motion requires no "cause." What requires a "cause" is change from motion to rest or rest to motion, or a change in motion itself. But change in motion, for instance, can only be accounted for in terms of an unaltered or unchanged "state" of motion. And since, on the "Copernican" view, motion is defined in terms of velocity and direction, unaltered velocity is equivalent to equal distances covered in equal times (and unaltered direction then proves to be progression on a straight line). But equal distances covered in equal times presupposes homogeneity of one space-time, and more particularly of one space-time posited as infinite. Questions about the implications and rightful sense of this presupposition are raised in the next lines of the text.

24. Husserl indicates the view here that he will criticize in some detail in the *Crisis of European Sciences*, section 62: the "naturalistic method" of modern science is based on the dualism of "matter" and "mind" and so interpreted that the latter is conceived on the model of the former; the utter heterogeneity of "matter" and "mind" is thereby overcome and "mind" is understood by means of causal laws analogous to those that obtain in Nature—the "equalization of bodies and souls" according to which body and soul are "two real strata in this experiential world which are integrally and really connected similarly to, and in the same sense as, two pieces of a body. Thus, concretely, one is external to the other, is distinct from it, and is merely related to it in a regulated way"; "Cartesian dualism requires the parallelization of *mens* and *corpus*, together with the naturalization of psychic being implied in this parallelization, and hence also requires the parallelization of the required methods" by virtue of having "its roots in the consistent abstraction through which it [namely, modern natural science] *wants* to see, in the life-world, only corporeity." (*The Crisis of European Sciences and Transcendental Phenomenology*, trans. David Carr [Evanston: Northwestern University Press, 1970], pp. 215, 221, 227.)

25. The German text reads: "Aber da geht durch mein Leben die Einheit durch Wiedererinnerung—ich lebe noch, obschon im Anderssein, und lebe fort das Leben, das hinter mir liegt, und dessen Sinn des Hinter-mir in der Wiederholung und Wiederholbarkeit liegt. So lebt das Wir in der Wiederholbarkeit und lebt selbst fort in Form der Wiederholbarkeit der Geschichte, während der Einzelne 'stirbt,' d.i. nicht mehr von den Anderen einfühlungsmässig 'erinnert' werden kann, sondern nur in historischer Erinnerung, in der die Erinnerungssubjekte sich vertreten können." For a possible interpretation of this intriguing passage see Kersten, "Phenomenology, History and Myth," pp. 240f. Leaving aside all transcendental phenomenological trappings, Husserl's view bears a remarkable resemblance to the "l'unanimisme" of Jules Romains, such as expressed in his novel *The Death of a Nobody*; see the edition translated by Desmond MacCarthy and Sidney Waterlow, with an afterword by Maurice Natanson (New York: New American Library, 1961), and Natanson's afterword, pp. 122f.

26. The German text reads: "Die konstituierte Weltzeit birgt zwar in sich psychologische Zeit und das Psychologische weist zurück auf Transzendentales—aber doch nicht so, dass man nun das objektiv Psychische einfach ins Transzendentale umkehren und vor allem, dass man jede Weise wie man einstimmig unter irgendeinem abstrakten und relativ berechtigten Gesichtspunkt homogene Welt und näher Natur und darin psychophysisch gebundenes Psychisches voraussetzt und damit praktisch ganz gut operiert (für menschlich natürliche Praxis Wissenschaft ausbildend und verwertend), dass man das in Transzendentales umstülpt und nun die Paradoxien, die entspringen, gegen die Phänomenologie geltend macht."

This sentence ends the part of the manuscript published as supplement to *Essays in Memory of Edmund Husserl*; for the continuation of the manuscript see above, Introduction, pp. 213f. The themes developed at the end of this manuscript are not resumed in the continuation, the section headings of which are the following: "The different senses of space"; "Intentional reference of all experienced motions back to my kinaesthetic activity or holding still.—I have already formed my kinaesthetic system;" "Rest of a body—motion of the body"; "Constitution of motion belonging to what is at first at rest"; "The meaning of the reduction to pure primordial space."

13

Introduction to
"World of the Living Present"
FREDERICK A. ELLISTON

The title of this essay, provided by Alfred Schutz, aptly indicates its scope—the context of immediate experience, the world in which I live. It is one in a series of remarkable reflections by Husserl on the nature of space and the changes experienced within it. As such it should be read in conjunction with Fred Kersten's translation of "Foundational Investigations of the Phenomenological Origin of the Spatiality of Nature" (pp. 222–33 of this volume) and the intervening piece that supplements Kersten's translation and precedes the following: "Notes on the Constitution of Space" published in the first volume of *Philosophy and Phenomenological Research*.[1]

These texts illustrate Husserl's views on a fundamental philosophical theme—spatiality. It runs parallel to a second pervasive and consequential theme—temporality, which is also included in this volume (see excerpts from *The Phenomenology of Inner Time-Consciousness* and John Brough's Introduction, pp. 271–88 of this volume). But whereas time received systematic and coherent elaboration, space is dealt with far more tentatively and incompletely. Though these texts capture Husserl's major views they do not provide a mature theory.

Their style is much more exploratory, probing, and improvising. As a compensation for this roughness, the reader is privileged to witness phenomenology as Husserl practiced it, the process of philosophizing rather than its results. As such the following text is an opportunity to immerse ourselves in Husserl's daily work, his "meditations," in order to experience phenomenology in action.

The manuscript can be divided, as Schutz notes, into roughly two unequal parts: the first deals with changes; the second, with others. They are tied together by a common concept: apperception as a kind of coapprehending that makes it possible to experience something as the same though different—as one though changed, as like me though another.

I

The world of the living present has a spatial structure. All things experienced are situated relative to my body as center: they are near or far, to the left or right, above or below. None of them presents itself to me as a whole: at most I perceive only an aspect or part of each. Each aspect or adumbration points to others—aspects of the same thing or what Husserl terms the inner horizon, as well as to other things not immediately attended to but still present with the phenomenal field or what Husserl terms the outer horizon.[2]

The horizon, as a tie between actual and possible experiences, can be explored through physical movements, that is, a change of space or place whereby possible experiences become actual, empty intentions become fulfilled, and expectations are realized. In this process of fulfilling expectations, what

Husserl calls making evident (*Evidenz*)[3] or verification, an optimal point is reached: the thing is neither too close nor too far. Actuality is defined as the correlate of these optimal experiences, what is present when the situation is just right.

What holds for one thing holds also for pairs, and by extension for the entire world of immediate experience. What unifies it on the object or noematic side is its correlation to one perspectival style of fulfilled expectations on the subject or noetic side, the harmony that prevails within experience.

Against this analysis of spatial change, Husserl proceeds to a discussion of a second kind of change—qualitative. His earlier analysis continues to serve as a parallel, indeed as a paradigm.

In both cases he takes no change as the norm or standard against which all other changes are judged. Movement is understood in terms of rest, alteration in terms of rigidity.

At the lowest level of our experience of change is the phantom. Our perception of one thing *causing* another to change or appear to change represents a higher stratum of experience constituted on the basis of this more primordial phantom-experience.

Any qualitative change has three reference points: (1) the change of particular things or phantoms; (2) changes involving entire systems of things, for example my fall into the world of sleep; and (3) change in myself as animate organism. These changes can come about in different ways—slowly or quickly, from external impetus or my own volition. But in all cases the changes are intentional—that is, they take place within the nexus between self and world, experiencing and experienced.

Sometimes spatial and qualitative changes interact, as in the case of blurring: the discrete qualities of a thing merge as it recedes into the distance. The opposite also occurs: as something approaches, its particular properties become more distinct.

While a thing moves in and out of my perceptual field, its identity as the same thing is a function of the harmony of my experiences, the continuity of the process whereby expectations are fulfilled or conversely the discontinuity of my disappointments. Per-

fect harmony, the complete fulfillment of expectations, is an ideal, assumed as a condition for identity rather than achieved. Consider Husserl's simple example of spatial, periodic change, the swinging pendulum. When I glance away I assume continuous movement that I do not actually or immediately experience. When my glance returns to the pendulum again, my identification of it as the same is predicated on this assumption of continuity. As an assumption it could not in principle be verified for the infinitely varied contents of experience, for it is a condition for the very possibility of experience.

The identity of all things taken to be real cannot be verified by a phenomenological appeal to immediate experience or intuition. Husserl takes this fact not as a shortcoming of phenomenology, but as a proof that continuity is an a priori condition of experience, constitutive of space and time as structures of experience.

Husserl's phenomenology seeks to be a presuppositionless philosophy but falls far short of this ideal. Continuity is more assumed than demonstrated. Spatiality serves as a paradigm for qualitative change—a problematic and undefended assumption. Sight has served him as a paradigm for the other senses, and the generalizability of the results have yet to be proven. Husserl courageously acknowledges these and further difficulties. Perhaps most seriously, his analysis extends only to the phantom world, still divorced from the everyday world we live in and yet to be related to the world of science. And within this world his focus on physical things leaves out of account less material quasi-objects like rays of light, sound waves, and the radiating warmth of stoves.

Acknowledging these problems he pauses to take stock of what he has shown up to this point: "Actually, so far we have only given a justification for the constitution of unities from those subjective kinaesthetic-associative changes that occur in the living present."

II

To advance beyond this point, the living present in its narrow temporal sense requires a new term, a new kind of experience—recollection. But its introduction raises many problems too. Parallel to the earlier problem of the same thing midst spatial and qualitative change runs the new problem of the same present thing compared to the past recalled thing. The identification of something experienced now as numerically the same as something experienced earlier requires the repetition of past experiences, or at least this possibility. But how do I know that what I recall is identical to what I do or could experience?

To reexperience something now as identical to something experienced in the past but only recalled involves obstacles of various orders, as Husserl realizes. Some of the hurdles are empirical: lack of money, time, or opportunity may prevent me from repeating my experience of the same thing. Once these hurdles are cleared logical problems persist: things are never quite the same, but always somewhat different. Husserl's solution to the second is surprisingly semantic: the same sometimes means "perfectly alike in the present and in recollection" and at other times means altered yet numerically one and the same. That is, the same sometimes means *identical* in all respects and at other times only identical in some but not all—that is *similar*. In defense of this phenomenological distinction between numerically identical and qualitatively similar, Husserl invokes the fact that we do talk this way, a curious inversion of the normal phenomenological ordering of consciousness and language.

Ludwig Wittgenstein identifies a third problem Husserl appears to ignore: How do we know that our recollections are accurate? Their mere repetition, he points out, hardly suffices, and appealing to another memory provides inconclusive evidence. Internal checks do not guarantee veracity. In a telling analogue he suggests it is "as if someone were to buy several copies of the morning newspaper to assure himself that what it said was true."[4]

One problem of sameness is temporal. Another is the "same for me" versus "same for you." And a third is the problem of the same kind though numerically different. The second leads to a discussion of intersub-jectivity and empathy; the last, to an account of typification.

III

Once it is conceded that one thing can be more or less the same as it was before, the door is open for one thing to be more or less the same as a second presently existing thing. Their shared features whereby they can be grouped form a type. The latter is not a universal like space or time: its scope is more limited and it is logically less compelling. Types function as intermediaries between universals and particulars, grouping things with a "family resemblance," to use Wittgenstein's expression. Husserl's very detailed description of the formation of types is an incisive and illustrative piece of concrete phenomenological analysis.

The constitution of objects of different types involves a process of association or apperception: within a unitary experience one thing is grasped as like or unlike another, perhaps itself in the past or a second thing entirely. Empathy is an example of a higher level apperception whereby the type "alter ego" or another self is constituted.

IV

In the case of empathy, used in Husserl's all inclusive sense for all my experiences of another, what is conjoined or paired in apperception is myself as animate organism (*Leib*) and another. This apperception proceeds on the basis of a sphere of "ownness," as Husserl termed it in the Fifth Cartesian Meditation, an abstract stratum of experience consisting of myself as body-subject together with its kinaesthetic activities but nothing more. For the "more" had explicitly been put aside by a new kind of epoche, not overtly present in the following text but necessarily operative.

My body is a privileged physical thing intimately tied to a sensory field in which it moves and acts—touching, feeling, tasting, hearing, smelling, seeing, and performing what Arthur Danto calls "basic actions."[5] The kinaesthetic sensations are directly tied to movements of my body in a unique way. Moving my eyes, for example, correlates with a shift in the visual field, but nothing similar happens when I move any other eyes.

The core-world of things directly apprehendable is surrounded by a more distant world of things less directly grasped—the things I could experience on the horizon if I walked to them. At the centre of everything is myself as animate organism (*Leib*), a stationary object or null point in relation to everything else experienced as moving.

The constitution of others is secondary to its basis—the animate organism, which is here analyzed in more detail than in the Fifth Cartesian Meditation. In keeping with Husserl's theme, identity, the following text places far more emphasis on sameness. The Fifth Cartesian Meditation places considerable emphasis on otherness in order to rebut the charge of solipsism that threatens Husserl's entire philosophy.[6] The delightful vignette on typification offered earlier is now supplemented with an extraordinarily detailed phenomenological description of walking that unites many of the earlier themes. In walking spatial and qualitative changes are continuously taking place, along with an ongoing process of identification as perceived places and properties shift relative to me and one another.

V

This rich analysis is not a mere exercise in Husserl's peculiar style of philosophizing. Rather the analysis lays bare the very foundations of phenomenology and all experience. Husserl has attempted to peel off all the layers of consciousness in order to disclose what is more primordial, the very core of our existence.

This core is noteworthy for its contrast with both rationalism and empiricism. At the level of what is most basic, certain, and essential, Husserl speaks not of a *res cogitans* like Descartes or a "bundle of perceptions" like Hume but of an animate organism located at the very center of a kinaesthetic field that it explores by *walking*. It is distinguished by its duality: it senses and is sensed, moves and is moved. As an ambulatory null point it marks the opening on all that is and the locus of Husserl's triumph over both subjectivism and objectivism, over idealism and realism.

NOTES

1. Edmund Husserl, "Notizen zur Raumkonstitution," *Philosophy and Phenomenological Research* 1 (Sept. 1940): 21ff.

2. The inner, outer, and temporal horizons are briefly discussed in section 19 of *Cartesian Meditations*. For useful and insightful elaborations see the following: Helmut Kuhn, "The Phenomenological Concept of Horizon" in *Philosophical Essays in Memory of Edmund Husserl*, ed. Marvin Farber (Cambridge: Harvard University Press, 1940), pp. 106–23; Henry Pietersma, "The Concept of Horizon," *Analecta Husserliana* 2 (1972): 278–82; Cornelius van Peursen, "The Horizon" in *Husserl: Expositions and Appraisals*, ed. F. A. Elliston and Peter McCormick (Notre Dame: University of Notre Dame Press, 1977), pp. 182–201.

3. For Husserl's characterization of this process see his Third Cartesian Meditation; *Ideas*, sections 137–42; and *Experience and Judgment*, sections 2–13.

4. Ludwig Wittgenstein, *Philosophical Investigations* trans. G. E. M. Anscombe (Oxford: Blackwell, 1965), p. 94e.

5. Arthur Danto, "Basic Actions," *American Philosophical Quarterly* 2 (1965): 141–48.

6. For an explanation of the significance and urgency of this threat see F. A. Elliston, "Husserl's Phenomenology of Empathy" in *Husserl: Expositions and Appraisals*, pp. 213–15.

13

The World of the Living Present
and the Constitution of the Surrounding World
External to the Organism*

Translated by Frederick A. Elliston and Lenore Langsdorf

Editor's Preface:

The following pages are based upon an authorized typewritten transcription of an original manuscript of Edmund Husserl which shows the following introductory remark:

D 12 IV; No date (but clearly 1931) — The original manuscript consists of 19 typed pages. It is actually a double manuscript, but put by Husserl into one envelope as belonging together; it carries this inscription:

"1) The concrete present as unity of configuration of what is given in perception, the 'primary' world;

2) Constitution of others, of the organism as primary object of the surrounding world external to the organism."

Based upon these indications the undersigned has added the title under which this manuscript is herewith published. As to the genesis of Husserl's manuscripts and the problems arising therefrom for their editing he wishes to refer to his preface to Husserl's "Notizen zur Raumkonstitution" in vol. 1 of this journal (*Philosophy and Phenomenological Research*), September 1940, pp. 21ff.

Also in the following, additions made by the editor for logical or linguistic reasons are marked with [brackets] and have frequently the character of philosophical conjectures, admittedly open to criticism. By disregarding them, however, the reader will find the original text of Husserl's manuscript.**

Alfred Schuetz

III***

Have I already taken into consideration everything that could be significant for our question? Every perspectival "distant thing" indicates an existing thing and the whole system of perspectives that has its optimal domain in what is nearby and close. This indication is not isolated for the particular close and distant perspectives, and for the particular things which show themselves in fact in an optimal way. We could completely prove their actuality in practice by bringing them close to us.

The entire present world which appears as actual is rather a totality of perspectives for me. Not only is every particular thing a

---

*This article originally appeared as "Die Welt der lebendigen Gegenwart und die Konstitution der ausserleiblichen Umwelt", edited with a preface by Alfred Schuetz, *Philosophy and Phenomenological Research* vol. 6, no. 3 (March 1946): 323–43. Reprinted with permission of the publisher.

**For stylistic reasons, the translators have omitted these brackets. Scholars who wish to identify Schuetz's emendations may refer to the original.

***The typescript states as follows: "In connection with another manuscript — not indicated, but probably D 12, Husserl begins:"

unity in the change of its perspectivations, but every pair or simultaneously present group of things presents itself in one perspective. The entire physical perceptual field as a constituted manifold of things that appear in perspectives is a harmonious unity of perspectivity; *one* perspectival style governs and continues to govern throughout the changing perceptual field. Its changes can occur by the entry of the perceptual appearance of things not already in the field, or by the withdrawal of those previously in the field. Furthermore, it governs not just in each instantaneous present, but in the concrete and flowing present with its continuous synthesis. This synthesis is also concerned with the perspectival coexistences and successions as they pass over into one another and thereby suitably fit together with one another.

This style is continually prescribed and maintained, constantly being verified harmoniously such that particular appearances may indeed enter that violate the style, whether they occur internally and inconsistently — "counter to the style" — (in that they do not allow the usual transition from distant thing to close thing or its reverse) or, whether they do not progress as expected in a style of totality. Doubt, correction, and illusion grow, should such appearances occur.

What has been described so far is not, however, the entire, the concrete style of appearance in which the world as existent is harmoniously experienced for me, the perceiver, who originally experiences the living present. For there was no discussion of quality. It should be shown more precisely too that the concrete total style in its stratification continually constitutes a stratum of pluralistic "unchanged" things, and accordingly has a core stratum of primary normality. To this belongs the stratum of things which are "at rest with qualitative nonalteration." Only later does the stratum become explicit; the stratum of various "stably rigid" bodies becomes explicit by means of qualitative change as a continually unitary association and in full qualitative identity. The rigid body is the normal body, for even deformation of the body can, at any phase, turn into rigidity. The unchanged body as normal can be seen the very same way as qualitative change. In addition even the

causal style that constitutes the physical-thing appearance is to be construed as a founded level, for it must still be taken into consideration that this causal style is founded in the style of appearance just described: the lower level constituted the phantom [*Phantome*] and a constituted thing only arises through the founded standard causal style — which is founded in the usual behavior of the phantom under phantom circumstances.

Causality, the integrity of the style, has an integral form which runs through the "nonalteration" or "alteration" of perspectives (as merely spatial perspectives). This is an alteration and nonalteration not of things, nor perspectives perceived in the temporality of things, but is experienced within the temporality of immanent life.

The style of change, in its "rest" (in its momentary nonalteration) and "motion," is inseparably connected to my possible resting or moving. Accordingly, it can temporarily (in immanent temporality) change "of itself." We must then distinguish on the one hand the change of appearances in the system of appearances (*i.e.,* the system of the subjective presentations up to the causalities that are presenting themselves) and change of the entire system of appearances, a change accomplished "by itself" — including changes not accomplished "by themselves." And on the other hand we must distinguish change which I bring about as a result of my doing, that has begun with my kinaesthetic doing. However, it is always a doing and a doing within a system of capacities for doing. With respect to appearance of space, this sort of ability is related to my changing myself, that to the fact that in the closest familiar sphere, generally speaking, I can compensate (more or less completely) for every change in myself. Thus the total style of change, including each particular physical harmonious style of change of appearances in the mode of "by myself," is for its part changeable by virtue of my relevant capacity. In this way the entire style left to the ego or freely influenced by the ego is arranged so as to be able to experience each particular that appears in it (and appears in continuously, harmoniously changing appearances) as one and the same, preserving its harmony. Indeed in accord with the particular circumstances, each particular is experienced in a particular way as "objectively" changed or not, as retaining the same place and spatial extension or as moving in it, as being deformed and qualitatively altered or not.

One feature of this universal style of experiencing the world in the form of "living present" is that sometimes it already has or (unless contingent restrictions are involved) can have a capacity for extreme distance — a blurring of the experienced things due to themselves or due to me. This distance is continually extended to zero as a limit — such that all differences in configuration, all qualitative differences, all internal prominence of parts completely disappear. And yet in its continual identification, the same thing ultimately appears as a "point." The reverse can also occurr: a most distant point can, through itself or my effort (though in fact this does not always lie within our actual capacity), pass over into a continuity appropriate to a distant thing in which, as a distant thing, it is shown to be increasingly differentiated. Remote distance can also be like the blue sky or a distant monotonous background, so that when blurring occurs what is differentiated loses its prominence and blends into its background.

This also holds for the perspectival style of appearance: in changes appropriate to its style, it indicates possibilities for the dissolution of appearances which, as appearances that adapt themselves harmoniously to the universal style of appearance, would be experiences of Objects belonging to the world — without any question arising as to "whether I can really go there or not." This style indicates (or as we could also say induces) the world as a world having an existential sense by means of this style, this world continually appears with a co-given or (if I am perhaps in a room or cave and not exactly involved) factually producible range of distance (a horizon) and, moreover, appears as articulated into nearness and distance.

This world appears in such a way that there is an attendant possibility that objects could approach of themselves from the farthest distance (which for that very reason is still called distance), just as very commonly occurs: a horizonal point begins to be distinguished in accordance with appearances, is changed into a distant appearance and continuity of appearances whereby the existential sense "approaching thing" arises; correlatively, there is the attendant possibility that by means of my going off into the distance — in any direction of orientation — the horizon, no matter how much it may at first remain unaffected, is dissolved correspondingly into a horizon of appearances of things, at least in part.

These possibilities are "predelineated" through experience; they are possibilities which include existential validities and not merely imaginary possibilities. They are in fact induced possibilities for which something speaks, in accordance with the style, from earlier experience and also from the whole course of the living present — although no particular existential certainty is thereby motivated, in particular or in general.

The style of the perspectives, including spatial and then qualitative perspectives, is already constituted in spatiotemporality, which is the form of realities, indeed of realities as they are intrinsically; we have here already a difference between "immanent time," the "time of perspectival progressions," and the "phantom time of the perspectively appearing unities."

But how far does this extend? We must first ask about immanence: Do we not pause for sleep? What makes these pauses interruptions of a single time that connects the interrupted streams of perspectival appearances? We can say that we have here the hidden primal constitution as temporal, which becomes temporal in the distant reaches of memory. But what about phantoms? Is it not the case that phantom perceptual fields and temporal fields are not separate and only combined by immanent time; and that immanent time and phantom time are still undivided even though the phantom as a possibly constituted unity of appearances and time itself is already separated? What about space? Coexistence could be phantomly constituted, as distant from that coexistence which occurs in perspectives. Each phantom already has spatiality in itself, already has something coexistent, has something that now is, but is not now given together in accordance with perception. Illusions could be moving of their own accord or mine, and also with one another—several as a unity moving in space as their form.

But to what extent can I maintain the unity of a phantom? I can maintain it naturally by means of perception and recollection which extends within a sphere of continually advancing perception (hence, so to speak, in a present lengthened at will). But what about pauses, interruptions in which immanent time may well continue, but not the unity of phantom perception?

We need not touch on the problem of "sleep" or "unconsciousness" for prior to it is the manner of the living flowing phantom present: the problem is that phantoms come in and pass out of the present, can reenter it and so forth. But do the phantoms still *exist*, after their "withdrawal," as the word indicates; does it indeed make any sense if we say that the newly entering phantom is "the same" as before?

Within certain limits I have the capacity to see the lost phantom again. My given field of phantoms, which continually (in a change of perspectives) persists as perceived, extends to a field broadened by the phantoms, with the capacity to return at will to the earlier field with the previous phantoms. In the transition from phase to phase, a core of persistently perceived phantoms thereby mediates. In the continuous perceptual transition from the first field to the second I simply identify the newly perceived phantom with the same one perceived earlier, that is with what is remembered as present in the previous field. This transition has the character of a continuous total perception in which a unity of total experience of a phantom "world" is grounded. The phantom is continually perceptually present for me, even though I genuinely perceive (and perceived) only a sector of it in the momentary present. A perceptual style is attained here of the sort in which a horizon of possibly perceivable and coexistent copresent objects belongs to each perceptual present, whether known or unknown. Every manner of bringing my kinaesthetic activities into play brings to perception something which could have been previously perceived.

But is this not valid only for a normal sphere of unaltered (at rest and qualitative nonalteration) phantoms that persist in the continuity of experience? And if I concern myself in this investigation only with phantoms (thus with unities of perspectives) have I not merely taken into consideration corporeal nature as it is given to me in perception, and indeed precisely from the point of view of what may be said within the restriction to the perspectival mode of appearance of nature (thus, abstractly)? Have I not restricted myself to what may be genuinely said about nature perceptually or purely on the basis of the sensuous, intuitional present? Otherwise stated, I have then experienced the world as primordially reduced pure nature, as oriented around my functioning animate organism (which itself is a purely reduced animate organism). In the change of orientations within my unbroken continuity of living experience, this animate organism is experienced as identical, that is as persisting in changing perspectives, a change proceeding of itself which is also a change that it is within my power to direct.

The broader problems which result must naturally be those that take as their object the synthesis of this primordial world with the world of others who exist for me, and on the other hand the problem of "pauses," sleep and even death.

But now, how do we get past the normal case of rest and nonalteration, and how do we get to the already constituted form of space as the form of unchangeable phantoms that are endlessly open by virtue of the always predelineated horizon of possibly coexistent phantoms? No difficulty is caused by the constitutive unity-formation of a transition from unchanged phantom into the same one altered in such-and-such a way, and then again to the persistent unchanged phantom—a transition that leads sooner or later to nonalteration and can terminate there. The capacity for various kinds of alteration causes no difficulty when these are construed as a continuity of phases, to each of which corresponds a determinately pertinent nonalteration (structure of differentials). Hence rest and movement, the latter in different formations of movement in space, are experienced in the forms of uniform and dissimilar movement, etc.; similarly for the different modes and qualitative directions of alteration.

However, with reference to different "senses," etc., all that is not so simple. If we carry out the needed clarification we understand the abstract layer, phantom, in alteration or nonalteration. It persists at first as the same so long as the perception of this phantom (and any group of phantoms at all) continues unbroken and the withdrawal and entrance of illusions into the field of perception proceeds according to a certain style. When I see a pendulum swing, repeatedly look away and back again and always see the same undisturbed clock and surroundings, I "experience" the pendulum moving regularly throughout the unseen intervals — even though it would be possible to think that meantime it had moved otherwise. Furthermore, I know that movement can change into rest and alteration into nonalteration in very different ways. But when I experience enduring rest, I expect continuous rest, so long as nothing indicates that movement may be anticipated — as is the case if I had been able to experience this object or sort of object resting partially within a periodic change of rest and movement. The same is true for any sequences whatever, typical sequences of any processes of any alteration whatever.

Each phantom in its mode of alteration (including the limiting case of rest) intrinsically predelineates its future continuation and future alteration — within certain limits, even the very mode of change. However the predelineation takes place in such a way that the possibility of occuring otherwise remains open, and not just as a possibility for imagination. Rather starting and stopping occur, interrupting these anticipations. As a familiar matter, this itself belongs to the style of this illusory experience.

Entire fields, rather than just particulars, are thereby involved, but then qualities come into consideration in the already constituted space — the visual, tactile space. And we have the further problem of the constitution of space as empty of physical things though infused with rays, space as resounding object, rays of sound in space, warmth of an object, rays of warmth — and the manner in which radiation is experienced without a radiating object. How it is that this experience, which is not directly aimed at a spatial object, indicates its object

and indicates it in genuine perspective — the stove's warmth, perspectivally adumbrating itself in changing rays at different spatial locations in which my body is located. What is experienced together under identical kinaesthetic conditions makes available what is identical, constitutes the same as a unity of adumbrations.

The constitution of the phantom world takes place in the perception that flows uninterruptedly — the constitutive production that already lies within its sense, continually affirming, verifying. This is genuinely continuous constitution. Spatiotemporality is already form, the form for *res extensa*.

When we summarize the investigation thus far, we find: that rest and movement, alteration and nonalteration are in a certain sense already there in the constituted phantom world; that is, they are clarified in accordance with a determinate sense, by means of what our clarifying explication has shown.

And yet we have given no justification for what makes phantoms into real objects, into objects that persist in objectively real alteration and nonalteration, and as such are persistent in themselves.

Actually, so far we have only given a justification for the constitution of unities from those subjective kinaesthetic-associative changes that occur in the living present. Accordingly they yield only those unities immediately available kinaesthetically that are constituted in the perspective of their adumbrations as particulars and as entire perceptual fields with entrances and withdrawals of particulars, but always in the manner of continually presumed entities of which we are constantly conscious as immediately available. By virtue of their mode of constitution, these unities are already unities of alteration and nonalteration. At rest the thing (the phantom, as we said) is one-sidedly given; each side is given as available from the just-elapsed variation of sides and, thereby, it always carries with it the anticipating horizon of the opposite side — that is, furthermore, anticipated in the style of nonalteration. If the one-sidedly given illusion is in a process of change, change is also anticipated for the unseen side. Admittedly, the possibility always remains open that what is anticipated, what is posited as a genuinely nonexperienced copresence in a case where it was anticipated as resting may show itself as movement and alteration when we come to experience it. Or the reverse may occur: where movement and alteration were anticipated, it shows itself as unchanged and at rest. Nevertheless I can always convince myself, at least within limitations, whether for example the reverse side has remained unmoved in respect to its parts, or whether the body has been deformed in some way, qualitatively changed there—and I can provide an increasingly stronger certainty by walking around it repeatedly. It is the same too for alteration—but all of this holds only in the original living streaming present and the spatiotemporal present filled with objects and constituted within it. Of course this also holds for each past present as well as each future present.

But is all this enough for a satisfactory account of the constituted structure of experiencing the world that exists for me, does it satisfy the sense which it has for me in this experiential life of the one world which continues to endure through time? How does it happen that the flowing advance of my experiential life can have this peculiar sense? What universal structure does it have? And which sedimentations of the sense of experience within each living presence point back to it? How does the specific structure of living present experience in which this sense is grounded comport itself, and what is the verification effected there like?

It is certainly the case that recollection enters into the living present, and having developed within that present, reproduces for me my previous life, my previous living present, and thus the world experienced in it as spatiotemporally present. But to what extent is this world simply experienced as the same that I still experience now—even though the range of things which I now experience, my present surrounding world, is in general quite other than what was previously actually present? In the living present I have the change of phases, of stretches of present time, in which on the one hand things become experienced which were not yet there and on the other things disappear from actual experience which are taken as having already been there earlier or persist-

ing after their disappearance. This depends upon it being possible for us repeatedly to recover what has disappeared, in ordinary experience, arbitrarily and at will, and to be able to experience it again. It depends upon the apperceptions founded in this possibility. This seems easily understandable, as does the fact that in the process of flowing to a present that has already been closely reproduced with respect to the things it offered and that my current present does not offer I say: "I just don't see the things now, but they are still there, and with appropriate measures I can see them again." Similarly it is easily understandable that I can say, "I could have already experienced as something new—if only I had allowed my kinaesthetic activities appropriate play."

But is this such a simple matter, even in this narrow sphere? Doesn't this elucidation structurally presuppose something whereby it can arrive at such experiences of identity which depend upon always being able to do it again? And how can this occur for present surrounding worlds that lie in the distant past? The cities, countries, and mountains with which I became acquainted long ago while traveling, for instance, still exist even though I am now here, at home. I can of course visit them again, I can see the places of my childhood again—but how can I say that? How is it that I experience what is seen again as the same? How can it be experienced as the same? In fact I realize, and usually experience accordingly, that what is the same is more or less changed, perhaps much is completely gone; the familiar house no longer stands there, but has been replaced by another, and so forth. But on what basis can we say all this? In terms of what experiences does this become possible? I say "the same," and not "perfectly alike"; "the same, only changed." I call things that are perfectly alike in the present and in recollection: the same. But also I call something that is different and "looks entirely otherwise" by the name: "altered" one-and-the-same. I differentiate, and indeed do so experientially, things that are perfectly alike and the same identical things. Admittedly I cannot always differentiate; I cannot always be certain of the supposed identity. And yet I say: "the same world . . ." and say it even in situations of such undecided, and in fact for me undecidable, uncertainty—I only doubt whether it is identical or similar, or I doubt whether it is the same thing with a more extensive change or another thing. In any case, and this also underlies such doubts, the thing that I recall has not just become something which subjectively appears during my past experience, a thing to be confirmed in it only subjectively and temporally. In that it was objective, it was experienced as persisting, perhaps as changing in the manner of disintegration (which is only a way of persisting in the form of disintegrated pieces for which further occurrence of the same sort can take place). Perhaps this apprehension which governs our life, at least in its strict form as apprehension of an absolutely persistent nature, is already a mediated, artificial product of science. Perhaps the possibility is initially to be left open of an actual disappearance, of a becoming nothing—especially if we primordially consider the world abstractively and make no constitutive use of the achievement of coexperiencing others.

But in any case we must understand, and indeed understand as a preliminary stage, how the constitution of the unity of a temporal world as a persistent world occurs, complete with the constitution of the living present belonging to it, and with the experienced identification of things connecting my past with this present. Then we may ask how we come to this "idealization" that permits no disappearance and no wonder about the origin of things.

We see that the question of the constitutive possibility of a unified objective world (and of nature first of all) is closely tied with and indeed is equivalent to the problem of the possibility of being able to experience the same object at different times (and then also, by different human beings); or, with the question of the transcendental possibility of experiencing the same as the same.

Again this goes together with the problem of recognition of the concrete typicality of the objects, and of the objects themselves in their type. On the one hand, we distinguish the general characteristic or the general types (house, tree, animal, etc.), or the experience of an object, even an unknown one, as "a tree," "an animal," etc. Its type is

known and recognized, though not as a universal, as something objective for itself; but the individual object is unknown in its individuality. On the other hand, we distinguish the individual type by which the concrete individuality of the object as such is recognized. For example, a person has a body; but if he is not thematically divided as body and as person, he has his general universal characteristic in the unified construal as a person. But he also has his immediately construed individuality, however, incompletely—his mannerisms and behavior, which characterize him without comparison to others and by which he is simply recognized as this person. (Likewise indeed, the general type is not grasped by comparison and abstract generalization, but is itself given to consciousness as a moment of experience.) The world familiar to us from our experiences, our life-world, is in every present; and in every survey is found the unity of spatiotemporality, which is the unity of our experience, in the unified world which is ours. It is ours not only as flowingly present, but as our spatiotemporal world of experience. Thanks to recoverable pasts given through memory and also to expectations which predelineate the living future for us it is a thoroughly typified world. All that exists within it, whether known or unknown, is an object of experience with the form: an A, and, this A.

All real relations, connections, wholes, and parts are themselves relations and connections of these typifying forms, which here are to be understood, if you will, as "appearing forms" or "experiential forms"—rather than, so to speak, as artificial forms created by logic which all traditional logic already implicitly presupposes.

However, here the problem must be clarified as to the way and levels at which the typification is built up; that belongs essentially to the constitution of objects as mundane objects of possible experience. How is typification structured or founded in its sense-bestowing as belonging to "finished" objects, and indeed to the experience of objects that have been finished all along? And from that point one must then understand how individuals at different experiential times, to which however the objective times of what is experienced correspond, can be identified and recognized as the same, and verified in experience as the same, which has all along been something typified. Furthermore, this yields the problem of the way merely perfectly alike things, which already have the form of two or several As, can be experienced as different individual objects that are perfectly alike over a span of time.

The objects are constituted as persistent unities of nonalteration and alteration. At all levels reduction to types encompasses the constitutive formation of unities of alteration and the different "concepts" or types of alteration; finally, objective alteration. How does this constitution of types govern in a way that enables objects to be always repeatedly recognizable in experience, and always repeatedly verifiable as the same, still continually existing even though in entirely different conditions of alteration in the different conditions of alteration existing at different times, persisting as the same throughout these times?

If we think abstractly of a perceptual world, a living perceptual present, at rest, what must our procedure be? (A) The reduction of intersubjectivity to subjectivity as my own. (B) Every realteration has its sense of rest; thus the constitution of "rest" must found that of "alteration." (C) All of the past gains its sense in the flowing present and indeed constitutes itself out of that flow; all of the objective past constitutes itself out of the objective present, and the objective present constitutes itself ultimately, in the structure of the "living present," whereby it carries in itself, flowingly, a primal present. In this genuine perceptual present is constituted the perceptual world-present—thus the first perceptual world—and therein, the constitution of rest.

Every present is a situation, however much change has taken place in it—kinaesthetic and directional changes, changes in perspective, rest and movement, qualitative alteration and nonalteration. And it retains unity during and despite all the change in this present. Not only is the unity of the spatio-temporal thing as "the same, that thereby moves itself" experienced, etc., but even the entire situation has unity; or rather what is coexistently experienced in the unity of a living present has a unity, that of the situation.

(1) Let us take as the primary, normal case from which we can go on to others the situation of a "surrounding world at rest." Nonalteration is always experienced in the change of kinaesthetic activity, a nonalteration in the process of repeated identification of the same thing, the harmonious experiences of it, the becoming acquainted with it. In this way we have continually cogiven to us the horizon of what we are to become acquainted with for the first time, and perhaps of mere reapprehension, of "being able to perceive again as already known." In this temporal process (immanently-temporal physical time, presented therein as the persistence of all things in nonalteration), each thing has not only its persistent shape, but all things have at once a persistent spatial configuration that is presented by means of the configuration of presentations in their sense-fields.

It is characteristic of this change that in every phase of this streaming present a determinate configuration is perceptually actualized from a momentary side. But in the flowing transition from phase to phase, things enter into perception and others withdraw in such a way that if I stop the kinaesthetic activity, change of this sort does not occur. But stopping the kinaesthetic activity, as important as it is constitutively, is still only a transitory phase of the normal elapsing or arbitrary determinate direction of the kinaesthetic activity. The flowing progress of perception connects itself into the unity of a perception which reaches far enough so that the elements which have flowed past what is past, in the living process are still made prominent in the present precisely as a freshly living "retentional past" —despite its "dimness." Potentially in this stream, a living future in its flowing transition is likewise predelineated within the livingly actualized present. What flows therein, constituted as a unity, is a continually persistent "spatial field" of unchanged things—or, what says the same thing, an open spatial configuration of unchanged things that always comes to cognizance and expands in the act of taking cognizance in streamingly continual experience. The "ensemble" of things experienced at once in the living present is not a mere "being experienced together," but a unity of a spatiotemporal "ensemble," of one configuratively bound up in spatiotemporality. One must not think merely of spatiality in connection with the term "configuration" but also think of what is qualified. Thus, one must think of the phenomenological unity that here keeps the particular concreta united concretely. Just as association in a particular structural shape constitutes the thing at rest, (perspectives of kinaesthetic activity), so too the universal structure of the bound-together ensemble, is also an associative structure that delivers a peculiar and whole field of perception in the stream of the whole living present, assuming we understand what association as intentional synthesis means.

Association is thus at work here—and this includes continual apperception, the synthetic unity which forms at *one* place as the formation of adumbrations, as adumbrations that kinaesthetic transition in are appearances of the same thing, and carries itself over to all places in the sense-fields. In the simultaneous process of formation there is a process of association of formations. This process occurs in, so to speak, reciprocal apperceptive transfer and coincidence; that is, coincidence that has the character of transferred synthetic unities. Each newly entering object is already apperceived as an object, as a unity of appearances to be formed in such and such a way, and in that way to be brought into the temporal flow. Taken universally, this apperceiving of the object as object is the primary universal typification— precisely the typification of the object as experiential object, perceptual object, and the typification of the unities as a configuration of objects. Also included here in this primary universal typification is the typicality of self-expansion of the configuration by remaining-in-one's-grip; the readmission of genuinely perceivable objects and the loss of these—a loss that is however a preservation by way of remaining in living validity, the merely retentional modification.

Every object for itself is just a patterned thing; it is a configuration closed in on itself —that is, a configuration of the extensive parts stressed within it. We could just as well speak of a configuration of objects arranged

as a partial configuration of the totality. For in truth, the object is not yet constituted by this constitution of unities of mere rest.

(2) The constitution of alteration in terms of nonalteration is already presupposed for the perspectival constitution of physically spatial nonalteration, including first of all the constitution of spatial rest. I will dispense with any closer look at the constitution of the alteration of particular things here. This would have to be clarified as the constitution, under present, is a persistent total unity—not that of an object but that of a configurative connectedness of all immanent, conjointly experienced objects. It is, so to speak, the primary world as world of experience (here, to mere experience of the living present and indeed, more exactly the experiences of its objective perceptual structure alone). This implies that the multiplicity of alteration, which endures through the ongoing continuance (the duration of the perceptual object) and in which the object has its factual existence as a persistently identical unity, is not, and also cannot, be isolated. This multiplicity of alterations is rather correlated to the universal multiplicity of alterations of the totality of perceived objects that are together in the unity of the flowing perceptual present. They do not persist alone, but in a community within the persisting form of objective time (which persists in a way entirely different from that of persistence in the flowing perceptual present).

But here we must not overlook spatiotemporal configuration (every object too has its endurance, begins, ceases, and is no longer the same object when it has disintegrated into several objects—this spatiotemporal configuration is no longer an object at all in our present sense). It is prior to space and time themselves insofar as these are understood as identical persistent forms within which (as the form of space demands) all objects are spatial, are in their places, having a situation, by virtue of their spatial shape; as object-determining, this configuration is "spatial form in situation"—and (as the form of time demands) within which all times are durations, peculiar to the objects as determinations. The "presentation" of these forms first arises on the basis of the constantly changing configurations.

We have thereby achieved, as the primary world, the world which is experienced in the living perceptual present and is, simply in terms of that intentionality, a filled world. It extends as far as my retention reaches—indeed, as far as my available retention. The just-experienced is not lost; it still belongs to the world which is for me. Yet here we must not go beyond the problem too quickly . . .

Apperception is construing of similar existing things in accordance with what already exists for me as similar. The newly experienced thing is; this I have simply, experientially, in accord with the experiential sense that derives from the similarity with my earlier acquisition of similar things that exist for me. The construing sense is an existential validity with an anticipated horizon of possible validation. Apperception points toward earlier primal instituting, but apperception is also a constant process in coexistence, that is, in the sphere of the living present. If I have a plurality of things which are perfectly alike (sensuously similar) in original association in my field of the present, each new sense-fashioning transfers, in passive association, to all others as a new apperception of something which is perfectly like another, so long as the perfect likeness [Gleichheit] persists: passive-associative transfer accomplished analogously in accordance with similarity [Ähnlichkeit].

Our objects of experience and pluralities (alike things, similar things) are then usually very complicated formations out of apperceptions. Involved in them (in the manner of intentional modifications) are anticipations of apperceptions which build up sense —which are not actually accomplished, but implied. This is the case, for example, if we experience the likeness of two things, one of which is given as close and the other as distant. Apperception continues to work by means of intentional modification and increased similarity; motivation by means of similarity is itself something which generates intentional modification.

Association or apperception then constitutes existing things of a type, often in levels, so that the apperception of similar things in conformity with other similar things still remains in effect in a certain way even when typical similarity is violated; that is, insofar as one segment takes on, in addition to the typical similarity which remains preserved, an additional superimposed sense which the other segments do not have; and insofar as all these others have an apperceptive commonness among each other which the exceptional segment, for its part, does not have.

But surely that is too formal. I am concerned with the formation of apperceptions by means of intentional modification of already formed apperceptions, thus with the formation of perceptions from presentifications, etc., of different levels; or with those which in their higher sense-fashioning are peculiar sorts of intentional modifications of the lower-level, more original experiences, but which are still always experiences of the higher-level sort constitutive of existent things.

A special case of such higher-level apperceptions is formed by empathy, the experience of someone else or the perception of another human being. Here, animate organism [Leib] which subsequently is revealed as "other organism" is experienced as such in conformity with the apperception of my own organism. That seems simple; it is apprehension of something similar by means of and in accord with what was previously experienced as similar. But it is not exactly the kind of apperceptive transfer that is present if, within the already constituted field of existing things external to me, I simply apperceptively transfer what I come to know about one thing to another which is like it. First of all, my organism does not yet have any organism like it in the field of preconstituted external things. And it achieves such a thing only by means of a novel apperception of the organism, which indeed presupposes the apperception of external things but transforms it into something novel. In other words, the constitution of my organism as a bodily thing like any other bodily external thing is presupposed for the constitution of others existing for me. The above first makes possible the experience of things like my own organism, and then makes it possible that a thing similar to my organism is an organism, though another's organism —and can be experienced by me as such.

What is foremost here is the constitution of the primordial world external to my organism as a spatiotemporal world whereby my organism with its kinaesthetic activities is a functioning organism. In the change of kinaesthetically motivated modes of appearance every external thing is constituted as the same, and thus every ensemble is constituted configuratively as the same, and indeed as persisting in rest and movement as well as qualitative nonalteration and alteration.

What is presumed thereby, and is in itself primary, is constitution of movement (including deformation) and rest, and also that within the spatial field which functions as an invariant system of possible positions. This constitution takes place on two levels.

(1) On the first level the kinaesthetic activities of walking are still out of play; we abstract from "I walk" and from the sense of this "I walk" as "I am in motion in space." Together with that we also abstract from my being in motion in space "mechanically," that is, without my walking. All that remains in play at this level are my various other kinaesthetic activities, such as arm, finger, and eye movements, etc.

(2) Only after we have considered the productivity of this sphere does walking come into question. The "I rest" precedes constitutively the "I move myself" insofar as the latter must acquire its meaning as a continuum of possible resting-points. In the system "I move myself," taken purely in its subjective kinaesthetic sense, we now consider the special stillness of standing, of sitting, of "not-moving-myself-forward," as it is called in the language of an already objectified construal that is here first to be built up constitutively. All other kinaesthetic activities are in play, in their unconstrained elapsing as "rest" and "movement." The appearing external world of things in their movement and rest is thereby constituted. So too my organism constitutes itself: by means of its relation to itself as an animate organism it is also constituted as moveable, along with the "I stretch out my arm," the "I move my eyes," along with spatially rolling my eyes in their sockets, etc. The kinaesthetic activities and the spatial movements stay in union by means of association, and thus yield a combination of different movements in a double sense: the head moves itself conjointly with the eyes in the head, together with hand, upper arm, finger, etc. If we disregard the kinaesthetic activities, then the organs and their unity, the animate organism, are just a body like any other bodies of the external world; they are constituted like the others as bodies in relation to the modes of appearance. But these for their part are motivated by the kinaesthetic activities functioning at a given time, which as functioning at any given time do not belong to spatial things but to the subjective ways they are given. Likewise for the corporeal, physical body; the body as animate organism is constituted at any given time by means of the functioning kinaesthetic activities together with the manners of appearance belonging to each, which in a change of orientation are of course experienced as kinaesthetic flow localized in the hands, the eyes, the parts of the body, and as parallels to the external spatial movements of those parts.

In this constitutive interconnection we have things given as close and distant; we have movements and alteration given in different modes of appearance that are related to the different particular kinaesthetic systems. We have a system of ways of appearing for rest and movement and for alteration and nonalteration for each system; but all this is changed when other kinaesthetic systems enter as cofunctioning. In the total situation, however, they already constitute the changeable physically existent "world" in a manner still to be clarified though with very strict limitations.

I have here a core sphere of fully original constituted things, a core world, so to speak. It is a sphere of things to which I can go by virtue of my kinaesthetic activity, which I can experience in the most favorable form: handle them, see them, etc., where I thus have available systems of appearance for them, which I have the ability to transform into the optimal modes of appearance. There I would also have a possible realm of practice, indeed one to be brought about immediately by means of my thrusting, pushing, etc. organism.

But I also have apperceived things outside of this core-sphere. What is at issue here? "Things" distance themselves in perspectives up to the farthest edge of the horizon; from there to here, in the reverse process, these things show a perspectival approaching; they enter the core-filled. The distant things comport themselves perspectivally like things which belong to the core-spheres. In their unfamiliarity very "distant" things are similar to close things in a reduced formal way, as compared to the familiar and, by virtue of their completely original constitution, primarily familiar sphere of closeness, the core-sphere. But then again they are not entirely similar in that they are not noticeably put into perspective by bringing kinaesthetic activities into play. They resemble close things only if they move and finally leave the horizon: they can then be seen like pictures in a picture-book.

Of course this is not questioned if the experience occurs in an "enclosed space" such as a room: the "unfamiliar distance" with its horizon is lacking there. Phenomena such as the sun, moon, northern lights, rainbow, clouds, constellations and such, which are not constituted perspectively in the interplay of all kinaesthetic activities, are also not taken into consideration here.

However, walking is involved from the very beginning, even in an enclosed space in which, normally, everything is accessible, and hence is spatiotemporally constituted in the same manner as real, mutually external entities. Enclosed space is, and so the apperceptive enlargement of the sphere of closeness (the original core-sphere) into a homogeneous, endlessly open world of space is accomplished.

Distant appearances are first perspectivally transformed into close appearances in the activity of walking, as it acts together with other kinaesthetic activities and the things of a "core world" that are already constituted by these activities. They are thus grasped from the beginning with the possibility of being legitimized as things; to this also belongs the possibility of being actively (immediately actively) associated with them.

This is the situation for all things which are external to my animate organism. From the beginning the animate organism has constitutively an exceptional position. This is already apparent if I consider the constitution of the organism when it is stationary. The organism (by analogy with the wall of the enclosed room) is not experienced as possibly being, and capable of being, now resting, now moving itself—in any case, it is not so experienced. Rather only the parts of the body are so experienced, and even these only in a restricted sense. I can very well experience my hand as moving, and in the perspectivistic manner, experience this, just like above, any similar movement of a thing. And yet it cannot be moved arbitrarily, and cannot be moved like any other thing, that is arbitrarily far in all directions; I cannot throw my hand so that it flies far away, etc.

However, what concerns the animate organism is that its manner of appearance, notwithstanding all movements of parts of the body, resembles rest—similar to the rest of the tree as a whole even when its branches move. And yet all physical rest, according to its sense, is only experienced as rest through the power of those changes of appearance whereby physical movement is constituted. However, just this is not the case for the animate organism. As my animate organism, it is unique in that it is experienced as my total organ, articulated into organs in which I am the functioning ego—and this in such a way that in this functioning all perception of physical things takes place, even the perception of the organism itself which sees itself by means of itself-but disregarding all that, the organism is also uniquely constituted in that it is, so to speak, constituted as almost a thing and yet cannot be experienced for itself in physical movement—as this is itself originally constituted in perspectivating phenomena.

None of this is changed if we bring in the activity of walking. First of all this kinaesthetic activity brings about something new in that a change in orientation of the coexistent subjective appearances begins. We have seen that this primary "world" which is constituted in stationary kinaesthetic activity, in the inaction of "walking kinaesthetics" is a world which is firmly oriented around my physical animate organism (or the null-point constituted in it). If walking begins, all worldly things there for me continue to appear to me to be oriented about my phenomenally stationary, resting organism. That is, they are oriented with respect to here and there, right and left, etc., whereby a firm zero of orientation persists, so to speak, as absolute here. Now, however, that is "appearance," and so it happens that everything in arbitrary interruption of walking and reversal of kinaesthetic doing (in going back) shows itself as an object at rest; and in remaining stationary, it is legitimated as at rest. All this now is shown as changing orientation, and accordingly as in a phantom movement. By contrast movement at a standstill presents itself either as rest or, phenomenally, as modified movement. Walking thereby receives the sense of a modification of all coexistent subjective appearances whereby now the intentionality of the appearance of things first remains preserved, as a self-constituting in the oriented things and in the change of orientation, as identical things.

Every kinaesthetic activity functions as sense-bestowing by virtue of the fact that it has its modes of "keeping still" and "keeping-in-operation" ("I move"); and kinaesthetic movement which has become a continuum (constitutively) is the continuum of places of possible standing still. This is likewise also the case for the, so to speak, concluded kinaesthetic activity of walking, which has a special manner of functioning by means of its relation back to the already synthetic production of all other associated kinaesthetic activities. Each of these has already taken on the sense of being able to be combined with every other stationary and self-moving thing, and so to be a partial function of a whole function, so to speak, to be in a unity of organized functions. New movement and rest of the experienced surrounding world (perceptual world) in its flowing manner, like all other nonalteration and alteration, constitute themselves in walking. First to be constituted, then, is the fixed system of places with fixed distances, fixed configurations, arrangements of resting things—and also the objective change in these configurations by means of changes of distances of movement.

I ask myself: Does the homogeneous objective world, homogeneous spatiotemporality, in contrast to which the oriented primordial world is mere appearance, constitute itself first by means of the interplay of self-moving and having-moved, mechanically having-moved? Let us consider this in regard to mere oriented space: Does every thing in this "world" have its persistent or fixed distance from every other? My animate organism, like its parts, also has a changing distance from the things oriented about it, but it cannot bring about any change in position—it remains a stable null-object. Only other objects can bring about changes in position, take on other distances relative to it, be at changing distances relative to it. In walking, however, I myself change my distance to the objects which are persistent and identically resting in the change of orientation, and just as two external objects could ultimately be contiguous to each other so that their distance from the point of contiguity becomes zero, so can my organism also make itself contiguous with any other external object. Cannot I then, in this manner, get anywhere within the range of my capacity for walking? And thus is not space already a system of places (not just a system of orientation, orientation-space) and my organism constituted as object just like any other external object—as occupying and including a part of space, as having a place in space and being moved, spatially moved, like other objects?

Clearly the fixed system of places of all external things available perspectively to me is already constituted by means of self-moving, as is also the fact that I can bring myself as animate organism close to every thing and object at first directly, on the "surface of the earth" but indirectly also: by way of empathy for birds, I understand flying and have then the ideal possibility of being able to fly before my eyes as an idealization. (But that does not belong to the present constitutive level.) I can come to any place and be in it; thus my organism is also a thing, a *res extensa,* etc., movable.

But now, does becoming moved mechanically (being moved, being carried, etc.) in space accomplish nothing essential for the possibility of empathy?

14

Introduction to
"The Origin of Geometry"
DAVID CARR

According to Walter Biemel, editor of the posthumous *Husserliana* edition of *The Crisis of European Sciences and Transcendental Phenomenology*, "The Origin of Geometry" was written by Husserl in 1936. Thus its composition coincides with the preparation of *Crisis* for publication in the Belgrade yearbook *Philosophia*. There are clear indications that it was originally intended as part of *Crisis*, probably the section on Galileo, but it was finally not included in the text as published by *Philosophia*.[1] Eugen Fink edited and published this manuscript separately, beginning with the third paragraph, in the *Revue Internationale de Philosophie*, vol. 1, no. 2 (1939), giving it a title derived from the first sentence of that paragraph, "Der Ursprung der Geometrie als intentional-historisches Problem."

This title is slightly misleading, since the text is concerned less with the origination of disciplines like geometry than with their status for those who do not originate them but take them over as part of an already existing tradition of inquiry. The context is set by the discussion of Galileo, who is depicted as the originator of modern science through the "mathematization of nature."[2] But Galileo did not originate the science of geometry; he inherited it from the Greeks and took it for granted. To be sure, just as we take modern science for granted and must seek its origination in a figure like Galileo, so his taking for granted of geometry calls for a search for its origin. But it is the reason why

such a search for origins is called for, as an essential element in our understanding of these disciplines and the knowledge they contain, that concerns Husserl above all in this text. Why should the epistemology of natural science and even geometry require an apparently historical procedure such as this?

The answer is to be found by considering the way in which we—who are not the originators but the inheritors of geometry—acquire such a discipline and are initiated into its truths. It comes to us in the form of language, both written and spoken; it exists as a body of sentences organized in a certain way. This fact leads Husserl to a discussion of language that is probably more detailed than any he produced since the First Logical Investigation. In what sort of context does such a linguistic entity as geometry exist? A social context, obviously: the community of persons in which a common language is our primary medium of communication. As a linguistic entity, geometry is in some sense a human product. In this respect it resembles the artifacts that we and our fellows manufacture for our use or enjoyment. Each of these, we know, would not exist but for some human agency. But geometry is unlike artifacts in that it is a single entity, no matter how many times its propositions may be uttered or written down. This, of course, derives from its linguistic character: in this it is like *War and Peace*, or the sentence "How do you do?" or, to use Husserl's example,

251

the word 'lion'. Unlike these, however, geometry exists as a set of truth-claims, and it may be enlarged by sentences that are related by logic and subject matter to those already given.

Now our cultural space abounds with such truth-claims, not only scientific ones like those of geometry but also everyday factual claims, narratives about the past, etc. We encounter them in written form and in the spoken remarks of other people. What status do they have for us? According to most of Husserl's earlier analyses two possibilities exist: either such claims are simply *understood* and have no further status for us than that of *mere* claims; or we possess or acquire the corresponding evidence which justifies our assent to such claims so that they become part of our belief. Now Husserl recognizes the importance of a third possibility: that we assent to such claims without the corresponding evidence. This is by no means uncommon: it happens when we read a reliable newspaper or accept the assurances of a trustworthy friend. Many of our most fundamental and unshakable beliefs are acquired in this way. Our belief that the earth is round, for example, is one that almost all of us (a few astronauts excepted) have on hearsay alone. Do such beliefs have a "degree" of acceptance that is a shade less firm than those we have verified with our own eyes? It is hard to say. In any case it is clear that a great many, very important elements of the vast tissue of our beliefs about the world are of just this sort.

With this a new and important dimension is added to Husserl's theory of consciousness. He had previously used the metaphor of *sedimentation* to describe the ongoing, cumulative character of individual experience. Every case of self-evidence in my experience, he writes in *Cartesian Meditations,* "'sets up' or 'institutes' for me an *abiding possession*."[3] It is something to which I can return and which I can "reactivate." And even if I do not do so, such a self-evidence remains as an element of the structure of my beliefs and as such has its effect on my ongoing experience. But now Husserl introduces the notion of *social* and *historical* sedimentation. As we saw in the last paragraph, not every "abiding possession" of mine is traceable to a self-evidence of my own. Those taken over from the social context claim, as it were, to be the sedimentation of someone else's experience which I could conceivably repeat given the appropriate circumstances. But in the course of everyday life it rarely occurs to me to do so.

To be sure, it is precisely the ideal of the *scientific* attitude toward our beliefs that we not be satisfied with this situation, that we withhold judgment until truth claims are verified by the appropriate evidence, whether empirical or, in the case of disciplines like geometry, mathematical. It is symptomatic of Husserl's earlier, primarily scientific conception of cognition that it was this attitude which figured most heavily in his previous descriptions of experience. Now, with his interest in the life-world and everyday experience, the fact of social and historical sedimentation comes to the fore.

But in "The Origin of Geometry" yet a further twist is added to this analysis. For while it is true that the scientific attitude requires the evidential justification of all claims as an ideal, this ideal is seldom realized in practice, Husserl maintains. Indeed, in a vast and cumulative enterprise like geometry, especially in its more advanced stages, it would be counterproductive for such an ideal to be realized. If each geometer tried seriously to repeat all the mental processes on which the work of his predecessors was based, he would have no time or energy left for advancing the discipline. In point of fact, he acquires and uses many fundamental tenets of his discipline with no more evidential warrant than that attaching to many extrascientific, everyday beliefs; and it is thanks to this sort of acquisition that he is able to make progress and build upon the work of his predecessors. Much of his work consists in merely "explicating" —that is, tracing the logical implications of—truths whose establishment he takes for granted. Thus, what may appear a defect with respect to the ideal is actually a condition for the factual existence and development of the discipline. Within the community of researchers, and with respect to a particular subject matter, geometry thrives on its own sort of historical sedimentation.

Now if it is true that the practice of geometry, and of disciplines like it, exhibits such a form, then the epistemological understanding of such disciplines requires that we come to terms with this form. Science is a social enterprise and exists as a historical tradition. The individual scientist does not acquire the knowledge of his discipline through personal activity from the ground up but inherits the underlying framework for his own continuing work. The philosophy of science must become conscious of the history of science. Put in this way, Husserl's ideas have some similarity to those of more recent philosophers of science such as Thomas Kuhn. In important respects, of course, they differ. For one thing, Husserl views a scientific discipline as progressing in a cumulative manner and does not make much of the revolutionary upheavals that have so captured the attention of recent theorists.[4] This may be because mathematics seems to serve as his model even when he is speaking of natural science. Partly because he views science as cumulative rather than revolutionary, Husserl also avoids, or thinks he can avoid, the relativistic implications of recent philosophy of science. Epistemology must become historical, he says toward the end of this manuscript, but not historicist. Science may exist as a tradition in which fundamental assumptions and even theories are taken over unquestioningly, but it does not follow from this that these assumptions are arbitrary and could as easily be replaced by others. The principles of geometry reflect insights into the nature of its subject matter, and if the tradition were broken, the whole process of traditionalization could be started up again.

This may seem to reduce the significance of Husserl's remarks on geometry to that of a psychological description of the mental processes of its practitioners. In fact, they are meant as an epistemological and even metaphysical reflection on the status of the truth-claims of geometry and natural science. The traditional-historical character of the practice of geometry may aid in its forward development, but it stands in the way of a proper philosophical understanding of its status. Space, as conceived by geometry and dealt with deductively, acquires an autonomy and independence which obscures its relation to the experienced world around us. What is forgotten is that this conception of space is an idealization of the spatial aspects of the everyday life-world. When physical reality, through Galileo's "mathematization of nature," is in turn conceived in terms of such idealizations, serious philosophical misconstructions may follow. Knowledge may be approached as involving a causal relation between "true" reality, so conceived, and the mind. The life-world becomes a shadow-world of "mere appearance" in between. The stage is set for the insoluble paradoxes of modern philosophy which culminate in Hume's skepticism. What is forgotten is that the "true reality" whose nature and ontological status are being presupposed is the accomplishment of an idealizing mental activity on the part of theorists whose taken-for-granted reality was the life-world. It is for this reason that we must place ourselves in the position of the originators of these conceptions by reconstructing the accomplishment of Galileo for natural science and, further back, even that of a putative originator of geometry itself.

Husserl devotes little space here to an actual reconstruction of what he calls the "Thales of geometry." His reconstruction of Galileo in Crisis is much more detailed. What he does here is set the problem in a way which contributes to our understanding of Crisis and in some ways goes beyond it. Husserl's remarks on science and its relation to the life-world and the cultural world, on history and historicism, and on language both written and spoken, justify the wide attention this short manuscript has attracted.

NOTES

1. The reader may wish to consult a reconstruction of the composition of Crisis found in David Carr, Phenomenology and the Problem of History (Evanston: Northwestern University Press, 1974), pp. 181–85.

2. See Crisis, section 9, pp. 23ff.
3. Cartesian Meditations, trans. D. Cairns (The Hague: Nijhoff, 1960), p. 60.
4. See Crisis, p. 4.

FURTHER REFERENCES

Brand, Gerd. *Die Lebenswelt: Eine Philosophie des konkreten Apriori.* Berlin: de Gruyter, 1971.

Carr, David. *Phenomenology and the Problem of History: A Study of Husserl's Transcendental Philosophy.* Evanston: Northwestern University Press, 1974. See especially chapter 8.

Derrida, Jacques. Translator's introduction to *L'Origine de la géométrie,* by E. Husserl. Paris: Presses universitaires de France, 1964.

Hohl, Hubert. *Lebenswelt und Geschichte.* Munich: Alber, 1972.

Janssen, Paul. *Geschichte und Lebenswelt.* The Hague: Nijhoff, 1970.

Kern, Iso. "Die Lebenswelt als Grundlagenproblem der objektiven Wissenschaften." In *Lebenswelt und Wissenschaft in der Philosophie Edmund Husserls,* edited by E. Ströker, pp. 68–78. Frankfurt, Vittorio Klostermann, 1979.

Pazanin, Ante. *Geschichte und Wissenschaft in der Phänomenologie Edmund Husserls.* The Hague, Nijhoff, 1972.

Sokolowski, Robert. "Exact Science and the World in Which We Live." In *Lebenswelt und Wissenschaft,* pp. 92–106.

Ströker, Elisabeth. "Geschichte und Lebenswelt als Sinnesfundament der Wissenschaften in Husserls Spätwerk." In *Lebenswelt und Wissenschaft,* pp. 107–23.

14

The Origin of Geometry*

TRANSLATED BY DAVID CARR

The interest that propels us in this work makes it necessary to engage first of all in reflections which surely never occurred to Galileo. We must focus our gaze not merely upon the ready-made, handed-down geometry and upon the manner of being which its meaning had in his thinking; it was no different in his thinking from what it was in that of all the late inheritors of the older geometric wisdom, whenever they were at work, either as pure geometers or as making practical applications of geometry. Rather, indeed above all, we must also inquire back into the original meaning of the handed-down geometry, which continued to be valid with this very same meaning—continued and at the same time was developed further, remaining simply "geometry" in all its new forms. Our considerations will necessarily lead to the deepest problems of meaning, problems of science and of the history of science in general, and indeed in the end to problems of a universal history in general; so that our problems and expositions concerning Galilean geometry take on an exemplary significance.

*This manuscript was written in 1936 and was edited and published (beginning with the third paragraph) by Eugen Fink in the *Revue internationale de philosophie*, vol. 1, no. 2 (1939) under the title "Der Ursprung der Geometrie als intentional-historisches Problem." It appears in Biemel's edition of the *Crisis* as "Beilage III," pp. 365–86. The first paragraphs suggest it was meant for inclusion in the *Crisis*. Reprinted with permission from Edmund Husserl, *The Crisis of European Sciences and Transcendental Phenomenology*, trans. David Carr (Evanston: Northwestern University Press, 1970), pp. 353–78.

Let it be noted in advance that, in the midst of our historical meditations on modern philosophy, there appears here for the first time with Galileo, through the disclosure of the depth-problems of the meaning-origin of geometry and, founded on this, of the meaning-origin of his new physics, a clarifying light for our whole undertaking: namely, [the idea of] seeking to carry out, in the form of historical meditations, self-reflections about our own present philosophical situation in the hope that in this way we can finally take possession of the meaning, method, and beginning of philosophy, the *one* philosophy to which our life seeks to be and ought to be devoted. For, as will become evident here, at first in connection with one example, our investigations are historical in an unusual sense, namely, in virtue of a thematic direction which opens up depth-problems quite unknown to ordinary history, problems which, [however,] in their own way, are undoubtedly historical problems. Where a consistent pursuit of these depth-problems leads can naturally not yet be seen at the beginning.

The question of the origin of geometry (under which title here, for the sake of brevity, we include all disciplines that deal with shapes existing mathematically in pure space-time) shall not be considered here as the philological-historical question, *i.e.*, as the search for the first geometers who actually uttered pure geometrical propositions, proofs, theories, or for the particular propositions they discovered, or the like. Rather than this, our interest shall be the inquiry back into the most original sense in which geometry once arose, was present as the tradition of millennia, is still present for us, and is still being worked on in a lively forward development;[1] we inquire into that sense in which it appeared in history for the first time—in which it had to appear, even though we know nothing of the first creators and are not even asking after them. Starting from what we know, from our geometry, or rather from the older handed-down forms (such as Euclidean geometry), there is an inquiry back into the submerged original beginnings of geometry as they necessarily must have been in their "primally establishing" function. This regressive inquiry unavoidably remains within the sphere of generalities, but, as we shall soon see, these are generalities which can be richly explicated, with prescribed possibilities of arriving at particular questions and self-evident claims as answers. The geometry which is ready-made, so to speak, from which the regressive inquiry begins, is a tradition. Our human existence moves within innumerable traditions. The whole cultural world, in all its forms, exists through tradition. These forms have arisen as such not merely causally; we also know already that tradition is precisely tradition, having arisen within our human space through human activity, i.e., spiritually, even though we generally know nothing, or as good as nothing, of the particular provenance and of the spiritual source that brought it about. And yet there lies in this lack of knowledge, everywhere and essentially, an implicit knowledge, which can thus also be made explicit, a knowledge of unassailable self-evidence. It begins with superficial commonplaces, such as: that everything traditional has arisen out of human activity, that accordingly past men and human civilizations existed, and among them their first inventors, who shaped the new out of materials at hand, whether raw or already spiritually shaped. From the superficial, however, one is led into the depths. Tradition is open in this general way to continued inquiry; and, if one consistently maintains the direction of inquiry, an infinity of questions opens up, questions which lead to definite answers in accord with their sense. Their form of generality—indeed, as

one can see, of unconditioned general validity — naturally allows for application to individually determined particular cases, though it determines only that in the individual that can be grasped through subsumption.

Let us begin, then, in connection with geometry, with the most obvious commonplaces that we have already expressed above in order to indicate the sense of our regressive inquiry. We understand our geometry, available to us through tradition (we have learned it, and so have our teachers), to be a total acquisition of spiritual accomplishments which grows through the continued work of new spiritual acts into new acquisitions. We know of its handed-down, earlier forms, as those from which it has arisen; but with every form the reference to an earlier one is repeated. Clearly, then, geometry must have arisen out of a *first* acquisition, out of first creative activities. We understand its persisting manner of being: it is not only a mobile forward process from one set of acquisitions to another but a continuous synthesis in which all acquisitions maintain their validity, all make up a totality such that, at every present stage, the total acquisition is, so to speak, the total premise for the acquisitions of the new level. Geometry necessarily had this mobility and has a horizon of geometrical future in precisely this style; this is its meaning for every geometer who has the consciousness (the constant implicit knowledge) of existing within a forward development understood as the progress of knowledge being built into the horizon. The same thing is true of every science. Also, every science is related to an open chain of the generations of those who work for and with one another, researchers either known or unknown to one another who are the accomplishing subjectivity of the whole living science. Science, and in particular geometry, with this ontic meaning, must have had a historical beginning; this meaning itself must have an origin in an accomplishment: first as a project and then in successful execution.

Obviously it is the same here as with every other invention. Every spiritual accomplishment proceeding from its first project to its execution is present for the first time in the self-evidence of actual success. But when we note that mathematics has the manner of being of a lively forward movement from acquisitions as premises to new acquisitions, in whose ontic meaning that of the premises is included (the process continuing in this manner), then it is clear that the *total* meaning of geometry (as a developed science, as in the case of every science) could not have been present as a project and then as mobile fulfillment at the beginning. A more primitive formation of meaning necessarily went before it as a preliminary stage, undoubtedly in such a way that it appeared for the first time in the self-evidence of successful realization. But this way of expressing it is actually overblown. Self-evidence means nothing more than grasping an entity with the consciousness of its original being-itself-there [*Selbst-da*]. Successful realization of a project is, for the acting subject, self-evidence; in this self-evidence, what has been realized is there, *originaliter,* as itself.

But now questions arise. This process of projecting and successfully realizing occurs, after all, purely within the *subject* of the inventor, and thus the meaning, as present *originaliter* with its whole content, lies exclusively, so to speak, within his mental space. But geometrical existence is not psychic existence; it does not exist as something personal within the personal sphere of consciousness; it is the existence of what is objectively there for "everyone" (for actual and possible geometers, or those who understand geometry). Indeed, it has, from its primal establishment, an existence which is peculiarly supertemporal and which—of this we are certain—is accessible to all men, first of all to the actual and possible mathematicians of all peoples, all ages; and this is true of all its particular forms. And all forms newly produced by someone on the basis of pregiven forms immediately take on the same objectivity. This is, we note, an "ideal" objectivity. It is proper to a whole class of spiritual products of the cultural world, to which not only all scientific constructions and the sciences themselves belong but also, for example, the constructions of fine literature.[2] Works of this class do not, like tools (hammers, pliers) or like architectural and other such products, have a repeatability in many like exemplars. The Pythagorean the-

orem, [indeed] all of geometry, exists only once, no matter how often or even in what language it may be expressed. It is identically the same in the "original language" of Euclid and in all "translations"; and within each language it is again the same, no matter how many times it has been sensibly uttered, from the original expression and writing-down to the innumerable oral utterances or written and other documentations. The sensible utterances have spatiotemporal individuation in the world like all corporeal occurrences, like everything embodied in bodies as such; but this is not true of the spiritual form itself, which is called an "ideal object" [*ideale Gegenständlichkeit*]. In a certain way ideal objects do exist objectively in the world, but it is only in virtue of these two-leveled repetitions and ultimately in virtue of sensibly embodying repetitions. For language itself, in all its particularizations (words, sentences, speeches), is, as can easily be seen from the grammatical point of view, thoroughly made up of ideal objects; for example, the word *Löwe* occurs only once in the German language; it is identical throughout its innumerable utterances by any given persons. But the idealities of geometrical words, sentences, theories—considered purely as linguistic structures—are not the idealities that make up what is expressed and brought to validity as truth in geometry; the latter are ideal geometrical objects, states of affairs, etc. Wherever something is asserted, one can distinguish what is thematic, that about which it is said (its meaning), from the assertion, which itself, during the asserting, is never and can never be thematic. And what is thematic here is precisely ideal objects, and quite different ones from those coming under the concept of language. Our problem now concerns precisely the ideal objects which are thematic in geometry: how does geometrical ideality (just like that of all sciences) proceed from its primary intrapersonal origin, where it is a structure within the conscious space of the first inventor's soul, to its ideal objectivity? In advance we see that it occurs by means of language, through which it receives, so to speak, its linguistic living body [*Sprachleib*]. But how does linguistic embodiment make out of the merely intrasubjective structure the *objective* structure which, *e.g.,* as geometrical concept or state of affairs, is in fact present as understandable by all and is valid, already in its linguistic expression as geometrical speech, as geometrical proposition, for all the future in its geometrical sense?

Naturally, we shall not go into the general problem which also arises here of the origin of language in its ideal existence and its existence in the real world grounded in utterance and documentation; but we must say a few words here about the relation between language, as a function of man within human civilization, and the world as the horizon of human existence.

Living wakefully in the world we are constantly conscious of the world, whether we pay attention to it or not, conscious of it as the horizon of our life, as a horizon of "things" (real objects), of our actual and possible interests and activities. Always standing out against the world-horizon is the horizon of our fellow men, whether there are any of them present or not. Before even taking notice of it at all, we are conscious of the open horizon of our fellow men with its limited nucleus of our neighbors, those known to us. We are thereby coconscious of the men on our external horizon in each case as "others"; in each case "I" am conscious of them as "my" others, as those with whom I can enter into actual and potential, immediate and mediate relations of empathy; [this involves] a reciprocal "getting along" with others; and on the basis of these relations I can deal with them, enter into particular modes of community with them, and then know, in a habitual way, of my being so related. Like me, every human being—and this is how he is understood by me and everyone else—has his fellow men and, always counting himself, civilization in general, in which he knows himself to be living.

It is precisely to this horizon of civilization that common language belongs. One is conscious of civilization from the start as an immediate and mediate linguistic community. Clearly it is only through language and its far-reaching documentations, as possible communications, that the horizon of civilization can be an open and endless one, as it always is for men. What is privileged in consciousness as the horizon of civilization and as the linguistic community is mature normal civilization (taking away the abnormal and the world of children). In this sense civilization is, for every man whose we-horizon it is, a community of those who can reciprocally express themselves, normally, in a fully understandable fashion; and within this community everyone can talk about what is within the surrounding world of his civilization as objectively existing. Everything has its name, or is namable in the broadest sense, *i.e.,* linguistically expressible. The objective world is from the start the world for all, the world which "everyone" has as world-horizon. Its objective being presupposes men, understood as men with a common language. Language, for its part, as function and exercised capacity, is related correlatively to the world, the universe of objects which is linguistically expressible in its being and its being-such. Thus men as men, fellow men, world—the world of which men, of which we, always talk and can talk—and, on the other hand, language, are inseparably intertwined; and one is always certain of their inseparable relational unity, though usually only implicitly, in the manner of a horizon.

This being presupposed, the primally establishing geometer can obviously also express his internal structure. But the question arises again: How does the latter, in its "ideality," thereby become objective? To be sure, something psychic which can be understood by others [*nachverstehbar*] and is communicable, as something psychic belonging to this man, is *eo ipso* objective, just as he himself, as concrete man, is experienceable and namable by everyone as a real thing in the world of things in general. People can agree about such things, can make common verifiable assertions on the basis of common experience, etc. But how does the intrapsychically constituted structure arrive at an intersubjective being of its own as an ideal object which, as "geometrical," is anything but a real psychic object, even though it has arisen psychically? Let us reflect. The original being-itself-there, in the immediacy [*Aktualität*] of its first production, *i.e.,* in original "self-evidence," results in no persisting acquisition at all that could have objective existence. Vivid self-evidence passes — though in such a way that the activity immediately turns into the passivity of the flowingly fading consciousness of what-has-just-now-been. Finally this "retention" disappears, but the "disappeared" passing and being past has not become nothing for the subject in question: it can be reawakened. To the passivity of what is at first obscurely awakened and what perhaps emerges with greater and greater clarity there belongs the possible activity of a recollection in which the past experiencing [Erleben] is lived through in a quasi-new and quasi-active way. Now if the originally self-evident production, as the pure fulfillment of its intention, is what is renewed (recollected), there necessarily occurs, accompanying the active recollection of what is past, an activity of concurrent actual production, and there arises thereby, in original "coincidence," the self-evidence of identity: what has now been realized in original fashion is the same as what was previously self-evident. Also coestablished is the capacity for repetition at will with the self-evidence of the identity (coincidence of identity) of the structure throughout the chain of repetitions. Yet even with this, we have still not gone beyond the subject and his subjective, evident capacities; that is, we still have no "objectivity" given. It does arise, however — in a preliminary stage — in understandable fashion as soon as we take into consideration the function of empathy and fellow mankind as a community of empathy and of language. In the contact of reciprocal linguistic understanding, the original production and the product of one subject can be *actively* understood by the others. In this full understanding of what is produced by the other, as in the case of recollection, a present coaccomplishment on one's own part of the presentified activity necessarily takes place; but at the same time there is also the self-evident consciousness of the identity of the mental structure in the productions of both the receiver of the communication and the communicator; and this occurs reciprocally. The productions can reproduce their likenesses from person to person, and in the chain of the understanding of these repetitions what is self-evident turns up as the same in the consciousness of

the other. In the unity of the community of communication among several persons the repeatedly produced structure becomes an object of consciousness, not as a likeness, but as the one structure common to all.

Now we must note that the objectivity of the ideal structure has not yet been fully constituted through such actual transferring of what has been originally produced in one to others who originally reproduce it. What is lacking is the *persisting existence* of the "ideal objects" even during periods in which the inventor and his fellows are no longer wakefully so related or even are no longer alive. What is lacking is their continuing-to-be even when no one has [consciously] realized them in self-evidence.

The important function of written, documenting linguistic expression is that it makes communications possible without immediate or mediate personal address; it is, so to speak, communication become virtual. Through this, the communalization of man is lifted to a new level. Written signs are, when considered from a purely corporeal point of view, straightforwardly, sensibly experienceable; and it is always possible that they be intersubjectively experienceable in common. But as linguistic signs they awaken, as do linguistic sounds, their familiar significations. The awakening is something passive; the awakened signification is thus given passively, similarly to the way in which any other activity which has sunk into obscurity, once associatively awakened, emerges at first *passively* as a more or less clear memory. In the passivity in question here, as in the case of memory, what is passively awakened can be transformed back,[3] so to speak, into the corresponding activity: this is the capacity for reactivation that belongs originally to every human being as a speaking being. Accordingly, then, the writing-down effects a transformation of the original mode of being of the meaning-structure, [e.g.,] within the geometrical sphere of self-evidence, of the geometrical structure which is put into words. It becomes sedimented, so to speak. But the reader can make it self-evident again, can reactivate the self-evidence.[4]

There is a distinction, then, between passively understanding the expression and making it self-evident by reactivating its meaning. But there also exist possibilities of a kind of activity, a thinking in terms of things that have been taken up merely receptively, passively, which deals with significations only passively understood and taken over, without any of the self-evidence of original activity. Passivity in general is the realm of things that are bound together and melt into one another associatively, where all meaning that arises is put together passively. What often happens here is that a meaning arises which is apparently possible as a unity—*i.e.*, can apparently be made self-evident through a possible reactivation —whereas the attempt at actual reactivation can reactivate only the individual members of the combination, while the intention to unify them into a whole, instead of being fulfilled, comes to nothing; that is, the ontic validity is destroyed through the original consciousness of nullity.

It is easy to see that even in [ordinary] human life, and first of all in every individual life from childhood up to maturity, the originally intuitive life which creates its originally self-evident structures through activities on the basis of sense-experience very quickly and in increasing measure falls victim to the *seduction of language.* Greater and greater segments of this life lapse into a kind of talking and reading that is dominated purely by association; and often enough, in respect to the validities arrived at in this way, it is disappointed by subsequent experience.

Now one will say that in the sphere that interests us here—that of science, of thinking directed toward the attainment of truths and the avoidance of falsehood—one is obviously greatly concerned from the start to put a stop to the free play of associative constructions. In view of the unavoidable sedimentation of mental products in the form of persisting linguistic acquisitions, which can be taken up again at first merely passively and be taken over by anyone else, such constructions remain a constant danger. This danger is avoided if one not merely convinces oneself ex post facto that the particular construction can be reactivated but assures oneself from the start, after the self-evident primal establishment, of its capacity to be reactivated and enduringly maintained. This occurs when one has a view to the univocity of linguistic expression and to securing, by means of the most painstaking formation of the relevant words, propositions, and complexes of propositions, the results which are to be univocally expressed. This must be done by the individual scientist, and not only by the inventor but by every scientist as a member of the scientific community after he has taken over from the others what is to be taken over. This belongs, then, to the particulars of the scientific tradition within the corresponding community of scientists as a community of knowledge living in the unity of a common responsibility. In accord with the essence of science, then, its functionaries maintain the constant claim, the personal certainty, that everything they put into scientific assertions has been said "once and for all," that it "stands fast," forever identically repeatable with self-evidence and usable for further theoretical or practical ends—as indubitably reactivatable with the identity of its actual meaning.[5]

However, two more things are important here. First: we have not yet taken into account the fact that scientific thinking attains new results on the basis of those already attained, that the new ones serve as the foundation for still others, etc.—in the unity of a propagative process of transferred meaning.

In the finally immense proliferation of a science like geometry, what has become of the claim and the capacity for reactivation? When every researcher works on his part of the building, what of the vocational interruptions and time out for rest, which cannot be overlooked here? When he returns to the actual continuation of work, must he first run through the whole immense chain of groundings back to the original premises and actually reactivate the whole thing? If so, a science like our modern geometry would obviously not be possible at all. And yet it is of the essence of the results of each stage not only that their ideal ontic meaning in fact comes later [than that of earlier results] but that, since meaning is grounded upon meaning, the earlier meaning gives something of its validity to the later one, indeed becomes part of it to a certain extent.

Thus no building block within the mental structure is self-sufficient; and none, then, can be immediately reactivated [by itself].

This is especially true of sciences which, like geometry, have their thematic sphere in ideal products, in idealities from which more and more idealities at higher levels are produced. It is quite different in the so-called descriptive sciences, where the theoretical interest, classifying and describing, remains within the sphere of sense-intuition, which for it represents self-evidence. Here, at least in general, every new proposition can by itself be "cashed in" for self-evidence.

How, by contrast, is a science like geometry possible? How, as a systematic, endlessly growing stratified structure of idealities, can it maintain its original meaningfulness through living reactivatability if its cognitive thinking is supposed to produce something new without being able to reactivate the previous levels of knowledge back to the first? Even if this could have succeeded at a more primitive stage of geometry, its energy would ultimately have been too much spent in the effort of procuring self-evidence and would not have been available for a higher productivity.

Here we must take into consideration the peculiar "logical" activity which is tied specifically to language, as well as to the ideal cognitive structures that arise specifically within it. To any sentence structures that emerge within a merely passive understanding there belongs essentially a peculiar sort of activity best described by the word 'explication'.[a] A passively emerging sentence (e.g., in memory), or one heard and passively understood, is at first merely received with a passive ego-participation, taken up as valid; and in this form it is already our meaning. From this we distinguish the peculiar and important activity of explicating our meaning. Whereas in its first form it was a straightforwardly valid meaning, taken up as unitary and undifferentiated—concretely speaking, a straightforwardly valid declarative sentence—now what in itself is vague and undifferentiated is actively explicated. Consider, for example, the way in which we understand, when superficially reading the newspaper, and simply receive the "news"; here there is a passive taking-over of ontic validity such that what is read straightway becomes our opinion.

But it is something special, as we have said, to have the intention to explicate, to engage in the activity which articulates what has been read (or an interesting sentence from it), extracting one by one, in separation from what has been vaguely, passively received as a unity, the elements of meaning, thus bringing the total validity to active performance in a new way on the basis of the individual validities. What was a passive meaning-pattern has now become one constructed through active production. This activity, then, is a peculiar sort of self-evidence; the structure arising out of it is in the mode of having been originally produced. And in connection with this self-evidence, too, there is communalization. The explicated judgment becomes an ideal object capable of being passed on. It is this object exclusively that is meant by logic when it speaks of sentences or judgments. And thus the *domain of logic* is universally designated; this is universally the sphere of being to which logic pertains insofar as it is the theory of the sentences [or propositions] in general.

Through this activity, now, further activities become possible—self-evident constructions of new judgments on the basis of those already valid for us. This is the peculiar feature of logical thinking and of its purely logical self-evidences. All this remains intact even when judgments are transformed into assumptions, where, instead of ourselves asserting or judging, we think ourselves into the position of asserting or judging.

Here we shall concentrate on the sentences of language as they come to us passively and are merely received. In this connection it must also be noted that sentences give themselves in consciousness as reproductive transformations of an original meaning produced out of an actual, original activity; that is, in themselves they refer to such a genesis. In the sphere of logical self-evidence, deduction, or inference in forms of consequence, plays a constant and essential role. On the other hand, one must also take note of the constructive activities that operate with geometrical idealities which have been explicated but not brought to original self-evidence. (Original self-evidence must not be confused with the self-evidence of "axioms"; for axioms are in principle already the results of original meaning-construction and always have this behind them.)

Now what about the possibility of complete and genuine reactivation in full originality, through going back to the primal self-evidences, in the case of geometry and the so-called "deductive" sciences (so called, although they by no means merely deduce)? Here the fundamental law, with unconditionally general self-evidence, is: if the premises can actually be reactivated back to the most original self-evidence, then their self-evident consequences can be also. Accordingly it appears that, beginning with the primal self-evidences, the original genuineness must propagate itself through the chain of logical inference, no matter how long it is. However, if we consider the obvious finitude of the individual and even the social capacity to transform the logical chains of centuries, truly in the unity of one accomplishment, into originally genuine chains of self-evidence, we notice that the [above] law contains within itself an idealization: namely, the removal of limits from our capacity, in a certain sense its infinitization. The peculiar sort of self-evidence belonging to such idealizations will concern us later.

These are, then, the general essential insights which elucidate the whole methodical development of the "deductive" sciences and with it the manner of being which is essential to them.

These sciences are not handed down ready-made in the form of documented sentences; they involve a lively, productively advancing formation of meaning, which always has the documented, as a sediment of earlier production, at its disposal in that it deals with it logically. But out of sentences with sedimented signification, logical "dealing" can produce only other sentences of the same character. That all new acquisitions express an actual geometrical truth is certain a priori under the presupposition that the foundations of the deductive structure have truly been produced and objectified in orig-

inal self-evidence, *i.e.,* have become universally accessible acquisitions. A continuity from one person to another, from one time to another, must have been capable of being carried out. It is clear that the method of producing original idealities out of what is prescientifically given in the cultural world must have been written down and fixed in firm sentences prior to the existence of geometry; furthermore, the capacity for translating these sentences from vague linguistic understanding into the clarity of the reactivation of their self-evident meaning must have been, in its own way, handed down and ever capable of being handed down.

Only as long as this condition was satisfied, or only when the possibility of its fulfillment was perfectly secured for all time, could geometry preserve its genuine, original meaning as a deductive science throughout the progression of logical constructions. In other words, only in this case could every geometer be capable of bringing to mediate self-evidence the meaning borne by every sentence, not merely as its sedimented (logical) sentence-meaning but as its actual meaning, its truth-meaning. And so for all of geometry.

The progress of deduction follows formal-logical self-evidence; but without the actually developed capacity for reactivating the original activities contained within its fundamental concepts, *i.e.,* without the "what" and the "how" of its prescientific materials, geometry would be a tradition empty of meaning; and if we ourselves did not have this capacity, we could never even know whether geometry had or ever did have a genuine meaning, one that could really be "cashed in."

Unfortunately, however, this is our situation, and that of the whole modern age.

The "presupposition" mentioned above has in fact never been fulfilled. How the living tradition of the meaning-formation of elementary concepts is actually carried on can be seen in elementary geometrical instruction and its textbooks; what we actually learn there is how to deal with *ready-made* concepts and sentences in a rigorously methodical way. Rendering the concepts sensibly intuitable by means of drawn figures is substituted for the actual production of the primal idealities. And the rest is done by success — not the success of actual insight extending beyond the logical method's own self-evidence, but the practical successes of applied geometry, its immense, though not understood, practical usefulness. To this we must add something that will become visible further on in the treatment of historical mathematics, namely, the dangers of a scientific life that is completely given over to logical activities. These dangers lie in certain progressive transformations of meaning[6] to which this sort of scientific treatment drives one.

By exhibiting the essential presuppositions upon which rests the historical possibility of a genuine tradition, true to its origins, of sciences like geometry, we can understand how such sciences can vitally develop throughout the centuries and still not be genuine. The inheritance of propositions and of the method of logically constructing new propositions and idealities can continue without interruption from one period to the next, while the capacity for reactivating the primal beginnings, *i.e.*, the sources of meaning for everything that comes later, has not been handed down with it. What is lacking is thus precisely what had given and had to give meaning to all propositions and theories, a meaning arising from the primal sources which can be made self-evident again and again.

Of course, grammatically coherent propositions and concatenations of propositions, no matter how they have arisen and have achieved validity — even if it is through mere association — have in all circumstances their own logical meaning, *i.e.*, their meaning that can be made self-evident through explication; this can then be identified again and again as the same proposition, which is either logically coherent or incoherent, where in the latter case it cannot be executed in the unity of an actual judgment. In propositions which belong together in one domain and in the deductive systems that can be made out of them we have a realm of ideal identities; and for these there exist easily understandable possibilities of lasting traditionalization. But propositions, like other cultural structures, appear on the scene in the form of tradition; they claim, so

to speak, to be sedimentations of a truth-meaning that can be made originally self-evident; whereas it is by no means necessary that they [actually] have such a meaning, as in the case of associatively derived falsifications. Thus the whole pregiven deductive science, the total system of propositions in the unity of their validities, is first only a claim which can be justified as an expression of the alleged truth-meaning only through the actual capacity for reactivation.

Through this state of affairs we can understand the deeper reason for the demand, which has spread throughout the modern period and has finally been generally accepted, for a so-called "epistemological grounding" of the sciences, though clarity has never been achieved about what the much-admired sciences are actually lacking.[7]

As for further details on the uprooting of an originally genuine tradition, *i.e.*, one which involved original self-evidence at its actual first beginning, one can point to possible and easily understandable reasons. In the first oral cooperation of the beginning geometers, the need was understandably lacking for an exact fixing of descriptions of the prescientific primal material and of the ways in which, in relation to this material, geometrical idealities arose together with the first "axiomatic" propositions. Further, the logical superstructures did not yet rise so high that one could not return again and again to the original meaning. On the other hand, the possibility of the practical application of the derived laws, which was actually obvious in connection with the original developments, understandably led quickly, in the realm of praxis, to a habitually practiced method of using mathematics, if need be, to bring about useful things. This method could naturally be handed down even without the ability for original self-evidence. Thus mathematics, emptied of meaning, could generally propagate itself, constantly being added to logically, as could the methodics of technical application on the other side. The extraordinarily far-reaching practical usefulness became of itself a major motive for the advancement and appreciation of these sciences. Thus also it is understandable that the lost original truth-meaning made itself felt so little, indeed, that the need for the corresponding regressive inquiry had to be reawakened. More than this: the true sense of such an inquiry had to be discovered.

Our results based on principle are of a generality that extends over all the so-called deductive sciences and even indicates similar problems and investigations for all sciences. For all of them have the mobility of sedimented traditions that are worked upon, again and again, by an activity of producing new structures of meaning and handing them down. Existing in this way, they extend enduringly through time, since all new acquisitions are in turn sedimented and become working materials. Everywhere the problems, the clarifying investigations, the insights of principle are *historical*. We stand within the horizon of human civilization, the one in which we ourselves now live. We are constantly, vitally conscious of this horizon, and specifically as a temporal horizon implied in our given present horizon. To the one human civilization there corresponds essentially the one cultural world as the surrounding life-world with its [peculiar] manner of being; this world, for every historical period and civilization, has its particular features and is precisely the tradition. We stand, then, within the historical horizon in which everything is historical, even though we may know very little about it in a definite way. But it has its essential structure that can be revealed through methodical inquiry. This inquiry prescribes all the possible specialized questions, thus including, for the sciences, the inquiries back into origin which are peculiar to them in virtue of their historical manner of being. Here we are led back to the primal materials of the first formation of meaning, the primal premises, so to speak, which lie in the prescientific cultural world. Of course, this cultural world has in turn its own questions of origin, which at first remain unasked.

Naturally, problems of this particular sort immediately awaken the total problem of the universal historicity of the correlative manners of being of humanity and the cultural world and the a priori structure contained in this historicity. Still, questions like that of the clarification of the origin of geometry have a closed character, such that one need not inquire beyond those prescientific materials.

Further clarifications will be made in connection with two objections which are familiar to our own philosophical-historical situation.

In the first place, what sort of strange obstinacy is this, seeking to take the question of the origin of geometry back to some undiscoverable Thales of geometry, someone not even known to legend? Geometry is available to us in its propositions, its theories. Of course we must and we can answer for this logical edifice to the last detail in terms of self-evidence. Here, to be sure, we arrive at first axioms, and from them we proceed to the original self-evidence which the fundamental concepts make possible. What is this, if not the "theory of knowledge," in this case specifically the theory of geometrical knowledge? No one would think of tracing the epistemological problem back to such a supposed Thales. This is quite superfluous. The presently available concepts and propositions themselves contain their own meaning, first as nonself-evident opinion, but nevertheless as true propositions with a meant but still hidden truth which we can obviously bring to light by rendering the propositions themselves self-evident.

Our answer is as follows. Certainly the historical backward reference has not occurred to anyone; certainly theory of knowledge has never been seen as a peculiarly historical task. But this is precisely what we object to in the past. The ruling dogma of the separation in principle between epistemological elucidation and historical, even humanistic-psychological explanation, between epistemological and genetic origin, is fundamentally mistaken, unless one inadmissibly limits, in the usual way, the concepts of "history," "historical explanation," and "genesis." Or rather, what is fundamentally mistaken is the limitation through which precisely the deepest and most genuine problems of history are concealed. If one thinks over our expositions (which are of course still rough and will later of necessity lead us into new depth-dimensions), what they make obvious is precisely that what we know—namely, that the presently vital cultural configuration "geometry" is a tradition and is still being handed down—is not knowledge concerning an external causality which effects the succession of historical configurations, as if it were knowledge based on induction, the presupposition of which would amount to an absurdity here; rather, to understand geometry or any given cultural fact is to be conscious of its historicity, albeit "implicitly." This, however, is not an empty claim; for quite generally it is true for every fact given under the heading of "culture," whether it is a matter of the lowliest culture of necessities or the highest culture (science, state, church, economic organization, etc.), that every straightforward understanding of it as an experiential fact involves the "coconsciousness" that it is something constructed through human activity. No matter how hidden, no matter how merely "implicitly" coimplied this meaning is, there belongs to it the self-evident possibility of explication, of "making it explicit" and clarifying it. Every explication and every transition from making explicit to making self-evident (even perhaps in cases where one stops much too soon) is nothing other than historical disclosure; in itself, essentially, it is something historical, and as such it bears, with essential necessity, the horizon of its history within itself. This is of course also to say that the whole of the cultural present, understood as a totality, "implies" the whole of the cultural past in an undetermined but structurally determined generality. To put it more precisely, it implies a continuity of pasts which imply one another, each in itself being a past cultural present. And this whole continuity is a *unity* of traditionalization up to the present, which is our present *as* [a process of] traditionalizing itself in flowing-static vitality. This is, as has been said, an undetermined generality, but it has in principle a structure which can be much more widely explicated by proceeding from these indications, a structure which also grounds, "implies," the possibilities for every search for and determination of concrete, factual states of affairs.

Making geometry self-evident, then, whether one is clear about this or not, is the disclosure of its historical tradition. But this knowledge, if it is not to remain empty talk

or undifferentiated generality, requires the methodical production, proceeding from the present and carried out as research in the present, of differentiated self-evidences of the type discovered above (in several fragmentary investigations of what belongs to such knowledge superficially, as it were). Carried out systematically, such self-evidences result in nothing other and nothing less than the universal a priori of history with all its highly abundant component elements.

We can also say now that history is from the start nothing other than the vital movement of the coexistence and the interweaving of original formations and sedimentations of meaning.

Anything that is shown to be a historical fact, either in the present through experience or by a historian as a fact in the past, necessarily has its *inner structure of meaning;* but especially the motivational interconnections established about it in terms of everyday understanding have deep, further and further-reaching implications which must be interrogated, disclosed. All [merely] factual history remains incomprehensible because, always merely drawing its conclusions naïvely and straightforwardly from facts, it never makes thematic the general ground of meaning upon which all such conclusions rest, has never investigated the immense structural a priori which is proper to it. Only the disclosure of the essentially general structure[8] lying in our present and then in every past or future historical present as such, and, in totality, only the disclosure of the concrete, historical time in which we live, in which our total humanity lives in respect to its total, essentially general structure—only this disclosure can make possible historical inquiry [*Historie*] which is truly understanding, insightful, and in the genuine sense scientific. This is the concrete, historical a priori which encompasses everything that exists as historical becoming and having-become or exists in its essential being as tradition and handing-down. What has been said was related to the total form "historical present in general," historical time generally. But the particular configurations of culture, which find their place within its coherent historical being as tradition and as vitally handing themselves

down, have within this totality only relatively self-sufficient being in traditionality,
only the being of nonself-sufficient components. Correlatively, now, account would
have to be taken of the subjects of historicity, the persons who create cultural formations, functioning in totality: creative personal civilization.[9]

In respect to geometry one recognizes,
now that we have pointed out the hidden-
ness of its fundamental concepts, which
have become inaccessible, and have made
them understandable as such in first basic
outlines, that only the consciously set task of
[discovering] the historical origin of geometry (within the total problem of the a priori
of historicity in general) can provide the
method for a geometry which is true to its
origins and at the same time is to be understood in a universal-historical way; and the
same is true for all sciences, for philosophy.
In principle, then, a history of philosophy, a
history of the particular sciences in the style
of the usual factual history, can actually render nothing of their subject matter comprehensible. For a genuine history of philosophy,
a genuine history of the particular sciences,
is nothing other than the tracing of the historical meaning-structures given in the present, or their self-evidences, along the documented chain of historical back-references
into the hidden dimension of the primal
self-evidences which underlie them.[10] Even
the very problem here can be made understandable only through recourse to the historical a priori as the universal source of all
conceivable problems of understanding.
The problem of genuine historical explanation comes together, in the case of the sciences, with "epistemological" grounding or
clarification.

We must expect yet a second and very
weighty objection. From the historicism
which prevails extensively in different forms
[today] I expect little receptivity for a depth-
inquiry which goes beyond the usual factual
history, as does the one outlined in this
work, especially since, as the expression "a
priori" indicates, it lays claim to a strictly
unconditioned and truly apodictic self-
evidence extending beyond all historical facticities. One will object: what naïveté, to
seek to display, and to claim to have dis-

played, a historical a priori, an absolute, supertemporal validity, after we have obtained
such abundant testimony for the relativity
of everything historical, of all historically
developed world-apperceptions, right back
to those of the "primitive" tribes. Every people, large or small, has its world in which,
for that people, everything fits well together, whether in mythical-magical or in
European-rational terms, and in which everything can be explained perfectly. Every
people has its "logic" and, accordingly, if
this logic is explicated in propositions, "its"
a priori.

However, let us consider the methodology of establishing historical facts in general,
thus including that of the facts supporting
the objection; and let us do this in regard to
what such methodology presupposes. Does
not the undertaking of a humanistic science
of "how it really was" contain a presupposition taken for granted, a validity-ground
never observed, never made thematic, of a
strictly unassailable [type of] self-evidence,
without which historical inquiry would be a
meaningless enterprise? All questioning
and demonstrating which is in the usual
sense historical presupposes history [Ge-
schichte] as the universal horizon of questioning, not explicitly, but still as a horizon
of implicit certainty, which, in spite of all
vague background-indeterminacy, is the
presupposition of all determinability, or of
all intention to seek and to establish determined facts.

What is historically primary in itself is
our present. We always already know of our
present world and that we live in it, always
surrounded by an openly endless horizon of
unknown actualities. This knowing, as
horizon-certainty, is not something learned,
not knowledge which was once actual and
has merely sunk back to become part of the
background; the horizon-certainty had to be
already there in order to be capable of being
laid out thematically; it is already presupposed in order that we can seek to know
what we do not know. All not-knowing concerns the unknown world, which yet exists
in advance for us *as* world, as the horizon of
all questions of the present and thus also all
questions which are specifically historical.
These are the questions which concern men,

as those who act and create in their communalized coexistence in the world and transform the constant cultural face of the world. Do we not know further—we have already had occasion to speak of this—that this historical present has its historical pasts behind it, that it has developed out of them, that historical past is a continuity of pasts which proceed from one another, each, as a past present, being a tradition producing tradition out of itself? Do we not know that the present and the whole of historical time implied in it is that of a historically coherent and unified civilization, coherent through its generative bond and constant communalization in cultivating what has already been cultivated before, whether in cooperative work or in reciprocal interaction, etc.? Does all this not announce a universal "knowing" of the horizon, an implicit knowing that can be made explicit systematically in its essential structure? Is not the resulting great problem here the horizon toward which all questions tend, and thus the horizon which is presupposed in all of them? Accordingly, we need not first enter into some kind of critical discussion of the facts set out by historicism; it is enough that even the claim of their factualness presupposes the historical a priori if this claim is to have a meaning.

But a doubt arises all the same. The horizon-exposition to which we recurred must not bog down in vague, superficial talk; it must itself arrive at its own sort of scientific discipline. The sentences in which it is expressed must be fixed and capable of being made self-evident again and again. Through what method do we obtain a universal and also fixed a priori of the historical world which is always originally genuine? Whenever we consider it, we find ourselves with the self-evident capacity to reflect—to turn to the horizon and to penetrate it in an expository way. But we also have, and know that we have, the capacity of complete freedom to transform, in thought and phantasy, our human historical existence and what is there exposed as its life-world. And precisely in this activity of free variation, and in running through the conceivable possibilities for the life-world, there arises, with apodictic self-evidence, an essentially general set of

elements going through all the variants; and of this we can convince ourselves with truly apodictic certainty. Thereby we have removed every bond to the factually valid historical world and have regarded this world itself [merely] as one of the conceptual possibilities. This freedom, and the direction of our gaze upon the apodictically invariant, results in the latter again and again—with the self-evidence of being able to repeat the invariant structure at will—as what is identical, what can be made self-evident *originaliter* at any time, can be fixed in univocal language as the essence constantly implied in the flowing, vital horizon.

Through this method, going beyond the formal generalities we exhibited earlier, we can also make thematic that apodictic [aspect] of the prescientific world that the original founder of geometry had at his disposal, that which must have served as the material for his idealizations.

Geometry and the sciences most closely related to it have to do with space-time and the shapes, figures, also shapes of motion, alterations of deformation, etc., that are possible within space-time, particularly as measurable magnitudes. It is now clear that even if we know almost nothing about the historical surrounding world of the first geometers, this much is certain as an invariant, essential structure: that it was a world of "things" (including the human beings themselves as subjects of this world); that all things necessarily had to have a bodily character—although not all things could be mere bodies, since the necessarily coexisting human beings are not thinkable as mere bodies and, like even the cultural objects which belong with them structurally, are not exhausted in corporeal being. What is also clear, and can be secured at least in its essential nucleus through careful a priori explication, is that these pure bodies had spatiotemporal shapes and "material" [*stoffliche*] qualities (color, warmth, weight, hardness, etc.) related to them. Further, it is clear that in the life of practical needs certain particularizations of shape stood out and that a technical praxis always [aimed at][b] the production of particular preferred shapes and the improvement of them according to certain directions of gradualness.

First to be singled out from the thing-shapes are surfaces—more or less "smooth," more or less perfect surfaces; edges, more or less rough or fairly "even"; in other words, more or less pure lines, angles, more or less perfect points; then, again, among the lines, for example, straight lines are especially preferred, and among the surfaces the even surfaces; for example, for practical purposes boards limited by even surfaces, straight lines, and points are preferred, whereas totally or partially curved surfaces are undesirable for many kinds of practical interests. Thus the production of even surfaces and their perfection (polishing) always plays its role in praxis. So also in cases where just distribution is intended. Here the rough estimate of magnitudes is transformed into the measurement of magnitudes by counting the equal parts. (Here, too, proceeding from the factual, an essential form becomes recognizable through a method of variation.) Measuring belongs to every culture, varying only according to stages from primitive to higher perfections. We can always presuppose some measuring technique, whether of a lower or higher type, in the essential forward development of culture, [as well as] the growth of such a technique, thus also including the art of design for buildings, of surveying fields, pathways, etc.;[c] such a technique is always already there, already abundantly developed and pregiven to the philosopher who did not yet know geometry but who should be conceivable as its inventor. As a philosopher proceeding from the practical, finite surrounding world (of the room, the city, the landscape, etc., and temporally the world of periodical occurrences: day, month, etc.) to the theoretical world-view and world-knowledge, he has the finitely known and unknown spaces and times as finite elements within the horizon of an open infinity. But with this he does not yet have geometrical space, mathematical time, and whatever else is to become a novel spiritual product out of these finite elements which serve as material; and with his manifold finite shapes in their space-time he does not yet have geometrical shapes, the phoronomic shapes; [his shapes, as] formations developed out of praxis and thought

of in terms of [gradual] perfection, clearly serve only as bases for a new sort of praxis out of which similarly named new constructions grow.

It is evident in advance that this new sort of construction will be a product arising out of an idealizing, spiritual act, one of "pure" thinking, which has it materials in the designated general pregivens of this factual humanity and human surrounding world and creates "ideal objects" out of them.

Now the problem would be to discover, through recourse to what is essential to history [Historie], the historical original meaning which necessarily was able to give and did give to the whole becoming of geometry its persisting truth-meaning.

It is of particular importance now to bring into focus and establish the following insight: Only if the apodictically general content, invariant throughout all conceivable variation, of the spatiotemporal sphere of shapes is taken into account in the idealization can an ideal construction arise which can be understood for all future time and by all coming generations of men and thus be capable of being handed down and reproduced with the identical intersubjective meaning. This condition is valid far beyond geometry for all spiritual structures which are to be unconditionally and generally capable of being handed down. Were the thinking activity of a scientist to introduce something "time-bound" in his thinking, i.e., something bound to what is merely factual about his present or something valid for him as a merely factual tradition, his construction would likewise have a merely time-bound ontic meaning; this meaning would be understandable only by those men who shared the same merely factual presuppositions of understanding.

It is a general conviction that geometry, with all its truths, is valid with unconditioned generality for all men, all times, all peoples, and not merely for all historically factual ones but for all conceivable ones. The presuppositions of principle for this conviction have never been explored because they have never been seriously made a problem. But it has also become clear to us that every establishment of a historical fact which lays claim to unconditioned objectivity likewise presupposes this invariant or absolute a priori.

Only [through the disclosure of this a priori][d] can there be an a priori science extending beyond all historical facticities, all historical surrounding worlds, peoples, times, civilizations; only in this way can a science as *aeterna veritas* appear. Only on this fundament is based the secured capacity of inquiring back from the temporarily depleted self-evidence of a science to the primal self-evidences.

Do we not stand here before the great and profound problem-horizon of reason, the same reason that functions in every man, the *animal rationale,* no matter how primitive he is?

This is not the place to penetrate into those depths themselves.

In any case, we can now recognize from all this that historicism, which wishes to clarify the historical or epistemological essence of mathematics from the standpoint of the magical circumstances or other manners of apperception of a time-bound civilization, is mistaken in principle. For romantic spirits the mythical-magical elements of the historical and prehistorical aspects of mathematics may be particularly attractive; but to cling to this merely historically factual aspect of mathematics is precisely to lose oneself to a sort of romanticism and to overlook the genuine problem, the internal-historical problem, the epistemological problem. Also, one's gaze obviously cannot

then become free to recognize that facticities of every type, including those involved in the [historicist] objection, have a root in the essential structure of what is generally human, through which a teleological reason running throughout all historicity announces itself. With this is revealed a set of problems in its own right related to the totality of history and to the full meaning which ultimately gives it its unity.

If the usual factual study of history in general, and in particular the history which in most recent times has achieved true universal extension over all humanity, is to have any meaning at all, such a meaning can only be grounded upon what we can here call internal history, and as such upon the foundations of the universal historical a priori. Such a meaning necessarily leads further to the indicated highest question of a universal teleology of reason.

If, after these expositions, which have illuminated very general and many-sided problem-horizons, we lay down the following as something completely secured, namely, that the human surrounding world is the same today and always, and thus also in respect to what is relevant to primal establishment and lasting tradition, then we can show in several steps, only in an exploratory way, in connection with our own surrounding world, what should be considered in more detail for the problem of the idealizing primal establishment of the meaning-structure "geometry."

NOTES

1. So also for Galileo and all the periods following the Renaissance, continually being worked on in a lively forward development, and yet at the same time a tradition.

2. But the broadest concept of literature encompasses them all; that is, it belongs to their objective being that they be linguistically expressed and can be expressed again and again; or, more precisely, they have their objectivity, their existence-for-everyone, only as signification, as the meaning of speech. This is true in a peculiar fashion in the case of the objective sciences: for them the difference between the original language of the work and its translation into other languages does

not remove its identical accessibility or change it into an inauthentic, indirect accessibility.

3. This is a transformation of which one is conscious as being in itself patterned after [what is passively awakened].

4. But this is by no means necessary or even factually normal. Even without this he can understand; he can concur "as a matter of course" in the validity of what is understood without any activity of his own. In this case he comports himself purely passively and receptively.

5. At first, of course, it is a matter of a firm direction of the will, which the scientist establishes in him-

self, aimed at the certain capacity for reactivation. If the goal of reactivatability can be only relatively fulfilled, then the claim which stems from the consciousness of being able to acquire something also has its relativity; and this relativity also makes itself noticeable and is driven out. Ultimately, objective, absolutely firm knowledge of truth is an infinite idea.

6. These work to the benefit of logical method, but they remove one further and further from the origins and make one insensitive to the problem of origin and thus to the actual ontic and truth-meaning of all these sciences.

7. What does Hume do but endeavor to inquire back into the primal impressions of developed ideas and, in general, scientific ideas?

8. The superficial structure of the externally "ready-made" men within the social-historical, essential structure of humanity, but also the deeper [structures] which disclose the inner historicities of the persons taking part. ["Structures" is Biemel's interpolation.]

9. The historical world is, to be sure, first pre-given as a social-historical world. But it is historical only through the inner historicity of the individuals, who are individuals in their inner historicity, together with that of other communalized persons. Recall what was said in a few meager beginning expositions about memories and the constant historicity to be found in them [pp. 258f., above].

10. But what counts as primal self-evidence for the sciences is determined by an educated person or a sphere of such persons who pose new questions, new historical questions, questions concerning the inner depth-dimension as well as those concerning an external historicity in the social-historical world.

TRANSLATOR'S NOTES

a. *Verdeutlichung, i.e.,* making explicit.
b. Biemel's interpolation.
c. I have reverted to the original version of this sentence as given in the critical apparatus; I can make no sense of the emended version given in the text.
d. Biemel's interpolation.

15

The Phenomenology of Internal Time-Consciousness

JOHN B. BROUGH

1. Husserl's Writings on Time-Consciousness from the First Decade of the Century

Husserl once referred to time-consciousness as a "wonder," and said that it is the most important matter in phenomenology. He added, as if to trouble the reader, that it is also the most difficult of all phenomenological problems.[1] The choice of texts assembled here was governed by the intention to present the basic elements of Husserl's phenomenology of time-consciousness and by a desire to convey to the reader something of the breadth and richness of Husserl's reflections. The passages included therefore concern, among other themes: the manner in which temporal objects appear; retention, impression, and protention as the original forms of time-consciousness; secondary memory and expectation and the ways in which they differ from retention and protention; the relation of immanent (subjective) and objective time; and the absolute time-constituting flow of consciousness.

The selections are drawn from *The Lectures on Internal Time-Consciousness from the Year 1905*, first published in 1928. The dating is misleading, however. In fact, the texts in the publication of 1928 come not only from 1905 but from as early as 1901 and at least as late as 1911. They were originally stitched together from various manuscripts by Husserl's assistant Edith Stein. Apparently not until Husserl learned of Heideg-

ger's forthcoming *Being and Time* did he feel sufficiently motivated to have Stein's assemblage published in the *Jahrbuch*. And then he asked Heidegger to shepherd it through the press.[2]

The years from 1900 to 1911 or so saw significant development in Husserl's thought. The period opens with the *Logical Investigations* and closes on the eve of the publication of the *Ideas*. Husserl's thought about time-consciousness from these years shows a development as well; indeed, some dramatic upheavals in the phenomenological understanding of time seem to occur during this decade. These do not come through clearly in the edition of 1928, combining as it does without decisive order texts of earlier and later date which sometimes represent quite different positions. The present introductory remarks are intended in part to shed some light on these confusions.

While not all the texts we are considering come from 1905, the title of the lectures which Husserl gave in that year, and which were in part devoted to the investigation of time, is instructive concerning the significance the phenomenology of time-consciousness has for phenomenology as a whole. The lectures were entitled "Important Points from the Phenomenology and Theory of Knowledge." Now Husserl's theory of time-consciousness may justly be taken as a fundamental chapter in the phenomenology of knowledge or experience in general. It certainly is not simply a regional ontology or

271

the study of some dimension of consciousness which enjoys more or less limited importance. This should become clear as we survey the main features of Husserl's reflection.

2. The Fundamental Descriptive Features of Time-Consciousness

Of the major phenomenological themes which emerged between 1901 and 1911, none is more central than the phenomenological reduction. It therefore comes as no surprise that the reduction makes an appearance in the writings on time with which we are concerned. As we will observe in a later section, there are certain ambiguities involved in this early expression of the epoche, especially, in the lectures of 1905. But the main thrust of Husserl's analysis is clear enough. He commences with the notion that time-consciousness exemplifies that most general structure of conscious life, intentionality. This assumed, the phenomenologist in performing the reduction or epoche attempts to describe, on the one hand, the manner in which temporal objects appear through the time-constituting acts intending them and, on the other hand, the elements and features of those acts which constitute them as experiences of temporal objectivity. Whatever does not immediately appear or actually present itself to the phenomenologist as pertaining to the intending act and intended object, whatever might have to be inferred or attained through scientific measurement and the like, is set out of play. The reader will not find in Husserl the kind of quantitative psychological and physiological investigations with which William James laces his pure descriptions of time. To be sure, Husserl is not content simply to describe the phenomena of time-consciousness: he clearly seeks the *essential* structures or features of those phenomena. While the eidetic reduction of the *Ideas* is not mentioned by name in these early writings on time, Husserl has clearly put it to work in the cause of a phenomenology of the necessary and universal structures of time-consciousness.

Husserl shares the descriptive starting point of Augustine and James, whose reflections on time he respected greatly.[3] Objects of our experience appear to us to develop in some kind of succession, such as melodies, or to endure, such as a statue which we contemplate. In either case, the objects "take time"; they appear to us in the temporal modes "now, past, and future." Furthermore, these objects appear through acts of consciousness which are themselves steeped in temporality: they begin, they run off in a succession of phases, they end. It takes time to perceive a temporal object just as the object takes time when it is perceived. The question Husserl will address, then, concerns how it is that in acts of consciousness which unfold in a succession of phases, we become aware of temporally extended objects.

The cardinal descriptive feature of time-consciousness, the condition without which there would be no consciousness of time, is that every act which intends a temporal object reaches out beyond and intends more than the object's now-phase. Specifically, each phase of the act intends not only the now-phase of the object but its past and future phases as well. Imagine for a moment that each act-phase is aware exclusively of the now, say of the single word in a sentence or note in a melody which enjoys for an instant the greatest fullness of perceptual presence. Under that condition, no experience of the temporally extended object, of the sentence or melody as a whole of successively emerging parts, would ever arise; furthermore, since the now is a mode relative to past and future, one could not even claim that a genuine awareness of a *now*-point would be constituted under such circumstances.

That time-consciousness reaches out beyond the now may also be expressed in terms of presentation and modification. If elapsed phases of the temporal object are not in some sense preserved for consciousness, at least for awhile, awareness of temporally extended objectivity would be impossible. On the other hand, if the past phases were preserved in an unmodified way, that is, if they continued to stand forth for consciousness as now despite their being past, then once again there would be no experience of time. A melody, whose successive notes were heard all at once as now, would not appear as a melody at all, but as a crash of simultaneous sound. The necessity of preservation, then, is coupled with the necessity that what is perceived appear in the appropriate mode of the past.

A still more refined reflection on the relation between preservation and modification discloses that elapsed phases are preserved in a definite order and in definite temporal positions: note *a* as coming before note *b*, note *b* as before *c,* and so on. This order is fixed and unchanging. However, as these objective phases in their definite positions relative to one another recede further and further from the actual now, slipping into an always more distant past, they appear in constantly changing temporal modes. That is, note *b* will appear first as now, then as just past, then as still further past, all the while preserving the same position with respect to the *a* which precedes it and the *c* which follows it. The temporal object is an identity in the face of change, with the element of change supplied by the manifold of always different temporal modes.

The reaching out beyond the now which we have been discussing occurs in each and every phase of the temporally extended act of consciousness: we are aware in each such phase of an extended portion of the object and not simply of its now-point. Husserl claims that this is possible because of the threefold intentionality of *retention, primal impression,* and *protention* belonging to the act-phase. These three intentional modes are not themselves acts or even phases of acts; they are simply names for the three directions in which the intentionality of a given act-phase deploys itself. Primal impression is the original consciousness of the now, as opposed to the immediate past and immediate future. Retention is the original consciousness of the past, which at once preserves and modifies the just elapsed phases of the object. Husserl insists that retention or primary memory must not be confused with ordinary or, as he calls it, "secondary" memory. This was the mistake made by Brentano and probably by Augustine as well. Ordinary memory is directed towards objects in the more distant past, while retention intends moments of the object which have just elapsed and which form the past segment of what James called the "spe-

cious present." Furthermore, secondary memory re-presents or reproduces the past object rather than presenting or actually perceiving it. In retention, by contrast, the past is originally presented or perceived—not as now, of course, but as just past. Finally, secondary memory, as a form of representation, runs through the past object from beginning to end as if it were being perceived all over again, while retention simply hangs on to the just past phase as it slips away from the now, finally disappearing from retentional awareness altogether. That secondary memory is a derivative form of consciousness compared with retention does not imply that Husserl neglects it, however; on the contrary, some of his most interesting reflections on time-consciousness concern memory in this sense. The third mode of intentionality, protention, is the immediate consciousness of the future phase or phases of the object. It might aptly be described as the perpetual openness of consciousness to further experience. The intentionality here is also "presentational," but obviously its content will not enjoy the determinate and actual form of what is retained. Protention stands opposed to expectation, which would be the explicit representation of a future event.

3. The Constitution of Time-Consciousness

Having isolated the main descriptive features and conditions of time-consciousness, Husserl proceeds to consider the manner in which primal impression, retention, and protention are constituted. In the *Logical Investigations,* Husserl explains the constitution of various sorts of conscious acts in terms of intentional apprehensions which "animate" immanent sensory contents.[4] Thus the white apple blossoms outside my window are perceived through the animation of a complex of sensations by an appropriate perceptual apprehension. Between about 1901 and 1907, Husserl applies precisely this explanation to the constitution of retention, primal impression, and protention. Accordingly, references to special "now-apprehensions," "past-apprehensions," and the like dot the text of the 1928 edition. The difficulty is that after 1907 Husserl abandoned this way of interpreting the constitution of time-consciousness (though not of other forms of consciousness such as perception), and yet the text of 1928 is unclear about either the fact that the view was rejected or the reasons for the rejection. Compounding the confusion is the presence in the edition of 1928 of the new view which Husserl then adopted: time-consciousness intends its objects "directly" and without any animating of contents by apprehensions. The reader can only be advised to be cautious under these conditions and to consult Rudolf Boehm's critical edition (*Husserliana* 10) if things become too muddled.

One major piece of territory has so far been neglected in our survey. We have focused on the experience of the transcendent temporal object—the melody played on a piano, Rodin's *Balzac* inspected in a sculpture garden, and the like. But the act which intends such objects itself runs off, and is known or experienced as an *immanent* temporal object. This properly raises the issue of *internal* time-consciousness. Acts and the sensory contents which inhabit them are not perceived and are certainly not transcendent objects, but as immanent "objects" on the side of consciousness they are, in Husserl's language, "experienced" (*erlebt*), that is, we are aware of them as temporally extended in a marginal, nonthematizing way. While we *perceive* the external temporal object, the melody in the concert hall, we *experience* the act intending it, the immanent temporal object. How is this possible? On Husserl's mature view, which is included in sections 35 through 39 of the 1928 edition, retention, primal impression, and protention are understood as constituting not only the awareness of the melody but also of the act itself. It is in Husserl's attempts at explaining how this awareness comes about that time-consciousness really does seem to become the most difficult of all phenomenological problems. But it is also here that all the themes of Husserl's reflection come together. For Husserl seems to envision retention as preserving elapsed phases of the act and, *by so doing,* also preserving the elapsed phases of the transcendent object which the retained act-phases originally intended. Primal-impression is the conscious-

ness of the present or actual act-phase, and through it of the now-phase of the object, and protention is the consciousness of future act-phases. By these means, external and internal time-consciousness are supposed to be brought into harmony, the former constituted through the latter. Now the internal time-consciousness, understood as the experiencing of immanent temporal objects, requires no further consciousness to constitute it. As such, Husserl calls it "the absolute time-constituting flow of consciousness." Through the absolute flow, all of our acts are bound together into a single unified stream, and the foundation of the richly complex life of the ego is laid down.

4. Evaluation

We noted earlier that the phenomenological epoche appears in Husserl's lectures from 1905. It must be said, however, that the version of the reduction found in these texts is quite immature and even misleading, at least from the standpoint of the *Ideas* and still later works. Two formulations from the lectures of 1905 will serve to illustrate the point. First, Husserl sometimes seems to distinguish between a real and objective time about which the phenomenologist can talk and a second real and objective time about which he must remain silent.[5] The difficulty with this distinction is that it suggests that there is a domain of reality which the phenomenologist is powerless to penetrate. In terms of Husserl's later discussions of what the reduction makes available, this way of putting things is altogether too Kantian. There is even evidence that Husserl himself realized this in 1905, for in the midst of a text in which he apparently draws the line between the two objective times, we find the statement: "In truth, space and reality are not transcendent in a mystical sense. They are not 'things in themselves' but just phenomenal space, phenomenal spatio-temporal reality, . . . the appearing temporal form."[6] The time in which a melody, a conversation, or a building unfolds for me simply is the objective time of the perceptual world; it is not a crust hiding a further and noumenal time behind itself. By 1907 or so, Husserl seems to have settled on this view, and he no longer hints at a contrast between accessible and inaccessible times. There is a single time of the world we perceive, and it is this time, precisely as it appears, that the phenomenologist describes.[7]

The second disconcerting feature of the epoche as it is presented in 1905 involves Husserl's occasional suggestions that the phenomenologist is not concerned with objective time or temporal objects at all, but solely with the acts and contents positioned on the side of the intending consciousness.[8] If this were the case, then the phenomenologist's descriptive endeavors would never extend to the objects of intentional acts. In the terms of Husserl's *Ideas,* there would be no *noematic* phenomenology of time-consciousness. Now even in 1905, notwithstanding sporadic declarations to the contrary, Husserl's practice clearly includes descriptions of the way in which temporal objects appear and are constituted. And again, by 1907 or so, his ambivalence about what the phenomenologist is concerned with has been cleared up: intending act and intended temporal object are both perfectly appropriate subjects of phenomenological investigation. By the end of the decade, then, Husserl has largely overcome his early confusions and ambiguities, and has set the phenomenology of time-consciousness on a firm course.[9]

But it might be claimed that more serious and ultimately unresolved difficulties plague Husserl's understanding of time-consciousness. One could perhaps argue that his analysis is in some measure vitiated by a tendency to pulverize time into a series of isolated present and past "nows," and to spend too much energy on worrying about the constitution of immanent sensory contents which, from the standpoint of a consistently developed phenomenology, probably do not even exist. But Husserl does not atomize time; the whole thrust of his thought is in the opoosite direction. It is true that he is forced, as were Augustine and James, to resort to terminology which may suggest an atomistic view of time. But a careful reading of the Husserlian texts surely confirms that the now, past, and future are not atoms of experience but modes of appearance. And the absolute flow of consciousness breaks down into dependent phases woven into a tissue of intentionality, not into discrete bits and pieces of experience. As for his allegiance to sensory data, it can safely be said that one could reject the idea of a sensed tone in consciousness and still preserve virtually everything Husserl says about the constitution of time. And what he does say arguably represents the most thorough, careful, and insightful reflection on the phenomenon of the experience of time in the literature, whether ancient or modern.

NOTES

1. Edmund Husserl, *Zur Phänomenologie des Inneren Zeitbewusstseins (1893–1917),* ed. Rudolf Boehm, *Husserliana* 10 (The Hague: Nijhoff, 1966), pp. 279–80. This is the critical edition of Husserl's writings on time through 1917. Most of the texts come from the years 1901 to 1911.

2. In his editorial introduction to *Husserliana* 10 Rudolf Boehm outlines the history and composition of the text of 1928. There is an English translation of the 1928 edition: *The Phenomenology of Internal Time-Consciousness,* ed. Martin Heidegger, trans. J. S. Churchill (Bloomington: Indiana University Press, 1964).

3. Augustine's discussion of time and the role of memory in the experience of time is found chiefly in book 11, sections 14–30, of the *Confessions.* William

James takes up the themes of the perception of time and memory in chapters 15 and 16 of *The Principles of Psychology* (New York: Henry Holt & Co., 1890).

4. Edmund Husserl, *Logische Untersuchungen,* 5th ed. (Tübingen: Max Niemeyer, 1968), II, 1, p. 385.

5. Section 1 of the 1928 edition, *Husserliana* 10:5; English translation, pp. 23–24.

6. Section 1 of the 1928 edition, *Husserliana* 10:6; English translation, p. 24.

7. Section 34 of the 1928 edition, *Husserliana* 10: 73, 286ff.; English translation, p. 98.

8. Section 1 of the 1928 edition, *Husserliana* 10:6. English translation, p. 24.

9. Section 34 of the 1928 edition, *Husserliana* 10: 73, 286ff.; English translation, p. 98.

FURTHER REFERENCES

Brand, Gerd. *Welt, Ich, und Zeit.* The Hague: Nijhoff, 1955.

Brough, John. "The Emergence of an Absolute Consciousness in Husserl's Early Writings on

Time-Consciousness." *Man and World,* vol. 5, no. 3 (August 1972): 298–326; reprinted in *Husserl: Expositions and Appraisals,* edited by Frederick A. Elliston and Peter J. McCormick, pp. 83–100 (Notre Dame: University of Notre Dame Press, 1977).

————. "Husserl on Memory." *Monist* 59 (1975): 40–62.

Eigler, Gunther. *Metaphysische Voraussetzungen in Husserls Zeitanalysen.* Meisenheim a. Glan: Hain, 1961.

Findlay, John. "Husserl's Analysis of the Inner Time-Consciousness." *Monist* 59 (1975): 3–21.

Granel, Gerard. *Le sens du temps et de la perception chez E. Husserl.* Paris: Gallimard, 1968.

Gurwitsch, Aron. *Studies in Phenomenology and Psychology.* Evanston: Northwestern University Press, 1966.

Held, Klaus. *Lebendige Gegenwart.* The Hague: Nijhoff, 1966.

Sartre, Jean-Paul. *La Transcendence de L'Ego.* Paris: J. Vrin, 1966.

Seebohm, Thomas. *Die Bedingungen der Möglichkeit der Transzendental-Philosophie.* Bonn: Bouvier, 1962.

————. *Zur Kritik der hermeneutischen Vernunft.* Bonn: Bouvier, 1972.

Sokolowski, Robert. *The Formation of Husserl's Concept of Constitution.* The Hague: Nijhoff, 1964.

————. *Husserlian Meditations.* Evanston: Northwestern University Press, 1974.

Spicker, Stuart F. "Inner Time and Lived Through Time: Husserl and Merleau Ponty." *Journal of the British Society for Phenomenology* 4 (1973): 235–47.

15

The Lectures on Internal Time Consciousness
from the Year 1905*

TRANSLATED BY JAMES S. CHURCHILL

Introduction

Naturally, we all know what time is; it is that which is most familiar. However, as soon as we make the attempt to account for time-consciousness, to put Objective[a] time and subjective time-consciousness into the right relation and thus gain an understanding of how temporal Objectivity—therefore, individual Objectivity in general—can be constituted in subjective time-consciousness—indeed, as soon as we even make the attempt to undertake an analysis of pure subjective time-consciousness—the phenomenological content of lived experiences of time (*Zeiterlebnisse*)—we are involved in the most extraordinary difficulties, contradictions, and entanglements. . . .

A few general observations must still be made beforehand. Our aim is a phenomenological analysis of time-consciousness. In-

*From Edmund Husserl, *The Phenomenology of Internal Time-Consciousness*, edited by Martin Heidegger, trans. by James S. Churchill (Bloomington: Indiana University Press, 1964). Copyright © 1964 by Indiana University Press. Reprinted by permission of the publisher.

a. [Following the practice of Dorion Cairns, the translator of Husserl's *Cartesianische Meditationen* (Martinus Nijhoff, The Hague, 1960), to differentiate the terms *Objekt* and *Gegenstand*, both of which are used by Husserl, I have chosen to translate the word *Objekt* by *Object* and *Gegenstand* by *object*. The same applies, *mutatis mutandis*, in the case of words derived from *Objekt* and *Gegenstand*. If the English word *object* or any word derived from it stands first in a sentence, the German word is given in brackets. J.S.C.]

volved in this, as in any other such analysis, is the complete exclusion of every assumption, stipulation, or conviction concerning Objective time (of all transcendent presuppositions concerning existents). . . .

. . . Just as a real thing or the real world is not a phenomenological datum, so also world-time, real time, the time of nature in the sense of natural science including psychology as the natural science of the psychical, is not such a datum.

When we speak of the analysis of time-consciousness, of the temporal character of objects of perception, memory, and expectation, it may seem, to be sure, as if we assume the Objective flow of time, and then really study only the subjective conditions of the possibility of an intuition of time and a true knowledge of time. What we accept, however, is not the existence of a world-time, the existence of a concrete duration, and the like, but time and duration appearing as such. These, however, are absolute data which it would be senseless to call into question. To be sure, we also assume an existing time; this, however, is not the time of the world of experience but the *immanent time* of the flow of consciousness. The evidence that consciousness of a tonal process, a melody, exhibits a succession even as I hear it is such as to make every doubt or denial appear senseless. . . .

. . . We also understand the difference between the phenomenological question (*i.e.*, from the standpoint of theory of knowledge) and the psychological with regard to the origin of all concepts constitutive of experience, and so also with regard to the question of the origin of time. *From the point of view of theory of knowledge, the question of the possibility of experience* (which, at the same time, is *the question of the essence of experience*) necessitates a return to the phenomenological data of which all that is experienced consists phenomenologically. . . .

Accordingly, the question of the essence of time leads back to the question of the "origin" of time. The *question of the origin* is oriented toward the *primitive* forms of the consciousness of time in which the primitive differences of the temporal are constituted intuitively and authentically as the originary (*originären*) sources of all certainties relative to time. The question of the origin of time should not be confused with the *question of its psychological origin*—the controversial question between *empiricism and nativism*. With this last question we are asking about the *primordial material of sensation out of which arises Objective intuition of space and time* in the human individual and even in the species. We are indifferent to the question of the empirical genesis. What interests us are lived experiences as regards their objective sense and their descriptive content. . . . We are concerned with reality only insofar as it is intended, represented, intuited, or conceptually thought. With reference to the problem of time, this implies that we are interested in *lived experiences* of time. . . .

It is indeed evident that the perception of a temporal Object itself has temporality, that perception of duration itself presupposes duration of perception, and that perception of any temporal configuration whatsoever itself has its temporal form. And, disregarding all transcendencies, the phenomenological temporality which belongs to the indispensable essence of perception according to all its phenomenological constituents still remains. Since Objective temporality is always phenomenologically constituted and is present for us as Objectivity and moment of an Objectivity according to the mode of appearance only through this constitution, a phenomenological analysis of time cannot explain the constitution of time without reference to the constitution of the temporal Object. By *temporal Objects,* in this *particular sense,* we mean Objects which not only are unities in time but also include temporal extension in themselves. When a tone sounds, my Objectifying apprehension can make the tone which endures and sounds into an object, but not the duration of the tone or the tone in its duration. The same also holds for a melody—for every variation and also for every continuance considered as such. Let us take a particular melody or cohesive part of a melody as an example. The matter seems very simple at first; we hear a melody, *i.e.,* we perceive it, for hearing is indeed perception. While the first tone is sounding, the second comes, then the third, and so on. Must we not say that when the second tone sounds I hear *it,* but I no longer hear the first, and so on? In truth, therefore, I do not hear the melody but only the particular tone which is actually present. That the expired part of the melody is objective to me is due—one is inclined to say—to memory, and it is due to expectation which looks ahead that, on encountering the tone actually sounding, I do not assume that that is all.

We cannot rest satisfied with this explanation, however, for everything said until now depends on the individual tone. Every tone itself has a temporal extension: with the actual sounding I hear it as now. With its continued sounding, however, it has an ever new now, and the tone actually preceding is changing into something past. Therefore, I hear at any instant only the actual phase of the tone, and the Objectivity of the whole enduring tone is constituted in an act-continuum which in part is memory, in the smallest punctual part is perception, and in a more extensive part expectation. However, this seems to lead back to Brentano's theory. At this point, therefore, we must initiate a more profound analysis.

Immanent Temporal Objects (Zeitobjekte) and Their Modes of Appearance

We now exclude all transcendent apprehension and positing (*Setzung*) and take the sound purely as a hyletic datum. It begins and stops, and the whole unity of its duration, the unity of the whole process in which it begins and ends, "proceeds" to the end in the ever more distant past. In this sinking back, I still "hold" it fast, have it in a "retention," and as long as the retention persists the sound has its own temporality. It is the same and its duration is the same. I can direct my attention to the mode of its being given. I am conscious of the sound and the duration which it fills in a continuity of "modes," in a "continuous flux." A point, a phase of this flux is termed "consciousness of sound beginning" and therein I am conscious of the first temporal point of the duration of the sound in the mode of the now. The sound is given; that is, I am conscious of it as now, and I am so conscious of it "as long as" I am conscious of any of its phases as now. But if any temporal phase (corresponding to a temporal point of the duration of the sound) is an actual now (with the exception of the beginning point), then I am conscious of a continuity of phases as "before," and I am conscious of the whole interval of the temporal duration from the beginning-point to the now-point as an expired duration. I am not yet conscious, however, of the remaining interval of the duration. At the end-point, I am conscious of this point itself as a now-point and of the whole duration as expired (in other words, the end-point is the beginning point of a new interval of time which is no longer an interval of sound). "During" this whole flux of consciousness, I am conscious of one and the same sound as enduring, as enduring now. "Beforehand" (supposing it was not expected, for example) I was not conscious of it. "Afterward" I am "still" conscious of it "for a while" in "retention" as having been. It can be arrested and in a fixating regard (*fixierenden Blick*) be fixed and abiding. The whole interval of duration of the sound or "the" sound in its extension is something dead, so to speak, a no longer living production, a structure animated by no productive point of the now. This structure, however, is continually modified and sinks back into emptiness (*Leere*). The modification of the entire interval then is an analogous one, essentially identical with that modification

which, during the period of actuality, the expired portion of the duration undergoes in the passage of consciousness to ever new productions.

What we have described here is the manner in which the immanent-temporal Object "appears" in a continuous flux, *i.e.,* how it is "given." To describe this manner does not mean to describe the temporal duration itself, for it is the same sound with its duration that belongs to it, which, although not described, to be sure, is presupposed in the description. The same duration is present, actual, self-generating duration and then is past, "expired" duration, still known or produced in recollection "as if" it were new. The same sound which is heard now is, from the point of view of the flux of consciousness which follows it, past, its duration expired. To my consciousness, points of temporal duration recede, as points of a stationary object in space recede when I "go away from the object." The object retains its place; even so does the sound retain its time. Its temporal point is unmoved, but the sound vanishes into the remoteness of consciousness; the distance from the generative now becomes ever greater. The sound itself is the same, but "in the way that" it appears, the sound is continually different.

The Consciousness of the Appearances of Immanent Objects (Objekte)

On closer inspection, we are able to distinguish still other lines of thought with reference to the description: (1) We can make self-evident assertions concerning the immanent Object in itself, *e.g.,* that it now endures, that a certain part of the duration has elapsed, that the duration of the sound apprehended in the now (naturally, with the content of the sound) constantly sinks back into the past and an ever new point of duration enters into the now or is now, that the expired duration recedes from the actual now-point (which is continually filled up in some way or other) and moves back into an ever more "distant" past, and so on. (2) We can also speak of the way in which we are "conscious of" all differences in the "appearing" of immanent sounds and their content of duration. We speak here with reference to the perception of the duration of the sound which extends into the actual now, and say that the sound, which endures, is perceived, and that of the interval of duration of the sound only the point of duration characterized as now is veritably perceived. Of the interval that has expired we say that we are conscious of it in retentions, specifically, that we are conscious of those parts or phases of the duration, not sharply to be differentiated, which lie closest to the actual now-point with diminishing clarity, while those parts lying further back in the past are wholly unclear; we are conscious of them only as empty (*leer*). The same thing is true with regard to the running-off of the entire duration. Depending on its distance from the actual now, that part of the duration which lies closest still has perhaps a little clarity; the whole disappears in obscurity, in a void retentional consciousness, and finally disappears completely (if one may say so) as soon as retention ceases.

In the clear sphere we find, therefore, a greater distinction and dispersion (in fact, the more so, the closer the sphere to the actual now). The further we withdraw from the now, however, the greater the blending and drawing together. If in reflection we immerse ourselves in the unity of a structured process, we observe that an articulated part of the process "draws together" as it sinks into the past—a kind of temporal perspective (within the originary temporal appearance) analogous to spatial perspective. As the temporal Object moves into the past, it is drawn together on itself and thereby also becomes obscure. . . .

Primal Impression and Retentional Modification

The "source-point" with which the "generation" of the enduring Object begins is a primal impression. This consciousness is engaged in continuous alteration. The actual (*leibhafte*) tonal now is constantly changed into something that has been; constantly, an ever fresh tonal now, which passes over into modification, peels off. However, when the tonal now, the primal impression, passes over into retention, this retention is itself

again a now, an actual existent. While it itself is actual (but not an actual sound), it is the retention of a sound that has been. A ray of meaning (*Strahl der Meinung*) can be directed toward the now, toward the retention, but it can also be directed toward that of which we are conscious in retention, the past sound. Every actual now of consciousness, however, is subject to the law of modification. The now changes continuously from retention to retention. There results, therefore, a stable continuum which is such that every subsequent point is a retention for every earlier one. And every retention is already a continuum. The sound begins and steadily continues. The tonal now is changed into one that has been. Constantly flowing, the *impressional* consciousness passes over into an ever fresh *retentional* consciousness. Going along the flux or with it, we have a continuous series of retentions pertaining to the beginning point. Moreover, every earlier point of this series shades off (*sich abschattet*) again as a now in the sense of retention. Thus, in each of these retentions is included a continuity of retentional modifications, and this continuity is itself again a point of actuality which retentionally shades off. This does not lead to a simple infinite regress because each retention is in itself a continuous modification which, so to speak, bears in itself the heritage (*Erbe*) of the past in the form of a series of shadings. It is not true that lengthwise along the flux each earlier retention is merely replaced by a new one, even though it is a continuous process. Each subsequent retention, rather, is not merely a continuous modification arising from the primal impression but a continuous modification of the same beginning point.

Up to this point, we have been chiefly concerned with the perception of the originary constitution of temporal Objects and have sought analytically to understand the consciousness of time given in them. However, the consciousness of temporality does not take place merely in this form. When a temporal Object has expired, when its actual duration is over, the consciousness of the Object, now past, by no means fades away, although it no longer functions as perceptual consciousness, or better, perhaps, as impressional consciousness. (As before, we have in mind immanent Objects, which are not really constituted in a "perception.") To the "impression," "primary remembrance" (*primäre Erinnerung*), or, as we say, retention, is joined. Basically, we have already analyzed this mode of consciousness in conjunction with the situation previously considered. For the continuity of phases joined to the actual "now" is indeed nothing other than such a retention or a continuity of retentions. In the case of the perception of a temporal Object (it makes no difference to the present observation whether we take an immanent or transcendent Object), the perception always terminates in a now-apprehension, in a perception in the sense of a positing-as-now. During the perception of motion there takes place, moment by moment, a "comprehension-as-now"; constituted therein is the now actual phase of the motion itself. But this now-apprehension is, as it were, the nucleus of a comet's tail of retentions referring to the earlier now-points of the motion. If perception no longer occurs, however, we no longer see motion, or — if it is a question of a melody — the melody is over and silence begins. Thus no new phase is joined to the last phase; rather, we have a mere phase of fresh memory, to this is again joined another such, and so on. There continually takes place, thereby, a shoving back into the past. The same complex continuously undergoes a modification until it disappears, for hand in hand with the modification goes a diminution which finally ends in imperceptibility. The originary temporal field is obviously circumscribed exactly like a perceptual one. Indeed, generally speaking, one might well venture the assertion that the temporal field always has the same extension. It is displaced, as it were, with regard to the perceived and freshly remembered motion and its Objective time in a manner similar to the way in which the visual field is displaced with regard to Objective space.

Retention as Proper Intentionality

We must still discuss in greater detail what sort of modification it is that we designate as retentional.

One speaks of the dying or fading away, etc., of the content of sensation when veritable perception passes over into retention. Now, according to the statements made hitherto, it is already clear that the retentional "content" is, in the primordial sense, no content at all. When a sound dies away, it is first sensed with particular fullness (intensity), and thereupon comes to an end in a sudden reduction of intensity. The sound is still there, is still sensed, but in mere reverberation. This real sensation of sound should be distinguished from the tonal moment in retention. The retentional sound is not actually present but "primarily remembered" precisely in the now. It is not really on hand in retentional consciousness. The tonal moment that belongs to this consciousness, however, cannot be another sound which is really on hand, not even a very weak one which is qualitatively similar (like an echo). A present sound can indeed remind us of a past sound, present it, symbolize it; this, however, already presupposes another representation of the past. The intuition of the past itself cannot be a symbolization (*Verbildlichung*); it is an originary consciousness. Naturally, we cannot deny that echoes exist. But where we recognize and distinguish them we are soon able to establish that they do not belong to retention as such but to perception. The reverberation of a violin tone is a very weak violin tone and is completely different from the retention of loud sounds which have just been. The reverberation itself, as well as after-images in general, which remain behind after the stronger givens of sensation, has absolutely nothing to do with the nature of retention, to say nothing of the possibility that the reverberation must necessarily be ascribed to retention.

Truly, however, it pertains to the essence of the intuition of time that in every point of its duration (which, reflectively, we are able to make into an object) it is consciousness of *what has just been* and not mere consciousness of the now-point of the objective thing appearing as having duration. In this consciousness, we are aware of what has just been in the continuity pertaining to it and in every phase in a determinate "mode of appearance" differentiated as to "content" and "apprehension." One notices the steam whistle just sounding; in every point there is an extension and in the extension there is the "appearance" which, in every phase of this extension, has its moment of quality and its moment of apprehension. On the other hand, the moment of quality is no real quality, no sound which really is now, *i.e.*, which exists as now, provided that one can speak of the immanent content of sound. The real content of the now-consciousness includes sounds which, if the occasion should arise, are sensed; in which case, they are then necessarily to be characterized in Objectifying apprehension as perceived, as present, but in no wise as past. Retentional consciousness includes real consciousness of the past of sound, primary remembrance of sound, and is not to be resolved into sensed sound and apprehension as memory. Just as a phantasied sound is not a sound but the phantasy of a sound, or just as tonal sensation and tonal phantasy are fundamentally different and are not to be considered as possibly the same, except for a difference in interpretation, likewise primary, intuitive remembered sound is intrinsically something other than a perceived sound, and the primary remembrance of sound is something other than the sensation of sound. . . .

Whether A is the object of primary attention or not, it really is present as something of which we are conscious even if unnoticed or noticed only incidentally. If it is a question of an immanent Object, however, the following holds true: a succession, an alternation, a variation of immanent data, if it "appears," is absolutely indubitable. And within a transcendent perception, the immanent succession belonging essentially to the composition of this perception is also absolutely indubitable. It is *basically absurd* to argue: How in the now can I know of a not-now, since I cannot compare the not-now which no longer is with the now (that is to say, the memory-image present in the now)? As if it pertained to the essence of memory that an image present in the now were presupposed for another thing similar to it, and as with graphic representation, I could and must compare the two. Memory or retention is not figurative consciousness, but something totally different. What is re-

membered *is*, of course, not now; otherwise it would not be something that has been but would be actually present. And in memory (retention) what is remembered is not given as now: otherwise, memory or retention would not be just memory but perception (or primal impression). A comparison of what we no longer perceive but are merely conscious of in retention with something outside it makes no sense at all. Just as in perception, I see what has being now, and in extended perceptions, no matter how constituted, what has enduring being, so in primary remembrance I see what is past. What is past is given therein, and givenness of the past is memory.

If we now again take up the question of whether a retentional consciousness that is not the continuation of an impressional consciousness is thinkable, we must say that it is impossible, for every retention in itself refers back to an impression. "Past" and "now" exclude each other. Something past and something now can indeed be identically the same but only because it has endured between the past and now. . . .

Perception as Originary Presentation (Gegenwärtigung) *as Distinguished from Retention and Recollection*

Any reference to "perception" still requires some discussion here. In the "perception of a melody," we distinguish the tone *given now*, which we term the "perceived," from those which *have gone by*, which we say are "not perceived." On the other hand, we call the *whole melody* one that is *perceived*, although only the now-point actually is. We follow this procedure because not only is the extension of the melody given point for point in an extension of the act of perception but also the unity of retentional consciousness still "holds" the expired tones themselves in consciousness and continuously establishes the unity of consciousness with reference to the homogeneous temporal Object, *i.e.*, the melody. An Objectivity such as a melody cannot itself be originarily given except as "perceived" in this form. The constituted act, constructed from now-consciousness and retentional consciousness, is *adequate perception of the temporal Ob-*

ject. This Object will indeed include temporal differences, and temporal differences are constituted precisely in such phases, in primal consciousness, retention, and protention. If the purposive (*meinende*) intention is directed toward the melody, toward the whole Object, we have nothing but perception. If the intention is directed toward a particular tone or a particular measure for its own sake, we have perception so long as precisely the thing intended is perceived, and mere retention as soon as it is past. Objectively (*objektiver*) considered, the measure no longer appears as "present" but as "past." The whole melody, however, appears as present so long as it still sounds, so long as the notes *belonging to it,* intended in the *one* nexus of apprehensions, still sound. The melody is past only after the last note has gone.

As we must assert in accordance with the preceding statements, *this relativation* carries over to the individual *tones.* Each is constituted in a continuity of tonal data, and only a punctual phase is actually present as now at any given moment, while the others are connected as a retentional train. We can say, however, that a temporal Object is perceived (or intentionally known) as long as it is still produced in continuous, newly appearing primal impressions. . . .

Perception, or the self-giving of the actual present, which has its correlate in the given of what is past, is now confronted by another contrast, that of recollection, secondary remembrance. In recollection, a now "appears" to us, but it "appears" in a sense wholly other than the appearance of the now in perception. This now *is not perceived, i.e., self-given, but presentified.* It places a now before us which is not given. In just the same way, the running-off of a melody in *recollection* places before us a "just past," but does not give it. In addition, every individual in mere phantasy is temporally extended in some way. It has its now, its before and after (*sein vorher und Nachher*), but like the whole Object, the now, before, and after are merely imagined. Here, therefore, it is a question of an *entirely different concept of perception.* Here, *perception* is an act which brings something *other than itself before us,* an act which *pri-*

mordially constitutes the Object. *Presentification,* re-presentation, as the act which does not place an Object itself before us, but just presentifies—places before us in images, as it were (if not precisely in the manner of true figurative consciousness)—, is just the opposite of this. There is no mention here of a continuous accommodation of perception to its opposite. Heretofore, consciousness of the past, *i.e.,* the primary one, was not perception because perception was designated as the act originarily constituting the now. Consciousness of the past, however, does not constitute a now but rather a "*just-having-been*" (*ein soeben gewesen*) that intuitively precedes the now. However, if we call perception *the act in which all* "*origination*" lies, which *constitutes originarily,* then *primary remembrance is perception.* For only in *primary remembrance do we see what is past;* only in it is the past constituted, *i.e., not in a representative but in a presentative way.* The just-having-been, the before in contrast to the now, can be seen directly only in primary remembrance. It is the essence of primary remembrance to bring this new and unique moment to primary, direct intuition, just as it is the essence of the perception of the now to bring the now directly to intuition. On the other hand, recollection, like phantasy, offers us mere presentification. It is "as-if" the same consciousness as the temporally creative acts of the now and the past, "as-if" the same but yet modified. The phantasied now represents a now, but does not give us a now itself; the phantasied before and after merely represents a before and after, etc. . . .

In order now to understand the disposition of this constituted unity of lived experience, "memory," in the undivided stream of lived experience, the following must be taken into account: every act of memory contains intentions of expectation whose fulfillment leads to the present. Every primordially constitutive process is animated by protentions which voidly (*leer*) constitute and intercept (*auffangen*) what is coming, as such, in order to bring it to fulfillment. However, the recollective process not only renews these protentions in a manner appropriate to memory. These protentions were not only present as intercepting, they have also intercepted. They have been fulfilled, and we are aware of them in recollection. Fulfillment in recollective consciousness is re-fulfillment (*Wieder-Erfüllung*) (precisely in the modification of the positing of memory), and if the primordial protention of the perception of the event was undetermined and the question of being-other or not-being was left open, then in the recollection we have a pre-directed expectation which does not leave all that open. It is then in the form of an "incomplete" recollection whose structure is other than that of the undetermined, primordial protention. And yet this is also included in the recollection. There are difficulties here, therefore, with regard to the intentional analysis both for the event considered individually, and, in a different way, for the analysis of expectations which concern the succession of events up to the actual present. Recollection is not expectation; its horizon, which is a posited one, is, however, oriented on the future, that is, the future of the recollected. As the recollective process advances, this horizon is continually opened up anew and becomes richer and more vivid. In view of this, the horizon is filled with recollected events which are always new. Events which formerly were only foreshadowed are now quasi-present, seemingly in the mode of the embodied present. . . .

The foreground is nothing without the background; the appearing side is nothing without the non-appearing. It is the same with regard to the unity of time-consciousness—the duration reproduced is the foreground; the classifying intentions make us aware of a background, a temporal background. And in certain ways, this is continued in the constitution of the temporality of the enduring thing itself with its now, before, and after. We have the following analogies: for the spatial thing, the ordering into the surrounding space and the spatial world on the one side, and on the other, the spatial thing itself with its foreground and background. For the temporal thing, we have the ordering into the temporal form and the temporal world on the one side, and on the other the temporal thing itself and its changing orientation with regard to the living now.

The Difference between Memory and Expectation

We must further investigate whether memory and expectation equal each other. Intuitive remembrance offers me the vivid reproduction of the expiring duration of an event, and only the intentions which refer back to the before and forward to the living now remain unintuitive.

In the intuitive idea of a future event, I now have intuitively the productive "image" of a process which runs off reproductively. Joined thereto are indeterminate intentions of the future and of the past, *i.e.,* intentions which from the beginning of the process affect the temporal surroundings which terminate in the living now. To that extent, expectational intuition is an inverted memorial intuition, for the now-intentions do not go "before" the process but follow after it. As empty environmental intentions, they lie "in the opposite direction." . . .

The principal differences between memory and expectation, however, are to be found in the manner of fulfillment. Intentions of the past are necessarily fulfilled by the establishment of nexuses of intuitive reproductions. The reproduction of past events permits, with respect to their validity (in internal consciousness) only the confirmation of the uncertainties of memory and their improvement by being transformed in a reproduction in which each and everything in the components is characterized as reproductive. Here we are concerned with such questions as: Have I really seen or perceived this? Have I really had this appearance with exactly this content? All this must at the same time dovetail into a context of similar intuitions up to the now. Another question, to be sure, is the following: Was the appearing thing real? On the other hand, expectation finds its fulfillment in a perception. It pertains to the essence of the expected that it is an about-to-be-perceived. In view of this, it is evident that if what is expected makes its appearance, *i.e.,* becomes something present, the expectational situation itself has gone by. If the future has become the present, then the present has changed to the relatively past. The situation is the same with regard to environmental intentions.

They are also fulfilled through the actuality of an impressional living experience. . . .

Memory as Consciousness of Having-Been-Perceived

What follows is of the greatest significance with regard to the characterization of the positing reproductions which have been analyzed. What pertains to their essence is not the mere reproductive positing of temporal being but a certain relation to internal consciousness. It belongs primarily to the essence of memory that it is consciousness of having-been-perceived. . . .

. . . The memory really implies, therefore, a reproduction of the earlier perception, but the memory is not in the true sense a representation of the perception. The perception is not meant and posited in the memory. What is meant and posited in the memory is the object of the perception together with its now, which last, moreover, is posited in relation to the actual now. I remember the lighted theater of yesterday, *i.e.,* I effect a "reproduction" of the perception of the theater. Accordingly, the theater hovers before me in the representation as something actually present. I mean this, but at the same time I apprehend this present as lying back in reference to the actual present of perceptions now extant. Naturally, it is now evident that the perception of the theater was; I have perceived the theater. What is remembered appears as having been present, that is, immediately and intuitively. And it appears in such a way that a present intuitively appears which is at an interval from the present of the actual now. The latter present is constituted in the actual perception. The intuitively appearing present, the intuitive representation of the not-now, is constituted in a counter-image of perception, in a "presentification of the earlier perception" in which the theater comes to be given "as if now." This presentification of the perception of the theater is therefore not to be understood as if it were a re-living of the perception. What I intend in the presentification, rather, is the being-present of the perceived Object. . . .

. . . An impression, in contrast to a phantasm, is distinguished by the character of originarity. Now, within the sphere of impressions we must lay stress on primal impressions, which, over against the continuum of modifications, are present in the consciousness of primary remembrance. Primal impressions are absolutely unmodified, the primal source of all further consciousness and being. Primal impressions have for content what is signified by the word *now,* insofar as it is taken in the strictest sense; every new now is the content of a new primal impression. Constantly, a new and ever new impression flares up with ever new matter, now the same, now changing. What separates primal impression from primal impression is the individualizing moment of the primordial impression of temporal positions, which moment is basically different from the moment of quality and the other moments of the content of sensation. The moment of primordial temporal position naturally is nothing for itself. Individuation is nothing in addition to what has individuation. The entire now-point, the whole originary impression, undergoes the modification of the past, and through the latter we have first exhausted the complete concept of the now so far as it is a relative one and points to a "past," as "past" points to the "now." In addition, this modification, to begin with, affects the sensation without nullifying its universal, impressional character. It modifies the total content of the primal impression both in its matter and its temporal position. It modifies in exactly the sense that a modification of phantasy does, namely, modifying through and through and yet not altering the intentional essence (the total content).

Therefore, the matter is the same matter, the temporal position the same temporal position; only the mode of givenness has been changed. It is givenness of the past. On this material of sensation is erected the entire Objectifying apperception. . . .

The Levels of Constitution of Time and Temporal Objects (Objecte)

The Differentiation of the Levels of Constitution

Proceeding from the most obvious phenomena, after we have studied time-consciousness according to several principal lines of thought and in different strata, it would be wise to determine the different levels of constitution in their essential structure and go through them in a systematic way.

We discovered:

1. The things of experience in Objective time (whereby still different levels of empirical being were to be differentiated which hitherto had not been taken into account: the experiential thing of the individual subject, the intersubjectively identical thing, the thing of physics).

2. The constitutive multiplicities of appearances of different levels, the immanent unities in pre-empirical time.

3. The absolute, temporally constitutive flux of consciousness.

Differences between the Constituted Unities and the Constitutive Flux

. . . Every individual Object (every Object in the stream of constituted unity, be it immanent or transcendental) endures, and necessarily endures, i.e., it is continuous in time and is identical in this continuous being, which also can be considered as process. . . .

If, in comparison therewith, we now consider the constitutive phenomena, we find a flux, and every phase of this flux is a continuity of shading. However, in principle, no phase of this flux is to be broadened out to a continuous succession; therefore, the flux should not be thought to be so transformed that this phase is extended in identity with itself. Quite to the contrary, we find necessarily and essentially a flux of continuous "alteration," and this alteration has the absurd property (*das Absurde*) that it flows exactly as it flows and can flow neither "more swiftly" nor "more slowly." Consequently, any Object which is altered is lacking here, and inasmuch as in every process "something" proceeds, it is not a question here of a process. There is nothing here which is altered, and therefore it makes no sense to speak here of something that endures. It is also senseless, therefore, to wish to find anything which in a duration is not once altered.

The Temporally Constitutive Flux as Absolute Subjectivity

It is evident, then, that temporally constitutive phenomena are, in principle, objectivities other than those constituted in time. They are not individual Objects, in other words, not individual processes, and terms which can be predicated of such processes cannot be meaningfully ascribed to them. Therefore, it can also make no sense to say of them (and with the same conceptual meaning) that they are in the now and have been previously, that they succeed one another temporally or are simultaneous with respect to one another, etc. To be sure, one can and must say that a certain continuity of appearance, namely, one which is a phase of the temporally constitutive flux, belongs to a now, namely, to that which it constitutes, and belongs to a before, namely, as that which is (one cannot say was) constitutive of the before. But is not the flux a succession? Does it not, therefore, have a now, an actual phase, and a continuity of pasts of which we are conscious in retentions? We can only say that this flux is something which we name in conformity with what is constituted, but it is nothing temporally "Objective." It is absolute subjectivity and has the absolute properties of something to be denoted metaphorically as "flux," as a point of actuality, primal source-point, that from which springs the "now," and so on. In the lived experience of actuality, we have the primal source-point and a continuity of moments of reverberation (*Nachhallmomenten*). For all this, names are lacking.

Appearances of Transcendent Objects (Objekte) as Constituted Unities

It is further to be noted that when we speak of the "act of perception" and say that it is the point of authentic perceiving to which a continuous sequence of retentions is joined, we have described thereby no immanent temporal unities but precisely moments of the flux. That is, the appearance, let us say, of a house is a temporal being which endures, is altered, etc. This is also the case with the immanent sound which is not an appearance. But the appearance of a house is not the perceptional consciousness and the retentional consciousness [of the house]. These can be understood only as temporally constitutive, as moments of the flux. In precisely the same way, memorial appearance (or the remembered immanent [*Immanent*], perhaps the remembered immanent primary content) is to be distinguished from memorial consciousness with its retentions of memory. We must distinguish at all times: consciousness (flux), appearance (immanent Object), and transcendent object (if it is not the primary content of an immanent Object). . . .

The Double Intentionality of Retention and the Constitution of the Flux of Consciousness

The duality in the intentionality of retention gives us a clue to the solution of the difficulty of determining how it is possible to have knowledge of a unity of the ultimate constitutive flux of consciousness. There is no doubt that there is a difficulty here. If a complete flux (one belonging to an enduring process or Object) has expired, I can still look back on it. It forms, so it appears, a unity in memory. Obviously, therefore, the flux of consciousness is also constituted in consciousness as a unity. In this flux, for example, the unity of the duration of the sound is constituted. The flux itself, however, as the unity of the consciousness of the duration of the sound, is again constituted. And must we then also not say further that this unity is constituted in a wholly analogous fashion and is just as good a constituted temporal series and that one must still speak, therefore, of a temporal now, before, and after?

In conformity with the preceding statements, we can give the following answer: It is the one unique flux of consciousness in which the immanent temporal unity of the sound and also the unity of the flux of consciousness itself are constituted. As startling (if not at first sight even contradictory) as it may appear to assert that the flux of consciousness constitutes its own unity, it is still true, nevertheless. And this can be made intelligible through the essential constitution of the flux itself. The regard can on occasion be guided by the phases which "coincide" as intentionalities of sound in the continuous development of the flux. But the regard can also focus on the flow, on a section of the flow, or on the passage of the flowing consciousness from the beginning to the end of the sound. Every shading off of consciousness which is of the "retentional" kind has a double intentionality: one is auxiliary to the constitution of the immanent Object, of the sound. This is what we term "primary remembrance" of the sound just sensed, or more plainly just retention of the sound. The other is that which is constitutive of the unity of this primary remembrance in the flux. That is, retention is at one with this, that it is further-consciousness [*Noch-Bewusstsein*]; it is that which holds back, in short, it is precisely retention, retention of the tonal retention which has passed. In its continuous shading-off in the flux, it is continuous retention of the continuously preceding phases. If we keep any phase whatsoever of the flux of consciousness in view (in the phase appears a tonal now and an interval of duration in the mode of just-having-flowed-away [*Soeben-Abgeflossenheit*]), this phase is concerned with a uniform continuity of retentions in the before-all-at-once. This is retention of the entire momentary continuity of continuously preceding phases of the flux. (In the beginning member it is a new primal sensation; in each leading member that now continuously follows, in the first phase of shading-off, it is immediate retention of the preceding primal sensation. In the next momentary phase it is retention of the retention of the preceding primal sensation, and so on.) If we now let the flux flow away, we then have the flux-continuum as running-off, which allows the continuity just described to be retentionally modified, and thereby every new continuity of phases momentarily existing all-at-once is retention with reference to the total continuity of what is all-at-once in the preceding phase. Hence, a longitudinal intentionality (*Längs-intentionalität*) goes through the flux, which in the course of the flux is in continuous unity of coincidence with itself. Flowing in absolute transition, the first primal sensation changes into a retention of itself, this retention into a retention of this retention, and so on. . . .

Consequently, like two aspects of one and the same thing, there are in the unique flux of consciousness *two* inseparable, homogeneous *intentionalities* which require one another and are interwoven with one another. By means of the one, immanent time is constituted, i.e., an Objective time, an authentic time in which there is duration and alteration of that which endures. In the other is constituted the quasi-temporal disposition of the phases of the flux, which ever and necessarily has the flowing now-point, the phase of actuality, and the series of pre-actual and post-actual (of the not yet actual) phases. This pre-phenomenal, pre-immanent temporality is constituted intentionally as the form of temporally constitutive consciousness and in the latter itself. The flux of the immanent, temporally constitutive consciousness not only *is,* but is so remarkably and yet so intelligibly constituted that a self-appearance of the flux necessarily subsists in it, and hence the flux itself must necessarily be comprehensible in the flowing. The self-appearance of the flux does not require a second flux, but *qua* phenomenon it is constituted in itself. The constituting and the constituted coincide, yet naturally they cannot coincide in every respect. The phases of the flux of consciousness in which phases of the same flux of consciousness are phenomenally constituted cannot be identical with these constituted phases, and they are not. What is caused to appear in the momentary-actual (*Momentan Aktuellen*) of the flux of consciousness is the past phase of the flux of consciousness in the series of retentional moments of this flux.

16

On Experience and Judgment
KARL AMERIKS

I

In 1928 Husserl made plans for an extensive book on transcendental logic, and he charged his assistant Ludwig Landgrebe with the project of compiling and ordering various relevant manuscripts, some going back to 1910. With the original aim of presenting an introduction to that book, Husserl then wrote some new material which became a book of its own: *Formal and Transcendental Logic.* Landgrebe meanwhile continued with his project, now having to take into account the new book as well as additional earlier material Husserl felt was relevant. In 1930 Husserl reviewed Landgrebe's work but did not himself bring it to completion, and in 1935 he authorized Landgrebe to put the material into final form for an independent volume. Landgrebe again made additions from earlier manuscripts and tried to take into account Husserl's later work, which now focused on the themes found in the *Crisis.* The result was the book *Experience and Judgment,* a work described by Landgrebe (in his "Editor's Preface") as resulting from a "collaboration of a unique kind."

The "material" of *Experience and Judgment* is said to stem entirely from Husserl (*i.e.,* his manuscripts, notes, and conversations), but the "literary form," the phrasing and organization, is to be ascribed to Landgrebe. Except for a few sections, such as "Appendix I" (a practically unchanged manuscript from 1919 to 1920), it is difficult to tell with certainty which parts of *Experience and Judgment* are to be traced entirely to

Husserl or precisely what phase of Husserl's thought is being presented. It is also difficult to say whether the book is fully successful in its main aim, namely, to present a set of specific "analytic-descriptive" contributions to transcendental logic that would complement and complete the more general and architectonic work of *Formal and Transcendental Logic.* The contributions hardly fill out the whole field of questions in transcendental logic, and the issues they do treat are sometimes only sketched. Moreover, the individual analyses are generally pursued on the basis of various systematic doctrines that underwent change in the period from 1910 to 1935 from which the underlying manuscripts of *Experience and Judgment* were drawn. On the other hand, the style and the main message of the book are relatively straightforward, and for the most part the intricacies of the phenomenological method and the peculiarities of Husserl's transcendental idealism[1] are kept offstage. In sum, although the book is an incomplete work with a curious origin, it is quite clear, and Husserl himself would probably have judged it a fair introduction to his views on experience and judgment.

II

Experience and Judgment is said in its subtitle to be a study in the "genealogy of logic." The general aim of that study can be outlined in terms of some familiar problems of the empiricist tradition. "Logic" as Husserl understands it can be taken to include not only the sheerly symbolic discipline we know today but also—and primarily—the realm of all objective judgments and so all scientific knowledge. It is only natural to seek for that knowledge some kind of foundation in experience, and so to seek its origins or "genealogy." However, at least two serious and related problems immediately arise here. First of all, there are various ways to treat the idea of a foundation of science, especially in view of the prima facie multi-layered nature of our knowledge, in which systematic scientific judgments appear to be built upon or at times even conflict with the more imprecise judgments of the common man. Second, the question arises of how judgment can be based on anything that is purely experiential rather than already partially judgmental. We seem to move always within a set of judgments, and any move to a truly distinct realm of experience would seem to bring us only to mute and unhelpful bare givens.

The first problem, which involves what might be called the conflict of the manifest and scientific images,[2] is treated by Husserl in his discussions of the relation of the "life-world" to the "Galilean world-view."[3] That discussion is referred to in *Experience and Judgment* primarily only in its long introductory section, but it provides a framework for the work as a whole, for it involves a basic problem that concerned Husserl not only in his last years but already in the period of the earliest manuscripts upon which *Experience and Judgment* is based.[4] The second problem, on the other hand, can be seen primarily as a special theme of *Experience and Judgment* alone, especially as regards its central claim that there is a "prepredicative" realm of experience at the basis of all predicative activity, hence underlying all logic in the broadest sense.[5] The primary answer that Husserl presents here to the second problem —that phenomenology reveals a totally isolated ego presented with a structured flow of individual nonconceptualized bodies—may seem naïve and has some features that are rejected by many phenomenologists.[6] However, if Husserl's approach here is understood in the light of what he believes about the first problem, it may be taken to be much more sophisticated than it at first appears.

It is possible to divide the major approaches to the first problem into two groups: "noncompatibilist" and "compatibilist." The noncompatibilists see a deep conflict between what is asserted by the common man and what is (or at least seems to be) asserted by modern science. The more conservative, or instrumentalist, wing here resolves the problem by eventually denying that science has any distinct truths to offer. The more radical, or scientific realist, wing takes the opposite path of denying that the manifest image is ultimately true. A division can also be made among compatibilist views on this issue, but here the alternatives are not so much opposites as rather a series of relatively naïve views that can be contrasted with the more complex and ultimately Husserlian view. On the most naïve view there is no conflict between the scientific and manifest images because no basic contrast is even recognized. Here it may be believed that the categories by which we immediately experience the world are simply the general categories of modern science, as if there were no other way the world could appear (see *Experience and Judgment,* section 10). Less naïvely, it may be believed that between the manifest and scientific images there is a rather simple foundational relation, such as Carnap presented, for example, in *The Logical Structure of the World.*

Now Husserl is in one way closest to this last view because it is at least definitely foundationalist. Sometimes Husserl is thought rather to be an instrumentalist because he speaks of science as a mere method throwing a "garment of ideas" over the life-world (see again *Experience and Judgment,* section 10). But usually it is clear that he does not mean thereby that science itself distorts what is true; he means only that we are philosophically misled if we believe the scientific realm requires no general foundation.[7] Husserl does not think we should divorce the scientific realm from the experiential one as extremely as the noncompatibilists do, but he also sees that if a foundational relation is to be posited, it must not be conceived in a naïve empiricist manner. In particular, he holds that (i) the givens at the base of the foundation are not synchronically atomic but are necessarily relative to a surrounding field of experience; (ii) this field in turn is not diachronically atomic in that it becomes cognitive not by any mere accumulation of distinct impressions but only via an active process of synthesis and interpretation; (iii) and the field is to an extent historically relative, and it becomes related to science proper only when the most basic synthetic processes are transcended by the projection of theories and idealizations of a mathematical nature.

This last point bears on the "more sophisticated" approach promised earlier to the problem of a nonconceptual foundation for judgments. By reflecting on the field of experience from a historical perspective, Husserl demonstrates especially clearly that he does not take the ultimately fundamental and prepredicative realm to be an explicit part of our consciousness. On the contrary, he believes that not only that realm but also elementary predications have been covered over by the influence of science. Thus *Experience and Judgment* is hardly a mere search for the prepredicative; it is also from the beginning (see, *e.g.*, section 1) largely a disclosure of the predicative realm and a demonstration of how deeply logic has penetrated even the lower levels of our experience. Because of the complexity of this insight Husserl's criticism of his opponents can take on an apparently contradictory form. Sometimes he seems to charge them with forgetting the fact that what we are originally oriented to are ordinary-sized perceptual objects and not the peculiar entities and properties of science or even the idea of their possibility (as providing in a readily accessible way a fully determinate ultimate structure for natural objects). Yet at other times his criticism presupposes that this is precisely not a fact (at least if "originally oriented to" means "consciously aware"), and that on the contrary modern man is already oriented toward objects primarily as possibly theoretically determinable entities. The scientific viewpoint is then to be countered not because it does not reflect our common experience, but, rather, precisely because it does reflect so much of that experience it must be countered since it has covered over a realm that is "original" in a special sense, namely, as epistemologically fundamental

even if not necessarily consciously first-present or even ever-known by itself. Prepredicative experience (and the "genealogy" of logic as a whole) is then a necessary theoretical posit (see *Experience and Judgment,* section 11) introduced to account for the justification that we believe the judgmental and scientific realm has.

Such an idea is not unique to Husserl, and notable analogues to it can be found in the American philosophical tradition. What distinguishes Husserl is his Cartesian methodology, his belief that the ultimate layer of experience that the philosopher must posit is revealed through a special form of phenomenological reflection and is not purely theoretical but can be brought to a kind of intuition. Moreover, Husserl assumes this layer has a specifically mental (though not psychological, in the ordinary sense) nature, and that it could not be accounted for merely in terms of some kind of material substrate underlying linguistic dispositions. It is obvious that there are alternatives to this position. One might contend, as recent scientific realists do, that once a turn to theoretical considerations is taken, it need not be inconsistent to understand the ultimate knowledge-generating states of knowers themselves in terms of the most complicated features of the natural objects that we know. On the other hand, as some recent Continental philosophy has suggested, it is also possible to reject the theoretical approach in favor of a more radically phenomenological and historical method, and so to treat as a fateful aberration the whole notion that the justification of natural science is a legitimate primary goal of philosophy. A large part of the continuing appeal of Husserl's philosophy may lie in the fact it attempts a sophisticated account of the central significance of modern science without opting for such an extreme positive or negative position.

III

The following excerpt from *Experience and Judgment* comes from near the end of the last part of its discussion of the prepredicative realm. It attempts to illuminate the relation between what for Husserl is the most complex aspect of that realm, the various kinds of passive temporal experiences, and the basic feature of the judgmental realm, the construction of an objective temporal framework. The move from experience to judgment here requires first of all that a plurality of temporal impressions be combined into a unity. Not every such unity directly reflects an objective temporal unity, and thus arises the question of how the various kinds of intuitive unity that may subjectively develop relate to unity that can be objectly asserted. At the simplest level this is the problem of how mental acts of a "positional" nature—*i.e.*, of a kind that posits genuine individuals, such as memory and perception—are to be sorted out. A broader issue arises when it is seen that a subjective unity of positional and nonpositional consciousness, such as phantasy, is possible. This raises the problem not only of better specifying the distinct trait of objective unities but also of determining whether this trait implies any limits for the possible worlds that can occur in a purely subjective phantasy consciousness.[8]

Throughout these analyses Husserl manifests his commitment to doctrines that for contemporary readers may have a strong Strawsonian flavor. Not only does Husserl believe that predicative judgments concerning spatial particulars are basic, but he also takes objectivity to consist in the possibility of asserting such judgments by tracing a temporal path through experiences such that the unity of one's path can be distinguished from a spatiotemporal unity that constitutes the world at large.[9] Here Husserl goes into considerable helpful detail in trying to give a relatively nonidealistic rendering of what he calls the "inner truth" of the Kantian doctrine that time is the universal form of experience. He discusses how it is the form of each individual intuited (object), of each particular connection of intuiteds, and of the total realm of all intuiteds (for all intuitors), as well as how it is the form of each individual intuiting, of each particular connection of intuitings (*e.g.*, in the experience of a duration), and of each total set of intuitings as the stream of consciousness of an ego. With respect to the last unity Husserl states that this stream constantly constitutes a total memory field that is potentially accessible to one, although at any moment only a smaller given field may be intuitive. In this way Husserl takes the identity of the person to be constituted by not only a relation of continuity but also one of psychological connectedness to all its acts.[10]

As is often the case, it is not clear whether these phenomenological claims really establish general truths about our situation, let alone necessary truths about all possible experiencers. But the value of Husserl's work cannot be measured by the strength of support for such particular claims here; it lies rather in the provocative and broad nature of his analyses as a whole. A good sample of these analyses, I believe, is to be found in the following extract concerning the difficult and still largely uncharted area of the nature of the experience of temporality.

NOTES

1. For a recent treatment of this crucial problem see Karl Ameriks, "Husserl's Realism," *Philosophical Review* 86 (1977): 498–519.

2. See Wilfrid Sellars, "Philosophy and the Scientific Image of Man," in *Science, Perception and Reality* (London, 1963), chapter 1.

3. See Husserl's *The Crisis of European Sciences and Transcendental Phenomenology*, trans. David Carr (Evanston, 1973), section 9, pp. 29ff., and "Translator's Introduction."

4. See, *e.g.*, Husserl's "Philosophy as a Rigorous Science" (1910) and *Ideas* (1913), section 40.

5. A good treatment of this problem is given in Ross Harrison, "The Concept of Pre-Predicative Experience," *Phenomenology and Philosophical Understanding*, ed. E. Pivcevic (London, 1975), pp. 93–107.

6. See G.T. Null's helpful "Review of *Experience and Judgment*," *Man and World* 2 (1974): 182–92.

7. A helpful article here is J.J. Compton's "Natural Science and the Experience of Nature," in *Phenomenology in America*, ed. J.M. Edie (Chicago, 1967), pp. 80–96.

8. Husserl's view here may be compared with N. Wolterstorff, "Worlds of Works of Art," *Journal of Aesthetics and Art Criticism* 35 (1976): 121–32.

9. See especially Peter Strawson's *Subject and Predicate in Logic and Grammar* (London, 1974) and *The Bounds of Sense* (London, 1966), pp. 97–112.

10. For a recent discussion of these characteristics see D. Parfit, "Personal Identity," *Philosophical Review* 80 (1971): 3–27.

FURTHER REFERENCES

Derrida, Jacques. *Speech and Phenomena and Other Essays on Husserl's Theory of Signs.* Translated by David Allison. Evanston: Northwestern University Press, 1973.

Eley, Lothar. "Life-World Constitution of Propositional Logic and Elementary Predicate Logic." In *Analecta Husserliana,* vol. 2, pp. 333–53. Dordrecht: Reidel, 1972.

Findlay, John. "Husserl's Analysis of the Inner-Time Consciousness." *Monist* 59 (1975): 3–20.

Gurwitsch, Aron. "Phenomenological Presuppositions of Logic." In *Studies in Phenomenology and Psychology,* pp. 350–58. Evanston: Northwestern University Press, 1966.

Haglund, A.R. "Perception, Time and the Unity of Mind." Ph.D. dissertation, Institute for Philosophy, Goteborg, 1977.

Kohák, Erazim. *Idea and Experience.* Chicago: University of Chicago Press, 1978.

Landgrebe, Ludwig. *Der Weg der Phänomenologie.* Gütersloh: Gütersloher, 1963.

Ströker, Elisabeth. "Edmund Husserl's Phenomenology as a Foundation of Natural Science." In *Analecta Husserliana,* vol. 2, R245F. Dordrecht: Reidel, 1972.

Tragesser, Robert. *Phenomenology and Logic.* Ithaca: Cornell University Press, 1977.

Welton, Donn. "Intentionality and Language in Husserl's Phenomenology." *Review of Metaphysics* 27 (1973): 260–93.

16

Experience and Judgment* **

Translated by J. S. Churchill and Karl Ameriks

The Passive (Temporal) Unity of Perception

In order for a *unity of the perception of a plurality of individuals* to be possible, it must be given as simultaneously affecting in a *single* now of consciousness. This means that the unity of a sensuous perception, the unity of an intuitive object of consciousness, is the *unity of a sensuous consciousness* in which everything objective, whether it is a self-enclosed individual or a plurality of such individuals, attains original givenness in and with the *form of a temporal duration,* rendering an encompassing and objective unity possible.

If we assume, to begin with, *one* individual that comes to intuition, then the unity of the intuition of this individual extends exactly as far as the unity of its original duration, *i.e.,* of the original duration which is constituted in original time-consciousness. The individual emerges anew from the intuition, even though it may also further endure in itself and may even be intended relative to consciousness, although not intuitively, as enduring somehow or other—if the continuing original constitution of time does not constitute this duration as the du-

ration of the individual in question, therefore as duration filled with the individual plenitude of the moments of its material content.

The same thing holds for a plurality of individuals. But they are then present together to consciousness in the unity of an intuition only if a unity of the consciousness constituting original duration and temporality in general includes this plurality according to the modes of the simultaneous and the successive. Then, not only is each of these individuals intuited and each present to consciousness with its companions in a temporal duration, but they are originally present to consciousness *all together,* in *one duration:* they form a sensuous unity all together, in that the duration which connects them is constituted intuitively in the original sensuous form. As far as originally constituted time extends, thus far extends the originally and sensuously (that is, passively, prior to all activity) constituted unity of a possible objectivity, which is either a single individual or a plurality of coexisting independent individuals. Such an originally given plurality is not a collection merely snatched together by an act of colligation but a unity of objectivity, which, to be sure, as a merely temporally established unity, is not a new, somehow consolidated "individual."

With these comments, it has become evident that a *plurality,* a mere coexistence of pregiven individual objects, is a *unity of connection:* not a categorial unity produced in a creative spontaneity, but a unity of the same sort as that of a particular individual.

*Reprinted with permission of the publisher from E. Husserl, *Experience and Judgment,* trans. by J. S. Churchill and Karl Ameriks (Evanston: Northwestern University Press, 1973), pages 157–82.

**Husserl's footnote references to other parts of *Experience and Judgment* have been deleted here. The reader should be aware, however, that Husserl meant his comments to be related directly to other parts of his full text.

Certainly, it is not itself an individual, but it has the basic phenomenological property of all simply given objectivities: namely, that it must be given originally and as a sensuous unity and that, for it, all active apprehension requires a unitary pregivenness of sensuousness. To be sure, what has already been originally preconstituted in passivity first becomes a theme only through active apprehension. Accordingly, the temporal form is not only a form of individuals, insofar as these are enduring individuals, but it also has, further, the function of uniting individuals in a unity of connection. *The unity of the perception of a plurality of individuals is thus a unity on the basis of a connecting temporal form.* It is the unity which is at the bottom of the relation already alluded to, namely, that of "lying-beside-one-another," hence, of *relations of spatial position.* Individual objects of perception have their reciprocal spatial position on the basis of their being-together in a single time.

More precisely, the time by which objects are united is not the subjective time of perceptual lived experience but *the objective time* conjointly belonging to the objective sense of this experience; not only are the lived experiences of perception immanently simultaneous, in other words, in general linked to a single perception of the plurality, but the objectivities intended in these experiences as actually being are also intended as objectively and simultaneously enduring. The unity of intuition which is present here is thus not only a unity on the basis of the intuitive intention of the plurality in a present lived experience but a *unity of objective togetherness.* This will become clearer in contrast to other cases in which intuitive unity is also present but where the objects united intuitively are objectively intended as existing at different times or, as in the case of imagined objectivities, as in general existing at no objective time.

These cases will compel us to go a little beyond the domain of that which is proper to oneself alone, a domain to which in other respects our study remains limited (cf. Introduction, pp. 57ff.). If, up to now, it has been a question of perception, thus of a positional consciousness intending objects as *existing,* these objects were thought of only

as objects *for me,* as objects of a world only for me. But the reference to objective time —which is unavoidable here and in the following if we are to understand in depth the contrasts between perception and memory, on the one hand, and the lived experiences of imagination, on the other, and the differences conditioned by the unity founding the relation—already leads beyond this domain of being-only-for-me. Objective time, objective being, and all determinations of existents as objective certainly designate a being not only for me but also for others.

The Unity of Memory and Its Separation from Perception

In connection with the question about the other kinds of intuitive unity which can still exist beyond the immediate unity of perception, we will, for the present, hold ourselves within positional consciousness. Consequently, the most immediate question will concern above all the *connection of perception with memory* as positional [*setzender*] presentification and *the mode of their intuitive unity,* of a unity, therefore, which can also appear when the unified objects, which are in reciprocal relation, are not given simultaneously in a perception but are given partly in perceptions, partly in presentifications.

The following serves as an example: through perception I see a table before me, and at the same time I am reminded of another table, which formerly was in its place. Although I can, as it were, "place" the remembered table beside the perceived table, it is still not beside the latter in the unity of an actual duration; it is in a certain manner separated from the perceived table. The world of perception and the world of memory are separate worlds. But, on the other hand, there is still a unity, and this, as will become apparent, in a multiple sense, insofar as I have both tables before me in a single intuitive presence. *In what sense are we talking here of separation, and in what sense of unity?*

Certainly, there is a legitimacy to talking about the *separateness* of the perceived and the remembered. If I live in memory, I have a unity of intuition of memory; what is remembered is there *before* all acts of comparing, distinguishing, relating; the remembered is "sensuous" and made of flowing parts, "intuitive," unitary, and self-enclosed — just as long as I live in *one* intuition of memory which persists uninterrupted, as long as I don't "leap" from memory to memory in a chaos of sudden "whims." Every uniform memory is in itself continuously uniform and in itself constitutes for consciousness a unity of objectivities, which is an intuitive-sensuous unity: intuitive in flowing parts, we said. That is, the running-through in memory of an event of sufficiently long duration has exactly the same structure as its apprehension in original perception. Just as in perception there is always only a single phase intuitively present to consciousness in the original, which phase, immediately detached from the next and retained in grasp, is united synthetically with it, so, in the memory of the event, the whole event is, to be sure, intuitively intended in its unity, namely, in all of its phases, although always only a single stretch of its flowing temporality is "really intuitive."

The principle of the closed nature [Geschlossenheit] of memory is naturally exactly the same as that which we have determined previously for perception, namely, it is based on a unity of temporal duration. It is a unity, not only in relation to the extraction and thematic contemplation of a perceived individual thing or event, but in relation to the unitary phenomenon of the "impression" which founds this activity, a phenomenon in which a unity of objectivity (however numerous its components may be) is sensuously pregiven to us, is already passively there for us. It is an originally constituted structure which flows along continuously. This structure, whether of perception (first-hand sensuous givenness) or of memory, is always for itself, and only the horizon-intentions give it a connection with the objectivity which extends beyond it, with the objective world of which it is a constituent part.

In such memory there can occur, on the basis of these horizon-intentions, what we call *continuous running-through* in memory, for example from a more recent past up to the incipient present. The memory which

first appears in isolation admits of being "freely" extended; we press on in the horizon of memory away from the present, we progress continuously from memory to memory. All the memories which thereby appear are now stretches, flowing into one another, of one interconnected, homogeneous memory. As a rule, the process undergoes at the same time a loss of detail and curtailment (contraction) by the omission of unessential parts of the memory. It is necessary, therefore, to distinguish:

1. The unity of the specific (always flowing) memory-field, which is an *intuitive unity in the narrow sense:* the running-through in memory of an event of longer duration is *one* memory insofar as in every phase of this recollective lived experience what has been intuited in the preceding phase, the earlier past, is "still" intuitive, still retained in grasp, while what newly appears in it is just attaining "primary" intuitiveness.

2. The *total intuitive memory-field in the broad sense:* to this belongs, first of all, the continuum "run through" in a unity of consciousness, a continuum of truly intuitive memory-fields, among which the no longer truly intuitive still have a retentional vividness and are not "absorbed." Further, to this also belongs everything which, though not recollected anew, is still included in the horizons of the past — included as the mere potentiality of bringing intentions in the form of recollections to fulfillment, at first in the form of intuitive recollections which then themselves dwindle away retentionally, becoming retentions which are nonintuitive but still vivid, which are absorbed but still not lost.

All these unities of recollection are *separate from one another* (if they are not traced back to an original perception in separate and individually structured processes or bound together by a continuous bond into an interconnected unity of one recollection). The sensuous unities, objects, and connections that appear in recollection are separate from one another and also separate from whatever appears in the respective world of perception. Therefore, we obviously cannot say that the given makes its appearance here [in recollection] and there [in perception] in a false or in a genuine "intuitive," "sensuous" connection. An object of perception, for example the fountain pen which I now perceive lying on the table here, is not connected intuitively with the book which a year ago lay in the same place on the table and which I now remember. The book is not "beside" the fountain pen; it has no relation of spatial unity with it at all, because, for such a relationship, precisely the unity of what is intuited within *one* temporal duration is required. Such relations, and the act of relational contemplation directed on them, the *relations of the spatial situation* of objects to one another, are therefore not possible in the case of objects which appertain to intuitions separated in such a manner.

The Necessary Connection, on the Basis of Time as the Form of Sensibility, between the Intentional Objects of All Perceptions and Positional Presentifications of an Ego and a Community of Egos

Nevertheless, despite this separation, there is still a *unity* here, and *relations of unity* based on it. Of what sort they are will become clear to us when we recall the *horizon-intentions* already mentioned. Every perception, as a consciousness intending an actual objectivity, has its horizon of before and after. It refers back to what was perceived before, which can be presentified in memories, even when these are not immediately connected with the respective perception but are separated from it by obscure unremembered stretches. Apart from the connection, to be considered later, that everything perceived "reminds" one of something past that is similar or like even though temporally separated—a connection which is therefore a relation of likeness and similitude—there is also still another kind of unity, lying at a deeper level: when through memories, starting from a perception, I am led back into my own past, this past is precisely *my* own, the past of this same subject who is present and living. And the past environing world [*Umgebungswelt*] which is now remembered belongs to the *same world* as the world in which I now live, only it is presentified in a fragment of its past.

To introduce the matter of intersubjectivity, what we have said also holds true if another person tells me about his past experiences, communicates his memories: what is recalled in them belongs to the same objective world as that which is given in my and our common present lived experience. The remembered environing world of the other, about which he tells us, may certainly be another world than that in which we find ourselves at present, and likewise the environing world which I myself remember may be another world; I can have changed my place of residence, have come to another country, with other men and other customs, etc., or this same geographical neighborhood with its inhabitants may have so changed in the course of a human life that it has simply become another; but, despite all this, all these different remembered environing worlds are *pieces of one and the same objective world.* This world is, in the most comprehensive sense, as the *life-world* for a human community capable of mutual understanding, *our earth,* which includes within itself all these different environing worlds with their modifications and their pasts—the more so since we have no knowledge of other heavenly bodies as environing worlds for possible human habitation.[1] In this unique world, everything sensuous that I now originally perceive, everything that I have perceived and which I can now remember or about which others can report to me as what they have perceived or remembered, has its place. Everything has its unity in that it has its fixed temporal position in this objective world, its place in objective time.

This holds for every object of perception as such, *i.e.,* as an intended object, as an object alleged to actually exist. This signifies that in perception, in the sphere of the living present, there is conflict, the sudden change of one perception into a second which is in a conflict of interpenetration with it (cf. above, section 21), and this is also true of every past perception which has emerged. Conflict occurs in sensibility itself (therefore, prior to all activity). But at the same time it should be noticed that *intentional time,* the time which pertains to what is intended as objective as such, is *not affected* by conflict, insofar as the intentional objects which are in conflict and which interpenetrate are not in conflict with respect to the temporal moment itself; as if, for example, two temporal situations with the same coloring were to come into conflict in the same way as the colors of an object can come into conflict as two different colors at variance with each other in the same temporal situation. Sensuous conflict, originally occurring as passive, necessarily involves two objects of the same temporal determination and presupposes this identity of temporal determination.

Thus the sensuously constituted temporal series is unique in every respect: it is in it that everything intentional as such which is sensuously constituted (appears originally) is ordered, irrespective of further characteristics of unity and independence already constituted or to be constituted. Therefore, all *that appears originally,* even if it appears in conflict, *has its determinate temporal position, i.e.,* it has not only a phenomenal time, that is, one given in intentional objectivity as such, but also *its fixed position in the one objective time.* More precisely, even if objects, in the mode of their reciprocal suppression, can appear only one after the other, and, when the one appears, the other is present to consciousness in the mode of concealment, still, every such object, whether given as concealed or manifest, must have its intentional temporal situation and its own position in the one time.

We now understand the inner truth of the Kantian thesis: *time is the form of sensibility,* and thus it is the form of every possible world of objective experience. Prior to all questions about objective reality—prior to the question concerning what gives priority to certain "appearances," to intentional objects which are self-giving in intuitive experiences, by reason of which we bestow on them the predicate "true" or "real object"— is the fact of the essential characteristic of all "appearances," of the true as well as those shown to be null, namely, that they are *time-giving,* and this in such a way that all given times become part of *one time.* Thus, all perceived, all perceptible, individuals have the common form of time. It is the first and fundamental form, the form of all forms, the presupposition of all other connections capable of establishing unity. But, from the first, "form" designates here the character which necessarily precedes all others in the possibility of an intuitive unity. Temporality as duration, as coexistence, as sequence, is the necessary form of all objects of intuition as unities and in this respect is the form of their intuition (the form of concrete, individual intuitivities).

At the same time, the expression "form of intuition" has still a second sense: every individual intuited in the unity of an intuition is given in a *temporal orientation,* which is the form of the givenness of all that is present in one presence. But, in addition, it is also true that all concrete individuals (abstract individual moments are affected by this in an obvious consequence), which are first given to consciousness in unconnected intuitions, pertain to the unity of a single time (which is certainly not intuitive but can become intuitive in free development, *i.e.,* in the fulfillment of the intentions which are in the intuitions and which must be brought to givenness). *The one time is the form,* the one unique form, *of all individual objectivities* which an ego has given or may have given in intuitions at first unconnected, *e.g.,* in perceptions and in memories separated from them. Or: every perception has its horizon, which is capable of being developed in an infinity of intuitions to which correspond objectivities, presented to consciousness through this development as given in a single time; it is one time, which, in its development and therefore in its givenness, appears as the same, to which also pertain the intuitive lived experiences themselves and the lived experiences of the ego in general.

This is then continued in *empathy.* In empathy an objective, intersubjectively common time, in which everything individual in lived experiences and temporal objectivities must be capable of being ordered, is constituted. This constitution can be reduced to the fact that for every ego empathy is nothing other than a special group of positional presentifications in relation to memories and expectations and that, like all positional intuitions, the ego can unite these intuitions in the way already mentioned.

When we inquired about the connection

which makes possible the unity between all the perceptions and positional presentifications of an ego, this was found to be the *temporal connection*. It is established in the sphere of passivity, and this implies in sensibility. Any perceptions whatsoever within an ego-consciousness necessarily have a connection, whether the ego actively combines them, putting them into relation with others, to which it links them, or whether it does not live in them at all and is occupied with other objects, no matter what they may be—they have this connection in themselves: they constitute an all-embracing connection of their intentional objects. Each perception has its retentional horizon and provides the possibility of entering into this horizon and of developing it in memories. Thus all connections not given intuitively in the unity of a perception refer back to enchainments [*Verkettungen*] of connections in the unity of actual intuition, that is, to the possibility of continuous recollections which reproduce the enchainment intuitively. On the other hand, what is actually intuited exhibits new actual intuitions, and this exhibition is protentional expectation. It pertains to the nature of the perceptions of an ego that they occur only in continuous enchainment. The unity of an ego extends, and can extend, only as far as we have a unity of internal consciousness; and all intentional objects of the perceptions which appear in this consciousness must, to the same extent, also constitute a temporal connection which coincides with that of the immanent time of the acts. Every perception and every recollection as the reproduction of a perception must, therefore, set up for their objects a *temporal relation which on principle is capable of being made intuitive*. They are connected with each other as referring to objects, either actual or intended, within one world. This connection serves as the basis for a certain kind of relation, for relations of the temporal location of all perceived objectivities intended in perceptions as actually existing.

In a general way, and formulated as a law, we can say: *all perceptions and experiences of an ego are in connection with regard to their intentional objects; they are related* (even where they enter into conflict) *to a single time*. And, similarly: *all perceptions and experiences of all ego-subjects which are in mutual understanding are in connection with regard to their intentional objects*—a connection which is that of an objective time being constituted in all their subjective times and of an objective world itself being constituted in objective time.

It is, to be sure, a fundamental problem of phenomenology to explain fully how every experience (*e.g.*, every recollection) comes to have this connection with every other (*e.g.*, a recollection has a connection with the corresponding actual perception) of the same ego or in the stream of consciousness of the same ego, a connection which produces the association of everything that is experienced in one time; and it is also a problem to understand the kind of necessity which claims to hold good for every possible ego and its experiences.

If one speaks of the stream of consciousness, then in a certain way one already presupposes infinite time, under the guidance of which, so to speak, one goes back or moves forward from consciousness to consciousness. If a consciousness is actually given (or represented as given in possibility) and if it necessarily continues to flow on, then the possibility exists that recollections of consciousness arise which lead to a stream of consciousness unified in memory. These difficult problems, and in particular that which concerns how the apprehension of absolute temporal determinations of objects, the constitution of their location in objective time, comes about, and how in general this continuity of absolute, objective time manifests itself in the subjective times of lived experiences: all this is the great theme of a more worked-out phenomenology of time-consciousness.

Transition to Quasi-Positionality. The Unconnectedness of Intuitions of Imagination

If, until now, we have considered only the possibilities of intuitive unity within *positional consciousness*, within the unity of perceptions in respect of one another and of perceptions in respect of positioning presentifications, we now pass to quasi-positionality, that positionality appertaining to perceptive or to reproductive imagination; we ask what possibilities of intuitive unity can exist within it (considered as the unity of its intentional objects) and likewise between it and the intentional objects of positional lived experiences.

In between the lived experiences of the perceptive intention of objects in the actual world there can appear—without connection with them—lived experiences of imagination, which are directed toward fictions, toward objectivities intended as fictions. These have *no connection with the perceptions;* this means: while all perceptions with regard to the objects intended in them are joined together in a unity and have reference to the unity of a single world, the objectivities of imagination fall outside this unity; they do not join together in the same way with the objectivities of perception in the unity of a world intended as such.

Certainly, the imaginings [*Phantasien*] of one ego have a connection, not only among themselves but also with the perceptions of this ego, *as lived experiences,* as do all the lived experiences of internal consciousness, which, relative to them, is perceptional. As lived experiences, imaginings are ordered in the unity of the ego, just as all acts are— which means that internal consciousness constitutes intentional connection. But they still have no connection in their *objective relations,* either among themselves or with perceptions. The centaur which I now imagine, and a hippopotamus which I have previously imagined, and, in addition, the table I am perceiving even now have no connection among themselves, *i.e.,* they have *no temporal position in relation to one another.* Though all experiences, past and present, are united in the connection of *one* experience, and though they have therein the unequivocal temporal order in absolute time of the before, the after, and the simultaneous, this is not true of the objectivities of the imagination; the centaur is neither earlier nor later than the hippopotamus or than the table which I now perceive.

In a certain sense, to be sure, every objectivity of imagination has its time; it is present to consciousness as a unity of temporal duration. Thus time also functions here as constituting a unity, exactly in the same way

as was shown for a perception or a memory complete in itself. *What is imagined is always something temporal; e.g.,* all sensuous imagination imagines a sensuous object, and intentional temporality pertains to this merely by its being an intentional object. The object of imagination is present to consciousness as temporal and temporally determined, enduring in time; but its time is a *quasi-time.* Consider, for example, the imagining of a red-colored triangle such as it appears in my mind. I can describe it and, by describing it, also arrive at its duration. It is a temporal object, it has its time. And yet it is not in time. This means: the temporal duration of the triangle, with all of its points of time, is modified in the same way that the quasi-coloration which it has is a modification of the color of an actual red triangle. Everything has a color. A thing of imagination is an imagined thing; it is imagined as colored in such and such a way, etc. The imagined color is the intentional correlate of the imagination and as such has the mode of as-if. Nevertheless, it makes good sense to say that what is merely represented (or, in general, represented, perceived, remembered, imagined, etc.) might also be actual, or that it might not be actual: namely, that something unreal, given in a representation or presented to the mind, and being identified according to rule, might conform, point by point, determination by determination, to something actual. The same thing holds in reverse, namely, that for each thing given regularly in normal perception we could construct a pure fiction which represented exactly the same object in exactly the same manner of representation. But one thing which distinguishes actually existing objects is necessarily lacking in the mere fiction: *absolute temporal position,* "actual" time, as absolute, rigorous uniqueness of the individual content given in temporal form. To put it more plainly: time is certainly represented in imagination, and even represented intuitively, but it is *a time without actual, strict localization of position*—it is, precisely, a *quasi-time.*

To be sure, we also have intuitively in imagination phenomenal places and distances, references relative to place or position. But imagination still offers us no positions which allow themselves to be identified in the sense of an "in-itself" and which can be distinguished accordingly. We can represent to ourselves a red-colored triangle in as many completely detached imaginings as we wish, [and we always represent it] in a complete self-identity, in a duration completely the same: each triangle is then different from every other as the content of a different imaginative consciousness, but *qua individual object* it differs in no way. If the things imagined are actually without connection, then it is impossible to speak of several objects or even of one and the same object represented repeatedly. In view of this, we want to assume, in order to be exact, that the imaginings in question present their objects within exactly the same "horizons," hence, that when one represents object A in a context of temporal objectivity, determined or undetermined as so and so, the other does it in exactly the same context, determined or undetermined in exactly the same way. With the freedom of imagination, this possibility of imaginings being exactly the same is given a priori.

Thus the *sense of the affirmation of the disconnectedness of the intuitions of imagination* has become clear. *Objectivities of imagination lack absolute temporal position,* and so they also cannot have a temporal unity among themselves, a unique temporal order like the objects of perception—that is, insofar as we speak, as previously, of imaginings which do not constitute among themselves a cointended connection relative to consciousness, [which do not constitute] a unity of imagination. *Such a possible constitution of unity is external to the essence of imaginings.* It is not part of their essence that they must appear in a continuous enchainment, which would be, as [a form of] unity, a continuity of imagination. Imaginings separate from one another have no necessary connection a priori and, as a rule, also have none in our actual experience. Hence, in such cases there is no sense in asking whether the object of the one precedes or follows that of the other. Every act of imagination, being divorced from all [temporal] connection, has its own *imagination-time*, and there are as many such, incomparable with one another (disregarding their general form, their con-

crete essence, in general), as there are or can be such imaginings, thus, infinitely many. No absolute position of one can be identical with that of another. However, what other relations are possible between them is still to be examined.

Note: If we speak of several disconnected imaginings of a completely like objectivity, with respect to which, despite this likeness, we can talk of neither individual identity nor nonidentity, it is to be remarked that we do not mean by this a plurality of imaginings of one and the same imagined thing, in the rigorously positive sense which implies that, relative to consciousness, these imaginings are imaginings of the same. For if I imagine A, then I can, forming an image of the content A, completely similar, intend this imagined A a second time as the same thing that I had imagined earlier. This takes place in a very simple way in an act which is related to the first act of imagination exactly as a recollection is to an earlier perception of the same thing. We thus behave "as if" we called to mind again a quasi-perception; and such a quasi-recollection (which in the change of attitude [of consciousness] involves an actual recollection of the previous act of imagination and what was imagined as such) can be linked as often as we like to the first act of imagination, possibly having at the same time the character of a recollection of what was previously already recollected, etc. We then have a chain of imaginings, not of unconnected but of intentionally interrelated imaginings, which on their part can be transformed into a unity of interrelated recollections in which what is repeatedly intuited is present to consciousness and given intuitively as the same. However, this is already a case of the constitution of a connection between imaginings, which must now be examined in greater detail.

The Unity of Time and Connection [Instituted] in Imagination by the Combination of Imaginings into the Unity of a World of Imagination. Individuation as Possible Only within the World of Actual Experience

In spite of the essential disconnectedness of all intuitions of imagination, unity is still possible to some degree even here, namely, as far as in all imaginings—speaking in terms of the modification of neutrality— there is constituted a single *quasi-world* as a unique world, partly intuited, partly intended in empty horizons. To be sure, it remains within the province of our freedom to allow the indeterminateness of these horizons to be quasi-fulfilled in an arbitrary way by imaginings. But this changes nothing regarding the fact that, so far as this is the case, all these imaginings have a connection in the unity of an object-consciousness which encompasses all of them, a consciousness actual and possible. The "unity of an imagination" is manifestly nothing other than *the unity of a possible experience or the modification of neutrality of a unity of experience.* But this unity affords precisely the ground for the *essence:* unity of experience.

There is thus a formation of unity in all free imaginings belonging to a fairy tale, which, in order to have an unencumbered imagination, we conceive to be free from all relation to the actual world. Whether our imagination runs through the story at one stretch or in separate sections, each new stretch is linked to the preceding one by an obscure horizon, but one capable of further development, whereby the obscure memories are for me, the continuing reader of the tale, actual memories of what I have already read and which have been imagined by me, while in the course of my engagement in the tale the linkage takes place in "memories in imagination," which are themselves quasi-memories.

A *single* act of imagination—this encompasses, therefore, an arbitrary "complex" of imaginings which, precisely by their specific sense, converge to form an intuitively possible, unitary act of imagination in which, concordantly, a unitary world of imagination is constituted as a correlate. Within such a world of imagination we have, for every individual object of imagination (as quasi-actuality), an "individual" singularization [*Vereinzelung*] for every temporal point and every duration. We have it first of all in the most strictly defined unity of an act of imagination, namely, within a single

presence; in it, like is distinguished from like on the basis of individuality. But, in addition, there is an "individual" singularization in imagination, *as far as* it is possible in general (in the unity of interrelated individual imaginings) to convert this act into an intuitive unity, into the unity of a single presence in the extended sense (as a continuum of flowing presents), without supplementation by new imaginings relative to new objects and extending the imagined world.

But how is it possible to make this conversion if we pass from one imaginary world to another to which it is unrelated? In the nature of any two imaginings there is nothing at all to imply that they *require* to be unified in a single act of imagination. As soon as we move intentionally within a single complex of imaginings, correlatively, within a single imaginary world, there is agreement and contradiction, there is incompatibility, and all the relations of spatial and temporal position which we have pointed out for objects within an actual world are also equally possible here: everything is now carried over to the quasi. But between complexes of disconnected imaginings there is nothing like this. For the "things," the events, the "actualities" of one world of imagination have "nothing to do" with those of the others. Better: the fulfillments and disappointments of intentions constitutive of one of these worlds can never extend to intentions which are constitutive of another, in connection with which it does not matter that we are dependent on quasi-intentions. Here the unity of time plays its special role as the condition of the possibility of a unity of the world, as the correlate of the unity of "one" experience and, so to speak, of the ground on which all incompatibilities occur in the form of "conflict."

How are the singularizations of temporal points, temporal durations, etc., related to one another within different imaginary worlds? We can speak here of the likeness and similarity of the components of such worlds but never of their *identity,* which would have absolutely no sense; hence, no connections of incompatibility can occur, for these would indeed presuppose such identity. It makes no sense, *e.g.*, to ask whether the Gretel of one fairy tale and the Gretel of another are the same Gretel, whether what is imagined for the one and predicated of her agrees or does not agree with what is imagined for the other, or, again, whether they are related to each other, etc. I can stipulate this—and to accept it is already to stipulate it—but then both fairy tales refer to the same world. Within the *same* tale I can certainly ask such questions, since, from the beginning, we have a *single* imaginary world; but the question ceases to make sense where the imagination ceases, where it does not supply more precise determinations; and it is reserved to the development of imagination, in the sense of the pursuance of the unity of a complex of imaginings, to seize upon determinations arbitrarily (or, in the case of instinctively continuing again, to leave open the possibility of such determinations).

In the actual world, nothing remains open; it is what it is. The world of imagination "is," and is such and such, by grace of the imagination which has imagined it; a complex of imaginings never comes to an end that does not leave open the possibility of a free development in the sense of a new determination. But, on the other hand, there is still, in the essence of the connection which constitutes the "unity" of imagination, an abundance of *essential limitations,* which must not be overlooked. They find their expression in this: that in the continuation, although free and open, of the unity of a complex of imaginings, it is the unity of a "possible world" which is constituted with an encompassing form of the time of imagination pertaining to it.

In what has been pointed out, the implication is that *individuation* and *identity of the individual,* as well as the identification founded on it, *is possible only within the world of actual experience, on the basis of absolute temporal position.* We may call attention to this only very briefly here, for a complete theory of individuation is not now our intention.[2] Accordingly, the experience of imagination in general provides no individual objects in the true sense but only *quasi-individual* objects and a *quasi-identity,*

namely, within the fixed unity of an imaginary world. Thus our initial exclusion of the sphere of neutrality for the purpose of laying the foundation of a theory of judgment proves to be justified, insofar as a theory of judgment must begin precisely with the experience of the individual as yielding ultimate self-evidence, and such experience of the individual does not occur in imagination or in general in a neutral consciousness.

The Problem of the Possibility of an Intuitive Unity between Objects of Perception and Objects of Imagination of One Ego

If, nonetheless, the experience of imagination has been taken into consideration within the field of our inquiry, this has its ground in that imagination involves more than a merely indifferent parallel to actual experience and the determinations being realized therein. It is therefore not enough merely to transfer everything which has appeared in the domain of positionality to the quasi. Rather, in spite of the lack of connection between objects of perception and objects of imagination, an intuitive unity of a kind which can contribute to the (relative) determination of individual objects given in experience is still possible even here. The pursuance of this question concerning the unity which remains possible here will lead us to the *broadest concept of the unity of intuition*—broader than those set forth up to now—and to the most inclusive kind of relations, namely, the relations of likeness and similarity, which are possible between all objectivities capable of being united in such a unity of intuition, whether they are objects of perception or of imagination.

By way of anticipation, we call attention to the fundamental function of these relations and hence also of free imagination in the higher dimension of the consciousness of generality and, in particular, the intuition of essences. This function will be discussed in detail in Part III. Here we remain in the sphere of the experience of the individual, and we now ask: what sort of unity of intuitions makes these relations possible, and on what does it rest?

The Possibility of the Establishment of an Intuitive Connection between All Objectivities Constituted in One Stream of Consciousness by Association

a. The Temporal Unity of All the Lived Experiences of an Ego.

The unity we inquire about here cannot be the *unity of objectivities* in absolute world-time as the unity of simultaneity or succession. For it has been shown that objects of imagination have no temporal connection, either with objects of perception or among themselves, and consequently also no possible unity *based on* such a connection. Therefore, if the unity is not a unity of objectivities, it can only be a *unity of the lived experiences constituting objectivities,* of lived experiences of perception, of memory, and of imagination.

All the lived experiences of an ego have their temporal unity; they are constituted in the absolute flow of internal time-consciousness and in it have their absolute position and uniqueness, their unique appearance in an absolute now, after which they retentionally fade away and sink back into the past. Naturally, this *time of the lived experiences is not the time of the intentional objectivities in the lived experiences.* If, e.g., while I perceive my material environment, a flash of memory comes to me and I devote myself entirely to it, this world of perception does not then disappear; no matter how much this world may lose its "actuality," may "withdraw from me," perceptively it is always there, perceived, in the broader sense of the term. The memory in which I now live furnishes me a time for what is remembered, which is implicitly oriented toward the present of perception. But what is remembered is past and even "lies far behind" in relation to the perceived (a character which is not an immediately intuitive, temporal character but refers to a deployment in chains of intuitions), while the memory as a lived experience is contemporaneous with the lived experience of perception. And if we form a foreseeing expectation, the expected is then characterized as futural, as becoming (although this is also not intuitive),

while the lived experiences of expectation and perception are partly contemporaneous and partly successive, the perception in one part preceding, the expectation following. Since here it is a question of positional lived experiences, all these intentional objectivities, the individual objectivities intended in them, have an absolute position in objective time, in world-time, and this position is in principle capable of being made intuitive by the establishment of a series of memories, going back from the present perception. More precisely: it belongs to their objective sense; they are intended as determined by their absolute position in objective time. Leaving this out of account here, the constitutive *lived experiences, as lived experiences* in internal time-consciousness, have, in addition, *their absolute temporal position relative to one another,* their before and after. The like is true of the lived experiences of imagination which appear in this stream, but the imaginary objectivities intended in them have no absolute, identifiable temporal position.

Thus, there is a temporal unity among all the lived experiences of an ego, a unity which, to be sure, is not yet a unity of intuition. For what is intended, intuited, in the lived experiences, namely, the objectivities perceived, remembered, or imagined, are separated from one another. And although among all perceived and remembered individual objectivities of *positional* lived experiences there is the unity which it is possible to render intuitive and which these experiences have, on the basis of their absolute temporal position in the objective world, *this* possibility of connection disappears for imaginary objectivities. Nevertheless, on the basis of being constituted together in the flux of *one* time-consciousness, there is the *possibility of the establishment of an intuitive connection among all objectivities constituted in it.*

b. The Double Function of Association for the Connection of Positional Consciousness.

However, in order to actually establish such an intuitive connection, *i.e.,* a unity of intuition between the intentional objects of the same ego, temporally separated from one another, the fact of their being constituted together in one ego-consciousness is not yet sufficient. Time-consciousness is, after all, a consciousness which establishes only a general form (cf. sections 16 and 38). The *actual awakening*, and, therewith, the actual intuitive unification of perceptions and memories or, correlatively, of intentional objects of perception and memory, is the achievement of association, that mode of passive synthesis founded on the lowest syntheses of time-consciousness. We have already had to go back to the regularities of association and affection in order to understand the structure of a sensuous field, a field of pregivens actively affecting us, which are together in a single presence, and in order to understand, further, both the possibility that particular givens stand out from this field and that the ego is induced to turn toward them and apprehend them objectively (homogeneous association) and the possibility of the unification of data from different sensuous fields given in a single presence (heterogeneous association). But beyond this function of unification within a presence, association has a broader one, namely, that of uniting what is separated, insofar as this was ever at all constituted within a single stream of consciousness, thus, of uniting the present with the not-present, the presently perceived with remote memories separated from it, and even with imaginary objects: the like here recalls what is like there, the similar recalls the similar. Hence a unique reciprocal relationship takes place, though, to be sure, in this sphere of passivity and in the sphere of receptivity which is constructed on this, it is not yet a relation in the logical sense of a spontaneous, creative consciousness in which a relation as such is constituted.

If we still limit ourselves for the time being to positional consciousness, it is thus the function of association first of all to vivify the connection which all perceptions, past and present, of one ego have with one another on the basis of their being constituted in one time-consciousness and to establish among them an actual unity relative to consciousness. Only on the basis of an as-

sociative awakening can separated memories be related to one another and be inserted, as we move back from one member to the next, into *one* intuitive nexus of memory. This means that, once memories are associatively awakened, they can then be ordered in the temporal connection, the *before* and *after* "as they actually were," and their temporal position in the past can be determined. Associative awakening thus constitutes the *presupposition for the constitution of temporal relations,* of the "earlier" and "later." To be sure, in the domain of receptivity, to which we now limit ourselves, nothing more occurs than the establishment of a unified connection of memory; the connection of memory, as it is awakened by association, is run through and presentified. It is on the basis of this that, at a higher level, the temporal relations which find their expression in the temporal modalities of the predicative judgment can then be apprehended.

Through associative linkage, the no longer living worlds of memory also get a kind of being, despite their no longer being actual; the present "awakens" a past, flows over into a submerged intuition and its world. From the like or the similar the tendency goes in the direction of a complete recollection, and, even before anything actually emerges in memory, "remembering" has a peculiar "intention going back into the past to the like or the similar"; it calls the similar to mind, which thereby is not an empty nothing but for consciousness is comparable to the horizon, which has receded, of the just-now-intuited, or (what amounts to the same thing) of the just-having-been-intuited past, which persists obscurely in the horizon of what is still actually intuitive. It is, therefore, an inverse process. From what is given intuitively (perception or memory) emanates an intention, an intentional tendency, in which, gradually and uninterruptedly, what is submerged and no longer living seems to steadily change over to the vivid and ever more vivid, until, at a tempo now more deliberate, now more rapid, what has receded appears again as intuition. When the tempo is very rapid, we speak of a "sudden" appearance, whereas in fact the difference is only in degree. *Complete submergence* is thus only *a limit of what has receded,* as, on the other hand, the opposite limit is complete intuitiveness; thus, intuitiveness does not really denote a breach. Linked to this, to be sure, are the processes of overlapping and interpenetration, of the fusion of memories belonging to different "awakened" worlds of memory.

That such "awakening," radiating out from the present and directed toward the vivifying of the past, is possible must have its ground in the fact that between the like and the similar a *"sensuous"* unity is already passively constituted in advance, a unity in "subconsciousness," which unites the different situations of actual and submerged intuitions. Thus, in all situations, and in conformity with all likenesses and similarities, there are constant connections, and the "awakening," the calling-to-mind of the earlier, is only the vivifying of something which previously was already there. To be sure, this vivifying does bring in something new, in that now a new intention, radiating from the awakening situation, goes to what is awakened, an intention which, after this irradiance, changes its state to neutrality and thus to a phenomenal persistence.

All these occurrences of associative awakening and linkage take place in the domain of passivity without any participation by the ego. The awakening radiates from what is presently perceived; the memories "rise up," whether we will or no. But the ego can also have the desire *to remember,* the desire, for example, to presentify again a past event in its order of occurrence. At first it may be that only pieces are presentified, still not ordered as to earlier and later. It may be that the intermediate parts are missing, which the ego, by the probative presentification of connecting members having an awakening function, seeks again to vivify until it finally has the entire occurrence before itself in a closed sequence of memories in which each individual part can be assigned its temporal position. But even this *active remembering* is possible only *on the basis of the associative awakening which has already taken place;* the awakening itself is an event which always occurs passively. The activity of the ego can provide only the conditions for this; it

can discover the appropriate intermediate members by tentative actualization of the stretches of memory not forgotten, and from these members the associative awakening ray can go toward what is submerged and make it again living. The analysis of all this is the theme of a phenomenology of presentifying consciousness, which cannot here be further carried out.

Association thus has a *double function* for positional consciousness; on the one hand, it establishes, on the basis of absolute position in the stream of time-consciousness, the actual connection of all perceptions of an ego, present and past, in the unity of one memory, and, on the other hand, it establishes an intuitive unity of the remembered, in that it brings the awakened into the unity of an intuition with the awakening, in a way to be discussed forthwith.

c. The Intuitive Unification of the Intuitions of Perception and Imagination on the Basis of Association, and the Broadest Concept of the Unity of Intuition.

All this is of particular importance if we consider that this associative connection exists among *all* the lived experiences of an ego as far as they at all objectively constitute in themselves anything similar and anything comparable, therefore that this connection includes not only the positional intuitions but also those of imagination, which in themselves are unconnected with regard to their temporality. Consequently, not only is there a unified correlative objectivity constituted within every section, present in the broadest sense (present, whether in a perception, a memory, or even in an imaginary perception), of the stream of consciousness, and, furthermore, not only is a cohesive unity constituted in the flux of these presences; there is also, beyond these connections which unify sections of individual presence, a *connection which is instituted between arbitrarily different presences,* of which one is actual, the other submerged. The submerged is reawakened by association and presentified in intuition and is thus intuitively unified with the awakening in a new presence.

On this depends the possibility of a unity

between the present and the presentified, between perception and associatively awakened memory or imaginary intuition. It is an intuitive, sensuous unity, constituted in an actual and proper field of intuition and, beyond this, in a living temporal field, *i.e.*, a *unity founded in intuitive singularities*. This unity presupposes a unity of consciousness in which is constituted an original temporal field with content, or in which a modified, quasi-original field is constituted in the unity of a memory or of a memory leading back to a perception. Here we always have, not only some connection or succession of intuitions, but *one* intuition with one correlative unity of the objective. To the intuition belongs the form of time—as the form which connects and at the same time makes all further connection possible—and (with transcendent objectivities) the form of space which is ordered with time; naturally, in the case of the unitive intuition of elements not actually coexistent, the form of space does not appear as the form of objective space but as the form of apparent space, in which things that appear are not actually constituted as connected in the unity of an objective duration but are collected on the basis of the associative awakening.

If we place the remembered table beside this perceived table, then we have a space with a spatial plenitude and, giving itself in it, a vivid second table and a time in which this juxtaposition of both tables appears for a while. Here it does not matter that the remembered table in itself "belongs" to another objective time than the perceived table. We have a unity of "image," and this is the image of a present, of a duration with a coexistence to which pertains a spatial unity. Thus we can spatially "bring together" objects belonging to different fields of presence if they are physical objects, "juxtapose" them in an apparent space; we can also juxtapose them or bring them together temporally, and this last in every case, even in that of nonspatial objects, or where objects are not capable of coexistence. We can then say: we bring objects which belong to different fields of presence together by transposing them to *one temporal field*; we move the first objects to the intuitive temporal field of the others. In this way we bring them into one intuitive succession or into an intuitive coexistence (that is, into a unity of simultaneous duration). If they are spatial objects, they then appear *eo ipso* in the unity of the one same space, in fact in the unity of the part of infinite space which includes the objects of the privileged intuition, and they appear in the case of contemporaneity as enduring side by side or as appearing one after another in this space and remaining there. A *unity of intuition,* a unified assemblage of objects of intuition (it being of small importance whether perceived or presentified), means, therefore (since we are in the sphere of individual or quasi-individual objects), a *unity of time in which these objects are intuitively together.* To be sure, we must also distinguish here between what is the business of passivity—being awakened—and what, built on this, is the business of (receptive) activity—the apprehension of what is awakened, the act of turning toward what has been pregiven in the unity of an intuition.

This unity of intuition, originally established by association, is such, therefore, that it is possible, not only between perceptions and memories of the same ego, but also between positional and imaginary intuitions. With this we have attained the *broadest concept of the unity of intuition,* which we can define as follows:

The unity of intuition is the unity of an intuitive object-consciousness and has as a correlate the intuitive unity of objectivity. Different individuals (or quasi-individuals of imaginary intuitions) *can, however, attain the unity of an intuition,* or, correlatively, can in general form a unified intuitive objectivity, only insofar as *they are encompassed by the unity of an intuitively constituted time,* insofar, therefore, as they appear phenomenally as simultaneous or consecutive (or in reciprocal temporal displacement, partly simultaneous, partly consecutive) in the unity of an intuitive presence.

This implies: *the unity of the intuition of time is the condition of the possibility of all unity of the intuition of a plurality of objects connected in any way, for all are temporal objects;* accordingly, every other connection of such objects presupposes the unity of time.

NOTES

1. In view of this, the objective world is, to be sure, equated with the life-world of humanity, the all-embracing community wherein mutual understanding is possible. In our context we can disregard the problem of knowing how the world, taken concretely as the life-world of humanity, stands with regard to the objective world in the strict sense, *i.e.*, to the world as determined in the sense of natural science.

2. For a few supplementary observations see section 42.

PART FIVE

Husserl on the Social and the Personal Worlds

Besides the lifelong reflections on questions about logical psychologism, the status of phenomenology as a science, and the repeated investigations into the varied philosophical problems of space and time, Husserl returned often in his later philosophy to the peculiarly difficult problems which the existence of other minds posed for the transcendental concern of his philosophy. These difficulties are explained with enormous ingenuity in a variety of later texts, most notably perhaps the *Cartesian Meditations* and the extensive materials gathered in the three volumes in the *Husserliana* series on the complex topic of intersubjectivity. Part of Husserl's concerns with intersubjectivity included the nature of the social sciences and especially the kinds of questions which are often discussed today in the context of moral philosophy.

Part Five includes a selection of materials which illustrate many of these later concerns of Husserl. The materials once again comprise both more comprehensive statements, such as those to be found in Husserl's texts on "Phenomenology and Anthropology" and "Renewal," as well as more fragmentary texts, such as the reflections on "Universal Teleology." In addition, some materials are added from Husserl's recollections and correspondence.

It is essential to notice here the continuity between the issues raised in these texts and those discussed earlier in this collection. In both places we find Husserl dealing with the questions of psychologism, the nature of science, and, above all, the coherence of his basic project, phenomenology as a truly rigorous science. But the present texts are discontinuous with these common concerns in that they show a new philosophical awareness of and a striking sensitivity to the difficulties not simply of making one more new beginning but especially of finding an adequate starting point in the phenomenology of intersubjectivity that will allow Husserl finally to skirt the insolvable difficulties of his earlier transcendental phase. This later concern with the intersubjective realm would lead to a series of new insights not only into the cultural and historical situation of philosophy itself but also into the most important critical work of his final years, the *Crisis*.

Despite the summary character of much of the work to be found in these texts, what we discover is an unusual startling sensitivity to the ethical domain which is hardly to be found at all in the more systematic and, in some ways, more impressive earlier texts.

The historical is one helpful perspective on Husserl's phenomenology and especially on the philosophical ideals which motivated his work throughout his life. In Husserl's case—as in the case of other difficult German philosophers such as Leibniz, Kant, Hegel, Nietzsche, and Heidegger—knowing something about the intellectual debts to teachers and the interests discussed in the correspondence helps fill in some of the necessary background to the philosophical work itself. Sometimes, as in several of the letters included in these materials, the critical reader not only achieves a better grasp of the context of Husserl's work but also finds detailed comments on topics of central importance in the development of Husserl's own work.

The historical materials included are of two kinds.

The first text is an attempt on Husserl's part to set down his recollections of his Vienna teacher, Franz Brentano. These recollections are valuable, not so much for the light they throw on the substance of Husserl's own philosophy, but for the reflections they provide of certain personal and professional ideals which Husserl assimilated partly because of his studies and friendship with Brentano. These ideals, although necessarily modified as Husserl's work moved further away from Brentano's preoccupations especially with phenomenological psychology, nonetheless remained a constant and strong influence on Husserl.[1]

The second set of materials is much poorer in information about Husserl's intellectual and personal ideals but correspondingly richer in details on correlations between Husserl's philosophical work and its cultural context. The correspondence with Arnold Metzger, for example, not only provides us with some important insight into how Husserl at this time understood the relationship between phenomenology and Kantianism but also is an excellent example in its early paragraphs of the intellectual and personal ideals which animated his researches. And the remarks on Eucken, Reinach, and Shaw as well as the letter to Munsterberg also add several details to our understanding and appreciation of Husserl's intellectual background and historical milieu.

With such materials in hand those interested in deepening their understanding of Husserl's work will be increasingly sensitive to the peculiar mix of theoretical ideals and philosophical practice that comprises Husserl's phenomenology.

NOTE

1. For a detailed survey and discussion of the extensive correspondence between Husserl and Brentano see H. Spiegelberg, "On the Significance of the Correspondence Between Franz Brentano and Edmund Husserl," *Grazer Philosophische Studien* 5 (1978): 95–116.

17

A Transcendentalist's Manifesto:
Introduction to
"Phenomenology and Anthropology"[1]

JOHN SCANLON

The Question

Can concrete human existence in the world be the true foundation for philosophy? This is the question which Husserl asks in his 1931 lecture "Phenomenology and Anthropology."

At first it might look as if the growing trend toward a general philosophy whose methodological foundation is a philosophical anthropology had prompted Husserl merely to review a question which he had already answered to his own satisfaction more than thirty years earlier, in the "Prolegomena to Pure Logic" in his *Logical Investigations*.[2] But, surprisingly, Husserl takes up the question anew. And a closer look shows why he has to: the current philosophical anthropology is itself significantly novel.

Husserl's earlier arguments against psychologism and anthropologism had emphasized two basic fallacies: the formal fallacy of founding ideal sciences like logic upon factual, empirical sciences like psychology or anthropology ("naturalizing ideas"), and the material fallacy of construing consciousness as reducible to physical elements and principles ("naturalizing consciousness").[3] But the new philosophical anthropology rests upon Dilthey's emancipation of the human sciences from the domination of the physicalistic model;[4] thus, it can not be faulted for naturalizing consciousness or human existence. And the new philosophical anthropology rests upon Husserl's own phenomenology; hence, it is neither empirically factual nor naively objective, but eidetic and reflective in its approach to human existence.[5]

Thus, the new question which the philosophical situation in Germany raises for Husserl is more specific: "Can a phenomenological (reflective and eidetic) interrogation of concrete human existence in the world serve as the true foundation for philosophy?" If Husserl's answer to this question is still negative, as it is, his reasons must lie in his conception of the distinctive character of philosophy itself and the consequent requirements for founding it. And, since Husserl views the current formulation, despite its novelty, as only the latest version of a question which has disturbed all of modern, post-Cartesian, philosophy, his procedure is to reset the question within its original Cartesian context and then to propose a negative response based upon insights yielded by his own transcendental or constitutive phenomenology.

The Answer

In the European tradition, philosophy has been understood as the science of all that is, in two senses: collectively, as comprising the ideal unity of all the special sciences, each investigating its restricted domain of entities, and distinctively, as including only those sciences whose questions refer, not to limited domains of entities, but universally to all entities.

Descartes transforms the very idea of philosophy, and post-Cartesian philosophy can be seen as striving to overcome the pre-Cartesian idea by preserving it while clarifying it in relation to a new methodological foundation. Retrospectively, pre-Cartesian objectivistic philosophy had identified without question the formal concept "entity" [*Seiendes*] with the materially determinate concept "real entity" [*Reales*] or "entity of the world" [*weltlich Seiendes*]. Cartesian philosophy, by discovering a new fundamental dimension of philosophical questioning, that of subjectivity as experiencing the world, made it possible and necessary to distinguish those previously indistinguishable concepts.

Post-Cartesian philosophy has inherited and attempted to resolve the basic conceptual confusions which resulted from the discovery of this new fundamental dimension, to which the familiar concepts of objectivistic philosophy were inadequate. Specifically, the question of Husserl's lecture concerns the sense of this newly discovered subjectivity. Is it to be interpreted as "human," "anthropological"? Or, is it to be differentiated as "transcendental"?

Descartes was led to his discovery only because he transformed the very spirit of philosophizing by injecting into it the demand for utmost scientific radicalism. Scientists in general are responsible for autonomy of judgment, for basing their statements solely on the evidence of their own findings. The philosopher's responsibility goes further: he must trace all such findings back to their ultimate foundation of meaning and knowledge, a foundation which, to qualify as ultimate, must itself be immediately and apodictically given. Thus, the very question of the true methodological foundation for philosophy stems from the Cartesian and post-Cartesian spirit of utmost radicalism in science.

Guided by this radical demand, I discover as a previously unnoticed and unexpressed presupposition of all scientific activity and nonscientific life my constant acceptance of the given world. The source of this undisturbed certainty is pervasive experience, which provides such an unshakable conviction that I cannot reasonably deny or doubt the existence of the given world. But if I am to be radically responsible, I can not simply go on accepting this certainty as unquestioned. I must clarify, explicate, and articulate this fundamental certainty and its multiple sources in experience. To do that, I can not base my findings on what that experience itself presents as certainly existing, namely, the actual world. Hence, I must perform an epoche with regard to the being of the world in order to interrogate and clarify experience as the source of certainty concerning it. The exercise of this epoche furnishes as a new, immediate and apodictic source of evidence, the essentially new experience of myself not as an entity of the world but as a conscious life which continues to experience entities of the world even though I do not base any philosophical assertions upon what that experience presents as existing. I now experience myself as "transcendental ego," as "transcendentally reduced consciousness."

Without entering into any of the complexities of constitutive phenomenology, Husserl is confident that careful reflection upon the very sense of this epoche suffices to provide a definitively negative answer to the main question of his lecture.

I experience myself as a human being among other human beings and among other entities of the world. However different in detail the apperception of myself or of another human being as an identical individual may be from the apperception of other types of individual entities like trees or buildings, that apperception still fits within the genus of apperceiving an entity of the given world whose existence is presupposed without question.

By contrast, to apperceive myself as transcendental ego requires a different kind of apperception by which I apperceive myself not as an individual entity of the given world but, by virtue of this epoche, as a conscious life in which the apperceiving of entities of the world (including that of myself as a human being) takes place.

When the respective apperceptions are

made reflectively and raised to the eidetic level, the contrast still stands. The transcendental reduction does not yield consciousness as an abstract layer of concrete human existence, as what is essential to human mental or spiritual life (a theme of interest to a phenomenological psychology or anthropology[6] as well as to *Lebensphilosophie*). What transcendental or constitutive phenomenology presents as the true methodological foundation of philosophy must be understood from the very sense of its task of radically interrogating the meaning and legitimacy of science as genuine knowledge. What it presents can be formulated most generally as the essential regularities of correlation between entities of every sort and the various species of lived experiences by which such entities can be meant and known.

Comment

The question of the methodological foundation for philosophy has its own logic. On Husserl's account, that logic requires a conceptual distinction between my own conscious life reflected upon as the conscious life of a human being and my own conscious life reflected upon as an instance of the formations of meaning which are necessary for any entities to be given. Husserl presents that distinction as involving not specific details or isolated results of reflective interrogation but the total nexus of interpretation in terms of which single details are experienced. In other words, "transcendental ego" or "transcendentally reduced consciousness" on the one hand and "concrete human existence" on the other hand designate two essentially distinct "hermeneutic"[7] totalities corresponding to two different stances of reflective questioning.

Husserl, who has carried through the *transcendental* reduction with all possible thoroughness, speaks of the resultant position in terms which should warn us against taking it as an unambiguous perspective for reflection upon mundane human existence: it is a stance "above all worldly existence, above my own human life and existence as man." Philosophical questioning at a methodologically fundamental level is by its own internal logic supremely indifferent to specifically human affairs and human material concerns, whether the fundamental emphasis is placed upon transcendental subjectivity or upon the meaning of being. If that fundamental philosophical perspective is itself taken as the vantage point from which to interpret concrete human existence, then the result, besides being a conceptual confusion as Husserl has indicated, may readily become, as Sartre has charged, a subordination of the human to the nonhuman, in effect, a "hatred of man."[8]

NOTES

1. A lecture delivered in Berlin, June 10, 1931. Published in *Philosophy and Phenomenological Research* 2 (1941): 1–14. English translation by Richard G. Schmitt, in Roderick M. Chisholm, ed., *Realism and the Background of Phenomenology* (Glencoe, 1960), pp. 129–42. Reprinted here.

2. Tr. J. N. Findlay (New York, 1970).

3. Edmund Husserl, "Philosophy as Rigorous Science," tr. Quentin Lauer, in Edmund Husserl, *Phenomenology and the Crisis of Philosophy* (New York, 1965), pp. 79–122 (see pages 166–97 above). Also "Naturalistic Misconstructions" in Edmund Husserl, *Ideas*, tr. W. R. Boyce Gibson (New York, 1962), pp. 72–88.

4. Between 1914 and 1931 the first seven volumes of Wilhelm Dilthey's *Gesammelte Schriften* had been published.

5. Apparently the main proponents of the position in question were too well known to require their being mentioned by name. On April 19, 1931, Husserl wrote,

in a letter to Ingarden, "I am to speak in Berlin (June 6), in Halle and in Frankfurt on Phenomenology and Anthropology (Kant-Gesellschaft), and I must carefully read my antipodes Scheler and Heidegger." Edmund Husserl, *Briefe an Roman Ingarden* (The Hague, 1968), p. 67.

6. Husserl took up the question of the difference between a phenomenological psychology, with its own distinctive epoché, and transcendental phenomenology in at least three places: "Author's Preface to the English Edition," *Ideas*, pp. 5–22 (see pages 43–53 above); "'Phenomenology': Edmund Husserl's Article for the Encyclopaedia Britannica (1927): New Complete Translation by Richard E. Palmer," *Journal of the British Society for Phenomenology* 2 (1971): 77–90 (see pages 21–35 above); *Phenomenological Psychology: Lectures, Summer Semester, 1925*, tr. John Scanlon (The Hague, 1977).

7. In this lecture Husserl does not reject, but en-

dorses, a hermeneutical understanding of phenomenology, "a hermeneutic of the life of consciousness."

8. Jean-Paul Sartre, *Critique de la raison dialec-* *tique* (Paris, 1960), p. 248; English translation: *Critique of Dialectical Reason*, tr. Alan Sheridan-Smith (Atlantic Highlands: Humanities Press, 1976), p. 181.

FURTHER REFERENCES

Carr, David. *Phenomenology and the Problem of History.* Evanston: Northwestern University Press, 1974.

Elveton, R. O., ed. *The Phenomenology of Husserl: Selected Critical Readings.* Chicago: Quadrangle, 1970.

Kohak, Erazim. *Idea and Experience: Edmund Husserl's Project of Phenomenology in Ideas I.* Chicago: University of Chicago Press, 1978.

Ricoeur, Paul. *Husserl: An Analysis of His Phenomenology,* translated by Edward G. Ballard and Lester Embree. Evanston: Northwestern University Press, 1967.

Scanlon, John. "The Epoche and Phenomenological Anthropology." *Research in Phenomenology* 2 (1972): 95–109.

Schmitt, Richard. "Husserl's Transcendental-Phenomenological Reduction." *Philosophy and Phenomenological Research* 20 (1959–60): 238–45; reprinted in *Phenomenology: The Philosophy of Edmund Husserl and Its Interpretation,* edited by Joseph J. Kockelmans (Garden City, N.Y.: Doubleday, 1967).

Sokolowski, Robert. *The Formation of Husserl's Concept of Constitution.* The Hague: Nijhoff, 1964.

Phenomenology and Anthropology*

Translated by Richard G. Schmitt

It is a well-known fact that the younger German philosophers have during the last decade become increasingly interested in philosophical anthropology. Wilhelm Dilthey's *Lebensphilosophie,* a new kind of anthropology, which is very influential at present and has even affected the so-called phenomenological movement, maintains that true philosophy should seek its foundations exclusively in man and, more specifically, in the essence of his concrete worldly existence. This reform is considered indispensable if the original constitutive phenomenology is ever to reach the truly philosophical dimension.

A complete reversal of principles has here taken place. The original phenomenology, in its mature transcendental form, refused to derive any part of the foundations of philosophy from any science of man and opposed, as "anthropologism" and "psychologism," all attempts in this direction. But now, on the contrary, one looks to human existence as the sole basis for the reconstruction of phenomenological philosophy. The old contrasts which have always agitated all of modern philosophy recur in a contemporary guise in this dispute. From the very beginning the subjectivistic tendency which characterizes our period of history develops in two opposite directions: one is anthropologistic (or psychologistic); the other, transcendentalistic. While everyone feels that philosophy

needs to be subjectively grounded, one party claims that this must, of course, be done by psychology; the other demands a science of transcendental subjectivity, a science of a completely new kind, without which psychology and the other sciences cannot be grounded philosophically.

Should we accept it as destiny that this controversy must reappear in every age, differing only in its historic guise? We cannot accept this. Philosophy needs its own method of grounding its statements; this method must be implicit in the essence of philosophy and in the fundamental meaning of its task. If this meaning is necessarily subjective, the specific meaning of this subjectivity must also be determined a priori. Therefore, a fundamental decision between anthropologism and transcendentalism must be possible, one which transcends all historical forms of philosophy and anthropology (or psychology).

Yet everything depends on whether we really possess the *insights* which this decision presupposes and for the lack of which the controversy has continued unabated. Do we have these insights at our disposal today? Has the fundamental essence of philosophy and of its method already been given so radical a clarification and apodictic conceptual definition that we can base a conclusive decision on it?

I shall try to convince you that, indeed, the results of the development of constitutive phenomenology enable us to do so. Without tracing the development itself, I wish to try to outline the transcendental-

*Printed with permission of the publisher and translator from *Philosophy and Phenomenological Research* 2 (1941): 1–14.

philosophical method whose purification it brought about and to present you at least with the idea of the transcendental philosophy which this method enabled us to begin to work out systematically. The fundamental, that is to say, definite, decision of the question under discussion, how far philosophy and, specifically, phenomenological philosophy can derive its method from "philosophical" anthropology will accrue to us automatically on the basis of the acquired insight.

Let us begin by contrasting pre-Cartesian and post-Cartesian philosophy. The former was dominated by the original objectivistic idea of philosophy; the latter, by the tendency toward a new subjectivistic-transcendental idea. The modern struggle for a true philosophy (and the methodological controversies mentioned above) conceals the struggle to overcome the old idea of philosophy and science in favor of the new idea: here, genuine overcoming means at the same time conserving by clarifying its true sense as one that is transcendentally relative.

It is well known that science, as we Europeans understand it, was created, in its general outlines, by the Greek spirit. Its original name is philosophy; its object is the universe of whatsoever exists. It branches out into the special disciplines whose main branches are called sciences, while only those disciplines are called philosophical which deal universally with questions that apply equally to all that exists. Nevertheless, the ancient concept of philosophy as the concrete totality of the sciences will always remain indispensable.

The final idea of philosophy and of science, conceived only dimly at first, is clarified, shaped, and established step by step in the course of a long period of development. Cognition in the attitude of θαυμάζειν, of purely "theoretical" interests, yields science in a first sense, which, however, soon proves insufficient. Merely empirical, descriptively classificatory (inductive) knowledge is not yet science in the full sense of the word. It merely furnishes relative truth, tied to specific situations. Philosophy, genuine science, aims at absolute, ultimately valid truths which transcend all relativity. Such truth defines what exists, as it exists in itself. Of course, an actually existing world manifests itself in the intuitive world, the world of prescientific experience, in spite of its relativity; but its properties which are true in themselves transcend plain experience. Philosophy, genuine science, attains them, though only in degrees of approximation, by its appeal to the pure a priori which is accessible to everyone in apodictic insight.

The development tends toward the following idea. Philosophical cognition of the given world requires, first, universal a priori cognition, or, one might say, a universal *ontology* which is not only abstractly general but is concretely rational, which grasps the changeless essential form, the pure *Ratio* of the world down to all its regional spheres of existence. In other words, the cognition of the actual world presupposes universal cognition of the essential possibilities, without which neither any possible world nor the actual world can be conceived as existing.

This a priori places within our reach a rational method of knowing the actual world in the form of rational factual sciences. Experience will remain, but will be rationalized so as to share in the pure *Ratio* which grounds cognition on its foundation to produce a rational explanation and cognition of facts. In physical nature (for instance), pure mathematics as a priori of any conceivable nature makes genuine philosophical, *i.e.,* mathematical, natural sciences possible. Yet this is more than just an example: pure mathematics and mathematical natural sciences first brought to light, albeit only within a limited sphere, the goals of the original, objectivistic idea of philosophy and science.

Only more recent developments showed the need for a further distinction which we must now introduce, that between the formal and the material aspects of this conception. Formally, it is a conception of universal cognition of the totality of being, which is also rational cognition in the sense specified above. But in the entire tradition the formal concept of "what is" or of "something" has always had, as a matter of course, a materially limiting sense, namely, the sense of "being in the world," *i.e.,* of being real and deriving its existential meaning from the existing world. It is the aim of philosophy to be the science of the sum total of reality, but, as we shall see immediately, the dedication to this aim has begun to waver in modern times.

The modern philosophic development which begins with Descartes differs sharply from all preceding developments. A new kind of motive begins to function which attacks, not philosophy's formal ideal of being a rational science, but its material meaning, which, in the end, it changes completely. No longer is the world naïvely presupposed as obviously existing and obviously given in experience: its obviousness becomes a great enigma.

The Cartesian regress from this given world, to the subjectivity experiencing the world and thus to the subjectivity of consciousness in general, opens up an entirely new dimension of scientific questioning which we shall call *transcendental* even before investigating it. As a basic philosophic problem this new dimension is expressed in various ways: as the problem of cognition or of consciousness, as the problem of the possibility of objectively valid science, or of the possibility of metaphysics, etc.

In all these expressions the problem is never precisely formulated in scientific concepts of original coinage. It always retains an aura of ambiguity and, being vague, permits absurd formulations. It is difficult to state and express the new dimension of cognition; traditional concepts are too alien to its nature to do anything but misrepresent it. Thus, modern philosophy constantly strives to enter into this new dimension, to formulate the proper concepts, ask the proper questions, develop the proper methods. This is a distant goal and thus it is understandable that all serious dedication to the scientific ideal has failed to replace the existing plurality of mutually contradictory systems with one single philosophy which satisfies the transcendental motivation.

Has this situation improved in our time? Dare we hope that in the confusion and in the rapid coming and going of fashionable philosophies, there is one in which the transcendental tendency of the modern period has been completely clarified and which has produced a definitely established, apodictically necessary idea of transcendental philosophy? Has it produced a method of autonomous, strictly scientific work? Has this work

been begun, and is it being carried on systematically? I answered these questions in my introductory remarks. I cannot help regarding transcendental or constitutive phenomenology as that transcendental philosophy which is established free from impurities and is now being worked out in a genuinely scientific manner. Although much discussed and much criticized, it is, in fact, still *unknown*. Natural and traditional prejudices act as a screen which does not allow the real meaning of phenomenology to penetrate. Criticism, far from helping or improving, has, therefore, not yet touched it.

My task is now to make this true meaning of transcendental phenomenology evident to you. This will lead us to those fundamental insights which will help us decide whether philosophical anthropology is possible.

The most convenient starting point is the Cartesian *Meditations*. We shall be guided only by their form and by the will to utmost scientific radicalism which emerges in them, while disregarding the content which is vitiated, in many respects, by unnoticed prejudices. We shall try to practice an unsurpassable scientific radicalism. All modern philosophy originates in the Cartesian *Meditations*. Translated into material terms, this historical proposition means that every genuine beginning of philosophy issues from meditations, from solitary reflections. Autonomous philosophy (in an age like ours, incidentally, in which mankind has awakened to autonomy) comes into being in the solitary and radical attempt of the philosophizing individual to account and to be accountable only to himself. Isolation and meditation alone make him a philosopher and make philosophy necessarily begin in him. Accepting only what is evident to me, I, as an autonomous ego, must pursue to its ultimate grounds what others, following the tradition, regard as scientifically grounded. These ultimate grounds must be immediately and apodictically evident. Only in that way can I account for and justify my thought absolutely. There is no prejudice, therefore, however obvious it might be, which I can allow to pass unquestioned and ungrounded.

When I seriously try to fulfill this task, I am amazed to discover an obvious belief never before noticed or made explicit, a universal belief in existence, which pervades and supports my entire life. Imperceptibly, it also permeates my philosophical project, the creation of a universal science of the world and, later, of special sciences of the separate spheres of the world. *The* world and its existence is always obvious, is always an unexpressed presupposition.

The source of this assumption is, of course, universal experience with its constant certitude of existence. What is the status of its evidence? As far as individual realities are concerned, its evidence frequently cannot withstand scrutiny. Its certitude of existence occasionally becomes dubious and is sometimes even cancelled because it is invalid and illusory. Why is it, on the other hand, that the certitude of my experience of the world as the totality of those realities which really exist for me, remains unshaken? It really is quite impossible for me to ever doubt, let alone deny, it.

Does this supply sufficiently radical grounds for this certitude? Is not, perhaps, the certitude of existence which inheres in the continuity of the experience of the world based on many different grounds? Have I ever pursued and explicated this certitude by questioning and by trying to account for the sources and the scope of the validity of experience? No! I have based my previous life and scientific activities on it without ever justifying it. But it may not remain unjustified; it must be questioned. I cannot even begin a seriously autonomous science without first having justified it apodictically and ultimately in an activity of grounding by questioning and answering.

After the certitude of existence, implicit in the experience of the world, has become questionable, it can no longer serve to support judgments. This imposes upon us, upon me as the meditating, philosophizing ego, the obligation to practice a universal epoche of the existence of the world with all its individual realities which experience, even consistently coherent experience, offers as realities.

What remains? Is not the world the universe of all existents? Am I left with nothing? Can I still make judgments, and can they be supported by any experience in which I perceive existents originally, before they are made the objects of judgments? Our answer is similar to, but not identical with, that of Descartes: Let the existence of the world be questionable for me now because it is not yet grounded, let it be subject to the epoche; I who question and practice the epoche, I exist nonetheless. I am conscious of my existence and can grasp it immediately and apodictically. I experience myself as this being who practices the epoche, an experience which I can justify immediately and actively. This is not experience of the world, because the validity of the experience of the world has been suspended — yet it is experience. In it I apprehend myself as the ego in the world-epoche, with all that is inseparable from it. As this apodictic ego, therefore, I am prior to the existence of the world because I exist as this ego whether or not the world's existence can be accepted and accounted for. Only as such an ego, obviously, can I justify the existence of the world ultimately and can I, if at all, practice a science which requires radical justification.

We must now take a further important step: I have deliberately emphasized the term, 'this ego.' Having reached this point, I notice that my philosophizing ego has been genuinely revolutionized. At first, when I began my meditation, I regarded myself as this individual who sought philosophic solitude only for a time in order to liberate himself from the judgments of his fellow men. In spite of everything, I lived in the world of experience whose existence I took for granted. But since this world of experience must now remain in question, my being as man among men and among other realities of the world has become questionable too and is also subject to the epoche.

Due to this epoche, human solitude has been transformed into something radically different: the transcendental solitude, the solitude of the ego. As an ego I am not this man in the existing world, but the ego who questions the existence of the world, as well as its being thus-or-so, without reservations, or, in other words, the ego which still has its universal experience but has bracketed its existential validity. The same applies to all those non-experiential modes of consciousness in which the world possesses practical or theoretical validity. The world still appears as it appeared formerly; the life in and of the world is not interrupted: the world is now a bracketed "world," a mere phenomenon; it is the flow of experience and consciousness, in general—which now, however, is transcendentally reduced consciousness—possessing only phenomenal validity. This "world" with phenomenal validity is manifestly inseparable from transcendentally reduced consciousness.

This completes the description of the phenomenological reduction in transcendental phenomenology. It is not a temporary, but a permanent, deliberate abstention from belief in the existence of the world, an abstention which I, as phenomenologist, am bound to observe permanently. In this sense it is only the indispensable prerequisite for the reflective activity of experiencing and of theoretical judgment in which an essentially new field of experience and cognition, the transcendental field, opens up. Our new theme, which can become thematic only through the epoche, is my transcendental ego, its transcendental *cogitationes, i.e.,* the transcendentally reduced conscious lived experiences in all their typical forms, and also the corresponding *cogitata:* whatever I am conscious of in the modalities of such consciousness—all this while maintaining the epoche. All this constitutes the ego's transcendental domain of consciousness, which, though changing, remains unitary at all times. But this is only the beginning, although a necessary one. Transcendental reflection, if continued, soon leads us to the transcendental property, "I can," and to habitual dispositions and to many other things, as (for example) the universal phenomenal validity of the "world" as a permanent universe in contrast to the varieties of consciousness of that world.

The phenomenological reduction discloses an entirely unsuspected, vast field of research. This is, first, a field of immediate and apodictic experience, the soil in which all transcendental mediate and immediate judgments are rooted. Descartes and his followers were, and remained, blind to this. It was, of course, extremely difficult to elicit the pure meaning of the transcendental change of attitude and to bring out the fundamental contrast between the transcenden-

tal ego and its transcendental sphere, on one hand, and the worldly sphere with the human ego and the psychical sphere, on the other. Even after the contrast had been perceived and the pure meaning of the task of a transcendental science understood, as *e.g.,* by Fichte and his successors, the infinite transcendental ground of experience was difficult to perceive and to exploit. Since German Idealism failed at this point, it lost its way in a mire of speculations whose unquestionably unscientific character is by no means to its credit, notwithstanding contemporary opinion to the contrary. It is, of course, extremely difficult to do justice to the entirely new problem of a philosophical method intended as the method of a scientific philosophy, *i.e.,* a science which is ultimately accounted for. But, in the final analysis, everything depends on the method of beginning with the phenomenological reduction.

If we miss the meaning of the reduction, which is the unique entrance to this new realm, everything is lost. The temptations to misunderstand are almost irresistible. What is more obvious than saying that it is I, this human being, who employs the method of the transcendental change of attitude and who thus retreats to his pure ego? What else is this ego but an abstract stratum in the concrete human being, what else but his pure spiritual being in abstraction from the body? To say this is to obviously relapse into the naïve and natural attitude and to think in terms of the given world rather than of the epoché. If I regard myself as a human being, I presuppose the validity of the world. The epoche, however, makes it clear that the apperception, "human being," receives its existential meaning within the universal apperception, "world," only in the life of the ego.

But even if one has reached the point which we have now reached, even if he can keep the transcendental fields of experience and judgment strictly separated from the natural and worldly field, and even if he observes that a vast region of possible research opens up here, it is not easy to see what purpose such research might serve, to see, in other words, that it is destined to launch a genuine philosophy. How could investigations of a purely egological nature, which are subject to a consistent and strictly maintained epoche, have any philosophical relevance? As *man in the world* I address all theoretical and practical questions, all questions concerning my destiny, to the world. Can I set these questions aside? But must I not do so, if the existence of the world is and remains subject to the epoche? In that case, it seems that I shall never return to the world and to all those problems of life which led me into philosophy in quest of science as the rational and radical reflection on the world and human existence.

Let us consider whether the consistent renunciation of the world through transcendental reduction is not the necessary way to a true and ultimately valid cognition of the world, since such cognition can only be sought within this epoché. Let us not forget how all this is connected with the meaning of the meditations in which the epoché acquired its significance and its cognitive function. Renouncing the world or "bracketing the world" does not mean that the world ceases henceforth to be thematic, but rather that it must now be our theme in a more profound way because a whole new dimension has been added. We merely relinquished the naive attitude in which we allowed universal experience to present the world as existing and being thus-and-so. This naive attitude disappears as soon as we obey our motivating impulse to interpret, as autonomous and responsible subjects, the validity conferred by experience, and to seek the rational insight which allows us to justify this validity and to determine its scope. Instead of accepting the world naively and asking naive questions about it (about truth in the ordinary sense of the word), we now ask new questions about the world. These are questions about the world purely as experienced or as an object of other modes of world consciousness, *i.e.*, a world which has received meaning and validity purely in us and, first and foremost, purely from me and in me, specifically in me as the transcendental ego.

But we must bring this to a clearer focus: The existence of this world is obvious for me because it is obvious only in my own experience and consciousness. This consciousness is the source of the meaning of the world

and of any worldly objective facts. But, thanks to the transcendental epoché, I perceive that whatever belongs to the world, including my existence as a human being, exists for me only as the content of a certain experiential apperception in the mode of certitude of existence. As a transcendental ego I am the ego which apperceives actively and passively. This happens in me although it is concealed prior to reflection. In this apperception the world and the human being are first constituted as existing. Any evidence gained for worldly things, any method of verification, whether pre-scientific or scientific, lies primarily in me as transcendental ego. I may owe much, perhaps almost everything, to others, but even they are, first of all, others for me who receive from me whatever meaning or validity they may have for me. They can be of assistance to me as fellow subjects only after they have received their meaning and validity from me. As transcendental ego I am thus the absolutely responsible subject of whatever has existential validity for me. Aware of myself as this ego, thanks to the transcendental reduction, I stand now above all worldly existence, above my own human life and existence as man. This absolute position above everything that is or might ever be valid for me, including all its possible content, is necessarily the position of the philosopher. It is the position which the phenomenological reduction assigns to me. I have lost nothing of what existed for me in the naive attitude, nothing, in particular, whose real existence was shown. In this absolute attitude, I know the world itself and know it now, for the first time, for what it always was and had to be by its very essence: a transcendental phenomenon. In this way I have brought into play a new dimension of questions never asked before about just this existing reality. Only the answers to these questions will bring to light the concrete and full existence of the world and its complete and ultimate truth.

Is it not certain in advance that the world, which for the natural attitude is the universe of all that exists without qualification, possesses only transcendentally relative truth, and that only transcendental subjectivity exists without qualification?

But here an objection occurs to me: It is

true that I had ideas about the world and spoke about it meaningfully because it had meaning and validity for me by virtue of my own apperceptive acts, such as my thinking. But is it not insane to suggest that the world exists only through an act of mine? Perhaps it would be a more correct formulation to say that my "idea or image of the world" takes shape in my ego through its own transcendental activity and passivity, while the world itself is, of course, outside myself.

But is this an adequate solution? Is not the meaning of these terms, 'outside' and 'inside', if they have any meaning at all, conferred and verified by me? I must not forget that nothing that I could ever conceive as existent lies outside the universal scope of the possible and actual consciousness of myself, the ego.

This answer is cogent, but nevertheless unsatisfactory. It may be absolutely necessary to acknowledge that all existents and, accordingly, the entire existing world is transcendentally relative, but if presented only formally as it is here, this statement is completely incomprehensible, and will remain so if we allow ourselves to be drawn into speculative arguments which have always been the bane of so-called epistemology.

But was not transcendental subjectivity revealed as a field of experience and of cognitions referring to it? Does this not, in fact, open the way to a solution of the new transcendental puzzle about the world? Differing *toto caelo* from any ordinary puzzle about the world, this transcendental puzzle lies in the fact that transcendental relativity, as it confronts us *at the beginning,* as soon as we discover the transcendental attitude and the transcendental ego, is incomprehensible. But this initial incomprehensibility is not final. It is clear, at least, what must be done to make comprehensible what is incomprehensible and to attain really concrete and radically grounded cognition of the world. We must undertake a systematic study of concrete transcendental subjectivity. The question is how this subjectivity confers meaning and validity upon a world objective in itself. My own self, the essential structures of my entire sphere of consciousness together with the structures of actual and potential meanings, and the conferring

of validity, must all be made the themes of an eidetic science by me, the ego. As a philosopher, of course, I do not want to remain on the level of transcendental facts. My first task is, therefore, to grasp the eidetic typology of my conscious lived experiences in their immanent temporality. This is what Descartes called the stream of my *cogitationes.* The fact that they are intentional makes them what they are. Every single *cogito,* and every combination of them into the unity of a new *cogito* has its corresponding *cogitatum.* And the latter, qua *cogitatum,* taken exactly as it appears, is essentially inseparable from the *cogito.* On the other hand, I must, of course, also trace the essential bond between the *cogitationes* and the corresponding dispositions. Also, dispositions like "I can," "I do," "I have a permanent disposition," have the character of essences, as do all of the ego's dispositions for conscious activity. The ego, which makes its appearance at first as a center without content, brings with it problems of its own, namely, the problems of dispositional qualities. But the correlation between consciousness as lived experience and that which it is conscious of (the *cogitatum*) must be investigated first of all. Here it is important not to overlook crucial points. As ego I must, therefore, center my attention on the connected manifold of subjective modes of consciousness which belong together because they are modes of consciousness of one and the same supposed object. For instance, the manifold modes of appearing which compose the perception of a thing and through which we become immanently conscious of the thing belong together by virtue of the syntheses of identity which necessarily occur in the transition. The thing which presents itself unified and perhaps even unchanged to the naive observer becomes the transcendental guide for the systematic and reflective study of the manifolds of consciousness which belong to this one thing. This is true of every single real something and also of the world as total phenomenon.

The existence of these apodictic essential laws of correlation was an entirely new discovery of far-reaching importance.

All this requires very extensive descriptive studies, but nevertheless merely begins the ascent to ever new levels of transcendental investigations which derive their concrete apodictic evidence and autonomy from concrete experience and description. All these investigations are possible only if we understand the method of questioning regressively, starting from the intentional object by means of concrete discovery, which is the method for studying correlations.

Genuine analysis of consciousness is, so to speak, hermeneutic of the life of consciousness insofar as this consciousness intends something which always exists (something identical), which constitutes itself intentionally in its essential manifolds of consciousness. Rather than "interrogate" nature, as Bacon recommended, we must, therefore, interrogate consciousness or the transcendental ego, in order to force it to betray its secrets.

Due to an essential characteristic of the life of consciousness itself, these problems and methods could remain entirely hidden. In the natural attitude the ego's attention is always engrossed by some given object, so that the essential features of the stream of consciousness, in which syntheses are effected, remain, so to speak, anonymous and hidden. But what is hidden can be revealed. It is of the essence of the ego that it can reflect and that it can redirect its thematic attention; that it can ask intentional questions regressively and, through systematic explanation, bring to light and render intelligible the process of effecting syntheses.

Now we can also understand that when I turn away from the naive exploration of the world to the exploration of the self and its transcendental egological consciousness, I do not turn my back on the world to retreat into an unworldly and, therefore, uninteresting special field of theoretical study. On the contrary, this alone enables me to explore the world radically and even to undertake a radically scientific exploration of what exists absolutely and in an ultimate sense. Once the inadequacy of the naïve attitude has been realized, this is the only possible way of establishing science in its genuine radicality—more precisely, the way to the only possible, radically grounded philosophy.

It is true that this monumental task requires an extremely difficult procedure when we come to the abstract stratification of the transcendental sphere and to the corresponding problems. This procedure is necessary in order to proceed, in this work, from one level of problems to the next in a fixed order. This means, above all, that we abstract from the transcendental contributions of empathy on the first level of investigations. Only in this way can we apprehend the essential prerequisites for understanding just this contribution and, thus, for comprehending what was at first distressingly incomprehensible, *i.e.,* for dispelling the initial illusion of a transcendental solipsism, which perplexes us when we begin. But this is not achieved by empty argumentation, but by concretely intentional analysis.

In the course of these studies a fundamental distinction comes to light, within the ego's transcendental sphere of cognition, between that which belongs, so to speak, to his own person and that which is alien to him. Starting out from myself as ego constituting existential meaning, I reach the transcendental others, who are my peers, and at the same time the entire open, infinite transcendental intersubjective realm. In this transcendental community the world as "objective" and as the same for everybody is constituted.

This, then, is the path of transcendental phenomenology, from the naive attitude of everyday, natural life and from philosophy in the old style to absolute transcendental cognition of what exists as such.

We must never lose sight of the fact that this transcendental phenomenology does nothing but interrogate just that world which is, at all times, the real world for us; the only one which is valid for us, which demonstrates its validity to us; the only one which has any meaning for us. Phenomenology subjects this world to intentional interrogation regarding its sources of meaning and validity, from which sources, of course, its true existence also flows. Only in this way can we arrive at all conceivable problems about the world and, beyond those, at the problems of being which are only uncovered by the transcendental method and which are, therefore, not merely the old problems reinterpreted transcendentally.

If one has seriously understood our aims

and the systematic theory which is being worked out concretely with absolutely compelling evidence, one can no longer doubt that there can be only *one* ultimate philosophy, only one kind of ultimate science, the science inseparable from transcendental phenomenology's method of exploring origins.

Introduction to Husserl's
"Renewal: Its Problem and Method"

JEFFNER ALLEN

During the period from 1923 to 1924 Husserl wrote a series of articles concerning the ethical task that must be undertaken by practical reason, namely, that of establishing and developing a rational, a priori science of the socioethical sphere. Among the first of these articles was "Renewal: Its Problem and Method," which showed the need for an a priori normative science by means of which the ethical values of a culture could be given a new life, and the renewed culture could, in turn, become a genuine humanity. During the same year, in "The Idea of a Philosophical Culture: Its First Dawn in Greek Philosophy" (*Japanisch-deutsche Zeitschrift für Wissenschaft und Technik* [Lübeck] 1 [1923]), Husserl uncovered the historical origins, in the early Greeks, for such ideas of science, ethics, and genuine, that is, philosophical, culture. Husserl's concern for the development of a method of inquiry that would be appropriate to this realm of human, cultural accomplishments and, in particular, to the revitalization and actualization of ethical values, was set forth in the following year, in "The Method of Eidetic Inquiry" ("Die Methode der Wesensforschung," *The Kaizo* 2 [1924]). Finally, the special role of the individual, who, above all, bears the responsibility for regenerating his culture in a rational, ethical manner, was expressed in "Renewal as an Individual Ethical Problem" ("Erneuerung als individualethisches Problem," *The Kaizo,* special supplementary issue [1924]). It is

interesting to note that not only did these articles share a common theme, that of a phenomenological uncovering of the foundations for the normative study of contemporary culture, but they also appeared in similar types of journals, that is, in Japanese journals which themselves were striving to present an internationally acceptable ideal of cultural renewal. In fact, all of Husserl's articles in *The Kaizo-La rekonstruyo*—a widely circulated journal for Japanese intellectuals who were interested in opening Japan to Western, democratic ideas, and whose title, *The Kaizo,* means "to reform" or "to reconstruct"—appeared in Japanese translation, and his articles of 1924 appeared *only* in Japanese translation.

If we turn to Husserl's article "Renewal: Its Problem and Method," we find that from 1911 to 1923 he had continued to work through themes that were of interest to him in the "Dilthey-Husserl Correspondence," namely, themes arising from the need to establish a universal, a priori science of the particular human sciences. In his "Renewal" article such themes reappear in Husserl's analyses of the *problem* of renewal, a problem that is disclosed by a penetrating analysis of modern society and the ensuing criticism of this society, as well as in Husserl's investigation of the *method* of renewal, a method that emerges through his positive attempts to give modern society, and especially its ethical values, a new foundation in an a priori science of the ethicocultural domain.

We may ask: Why is renewal necessary? Yet, to answer this question is to see the necessity for a new birth of modern culture, is already to be on the way toward its renewal. Although humanity's faith in itself, which is formed by its faith in its ethicocultural life, has disappeared into the dark and vague horizons of the past, nonetheless, to see that this faith is absent is, for Husserl, already to see that something must be done about its absence, that something new, namely, the establishment of a scientific, rationally justified, foundation for the actual renewal of this faith, must take place.

However, the foundation for such a renewal has its own orderly, rational, internal structure. As Husserl shows in his "Renewal" article, what is most essential for cultural renewal is the development of an a priori science of the individual person and his community, a science having its own peculiar nature. Arising from this science there must, in turn, be constituted a scientifically developed nexus of those purely rational, a priori normative laws that are rooted in the very nature of the individual and the social group. And, to take a step further, such a closely interrelated system of laws must then be viewed as forming the "pure *logos*" for the method that makes possible the rational explanation of empirical, ethicocultural states of affairs. Ultimately, this method must be developed in such a way as to guide all aspects of actual praxis in the contingent domain of present-day culture.

Yet, as Husserl stresses throughout his essay, it does not suffice to merely be aware of the need for renewal and of the general way in which renewal may be accomplished. Rather, any genuine consideration of renewal must itself enter into the domain of practical reason, and work to bring about such renewal. Within this domain, Husserl's essay gives rise to two major problematics which must be dealt with. First, insofar as Husserl suggests that the distinguishing characteristic of the socioethical realm is its "inwardness," that is, its life of consciousness which gives rise to a mutual understanding between its members, all attempts at renewal must strive to remain faithful to this "inwardness." Second, in that Husserl finds the attempt at renewal to be an infinite task, one that is directed to the revitalization of all aspects, both past and future, of human culture, any practical working out of ethicocultural considerations must attempt to renew the infinity of horizons present in the ethical domain and, at the same time, cannot avoid extending to all aspects of a genuine human culture.

18

Renewal: Its Problem and Method*

Translated by Jeffner Allen

Renewal is the universal call in our present, sorrowful age, and throughout the entire domain of European culture. The war which has devastated Europe since 1914, and which since 1918 has merely chosen to employ the "refinements" of psychological tortures, of moral depravation and economic need, instead of military force, has revealed the internal untruthfulness and senselessness of this culture. And it is precisely this revelation which drains it of its vital energy. A nation or people [*Menschheit*] lives and creates in the fullness of its power when it is sustained by a perpetual faith in itself and in an aesthetic and moral sense of its cultural life—when a nation does not merely strive to keep alive, but instead, lives for what is great in its own eyes and is pleased with its increasing success in actualizing genuine and enriching values. To be a worthy member of such a people, to contribute to such a culture and to be instrumental in forming its heart-stirring values, is the good fortune of every able-bodied person and raises him above his personal troubles and misfortunes.

We, as well as the largest part of the population, have lost this faith which upheld us

*Translator's note: "Erneuerung: Ihr Problem und ihre Methode," *The Kaizo-La rekonstruyo* (Tokyo) 3 (1923): 84–92.

I would like to thank Professor Elmar Bund, executor of Husserl's estate, for granting permission to publish this translation. I would also like to thank Professors Frederick Elliston, David Carr, and Joseph J. Kockelmans for their helpful comments and suggestions on the translation. In addition, I am grateful to the Husserl Archives for their help with this project.

and our ancestors, and which also spread to nations which, like Japan, have only recently joined the European cultural endeavor.

If this faith had already been weakened before the war, now it has completely collapsed. As free men, we stand before this fact; it must determine our practical affairs.

And thus we feel compelled to say: *Something new must happen.* It must take place *within* us and be carried out by us, as members of humanity who live in this world, forming the world and being formed by it. Shall we wait to see whether this culture will recover of itself, in the chance play of forces which create and destroy values? Shall we let the "decline of the West" happen to us as our fate? This *is* our fate only if we stand along the sidelines and passively observe its occurrence. But even those who proclaim this fate to us cannot do this.

We are men, free-willing subjects who are actively engaged in our surrounding world, constantly involved in shaping it. Whether we want to or not, whether it is right or wrong, we act in this way. Could we not also act *rationally*? Do not rationality and efficiency stand within our power?

The pessimists and the supporters of "realpolitik" will, of course, protest that these are chimerical goals. If the idea of the individual shaping his personal life according to a life of reason is an unattainable ideal, then how are we supposed to undertake a similar task for community life [*Gemeinschaftsleben*], national life, and indeed, for all of Western mankind?

And yet, what would we say to a man

who, because of the unattainability of the ethical ideal, wants to abandon this ethical goal and is not willing to take up the ethical struggle? We know that insofar as this struggle is an earnest and constant one, it always has a value-creating significance—indeed, that it already elevates the struggling personality to the level of true humanity. Besides, who would deny the possibility of constant ethical progress under the guidance of the rational ideal?

Not allowing ourselves to be led astray by a feeble pessimism and a "realism" without ideals, we shall not unquestioningly consider such progress to be impossible, even for "man writ large," for larger and even the largest communities. We shall have to recognize, as an absolute ethical demand, the similar posture which struggles for a better humanity and a genuine humane culture.

Thus from the very first a natural feeling arises which is obviously rooted in the Platonic analogy between the individual man and the community. This analogy is by no means the ingenious invention of the eccentric philosopher who soars far beyond natural thinking; rather, it is nothing but the expression of an everyday apperception which naturally arises from the passing events of human life. For in its naturalness, this analogy always proves to be decisive as, for instance, in nearly all national and international value judgments of a political nature, and as the motive for actions corresponding to these judgments. But are such natural apperceptions and the emotional attitudes that arise from them a sufficient foundation for rational communal reforms? Can they possibly form the basis for the greatest of all reforms—the radical renewal of an entire human culture, such as the European culture? The faith that sustains us—in our culture it *must* not rest here, it can and must be reformed by human reason and human willing—this faith can "move mountains," not merely in fantasy, but in reality, only if it is transformed into prudent, rationally insightful ideas, only if it is in them that it brings to complete determination and clarity the essence and possibility of its goal and of the method by which it is to be attained. In this way, our faith first creates for itself its own rationally justified foundation. Only

such clarity of thought can summon joyful work and give the will, the resoluteness, and the all-pervasive power to carry out acts of liberation. Only such knowledge can become the enduring possession of all men, so that finally, through unlimited acts of cooperation by those who are convinced by this rationality, mountains will be moved—that is, the mere feeling of renewal will turn into the actual process of renewal.

However, such clarity is by no means easy to attain. The sceptical pessimism and the shamelessness of the political sophistry which so ominously dominates our age, and which only uses socioethical argumentation as a disguise for the egotistical goals of an utterly degenerate nationalism, would not be possible at all if the community's concepts, which have arisen naturally, were not, despite their naturalness, afflicted with dark and unclear horizons and with intricate and hidden implications whose clarification lies completely beyond the powers of untrained thinking. Only rigorous science can provide us with reliable methods and sound results; it alone can thereby provide the preparatory theoretical work upon which a rational reform of culture depends.

But now we are in a deplorable situation: We are searching in vain for the science that is supposed to serve us. We fare here in the same way as in the rest of the practical domain of community life, namely, whenever we would like to conscientiously ground our sociopolitical, international, and national views on a special type of knowledge, and when, in order to do so, we go to a lot of trouble to find some form of scholarly instruction which, in this fateful world of community life, could possibly release us from the primitive position of following our instinctive, vague, and traditionalistic ideas and actions. Our age is more than rich in great and serious sciences. We have "exact" natural sciences, and owing to them, we have that greatly admired applied science of nature which has given our modern civilization its powerful superiority, and of course has also resulted in much-lamented disadvantages. But in any case, in this natural, technological sphere of human activity, science made a truly practical rationality possible, and it provided the paradigm for how science in general must become a model of practical action. But we entirely lack a rational science of man and of the human community, a science that would establish a rationality in social and political activity and a national, political technique.

This is also the case with respect to the problems of renewal, which are of such great interest to us. More precisely, we lack the science which, with respect to the *idea of man* (and consequently, also with respect to the a priori inseparable pair of ideas: the individual man and his community), would have to undertake to accomplish something similar to what the pure mathematical science of nature has undertaken for the *idea of nature* and, in its principal divisions, has actually accomplished. Just as the latter idea —nature in general, as a universal form— encompasses the universe of the natural sciences, so too, the idea of a spiritual being —and especially or a rational being, man— encompasses the entire universe of the human sciences, and especially all humane social sciences. Since, on the one hand, the mathematical science of nature, in its a priori disciplines of time, space, movement, and moving force, exhibits the a priori necessities included in such essential constituents of nature in general (*"natura formaliter spectata"*), it makes possible, when applied to the facts of observed nature, an empirical science of nature with a rational, that is, mathematical, method. Therefore, the mathematical science of nature, with its a priori, provides the principles for the rationalization of the empirical domain.

On the other hand, we now have many fruitful sciences related to the realm of the spirit, that is, humanity, but they are entirely and "merely" empirical sciences. The enormous abundance of facts that are arranged under temporal, formal, inductive, or practical viewpoints is not held together by any bond of rationality *concerning principles.* Here we lack the parallel a priori science, the *mathesis of spirit and of humanity,* as it were; we are also lacking the scientifically developed system of purely rational, "a priori" truths that are rooted in the "essence" of man. Such an a priori system of truths, which would form the pure *logos* of the method in the domain of the human sci-

ences, would also bring forth a theoretical rationality, and likewise, would make possible the rational explanation of empirical facts, just as the pure mathematical science of nature has made empirical, natural science possible as a mathematical, theoretical, and consequently, rational, mode of explanation.

But in the domain of the human sciences, it is not merely a matter of rational "explanation," as in the case of nature. With the human sciences, a very special manner of rationalizing the empirical domain appears: the normative *judgment according to universal norms,* which belong to the a priori essence of "rational" humanity, and the *guidance* of actual practical activity according to the very norms to which the rational norms of practical guidance also belong.

The state of affairs on both sides [that is, nature and the human] is fundamentally different by virtue of the essential differences between natural and spiritual realities; thus the ways in which both sides require the rationalization of their factual domains are most certainly not the same. Thus, in order that our further analyses of renewal will not be hindered by naturalistic prejudices, it will be helpful to clarify this point right away by means of a brief contrast which will bring us closer to the peculiar methodological character of what we have previously called the missing science for which our analyses are striving.

In its essentials, nature is merely factual existence, and moreover, a fact given only in external experience. Consequently, a fundamental consideration of nature as such leads a priori only to the rationality of external appearances, namely, to the essential laws of the spatiotemporal form, and to the necessity of there being an *exact*, inductive, lawful order of entities existing in the spatiotemporal realm—which we usually characterize simply as a "causal," lawful order.

By contrast, in the specific sense of the spiritual, there lie quite different forms, different and most universal, essential determinations of individual realities and the essential forms of connection between them. Apart from the fact that, within the realm of the spirit (for example, in history), the spatiotemporal form has an essentially different sense than it has in physical nature, it should also be pointed out that every single spiritual reality has its own inwardness, a self-contained life of consciousness which is related to an "ego," so to speak, as a centripetal pole of all particular acts of consciousness, whereby these acts stand in "motivational" connections.

Furthermore, the separate, individual realities, or rather, their ego-subjects, approach one another through relations of mutual understanding ("empathy"); through "social" acts of consciousness, they establish (immediately or mediately) an entirely new form of unification of these realities: the form of the community which is spiritually united through internal moments, through intersubjective acts and motivations.

And we must still make an extremely important point: Belonging to such acts and their motivations are the distinctions of rational and irrational, of thinking, valuing, and willing "rightly" or "wrongly."

To be sure, in a certain way we can also consider spiritual realities (as second nature), as being externally related: consciousness as being an external appendage to physical realities (to the physical bodies to which each belongs); men and animals as being mere occurrences in space, "in" nature. But in contrast to what is essentially the case for physical nature, the inductive regularities which emerge in such a study are not indications of exact laws, of laws which determine the objectively true "nature" of these realities, that is, laws which determine rational truth in accordance with the essential nature of such realities. In other words, in cases where the peculiar essence of spiritual phenomena is expressed in the inwardness of conscious life, it can be maintained on a priori grounds that no rational explanation of these activities can be obtained by way of an inductive, causal consideration (and consequently, it is nonsensical to seek such an explanation in the manner of our naturalistic psychology). For the actual rationalization of the empirical domain, what is needed (here, just as in the case of nature) is a return to essential determining laws, and thus, to the specific spirituality as the world of inwardness. Now the normative forms of "reason" belong to the forms of consciousness

and of motivation, which are predelineated a priori as possible by the essence of human spirituality. And there also exists a priori the possibility of thinking freely in universal terms, and of practically and universally determining oneself according to a priori normative laws which one recognizes oneself. Therefore, in accordance with what we said earlier, in the realm of the human spirit, unlike in the case of nature, we do not have solely the formation of so-called "theoretical judgments" (taken in the special sense) which are directed to "mere facts of existence" (matter of fact).[1] Consequently, we do not merely have the tasks of rationalizing these facts through so-called "explanatory theories," and in accordance with an a priori discipline which explores the essence of the spirit in a purely matter-of-fact manner. Rather, in this context there also appears an entirely new kind of critical evaluation and rationalization of everything spiritual— according to norms, or according to normative, a priori disciplines of reason, of logical, axiological and practical reason. But in practice, evaluative reason is followed, or can freely be followed, by a freely acting subject who recognizes the norm and is directed by it. Accordingly, the tasks of a rational *guidance* of practice do, in fact, emerge in the spiritual sphere; thus there again emerges a new method for the possible rationalization of spiritual facts on the basis of a scientific foundation, that is, by means of a preceding a priori study of the norms of practical rational guidance.

If we now return again to our main problem, it must be noted that, in this regard, in fact, the existing, merely empirical sciences of man (such as our historical, cultural sciences, or even the modern, merely inductive psychology), cannot offer us what we need in our striving for renewal; and actually, only the a priori science of the essence of human spirituality—if it were to exist—could be regarded as a rational helper. First we should note that sciences of mere facts are ruled out by us from the outset. To be sure, our questions concerning renewal do indeed start with mere matters of fact, for they really do involve present-day culture, and especially that of our European civilization. But these facts are going to be evaluated and subjected to a normative regulation by reason; what is asked is how a reform of this worthless cultural life is to be guided towards a *rational life*. In this context, every deeper reflection leads back to the *fundamental* questions of practical reason, which concern both the individual person and the community, and its rational life in its essential and purely formal universality, a universality which leaves far behind it all empirical matters of fact and all contingent concepts.

Little is needed to establish this, and thus at the same time to make evident that it is precisely that essential science of man in general which would be just the one that we would need to help us.

If we subject our culture—and thus ourselves and our culture's surrounding civilized humanity—to a judgment of condemnation, it then becomes apparent that we believe in a "good" humanity as an ideal possibility. Implicit in our judgment is our belief in a "true and genuine" humanity as an objectively valid idea; the obvious goal of our reformatory efforts must therefore be to reform our factual culture according to the meaning of that idea. Thus our first reflections should proceed to a clear sketch of this idea. If we are not embarking on some utopian fantasy, but rather are aiming at sober, objective truth, then our sketch of this idea must take the form of a purely conceptual determination of essences; in the same way, the possibilities for actualizing this idea should first be considered in strict scientific rigor a priori as pure possibilities of these essences. Which particular, normatively justified forms would then be possible and necessary within a mankind that is in accordance with this idea of a genuine humanity? Which forms would be possible and necessary for the individual persons who, as members of a community, constitute this humanity, as well as for the different types of associations, social institutions, cultural activities, etc?—All of this would belong together in a scientific, eidetic analysis of the idea of a genuine, rational mankind, and would lead to various individual investigations with numerous ramifications.

Even a cursory reflection makes it clear that the entire character and the particular themes of the investigations which compel our interest are, in fact, determined from the outset by the formal, universal structures which our culture, above and beyond all of its facticities, may have in common with an infinite number of ideally possible cultures. All concepts encountered by our investigation as it penetrates into the depths, and thus into basic principles, have an a priori formal universality in the positive sense. This applies to the concept of man in general as a rational being, to the concept of being a member of the community and that of the community itself, no less than to all particular social concepts, such as those of family, people, state, etc. It also holds for the concepts of culture and of particular cultural systems, science, art, religion, etc. (And, of course, this holds for their normative forms, such as "true" and "genuine" science, art, or religion.)

The original and classical training ground for pure eidetic research and for the eidetic abstraction pertaining to such research (abstraction of "pure" a priori "concepts") is mathematics; but our type of research and method is by no means tied to mathematics. So no matter how unaccustomed we may be to practicing such abstraction in the spiritual sphere and to investigating its "a priori" and the essential necessities of spirit and reason, from our standpoint such practices are entirely possible. Indeed, quite frequently we are already—but not consciously or methodically—in the midst of the realm of the a priori; for whenever we enter into *fundamental* considerations, our gaze comes of its own accord to rest on the pure form. The methodical, conscious disregard of the empirical content of specific concepts may omit the conscious formation of "pure" concepts, but such empirical content still does not play any motivating role in our thinking. One thinks of the community in general, of the state, the people in general, as well as of man, the citizen, etc., and of what belongs to the "genuineness," to the "reasonableness" that is present in such universal notions. Thus all empirical factual distinctions of corporeality and spirituality, of concrete earthly life, are obviously circumstantial, and likewise, "indeterminate" and "freely variable" in the same sense that pertains to the concrete features and to the contingent, empirical bonds of the unities that the arithmetician considers ideally, or of the magnitudes that the algebraist investigates. For fundamental considerations such as, for instance, those of pure reason, matters such as whether man's senses, eyes, ears, etc., are formed empirically in this or that way, whether he has two or more eyes, whether he has this or that organ for locomotion, be it legs or wings, etc., are entirely extraneous questions that always remain open. Only certain forms of corporeality and psychical spirituality are presupposed and are under consideration; to bring these matters to light as being necessary a priori, and to fix them conceptually, is the task for essential scientific investigation which is consciously worked out. This applies to all of the many ramifications of the conceptual system which emerges as the formal framework that permeates all thinking in the human sciences, and, in particular, that permeates the investigations into the kinds of norms which are in question for us.

If an a priori science of the essential forms and laws of the spiritual realm and of the rational spirituality which is of the greatest interest to us has not yet been systematically developed, and if we cannot draw on the already existing wealth of knowledge in order to give our striving for renewal a rational foundation, what should we do? Should we again proceed, as in political matters when, for instance, as citizens we prepare to vote? Are we supposed to judge only according to instinct and inclination, according to assumptions which we tend to overlook? Actions like these may be perfectly justified if the day comes on which such a decision is required, and with it the action is completed. But in our case there is a concern for a temporal infinity and for the eternal in the temporal—the future of mankind, the genesis of true humanity—for which we still feel ourselves to be responsible. And we who are scientifically educated also know that only science establishes ultimately

valid, rational distinctions, and that only science can be the authority that ultimately prevails; for us, then, there cannot be any doubt about what our duty is. It is a matter of personally searching for the scientific ways which, unfortunately, no previous science has prepared, and of beginning in earnest with preliminary methodological considerations and with an analysis of the problem, as well as with preparatory guiding thoughts of the sort which prove to be prerequisites for our task.

In this sense, the reflections which we have already undertaken with respect to such a science are preparatory, but hopefully, not useless preliminary considerations. Above all, they have been of use because they have methodically shown us that the only really fruitful type of reflection is the one that is an *essential reflection,* for only it can open up the way to a rational science that not only treats man as such, but also his "renewal." But it must still be made clear that a "renewal" of essential necessity belongs to the development of a man and a mankind toward true humanity. If this is made clear, it follows that the foundation for this science would itself be the necessary presupposition for an actual renewal, and indeed, would be a first beginning of its inception. In any case, the preliminary preparation for this renewal is all that we can do at present.

In the next article,[2] we shall attempt, in approaching the idea of a genuine humanity and renewal, to pursue a series of fundamental lines of thought which, when consciously carried out in the eidetic attitude, should decisively show how we are to think of the beginnings—tentative beginnings—of prudent and scientific, and thus, of a priori cultural investigations of the normative—socioethical—sphere. The interest in our scientific situation must, above all, be directed to the *problem and method* of renewal.

NOTES

1. This parenthetical expression appears in English in the German text (Trans.).

2. See page 324 above.

19

Introduction to "Universal Teleology"

F. A. ELLISTON

Along with a few terse remarks in his three volume work on intersubjectivity, the following text is one of the few occasions on which Husserl comments on a pervasive and consequential dimension of human experience—sexuality.[1] His taciturnity hardly distinguishes him from most turn-of-the-century thinkers, for with the notable exception of Bertrand Russell none of his continental or Anglo-American contemporaries said anything significant on this topic.[2]

Phenomenology's thrust toward the concrete eventually brought sexuality into Husserl's purview—to be further developed by his successors Jean-Paul Sartre, Simone de Beauvoir, Maurice Merleau-Ponty, and Ortega y Gasset.[3] The recent appearance of *Facets of Eros* marks its coming of age among American phenomenologists today.[4]

"Universal Teleology" explores two themes as they converge into the domain of human sexuality. First is the constitution of the social world, a recurring problem for Husserl because its intersubjectivity functions as the logically more primitive notion for explicating objectivity—whether in science, mathematics, logic, history or art: something exists "objectively" only insofar as it is "there for everyone."[5] Only if Husserl can explain how we come to experience something as another person, and hence a community of others, will he be in a position to explain how anything can be experienced as objectively existing. The problem of intersubjectivity is thus rightly termed by Paul Ricoeur the "touchstone" of Husserl's philosophy.[6]

Second is the notion of intentionality so central to Husserl's philosophy, as scholars and commentators have noted, that his entire corpus could be taken as an explication of it.[7] From his teacher and mentor Franz Brentano, Husserl adopted the thesis that consciousness is intentional—that is, it is always directed to something other than itself (though he did not adopt Brentano's representative realism).[8] Husserl's stratified view of consciousness, which parallels a stratified view of knowledge as old as Plato's divided line, poses for him as for many other epistemologists the question of the foundations of knowledge. In his Fifth Cartesian Meditation he answers this question in terms of the *Leib* or animate organism, there characterized as a body with a sensory field, a conjunction Husserl terms the "sphere of ownness." The sense "alter ego" is constituted through an apperceptive transfer—an imaginative projecting of oneself into another's situation which is motivated by perceived similarities in physical appearances and movements. This "pairing" of self and other forms the basis of all my experiences of others —empathy (*Einfüllung*) in Husserl's all inclusive sense.

In the following text intentionality becomes teleology—the goal directed character of consciousness, its drive. Consciousness is a system of drives seeking fulfillment, each of which can be located within a hierarchy. At the bottom are the most fundamental ones—hunger and sex. What satisfies the first is food and what satisfies the second is the other. Sexuality is thus a primordial form of intentionality that finds its consummation in copulation. So explicated, intentionality and sexuality become woven into the fabric of intersubjectivity. Sex is a social bond uniting the otherwise isolated monads into a community. It is essential not just to the meaning of social life but to its very existence: the other is the telos of my sexual drives, and the means whereby future generations are born.

Husserl's topology of human sexuality can be summarized into three theses:

T₁ Sex is a social act.
T₂ Sex seeks copulation.
T₃ Sex is heterosexual.

Taken as a whole they demarcate what could be termed the "reproductive model."

The first thesis locates the sexual drive squarely within the context of interpersonal relationships. Thereby excluded as nonsexual is all solitary, nonsocial, or antisocial behavior. But whatever one's moral scruples or reservations, masturbation (along with fetishism and bestiality) are clearly forms of sexual activity—however deviant or perverted some might regard them. Indeed Masters and Johnson take the ability to masturbate to orgasm as the test of healthy sexual development.[9] Under the rubric "No masturbation without representation" one could counter that this ostensibly solitary sexual activity is in reality phantasized social behavior. But such a strategy to rescue Husserl's first thesis flies in the face of some people's sexual phantasies. Conversely it could be interpreted as: All intersubjectivity is sex-

ual. But this pansexualism, reminiscent of Freud, introjects an incestuous element into innocent family play and denies the very possibility of purely platonic relationships.

Husserl's second thesis, even if it is not taken to identify the goal of all social encounters, overstates the goal of even those that are sexual. For if all sex seeks copulation, then flirting, petting, reading pornography, or watching a strip tease cannot be sexual when they are undertaken for their own sake. But, surely voyeurism and exhibitionism remain sexual even when intercourse is deliberately excluded. Husserl has built into his definition of what sex is undefended assumptions of what it ought to be.

His moral prescription becomes evident in the third thesis—that sex is engaged in by a man and a woman (perhaps a husband and a wife).[10] What is thereby ruled out by fiat is that homosexual encounters can qualify as sexual, or that group sex (however satisfying or dissatisfying) can even be counted as sex. Husserl's assumptions of heterosexuality and a binary framework for interpreting sex is more visible to our later culture that includes gay rights marches and the phenomenon of swinging, and they underscore the difficulty of freeing oneself from the culture milieu and its presuppositions—even when the thinker makes it his explicit ideal. To disengage oneself from such preconceptions in order to examine them critically is indeed an infinite task.

NOTES

1. See, for example, the following: *Husserliana,* vol. 14, p. 172, where love is treated as a dimension of communality; vol. 15, p. 171, where birth is treated as one limit to the (other) self, and p. 508, where lust is one way to be preoccupied with others.

2. Bertrand Russell, *Marriage and Morals* (New York: Liveright Publishers, 1928); "Sex Education," in *On Education* (London: Allen and Unwin, 1926); and "Our Sexual Ethics," *The American Mercury* 38 (1936): 36–41.

3. Jean-Paul Sartre, *Being and Nothingness* (1943), trans. Hazel E. Barnes (New York: Philosophical Library, 1956), pp. 478–91; Simone de Beauvoir, *The Second Sex* (1949), trans. H.M. Parshley (New York: Knopf, 1952); Maurice Merleau-Ponty, *Phenomenology of Perception* (1945), trans. Colin Smith (New York: Humanities Press, 1965), pp. 154–73; and Or-

tega y Gasset, *On Love* (1939), trans. Tolby Talbot (New York: Meridian, 1957).

4. *Facets of Eros,* ed. Erling Eng and F. Joseph Smith (The Hague: Nijhoff, 1969).

5. E. Husserl, *Cartesian Meditations,* p. 92.

6. Paul Ricoeur, *Husserl: An Analysis of His Phenomenology* (Evanston: Northwestern University Press, 1967), p. 115.

7. For especially insightful discussions of Husserl's notion of intentionality see the following: D. Carr, "Intentionality" in *Phenomenology and Philosophical Understanding* ed. E. Pivcevic (New York: Cambridge University Press, 1975), pp. 17–36; A. de Waelhens, "The Phenomenological Concept of Intentionality," *Philosophy Today* 6 (1962): 3–13; A. Gurwitsch, "Towards a Theory of Intentionality," *Philosophy and Phenomenological Research* 30 (1969–70): 354–67; and

J. N. Mohanty, *The Concept of Intentionality* (St. Louis: W.H. Green, 1972).

8. The philosophical relationship between Husserl and Brentano is treated by James C. Morrison in "Husserl and Brentano on Intentionality," *Philosophy and Phenomenological Research* 31 (1970–71): 27–46. For their personal relationship see "Recollections of Franz Brentano," pp. 342–48 of this volume.

9. William H. Masters and Virginia E. Johnson, *Human Sexual Response* (Boston: Little, Brown, 1966), pp. 12, 32, and 198. They extol the virtues of masturbation for relief of menstrual pain (p. 125), sexual fitness in old age (pp. 241, 246), and its greater intensity compared to coital orgasm (pp. 34, 53–55, 313–14). In their second work *Human Sexual Inadequacy* (Boston: Little, Brown, 1970) failure in women is treated as pathological (p. 240) but curable (pp. 248–9).

10. This bias is most evident in the official pronouncements of the Roman Catholic Church—Pius XI's *Casti Connubii* and Paul VI's *Humanae Vitae*. The study commissioned by the Catholic Theological Society of America is noticeably more tolerant and supportive: A. Kosnik et al., *Human Sexuality* (New York: Paulist Press, 1977), pp. 211–18.

11. Though heterosexuality has dropped out in recent alternative models, the binary framework has tended to persist. In "Sexual Perversion" [*Journal of Philosophy* vol. 66, no. 1 (January 16, 1969)] Thomas Nagel interprets sex as incarnate and dialectical awareness, but still between two people. Criticizing and expanding on Nagel, Robert Solomon develops a communicative model whereby sex is taken as body language which paradigmatically remains dyadic: "Sex and Perversion" in *Philosophy and Sex*, ed. R. Baker and F. Elliston (Buffalo: Prometheus Books, 1975), pp. 269–87.

19

Universal Teleology*

TRANSLATED BY MARLY BIEMEL

The intersubjective drive in each and every subject viewed transcendentally: Relative worlds of monads, each constituting for itself an objective temporal world and, ultimately, the human monadic world and the temporal world of men.

The being of the monadic *totality* as flowing being which arrives at self-consciousness and which is already in self-consciousness, gradual process *in infinitum*—universal teleology.

Marginal note

The intersubjective drive (particularly the sex drive) viewed transcendentally. The existence with and in each other of all monads in the unity of a universal development, development in the form of relative worlds of monads. Every such world has intentionally constituted within itself an objective world (temporal world) with ego-subjects living in it. Ultimately, the existent, monadic humanity or the humanity of the world, which is always in the process of constitution. The being of the monadic totality as flowing being coming to universal self-consciousness and already present in self-consciousness in an infinite gradual process—universal teleology.

Text

The internal of procreation. The drive towards the other sex. The drive in one indi-

vidual and the reciprocal drive in the other. The drive can be in the stage of the indeterminate hunger that does not yet contain within itself its object as its goal. Hunger in the ordinary sense is more determinate when there is a drive toward the food—determinately directed in the original mode (even before the hunger has been satisfied by such a food and this food already has that certain character which allows its recognition, the typical character, of course, of a "food," of a familiar object which can satisfy a hunger). In the case of sexual hunger which directs itself in a specific way towards its enticing, exciting goal, this goal is the other. This determinate sexual hunger has its modality of realization in the mode of copulation. In the drive itself lies the relation to the other as other and to its correlative drive. Both drives can be present in the mode—in the modified mode of abstinence of repugnance. In the original mode the drive is "uninhibited," an unmodified drive, which forces itself within the other and has constituted its own intentionality through the correlative intentionality of the other.

In the simple fulfillment of the primary mode we never have two separate fulfillments of each drive in the one and in the other primordiality, but rather one unity arises through the reciprocal fulfillment of the two primordialities. If I, in my worldli-

*This is a translation of manuscript E-III-5. It was transcribed by Marly Biemel in August 1952. It has appeared as an "Appendix" to Enzo Paci, *Tempo e Verità nella Fenomenologia di Husserl* (Bari, 1961), pp. 256–69. Reprinted with permission of the publisher from *Telos* 4 (Fall 1969): 176–80.

ness, explicate this in its most profound originality, I can do so only as a sexual man — *i.e.*, as a man, as a man in the actual reciprocal feeling or empathy (*Einfühlung*) with the woman (which, generally speaking, is naturally already mediate).

We go from there through a mediate interpretation to "higher" animals, which I can and must view as bound to one another through reciprocal feelings, essentially through the motivation of the "perceptions of the strange," precisely as it happens among men. It is, therefore, according to a representation of their world in which the animal experiences itself as having a world, as an animal of his species.

We are also faced with the question whether the intentionality of the drive, including that directed towards others (sexual-social), does not necessarily have a preceding stage obtaining before a developed constitution of the world — even if this constitution does not reach so far as it does for humans who are "reasonable creatures" (*Vernunftwesen*). Here I have in mind the problems of parents, above all those of mother and child. These problems, however, arise also in connection with the problematic of copulation.

Primordiality is a system of drives — and if we understand it as an originally constant stream, every drive in it is also in other streams, and eventually it is together with the drive of other ego-subjects. This intentionality has its transcendent "goal," transcendent insofar as it is felt as foreign in reciprocal feeling. Yet, primordially, this goal is its own — *i.e.*, it is the goal of the originary modal intention which simply emerges and constantly fulfills its own nucleus. In my old theory of the internal consciousness of time, I dealt with the intentionality introduced here precisely as intentionality — set up as protention and retention, self-modifying yet preserving the unity; but I did not talk about the ego, and I have not characterized this intentionality as egological (in the broadest sense of intentionality of the will). Later I introduced the latter as founded in an egoless intentionality ("passivity"). But isn't the same ego of actions and habits deriving from it, a developing ego?[1] Shouldn't we or musn't we posit a universal intention-

ality of the drive which unifies every original presence as permanence of a temporalization which concretely moves it forward from presence to presence in such a way that all content is the content of the realization of the drives and it is determined by the goal toward which the drive aims and in such a manner that the superior drives in every primordial presence are transcended and force themselves within every other presence thus connecting all of the presences as monads, while they are all implied in each other— intentionally? The reconsideration and the reconstruction leads us to the permanent centrality of every primordiality through the ego-pole: the pole that remains permanent in the constant movement of objectification in which, from the side of the world, stands the objectified ego with its body.

That could lead us to the conception of a universal teleology as a universal intentionality always in the process of fulfilling itself in accordance with the unity of a total system of fulfillment.

The question then is how to conceive of the centrality of the ego (*Ichzentrierung*) in the universality of the intentional implication, in the constantly constituted, all-primordial, original living presence, in the absolute "simultaneity" of all monads, of the changing immediate and mediate reciprocal transcending of the drives of the community of the monads. This open infinity, as open infinity of the mediacy of transcendence, has the essential characteristic that an infinity of monadic degrees belong to it — as degrees of the development of the ego and of the world. Here also belong the infinity of the degrees of animal monads of the animal, pre-animal monads up to man, of the infantile and pre-infantile monads — in the permanence of the "ontogenetic" philogenic development.

The new awakening of the egos as self-sufficient, as the center of acts which are realized in a surrounding world and therefore the awakening of the constitutions of "beings," and lastly of an horizon of the world — as teleology included in the universal teleology, as a universal intentionality is always "prior" in the continual vitality of a unitary and conscious community of monads. This is the community of universally constituted drives which has, corresponding to it, a world which always brings anew the monads to a new formation and to their "development." *In this form the totality of the monads* gradually *comes to self-consciousness* and attains its maximum universality as a human community.

This community has the unique universal world in which it finds itself as world-perceiving and in which it has climbed to the will of the knowledge of the world in the cultural European humanity, which has created a universal positive science. Only from this follows the possibility of a transcendental reduction through which the monads discover themselves as human monads and therefore in the form of the generative connection of all degrees of monads: the higher and lower animals, the plants and their lower forms and all in the connection of their ontogenetic development. Every monad is essentially in such a development and all monads are essentially in the generative development.

I start from myself as a man and from my human monad which contains implicitly my immediately surrounding human world. The question arises concerning the intentionality of copulation. In the fulfillment of the drive, immediately viewed, there is nothing concerning the child which is created, nothing concerning what will have the well-known consequences in the other subject: the fact that the mother will give birth to the child.

But the fulfillment of the drive as penetration into the other "soul" is not a reciprocal feeling oneself in the other as an uninterrupted experience of the life of the other, of what follows as the act of reproduction as a worldly event, and thus it is not all related to the other, as an act of copenetration which is in the life of the world.

The unity of my concrete being as constant being based in the temporalization of the ego is also a unity of intentionality and, considered from within, it is such that the original constitutes itself in it. However, it does not come into question since it is in the world and becomes explicit in the experience of the world and in knowledge. "Before" the world there is the constitution of the world, my self-temporalization in pre-time, the intersubjective temporalization in pre-time, and the intersubjective temporalization of intersubjective pre-time. The intersubjective "act of reproduction" "motivates" natural processes in the life of the other — processes that are different from self-temporalization and, in the explication from the side of my being in the world as man, I experience what in the world reveals itself through further inductions, I experience what concerns the physiology of pregnancy.

Teleology encompasses all of the monads. What occurs in the motherly domain (*in der mutterlichen*) is not limited to it, but "is reflected throughout." But I arrive at this only as an ego that recognizes itself as a scientific man in mundane life and questions my and our monadic being and from there goes systematically further.

The reconsideration begins from me and from the world in which I live concretely and naturally — the world of my and our experience, which is at the same time the world for the sciences, which in turn belong to my world and in their own way they can be experienced and are experienced as the being (*seiendes*) of this world.

NOTE

1. The ego, as a pole in which it operates in temporalization constantly constituting objectivity in the process, temporalizes and objectifies itself, along with its peers, in corresponding degrees.

20

Introduction to
"Recollections of Franz Brentano"
RICHARD HUDSON

The "Erinnerungen an Franz Brentano," which is presented here in English translation, was first published in 1919 in *Franz Brentano: Zur Kenntnis seines Lebens und seiner Lehre,* a book put together by one of Brentano's more faithful students, Oskar Kraus, to consecrate the memory of Brentano, who had recently (1917) passed away.[1] Half of the book consists of an essay by Kraus attempting to show that "Brentano is an author not of the past but of the future";[2] the other half consists of recollections of Brentano by Husserl and by Carl Stumpf, the two most famous of Brentano's students.

Husserl's article thus contains for the most part recollections of his personal relationship to the man who introduced him to philosophy, and it does not contain much in the way of philosophic analysis either of Brentano's work or of those of Brentano's ideas which particularly influenced the young Husserl.

Although Husserl is writing in a book which aims at commemorating Brentano, in talking of his own relation to the master, Husserl does not hide the disagreements he had with Brentano's ideas nor the problems he had in relating to his professor—problems which severely reduced the amount of contact between them (Husserl last saw Brentano some ten years before the death of the latter).

Despite their later differences, there can be no doubt that Husserl was deeply impressed by Brentano from the start. In his "Recollections" Husserl talks of the physical impression Brentano left—his presence before a class, the otherworldliness of his view, his sense of having a great mission, etc.—as well as the impression of seriousness coming from the strictness and rigor with which he proceeded and the sharpness and clearness of his arguments. Husserl claims that it was this personal example which led him to believe philosophy too could be scientific and that it would be worthwhile for him to abandon mathematics and take up philosophy as his life's work.

At the time of this first meeting (1884) Husserl was a young mathematician who had received his doctorate in philosophy in 1883 for his dissertation "Beiträge zur Theorie der Variationsrechnung"[3] and had just finished his year of military service.[4] Upon finishing his time in the army, Husserl returned to Vienna to go to Brentano's lectures. In the "Recollections" Husserl says he went to the lectures out of curiosity aroused by all the talk about the famous Brentano; however, in fact it was more than mere idle curiosity which motivated him—for years friends, particularly Thomas Masaryk (who later became president of Czechoslovakia), had urged him to study under Brentano.[5]

Brentano, although famous for his original work in philosophy, was much better known for the various scandals which had touched his life. In 1873 Father Brentano quit the church because he could not accept the newly proclaimed doctrine of papal infallibility. At that time he went to Vienna and received a chair in philosophy, which he had to give up when he married in 1880. Husserl recounts how sorely Brentano felt the loss of his chair, since as a mere "Privat-dozent," although he could continue to teach, he could not direct theses nor have a say in the *Habilitation* of young professors.

Despite these difficulties Brentano continued to teach and to deeply influence his students. Husserl discusses briefly the subjects of the various courses he took from Brentano, and the other philosophic subjects Brentano was working on at that time. However, what seems to have most impressed Husserl was Brentano's teaching ability— Husserl exclaims that Brentano was an expert at Socratic maeutic, *i.e.,* that Brentano knew how, by using the Socratic method of questions and answers, to draw out of a serious student things the student was not aware of knowing, and how conversely, through irony, etc., he knew how to shut up pretentious show-offs.[6] What also impressed Husserl was Brentano's openness with his students: inviting them to go on walks with him in Vienna, and to go to his house for dinner, and speaking openly with them of his innermost concerns, his political and religious ideas, his personal fate. Brentano seems to have been especially friendly with the young Husserl (25 years old in 1884), inviting him to his summer residence and even painting his portrait (a painting which unfortunately was destroyed in the Second World War).[7]

Exactly in what ways and how much Brentano influenced Husserl is not a matter of total agreement among experts and is perhaps a question which, as Spiegelberg claims, cannot be resolved without thorough study of the correspondence between the two men.[8]

That, as Husserl claims in this article, Brentano's personality was a decisive influence on him is generally accepted.[9] What is at times questioned, however, is how much Brentano's ideas influenced Husserl. The late Father Van Breda, founding director of the Husserl Archives, said in a 1959 discussion:

I think that in general the influence of Franz Brentano on Husserl is overestimated. That there

was congeniality, I do not doubt at all. I think that Husserl borrowed from Brentano primarily a series of philosophical terms, of which several come originally from Aristotle and the Scholastics. Husserl furthermore quite often transformed these terms right from the beginning. For my part, I do not really believe that we can see in Brentano the precurser of Husserlian Phenomenology. I think as well that Brentano himself would be the first to reject this title.[10]

According, then, to Van Breda, and to Jean Wahl, who agreed with him that the relation was more of congeniality than influence,[11] Brentano did not influence Husserl all that much in his ideas, though perhaps he did in his vocabulary.

However, the opposite view that Brentano's influence on Husserl was very real, at least at the beginning of Husserl's career, seems to be more generally held. As Walter Biemel says: "It is beyond doubt that Brentano's influence was decisive for Husserl."[12] Th. de Boer in his exhaustive study of the early Husserl says: "When we look over Husserl's early work, we notice a dominating influence from his master, Brentano."[13] Spiegelberg also recognizes this influence by starting his famous history of the phenomenological movement with a chapter on Brentano, who he admits was never a phenomenologist.

Those who see an influence of Brentano on Husserl (and particularly on the early Husserl) do not always agree on the precise points in which this influence can be found; however, all seem to admit that the most important of Brentano's ideas for Husserl was that of intentionality. Thus de Boer writes:

In his earliest work [*i.e.,* before the *Logical Investigations*] Husserl is in certain ways dependent on Brentano. This is the case particularly for the theme of intentionality, which plays such a central role in phenomenological philosophy. Brentano's well-known definition of intentionality is presented by Husserl and is at first simply taken over unchanged.[14]

Biemel, Tatarkiewicz, and Illemann also stress that the concept of intentionality is one which Husserl without much doubt derived from Brentano's reformulation of the Scholastic concept.[15]

Many authors who see an influence of Brentano on Husserl believe that Husserl was indebted to Brentano for concepts other than that of intentionality. Thus de Boer claims:

The dependence on Brentano is not limited, as most people think, to the theme of intentionality, but rather it goes much deeper and wider. One of the most urgent problems which Brentano set before Husserl is that of the relation of genetic to descriptive psychology.[16]

Illemann also sees several of Brentano's ideas in Husserl, particularly in the *Logical Investigations,* where, Illemann believes:

In fact Husserl takes over several things that Brentano had already noticed: *e.g.,* the distinction between act and content, the concept of intentionality, the refusal of an unconsciousness in the psyche . . . , and the immediate evidence of inner perception.[17]

Illemann, however, sees so many influences of Brentano in Husserl that he believes that the *Logical Investigations* was basically in accord with Brentano's philosophizing—a viewpoint held by very few, and almost certainly not by Brentano.

In fact, although in 1886 Husserl left Vienna probably very much influenced by Brentano in several ways, a gap soon developed between the two men due to differences in the way they saw philosophy. Husserl recounts in the "Recollections" that in his work, which he says was at first heavily influenced by Brentano, he developed themes which were originally those of Brentano; that, however, in his own hands these themes went in directions that Brentano did not want to go; and that, although Brentano tried to educate his students to think for themselves, he could not accept that they think something different from him.[18] Thus relations between the two thinkers became strained—with the younger man seeing himself as being faithful to the spirit of the older man's thought, and the older professor seeing his student as incapable of rising to the high level he had already attained.

The strained relations began soon after Husserl left Vienna. Although Husserl sent Brentano copies of his writings and dedicated his 1891 book, the *Philosophie der Arithmetik,* to him, Brentano never read Husserl's work very closely. Spiegelberg reports that Brentano did not even read Husserl's works "slantingly"—that Brentano's copy of the *Philosophie der Arithmetik* did not even have the pages cut open, and that neither his copy of this book nor his copy of the *Logical Investigations* had any markings in it.[19] Brentano's failure to read Husserl's books was perhaps partly due to Husserl's concerns with mathematics, concerns which Brentano did not share, and partly, at least after 1902, to Brentano's failing eyesight which made reading anything extremely difficult.[20]

Whatever the cause—whether a failure by Brentano to understand Husserl's work, or a correct assessment by Brentano that this work was opposed to his own aims—Brentano seems not to have been very pleased with the writings of his star pupil, and he quite probably saw, as did others, that Husserl's *Logical Investigations* with its attack on "psychologism" was an attack on himself.[21] Husserl, as he says in the "Recollections," felt that Brentano did not understand what he was attempting to do, and he thought that Brentano was unfair to him. He felt the older man was rigid, set in his ways, and closed off against any new ideas. Husserl particularly disliked what he saw as Brentano's lack of sympathy for those who, like the German Idealists and like Husserl himself, try to work out ideas which at the beginning lack clearness and preciseness, but which give the possibility of new and original ways of thinking. While it is easy for a master logician like Brentano to make fun of people caught in such a predicament, Husserl felt it was unfair, and he thus found it difficult to continue to communicate with the master.

Despite these later difficulties however, Husserl never lost his respect for his master nor his memories of all that Brentano had done for him when he was a young student in Vienna. It was Brentano's personality, his strict scientific way of proceeding, his otherworldly attitude, and his sense of purpose which persuaded Husserl of the value of philosophy and which enabled him to decide what he would do with his life.

NOTES

1. Oskar Kraus, *Franz Brentano: Zur Kenntnis seines Lebens und seiner Lehre*, Mit Beiträgen von Carl Stumpf und Edmund Husserl (Munich: C.H. Beck'sche Verlagsbuchhandlung, 1919).

2. Kraus, *Franz Brentano*, p. iv.

3. Karl Schuhmann, *Husserl-Chronik. Denk-und Lebensweg Edmund Husserls*, Husserliana Dokumente 1 (The Hague: Nijhoff, 1977), p. 11.

4. Ibid.

5. Ibid., p. 5. Herbert Spiegelberg in his *The Phenomenological Movement: A Historical Introduction*, Phaenomenologica 5, (The Hague: Nijhoff, 1960), 1: 92, also reports that it was on Masaryk's recommendation that Husserl went to Vienna to hear Brentano.

6. See "Recollections," p. 343.

7. Herbert Spiegelberg, "The Lost Portrait of Edmund Husserl by Franz and Ida Brentano," in *Philomathes: Studies and Essays in the Humanities in Memory of Philip Merlan*, ed. Robert B. Palmer and Robert Hamerton-Kelly (The Hague: Nijhoff, 1971), pp. 341–45. In this brief article Spiegelberg gives details on the picture, and he makes a couple of corrections of minor errors in Husserl's account (*e.g.*, he shows that Husserl got the name wrong of the art critic who thought the painting "lovely".

8. Ibid., pp. 343–44: "The entire relation between the always revered master and the emancipated pupil would require a full-scale study, in which their voluminous correspondence between 1891 and 1915 would have to be a center piece." It is to be noted that in the "Recollections" Husserl says (p. 346): "I did not exchange many letters with Brentano."

9. As Lothar Kelkel and René Schérer say in their book *Husserl: Sa vie, son oeuvre* (Paris: P.U.F., 1964), pp. 2–3: "Without doubt, no other personality marked him [*i.e.*, Husserl] more, toward no other thinker did he recognize a greater debt" than toward Brentano. See also Spiegelberg, *Phenomenological Movement* p. 28.

10. *Husserl*, Cahiers de Royaumont, Philosophie no. 3 (Paris: Les éditions de Minuit, 1959), p. 29.

11. Ibid. Van Breda's and Wahl's comments come in a discussion of an article by V. Tatarkiewicz.

12. Ibid., p. 70.

13. Th. de Boer, *De Ontwikkelingsgang in het Denken van Husserl* (Assen: Van Gorcum & Comp., 1966), p. 147.

14. Ibid., p. 577.

15. See Biemel, *Husserl*, Cahiers de Royaumont, p. 70, Tatarkiewicz, ibid., p. 21, and Werner Illemann, *Husserls vor-phänomenologische Philosophie*, mit einer Monographishen Bibliographie Edmund Husserl (Leipzig: Verlag von S. Hirzel, 1932), p. 59.

16. De Boer, *De Ontwikkelingsgang*, p. 580.

17. Illemann, *Husserls*, p. 59.

18. See "Recollections," p. 345: "Completely under Brentano's direction in my beginnings . . ."; p. 345: "No one surpassed [Brentano] in educating students to think independently, yet no one took it harder when such thinking was directed against his own entrenched convictions"; p. 346: "I knew, however, how much it bothered him when someone took another path even though it emanated from his own"; p. 347: "I was hindered by the inner conviction that . . . Brentano was no longer adaptable enough to be able to understand the necessity which had forced me to transform his basic intuitions."

19. Spiegelberg, "The Lost Portrait," p. 344. Spiegelberg in this article corrects Husserl's claim that Brentano never responded to the dedication of the *Philosophy of Arithmetic*—apparently Brentano wrote a short note at that time, and then years later, as Husserl recounts, noticed that the book was dedicated to him, and feeling that he might not have written Husserl, wrote a letter apologizing and thanking him for the dedication.

20. Spiegelberg makes these suggestions in *Phenomenological Movement*, pp. 27 and 92.

21. See ibid., p. 49.

20

Recollections of Franz Brentano*

TRANSLATED BY R. HUDSON AND P. McCORMICK

The good fortune of attending Brentano's lectures was mine for only two years. During this time, the only whole semesters were the winter semesters of 1884–85 and 1885–86. Brentano lectured five hours a week on "practical philosophy" both times and, besides the discussion groups, another one or two hours on selected philosophical questions. In the corresponding summer semesters he continued these shorter lecture courses which were exclusively for advanced students, but the courses would end early, by the first week in June. The first of these lecture courses, "Elementary Logic and Its Necessary Revisions," concerned systematically connected basic elements of a descriptive psychology of the intellect. Parallels in the mental sphere were pursued in a chapter devoted to them. The other lecture course, "Selected Psychological and Aesthetic Questions," mainly offered descriptive fundamental analyses of the essence of phantasy representations. About the middle of June, Brentano went to the Wolfgangsee, which he liked so much then, and at his friendly request I accompanied him there (to St. Gilgen). It was particularly during these summer months, in which I had a standing invitation to visit his home and to go along on his short walks and boat outings (even on the only large excursion of the two years), that I was able to get somewhat close to him —as much as the great difference in age and

maturity allowed. At that time I had just finished my university studies and was still a beginner in philosophy, which was the minor subject for my doctorate in mathematics.

At a time when my philosophical interests were increasing and I was uncertain whether to make my career in mathematics or to dedicate myself totally to philosophy, Brentano's lectures settled the matter. At first I attended these lectures just out of curiosity, simply to hear the man who was then being talked about so much in Vienna. Some admired and highly respected Brentano, but just as many others polemicized against him as a disguised Jesuit, a speechifier, sham, sophist, and scholastic. The very first impression Brentano made upon me struck me quite a bit. This haggard figure with the massive head framed by curly hair, the energetic boldly soaring nose, the expressive facial lines which spoke not only of mental work but also of deep spiritual battles, was completely beyond the scope of ordinary everyday life. Brentano expressed the consciousness of a great mission in each trait, in every movement, in the upward and inwardly turned look of the soulful eyes, in his entire way of behaving. The language Brentano used in his lectures was formally perfect. It was in no way artificial, neither cleverly ornamental nor rhetorical, but nothing less than sober scientific discourse. The style throughout was elevated and artistic, a style which expressed Brentano's personality in a completely appropriate and natural way. When he spoke in his peculiarly soft and husky undertone, all the while gestur-

*Translated and printed with the permission of the publisher and translators from Kraus, *Franz Brentano* (Munich: C.H. Beck, 1919), pp. 153–67.

ing in his priestly way, Brentano stood before his young students like a seer of eternal truths and a herald of a celestial world.

Despite all the prejudices against him, I did not resist the strength of this personality very long. Sometimes it was the subject matter which overcame me, other times the quite singular clearness and dialectical sharpness of his expositions, the cataleptic power as it were of his way of developing problems and of his theories. Brentano's lectures gave me for the first time the conviction that encouraged me to choose philosophy as my life's work, the conviction that philosophy too was a serious discipline which also could be and must be dealt with in the spirit of the strictest science. What made me marvel and filled me with confidence was the completely impartial way Brentano attacked all problems, his treating problems in terms of *aporiai,* his finely dialectical measuring of various possible arguments, his clarifying of equivocations, and retracing of every philosophical concept to its original intuitive sources. His serious, complete, even holy submission to his subject matter kept his lectures free from common academic witticisms and jokes. Brentano avoided too any kind of clever antitheses whose linguistic point requires violent intellectual simplifications as payment. In ordinary conversation however and when he was in a good mood, Brentano was very clever with an effervescent wit and humor. Most impressive was his activity in the unforgettable discussion groups. (I remember the following subjects: Hume's *Enquiry Concerning Human Understanding* and *Enquiry Concerning the Principles of Morals,* Helmholz's *The Facts of Perception,* Dubois-Reymond's *Boundaries of Natural Knowledge.*) Brentano was a master of socratic maieutic. How well he knew how to use questions and objections to guide the unsure groping beginner, to encourage sincere efforts, and to transform the unclear beginnings of vaguely felt truths into clear thoughts and insights. And how well too he was able to silence the empty chatterers without ever insulting them. After the discussions Brentano used to invite those who had read papers together with three or four of the most active participants to go home with him where his wife, Ida

Brentano, had supper prepared. These suppers were never occasions for small talk. Discussions continued. Speaking tirelessly, Brentano would raise new questions or give whole talks opening huge and novel perspectives. Shortly after the meal was over, and after having tried hard to make the shy students feel at home and help themselves (something which Brentano never thought of), Frau Ida would vanish. Once by chance the famous politician and a close friend of the household, E. von Plener, dropped in on one of these groups. Brentano however was not to be diverted; on this evening he belonged entirely to his students and the subject for discussion.

His students found Brentano easy to speak with. He freely invited them for walks where, totally unperturbed by the noises of the city streets, he answered their philosophical questions. In a self sacrificing way he took an interest in his students, not only in their scholarly but also in their personal needs, and he became their most benevolent advisor and educator. To those he viewed as trusted friends, Brentano would even talk about his political and religious convictions and his personal fate. Everyday politics he kept at a distance. But Brentano was keenly interested in the idea of a Greater Germany in the old south German understanding of the matter which he grew up with and held on to tenaciously. He also kept his antipathy toward Prussia, a point on which I could never agree with him. Clearly, Brentano never experienced the Prussian manner and had no significant personal or worthwhile social impression of it. I however, with more luck, had had such experience and had learned to appreciate it highly. The result was that Brentano was insensitive to the peculiar greatness of Prussian history. A similar case was Protestantism which, in withdrawing from the Catholic church, he had not approached in any way. As a philosopher he had freed himself from Catholic dogma. No relation however to Protestant ideas played any role in this process. The sympathetic historical-political understanding and the appreciation of historical value which could arise from such an understanding were simply lacking in Brentano. I never heard him speak of Catholicism without the greatest respect. Sometimes he would vigorously defend the religious and ethical powers linked with Catholicism against injudicious deprecating talk. The theistic world view which he treasured linked him philosophically to the old church, so that he liked to discuss questions about God and immortality. Brentano thought through his two-hour lecture course on the proofs for the existence of God with the greatest care (this was a part of the larger course on metaphysics which he had given in earlier years at both Würzburg and Vienna). As I was leaving Vienna he started working on these problems freshly. I know that he was concerned with such problems until his last years.

What mainly occupied him in these years however were the questions of descriptive psychology (the theme of the lectures mentioned) and the investigations into the psychology of the senses. The latter were first published a few years ago and I still remember at least the major parts from the talks in Vienna and St. Gilgen. Brentano dealt particularly thoroughly in the elementary logic lectures in what are clearly creative new formulations, with the descriptive psychology of the continua. He dealt exhaustively with Bolzano's *Paradoxes of the Infinite*. He did the same with the distinctions between "intuitive and nonintuitive," "clear and unclear," "distinct and indistinct," "authentic and inauthentic," and "concrete and abstract" representations. That summer semester Brentano tried to investigate in a fundamental way all the descriptive moments which underlie the traditional distinctions of judgments and which are exhibited in the immanent nature of the judgment. Just afterwards, and as the theme in one of the lecture courses mentioned above, he investigated descriptive problems about phantasy, especially the relationship between phantasy representations and perceptual representations. These lectures were particularly stimulating because the problems were exhibited in the course of their investigation. The lectures, however, on practical philosophy or on logic and metaphysics (from which I could use accurate notes), despite the critical-dialectical presentation, were somewhat dogmatic; they were supposed to and in fact did arouse the impression of final truths and theories. My impression then and later was that Brentano thought of himself as the creator of a *philosophia perennis*. He was completely certain of his method and he strove constantly to satisfy the highest claims of an almost mathematical strictness. Brentano believed that his sharply polished concepts, his strongly constructed and systematically ordered theories, and his all round aporetic refutation of alternative interpretations, captured final truths. For all his determined defense of his doctrines, Brentano did not, although I believed so for a long time, rigidly cling to them. He later abandoned various favorite theses of his earlier years. He was never at a standstill. Although his intuitive analyses were deeply penetrating and often ingenious, Brentano relatively quickly moved from intuition to theory, to the delimitation of sharp concepts, to theoretical formulation of working problems. He constructed a systematic aggregate of possible solutions, the choice among which was to be made through criticism. If my judgment of his philosophy is correct, then at each phase of his development Brentano had quite definite theories defended with well considered arguments, which allowed him to feel himself the match of anyone else's doctrines. Brentano had little esteem for thinkers like Kant and the post-kantian German Idealists, for whom the value of original intuition and anticipatory presentments stood so much higher than the value of logical method and scientific theory. Brentano would not concede evaluating a philosopher as great when all his theories taken strictly were unscientific and when even all his basic concepts left almost everything to be desired in "clearness and distinctness." He would not concede that a philosopher's greatness, instead of lying in the logical perfection of his theories, could lie in the originality of highly meaningful, although vague and barely clarified basic intuitions, in a prelogical resoluteness which first of all pushes towards the *logos*, in short, in fully new-fashioned thought *motifs*, which are ultimately decisive for the goals of all philosophical work and yet which are far from taking effect in theoretically strict insights. Brentano was entirely devoted to the austere ideal of a strict philosophic science, an ideal he saw in the exact natural sciences. He regarded the systems of German Idealism as degenerate. Completely under Brentano's direction in my beginnings, I developed rather late the conviction which is shared today by so many scholars intent on a strict scientific philosophy, namely that the Idealistic systems, which are basically no different from all the previous philosophies of the era which Descartes inaugurated, must be seen rather as immature and yet of the highest value. Kant and the other German Idealists offer little which is satisfactory and stable for a scientific and rigorous development of the problems which truly motivated them. Yet those who manage to understand and become familiar with the intuitive content of their themes are certain that entirely new and totally radical dimensions of philosophical problems are illuminated in the Idealist systems. Moreover the ultimate and highest goals of philosophy are opened up only when the philosophical method which these peculiar systems require is clarified and developed.

Brentano's preeminent and admirable strength was in logical theory. Yet the extraordinary and far from concluded effect of Brentano's philosophy in the long run rests on his having drawn as an original thinker from original intuitive resources. He thereby conveyed new and vital themes to the German philosophy of the 1870s which had become so unproductive. How long his methods and theories will be preserved is not to be decided here. Brentano's themes in any case have grown differently in other minds than in his, but this is merely new proof of their original vitality. This however was not to his liking, for as I said Brentano was sure of his philosophy. In fact, his confidence in himself was total. His inner certainty of being on the right path and of founding a purely scientific philosophy never wavered. He felt called upon from within and from above to develop his philosophy more precisely inside the systematic and basic doctrines that he considered certain. I would like to stress this pure doubt free conviction of his mission as being plainly the basic fact of Brentano's life. Brentano's personality can neither be understood without this basic fact nor can it be correctly judged.

In this light it is easy to understand that a deeply penetrating teaching activity and even, in a good sense, a school was so important to him; it was important not only for the diffusion of the insights he achieved but also for further work on his thoughts. Brentano was sensitive about any deviation from his fixed convictions. He became spirited in the face of objection to these convictions. He remained rather rigid with the formulations and aporetic foundations which he had measured out long ago. And he claimed victory thanks to his masterful dialectic, which nonetheless was not always convincing when objections were based upon alternative original intuitions. No one surpassed him in educating students to think independently, yet no one took it harder when such thinking was directed against his own entrenched convictions.

The great value that Brentano put on regaining his professorship at the University of Vienna (something I understood very little of at the time) was undoubtedly linked with his conviction of inaugurating a new kind of philosophy. He spoke much of constantly renewed hopes, of promises made to him and never kept. Brentano found it difficult not being able any more to direct doctoral work, not to present such work to the faculty, and even more having to watch passively the inauguration of university lecturers he judged unacceptable. He often spoke bitterly about this. Except for the voluntary limitation of his summer lectures, however, his teaching did not suffer under these conditions. Even afterwards, his influence as before was decisive not only in Vienna but also in all of Austria. Each winter hundreds of first semester law students and students of all faculties used to attend his classically, finely polished lecture course on practical philosophy. After a few weeks, however, the numbers diminished a great deal since the continual amount of work required to keep up was not to everyone's liking. This lecture course always brought more talented young people into Brentano's discussion groups and proved that his efforts were well worthwhile.

Brentano complained much in these years, even in St. Gilgen which was supposed to strengthen them, about his weak nerves.

He always tried to relax from intensive mental effort in other activities which were just as intensive and which he pursued with no less zeal. In the Vienna Chess Club he was considered a particularly clever player—too clever, I was informed, and too often set on pursuing a guiding thought to be able to win very often—and at times he could be totally engrossed in a game. On other occasions he did wood-carvings or some painting and drawing—always passionately engaged. On the trip to St. Gilgen, he would quickly get out his practical, self-carved chess set and then play enthusiastically throughout the whole long trip. In St. Gilgen he participated in the portrait painting which his wife, an able painter, pursued, improving or entirely taking over her pictures in process. Of course she then had to help out and fix up several parts. In 1886 he and his wife did my portrait—"a lovely picture" was the verdict of the sensitive art historian Theodor Vischer. With similar enthusiasm he would play boccia afternoons in St. Gilgen in the "garden," a small piece of land behind the rented cottage near the lake. Hiking in the mountains did not interest him; he liked only moderate walks. In St. Gilgen as well as in Vienna his life style was very simple. It was unnecessary to know him long and observe his habits to see that the rumors about his having married his first wife for her money were ridiculous. Brentano did not like the pleasures of the rich, luxury, good food, and sumptuous living of any kind. He did not smoke and he ate and drank very moderately without any noticeable discrimination at all. I often ate at Brentano's house and I never heard him comment on the food or drink or noticed that he took any particular pleasure at meals. Once when we arrived in St. Gilgen before his wife and had to eat in a rather bad restaurant, Brentano was quite content; he was not even aware of the difference and was completely occupied with his thoughts or with the conversation. He ordered the simplest meals only, just as on the train when he travelled alone he was content with the lowest class. It was the same story with his clothes, which were overly simple and often worn out. In all these respects Brentano was frugal in things that touched his own person, but generous when

he could do a good turn for another. In his personal conduct toward younger people he was both very dignified, and yet exceedingly gracious and kind. He was continually concerned for their scholarly development, but also for their moral well-being. One could only submit oneself entirely to this higher guidance and feel its ennobling power constantly, even when one was far away. Even in his lectures, those who had let themselves be guided by him were affected most deeply, not just at a theoretical level by the subject matter but even more so by the pure ethos of his personality. And how personally he could give of himself! I cannot forget the quiet summer evening walks by the Wolfgangsee when he would often let himself go and speak freely about himself. He had the openness of a child, and in general the childlikeness of genius.

I did not exchange many letters with Brentano. To my letter in which I asked him to accept the dedication of my first philosophical writing, the *Philosophie der Arithmetik,* he replied warmly. He thanked me but earnestly tried to dissuade me from taking the rancor of his enemies on my back. I dedicated the book to him anyway, but received no further response to the sending of the dedicatory copy. Brentano never noticed that I had actually dedicated the book to him until fourteen years later. He then thanked me heartily and generously. Clearly he had either not looked at the book at all or at most he had only, in his way, read it "slantingly." I had too much respect for him of course and understood him too well to be irritated.

Something deeper was at the basis of our failure to exchange more letters. Initially I was his enthusiastic student, and I never ceased to respect him as a teacher. But I could not remain a member of his school. I knew, however, how much it bothered him when someone took another path even though it emanated from his own. In such a case he could easily be unfair, as he was towards me, and that was painful. Anyone who is inwardly driven by unclarified and yet overpowering thoughts or who tries to fulfill intuitions which cannot yet be conceptualized and which do not conform to the standard theories will not gladly open himself to those who remain certain of their own theories, and hardly to a master logician like Brentano. The torment of one's own unclearness is enough, and no new proofs or dialectical refutations are needed of one's logical incapability, which is precisely the driving force for investigative thought. Such proofs and refutations presuppose methods, concepts, and principles which must be suspected and eliminated right away as doubtful, and the misfortune lies precisely in the fact that one can neither clearly refute nor even make anything sufficiently clear to oneself nor exhibit anything definite. This was my case, and this explains if not a personal alienation, at least a certain distance between my teacher and me, a distance which even later on made scientific contact so difficult. I have to concede that it was never a lack on Brentano's part. He repeatedly took the trouble to enter again into scholarly contact. He surely felt that my great respect for him had not diminished in these decades. On the contrary my respect had only grown. As my own development continued I learned precisely to esteem more and more the power and the value of the impulse Brentano had given me.

When I was a university lecturer I visited him once in the summer vacation at Schönbühl on the Danube. Shortly before he had bought the "tavern," which was now being remodelled as a house. I will never forget the situation in which I found him. On arriving at the house I saw a group of bricklayers and among them a haggard, tall man with his shirt open, lime-sprinkled trousers, and slouch hat, using a trowel like the others —an Italian worker, like one used to see in streets and alleys everywhere at the time. It was Brentano. He came up to me in a friendly way, showed me his plans for the remodelling, complained about the incompetence of the foreman and bricklayers which had made it necessary for him to take everything in hand himself and to work along with them. Not long afterwards we were in the midst of a philosophical conversation, he was still wearing this outfit.

I did not see him again until 1908 in Florence in his apartment magnificiently situated on the Via Bellosguardo. I can only think of these days with the greatest emotion. It moved me greatly when, almost blind, he explained from the balcony the incomparable view of Florence and the countryside, or led me and my wife by the most beautiful paths to the two villas Galileo once lived in. I found him really very little changed in his outer appearance. But his hair was gray and his eyes had lost their shine and earlier expression. And yet how much he spoke even now through these eyes, what radiance and divine hope. We talked of course a good deal of philosophy. Even that was painful. He was filled with emotion to be able to speak philosophically once again. Being a teacher for Brentano was a necessity, and yet he had to live alone in Florence in no position to have a personal influence. He would become happy simply when someone from the North came who could listen to and understand him. At that time it seemed to me as though the decades since my student days in Vienna were a faint dream. I felt myself once again a shy beginner over against a towering and more powerful spirit. I preferred to listen rather than to speak. And how great, and beautifully organized, and firmly constructed was his talk. Once however he wanted to listen and without interrupting me with objections he let me report cohesively on the sense of the phenomenological way of investigation and my past struggle against psychologism. But we did not understand each other. Perhaps some of the fault was mine. I was hindered by the inner conviction that, with the rigid structure of his concepts and arguments and in his rigid way of viewing things, Brentano was no longer adaptable enough to be able to understand the necessity which had forced me to transform his basic intuitions.

Not even the smallest discord troubled these beautiful days. His second wife, Emilie, showed us every consideration and friendliness, she who in such a comforting and affectionate way cared for him in his old age and so handsomely adapted herself to the style of his life at that time. He wanted to be with me as much as possible. He felt that my gratitude for what he had been to me through his personality and through the living power of his teaching was inextinguishable. In his old age Brentano had become even more affectionate and mild. I did not find in him the embittered old man on whom his first and second homeland had conferred all too little assistance and had paid for his great gifts with ingratitude. He lived perpetually in the world of his ideas and he lived for the completion of his philosophy which, he said, had developed greatly in the course of the decades. There was a kind of radiance about him, as if he belonged no longer to this world, as if he lived half here and half already in that higher world in which he believed so firmly, and whose philosophical interpretation in theistic theories had occupied him so much even in these later years. This last image I have of him from that time in Florence has impressed itself most profoundly in my spirit. This is the way Brentano lives now always in my memory, an image from a higher world.

Introduction to
Selected Philosophical Correspondence
FREDERICK A. ELLISTON

Husserl's phenomenology serves as the prototype of pure philosophy—a rigorous scientific inquiry totally divorced from the vicissitudes and contingencies of everyday life. In large part this image is the result of his initial penchant for questions about the nature and foundations of logic and mathematics, whose answers led him to a broad critique of psychologism and anthropologism, Dilthey's *Lebensphilosophie* and Heidegger's existential analyses—all in the name of a transcendental philosophy that went beyond the flux of the mundane world. Yet at the same time Husserl was not unaware of the context within which he lived, lectured and wrote—his personal, cultural, and historical situation that became increasingly evident in the themes of his reflections. The quest for quasi-platonic mathematical and logical forms in his *Philosophie der Arithmetik* and *Logical Investigations* led him back to consciousness and its all-pervasive temporal structure. The attempt to avoid all presuppositions culminated in the life-world, only hinted at in the middle of his career when these letters were written but more fully developed later in the *Crisis*. And the growing need for a full explication of his distinctive style of philosophizing forced him to locate it within the western tradition in dialogues with its major thinkers like Plato, Descartes, Hume, and Kant. The following philosophical correspondence clarifies our picture of Husserl as a man at work in his times by shedding some light on his personal life, or at least on some contemporary figures and events prominent within it and on his responses to them.

The first letter, written in 1915, reveals Husserl's view of the most cataclysmic event of his time—World War I. The personal hardships are evident in the departure of his two sons (one of whom, Wolfgang, was later killed in action) as well as his empathy for their suffering and that of their comrades. What registers just as clearly is his feeling of disillusionment, bitterness, and betrayal at America's support of France despite its earlier proclaimed neutrality. These are intermingled with an almost Kierkegaardian sense of loneliness and abandonment: Germany stands isolated and alone. But any self-pity is quickly transformed into a Fichtean national calling. German Idealism, later rejected in his tribute to Euken, is invoked here as a source of consolation and fortitude. Deaths are seen in Hegelian terms as sacrifices on the "slaughter-bench of history," a necessary evil in the service of a divine mission. Heroism is unconditionally praised, at least on one side, as if the soldiers who make history act on a plane beyond ordinary morality. The individual gives way to the spirit of the nation which has become polarized in opposition to them: the enemy that is America too. In Nietzschean tones Husserl calls for an overcoming, a passionate striving and strength of will.

His unyielding and unqualified commitment to nationalism, with no doubts about the justification for so much death and destruction, stands in quixotic contrast to his philosophical demand that everything be called into question in the name of reason and truth. His adopting the commonplace rhetoric about "sacrifice for the fatherland," blind faith that God is on Germany's side, and total identification with his nation's hopes regardless of the political realities— these are the very antitheses of the openness, disinterestedness, and comprehensiveness Husserl sought as a philosopher.

Husserl's tribute to Rudolf Euken, the 1908 recipient of the Nobel prize in literature, serves to locate phenomenology in relation to one of its major contemporary alternatives. Under the influence of Hegelianism, a tradition from which Husserl now quickly disassociates himself, Euken had developed a philosophy of life with several phenomenological motifs: the opposition to the naturalism that Euken regarded as impoverished, falsely limiting human potentialities and providing no guide to the exercise of human freedom; the endorsement of science as a form of cooperation among men whereby nature could be controlled in pursuit of a peaceful society; the commitment to reason as the complement to religion and the basis of science; and the emphasis on temporal processes, the open-ended flux forever beyond the finite grasp of philosophical systems.

Despite these similarities Euken's philosophy of life operates at a different level— that of society, its institutions and cultural forms. Husserl's phenomenology contains nothing comparable to Euken's detailed critique in *Socialism: An Analysis*. His view that philosophy is an infinite task never quite approximates Euken's insistence à la Kierkegaard that philosophical systems can never fully encompass their subject matter. Nor does Husserl's limitation to consciousness, its contents and structures—whether cognitive, volitional or emotive—provide a framework for philosophical inquiry as comprehensive as life.

In a sense Husserl recognizes these differences by calling for a fusion of their two philosophies with phenomenology operating at the more fundamental level of origins. The appearance of the *Crisis* some 20 years later,

with its more detailed analyses of the life-world, could be taken as Husserl's effort to fulfill this call.

Adolf Reinach represents another dimension of phenomenology—its relevance to ethical and legal issues. He was warmly regarded by Husserl as a colleague at Göttingen, partly because he was the only one of his students to join him there but also because of his perseverance, determination, and originality. Though acknowledging Reinach's help in overcoming a Kantian misconception of analyticity, Husserl's eulogy somewhat misleadingly (though understandably) says little of their differences. For Reinach the a priori essences he sought to describe in cognitive judgements and moral decisions had an objective independent status. Husserl, on the other hand, had progressed beyond this Platonic realism reminiscent of his *Logical Investigations* to a transcendental idealism that traces their origin to the constituting activities of consciousness.

Despite this difference, Husserl appreciates Reinach's rejection of the natural law theory of legal essences. Whereas for Augustine an unjust law is no law at all, for Reinach the universal and necessary features of existing laws are independent of the moral norms used to evaluate them.

Husserl's panegyric underscores his personal tolerance for the enterprising work of a younger colleague who diverges sharply from him on a fundamental issue and the philosophical range of the methodology associated with his name that could range from epistemology to penology.

However, this extension requires the fiction of a legal consciousness in terms of which the sense of claim, property, and contract can be explicated. But its artificiality, grouping together so many disparate experiences, may raise doubts that more familiar phenomenological frameworks like perception are likewise abstractions with far less coherence than reputed.

Like Adolf Reinach, George Bernard Shaw struck Husserl as a kindred spirit. They were contemporaries in Schutz's sense, members of the same epoch defined by its paradoxical combination of decline and ascent, its superficial self-indulgence and resolute quest for spiritual rebirth. Husserl recognized the ties that united him with Shaw: the same method of self-reflection, an "I am" uttered with scientific rigor and conviction against all forms of naturalism; the same movement away from the sham of mundane life toward a transcendental idealism that sees the world as shaped by our collective strength or weakness, our selfishness or true freedom; the same perspective that identifies individuals not as isolated entities but as members of social networks that are all embracing and historical in their roots; and the same objective of unmasking the unreality and hypocrisy of the social world by bringing into relief contradictory images or ideas.

Husserl's letter to Arnold Metzger further emphasizes the paradoxical tensions within his life: his unwavering commitment to scientific rigor compared to his unquestioned faith in his divine mission; the methodological precision of phenomenological techniques and the Socratic-like trance in which he wrote; the Cartesian demand for clear and distinct ideas compared to the confusion and incompleteness of the world of action. Though dedicated totally to the problem of knowledge, Husserl acknowledges the greater urgency of more practical social and moral questions. His greatness lies not in his ability to resolve these contradictions, for they shape our human condition, but in his courage to confront them openly.

21

Selected Letters

Letter to Hugo Munsterberg*

. . . You are, of course, well informed about the happenings in Germany during the war. To be sure, no report can replace the personal experience—the tremendous experience of this war. Routine life continues its ordinary course. Seen from without the changes appear really insignificant. Not the least privation is felt. Industrial life has adjusted itself with astonishing rapidity to the war situation. Naturally there is much, far too much, mourning. But how different the way in which it is borne and endured! The feeling that every death means a sacrifice voluntarily offered gives a lofty dignity and raises the individual suffering into a sphere above all individuality. We hardly live any longer as private persons. Everyone experiences concentrated in himself the life of the whole nation, and this gives to every experience its tremendous momentum. All the tense, passionate striving, all the endeavoring, all the sorrowing, all the conquering and all the dying of the soldiers in the field—all enter collectively into the feeling and suffering of every one of us. All the poisonous calumnies, all the pestilent winds of a selfish neutrality, blow against every one of us. We believed at first that we should break down; and yet we have learned to bear it. The confidence too has become concentrated. A magnificent stream of national will to win floods through everyone of us and gives us an undreamt-of strength of will in this terrible national loneliness.

*Published in Hugo Münsterberg, *The Peace and America* (New York: D. Appleton & Co., 1915), pp. 222–24.

To bear and to overcome in ourselves this feeling of national isolation—that was the hardest test. Our splendid soldiers out in the field—my two sons, like all the able-bodied students in Göttingen, are in it too—are resisting the enemy in the mud of the trenches, under unspeakable hardships, no day without being under fire, no night in a bed, the wet clothes never changed, in the midst of ghastly impressions, surrounded by the bodies of the dead; and when they press forward they rush on with ringing song. Truly it is a marvelous heroism; and yet the defiling froth of calumny is dashed upon it. They have gone out to fight this war in the Fichtean spirit as a truly sacred war, and to offer themselves with full hearts as a sacrifice for the fatherland; and now they are pilloried before the world as atrocious barbarians. And America? Our astonishment was beyond measure. We did not expect any help, but understanding and at least justice. America! What an ideal image we had in our souls of the new America. We believed in a new idealism and dreamed of a new world period when the idealism of America would blend with the rejuvenated faith of Germany. The wave of our astonishment has ebbed. We have learned to bear this disappointment too. We no longer speak of it. It is understood that among the shells which the French used and of which originally sixty per cent were failures, now hardly ten per cent do not explode since they are imported from America. It accords with the reports from the front; the list of our dead and maimed is growing. They have to suffer. We say only: America! and remember the beautiful words of President Wilson, words of purest idealism, concerning neutrality. We have become so firm and hardened that we now do not fear even the neutrals—we have never feared the enemy. Hence we hope that we shall be able to carry it through and that God will continue to be with us, as we are so humbly endeavoring to prepare a worthy altar for him in our feelings and our intentions.

Phenomenology and Rudolf Eucken* **

Translated by Frederick Elliston and Theodore Plantinga

There are two possible ways to discover the primordial life that constitutes in itself the experiential world, two ways to penetrate to the essential difference between man in nature and man as mind or spirit (*Geist*), in order to catch sight of the unity of spiritual life increasingly manifest in the course of human history and to trace it back to its primordial sources. Rudolf Eucken has followed the first in his philosophy of spiritual life, and phenomenological philosophy has chosen the second.

Guided by some stimulating ideas in German idealism, Eucken derived the possibility of a new attitude completely opposed to that of naturalism from a comprehensive intuition that knowingly penetrates into the deepest motivations of the great unitary systems, an intuition of the becoming and self-development of the spiritual life of mankind, of the motivating intentions sometimes in harmony and sometimes in conflict, of an intuition of the increases in relative fulfillments, of the restrictions of the ensuing disappointments, of the tensions from unresolved contradictions, and so forth. Instead of regarding human spiritual life as a mere causal appendage to nature, Eucken saw in it the unity of a life-stream sustained by an immanent teleology in which the finality of motivation predominates, not the causality of its nature. In its

*The following lines were dedicated to Rudolf Euken for his seventieth birthday on May 1, 1916.

**Published originally in *Die Tatwelt* 3 (1927): 10–11.

richly meaningful and readily understandable play of superindividual propensities toward movement, the immanent rule of a unified rational power is revealed. Its pressure points are the individualities that develop within this process, with their rational striving and their free rational acts. The inestimable value of Eucken's philosophy of spirit and its animating power rest completely on the fact that he, unlike the proponents of logicistic ontologism, does not spin any metaphysical profundities out of concepts already given. Instead he always draws on life itself, on intuitions guided by history and on the superempirical necessities of motivation he sees in them.

On the other hand, as far as phenomenology is concerned, its origin had nothing to do with German idealism but was determined instead by the motive for a theory of reason that underlies the development of modern philosophy from Descartes to Kant. Phenomenology takes its point of departure in observation through intuition of the fundamental acts of conscious life, together with the objectivities we are aware of in these acts and their changing modes of appearance. Through systematic analysis and description it explores the acts of inner and outer experience, the acts of predicative judgment, and the acts of feeling and willing, investigating the conscious syntheses interwoven with all such acts, especially those of reason. It thereby follows the method of the "phenomenological reduction." It thereby rises to the apprehension of transcendental pure acts and gains the field of the "pure" life of consciousness as a whole. It studies the motivations dominant in this field and uncovers in consciousness the primordial and ultimate sources of all bestowal of meaning, the systematic levels of the phenomenological constitution of all fundamental kinds of objectivities, and so forth. In virtue of this, it believes it can solve all real problems of origins (always by way of a purely intuitive apprehension and never by way of constructing conceptually) and that it can trace all principal concepts back to their origins. Its procedure of intentional analysis and synthesis that starts from below and moves upward must result in reaching the heights at which Eucken's philosophy has operated up to now. Thus Eucken's philosophy and phenomenological philosophy must ultimately fuse into an harmonious agreement.

Phenomenology has its special reasons for bringing wreaths of honor to Rudolf Eucken on this day. Not only does it see in him the brightest exemplar of the noblest practical influences of our time, but in purely scientific respects it also sees in his works spiritual treasures which it gratefully accepts and hopes to utilize in its own subsequent labors.

Adolf Reinach: In Memoriam*

Translated by Frederick Elliston and Theodore Plantinga

Through the early death of *Adolf Reinach,* German philosophy has suffered a heavy loss. His growth was still far from complete when the war broke out, but he joined in as a volunteer, full of excitement, to fulfill his duty to the Fatherland. His first works already testified to the independence and power of his mind as well as the seriousness of his scientific efforts, which could be satisfied only through the most fundamental investigations. Those who were closer to him, who learned in scientific discussions to value his philosophical nature, who observed the scope of his studies and the manysidedness of his interest, might be surprised that he was so slow to publish. How easily he grasped complicated sequences of thoughts that he heard or read, and how quickly he recognized principal difficulties and surveyed the most remote consequences. And what a wealth of brilliant ideas he could draw on quickly whenever he was immersed in thought. But how he held in check these gifts that seemed to point him in the direction of quick and fascinating scholarly productions. He wanted to draw only on the most profound sources and only do work of abiding value. Because of his prudent restraint, he succeeded in this. The writings which he produced after receiving his doc-

*Translated and printed with the permission of Professor Elmar Bund, executor of Husserl's estate. Originally published in *Kantstudien* 23 (1918): 147–49.

torate (the last of which appeared when he was 30 years of age) are not great in number and size, but each of them is rich in concentrated thought-content and worthy of the most thorough study. The first of his writings[1] was composed under the determining influence of Theodore Lipps, from whom he received his initial philosophical education. Yet as a student in Munich he had already become receptive to the influence of the new phenomenology, and joined the group of this significant researcher's highly gifted students who opposed Lipp's psychologism by means of the standpoint of my *Logical Investigations*. Reinach did not follow the changes in thinking through which Lipps went in his writings after 1901 as a result of this opposition, however much he too prized them for their richness in valuable ideas. He was one of the first to understand fully the proper meaning of the new phenomenological method and to be able to survey its philosophical range. The phenomenological way of thinking and investigating soon became second nature to him, and from then on he was never shaken in the conviction bringing him so much joy that he had reached the true mainland of philosophy and was now as investigator surrounded by an endless horizon of possible discoveries that would be decisive for a rigorously scientific philosophy. Thus his Göttingen writings breathe a completely new spirit and at the same time announce his effort to make certain circumscribed problems his own and to make the ultimate basis fruitful through the work he had undertaken.

Only one of Reinach's essays is historical. Its topic is Kant's view of the Humean problem ("Kant's Auffassung des Hume'schen Problem" in the *Zeitschrift für Philosophie und philosophische Kritik*, volume 141, 1908). It deserves the most serious attention. For me, on the one hand, the immersion into the sense of cognition beyond "relations of ideas" and the insight that Kant's interpretation of them as analytic judgments represents a misunderstanding were on the way to pure phenomenology. Reinach, on the other hand, coming to Kant as an accomplished phenomenologist, immediately spotted the Kantian misunderstanding and devoted an instructive investigation to it.

The first of Reinach's systematic-phenomenological works—an essay written in honor of his earlier philosophical teachers—concerned the theory of negative judgments ("Zur Theorie des negativen Urteils"). It dealt in an extraordinarily penetrating way with difficult problems in the general theory of judgment. In this essay Reinach made the original attempt to draw a phenomenological distinction between "conviction" and "assertion," and in connection with this he also enriched the theory of negative judgment by way of a series of phenomenological distinctions. Some very important and—as it appears—little known phenomenological investigations appeared in 1912–13 in the *Zeitschrift für Philosophie und philosophische Kritik* (volumes 148 and 149) under the title "Die Überlegung: Ihre ethische und rechtliche Bedeutung" (Premeditation: Its Ethical and Legal Significance). The purely phenomenological analysis of the essence of theoretical ("intellectual") and practical ("voluntary") deliberation led Reinach in various directions, to fine and important distinctions in the area of intellectual and emotional-practical acts and states. The results were then made useful in ethics and penology. Of the same maturity and sterling quality, finally, is the best known and at the same time most comprehensive of Reinach's works "Über die apriorischen Grundlagen des bürgerlichen Rechts" (On the A Priori Foundations of Civil Law), with which he as coeditor introduced the first volume of my *Jahrbuch für Philosophie und phänomenologische Forschung* (1913)[3]. In contrast to all present and past outlines of a philosophy of law this work represents a completely new kind of attempt, on the basis of pure phenomenology, to realize the long tabooed idea of an a priori theory of law. With incomparable perspicuity Reinach brings to light a great variety of "a priori" truths upon which all actual and conceivable law is grounded. As he shows, they are a priori in exactly the same sense in which primitive arithmetical or logical axioms are a priori— that is, as truths preceding all experience that we can grasp through insight as valid without exception. These a priori principles of law, such as that a claim is terminated when it is fulfilled, or that property passes

from one person to the other when the transfer takes place, express nothing less than "determinations" (voluntary decisions that something ought to be), just as all principles of positive law do. But all such positive legal determinations presuppose such concepts as claim, liability, property, and transferral—concepts, then, that are a priori with regard to positive law. Thus Reinach's a priori principles of law are nothing other than expressions of unconditionally valid truths that are grounded purely in the meaning-content of these truths and accordingly are themselves a priori with regard to positive legal decisions. What is completely original about this work, a masterpiece in every respect, consists in the recognition that this a priori that belongs to the proper essence of all law as such is to be sharply distinguished from another a priori that bears on all law in the manner of evaluative norms: for all law can and must be subordinated to the idea of "just law" (*rechtiges Recht*)—"just" from the standpoint of morality or some kind of objective purposiveness. The unfolding of this idea led to an entirely new a priori discipline that is no more intended as a realization of the fundamentally false ideal of a "natural law" than is Reinach's a priori theory of law. This discipline can establish only formal legal norms from which we can no more derive positive law than we can derive a natural scientific truth about states of affairs from formal logic. No one interested in a rigorously scientific philosophy of law, or in an ultimate clarification of the fundamental concepts constitutive of the idea of a positive law as such (a clarification that will obviously be achieved only through a phenomenological immersion into the pure essence of legal consciousness), can afford to ignore this pioneering work by Reinach. For me it is beyond doubt that it will assure the name of its author a lasting place in the history of philosophy of law.

During the last years before the war Reinach concerned himself with fundamental problems of general ontology, and believed he had gained decisive phenomenological insights especially into the nature of movement. It is to be hoped that valuable parts of his uncompleted writings will be made available to the public. In the war itself he devoted his strength to the Fatherland with unfaltering joy. But his fundamental religious outlook was too deeply affected by the powerful war experiences for him to dare to make any attempt during relatively calmer periods at the front to elaborate his worldview in the form of a philosophy of religion. I heard that he did indeed succeed in reaching a clarity that satisfied him. The enemy bullet struck one at peace with himself and completely at one with himself and God.

Notes to Adolf Reinach

1. On the Concept of Cause in Positive Penology (Munich doctoral dissertation, 1905).
2. Cf. "Munich Philosophical Treatises. Dedicated to Theodore Lipps on his sixtieth birthday by earlier students. Leipzig 1911."
3. In the following I repeat the characterization given in my summary in the *Frankfurter Zeitschrift*, vol. 6, no. 12 (1917).

Shaw and the Vitality of the West* **

Translated by Frederick Elliston and Theodore Plantinga

How could "the decline of the West," this latest theory born of a faint-hearted philosophical skepticism, be a cause of great concern at a time when Shaw's comedies are winning hearts everywhere and implanting the very faith that supports all genuine science and authentic life and that makes all forms of skepticism vanish? *We,* indeed, are the ones in whom the West lives, whether in descent or ascent—it is up to *us.* Has God withdrawn his favor from us? God's power lives and is consumated nowhere else than in us, in our radical will. Where else does He, the living God, work than in our life, in our pure will, in those who are true down to their ultimate roots, in those who seek to do only what we cannot refrain from doing

*This manuscript from the literary remains of Edmund Husserl was made available most cordially by the Husserl-Archives through the mediation of Professor Ludwig Landgrebe of Kiel for a publication dedicated to the memory of Edmund Husserl.
**Published originally in *Hamburger Akademische Rundschau* 3 (1950): 743–44.

without being forced to give up our lives as meaningless?

George Bernard Shaw is not the only one in whom such convictions, transforming our inward will, have taken shape and seek to become a revolutionary force in European civilization. No one can come close to him in the extent and strength of his influence— thanks to his method. In the language of artistic creations, he reacts with passion against the naturalism that kills genuine humanity and all efforts to live on the basis of personal responsibility, as well as against such accompanying phenomena as the art of the aesthetes, the science of the specialists, and the religion of the conventional churches. With unheard-of force, his art breaks through the barriers between the life situation of the viewer and its imaginative forms. In his hands art becomes a power of life itself working toward the social-ethical and religious renewal of life. With the continual repetition of "de te fabula narratur" (the story to be told about you), it strikes home to us not as mere private persons but as members of a social world. No one matches Shaw's ability to arouse our social conscience and instill the belief that no world existing for us simply is, but that any world is what we make or let it become through strength or weakness, through unmitigated selfishness or the power of our true freedom. In a word, Shaw the artist is Europe's most effective preacher at present as well as its most radically critical taskmaster. He is indefatigable in unmasking all mendacity and wellmeant sham, all intellectual and practical prejudices in any conceivable disguise. Yet no one surpasses him in his pure love of humanity before which all hatred melts, and in his genuine truthfulness which does not spare even itself. His art is genuinely philosophical in the universality of his socialpsychological analyses and in its exemplary formulations. It does not become mired in indecisiveness by presenting persons and destinies in isolation, but places them in the concrete unitary context of the entire social culture as their social milieu and releases their universal significance and motivating power.

Shaw's rallying cry in opposition to naturalism is "I am," a phrase which—as a scientific theme—represents an entirely different method for renewing life, one that follows more the way of a genuine science serving life than that of a genuine art serving life. I am referring, of course, to that of "phenomenological philosophy." The field on which it labors lies in solitary regions difficult to reach—namely those of the "mothers" of all knowledge. It aims at the renewal of science based on the most radical self-reflection upon its ultimate sources in life, in the "I live" and the "We live in community." In other words, its basis is a radical self-explication of the life in which science itself arises and arises as a process which serves a genuine life. The task is to develop a science that thoroughly understands and justifies itself by way of the greatest possible advance to freedom from presuppositions, a science that returns to the ultimate conceivable limit of disbelief in order to secure the inviolable, what is necessary in principle to all beliefs, the *rhizōmata pantōn*. And we must show that the only genuine meaning of science is to impart to universal life the clarity of the mind's eye, so that this life understands itself and the meaning of its goals. It can thereby become in practice what George Bernard Shaw longs for and seeks on his part. Hence he and I are comrades in pursuit of the same goal, with the difference that I have the good fortune of being able to refresh myself through his art, to learn something from it and become stronger through it. Thus the philosopher far removed from the world has a right to join in as well as to offer heartfelt thanks.

Edmund Husserl's Letter to Arnold Metzger

Erazim Kohák

Edmund Husserl's letter to Arnold Metzger may be the most important single key to identifying the underlying thrust and significance of Husserl's life's work. In texts intended for publication Husserl generally remains in the background, presenting his thought as a rigorous inquiry, technically radical but existentially neutral. Conventional Husserlian scholarship has, for the most part, perpetuated that image. The passionate outcry of the Prague and Vienna lectures, published posthumously as *The Crisis of European Sciences and Transcendental Phenomenology,* appears, on such a reading, as a marginal outburst occasioned by the stress of the time. Husserl's letter to Metzger suggests a radically different reading: the fundamental impetus of Husserl's work was profoundly existential and moral, an urgent quest for a renewed moral orientation in a time of disintegrating values.

Husserl wrote his letter in the direct aftermath of the First World War, between *Ideas* and *Cartesian Meditations.* It is an intensely personal letter, written to a young man who had lived the full turmoil of his time. Arnold Metzger earned his doctorate on the eve of the war, with a dissertation in phenomenology.[1] In addition to frequent references to Husserl both in the text and the notes, Metzger here acknowledges his indebtedness explicitly:

"The perspective of this work stems mainly from the philosophical investigation of Professor Edmund Husserl of Göttingen. These investigations, more than anything else, helped me formulate the philosophical viewpoint out of which the present work grew, the viewpoint of phenomenology."[2]

Before Metzger's work appeared in print, however, the author had volunteered for military service. He served with distinction both on the western and the eastern front, was taken prisoner and escaped from Siberia, became the chairman of a soldiers' Soviet at Brest Litowsk as the German Army was collapsing—in short, experienced at firsthand the upheaval and collapse of the old world and the paucity of the new. What Metzger sought in phenomenology was not simply a solid epistemological foundation but a clear, fundamental insight into the essential value-structure of being-human.

The manuscript which provoked the present letter reflects that concern. Published in a collection of Metzger's early writings,[3] it bears the title *Die Phänomenologie der Revolution* and the significant subtitle "Eine politische Schrift über den Marxismus und die liebende Gemeinschaft." Metzger is here doing what Husserl, in his letter, explicitly refuses to do as a "pretentious philosophical ostentation," using phenomenology as a perspective for social critique. Yet Husserl encourages him warmly and, in fact, accepted him as his assistant at Freiburg in the following year and for three subsequent years. Though Husserl does not see social critique as a task of pure philosophy, he sees its significance in making such a critique possible. In *Crisis* this becomes evident—yet the letter to Metzger, dated 1919, suggests that the moral impetus underlay Husserl's work from the very start.

However, while Metzger's dissertation shows his high esteem for Husserl and his strong affinity for Husserl's phenomenology, it also suggests reasons for the divergence between the two men of which Husserl speaks in the letter. At the time when Metzger presented his dissertation Husserl's thought was already moving from the descriptive phenomenology of *Logical Investigations* to the transcendental idealism of *Ideas* and the egological concerns of *Cartesian Meditations*. The letter indicates that Husserl had already completed the second volume of *Ideas, Phänomenologische Untersuchungen zur Konstitution,* and was deeply concerned with the vistas opened by the transcendental turn of his inquiries. Metzger, on the other hand, was moving in the opposite direction. Even the title of his dissertation, *The Difference between Phenomenology and Kantianism,* suggests as much. While in Husserl's thought the convergence of Kant and phenomenology, which was to culminate in the rational humanism of *Crisis,* was gradually emerging, Metzger was becoming aware of the divergence and sought to establish the validity of phenomenology at the expense of Kantianism. The phenomenology he defends is that of *Logical Investigations* with a strong existential emphasis; the Kantianism he attacks is uncomfortably close to the transcendental idealism of *Ideas* and *Cartesian Meditations*.

Husserl mentions two Metzger texts in his letter. Both of them reflect Metzger's pressing involvement with the problems of his time. The first is *Die Phänomenologie der Revolution* with its critique of philosophies which become ideologies defending a bankrupt social order and its quest for genuine ideals of humanity which can serve as a basis of a social rebirth. The second text, in

which Husserl expresses interest, was "Der Zusammenbruch," which appeared as an article in *Die Neue Rundschau*[4] in 1919. Both the date and the journal are significant. *Die Neue Rundschau* sought to serve as an open forum and had a tradition of *engagé* social commentary, publishing both literary contributions and articles commenting on contemporary events from a generally socialist and socially responsible perspective. Metzger's article comments on the crisis of German society in the year after the revolution which challenged the entire self-understanding of Bismarck's Germany. Metzger sees in this crisis the result of the alienation of the society from its ideals. In identifying the ideal with the useful, German society had lost sight of authentic ideals. Metzger's concern is to use the clear vision of phenomenology to rediscover the authentic ideals in whose common service humans can rediscover their genuine humanity.

Husserl's comments on the unpublished manuscript could be applied no less to the published article. Here again there is that clear, burning dedication to the ideal which excited Husserl and to which he responded in the letter from the depth of his being. We encounter again that radical rejection of all pettiness, of all inauthentic existence in the grayness of the everyday. Even so, the opposition is one, not of thought and action, but rather of pure theoretical thought and thought practical in a Kantian sense. Metzger is not preoccupied with everyday tasks as much as with *Zielgebung,* setting goals for a desperately disoriented society.

This is the background against which we should read Husserl's letter. Its opening paragraphs are perhaps the most striking. In part it is due to their intensely personal tone, so unlike the tone of scientific rigor which characterizes Husserl's philosophical writings. Even more it is the purity, generosity, and fervor of spirit with which Husserl responds to the call of the ideal in his young colleague's writings. The intense personal dedication which sustained Husserl's pursuit of philosophy as a rigorous science shines through this response to the young visionary whom Husserl greets as a kindred spirit. The emphasis is unmistakable: Husserl here interprets his own work as stemming from a passion for the ideal, for a "way to God," as a truly Socratic philosophizing. As Husserl notes here, Metzger may have sensed more in Husserl's work than a theory and a methodology—its fundamentally moral thrust.

But, as Husserl also points out, personal dedication to his work does not yet imply what in later years came to be called "existential" philosophy. The division of labor of which he speaks may sound conventional, but the point he is making goes deeper than that. Existential philosophy, precisely because it is involved and thus constantly in danger of losing itself in the world, badly needs a rigorous methodological and philosophical foundation. The division which Husserl has in mind is clearly not one between the concerned and the indifferent philosopher. Rather, one of its poles is the concerned philosopher whose realm of endeavor is practical in a Kantian sense, the discerning of goals with which Husserl credits Metzger. The other pole, with which Husserl identifies, is that of the equally urgently concerned philosopher who, however, devoted his labors to providing a solid foundation for the practical philosopher's *Zielgebung*.

This distinction, I think, is the high point of the letter and the point which makes it important for Husserlian scholarship. Husserl presents himself here clearly as a concerned philosopher whose contribution is to provide a rigorous foundation for a socially involved philosophical *Zielgebung*, for moral philosophy in the most basic sense. The intended implications of such fundamental inquiries are thus not merely theoretical but moral. Husserl, just as Metzger in his article in *Die Neue Rundschau*, is keenly aware that the fundamental experiential matrices are more covered than uncovered in traditional philosophy, that humans have become blind to the reality of the depth of experience. Phenomenology thus cannot be merely a superficial observation: its insight must be a radical critique. Husserl explicitly agrees with Metzger's attempt to recognize the covering for what it is and to go beyond it. It is precisely this attempt which led Husserl beyond the purely descriptive phenomenology to a transcendental one and to the radical humanism of his

late works. He clearly recognizes the younger man's commitment as his own and, in the latter part of the letter, attempts to commend his own path to him with all the concern of a man seeking to share his insight with a fellow worker. There is something wistful in the way in which he seeks to convince him that what he himself had seen in transcendental philosophy is precisely the bedrock of the essential structures of being human, on which authentic moral philosophy can be built, and something poignant in his earnest invitation to his younger colleague to visit him and to search and find with him.

Arnold Metzger was to accept that invitation in more than the obvious sense of becoming Husserl's assistant. Fourteen years after the date of the letter, in *Phänomenologie und Metaphysik*, he testifies to Husserl's lasting influence both in his rejection of relativism and in his interpretation of phenomenology. In traditional terms, neither that work nor Metzger's subsequent works, *Freiheit und Tod* and *Sozialismus und Existentialismus*, searching out the ontological foundations of human existence and coexistence, would be considered strictly Husserlian. In a superficial sense they are not. Yet there is the testimony of Husserl's letter to Metzger, reinforcing the impression of Husserl's late work. Perhaps those of Husserl's pupils who used phenomenology in the service of moral concerns are profoundly faithful to Husserl's fundamental commitment. The letter to Arnold Metzger certainly suggests that it is time to reexamine our conventional interpretations.

Notes

1. Arnold Metzger, *Untersuchungen zur Frage der Differenz der Phänomenologie und des Kantianismus* (Jena: A. Kämpfe, 1915).

2. Ibid., p. 54.

3. Arnold Metzger, *Phänomenologie der Revolution: Frühe Schriften* (Frankfurt am Main: Syndikat Verlag, 1979), pp. 15–104.

4. "Der Zusammenbruch," *Die Neue Rundschau*, vol. 30, no. 9 (September 1919): 1069–82.

• • •

To Arnold Metzger*

Translated by Erazim Kohák

Bernau i. Baden
September 4th, 1919

Dear Mr. Metzger:

I have been letting your manuscript work on me in the past week, and have endevoured to submerge myself in your thoughts as much as the lack of quiet in a Schwarzwald inn would permit.

That is a testimony to the power of the response evoked in me by the very first sentences I glanced at, as well as to the power of the ongoing community of thinking along with you as well as by myself into which I have been drawn and in which I am firmly held. This means a lot in view of the condition of my eyes which makes even ordinary reading difficult and reading such faint and indistinct handwriting a torture. I was fortunate that I could also have my daughter read the manuscript to me, and so could witness the impact which your almost harsh, direct truthfulness that defied grim war experience and raised itself to a pure light, has on her young soul.—The tone makes the music, and we have heard—we who have learned to mistrust, we whom many evil experiences have made so sceptical, so sensitive to ourselves and others—have heard a clear tone, yes, truly, a completely pure tone, the tone of genuine dedication to the ideal. And we understood the radical determination to keep life from degenerating into a commercial enterprise viewed in terms of 'Debit' and 'Credit' sides of a ledger in which the debit is never more than a demand on credit. We understood the determination which is radically opposed to all "capitalism" which values possession—and thus its senseless accumulation—above all else, a dedication which corrects even all egotistic per-

*The German text of the letter first appeared in an unauthorized edition in *Philosophisches Jahrbuch der Görres-Gesellschaft,* vol. 62, no. 1 (April 1953): 195–200. Both the text and an English translation appeared subsequently in a version reviewed both by Dr. Gerhart Husserl and Dr. Wilhelm Szilasi in *The Philosophical Forum,* vol. 21, (1963–64): 48–68. The present text and commentary are a revision of that edition. Reprinted with the permission of the publisher and translator.

sonal values, whether honor, fame, or pride—yes, even the pride of reforming insights, goals, and tasks.

I hope we shall always feel joined to one another in the fellowship of the "friends of God" and the "brotherhood of true life." For I, too, can point to such determination as the final fruition of the unfolding of my own, often not easy, life. That you should have sent me your manuscript—especially this manuscript—shows a great faith which anticipates such determination on my part: and for this I should like to thank you sincerely. I can only think that you have sensed some of the sustaining ethos through the laconic sobriety and strict concentration on the matters at hand in my writings. You must have sensed that this ethos is genuine, because my writings, just as yours, are born out of need, out of an immense psychological need, out of a complete collapse in which the only hope is an entirely new life, a desperate, unyielding resolution to begin from the beginning and to go forth in radical honesty, come what may. I cannot claim to have recognized already then, that is, in the closing decade of last century, the inner emptiness of the guiding aims which dominated the entire European culture, or specifically, to have subjected their outstanding example, the rise of the new German empire, to a deeper critique, thereby reorienting my entire personal life as well. I had as yet no eyes for practical and cultural realities, I was unfamiliar with the ways of men and nations. I still lived in an almost exclusive dedication to my theoretical work—even though the decisive influences, which drove me from mathematics to philosophy as my vocation, may lie in overpowering religious experiences and complete transformations. Indeed the powerful effect of the New Testament on a 23-year-old gave rise to an impetus to discover the way to God and to a true life through a rigorous philosophical inquiry. Thanks to Weierstrass and his thoroughgoing mathematics, I was used to an intellectual neatness, but I found that contemporary philosophy, which makes so much of its scientific approach, in fact falls far short of it, and so brings contempt on the ideal of philosophy, which is to be the consummation of all sciences in the most basic sense. Nor was this true only of the philosophy of that day. All philosophy bequeathed to us by history proved a failure: marked everywhere by lack of clarity, immature vagueness, and incompleteness, if not actually intellectual dishonesty. There was nothing one could take from it, no fragment one could retain as a valid beginning of a more earnest inquiry. Criticism, boundless and worthless because it lacked solid foundation from which it could be fruitfully guided, was of no help.

As you can see, my beginnings, my most basic motives and difficulties, the absolute demands which have accrued to me, perhaps I can call it my mission—for as such it in fact presents itself and confronts me within —are other than yours. And yet we have encountered each other, and the theoretical work of my life is carried out also for you, for you who are a man of action by vocation and preference. The theoretical gains which I have achieved, I can say, in a passionate striving for honesty and in most detailed self-criticism, demand a study which you have yet to undertake; then comes the demanding task originally attributed to you, the study of human realities and their philosophical clarification and guidance. That is not my task; I am not called to lead humanity in striving for happy life. I had to acknowledge this in the sorrowful course of the war years: my *daimonion* warned me. I live consciously and by choice purely as a scientific philosopher (I have written no books concerning the war, since I regarded that as a pretentious philosophical ostentation). Not that I consider truth and science the highest values. Quite the contrary, "Intellect is the servant of the will," and so also I am the servant of those who shape our practical life, of the leaders of humanity.—Naturally you will not want to accept this apportioning of functions as valid. You are young, and full of the overflowing consciousness of your strength; you still believe that you can and must attempt both functions. But as long as God preserves you in the Socratic dedication and in the radicalism of truthful life, your *daimonion* will speak to you at the right time. Of course, you can only appropriate what you have earned by your own labour, what you have made profoundly your

own. Both in coming to terms with himself and in reaching forward in thought, a living soul, thinking individually and thus also thinking forward, only appropriates thoughts which have already been thought. But I would like to warn you, at least to be careful. You obviously do not know yet (I have reason for saying this!) how incredibly tangled is the domain of the primordial phenomenological grounds of ideal as well as practical goal-determination. You surely know how little resemblance there is between the realm of "mothers"[1] and the endless empty night where there spin gruesomely old wives animated with metaphysical spectres by a pure postulate phantasy. You are also aware of the worlds of ideas which the light of phenomenology revealed to the discerning eye. Yet so far you are not willing to see the infinite wealth of basic creative processes which I regard as the context in which a godly life, a life which "creates" worlds of objects and worlds of ideas, works itself out. The reason for this is that as an independent thinker you go forth along your own path, already quite confident that you are right, without having understood the constraining motives and pressing intentions which determined my philosophical development since the *Logical Investigations*, and which lead it to new, absolutely indubitable insights. Of course the tragic element in my situation is that I have produced no definitive publication, at first because of the shocks of the war and occasional overwork, but also because of the mass of ever new fundamental problems which, between the desire to strive forward and the need for spiritual self-preservation, press themselves on me overwhelmingly from year to year. Even the work I have already completed, as the second volume of *Ideas*, no longer satisfied me when I saw it clearly in the new light. But when I started to rework it, originally because I was aware of how excessively difficult my very concise presentation made it, the book expanded far beyond its original natural limits. Thus you naturally do not know how far into truth I have gone, and how far into the truth you could be. Naturally I do not mean to suggest by this that I already have a philosophy, a system, thought through from all aspects and ordered as a science—or that I shall ever have it. God forbid! That idea is and remains infinitely removed from my feeble powers. But I speak of an overpowering abundance of problems of an entirely new dimension, into which the *Ideas,* even the already published first volume, open access and for which they forge the foundations, the method, and the rigorous concepts. Thus they adumbrate at the same time a new type of the total world view and of practical goal-determination. All of this reflects the various serious doubts which your work awakened in me. But I find it impossible to express them in writing without producing a long dissertation. How gladly I would show you more closely, if only I could, how very much your splendid ethical radicalism or maximalism (for all genuine philosophy is maximalistic in a good sense) quickened my heart, even while for deep and definite reasons, pondered through several decades, I cannot help doubting and often even definitely rejecting much of what you say. Naturally, this does not apply to the overall orientation you have given to your work by focusing it firmly on ideas, nor to your demand, formal in its universality, for a complete rebirth of mankind in the dignity of true labour, made meaningful by the ideal for which it strives. Nor does it apply to your critical examination of marxism, or naturalism of every form and type, nor to the way you point out how every anthropologism, biologism, and positivism metamorphoses into an anti-ethical egoism, which is ethically without foundation because it is devoid of ideals, and whose social reverse side is capitalism in the broadest sense. Yet I cannot go along with you at all when you bring in rationalism and transcendental philosophy along the same line, and when you appear unaware of the greatness of the themes which remained vague in these traditions, and which emerged into light as definite working problems only in phenomenology. Anyhow, as a matter of fact it seems to me (as has been openly asserted on several occasions with regard to your discussions of history of ideas) that your sense for the spirit of history is not yet fully developed, just as it emerged and grew rather late in my own development. (To me

this suggests that you, too, started out from studies in the natural sciences.) God and God's world, man in search of God, living as a child of God, and so on—all of that will acquire a new and richer meaning for you as soon as you have developed a sensitive eye for history, and—and this is not far removed from it—a sensitive eye for an absolute contemplation of being, as well as for a contemplation of the "world" from the viewpoint of pure subjectivity. Most of all you need to look back to transcendental philosophy, relearn it and grasp it anew. I don't mean to suggest by this that I would like to recommend the maxim, "Back to Kant," which always remained strange to me. The only sense in which you should go back to Kant is quite different from the usual one. You need to become intimate with the major themes which dominated the Kantian struggles, seeing them from the clearly grounded viewpoint of phenomenology as scientific transcendental philosophy which in turn has grown from themes appropriate to it. (The same is true of post-Kantian idealism.) I have learned incomparably more from Hume than from Kant, against whom I felt the deepest antipathy, and who in fact, if judged rightly, did not influence me at all. Yet now I, too, regard him as one of the greats, and rate him high over Hume. But here I am defending my own views, and do not refrain from reproaching you, my spiritual kinsman. You willingly acknowledge how deeply your whole outlook on reality has been affected by my *Logical Investigations.* Why then did you not come to see me in person, to provide an effective and fruitful foundation of a "loving fellowship"? Why have the doubts you had when studying my *Ideas* crystallize so rapidly into a rejection, when you have not even discussed them with me personally? How do you account for the fact that I myself regard the *Logical Investigations,* which you treat as, in the main, a satisfactory termination, as only a passing stage on the way to a higher development, and that I am convinced, as sure as I live, that only in that stage will my true God-given mission come to fruition? I have lived through about a decade of passionate and often desperate work to struggle out the

Logical Investigations. But it took a decade of no less exhausting labour for the *Ideas.* The *Ideas* have grown out of pure inner motivation, a working out of a continuous, unswerveable inner will and growth, just as the *Logical Investigations.* I do not think there has been a development more straight, more certain of its goal, more predetermined, more "daimonic." When I published the *Logical Investigations,* I had only a painfully divided logical consciousness, so much so that those near me had almost to wrest the manuscript from my hands. I felt, though I did not know why, that I had as yet neither the fully clear philosophical foundation nor a pure method, a clear general perspective on the work involved. When, however, I wrote the *Ideas*—in six weeks, without even a rough draft to use as a foundation, as in a trance—read them over, and printed them right away, I humbly thanked God that I had been allowed to write this book, and could do no other than to stand by it, in spite of the many shortcomings of the work in details. And I must go on thanking him that he allows me to visualize ever new horizons of problems in the continuing unfolding of the old yet constantly growing themes, and allows me to open ever new doors. Yet you wrote a doctoral dissertation in which you thought that you could disprove transcendental idealism with all manner of arguments, and, to be sure, more ingenious ones (as I recall) than the admittedly less than renowned literature on the opposite side. The deeper meaning of my work remained foreign to you; you need to search for it anew in an admittedly painstaking study. There is not a sentence in the book which is not the pure expression of what I have truly beheld. If, however, you had really grown into the living spirit of the *Logical Investigations,* how you could, differently than now you do, grow through them into the *Ideas!* In any case, it is a serious matter. I, whose whole life was devoted to learning and practicing clear insight and to put forth its just primordial claim, say: he who, in a laborious accomplishment of intentions, has pushed through to clear insight, is fully certain of that which he beholds in repeating the process of accom-

plishment as the primordial datum and has, to that extent, a "clean conscience." Finally, with respect to method, perspective, and areas of work of the *Ideas,* I can say but a single word, 'See!' I truthfully believe that I can say it, in full awareness of my responsibility. This does not in any way preclude the possibility that much could be improved, that here and there there may be and is something false in the book. It is, I like to say, the pride of transcendental phenomenology and its hallmark as a rigorous science that false propositions can occur in it, statements false in a strict logical sense, which can be shown to be such in the light of and in contradistinction to true propositions. Nebulous lack of clarity is on the opposite of the logically true and false—and that scores against almost all philosophy up to now. Please take this all as well intended, in the spirit of genuine modesty. I speak of phenomenology as a mathematician speaks of mathematics: that it is a genuine science, forged out of clear evidence, a field of possible true and false propositions—he speaks this way in spite of all sceptics and confused philosophers, because he "sees."

But enough. I write you all this because of my great confidence in your honest and clean mind which appealed to me from your manuscript and moved me. That is why I cannot look on when you limit your field of vision and make so much that would inevitably have great significance for your world view and your ethical and political efforts inaccessible to yourself. And I write it because the faith which I must presume that you have in me assures me that you will not take this as if I spoke to you as a self-satisfied professor, in threadbare formulas and lectures, rather than as a perpetual seeker.

I must close, even though I have not been able to speak concerning much that concerned you especially, such as the striking relationship between the new revolutionary movement and phenomenology—I, too, have thought of this relationship repeatedly, but have come to no definite conclusion about it. Nor have I spoken about the denial of all hierarchic ordering among regions of value—which I would not wish to adopt, at least in the way you seem to have in mind. Yet I should be glad to tell you what I think about all this when you will call on me in Freiburg, as I hope you will. I should also like to see the articles in the *Neue Rundschau* to which you refer; perhaps you could send them to me. These few limited days of vacation which I could afford as Dean and which made this long letter to you possible, are now at an end, and I am returning to Freiburg.

My best regards, and wishes that your de-velopment may be such as I would hope that it will be.

Yours
(s) EDMUND HUSSERL

Note

1. The reference is to the "Finstere Galerie" scene, scene 5, act 1 of Goethe's *Faust*, part 2 (lines 1605–54), here used as metaphor for the rich primordial realm of experience which phenomenology uncovers. [Trans.]

Glossary*

Abschattung	aspect, perspective or adumbration: the one-sided view an object presents from any finite perspective.
absolute	the property of being immune to doubt and further phenomenological reduction.
act	any lived experience directed to an object; later restricted to actualized as opposed to habitual experiences.
Adequation	adequacy: property of experiences that present an object so fully that even in principle no improvement of presentation can be conceived; fulfillment of all expectations about an object.
Aktmaterie	matter of act; the object as referred to; for example, the emperor of Germany.
Aktqualität	quality of an act: the manner of referring to the object; for example, seeing, remembering, imagining the emperor of Germany.
Aktualität	actuality: (1) the property an act has of being fully realized; as opposed to potential. (2) the property an act has of not being an abiding disposition but fulfilled in present performance; as opposed to habituality.
analysis, intentional	(1) analysis of experiences into mental processes and their contents. (2) the method for showing how objects are constituted in modes of intentional consciousness.
analysis, real	an analysis which identifies the immanent parts of an act. (The pair "real-intentional" usually modifies "content.")

*With Herbert Spiegelberg's permission this glossary is adapted from his listing in *The Phenomenological Movement* (The Hague: Nijhoff, 1965).

analytic	term applied to formal structures in, for example, logic or mathematics; the usual opposition is "synthetic" or "material" as opposed to "formal."
Animalien	term which includes all animals and human beings.
Anschauung	intuition: the act or process whereby the object becomes fully present to consciousness.
apperception	the apprehension of one thing along with another; co-presentation.
Appräsentation	the process whereby something else is made present through what is immediately or directly given.
anthropologism	any attempt to found philosophical knowledge solely on an empirical study of man.
apodictic	indubitable, certain, beyond all reasonable doubt; applies to statements and experiences.
apophantics	propositional logic as formal inquiry.
appearance	see *Erscheinung*.
a priori	universal: holding throughout a fixed domain and necessary as forming a transcendental condition.
	formal: delineates structural characteristics of objects independent of the material content.
	material: delineates the necessary features of a range of objects.
archaeology	another name for phenomenology, used to connote the sedimented layers of meaning which constitute objects.
attitude	see *Einstellung*.
ausweisen	pointing out or exhibiting; for example, by fulfilling empty intentions.
Bedeutung	significance; namely, of words or statements.
Bewusstsein	consciousness or being conscious:
	(1) intentional act directed to object.
	(2) mental processes formed by continuous series of such acts.
body	see *Körper* and *Leib*.
categorial intuition	see *Anschauung*.
consciousness	see *Bewusstsein*.
cogito	the Cartesian 'I think'; conscious acts of ego which remain after phenomenological reduction; *noesis*.
cogitatum (pl. *cogitata*)	the object of consciousness strictly as it presents itself, *noema*.
constitution	the act of process whereby an object is created as meaningful; the origin of all sense (*Sinn*). See *genesis*.
doxa (adj. doxic)	belief or factors which qualify beliefs.

ego	the identical subject pole of several acts.
egology	study of ego, especially the transcendental ego; phenomenology as egology adopts the first person point of view.
eidos (adj. *eidetic*)	essence.
Einfühlung	empathy: generic term to cover all experiences directed towards others.
Einklammerung	bracketing: from mathematics; absolute numbers are bracketed; for example, [7] has neither positive nor negative value. See *reduction.*
Einstellung	attitude: *natürlich,* natural: everyday attitude which naïvely believes in a real independently existing world. *phänomenologische,* phenomenological: critical reflective standpoint which overcomes naïveté by seeing world as correlate of consciousness.
empathy	see *Einfühlung.*
epoche	abstention: negative moment in phenomenological reduction; abstaining from a stand on validity, value, or existence; sometimes used as synonym for the reduction.
Erfahrung	sensory experience.
Erfüllung	fulfillment: process whereby intentions receive content, and expectations are met.
Erlebnis	lived experience.
Erscheinung	appearance: the way an object presents itself; not opposed to noumenal thing in itself, not an apparition of illusion (*Schein*).
essence	what a thing cannot lack and be what it is; whatness as opposed to thatness (existence). See *Eidos.*
Evidenz	experience which makes evident; self-evidence; process of fulfilling expectations which confirms what or that an object is.
experience	see *Erfahrung* and *Erlebnis.*
Fülle, fullness	intuited concreteness whereby object is completely given.
Fundierung	establishing or founding; one level of consciousness is based on a lower founding level.
Fungieren	functioning or operative mode of consciousness whereby meaning is achieved.
genesis	conscious process whereby an object is constituted or synthesized.

active: through specific acts such as counting or judging, for example, numbers and judgements are constituted.

passive: the sensory process constitutes objects which provide the material for active genesis.

horizon
the context for experience.
inner: other aspects of the one thing.
outer: other objects which could be experienced.
temporal: other experiences within the one stream of consciousness.

Hyle
(hyletic)
stuff: the sensory immanent material of lived experience.

Ich
ego or subject of consciousness.

idealism,
transcendental or
phenomenological
the doctrine that the meaning constitutive of all objects is the production of transcendental consciousness.

ideation
the process that begins with particulars and imaginatively varies their content until invariant essence or *eidos* is obtained.

Idee
something which can be grasped only as the limit of approximations; idea in this Kantian sense.

Identifikationssynthese
synthesis of identification: the process of combining the objects of different intentions into one and the same thing.

immanent
forming an intrinsic component of an experience, as opposed to that which goes beyond it.

intention
the property of an act whereby the act refers to objects.

intentional
adjective applied to both acts and objects.

intentionality
property belonging to consciousness of being directed toward something other than itself.

intersubjectivity
several subjects existing for one another so as to form a community sharing a common objective world.

intuition
see *Anschauung*.

irreal
not belonging to or being a part of the real world; for example, phenomena.

Körper,
body
physical, material thing extended in space and enduring through time.

Lebenswelt
life-world: the surrounding world correlated to immediate experience which serves as the foundation for scientific world.

Leib
animate organism or human body to which a field of sensations belongs.

Leistung
achievement or performance; the productive function of transcendental consciousness in constituting meaning.

Leitfaden, *transcendentale*	transcendental clue; the intentional object is a clue to guide phenomenological inquiry back to transcendental consciousness.
moment	the dependent part of a concrete object reached by abstraction; can exist only in combination with other parts or pieces [*Stücke*].
monad	the totality ego-cogito-cogitatum: the self as subject of consciousness, together with its mental acts or processes, and the objects strictly as they present themselves in these acts to the self.
morphé	the form imposed upon the hyletic data.
natural attitude	see *Einstellung, natürliche.*

noema
    (pl. *noemata*)
    (adj. noematic)
	the strict correlate of a mental act or process; *cogitatum.*

noesis
    (pl. *noeses*)
    (adj. noetic)
	any mental act or process directed to *noema*; *cogito.*

nominalization or substantivization	the conversion of a propositional or complex thought into a noun thought; conversion of an adjective or verb into a noun.
objectivity (adj. objective)	the property of being accessible to everyone: there not just for me but for all.
ontology	study of the general a priori structures of all possible objects or worlds. formal: that part of pure logic which provides a general theory of any object which exists. material or regional: theory of the essence of a region of entities.
originär	original, direct or first-hand; intuition secures the object in the original.
Paarung	pairing: the emergence of two objects in direct association with reciprocal overlapping sense.
phenomenology	eidetic: study of essences and their relations. genetic: study of the genesis of phenomena, the dynamic processes whereby objects are constituted. mundane: study of worldly objects prior to transcendental reduction. transcendental: based on the phenomenological or transcendental reduction.
phenomenon	what is revealed by the phenomenological reduction; the object purified of naïve presuppositions.
psychologism	narrow sense: the attempt to derive principles of formal logic from contingent psychological laws.

	wider sense: an attempt to reduce nonpsychological entities to psychological phenomena.
	transcendental: confusion of pure immanent psychology with transcendental philosophy, based on a misinterpretation of the transcendental reduction.
reduction	eidetic: the act which leads from particulars to universal "pure" essences.
	phenomenological or transcendental: the act by which the general thesis of belief in factual existence characteristic of the natural attitude is inhibited, suspended, bracketed, or turned off, and which uncovers in transcendental subjectivity the acts which constitute pure phenomena.
reflection	the act by which consciousness turns inward toward itself to reverse its usual outward orientation.
region	a field of nonformal or "material" ontology unified by a common essence.
Sinn	meaning, as constituted by transcendental consciousness.
solipsism	the position that I alone exist or am known to exist; the theory that there are no other minds or persons.
subjectivity	the sphere of the subject and his or her consciousness.
teleology	(of consciousness) the purposive structure of consciousness.
theme (adj. thematic)	the focus of the field of consciousness.
thesis (adj. thetic)	the positing of existence implied in beliefs and other acts, absent only from neutral modifications of consciousness.
transcendent	status of an intentional object constituted by intentional acts and lying beyond their immanent constituents.
transcendental	term designating the sphere of consciousness which is not affected by the phenomenological reduction; the transcendent is constituted by transcendental consciousness.
Umwelt, surrounding world	the environment as experienced.
Vergegenwärtigung, presentification	act in which an object not actually present is made intuitively present; for example, imagination or recollection.
Vernunft, reason	consciousness which judges the validity of our claims to knowing reality in the light of evidence.
Welt, world	totality of intentional objects facing consciousness within horizon of other objects.
Wesenschau	apprehension of essence of thing.
Zeitigung, temporalization	constitution of time.

Husserl Bibliography

Abbreviations

AA	*Aut aut* (1959), 345–433.
AF	*Archivio di filosofia*. Rome.
AFSP	*Archiv für systematische Philosophie*. Berlin.
AGP	*Archiv für Geschichte der Philosophie*. Berlin.
AJ	*Ajatus*. Helsinki.
ANALH	*Analecta Husserliana*. Dordrecht.
ANTW	*Algemeen Nederlands Tijdschrift voor Wijsbegeerts*. Assen.
AP	*Archiv für Philosophie*. Stuttgart.
APQ	*American Philosophical Quarterly*. Pittsburgh.
APRIORI	*Apriori and World: European Contributions to Husserlian Phenomenology*. Edited by William McKenna, Robert M. Harlan, and Lawrence E. Winters. The Hague: Nijhoff, 1981.
ARP	*Archives de philosophie*. Paris.
AS	*The Aristotelean Society, Supplementary Volume*. London.
AUS	*Auslegung*. Lawrence, Kansas.
B	*Behaviorism Bijdragen*. Nijmegen.
BC	*Boston College Studies in Philosophy*. Boston.
BILANCIO	*Bilancio della fenomenologia e dell'esistenzialismo*. Relazioni di E. Carin, E. Paci, P. Prini. Padua: Liviana, 1960.
BSFP	*Bulletin de la Société francaise de philosophie*. Paris.
CH	*Cultural Hermeneutics*. Dordrecht.
CHISHOLM	*Realism and the Background of Phenomenology*. Edited by Roderick M. Chisholm. Glencoe: Free Press, 1960.
CIS	*Cahiers internationaux de sociologie*. Paris.
CJP	*Canadian Journal of Philosophy*. Edmonton.
COMPITO	*Il compito della fenomenologia*. Articles by G. Alliney, F. Bianco, S. Breton, C. Fabro, G. Funke, M. De Gandillac, R. Ingarden, R. Lazzarini, A. Plebe, E. Przywara, R. Pucci. Padua: Cedam, 1957.
CR	*Critique*. Paris.
D	*Dialogue*. Ottawa; Vancouver.
DG	*Diogenes*. Paris.
DH	*Dialectics and Humanism*. Warsaw.

DJ   *Dialogue*. Journal of Phi Sigma Tau. Milwaukee.

DN   *Dianoia*. Mexico.

EH   *Edmund Husserl: 1859–1959. Recueil commemoratif publie a l'oc-
                      casion du centenaire de la naissance du philosophe.* The Hague:
                      Nijhoff, 1959.

EHC   *Centenaire de Bergson et de Husserl. ARP* 22 (1959): 5–55.

EHG   *Gedenkfeier für den Philosophen E. Husserl. Universitas* 14 (1959):
                      993.

EHI   *Il verri* 4 (1960): 157.

EHR   *Edmund Husserl. RPF* 84 (1959): 433–576.

EHS   *Symposium on the 100th Anniversary of the Birth of Edmund Hus-
                      serl. PPR* 1959–60: 147–274.

EHSS   (E. Husserl). *Symposium sobre la nocion husserliana de la 'Lebens-
                      welt.* By Jose Gaos, Ludwig Landgrebe, Enzo Paci, John Wild.
                      Mexico: Centre de Estudios Filosoficos, 1963.

EHZ   (E. Husserl). *ZPF.* Meisenheim/Glan: Hain, 1959.

ELV   *The Phenomenology of Husserl: Selected Critical Readings.* Edited
                      by R.O. Elveton. Chicago: Quadrangle Books, 1970.

EP   *Les etudes philosophiques.* Paris.

ESSAYS   *Essays in Phenomenology.* Edited by M. Natanson. The Hague:
                      Nijhoff, 1966.

EXPLORATIONS   *Explorations in Phenomenology: Papers of the Society for Phenom-
                      enology and Existential Philosophy.* Edited by David Carr and
                      Edward S. Casey. The Hague: Nijhoff, 1973.

F   *Filosofia.* Lisbon.

FEN   *La Fenomenologia.* Atti del'XI Convegno del centro di studi filoso-
                      fici tra professori universitari. Brescia: Morcelliana, 1956.

FS   *Franciscan Studies.* St. Bonaventure, N.Y.

FZ   *Freiburger Zeitschrift für Philosophie und Theologie.* Freiburg.

GC   *Giornale critico della filosofia italiana.* Genoa; Turin.

GM   *Giornale di metafisica.*

HAR   *Hamburger akademische Rundschau.* Hamburg.

HC   *Human Context.* Brighton, England.

HEA   *Husserl: Expositions and Appraisals.* Edited by Frederick Elliston
                      and Peter McCormick. Notre Dame: University of Notre Dame
                      Press, 1977.

HJ   *Heythrop Journal.* Oxford.

HPM   *Husserl et la pensée moderne. Husserl und das Denken der Neu-
                      zeit.* Actes du deuxieme Colloque international de phenome-
                      nologie, Krefeld, 1–3 novembre 1956, edites par les seins de II.
                      L. Van Breda et J. Taminiaux. Akten des zweiten internation-
                      alen phänomenologischen Kolloquiums, Krefeld, 1–3 Novem-
                      ber 1956, edited by H.L. Van Breda und Jacques Taminiaux.
                      The Hague: Nijhoff, 1959.

HS   *Human Studies.* Norwood, N.J.

HSW   *Husserl: Shorter Works.* Edited by Peter McCormick and Frederick
                      Elliston. Notre Dame: University of Notre Dame Press, 1981.

HUSSERL   *Husserl.* Cahiers de Royaumont. Troisieme Colloque philoso-
                      phique de Royaumont, 23 au 30 avril 1957. L'oeuvre et la pensée
                      de Husserl. Paris: Les Editions de Minuit, 1959.

ID	*Der Idealismus und Seine Gegenwart.* Edited by Ute Guzzon, Bernhard Rang, and Ludwig Siep. Hamburg: Felix Meiner, 1976.
IJLP	*International Journal of Language and Philosophy.*
ILR	*International Logic Review.* Bologna.
INGARDEN	*For Roman Ingarden: Nine Essays in Phenomenology and Literature, Philosophy and the Social Sciences.* The Hague: Nijhoff, 1959.
INPQ	*Indian Philosophical Quarterly.* Poona, India.
INQ	*Inquiry.* Oslo.
INVITATION	*An Invitation to Phenomenology.* Edited by James M. Edie. Chicago: Quadrangle Books, 1965.
IPQ	*International Philosophical Quarterly.* New York.
IS	*Idealistic Studies.* Worcester, Massachusetts.
JBSP	*The Journal of the British Society for Phenomenology.* Manchester.
JCA	*Journal of Critical Analysis.* Jersey City.
JCP	*Journal of Chinese Philosophy.* Hawaii.
JE	*Journal of Existentialism.* New York.
JHP	*Journal of the History of Philosophy.* Claremont, CA.
JP	*The Journal of Philosophy.* New York.
JPP	*Journal of Phenomenological Psychology.* Pittsburgh, PA.
K	*Kantstudien.* Bonn.
KN	*Kinesis.* Carbondale, IL.
LEE	*Phenomenology and Existentialism.* Edited by Edward Lee and Maurice Mandelbaum. Baltimore: Johns Hopkins University Press, 1967.
LIFE-WORLD	*Life-World and Consciousness: Essays for Aron Gurwitsch.* Edited by Lester E. Embree. Evanston: Northwestern University Press, 1972.
LTP	*Laval theologique et philosophique.* Quebec.
M	*Mind.* Oxford.
MJP	*Midwestern Journal of Philosophy.* Murray, Kentucky.
MO	*The Monist.* La Salle.
MOHANTY	*Readings on Husserl's "Logical Investigations."* Edited by J. N. Mohanty. The Hague: Nijhoff, 1977.
MS	*The Modern Schoolman.* Saint Louis.
MT	*Metaphilosophy.* Albany.
MÜN PHÄN	*Die Münchner Phänomenologie.* Edited by H. Kuhn, Eberhard Are-Lallemant, and Reinhold Gladiator. The Hague: Nijhoff, 1975.
MW	*Man and World.* The Hague.
NDJ	*Notre Dame Journal of Formal Logic.* Notre Dame.
NEP	*New Essays in Phenomenology.* Edited by James M. Edie. Chicago: Quadrangle Books, 1969.
NH	*Neue Hefte Philosophie.*
NO	*Noûs.* Bloomington, Indiana.
NOACK	*Husserl.* Edited by H. Noack (Wege von Forschung 10). Darmstadt: Wissenschaftliche Buchgesellschaft, 1973.
NS	*The New Scholasticism.* Washington, D.C.
OMAGGIO	*Omaggio a Husserl.* Saggi di Antonio Banfi, Enrico Filippini, Giorgio Guzzoni, Leo Lugarini, Enzo Melandri, Guido D. Neri, Enzo

Paci, Guido Pedroni, Raffaele Pucci, Giuseppe Semarari, Sofia Vanni-Rovighi. A cura di Enzo Paci. Milan: Il Saggiatore, 1960.

P *Pensiero*. Rome.

PATTERNS *Patterns of the Life-World: Essays in Honor of John Wild.* Edited by James M. Edie, Francis H. Parker, and Calvin O. Schrag. Evanston: Northwestern University Press, 1970.

PC *Proceedings of the Catholic Philosophical Association.* Washington.

PE *The Personalist.* Los Angeles.

PERSPECTIVE *Phenomenology in Perspective.* Edited by F. Joseph Smith. The Hague: Nijhoff, 1970.

PEW *Philosophy East and West.* Honolulu.

PF *Philosophische Forschung.*

PFB *Philosophical Forum.* Boston.

PHA *Phenomenology in America.* Edited by James M. Edie. Chicago: Quadrangle Books, 1967.

PHÄN H *Phänomenologische Heute.* Edited by E. W. Orth. Freiburg: Verlag Karl Alber, 1975.

PHCC *Phenomenology: Continuation and Criticism: Essays in Memory of Dorion Cairns.* Edited by Fred Kersten and Richard Zaner. The Hague: Nijhoff, 1973.

PHEX *Phénoménologie-Existence.* Recueil d'études par Henri Binault, H. L. Van Breda, Aron Gurwitsch, Emmanuel Levinas, Paul Ricoeur, Jean Wahl. Paris: Armand Colin, 1953.

PHIL ESSAYS *Philosophical Essays in Memory of Edmund Husserl.* Edited by Marvin Farber. Cambridge, MA: Harvard University Press, 1940.

PHNE *Phenomenology and Natural Existence: Essays in Honor of Marvin Farber.* Edited by Dale Riepe. Albany: State University of New York Press, 1973.

PHNS *Phenomenology and the Natural Sciences.* Edited by Joseph J. Kockelmans and Theodore Kisiel. Evanston: Northwestern University Press, 1970.

PHPA *Phenomenology: Pure and Applied.* The first Lexington Conference. Edited by Erwin W. Straus. Pittsburgh: Duquesne University Press, 1964.

PHSR *Phenomenology and Social Reality: Essays in Memory of Alfred Schutz.* Edited by Maurice Natanson. The Hague: Nijhoff, 1971.

PJ *Philosophisches Jahrbuch.* Munich.

PL *Philosophie et logique.* Bucharest, Romania.

PM *Philosophia mathematica.* Hauppage, N.Y.

PN *Philosophia naturalis.* Meisenheim/Glan.

PP *Phenomenological Perspectives.* Edited by Philip J. Bossert. The Hague: Nijhoff, 1975.

PPE *Proceedings in the Philosophy of Education.* Society of Australia. Kensington, Australia.

PPEH *Phenomenology: The Philosophy of Edmund Husserl and Its Interpretation.* Edited by Joseph J. Kockelmans. New York: Doubleday, 1967.

PPR *Philosophy and Phenomenological Research.* Buffalo.

PPU *Phenomenology and Philosophical Understanding.* Edited by Edo. Pivčević. New York: Cambridge University Press, 1975.

PQA	*Philosophical Quarterly.* Asualner, India.
PR	*Philosophische Rundschau.* Heidelberg.
PRC	*The Philosophical Review.* Cornell.
PROBLÈMES	*Problèmes actuels de la phénoménologie.* Textes de P. Thévenaz, H.J. Pos, P. Ricoeur, E. Fink, M. Merleau-Ponty, J. Wahl. Edités par H.L. Van Breda. Actes du Colloque international de phénoménologie. Paris: Desclée, 1952.
PRS	*Process Studies.* Claremont, California.
PS	*Philosophical Studies.* Dordrecht.
PSM	*Pensamiento.* Madrid.
PSP	*Philosophische Perspectiven.* Frayenlobstr, West Germany. (Superseded by *Perspektiven der Philosophie.*)
PST	*Philosophical Studies.* Ireland.
PT	*Philosophy Today.* Celina.
PTPF	*Perspectiven Transcendental Phänomenologische Forschung.* Utrecht: Patmos, 1972.
PY	*Philosophy.* London, England.
RA	*Ratio.* Oxford, England.
RBF	*Revista brasileim de filosofia.* São Paulo.
RE	*Revue d'esthetique.* Paris.
READINGS	*Readings in Existential Phenomenology.* Edited by Nathaniel Lawrence and Daniel O'Connor. Englewood Cliffs: Prentice-Hall, 1967.
REPP	*Review of Existential Psychology and Psychiatry.* New York.
REX	*Review of Existential Psychology and Psychiatry.*
RFN	*Rivista di filosofia neo-scholastica.* Milan.
RFS	*Revista de filosofia.* Madrid.
RIP	*Revue internationale de philosophie.* Paris.
RM	*Review of Metaphysics.* Washington.
RMM	*Revue de metaphysique et de morale.* Paris.
RP	*Rassegna di scienze filosofiche.* Naples.
RPF	*Revue philosophique de la France et de l'etranger.* Paris.
RPH	*Research in Phenomenology.* Pittsburgh.
RPL	*Revue philosophique de Louvain.* Louvain.
RPOR	*Revista Portuguesa de filosofia.* Braga.
RS	*Revue des sciences philosophiques et théologiques.* Paris.
RT	*Revue Thomiste.* Toulouse; Cedex.
RTP	*Revue de theologie et de philosophie.* Lausanne.
RUO	*Revue de l'Universite d'Ottawa.* Ottawa.
S	*Scientia.* Milan.
SE	*Sciences ecclesiastiques.*
SG	*Studium generale.* Berlin.
SH	*Scripta Hierosolynutana.* Jerusalem.
SJ	*Salzburger Jahrbuch für Philosophie.* Salzburg.
SJP	*Southern Journal of Philosophy.* Memphis.
SOLOMON	*Phenomenology and Existentialism.* Edited by Robert C. Solomon. New York: Harper and Row, 1972.
SPS	*Studia philosophica Basel.* Switzerland.
SR	*Social Research.* New York.
SSP	*Soviet Studies in Philosophy.*

SST	*Studies in Soviet Thought*. Dordrecht.
SWJP	*Southwestern Journal of Philosophy*. Norman.
SZ	*Sapienza*. Rome.
T	*Telos*. St. Louis.
TELEOLOGIES	*The Teleologies in Husserlian Phenomenology*. Analecta Husserlian, vol. 9. Edited by Anna-Teresa Tymieniecka. Dordrecht: Reidel, 1972.
TEMPO	*Tempo e intenzionalità*. Husserliana. Scritti di E. Husserl, E. Paci, P. Caruso, E. Renzi, F. Bosio, V. Fagone, G. Piana, W. Biemel, L. Lugarini, A. Plebe, F. Bianco, J. Wyrsch. Padua: Cedam, 1960.
TF	*Tijdschrift voor Filosofie*. Leuven.
TH	*Theoria*. Lund.
TPS	*Transactions of the Charles S. Peirce Society*. South Hadley, MA.
TSP	*Tulane Studies in Philosophy*. Tulane.
TT	*Thought*. New York.
TVP	*Tijdschrift voor Filosofie*. Leuven.
VFWP	*Vierteljahrschrift für wissenschaftliche Philosophie*. Leipzig.
VV	*Vérité et vérification*. Edited by Hermann L. Van Breda. The Hague: Nijhoff, 1974.
WANN	*Behaviourism and Phenomenology*. Edited by T.W. Wann. Chicago: University of Chicago Press, 1964.
WELT MEN	*Die Welt des Menschen*. Festschrift für Jan Patočka. Edited by Walter Biemel and the Husserl Archives at Louvain. Phänomenologica 72. The Hague: Nijhoff, 1976.
WILD	*The Return to Reason*. Edited by John Wild. Chicago: Henry Regnery, 1953.
ZPF	*Zeitschrift für Philosophische Forschung*. Postfach, West Germany: Meisenheim/Glan.
ZPPS	*Zeitschrift für Psychologie der Sinnesorgane*. Leipzig.
ZRG	*Zeitschrift für Religions und Geistesgeschichte*. Leiden.

Husserl's Works and English Translations
in Chronological Order

"Beiträge zur Variationsrechnung." Dissertation. Vienna, 1882.

Über den Begriff der Zahl. Habilitationsschrift. Halle Heynemann'sche Buchdruckerei (F. Beyer), 1887. English translation by D. Willard: "On the Concept of Number." *PM* 10 (1972): 44–52; 11 (1973) 37–87; and in *HSW*, pp. 92–119.

Philosophie der Arithmetik. Vol. 1. Halle: C.E.M. Pfeffer (Robert Stricker), 1891.

"Notice of *Philosophie der Arithmetik.*" *VFWP* 15 (1891): 360–61.

"Der Folgerungscalcul und die Inhaltslogik." *VFWP* 15 (1891): 168–89. English translation: "The Deductive Calculus and Intensional Logic." *PE* 60 (1979): 7–25.

"Der Folgerungscalcul und die Inhaltslogik." *VFWP* 15 (1891): 351–56.

"Review of Schröder: *Vorlesungen über die Algebra der Logik.*" *GGA* (1891): 243–78. English translation: "A Review of Volume I of Ernst Schröder's *Vorlesungen über die Algebra der Logik.*" *PE* 59 (1978): 115–43.

"A Voigt's 'elementare Logik' und meine Darlegungen zur Logik des logischen Calculs." *VFWP* 17 (1893): 111–20. English translation: "Remarks on A. Voigt's 'Elementary Logic' in Relation to My Statements on the Logic of the Logical Calculus." *PE* 60 (1979): 26–35.

"Antwort auf die vorstehende 'Erwiderung' des Herrn Voigt." *VFWP* 17 (1893): 508–11.

"Psychologische Studien zur elementaren Logik." *PM* 30 (1894): 159–91. English translation by P. McCormick and R. Hudson: "Psychological Studies for Elementary Logic." In *HSW*, pp. 126–42.

"Bericht über deutsche Schriften zur Logik aus dem Jahre 1894." *AFSP* 3 (1897): 216–44.

Logische Untersuchungen: Prolegomena zur reinen Logik. Halle: Max Niemeyer, 1900.

"Notice of *Logische Untersuchungen: Prolegomena zur reinen Logik.*" *VFWP* 24 (1900): 511–12.

Logische Untersuchungen: Untersuchungen zur Phänomenologie und Theorie der Erkenntnis. Halle: Max Niemeyer, 1901.

"Notice of *Logische Untersuchungen: Untersuchungen zur Phänomenologie und Theorie der Erkenntnis.*" *VFWP* 25 (1901): 260–63.

"Melchior Palàgyi's *Der Streit der Psychologisten und Formalisten in der modernen Logik.*" *ZPPS* 31 (1903): 287–94. English translation by D. Willard: "A Reply to a Critic of My Refutation of Logical Psychologism." *PE* 53 (1972): 5–13; and in *HSW*, pp. 152–58.

"Bericht über deutsche Schriften zur Logik in den Jahren 1895–1899." *AFSP* 9 (1903): 113–32, 237–59, 393–408, 523–43; 10 (1904): 101–25.

[Notes on] "'Faculté', 'Fait', 'Fantaisie'" in A. Lalande, *Vocabulaire philosophique*, fascicule no. 9, F et G, in *BSFP* 6 (1906): 293, 296, 299.

[Notes on] "'Individu' and 'Intention'" in A. Lalande, *Vocabulaire philosophique*, fascicule no. 12, in *BSFP* 9 (1909): 235, 263.

[Review of] "Anton Marty's *Untersuchungen zur Grundlegung der allgemeinen Grammatik und Sprachphilosophie.*" *DL* 31 (1910): 1106–10.

"Philosophie als strenge Wissenschaft." *Logos* 1 (1910–11): 289–341. English translation by Q. Lauer:

"Philosophy as Rigorous Science." In *Phenomenology and the Crisis of Philosophy*, pp. 71–147; and in *HSW*, pp. 166–97.

Logische Untersuchungen. Vols. 1 and 2. 2nd ed. Halle: Max Niemeyer, 1913. English translation by J. Findlay: *Logical Investigations*, 2 vols. London: Routledge and Kegan Paul, 1970.

Jahrbuch für Philosophie und phänomenologische Forschung. Edited by E. Husserl *et al.* 11 vols. Halle: Max Niemeyer, 1913–30.

"Vorwort. *Jahrbuch für Philosophie und phänomenologische Forschung*." In *Jahrbuch*, vol. 1 (1913), pp. v–vi.

"Ideen zu einer reinen Phänomenologie und phänomenologischen Philosophie." In *Jahrbuch*, vol. 1 (1913), pp. 1–323. English translation by Boyce Gibson in: *Ideas*. London: Routledge and Kegan Paul, 1931; and in *HSW*, pp. 43–53.

[Contribution to Discussion of] "Maier's 'Philosophie und Psychologie.'" In *Bericht über den VI. Kongress für experimentelle Psychologie vom 15. bis 18. April 1914*. Zweiter Teil. Edited by Schumann, pp. 144–45. Leipzig: J.A. Barth, 1914.

"Letter to Hugo Münsterberg." In Hugo Münsterberg, *The Peace and America*, pp. 222–24. New York: Appleton, 1915.

"Vorwort." In *Jahrbuch*, vol. 2 (1916), pp. v–vi.

"Adolf Reinach." *Frankfurter Zeitung*, December 6, 1917.

"Adolf Reinach: Ein Nachruf." *K* 23 (1918): 147–49.

"Erinnerungen an Franz Brentano." In Kraus, *Franz Brentano: Zur Kenntnis seines Lebens und seiner Lehre*, pp. 153–67. Munich: C.H. Beck, 1919. English translation by P. McCormick and R. Hudson: "Recollections of Franz Brentano." In *HSW*, pp. 342–48.

Logische Untersuchungen. Vol. 2, part two. 2nd ed. Halle: Max Niemeyer, 1921.

"Vorwort." In *Jahrbuch*, vol. 4 (1921), p. v.

Logische Untersuchungen. Vols. 1; 2: part one; 2: part two. 3rd ed. Halle: Max Niemeyer, 1922.

Ideen zu einer reinen Phänomenologie und phänomenologischen Philosophie. Vol. 1. Halle: Max Niemeyer, 1922.

"Die Idee einer philosophischen Kultur: Ihr erstes Aufkeimen in der griechen Philosophie." *Japanisch-deutsche Zeitschrift für Wissenschaft und Technik* (Lübeck) 1 (1923): 45–51.

"Erneuerung: Ihr Problem und ihre Methode." *The Kaizo* (Tokyo) 3 (1923): 84–92. English translation by Jeffner Allen: "Renewal: Its Problem and Method." In *HSW*, pp. 326–31.

"Die Phänomenologie und Rudolf Eucken." *Die Tatwelt* (Jena) 3 (1927): 10–11.

Logische Untersuchungen. Vols. 1; 2: part one. 4th ed. Halle: Max Niemeyer, 1928.

Ideen zu einer reinen Phänomenologie und phänomenologischen Philosophie. 3rd ed. Halle: Max Niemeyer, 1928.

"Vorlesungen zur Phänomenologie des inneren Zeitbewusstseins." Edited by Martin Heidegger. In *Jahrbuch*, vol. 9 (1928), pp. 367–498. English translation by J. S. Churchill: *Lectures on Internal Time-Consciousness*. Bloomington: Indiana University Press, 1964.

"Formale und transzendentale Logik: Versuch einer Kritik der logischen Vernunft." In *Jahrbuch*, vol. 10 (1929), pp. 1–298. English translation by Dorion Cairns: *Formal and Transcendental Logic*. The Hague: Nijhoff, 1969.

"Phenomenology." Translated by R. Palmer. In *The Encyclopaedia Britannica*, 14th ed., vol. 17 (1929), pp. 699–702; in *JBSP* 2 (1971): 77–90; and in *HSW*, pp. 21–35.

"Nachwort zu meinen *Ideen zu einer reinen Phänomenologie und phänomenologischen Philosophie*." In *Jahrbuch*, vol. 2 (1930), pp. 549–70. English translation by Boyce Gibson: "Author's Preface to the English Edition." In *Ideas* and in *HSW*, pp. 43–53.

Méditations cartésiennes. Translated by G. Peiffer and E. Levinas. Paris: Colin, 1931.

"Vorwort to 'Die phänomenologische Philosophie Edmund Husserls in der gegenwärtigen Kritik'." *K* 38 (1933): 319–20.

"Lettre: An den Präsidenten des VIII. internationalen Philosophen-Kongresses." In *Actes du huitième Congrès international de Philosophie à Prague 2–7 septembre 1934*, pp. xli–xlv. Prague, 1936.

"Die Krisis der europäischen Wissenschaften und die transzendentale Phänomenologie: Eine Einleitung in die phänomenologische Philosophie." *Philosophia* (Belgrad) 1 (1936): 77–176.

Erfahrung und Urteil: Untersuchungen zur Genealogie der Logik. Edited by Ludwig Landgrebe. Prague: Academia, 1939. English translation by James S. Churchill and Karl Ameriks: *Experience and Judgment*. Evanston: Northwestern University Press, 1973.

"Die Frage nach dem Ursprung der Geometrie als intentional-historisches Problem." *RIP* 1 (1939): 203–25. English translation by David Carr: "The Origin of Geometry." In *The Crisis of Euro-*

pean Sciences and Transcendental Philosophy, pp. 353–79. Evanston: Northwestern University Press, 1970; and in *HSW*, pp. 255–70.

"Entwurf einer 'Vorrede' zu den *Logischen Untersuchungen.*" *TVP* 1 (1939): 106–33; 319–39.

"Grundlegende Untersuchungen zum phänomenologischen Ursprung der Räumlichkeit der Natur." In *PHIL ESSAYS*, pp. 307–25. English translation by Fred Kersten: "Foundational Investigations of the Phenomenological Origin of the Spatiality of Nature." In *HSW*, pp. 222–33.

"Letter to Marvin Farber." In Marvin Farber, "Edmund Husserl and the Background of His Philosophy." *PPR* 1 (1940): 13.

"Notizen zur Raumkonstitution." Edited by Alfred Schutz. *PPR* 1 (1940): 21–37, 217–26.

"Phänomenologie und Anthropologie." *PPR* 2 (1941): 1–14. English translation by R. Schmitt: "Phenomenology and Anthropology." In *CHISHOLM*, pp. 129–42; and in *HSW*, 315–23.

"Phänomenologie und Psychologie." *TVP* 3 (1941): 481–98.

"Die Welt der lebendigen Gegenwart und die Konstitution der ausserleiblichen Umwelt." *PPR* 6 (1945): 323–43. English translation by Lenore Langsdorf: "The World of the Living Present." In *HSW*, pp. 238–50.

"Rapport entre la Phénoménologie et les sciences." *EP* 4 (1949): 3–7.

Cartesianische Meditationen und Pariser Vorträge. Husserliana, vol. 1. Edited by Stephan Strasser. The Hague: Nijhoff, 1950. English translation by Dorion Cairns: *Cartesian Meditations*. The Hague: Nijhoff, 1960. English translation by Peter Koestenbaum: *The Paris Lectures*. The Hague: Nijhoff, 1967.

Die Idee der Phänomenologie: Fünf Vorlesungen. Husserliana, vol. 2. Edited by Walter Biemel. The Hague: Nijhoff, 1950. English translation by Walter P. Alston and George Nakhnikian: *The Idea of Phenomenology*. The Hague, Nijhoff: 1964.

Ideen zu einer reinen Phänomenologie und phänomenologischen Philosophie: Erstes Buch: Allgemeine Einführung in die reine Phänomenologie. Husserliana, vol. 3. Edited by Walter Biemel. The Hague: Nijhoff, 1950.

"Shaw und die Lebenskraft des Abendlandes." *HAR* 3 (1950): 743–44.

"Persönliche Aufzeichnungen vom 25. September 1906." *PS* (Berlin) 2 (1951): 306–12.

Ideen zu einer reinen Phänomenologie und phänomenologischen Philosophie. Zweites Buch: Phänomenologische Untersuchungen zur Konstitution. Husserliana, vol. 4. Edited by Marly Biemel. The Hague: Nijhoff, 1952.

Ideen zu einer reinen Phänomenologie und phänomenologischen Philosophie. Drittes Buch: Die Phänomenologie und die Fundamente der Wissenschaften. Husserliana, vol. 5. Edited by Marly Biemel. The Hague: Nijhoff, 1952. English translation by Ted E. Klein and William E. Pohl: *Phenomenology and the Foundations of the Sciences*. The Hague: Nijhoff, 1980.

"Das bewusstlose Ich—Schlaf—Ohnmacht." *TVP* 14 (1952): 261–63.

"Ein Brief Edmund Husserls von 1919." *PJ* 62 (1953): 195–200.

Die Krisis der europäischen Wissenschaften und die transzendentale Phänomenologie: Eine Einleitung in die phänomenologische Philosophie. Husserliana, vol. 6. Edited by Walter Biemel. The Hague: Nijhoff, 1954. English translation by D. Carr: *The Crisis of European Sciences and Transcendental Philosophy*. Evanston: Northwestern University Press, 1970.

Erste Philosophie (1923/24). Erster Teil: Kritische Ideengeschichte. Husserliana. vol. 7. Edited by Rudolf Boehm. The Hague: Nijhoff, 1956. English translation by Jeffner Allen: *First Philosophy*. The Hague: Nijhoff, 1978.

"Drei Briefe an Georg Misch." In Alwin Diemer, *Edmund Husserl: Versuch einer systematischen Darstellung seiner Phänomenologie*, pp. 393–94. Meisenheim am Glan: Anton Hain, 1956.

"Correspondencia entre Delthey y Husserl." *Revista de filosofia de la Universidad de Costa Rica* (San José de Costa Rica) 1 (1957): 101–24. English translation by Jeffner Allen: "The Dilthey-Husserl Correspondence." In *HSW*, pp. 203–9.

Erste Philosophie (1923/24). Zweiter Teil: Theorie der phänomenologischen Reduktion. Husserliana, vol. 8. Edited by Rudolf Boehm. The Hague: Nijhoff, 1959.

"Ein Brief von Husserl und Stoltenberg." *ZPF* 13 (1959): 179–80.

"Über psychologische Begründung der Logik." *ZPF* 13 (1959): 346–48. English translation by Thomas J. Sheehan: "On the Psychological Grounding of Logic." In *HSW*, pp. 146–47.

"Drei unveröffentlichte Briefe von Husserl an Ingarden." *ZPF* 13 (1959): 349–51.

Phänomenologische Psychologie. Husserliana, vol. 9. Edited by Walter Biemel. The Hague: Nijhoff, 1959. English translation by John Scanlon: *Phenomenological Psychology*. The Hague: Nijhoff, 1977.

Zur Phänomenologie des inneren Zeitbewusstseins (1893–1917). Husserliana, vol. 10. Edited by Rudolf Boehm. The Hague: Nijhoff, 1966. English translation by J.S. Churchill: *The Phenomenology of Internal Time-Consciousness.* Edited by Martin Heidegger. Bloomington: Indiana University Press, 1964.

Analysen zur passiven Synthesis. Husserliana, vol. 11. Edited by Margot Fleischer. The Hague: Nijhoff, 1966.

Briefe an Ingarden. The Hague: Nijhoff, 1968.

Philosophie der Arithmetik. Husserliana, vol. 12. Edited by Lothar Eley. The Hague: Nijhoff, 1970.

Zur Phänomenologie der Intersubjektivität. Husserliana, vols. 13, 14, and 15. Edited by Iso Kern. The Hague: Nijhoff, 1973.

Ding und Raum. Husserliana, vol. 16. Edited by Ulrich Claesges. The Hague: Nijhoff, 1973.

"Syllabus of a Course of Four Lectures on 'Phenomenological Method and Phenomenological Philosophy'" (London Lectures). Translated by Herbert Spiegelberg. *JBSP* 1 (1970): 18–23; and in *HSW,* pp. 67–74.

"E. Husserl Letter." Translated by P. Senft. *Human Context* 4 (1972): 244–63.

"Husserl's Inaugural Lecture at Freiburg im Breisgau." Edited by H.L. Van Breda; translated by R.W. Jordan. In *LIFE-WORLD,* pp. 3–18; and in *HSW,* pp. 9–17.

"Universal Technology." *Telos* 4 (1969): 176–80.

"A Letter to Arnold Metzger." *PF* 21 (1963): 48–68.

"Letter to Ernst Mach." *ZPF* 19 (1965): 134–38.

"Letter to Aron Gurwitsch." In *LIFE-WORLD,* p. xvi.

"Kant and the Idea of Transcendental Philosophy." Translated by T. Klein. *SWJP* 5 (1974).

"The Method of Clarification." Translated by T. Klein and W. Pohl. *SWJP* 5 (1974).

Formale und transzendentale Logik. Erster Band. Versuch einer Kritik der logischen Vernunft. *Husserliana,* vol. 17. Edited by Paul Janssen. The Hague: Nijhoff, 1974.

Introduction to the Logical Investigations. Translated with Introductions by Philip J. Bossert and Curtis H. Peters. The Hague: Nijhoff, 1975.

Logische Untersuchungen. Erster Band. Prolegomena zur reinen Logik. *Husserliana,* vol. 18. Edited by Elmar Holenstein. The Hague: Nijhoff, 1975.

"Husserl's Syllabus for the Paris Lectures on 'Introduction to Transcendental Phenomenology'." Translated by Herbert Spiegelberg. *JBSP* 7 (1976): 18–23; and in *HSW,* pp. 78–81.

Aufsätze und Rezensionen (1890–1910). Husserliana, vol. 22. Edited by Bernhard Rang. The Hague: Nijhoff, 1979.

Phantasie, Bildbewusstsein, Erinnerung. Zur Phänomenologie der anschaulichen Vergegenwärtigungen. *Husserliana,* vol. 23. Edited by Eduard Marbach. The Hague: Nijhoff, 1980.

Studien zur Arithmetik und Geometrie. Husserliana, vol. 21. Edited by Ingeborg Strohmeyer. The Hague: Nijhoff, 1981.

Logische Untersuchungen. Zweiter Band. Untersuchungen zur Phänomenologie und Theorie der Erkenntnis. *Husserliana,* vol. 19. Edited by Ursula Panzer. The Hague: Nijhoff, 1982.

Works on Husserl and Phenomenology

The following bibliography is a compilation of works in English, French, and German on Husserl and Husserlian phenomenology. We hope it will prove especially valuable to students and scholars working primarily but perhaps not exclusively in English.

Studies in Dutch, Italian, and other languages can be found in earlier bibliographies on which this one is partly based: Jean Patočka, "Husserl-Bibliographie," in *Revue Internationale de Philosophie,* 1939, pp. 374–97; R.P. Jean Raes, "Supplement à la bibliographie de Husserl," in *Revue Internationale de Philosophie,* 1950, pp. 469–75; E. Lothar, "Husserl-Bibliographie 1945–1959," in *Zeitschrift für Philosophische Forschung* 13 (1959): 357–67; Gerhard Maschke and Iso Kern, "Husserl-Bibliographie," in *Revue Internationale de Philosophie,* 1965, pp. 153–202; M. M. Van de Pitte, "Husserl Literature 1965–1971," in *Archiv für Geschichte der Philosophie* 57, heft 1 (1975): 36–53; and Jeffner Allen, "Husserl Bibliography of English Translations," in *The Monist* 59, no. 1 (Jan. 1975): 133–37.

The authors would be grateful for corrections and additions.

Abba, Boris. *Vor- und Selbstzeitigung als Versuch der Vermenschlichung in der Phänomenologie Husserls.* Meisenheim a. Glan: Hain, 1972.

Abustan, R.L. "Edmund Husserl's Epoché and St. Thomas' Metaphysical Abstraction." *Unitas* (Manila) 44 (1971): 55–94.

Actes du XIe Congrès International de Philosophie, vol. 2. Louvain: Nauwelaerts, 1953.

Acton, H.B. "Phenomenology." *AS* 11 (1932): 101–15.

Adorno, Theodore W. "Die Transzendenz des Dinglichen und Noematischen in Husserls Phänomenologie." Ph.D. dissertation, Frankfort, 1924.

———. "Husserl and the Problem of Idealism." *JP* 37 (1940): 5–18.

———. "Zur Philosophie Husserls." *AP* 3 (1949): 339–78.

———. *Zur Metakritik der Erkenntnistheorie: Studien über Husserl und die phänomenologischen Antinomien.* Stuttgart: Kohlhammer, 1956; and Frankfort: Suhrkamp, 1972.

———. "Spezies und Intention." *AP* 6 (1956): 14–41.

———. "Metacritique of Epistemology." *T* 38 (1978): 77–103.

Adriaanse, Hendrik Johan. *Zu den Sachen selbst. Versuch einer Konfrontation der Theologie Karl Barths mit der phänomenologischen Philosophie Edmund Husserls.* The Hague: Mouton, 1974.

Aguirre, Antonio. *Genetische Phänomenologie und Reduktion: Zur Letztbegründung der Wissenschaft aus der radikalen Skepsis im Denken E. Husserls.* The Hague: Nijhoff, 1970.

———. "Transzendentalphänomenologischer Rationalismus." In his *Perspektiven Transzendental Phänomenologischer Forschung,* pp. 102–28. Utrecht: Patmos, 1972.

Ales Bello, Angela, ed. *The Great Chain of Being and Italian Phenomenology.* Analecta Husserliana, vol. 11. Dordrecht: Reidel, 1981.

Alexander, Ian W. "What Is Phenomenology?" *JBSP* 1 (1970): 3.

———. "Maine de Biran and Phenomenology." *JBSP* 1 (1970): 24–37.

Alexander, Meena. "Inner Time and a Phenomenology of Existence." *INPQ* 2 (1975): 319–39.

Allen, Jeffner. "Husserl and Intersubjectivity: A Phenomenological Investigation of the Analogical Structure of Intersubjectivity." Ph.D. dissertation, Duquesne University, 1973.

_____. "Husserl: Bibliography of English Translation." *MO* 59 (1975): 133–37.

_____. "A Husserlian Phenomenology of the Child." *JPP* 6 (1975): 164–79.

_____. "Husserl's Philosophical Anthropology." *PT* 21 (1977): 347–55.

_____. "Husserl's Overcoming of the Problem of Intersubjectivity." *MS* 55 (1978): 261–71.

Allison, David B. "Derrida's Critique of Husserl: The Philosophy of Presence." Ph.D. dissertation, The Pennsylvania State University, 1974.

Almeida, Guido Antonio de. *Sinn und Inhalt in der genetischen Phänomenologie Edmund Husserls.* The Hague: Nijhoff, 1972.

Ameriks, Karl. "Husserl's Realism." *PRC* 86 (1977): 498–519.

Ames, Van Meter. "Mead and Husserl on the Self." *PPR* 15 (1954): 320–31.

Anzenbacher, Arno. *Die Intentionalität bei Thomas von Aquin und Edmund Husserl.* Munich: Oldenbourg, 1972.

Apel, Karl-Otto. "The Problem of (Philosophical) Ultimate Justification in the Light of a Transcendental Pragmatic of Language." *MW* 8 (1975): 239–75; *AJ* 36 (1974): 142–65.

Aquila, Richard E. "Husserl and Frege on Meaning." *JHP* 12 (1974): 377–83.

Armstrong, Edward G. "Intersubjective Intentionality." *MJP* 5 (1977): 1–11.

Aschenberg, Heidi. *Phänomenologische Philosophie und Sprache: Grundzüge der Sprachtheorie von Husserl, Pos und Merleau-Ponty.* Tübingen: Narr, 1978.

Asemissen, Hermann Ulrich. *Strukturanalytische Probleme der Wahrnehmung in der Phänomenologie Husserls.* Cologne: Kölner Univ.-Verlag, 1957.

_____. "Egologische Reflexion." *K* 50 (1958).

_____. "Phenomenality and Transcendence." *PPR* 20 (1959): 246–51.

Ashmore, Jerome. "Essence in Recent Philosophy: Husserl, Whitehead, Santayana." *PT* 18 (1974): 198–210.

Attig, Thomas W. "Cartesianism, Certainty and the Cogito in Husserl's *Cartesian Meditations.*" Ph.D. dissertation, Washington University, 1973.

_____. "How Definitive Is the Text of Husserl's *Cartesian Meditations.*" *JBSP* 1 (1976): 3–11.

_____. "Husserl's Interpretation and Critique of Descartes in His *Cartesian Meditations.*" *MS* 55 (1978): 271–81.

_____. "Husserl and Descartes on the Foundations of Philosophy." *MT* 11 (1980): 17–35.

Atwell, John Everett. *A Critical Exposition of Edmund Husserl's First Two Logical Investigations.* (1964). Ann Arbor: University Microfilms International, 1976.

_____. "Husserl on Signification and Object." *APQ* 6 (1969): 132–17; *MOHANTY*, pp. 83–93.

Avonson, P. "Interpreting Husserl and Heidegger: The Root of Sartre's Thought." *T* (Fall, 1972): 47–68.

Ayer, Alfred J. "Phenomenology and Linguistic Analysis." *AS* 32 (1959): 111–24.

Bachelard, Suzanne. *La logique de Husserl: Etude sur* Logique formelle et transcendentale. Paris: Presses Universitaires de France, 1957. English translation: *A Study of Husserl's Formal and Transcendental Logic.* Translated by Lester E. Embree. Evanston: Northwestern University Press, 1968.

Back, Wayne F. "Husserl's Conception of Philosophy." *KN* 8 (1977): 10–25.

Ballard, E. "Husserl's Philosophy of Intersubjectivity in Relation to His Rational Ideal." *TSP* 12 (1962): 3–38.

_____. "On the Pattern of Phenomenological Method." *SJP* 8 (1970): 421–31.

_____. "Objectivity and Rationality in Husserl's Philosophy." In his *Philosophy at the Crossroads,* pp. 172–215. Baton Rouge: Louisiana State University Press, 1971.

_____. "On the Method of Phenomenological Reduction: Its Presuppositions and Its Future." In *LIFE-WORLD,* pp. 101–24.

Banfi, A. "Husserl et la crise de la civilisation européenne." In *HUSSERL,* pp. 411–27.

Banja, John D. "Ego and Reduction: A Key to the Development of Husserl's Phenomenology." Ph.D. dissertation, Fordham University, 1975.

Bannes, J. *Versuch einer Darstellung und Beurteilung der Grundlagen der Philosophie Edmund Husserls.* Breslau: Borgmeyer, 1930.

Bar-Hillel, Yehoshua. "Husserl's Conception of a Purely Logical Grammar." *PPR* 17 (1956): 362–69; *MOHANTY*, pp. 128–36.

Barral, Marie-Rose. "Problems of Continuity in the Perceptual Process." *ANALH* 3 (1974).

———. "Teleology and Intersubjectivity in Husserl—Reflections." In *TELEOLOGIES*, pp. 221–33.

Bartels, Martin. "Identität und Individualität: Überlegungen zur Problematik der Egologie Edmund Husserls." *AGP* 61 (1979): 52–67.

Barth, E.M. "Phenomenology, Grammar, or Theory of Argumentation." *CH* 4 (1977): 163–82.

Bartlett, Steven. "Phenomenology of the Implicit." *Dialectica* 29 (1975): 173–88.

Baseheart, Sister Mary Catherine. "The Encounter of Husserl's Phenomenology and the Philosophy of St. Thomas in Selected Writings of Edith Stein." Ph.D. dissertation, University of Notre Dame, 1960.

Beaufret, Jean. "Husserl et Heidegger." In his *Dialogue avec Heidegger: Approche de Heidegger.* Paris: Editions de Minuit, 1974.

Beck, Maximilian. "The Last Phase of Husserl's Phenomenology." *PPR* 1 (1940): 479–91.

Becker, Oskar. "The Philosophy of Edmund Husserl." In *ELV*, pp. 40–72.

———. "Die Philosophie Edmund Husserls. Anlässlich seins 70. Geburtstags dargestellt." In *NOACK*, pp. 129–67.

Bednarski, Juliusz. "La réduction husserlienne." *RMM* 62 (1957): 416–35.

———. "Deux aspects de la réduction husserlienne: abstention et retour." *RMM* 64 (1959): 337–55 English translation: "Two Aspects of Husserl's Reduction." *PT* 4 (1960): 208–23.

———. "Vérité et temporalité: l'impossibilité du dogmatisme." *EP* 15 (1960): 491–502.

———. "La teneur phénoménologique du monde constitué chez Husserl." *EP* 19 (1964): 49–56.

Bénézé, Georges. "Au-delà de Husserl." *EP* 14 (1959): 191–201 and 449–68.

Bennett, John B. "Husserl's *Crisis* and Whitehead's *Process Philosophy.*" *PE* 56 (1975): 289–300.

Bense, Max. "Bemerkungen über die Gesamtausgabe der Werke Husserls." *Merkur* 5 (1951): 987–90.

Berger, Gaston. "Quelques aspects de la philosophie allemande contemporaine." *EP* 3 (1936): 68–74.

———. "Husserl et Hume." *RIP* 1 (1939): 342–53. Translation: "Husserl und Hume." Translated by Katharina Arndt. In *NOACK*, pp. 210–22.

———. *Le cogito dans la philosophie de Husserl.* Paris: Aubier, 1941, 1950.

———. "Le progrès de la réflexion chez Bergson et Husserl." In *Henri Bergson*, pp. 257–63. Neuchâtel: La Baconnière, 1943.

———. "Les thèmes principaux de la phénoménologie de Husserl." *RMM* 49 (1944): 23–42.

———. *Expérience et transcendence: La philosophie française L'Activité philosophique en France et aux Etats-Unis,* vol. 2, ed. Marvin Farber, pp. 96–112. Paris: Presses Universitaires de France, 1950.

———. "L'originalité de la phénoménologie." *EP* 9 (1954): 249–59.

———. "Approche phénoménologique du problème du temps." *Bulletin de la Société française de philosophie* 44 (1954): 89–132. English translation: "A Phenomenological Approach to the Problem of Time." Translated by D. O'Connor. In *READINGS*, pp. 187–204.

———. *Phénoménologie du temps et prospective.* Paris: Presses Universitaires de France, 1964.

———. *The Cogito in Husserl's Philosophy.* Translated by Kathleen McLaughlin. Evanston: Northwestern University Press, 1972.

———. "La phénoménologie transcendentale." *L'Encyclopédie française*, vol. 19.

Bergman, Samuel Hugo. *Edmund Husserl.* Davar, 1938.

———. "Metaphysical Implications of Husserl's Phenomenology." *SH* 2 (1955): 220–30.

Bergmann, Gustav. "The Ontology of Edmund Husserl." In his *Logic and Reality*, pp. 193–224. Madison: University of Wisconsin Press, 1964.

Berl, H.E. "Husserl oder die Judaisierung des Platonismus." *Menorah* 10 (1932).

Berlinger, R. "Inhaltsanalyze und Nachwort." In Edmund Husserl, *Philosophie als strenge Wissenschaft*, edited by R. Berlinger, pp. 75–101. Frankfort, 1965.

Bernet, Rudolf. "Phänomenologische Erkenntnistheorie und Semantik: Eine Untersuchung zu Husserls Lehre von der noematischen Intentionalität." Ph.D. dissertation, Louvain, 1976.

_____. "Endlichkeit und Unendlichkeit in Husserls Phänomenologie der Wahrnehmung." *TF* 40 (1978): 251–69.

_____. "Zur Teologie der Erkenntnis: Eine Antwort an Rudolf Boehm." *TF* 40 (1978): 662–68.

Bersley, William J. "The Origins of Consciousness: Husserl and Sartre on the 'Cogito'." Ph.D. dissertation, University of Colorado at Boulder, 1978.

Bertoldi, Eugene F. "Phenomenology of Phenomenology." *CJP* 7 (1977): 239–54.

Beyer, Wilhelm R. "Im Schatten Husserls." In *Vier Kritiken: Heidegger, Sartre, Adorno, Lukacs*, pp. 146–49. Cologne: Rugenstein, 1970.

Bidney, David. "Phenomenological Method and the Anthropological Science of the Cultural Life-World." In *Phenomenology and the Social Sciences*, edited by Maurice Natanson, pp. 109–40. Evanston, IL: Northwestern University Press, 1973.

Biemel, Walter. "Edmund Husserl: Persönliche Aufzeichnungen 1906–1908." *PPR* 3 (1942).

_____. "Edmund Husserl: Persönaliche Aufzeichnungen. Herausgegeben von Walter Beimel." *PPR* 16 (1955): 293–302.

_____. "Les phases décisives dans le dévelopment de la philosophie de Husserl." In *HUSSERL*, pp. 32–62.

_____. "Die entscheidenden Phasen der Entfaltung von Husserls Philosophie." *ZPF* 13 (1959): 187–213. English translation: "The Decisive Phases in the Development of Husserl's Philosophy." In *ELV*, pp. 148–73.

_____. "Einleitende Bemerkung zum Briefwechsel Dilthey-Husserl." *MW* 1 (1968): 428–46.

_____. "Réflexions à propos des recherches husserliennes de la Lebenswelt." *TF* 33 (1971): 659–83.

_____. "Husserls Encyclopaedia-Britannica Artikel und Heideggers Anmerkungen dazu." In *NOACK*, pp. 282–315. English translation: "Husserl's *Encyclopedia Britannica* Article and Heidegger's Remarks Thereon." In *HEA*, pp. 286–303.

_____. "Reflexionen zur Lebenswelt-Thematik." In *PHÄN H*, pp. 49–77.

_____. ed. *Die Welt Menschen*. Festschrift für Jan Patočka. Phänomenologica 72. The Hague: Nijhoff, 1976.

Biermann, K.R. "Did Husserl take his doctor's degree under Weierstrass' supervision?" *Organon* 6 (1969): 261–64.

Binswanger, Ludwig. "On the Relationship between Husserl's Phenomenology and Psychological Insight." *PPR* 2 (1941): 197–210.

_____. "Dank an Edmund Husserl." In *EH*, pp. 64–72.

Bjelke, J. "Der Ausgangspunkt der Erkenntnistheorie: Eine Auseinandersatzung mit Husserl." *K* 55 (1964): 3–19.

Blakeley, T. J. "N.V. Motrošilova on Husserl." *SST* 10 (1970): 50–52.

Blumenberg, Hans. "The Life-World and the Concept of Reality." Translated by Theodore Kisiel. In *LIFE-WORLD*, pp. 425–44.

Boboc, Alexandru. "Husserl and the Program of Modern Logic." *PL* 23 (1979): 461–63.

Bochenski, J.M. *Europäische Philosophie der Gegenwart*. 2nd ed. Bern: Francke, 1951. English translation: *Contemporary European Philosophy*, translated by Donald Nicholl and Karl Aschenbrenner, pp. 131–40. Berkeley: University of California Press, 1969.

Bodnar, Joanne. "Bolzano and Husserl: Logic and Phenomenology." Ph.D. dissertation, State University of New York at Buffalo, 1976.

Boehm, Rudolf. "Akten des internationalen phänomenologischen Kolloquiums zu Brussel." *ZPF* 7 (1953): 598–605.

_____. "Une introduction a la philosophie phénoménologique." *AF* 2 (1954): 169–72.

_____. "Husserl et l'idéalisme classique." *Convivium* 3 (1958): 53–93; *RPL* 57 (1959): 351–96.

_____. "Les ambiguïtés des concepts husserliens d' 'immanence' et de 'transcendance'." *RPFE* 84 (1959): 481–526.

————. "Zum Begriff des 'Absoluten' bei Husserl." *ZPF* 13 (1959): 214–42. English translation: "Husserl's Concept of the 'Absolute'." In *ELV*, pp. 174–203.

————. "Deux points de vue: Husserl et Nietzsche." In *Pascal e Nietzsche*, pp. 167–81. Padua: Dedam, 1962.

————. "Les sciences exactes et l'idéal Husserlien d'un savoir rigoureux." *ARP* 27 (1964): 424–38.

————. "Elementare Bemerkungen über Husserls 'phänomenologische Reduktion'." *Bijdragan* 26 (1965): 193–208. English translation: "Basic Reflections on Husserl's Phenomenological Reduction." *IPQ* 5 (1965): 183–202.

————. "La phénoménologie de l'histoire." *RIP* 71–72 (1965): 55–73.

————. "Die *Philosophie als strenge Wissenschaft*." In his *Vom Gesichtspunkt der Phänomenologie*, pp. 1–17. The Hague: Nijhoff, 1968.

————. "Die *Erste Philosophie* und die Wege zur Reduktion." In his *Vom Gesichtspunkt der Phänomenologie*, pp. 186–216. The Hague: Nijhoff, 1968.

————. *Vom Gesichtspunkt der Phänomenologie*. The Hague: Nijhoff, 1968.

————. "Zur Phänomenologie der Gemeinschaft: Edmund Husserls Grundgedanken." In *Phänomenologie, Rechtsphilosophie, Jurisprudenz: Festschrift für Edmund Husserl zum 75. Geburtstag*, pp. 1–26. Frankfort: Klostermann, 1969.

————. "On Truth, A Fragment." Translated by Osborne Wiggins Jr. In *LIFE-WORLD*, pp. 83–100.

————. "Bewusstsein als Gegenwart des Vergangenen." *MO* 59 (1975): 21–39.

————. "Das 'Ding-an-sich' als Erkenntnisziel." *TF* 40 (1978): 659–61.

Boirel, René. "Mathématique Appliquées: Philosophie du Concept et Phénoménologie." *EP* 24 (1969): 335–50.

Bonomi, A. "The Problem of Language in Husserl." *T* (Fall 1970): 184–204.

Bosanquet, B. "Review of *Ideen I*." *M* 23 (1914): 587–97.

Bosio, Franco. "The Teleology of 'Theoresis' and 'Praxis' in the Thought of Husserl." In *TELEOLOGIES*, pp. 85–90.

Bossert, Philip. "The Origin and Early Development of Husserl's Method of Phenomenological Reduction." Ph.D. dissertation, Washington University, 1973.

————. "The Sense of the 'Epoché' and 'Reduction' in Husserl's Philosophy." *JBSP* 5 (1974): 243–55.

————. "A Common Misunderstanding concerning Husserl's *Crisis* Text." *PPR* 35 (1974–75): 20–33.

————, ed. *Phenomenological Perspectives: Historical and Systematic Essays in Honor of Herbert Spiegelberg*. The Hague: Nijhoff, 1975.

————. "Paradox and Enlightenment in Zen Dialogue and Phenomenological Description." *JCP* 3 (1976): 269–80.

————. "Hume and Husserl on Time and Time-Consciousness." *JBSP* 7 (1976): 44–52.

Bourgeois, Patrick. "Phenomenology and the Sciences of Language." *RP* 1 (1971): 119–36.

Brancaforte, Antonio. "A Historical Note on the Presence of Brentano in Sicily and on the First Links of Italian Culture with the Phenomenology of Husserl." In *TELEOLOGIES*, pp. 429–39.

Brand, Gerd. "Der Rückgang auf das welterfahrende Leben und die Zeitlichkeit als seine Ur-Form: Nach unveröffentlichten Manuskripten Edmund Husserls." Ph.D. dissertation, Louvain, 1950.

————. *Welt, Ich und Zeit: Nach unveröffentlichten Manuskripten Edmund Husserls*. The Hague: Nijhoff, 1955.

————. "Husserl-Literatur und Husserl." *PR* 8 (1960): 261–89.

————. "Intentionality, Reduction and Intentional Analysis in Husserl's Later Manuscripts." In *PPEH*, pp. 197–220.

————. "Edmund Husserl: Analysen zur passiven Synthesis." *PR* 17 (1970): 55–77.

————. *Die Lebenswelt: Eine Philosophie des konkreten Apriori*. Berlin: De Gruyter, 1971.

————. "The Material A Priori and the Foundation for Its Analysis in Husserl." *ANALH* 2 (1972): 128–48.

————. "The Structure of the Life-World according to Husserl." *MW* 6 (1973): 143–62.

————. *Welt, Geschichte, Mythos*. Trier: NCO-Verlag, 1977.

————. "Edmund Husserl: Zur Phänomenologie der Intersubjektivität." *PR* 25 (1978): 54–79; in *Husserl, Scheler, Heidegger in der Sicht neuer Quellen*, edited by E.W. Orth, pp. 28–117. Freiburg: Aber, 1978.

Bréhier, Emile. *Histoire de la philosophie allemande.* Troisième édition mise à jour par P. Ricoeur. Paris: J. Vrin, 1954; pp. 183–96.

Breton, Stanislas. *Conscience et intentionnalité.* Lyon: Vitte, 1956.

_____. "Conscience et intentionnalité selon Husserl." *ARP* 19 (1956): 55–97.

Brocker, Walter. "Husserls Lehre von der Zeit." *PN* 4 (1957): 374–79.

Broekman, Jan M. *Phänomenologie und Egologie: Faktisches und transcendentales Ego bei Edmund Husserl.* The Hague: Nijhoff, 1963.

Brough, John Barnett. "A Study of the Logic and Evolution of Edmund Husserl's Theory of the Constitution of Time-Consciousness." 1893–1917." Ph.D. dissertation, Georgetown University, 1970.

_____. "The Emergence of an Absolute Consciousness in Husserl's Early Writings on Time-Consciousness." *MW* 5 (1972): 298–324; *HEA,* pp. 83–100.

_____. "Husserl on Memory." *MO* 59 (1975): 40–62.

Brueck, Maria. *Über das Verhältnis Edmund Husserl zu Franz Brentano, vornehmlich mit Rücksicht auf Brentanos Psychologie.* Würzburg: Konrad Triltsch, 1933.

Brüning, Walther. "Der Ansatz der Transzendental philosophie in Husserls *Cartesianischen Meditationen.*" *ZPF* 20 (1966): 185–96.

Bruzina, Ronald. *Logos and Eidos.* The Hague: Mouton, 1970.

Bubner, Rüdiger. "Responses to 'Hermeneutics and Social Sciences'." *CH* 2 (1975): 327.

Buck, Wayne F. "Husserl's Conception of Philosophy." *KN* 8 (1977): 10–25.

Burke, John P. "The Concept of World in Husserl's Transcendental Phenomenology." Ph.D. dissertation, University of California at San Diego, 1974.

Bush, Charles P. "Concerning Husserl's Apparent Metaphysical Idealism: A Critique of Roman Ingarden." Ph.D. dissertation, University of Southern California, 1977.

Buttemeyer, Wilhelm. "Der Streit um 'positivistische' Erzichungswissenschaft in Deutschland." *S* 110 (1975): 419–68.

Butts, Robert E. "Husserl's Critique of Hume's Notion of *Distinctions of Reason.*" *PPR* 20 (1959): 213–21.

_____. *Husserl's Criticisms of Hume's Theory of Knowledge* [1957]. Ann Arbor: University Microfilms International, 1976.

Buytendijk, F.J.J. "Husserl's Phenomenology and Its Significance for Contemporary Psychology." Translated by D. O'Connor. In *READINGS,* pp. 352–64.

Cairns, Dorion. "Some Results of Husserl's Investigations." *JP* 29 (1939): 236–38.

_____. "Abstract of Husserl's *Die Frage nach dem Ursprung der Geometrie.*" *PPR* 1 (1940): 98–109.

_____. "Phenomenology." In *The Dictionary of Philosophy,* pp. 231–34. New York: Philosophical Library, 1942.

_____. "Phenomenology." In *A History of Philosophical Systems,* ed. Vergilius Fern, pp. 353–64. New York: Philosophical Library, 1950.

_____. "The Many Senses and Denotations of the Word *Bewusstsein* (Consciousness) in Edmund Husserl's Writings." In *LIFE-WORLD,* pp. 19–32.

_____. "An Approach to Husserlian Phenomenology." In *PHCC,* pp. 223–38.

_____. "The Ideality of Verbal Expressions." In *PHCC,* pp. 239–50.

_____. "Perceiving, Remembering, Image-Awareness, Feigning-Awareness." In *PHCC,* pp. 251–62.

_____. "A Letter to John Wild about Husserl." *RIP* 5 (1975): 155–81.

_____. *Conversations with Husserl and Fink.* Edited by the Husserl-Archives in Louvain. With a Foreword by Richard M. Zaner. The Hague: Nijhoff, 1976.

Campbell, R. "Essai sur la philosophie des mathématiques selon Jean Cavaillès (II)." *CR* (1953): 48–66.

Canon, J.H. "The Phenomenology of Temporal Awareness." *JBSP* 1 (1970): 38–45.

Caputo, John D. "The Nothingness of the Intellect in Meister Eckhart's 'Parisian Questions'." *Thomist* 39 (1975): 85–115.

_____. "The Question of Being and Transcendental Phenomenology: Reflections on Heidegger's Relationship to Husserl." *RPH* 7 (1977): 84–105.

————. "Transcendence and the Transcendental in Husserl's Phenomenology." *PT* 23 (1979): 205–16.

Carentini, E. "La signification transcendantale de la psychologie chez E. Husserl." *Revue de Psychologie et des Sciences de l'Education* (Liège), 7 (1972): 471–93.

Carr, David. "Husserl's Problematic Conception of the Life-World." *APQ* 7 (1970): 331–39; *HEA*, pp. 202–12.

————, and Casey, Edward S., eds. *Explorations in Phenomenology: Papers of the Society for Phenomenology and Existential Philosophy.* The Hague: Nijhoff, 1973.

————. "The *Fifth Meditation* and Husserl's Cartesianism." *PPR* 34 (1973–74): 14–34.

————. *Phenomenology and the Problem of History: A Study of Husserl's Transcendental Philosophy.* Evanston: Northwestern University Press, 1974.

————. "Husserl's *Crisis* and the Problem of History." *SWJP* 5 (1974): 127–48.

————. "Intentionality." In *PPU*, pp. 17–36.

————. "Interpretation und Evidenz." *FZ* 23 (1976): 253–68.

————. "Kant, Husserl, and the Non-Empirical Ego." *JP* 74 (1977): 682–90.

————. "Zum Problem des Nichtempirischen Ich." *ZFPF* 32 (1978): 163–83.

Carrington, Peter J. "Schütz on Transcendental Intersubjectivity in Husserl." *HS* 2 (1979): 95–110.

Carruba, Gerald J. "Some Phenomenological Aspects of a Marxist Philosophy of Language." *Kinesis* 6 (1974): 95–111.

Casey, Edward S. "Reflections on Man's Relation to Truth." *PT* 16 (1972): 34–42.

————. "Art, Imagination, and the A Priori." *ANALH* 3 (1974).

————. "Toward a Phenomenology of Imagination." *JBSP* 5 (1974): 3–19.

————. "The Image/Sign Relation in Husserl and Freud." *RM* 30 (1976): 207–25.

————. *Imagination: A Phenomenological Study.* Bloomington: Indiana University Press, 1976.

————. "Imagination and Phenomenological Method." In *HEA*, pp. 70–82.

————. "Perceiving and Remembering." *RM* 32 (1979): 407–32.

Catesson, Jean. "A propos d'une pensée de l'intervalle." *RMM* 74 (1969): 74–90.

Celms, Theodor. *Der phänomenologische Idealismus Husserls.* Riga: Lettland, 1928.

Chandler, Albert R. "Plato's Theory of Ideas in the Light of Husserl's Theory of Universals." Ph.D. dissertation, Harvard University, 1913.

————. "Professor Husserl's Program of Philosophy Reform." *PRC* 26 (1917): 634–48.

Chandravarty, H. "Husserl, la phénoménologie et la recherche occidentale de soi." *Age nouveau* 110 (1960): 37–50.

Chapman, H.M. "Realism and Phenomenology." In *WILD*, pp. 3–35.

————. *Sensations and Phenomenology.* Bloomington: Indiana University Press, 1966.

————. "The Phenomenon of Language." In *PHCC*, pp. 14–23.

Chatterjee, Margaret. "Language as Phenomenon." *PPR* 30 (1969): 116–21.

————. "Towards a Phenomenology of Time-Consciousness in Music." *DG* 74 (1971): 49–56.

Chestow, Leo. "Memento mori: A propos de la théorie de la connaissance d'Edmund Husserl." In his *Le pouvoir des clefs,* translated by B. de Schlozer, pp. 307–96. Paris: Schriffin, 1928.

————. "A la memoire d'un grand philosophe: Edmund Husserl." *RPF* 129 (1940): 5–32. English translation: "In Memory of a Great Philosopher: Edmund Husserl." Translated by George L. Kline. *PPR* 22 (1961): 449–71.

Chisholm, Roderick M., ed. *Realism and the Background of Phenomenology.* Glencoe: The Free Press, 1960.

————. Introduction to *Realism and the Background of Phenomenology*, pp. 3–36. New York: The Free Press, 1960.

————. "Intentionality." In *Encyclopedia of Philosophy*, vol. 4, pp. 201–4. New York: Macmillan, 1970.

————. "Brentano on Descriptive Psychology and the Intentional." In *LEE*, pp. 1–24.

Cho, Kah Kyung. "Mediation and Immediacy for Husserl." In *PHNE*, pp. 56–82.

Christensen, Renate. "Einige Bemerkungen zur Problematik von Intentionalität und Reflexion bei E. Husserl." *Wiener Jahrbuch für Philosophie* 9 (1976): 73–87.

Christoff, Daniel. *Husserl ou le retour aux choses.* Paris: Seghers, 1966.

Christopher, Dennis. "Husserl and Mill: A Rejoinder." *Mill News* 14 (1979): 12–17.

Claesges, Ulrich. *Edmund Husserls Theorie der Raumkonstitution.* The Hague: Nijhoff, 1964.
_____. "Intentionalität und Transzendenz: Zur Konstitution der materiellen Natur." *ANALH* 1 (1971): 91–99. English translation: "Intentionality and Transcendence: On the Constitution of Material Nature." *ANALH* 2 (1972): 283–91.
_____. "Zweideutigkeiten in Husserls Lebenswelt Begriff." In *Perspektiven transzendentalphänomenologischer Forschung,* edited by Ulrich Claesges and Klaus Held, pp. 85–101. The Hague: Nijhoff, 1972.

Colette, J. "Chronique de phénoménologie." *RS* 59 (1975): 613–44.

Collins, James. "Husserl." In his *The Existentialists: A Critical Study,* pp. 26–38. Chicago: Henry Regnery, 1959.

Compton, John J. "Hare, Husserl and Philosophic Discovery." *D* 3 (1964): 42–51.
_____. "Natural Science and the Experience of Nature." In *PHA,* pp. 80–95.

Comrad, Theodor. *Zur Wesenslehre des psychischen Lebens und Erlebens.* The Hague: Nijhoff, 1968.

Connell, Desmond. "Substance and Subject." *PST* 26 (1979): 7–25.

Conrad-Martius, Hedwig. "Die transzendentale und die ontologische Phänomenologie." In *EH,* pp. 175–84.

Cranaki, Mimica. "De Husserl à Heidegger." *CR* 10 (1954): 676–88.

Crosson, F.J. "The Concept of Mind and the Concept of Consciousness." In *PHA,* pp. 186–96.

Cunningham, Suzanne M. "Language and Intersubjectivity in the Phenomenology of Edmund Husserl." Ph.D. dissertation, Florida State University, 1972.
_____. *Language and the Phenomenological Reductions of Edmund Husserl.* The Hague: Nijhoff, 1976.

Curtius, Jerry L. "A Camus Commentary: Sartre's Debt to Husserl." *South Atlantic Bulletin* 40 (1975): 1–6.

Dallmayr, Fred R. "Phenomenology and Critical Theory." *CH* 3 (1976): 367–406.
_____. "Phenomenology and Social Science: An Overview and Appraisal." In *EXPLORATIONS,* pp. 133–66.
_____. "Husserl, Subjectivity and Constitutive Consciousness vs. Heidegger's 'Theory of Being'." In *From Contract to Community: Political Theory of Community,* edited by Fred Dallmayr. New York: M. Dekker, 1978.

Danek, Jaramir. *Die Weiterentwicklung der Leibnizschen Logik Bolzano.* Meisenheim a. Glan: Hain, 1970.
_____. "Kant, Husserl et l'histoire de la logique." *Dialogue* 12 (1973): 110–15.
_____. "Méditation husserlienne sur *Alter Ego.*" *LTP* 31 (1975): 175–91.

Dauenhauer, Bernard P. "On Speech and Temporality: Jacques Derrida and Edmund Husserl." *PT* 18 (1974): 171–80.
_____. "A Comment on Husserl and Solipsism." *MS* 52 (1975): 189–93.
_____. "Husserl's Phenomenological Justification of Universal Rigorous Science." *IPQ* 16 (1976): 63–80.
_____. "The Teleology of Consciousness: Husserl and Merleau-Ponty." In *TELEOLOGIES,* pp. 149–68.

David, G.E. "Edmund Husserl and 'The As Yet, in Its Most Important Respect, Unrecognized Greatness of Hume'." In *David Hume: Bicentennary Papers,* edited by G.P. Morise, pp. 69–76. Edinburgh: Edinburgh University Press, 1977.

De Boer, Theodorus. *Das Verhältnis zwischen dem Ersten und dem zweiten Teil der 'Logischen Untersuchungen' Edmund Husserls.* Turin: Edizrans di 'Filosofia', 1967.
_____. "The Meaning of Husserl's Idealism in the Light of His Development." *ANALH* 2 (1972): 322–32.
_____. "Die Begriffe 'absolut' und 'relativ' bei Husserl." *ZFPF* 27 (1973): 514–33.
_____. *The Development of Husserl's Thought.* Translated by Theodore Plantinga. The Hague: Nijhoff, 1978.

Debus, Ite I. "A Critical Analysis of Husserl's *Ideen I*." Ph.D. dissertation, Johns Hopkins University, 1971.

Declève, Henri. "La Lebenswelt selon Husserl." *LTP* 27 (1971): 151–61.

De Laguna, Grace. "The Lebenswelt and the Cultural World." *JP* 57 (1960): 777–91.

Delbos, Victor. "Husserl, sa critique du psychologisme et sa conception d'une logique pure." *RMM* 16 (1911); in his *La philosophie allemande au XIXe siècle,* chapter II. Paris: Alcan, 1912.

Del-Negro, Walter. "Von Brentano über Husserl zu Heidegger." *ZPF* 7 (1953): 571–85.

De Marneffe, J. "Bergson's and Husserl's Concepts of Intuition." *PQA* 33 (1960): 169–80.

Demetz, Peter. "Kafka, Freud, Husserl: Probleme einer Generation." *ZRG* 7 (1955): 59–69.

De Muralt, André. "Les deux dimensions de l'intentionnalité husserlienne." *RTP* 8 (1958): 188–202.

———. *L'idée de la phénoménologie: L'exemplarisme husserlien.* Paris: Presses Universitaires de France, 1958. English translation: *The Idea of Phenomenology: Husserlian Exemplarism.* Translated by Gary L. Breckon. Evanston: Northwestern University Press, 1974.

———. "La solution husserlienne du débat entre le réalisme et l'idéalisme." *RPF* 84 (1959): 545–52.

———. "Adéquation et intentions secondes. Essai de confrontation de la phénoménologie husserlienne et de la philosophie thomiste sur le point du jugement." *SPS* 20 (1960): 88–114.

———. "L'élaboration husserlienne de la notion d'intentionnalité: Esquisse d'une confrontation de la phénoménologie avec ses origines scolastiques." *RTP* 10 (1960): 265–84. English translation: "The 'Founded Act' and the Apperception of Others: The Actual Scholastic Sources of Husserlian Intentionality. An Essay in Structural Analysis of Doctrines." Translated by Gary L. Breckon. *ANALH* 6 (1977): 123–41.

———. "Epoché-Malin Génie-Théologie de la tout-puissance divine 'Husserl, Descartes, Occam'." *Studia Philosophica* 26 (1966): 159–91.

———. "La notion d'acte fondé dans les rapports de la raison et de la volonté selon le *Logische Untersuchungen* de Husserl." *RMM* 82 (1977): 511–27.

Dentoni, Francesco. "An Approach to the Philosophical Problems of the Early Husserl." *Phenomenology Information Bulletin* (Belmont, Mass.) 2 (1978): 58–64.

de Oliveira, Manfredo Araúgo. *Subjektivität und Vermittlung. Studien z. Entwicklung d. transzendentalen Denkens bei I. Kant, E. Husserl u. H. Wagner.* Munich: Fink, 1973.

Derrida, Jacques. "La forme et le vouloir-dire: note sur la phénoménologie du langage." *RTP* 21 (1967): 277–99.

———. *La voix et le phénomène.* Paris: PUF, 1967. English translation: *Speech and Phenomena.* Translated by David Allison. Evanston: Northwestern University Press, 1973.

———. *Edmund Husserl's Origin of Geometry: An Introduction.* Translated by John P. Leavy, Jr. New York: Nicholas Hays, 1978.

Desanti, Jean T. *Phénoménologie et praxis.* Paris: Editions Sociales, 1963.

Dessoir, Max. "La phénoménologie de Husserl." *RIP* 2 (1939): 271–76.

Deutscher, Max. "Husserl's Transcendental Subjectivity." *CJP* 10 (1980): 21–45.

Devaux, André-A. "La phénoménologie de Husserl, est-elle un néocartésianisme?" *EP* 9 (1954): 260–83.

Devettere, Raymond J. "Merleau-Ponty and the Husserlian Reductions." *PT* 17 (1973): 297–310.

De Vidovich, Silvana. "Husserl in USSR." *AA* 107 (1968): 104–6.

Devivaise, C. "Le testament philosophique de Husserl." *EP* 9 (1954): 352–59.

De Waelhens, Alphonse. "Descartes et la pensée phénoménologique." *Revue Néo-scolastique de Philosophie* 41 (1938): 571–89.

———. "La phénoménologie du corps." *RPL* 48 (1950): 371–97. English translation: "The Phenomenology of the Body." In *Readings in Existential Phenomenology,* edited and translated by N. Lawrence and D. O'Connor, pp. 149–67. Englewood Cliffs: Prentice-Hall, 1967.

———. "Husserl et la phénoménologie." *CR* 8 (1951): 1044–1057.

———. *Phénoménologie et vérité. Essai sur l'évolution de l'idée de vérité chez Husserl et Heidegger.* Paris: Presses Universitaires de France, 1953.

———. "Phénoménologie husserlienne et phénoménologie hégélienne." *RPL* 52 (1954): 234–49; in *Existence et Signification,* pp. 7–29. Louvain: Nauwelaerts, 1958.

————. "Husserl (1859–1938)." In *Les Philosophes célèbres*. Paris: Editions d'art Lucien Mazenod, 1956.

————. "L'idée phénoménologique d'intentionnalité." In *HPM*, pp. 115–29.

————. "Commentaire sur l'idée de la phénoménologie." In *HUSSERL*, pp. 143–56.

————. "Réflexions sur une problématique husserlienne de l'inconscient, Husserl et Hegel." In *EH*, pp. 221–37.

————. "Phenomenological Concept of Intentionality." Translated by A. Fisher. *PT* 6 (1962): 3–13.

————. "Descartes und das phänomenologische Denken." Translated by Klaus Stichweh. In *NOACK*, pp. 188–209.

Diemer, Alwin. "La phénoménologie de Husserl comme métaphysique." Translated by Jacques Ridé. *EP* 19 (1954): 21–49.

————. "Ziele und Aufgaben einer phänomenologischen Philosophie." *ZPF* 9 (1955): 315–19.

————. *Edmund Husserl: Versuch einer systematischen Darstellung seiner Phänomenologie*. Meisenheim a. Glan: Hain, 1956.

————. "Die Phänomenologie und die Idee der Philosophie als strenge Wissenschaft." *ZPF* 13 (1959): 243–62.

Dinan, Stephen A. "Intentionality in the Introduction to *Being and Nothingness*." *RP* 1 (1971): 91–118.

————. D'Ippolito, Bianca Maria Cuomo. "The Theory of the Object and the Teleology of History in Edmund Husserl." In *TELEOLOGIES*, pp. 271–74.

Dolgov, K.M. "The Philosophy and Aesthetics of Maurice Merleau-Ponty." *SSP* 14 (1975–76): 67–92.

Doran, R.M. "Sartre's Critique of the Husserlian Ego." *MS* 44 (1967): 307–17.

Dougherty, Charles J. "Phenomenological Critique of Empiricism: A Study in the Philosophies of Husserl and Peirce." Ph.D dissertation, University of Notre Dame, 1975.

————. "The Significance of Husserl's *Logical Investigations*." *PT* 23 (1979): 217–25.

————. "Common Root of Husserl's and Peirce's Phenomenologies." *NS* 54 (1980): 305–25.

Dovydaitis, P. "Ed. Husserl." *Logos* 18 (1939): 187–90,

Downes, Chauncey B. "Husserl's Theory of Other Minds: A Study of the *Cartesian Meditations*." Ph.D. dissertation, New York University, 1963.

————. "Husserl and the Coherence of the Other Minds Problem." *PPR* 26 (1965–66): 253–59.

————. "On Husserl's Approach to Necessary Truth." *MO* 49 (1965): 87–106; *MOHANTY*, pp. 162–78.

————. *Husserl's Theory of Other Minds. A Study of the Cartesian Meditations*. Ann Arbor: University Microfilms International, 1976.

Dreyfus, Hubert L. "The Priority of *the* World to *My* World: Heidegger's Answer to Husserl (and Sartre)." *MW* 8 (1975): 121–30.

————. "The Perceptual Noema: Gurwitsch's Crucial Contribution." In *LIFE-WORLD*, pp. 135–70.

————. "*Sinn* and Intentional Object." In *SOLOMON*, pp. 196–210.

———— and Haugeland, John. "Husserl and Heidegger: Philosophy's Last Stand." In *Heidegger and Modern Philosophy: Critical Essays*, edited by Michael Murray, pp. 222–38. New Haven-London: Yale University Press, 1978.

————. *Husserl's Phenomenology of Perception*. Evanston: Northwestern University Press, 1979.

Drüe, Hermann. *Edmund Husserls System der phänomenologischen Psychologie*. Berlin: De Gruyter, 1963.

Drummond, John J. "Husserl on the Ways to the Performance of the Reduction." *MW* 8 (1975): 47–69.

————. "Presenting and Kinaesthetic Sensations in Husserl's Phenomenology of Perception." Ph.D. dissertation, Georgetown University, 1975.

————. "On the Nature of Perceptual Appearances, or Is Husserl an Aristotelian?" *NS* 52 (1978): 1–22.

————. "The Phenomenology of Perceptual Sense." *SJP* 10 (1979): 139–46.

Dufrenne, Mikel. *Phénoménologie de l'expérience esthétique*. Paris: Presses Universitaires de France, 1953.

————. "Wittgenstein et Husserl." In *Jalons*, pp. 188–207. The Hague: Nijhoff, 1966.

————. *The Notion of the A Priori.* Translated by Edward S. Casey. Evanston: Northwestern University Press, 1966.

————. "Intentionality and Aesthetics." *MW* 11 (1978): 401–10.

Dunker, Karl. "Phenomenology and Epistemology of Consciousness of Objects." *PPR* 7 (1946–47): 505–41.

Dupré, Louis. "The Concept of Truth in Husserl's *Logical Investigations.*" *PPR* 24 (1963–64): 345–54.

————. "Husserl's Notion of Truth—Via Media between Idealism and Realism? Four Lectures on the *Logical Investigations* and *Ideas.*" In *Teaching Theology Today,* pp. 405–17. Washington, D.C.: The Catholic University of America Press, 1964.

————. "Husserl's Thoughts on God and Faith." *PPR* 29 (1968): 201–15.

————. "Phenomenology and Systematic Philosophy." *PT* 13 (1969): 284–95.

Durfee, Harold A., ed. *Analytic Philosophy and Phenomenology.* The Hague: Nijhoff, 1976.

Düsing, Klaus. "Das Problem der Denkökonomie bei Husserl und Mach." In *Perspektiven Transzendental Phänomenologischer Forschung,* pp. 225–54. Utrecht: Patmos, 1972.

Dussort, Henri. "Brentano et Husserl." *RPF* 84 (1959): 553–59.

————. "Husserl juge de Kant." *RPF* 84 (1959): 527–44.

————. "Introduction au 'Projet d'un livre sur Husserl'." *RMM* 66 (1961): 233–36.

Duval, R. "Parole, expression, silence: Recherche sur la parole comme révélatrice d'autrui." *RS* 60 (1976): 226–60.

Earle, William. "Phenomenology and Existentialism." *JP* 57 (1960): 75–84.

————. *Objectivity.* Chicago: Quadrangle, 1968.

Edie, James M. "Transcendental Ontology and Existentialism." *JP* 59 (1962): 681–82.

————. "Recent Work in Phenomenology." APQ 1 (1964): 115–28.

————. "Transcendental Phenomenology and Existentialism." *PPR* 25 (1964–65): 52–63.

————, ed. *An Invitation to Phenomenology.* Chicago: Quadrangle Books, 1965.

————. "Phenomenology as a Rigorous Science." *IPQ* 7 (1967): 21–30.

————, ed. *Phenomenology in America.* Chicago: Quadrangle Books, 1967.

————, ed. *New Essays in Phenomenology.* Chicago: Quadrangle Books, 1969.

————; Parker, Francis H.; and Schrag, Calvin O., eds. *Patterns of the Life-World: Essays in Honor of John Wild.* Evanston: Northwestern University Press, 1970.

————. "William James and Phenomenology." *RM* 23 (1970): 481–526.

————. "Revolution in Philosophy: What Is Phenomenology?" *SWJP* 2 (1971): 73–91.

————. "Husserl's Conception of *The Grammatical* and Contemporary Linguistics." In *LIFE-WORLD,* pp. 233–60; in his *Speaking and Meaning: The Phenomenology of Language,* pp. 45–71. Bloomington: Indiana University Press, 1976; in *MOHANTY,* pp. 137–61.

————. "Phenomenology in the United States (1974)." *JBSP* 5 (1974): 199–211.

————. "Husserl's Conception of the Identity of Language." *Humanitas* 11 (1975): 201–17.

Ehman, Robert R. "The Phenomenon of World." In *PATTERNS,* pp. 85–106.

Ehrhardt, Walter E. "Die Leibniz-Rezeption in der Phänomenologie Husserls." In *Akten des Internationalen Leibniz-Kongresses,* pp. 146–55. Hannover, 1966.

Ehrlich, W. *Kant and Husserl: Kritik der transzendentalen und phänomenologische Methode.* Halle, 1923.

————. *Intentionalität und Sinn: Prologomena zur Normenlehre.* Halle, 1934.

Eigler, Gunther. *Metaphysische Voraussetzungen in Husserls Zeitanalysen.* Meisenheim a. Glan: Hain, 1961.

Eley, Lothar. "Zum Begriff des Transzendentalen, eine kritische Studie zu Th. W. Adorno." *ZPF* 13 (1959): 351–57.

————. *Die Krise des Apriori in der transzendentalen Phänomenologie Edmund Husserls.* The Hague: Nijhoff, 1962.

————. "The Life-World Constitution of Propositional Logic and Elementary Predicate Logic." *PPR* 32 (1971): 322–40; *ANALH* 2 (1972): 333–53.

————. "Logik und Sprache." *K* 63 (1972): 247–60.

_____. "Afterword to Husserl's 'Experience and Judgment': Phenomenology and Philosophy of Language." In *Experience and Judgment*, pp. 399–429. Evanston: Northwestern, 1973.

Elie, Hubert. "Etude logico-grammaticale sur les *Logische Untersuchungen* de Husserl." *SPS* 23 (1963): 51–83.

Elkin, Henry. "Towards a Developmental Phenomenology: Transcendental-Ego and Body-Ego." *ANALH* 2 (1972): 258–66.

Ellis, Ralph. "Directionality and Fragmentation in the Transcendental Ego." *AUS* 6 (1979): 147–60.

Elliston, Frederick. "Phenomenology Reinterpreted: From Husserl to Heidegger." *PT* 21 (1977): 273–83.

_____. "Husserl's Phenomenology of Empathy." In *HEA*, pp. 213–31.

_____ and McCormick, Peter, eds. *Husserl: Expositions and Appraisals.* Notre Dame: University of Notre Dame Press, 1977.

Elveton, R.O., ed. *The Phenomenology of Husserl: Selected Critical Readings.* Chicago: Quadrangle Books, 1970.

Embree, Lester E., ed. *Life-World and Consciousness: Essays for Aron Gurwitsch.* Evanston: Northwestern University Press, 1972.

_____. "Reflection on the Ego." In *EXPLORATIONS*, pp. 243–52.

_____. "Toward a Phenomenology of Theoria." In *LIFE-WORLD*, pp. 191–208.

_____. "An Interpretation of the Doctrine of the Ego in Husserl's *Ideen.*" In *PHCC*, pp. 24–32.

_____. "A Note on 'Is' and 'Ought' in Phenomenological Perspective." *JBSP* 10 (1979): 101–9.

Eng, Erling. "Body, Consciousness, and Violence." *ANALH* 2 (1972): 267–77.

_____. "Constitution and Intentionality in Psychosis." *ANALH* 3 (1974).

Engel, W. "Zur Kritik der Phänomenologie Husserls." Ph.D. dissertation Prague, 1929.

Engelhardt, H. Tristram, Jr. "Husserl and the Mind-Brain Relation." In *Interdisciplinary Phenomenology,* edited by Don Ihde and Richard M. Zaner, pp. 51–70. The Hague: Nijhoff, 1977.

Erckmann, R. "Husserl und Hans Hörbiger." *Schlüssel zum Weltgeschehen* 5 (1919): 150–54 and 184–88.

Eschke, Hans-Günter. "Bemerkungen zur Phänomenologie Edmund Husserls." *Deutsche Zeitschrift für Philosophie* 12 (1964): 596–611.

Eyser, Ulrich. "Phänomenologie: Das Werk E. Husserls." *Mass und Wert* 2 (1938): 8–30.

Farber, Marvin. *Phenomenology as a Method and a Philosophical Discipline.* Buffalo, 1928.

_____. "Theses concerning the Foundation of Logic." *PRC* 38 (1929).

_____. "Relational Categories and the Quest for Unity." *PRC* 44 (1934).

_____. "Edmund Husserl and the Background of His Phenomenology." *PPR* 1 (1940): 1–20.

_____. "The Function of Phenomenological Analysis." *PPR* 1 (1940): 431–41.

_____. "The Ideal of a Presuppositionless Philosophy." In *PHIL ESSAYS*, pp. 44–64.

_____. *Philosophical Essays in Memory of Edmund Husserl.* Cambridge: Harvard University Press, 1940.

_____. *The Foundation of Phenomenology.* Cambridge: Harvard University Press, 1943.

_____. "Remarks about the Phenomenological Program." *PPR* 6 (1945): 1–10.

_____. "Concerning Freedom from Presuppositions." *PPR* 7 (1946): 367–68.

_____. "Modes of Reflection Inscribed to the Memory of Ed. Husserl." *PPR* 8 (1947): 588–600.

_____. "Phenomenology." In *Twentieth Century Philosophy*, ed. D.D. Runes, pp. 5–27. New York: Philosophical Library, 1947.

_____. "La philosophie descriptive et la nature de l'existence humaine." In *L'activité philosophique contemporaine en France et aux Etats-Unis*, pp. 67–94. Paris: Presses Universitaires de France, 1950. English translation: "Descriptive Philosophy and the Nature of Human Existence." In *Philosophic Thought in France and the United States*, pp. 419–41. New York: Philosophical Library, 1950.

_____. "Experience and Transcendence." *PPR* 12 (1951): 1–23.

_____. *Naturalism and Subjectivism.* Springfield: Charles C. Thomas, 1959.

_____. "On the Meaning of Radical Reflection." In *EH*, pp. 154–66.

————. "Phenomenological Tendency." *JP* 59 (1962): 429–39.

————. "First Philosophy and the Problem of the World." *PPR* 23 (1962–63): 315–34.

————. "The Phenomenological View of Values." *PPR* 24 (1963): 552–60.

————. "Edmund Husserl." In *Collier's Encyclopedia*, vol. 12, 1965.

————. *The Aims of Phenomenology*. New York: Harper, 1966.

————. "The Idea of a Naturalistic Logic." *PPR* 29 (1969): 598–601.

————. "The Goal of a Complete Philosophy of Experience." In *Phänomenologie heute: Festschrift für Ludwig Landgrebe*, pp. 14–26. The Hague: Nijhoff, 1972.

————. "The Philosophic Impact of the Facts Themselves." In *PHCC*, pp. 33–61.

Fein, Hubert. *Genesis und Geltung in E. Husserls Phänomenologie*. Frankfort: Europäische Verlags, 1970.

Fels, H. "Bolzano und Husserl." *PJ* (1926): 410–18.

Filipovic, Vladimir. "Die Sendung der Philosophie in unserer Zeit nach Marx und Husserl." *Praxis* 3 (1967): 346–51.

Findlay, John N. "Phenomenology." *Encyclopaedia Britannica*, 1964 ed., XVII, 699–702.

————. "Meinong: The Phenomenologist." *RIP* 27 (1973): 161–77.

————. "Phenomenology and the Meaning of Realism." In *PPU*, pp. 143–58.

————. "Husserl's Analysis of Internal Time-Consciousness." *MO* 59 (1975): 3–20.

Fink, Eugen. "Die Phänomenologische Philosophie Edmund Husserls in der gegenwärtigen Kritik." *K* 38 (1933): 319–83.

————. "Das Problem der Phänomenologie Edmund Husserls." *RIP* 1 (1938): 226–70.

————. "Das Problem der ontologischen Erfahrung." In *Actas del Primer Congresso de Filosofia* (Mendoza) 2 (1949): 733–49.

————. "L'analyse intentionnelle et le problème de la pensée spéculative." In *PROBLÈMES*, pp. 53–87.

————. "Operative Begriffe in Husserls Phänomenologie." *ZPF* 2 (1957): 321–37.

————. *Sein, Wahrheit, Welt: Vor-Fragen zum Problem des Phänomen-Begriffs*. The Hague: Nijhoff, 1958.

————. "Les concepts opératoires dans la phénoménologie de Husserl." In *HUSSERL*, pp. 214–30.

————. "Welt und Geschichte." In *HPM*, pp. 143–59. Translated: "Monde et histoire." In *HPM*, pp. 159–72.

————. "Die Spätphilosophie Husserls in der Freiburger Zeit." In *EH*, pp. 99–115.

————. *Studien zur Phänomenologie 1930–1939*. The Hague: Nijhoff, 1966.

————. *Phänomenologie: Lebendig oder Tot? Zum 30. Todesjaht Edmund Husserls*. Karlsruhe: Badeniaz, 1969.

————. "The Phenomenological Philosophy of Edmund Husserl and Contemporary Criticism." In *ELV*, pp. 73–147.

————. "Reflexionen zu Husserls Phänomenologischer Reduktion." *TF* 33 (1971): 540–58.

————. "What Does the Phenomenology of Edmund Husserl Want to Accomplish?" Translated by Arthur Grogan. *RP* 2 (1972): 5–27.

————. *De la phénoménologie*. Foreword by Edmund Husserl. Collection Arguments. Paris: Editions de Minuit, 1974.

————. "Totenrede auf Edmund Husserl bei der Einäscherung am 29 April 1938." *PSP* 1 (1975): 285–86.

————. *Nähe und Distanz: Phänomenologische Vorträge und Aufsätze*. Edited by Franz-Anton Schwarz. Freiburg: Alber, 1976.

————. "Operative Concepts in Husserl's Phenomenology." In *APRIORI*, pp. 56–70.

————. "The Problem of the Phenomenology of Edmund Husserl." In *APRIORI*, pp. 21–55.

Fische, M.P. *Husserls Intentionalitäts und Urteilslehre*. Bale, 1942.

Fischer, Gilbert R. "A Study in the Philosophy of Husserl." Ph.D. dissertation, University of Chicago, 1962.

Fischl, Johann. *Geschichte der Philosophie*. Bd. 5: *Idealismus, Realismus und Existentialismus der Gegenwart*, pp. 194–204. Cologne: Verlag Styria, 1954.

Fisher, A. "Some Basic Themes in the Phenomenology of Edmund Husserl." *MS* 43 (1965–66): 347–63.

Fleming, R. "Dramatic Involution: Tate, Husserl, and Joyce." *Sewanee Review* 60 (1952): 445–64.

Flynn, Bernard C. "Michel Foucault and the Husserlian Problematic of a Transcendental Philosophy of History." *PT* 22 (1978): 224–28.

Föllesdal, Dagfinn. *Husserl und Frege: Ein Beitrag zur Beleuchtung der Entstehung der phänomenologischen Philosophie.* Oslo: Aschehoug, 1958.

———. "Husserl's Notion of Noema." *JP* 66 (1969): 680–87.

———. "Husserl's Theory of Perception." *Ajatus* 36 (1974): 95–103.

———. "The Phenomenological Theory of Perception." In *Handbook of Perception I,* edited by E. C. Carterette and M. P. Friedman, pp. 381–85. New York: Academic Press, 1974.

———. "Brentano and Husserl on Intentional Objects of Perception." *Grazer Philosophische Studien* 5 (1978): 83–94.

———. "Husserl and Heidegger on the Role of Actions in the Constitution of the World." In *Essays in Honour of Jaakka Hintikka,* edited by E. Saarinen, I. Niiniluate, R. Hilpinen, and M. Provence, pp. 365–78. Dordrecht: Reidel, 1979.

Folwart, Helmut. "Kant, Husserl, Heidegger (Kritizimus, Phänomenologie, Existenzialontologie)." Ph.D. dissertation, Breslau, 1936.

Forrest, W. "Doubt and Phenomenological Reduction." *PPR* 18 (1957): 379–81.

Fouché, Fidela. "Phenomenological Psychology and Natural Science." *Philosophical Papers* 9 (1980): 1–14.

Foukes, William. "The Concept of the Self in Husserl and Beyond: The Transcendental Ego Reconsidered." *PT* 24 (1980): 44–54.

Frege, Gottlob. *Begriffsschriff und andere Aufsätze.* Hildesheim: Olms, 1964.

———. "Review of Dr. E. Husserl's *Philosophy of Arithmetic.*" *M* 81 (1972): 321–37; *MOHANTY,* pp. 6–21; *HEA,* pp. 314–24.

"Frege-Husserl Correspondence." *SWJP* 5 (1974): 83–96.

Friess, H.-L. "Husserl's Unpublished Manuscripts." *JP* (1939): 238–39.

Frings, Manfred S. "Husserl and Scheler: Two Views on Intersubjectivity." *JBSP* 9 (1978): 143–49.

Fritsch, W. *Die Welt 'einklamern', eine philosophische Frage an Edmund Husserl.* Reclams Universum, 1931.

Fuchs, Wolfgang Walter. *Phenomenology and the Metaphysics of Presence: An Essay on the Philosophy of Edmund Husserl.* The Hague: Nijhoff, 1976.

Fulda, Hans Friedrich. "Husserls Wege zum Anfang einer transzendentalen Phänomenologie." In *ID,* pp. 147–65.

Fulton, J.S. "The Cartesianism of Phenomenology." *PRC* 49 (1940): 285–308.

Funke, Gerhard. "Mundane Geschichte: ontologische Erfahrung und transzendentale Subjektivität: Eine transzendental-phänomenologische Untersuchung." *PJ* 64 (1956): 361–74.

———. "Geschichte als Phänomen." *ZPF* 11 (1957): 188–234.

———. *Zur transzendentalen Phänomenologie.* Bonn: Bouvier, 1957.

———. "Transzendental-phänomenologische Untersuchung über 'Universalen Idealismus', 'Intentionalanalyse' und 'Habitusgenese'." In *COMPITO,* pp. 117–54.

———. "Transzendentale Phänomenologie als erste Philosophie." *SG* 11 (1958): 564–82; 632–47.

———. *Phänomenologie — Metaphysik oder Methode?* Bonn: Bouvier, 1966.

———. "Bewusstseinswissenschaft: Evidenz und Reflexion als Implikate der Verifikation." *K* 61 (1970): 433–66.

———. "A Crucial Question in Transcendental Phenomenology: What Is Appearance in Its Appearing?" *JBSP* 4 (1973): 47–60.

———. "Husserl's Phenomenology as the Foundational Science." *SWJP* 5 (1974): 187–201.

———. "Die Diskussion um die metaphysiche Kantinterpretation." *K* 67 (1976): 409–24.

———. "Seinsgebundenheit der Erkenntnis und phänomenologische Kritik." *DH* 3 (1976): 78–89.

———. "A Transcendental-Phenomenological Investigation concerning Universal Idealism, Intentional Analysis and the Genesis of *Habitus.*" In *APRIORI,* pp. 71–113.

Gadamer, Hans Georg. *Wahrheit und Methode: Grundzüge einer philosophischen Hermeneutik.* Tübingen, J.C.B. Mohr, 1960.

————. "Die phänomenologische Bewegung." *PR* 11 (1963): 1–45.

————. "The Science of the Life-World." *ANALH* 2 (1972): 173–85.

————. *Kleine Schriffen III: Idee und Sprache: Platon, Husserl, Heidegger.* Tübingen: Mohr, 1972.

————. "Hermeneutics and Social Science." *CH* 2 (1975): 307–16.

Gagnebin, S. "La mathématique universelle d'après Edmund Husserl." In *Etudes de philosophie des Sciences,* pp. 99–114. Neuchâtel: Editions du Griffon, 1950.

Galay, Jean-Louis. "Essai sur le problème de l'intelligibilité d'après la *Critique de la raison logique* de Husserl." *SPS* 29 (1959): 25–53.

Gallagher, K.T. "Kant and Husserl on the Synthetic A Priori." *K* 63 (1972): 341–53.

Gallagher, Shaun. "Suggestions towards a Revision of Husserl's Phenomenology of Time-Consciousness." *MW* 12 (1979): 445–65.

Gauthier, Yvon, "La théorie de toutes les théories possibles est-elle possible?" *D* 14 (1975): 81–87.

Gendlin, Eugene T. *Experiencing and the Creation of Meaning.* New York: Free Press, 1962.

————. "A Phenomenology of Emotions." In *EXPLORATIONS,* pp. 367–98.

————. "Experiential Explication." In *SOLOMON,* pp. 160–67.

Geyser, Josef. *Neue und alte Wege der Philosophie: Eine Erörterung der Grundlagen der Erkenntnis in Hinblick auf Edmund Husserls Versuch ihrer Neubegründung.* Munster: Aschendorff, 1916.

Gibson, W.R. Boyce. "The Problem of Real and Ideal in the Phenomenology of Husserl." *M* 34 (1925): 311–27.

————. "From Husserl to Heidegger." *JBSP* 2 (1971): 58–62.

Gier, Nicholas F. "Intentionality and Prehension." *PRS* 6 (1976): 197–213.

Ginsburg, E. "Zur Husserlschen Lehre von Ganzen und Teilen." *Archiv für Systematische Philosophie,* 1929.

Glockner, Hermann. *Die europäische Philosophie von den Anfangen bis zur Gegenwart.* Stuttgart: Reclam, 1958.

Goel, Dharmendra. "Aesthetic Experience." *INPQ* 4 (1977): 349–61.

Golomb, Jacob. "Psychology from the Phenomenological Standpoint of Husserl." *PPR* 36 (1975–76): 451–71.

Gorner, Paul. "Husserl and Strawson." *JBSP* 2 (1971): 2–9.

————. "Husserl's *Logische Untersuchungen.*" *JBSP* 3 (1972): 187–94.

Gorsen, Peter. *Zur Phänomenologie des Bewusstseinsstroms: Bergson, Dilthey, Husserl, Simmel und die lebensphilosophischen Antinomien.* Bonn: Bouvier, 1966.

Gotesky, R. "Husserl's Conception of Logic as 'Kunstlehre' in the *Logische Untersuchungen.*" *PRC* 47 (1938): 375–89.

————. "Logic as an Independent Science: An Examination of E. Husserl's Conception of Pure Logic in the *Prolegomena zur reinen Logik* (First volume of the *Logische Untersuchungen*)." Ph.D. dissertation, New York University, 1939.

Granel, Gerard. *Le sens du temps et de la perception chez E. Husserl.* Paris: Gallimard, 1968.

————. "Remarques sur le rapport de *Sein und Zeit* et de la phénoménologie husserlienne." In *Durchbliche: Martin Heidegger zum 80. Geburtstag,* pp. 350–68. Frankfort: Klostermann, 1970.

————. "La gigantomachie." In his *Traditionis traditio: Essais.* Paris: Gallimard, 1972.

Graumann, Carl Friedrich. *Grundlagen einer Phänomenologie und Psychologie der Perspektivität.* Berlin: de Gruyter, 1960.

Graumann, Heinz. "Versuch einer historisch-kritischen Einleitung in die Phänomenologie des Verstehens." Ph.D. dissertation, Munich, 1924.

Grieder, Alfons. "Philosophy in a Technological Age." *JBSP* 6 (1975): 3–12.

————. "Geometry and the Life-World in Husserl's Later Philosophy." *JBSP* 8 (1977): 119–22.

————. "Husserl in the Thirties—the Hegelian Connection." *JBSP* 11 (1980): 255–70.

Grimme, A. "Die frohe Botschaft der Husserlschen Philosophie." *Der Falke* 1 (1917): 224–31.

Groethuysen, Bernard. *La philosophie allemande depuis Nietzsche.* Paris, 1926.

Groothoff, Hans H. "Edmund Husserl zu Gedächtnis." *Hamburger Akademische Rundschau* 3 (1950): 745–49.

Grünewald, Bernward. *Der phänomenologische Ursprung des Logischen: Eine krit. Analyse der phänomenologische Grundlegung der Logik in Edmund Husserls "Logische Untersuchungen."* Kastellaun: Henn, 1977.

Grundwaldt, H.H. "Über die Phänomenologie Husserls: Mit besonder Berücksichtigung der Wesenschau und die Forschungsmethode Gailieo Galileis." Ph.D. dissertation, Berlin, 1927.

Guilead, R. "Le concept de monde selon Husserl." *RMM* 82 (1977): 345–64.

Gurvitch, Georges. *Tendences actuelles de la philosophie allemande: E. Husserl, M. Scheler, E. Lask, M. Heidegger.* Paris: Vrin, 1930.

———. "La philosophie phénoménologie en Allemagne: Edmund Husserl." *RMM* 33 (1928).

Gurwitsch, Aron. "Phänomenologie der thematik und des reinen Ich." *Psychologische Forschung* 12 (1929): 19–38.

———. "Critical Study of Edmund Husserl 'Nachwort zu meinen Ideen zu einer reinen Phänomenologie und phänomenologischen Philosophie'." *Deutsche Literaturzeitung*, February 28, 1932.

———. "On the Intentionality of Consciousness." In *PHIL ESSAYS*, pp. 65–83; *PPEH*, pp. 118–36.

———. "A Non-Egological Conception of Consciousness." *PPR* 1 (1941): 325–38.

———. "Critical Study of James Street Fulton's 'The Cartesianism of Phenomenology'." *PPR* 2 (1942): 551–58.

———. "On the Object of Thought." *PPR* 7 (1947): 347–56.

———. "Gelb-Goldstein's Concept of 'Concrete' and 'Categorical' Attitude and the Phenomenology of Ideation." *PPR* 10 (1949): 172–96.

———. "L'approche phénoménologique et psychologique de la conscience." *Iyyun* (1953): 193–202. English translation: "The Phenomenological and Psychological Approach to Consciousness." *PPR* 15 (1955): 303–19.

———. "Beitrag zur Phänomenologische Theorie der Wahrnehmung." *PF* 13 (1953): 419–37; *ZPF* 13 (1959): 419–37.

———. "Présuppositions philosophiques de la logique." In *PHEX*, pp. 11–21.

———. "The Last Work of Edmund Husserl." *PPR* 16 (1956): 380–99; 17 (1957): 370–98.

———. *Théorie du champ de la conscience.* Paris: Desclée de Brouwer, (1957).

———. "La conception de la conscience chez Kant et chez Husserl." *BSFP* 54 (1960): 65–96. Paris: A. Colin, 1960.

———. "The Problem of Existence in Constitutive Phenomenology." *JP* 58 (1961): 625–32.

———. "On the Conceptual Consciousness." In *The Modeling of Mind*, edited by K.M. Sayre and F.J. Crosson, pp. 199–205. Notre Dame: University of Notre Dame Press, 1963.

———. "Der Begriff des Buwussteins bei Kant und Husserl." *K* 55 (1964): 410–27. Translated by Richard M. Zaner: "The Kantian and Husserlian Conception of Consciousness." In his *Studies in Phenomenology and Psychology*, pp. 148–74. Evanston: Northwestern University Press, 1966.

———. *The Field of Consciousness.* Pittsburgh, 1964.

———. "The Phenomenology of Perception: Perceptual Implications." In *INVITATION*, pp. 17–29.

———. "Critical Study of Husserl's *Nachwort*." Translated by Frederick Kerston. In Gurwitsch's *Studies in Phenomenology and Psychology*, pp. 107–15. Evanston: Northwestern University Press, 1966.

———. "Edmund Husserl's Conception of Phenomenological Psychology." *RM* 19 (1966): 689–727.

———. "Husserl's Noesis-Noema Doctrine." In his *Studies in Phenomenology and Psychology*. Evanston: Northwestern University Press, 1966; in *SOLOMON*, pp. 231–38.

———. *Studies in Phenomenology and Psychology.* Evanston: Northwestern University Press, 1966.

———. "Galilean Physics in the Light of Husserl's Phenomenology." In *Galileo, Man of Science*, edited by Ernan McMullin, pp. 388–401. New York: Basic Books, 1967.

———. "Husserl's Theory of the Intentionality of Consciousness in Historical Perspective." In *LEE*, pp. 25–58.

———. "The Husserlian Conception of the Intentionality of Consciousness." *The Isenberg Memorial Lecture Series, 1965–66*, pp. 145–62. East Lansing: Michigan State University Press, 1969.

———. "Towards a Theory of Intentionality." *PPR* 30 (1970): 354–67.

———. "Problems of the Life-World." In *PHSR*, pp. 35–61.

————. "Substantiality and Perceptual Coherence." *RP* 2 (1972): 29–46.

————. "Perceptual Coherence as the Foundation of the Judgment of Predication." In *PHCC*, pp. 62–89.

————. "Rezension von: Gaston Berger, *Das Cogito in Husserls Philosophie* (1941)." Aus dem Englischen übersetzt von Ursula Beul. In *NOACK*, pp. 222–30.

————. "Outlines of a Theory of 'Essentially Occasional Expressions'." In *MOHANTY*, pp. 112–27.

Gutting, Gary. "Husserl and Logical Empiricism." *MT* 2 (1971): 197–226.

————. "Husserlian Perspectives on Galilean Physics." In his *Phenomenology and the Theory of Science*, pp. 33–59. Evanston: Northwestern University Press, 1974.

————. "The Life-World and the Phenomenological Theory of Science." In his *Phenomenology and the Theory of Science*, pp. 3–32. Evanston: Northwestern University Press, 1974.

————. "Husserl and Scientific Realism." *PPR* 39 (1978): 42–56.

Guzzon, Ute; Rang, Bernhard; and Siep, Ludwig, eds. *Der Idealismus und Seine Gegenwart.* Hamburg: Felix Meiner, 1976.

Hachim, André. "Existentialisme et phénoménologie: Trois étapes: Husserl-Heidegger-Sartre." *Bulletin du Cercel Thomiste* (Caen) 15 (1953): 25–32.

Haddock, G.E. Rosado. "Edmund Husserls Philosophie der Logik und Mathematik im Licht der gegenwärtigen Logik und Grundlagensforschung." Ph.D. dissertation, Bonn, 1973.

Haglund, Dick A.R. *Perception, Time and the Unity of Mind: Problems in Edmund Husserls Philosophy, Part I.* Gothenburg: University of Gothenburg, Department of Philosophy, 1977.

Halda, Bernard. *Thematique phénoménologique et implications. Husserl, Edith Stein, Merleau-Ponty.* Louvain: Nauwelaerts; Paris: Diffusion Vander-Oyez, 1976.

Hall, Harrison. "Idealism and Solipsism in Husserl's *Cartesian Meditation.*" *JBSP* 7 (1976): 53–55.

————. "Intersubjective Phenomenology and Husserl's Cartesianism." *MW* 12 (1979): 13–20.

Hamilton, K.G. "Edmund Husserl's Contribution to Philosophy." *JP* 36 (1939): 225–32.

Harlan, Robert M. "The I and the Other: A Reformulation of Husserl's Fifth *Cartesian Meditation.*" Ph.D. dissertation, New School for Social Research, 1978.

Harris, Errol E. "The Problem of Self-Constitution for Idealism And Phenomenology." *IS* 7 (1977): 1–27.

Hartjes, John F. "The Critique of the 'Given' in Wilfrid Sellars and Edmund Husserl." Ph.D. dissertation, The Catholic University of America, 1974.

Hartmann, Klaus. *Husserls Einfühlungstheorie auf monadologischer Grundlage.* Bonn: Bouvier, 1953.

————. "Husserl und Kant." *K* 3 (1967): 370–75.

————. "Phenomenology, Ontology, and Metaphysics." *RM* 22 (1968): 85–112.

————. "Abstraction and Existence in Husserl's Phenomenological Reduction." *JBSP* 2 (1971): 10–19.

————. "The German Philosophical Science." *JBSP* 3 (1972): 11–14.

————. "Self-Evidence." *JBSP* 8 (1977): 79–93.

Hartmann, P. "Die Rolle der Sprache in Husserls Lehre von der Konstitution." *Der Deutschunterricht* 6 (1956).

Hartshorne, Charles. "The Method of Imaginative Variations." *JP* 36 (1939): 233–34.

————. "Husserl and the Social Structure of Immediacy." In *PHIL ESSAYS*, pp. 219–30.

————. "Husserl and Whitehead on the Concrete." In *PHCC*, pp. 90–104.

Hassell, Lewis. "Husserl's Theory of Meaning and Ordinary Language." *Graduate Faculty Philosophy Journal* 3 (1973): 32–41,

Heber, Johannes. "Die phänomenologisches Methode in der Religionsphilosophie: Ein Betrage zur Methodologie der Wesensbestimmung Religion." Ph.D. dissertation, Leipzig, 1929.

Hedwig, Klaus. "La discussion sur l'origine de l'intentionalité husserlienne." *EP* 3 (1978): 259–72.

————. "Intention: Outlines for the History of a Phenomenological Concept." *PPR* 39 (1979): 326–40.

Heffner, John. "Husserl's Critique of Traditional Empiricism." *JBSP* 5 (1974): 159–62.

Hegg, Hans. *Das Verhältnis der phänomenologischen Lehre von Husserl zur empirischen Psychologie.* Heidelberg: Hahn, 1919.

Heidegger, Martin. *Being and Time.* Translated by John Macquarrie and Edward Robinson. New York: Harper, 1962.
_____. "Phenomenology and Fundamental Ontology." In *PPEH,* pp. 294–312.
_____. "The Idea of Phenomenology." Translated by John N. Deely and Joseph A. Novak. *NS* 44 (1970): 325–44.

Hein, K.F. "Husserl's Criterion of Truth." *JCA* 3 (1971): 125–36.

Heinemann, F.H. "The Loneliness of the Transcendental Ego." In his *Existentialism and the Modern Predicament,* pp. 47–58 and passim. New York: Harper Torchbooks, 1958.

Held, Klaus. *Lebendige Gegenwart.* The Hague: Nijhoff, 1966.

Hemmendinger, David. "Husserl's Phenomenological Program: A Study of Evidence and Analysis." Ph.D. dissertation, Yale University, 1973.
_____. "Husserl's Concepts of Evidence and Science." *MO* 59 (1975): 81–97.

Hempolinski, M. "Epistemologie und Metaphysik bei Husserl und Ingarden." *Deutsche Zeitschrift für Philosophie* 24 (1976): 1546–55.

Hems, John M. "Husserl and/or Wittgenstein." *IPQ* 8 (1968): 547–78.

Henrich, Dieter. "Über die Grundlagen von Husserls Kritik der philosophischen Tradition." *PR* 6 (1958): 1–26

Henry, Michel. *L'essence de la manifestation.* Paris: Presses Universitaires de France, 1963.

Héring, Jean. "La phénoménologie de Husserl: il y a trente ans." *RIP* 1 (1939): 366–73.
_____. "Concerning Image, Idea and Dream." *PPR* 8 (1947): 188–205.
_____. "Malvine Husserl." *PPR* 11 (1950): 610–11.
_____. "Edmund Husserl, Souvenirs et réflexions." In *EH,* pp. 26–28.

Hermann, Friedrich-Wilhelm von. *Husserl und die Meditationen des Descartes.* Frankfort: Klostermann, 1971.
_____. "Lebenswelt und In-der-Welt-sein: Zum Ansatz des Welt problems bei Husserl und Heidegger." In *Weltaspekte der Philosophie,* pp. 123–41. Amsterdam: Rodopi, 1972.
_____. *Subjekt und Dasein: Interpretation zu "Sein und Zeit."* Frankfort: Klostermann, 1974.

Heyde, G. "Von philosophische Ausgang: Die Grundlegung der Philosophie untersucht am Beispiel der Lehre von J. Rehmke, H. Driesch, E. Husserl, J. Volkelt, H. Rickert." Ph.D. dissertation, Leipzig, n.d.

Hicks, G.D. "The Philosophy of Husserl." *HJ* 12 (1913): 198–202.

Hindess, Barry. "Transcendentalism and History: The Problem of History of Philosophy and the Sciences in the Later Philosophy of Husserl." *Economics and Society* 2 (1973): 309–42.
_____. "Husserl's Concept of the Nature of the Sciences and of Philosophy in *The Crisis.*" In his *Philosophy and Methodology in the Social Sciences.* Sussex: The Harvester Press, 1977.

Hines, Thomas J. *The Later Poetry of Wallace Stevens. Phenomenological Parallels with Husserl and Heidegger.* Lewisburg (Pa.): Bucknell University Press, 1976.

Hippolyte, J. "The Fichtean Idea of the Science of Knowledge and the Husserlian Project." *Auslegung* 1 and 2 (1973–75): 77–84.

Hirsch, Rudolf. "Edmund Husserl and Hugo von Hofmannsthal: Eine Begegnung und ein Brief [vom 12.1.1907]." In *Sprache und Politik,* edited by Carl-Joachim Freidrich and Benno Reifenberg, pp. 108–15. Heidelberg: Lambert Schneider, 1968.

Hoche, Hans-Ulrich. *Nichtempirische Erkenntnis: Analytische und synthetische Urteile a priori bei Kant und bei Husserl.* Meisenheim a. Glan: Hain, 1964.
_____. "Bemerkungen zum Problem der Selbst- und Fremd-erfahrung bei Husserl und Sartre." *ZPF* 25 (1971): 172–86.
_____. "Gegenwart und Handlung: Eine sprachanalytische-phänomenologische Untersuchung." In *PTPF,* pp. 189–224.
_____. "Phänomenologie und Sprachanalyse: Bemerkungen zu Wittgenstein, Ryle, und Husserl." In *Aufgaben und Wege des Philosophieunterrichts,* edited by Friedrich Borden. Neue Folge, Heft 4: Beiträge zu verschiedenen philosophischen Themes, 1972.

Hocking, William Ernest. "From the early days of the *Logische Untersuchungen*." In *EH*, pp. 1–11.

Hodges, H.A. "Phenomenology." *AS* 11 (1932): 84–100.

Hoeres, Walter. "Zum Begriff der verifizierenden Anschauung in Husserls *Logischen Untersuchungen*." *AP* 7 (1957): 325–34.

———. "Zur Dialektik der Reflexion bei Husserl." *SJ* 2 (1958): 211–30.

Hoffmann, Gisbert. "Zur Phänomenologie der Intersubjektivität. Kritische Bemerkungen aus Husserls Nachlass." *ZPF* 29 (1975): 138–49.

Hohl, Hubert. "Geschichte und Geschichtlichkeit. Ein Beitrag zur Spätphilosophie E. Husserls." *PJ* 69 (1961): 101–24.

———. *Lebenswelt und Geschichte: Grundzüge der Spätphilosophie E. Husserls.* Freiburg-Munich: Karl Albert, 1962.

Hohler, Thomas P. "Seeing and Saying: Phenomenology's Contention." *PT* 21 (1977): 327–46.

Holenstein, Elmar. "Passive Genesis: Eine begriffsanalytische Studie." *TF* 33 (1971): 112–53.

———. "Der Nullpunkt der Orientierung. Eine Auseinandersetzung mit der herkömmlichen phänomenologischen these der egozentrischen Raumwahrnehmung." *TF* 34 (1972): 28–78.

———. *Phänomenologie der Assoziation: Zu Struktur und Funktion eines Grundprinzips der passiven Genesis bei E. Husserl.* The Hague: Nijhoff, 1972.

———. "Jakobson und Husserl. Ein Beitrag zur Genealogie des Strukturalismus." *TF* 35 (1973): 560–607; in *History of Linguistic Thought,* edited by Herman Parret, pp. 772–810. Berlin and New York: Walter de Gruyter, 1976. English translation: "Jakobson and Husserl: A Contribution to the Genealogy of Structuralism." *HC* 7 (1975): 61–83.

———. *Jakobson ou le structuralisme phénoménologique.* Paris: Seghers, 1974.

———. "A New Essay concerning the Basic Relations of Language." *Semiotica* 12 (1974): 97–128.

———. "Jakobson phénoménologue?" *L'Arc* 60 (1975): 29–37.

———. *Roman Jakobsons phänomenologischer Strukturalismus.* Frankfort: Suhrkamp, 1975.

———. "Gewissen und rationale verantwortung." In *Gewissen.* Harsg. von Helmut Holzhey. Basel: Schwabe (in press).

———. *Jakobson and Structuralism. A Phenomenological Approach.* Bloomington: Indiana University Press (forthcoming).

Holmes, A.E. "Phenomenology and the Relativity of World-Views." *PE* 48 (1967): 328–44.

Holmes, Richard H. "Is Transcendental Phenomenology Committed to Idealism?" *MO* 59 (1975): 98–114.

———. "An Explication of Husserl's Theory of the Noema." *RIP* 5 (1975): 143–55.

Holveck, Eleanore W. "Edmund Husserl's Concept of the Ego in the *Cartesian Meditations*." Ph.D. dissertation, University of North Carolina at Chapel Hill, 1970.

Hook, Sidney. "Husserl's Phenomenological Idealism." *JP* 27 (1930): 365–80.

Horosz, William. "Does Husserl's Reach Exceed His Grasp? A Critique of the Transcendental Ego." *PT* 18 (1974): 181–97.

Hougaard, Esben. "Some Reflections on the Relationship between Freudian Psychoanalysis and Husserlian Phenomenology." *JPP* 9 (19--): 1–83.

Hoy, Ronald C. "Time and the Mental: An Examination of Broad's and Husserl's Theories of Temporal Consciousness." Ph.D. dissertation, University of Pittsburgh, 1974.

Hoyos Vasquez, Guillermo. "Zum Teleologiebegriff in der Phänomenologie Husserls." In *PTPF,* pp. 61–84.

———. *Intentionalität als Verantwortung. Geschichtsteleologie und Teleologie der Intentionalität bei Husserl.* The Hague: Nijhoff, 1976.

Huertas-Jourda, José. "On the Threshold of Phenomenology: A Study of Edmund Husserl's *Philosophie der Arithmetik*." Ph.D. dissertation, New York University, 1969.

———. "The Genetic Constitution of Reality from the Innermost Layer of the Consciousness of Time." *CH* 1 (1972): 225–49.

———. "Structures of the 'Living Present': Husserl and Proust." In *The Study of Time,* vol. 2, edited by J.T. Fraser and N. Lawrence, pp. 163–95. Berlin and New York: Springer-Verlag, 1975.

Hülsmann, Heinz. "Der Systemanspruch der Phänomenologie E. Husserls." *SJ* 7 (1963): 173–86.

_____. *Zur Theorie der Sprache bei Edmund Husserl.* Munich: Pustet, 1964.

Hutcheon, Peter. "Husserl's Problem of Intersubjectivity." *JBSP* 11 (1980): 144–62.

Hyppolite, Jean. "L'idée fichtéenne de la doctrine de la science et le project husserlian." In *HPM*, pp. 173–82; in *Figures de la pensée philosophique*, pp. 21–31. Paris: Presses Universitaires de France, 1971. Translated by Walter Biemel and E. Ch. Schröder: "Die fichtescht Idee der Wissen-schafts Lehre und der Entwurf Husserls." In *HPM*, pp. 182–92. English translation: "The Fich-tean Idea of the Science of Knowledge and the Husserlian Project." *AUS* 1–2 (1973–75): 77–84.

_____. "L'intersubjectivité chez Husserl." In *Figures de la pensée philosophique*, pp. 499–512. Paris: Presses Universitaires de France, 1971.

Ihde, Don. "Some Parallels between Analysis and Phenomenology." *PPR* 27 (1967): 577–86.

_____. *Hermeneutic Phenomenology.* Evanston: Northwestern University Press, 1971.

_____. *Sense and Significance.* New York: Humanities, 1974.

_____. "Under the Sign of Husserl and Heidegger." In his *Listening and Voice: A Phenomenology of Sound,* pp. 17–25. Athens, Ohio: Ohio University Press, 1976.

_____. *Experimental Phenomenology: An Introduction.* New York: G.P. Putnam's Sons, 1977.

Illeman, Werner. *Husserls vorphänomenologische Philosophie.* Leipzig: Hirzel, 1932.

Inciarte, Fernando. *Eindeutigkeit und Variation: Die Wahrung der Phänomen und das Problem des Reduktionismus.* Freiburg-Munich: Alber, 1973.

Ingarden, Roman. *Über die Stellung der Erkenntnistheorie im System der Philosophie.* Halle, 1926.

_____. "Bemerkungen zum Problem 'Idealismus-Realismus'." *Jahrbuch für Philosophie und Phä-nomenologische Forschung* (1929): 159–90.

_____. "Über die gegenwärtigen Aufgaben der Phänomenologie." In *COMPITO*, pp. 229–41.

_____. "Edmund Husserl zum 100. Geburtstag." In *EHZ*, pp. 459–63.

_____. "Le problème de la constitution et le sens de la réflexion constitutive chez Edmund Husserl." In *HUSSERL*, 242–70.

_____. "Über den transzendentalen Idealismus bei E. Husserl." In *HPM*, 190–204. Translated: "De l'idéalisme transcendental chez E. Husserl." In *HPM*, pp. 205–15.

_____. "Edith Stein on Her Activity As an Assistant of Edmund Husserl." *PPR* 23 (1962): 155–75.

_____. *Der Streit um die Existenz der Welt.* Bd. I: *Existentialontologie.* Tübingen: Niemeyer, 1964.

_____. "Husserls Betrachtungen zur Konstitution des physikalischen Dinges." *AP* 27 (1964): 355–407.

_____. *Time and Modes of Being.* Translated by H.R. Michejda. Springfield: Charles C. Thomas, 1964.

_____. "Die vier Begriffe der Transzendenz und das Problem des Idealismus in Husserl." *ANALH* 1 (1971): 36–74.

_____. "Letter to Edmund Husserl." *ANALH* 2 (1972): 357–74.

_____. "What Is New in Husserl's *Crisis*?" Translated by Rolf George. *ANALH* 2 (1972): 23–47.

_____. "A Priori Knowledge in Kant vs. A Priori Knowledge in Husserl." *DH*, Autumn (1973): 5–18.

_____. "Rezension von: Edmund Husserl, *Formale und transzendentale Logik*" (1929). In *NOACK*, pp. 168–73.

_____. *On the Motives Which Led Husserl to Transcendental Idealism.* Translated from the Polish by Arnor Hannibalsson. The Hague: Nijhoff, 1975.

_____. "The Letter to Husserl about the VI *Investigation* and 'Idealism'." Translated from the Ger-man by Helmut Girndt. *ANALH* 4 (1976): 418–38.

_____. "Probleme der Husserlschen Reduktion." Vorlesung gehalten an der Universität Oslo, Oktober/November 1967. *ANALH* 4 (1976): 1–71.

Jacques, J.H. "The Phenomenology of Temporal Awareness." *JBSP* 1 (1970): 38–45.

Jakowenko, B. "Edmund Husserl und die russische Philosophie." *Der Russische Gedanke* 1 (1929): 210ff.

Janssen, Paul. *Geschichte und Lebenswelt: Ein Beitrag zur Diskussion der Husserlschen Spätphiloso-phie.* Cologne, 1964; and The Hague: Nijhoff, 1970.

_____. "Ontologie, Wissenschaftstheorie und Geschichte im Spätwerk Husserls." In *PTPF*, pp. 145–63.

Jo Ja, Crizantema. "Intentionnalité et signification chez Husserl." *PL* 20 (1976): 119–26.

Johnson, Galen A. "Husserl and History." *JBSP* 11 (1980): 77–91.

Jolivet, Régis. "Le problème de l'évidence du jugement et l'évidence antéprédicative d'après Husserl." *RUO* 21 (1951): 235–53.

Jordan, Robert Welsh. "Husserl's Phenomenology as an 'Historical' Science." *SR* 35 (1968): 245–59.
———. "Being and Time: Some Aspects of the Ego's Involvement in His Mental Life." In *PHCC*, pp. 105–13.
———. "Vico and Husserl: History and Historical Science." In *Giambattista Vico's View of Humanity*, edited by Giorgio Tagliacozzo, pp. 251–61. Baltimore: The Johns Hopkins University Press, 1976.

Joseph de Saint Marie, O.C.D. "Le présupposé transcendental dans la phénoménologie de la perception de E. Husserl." *Doctor Communis* 25 (1972): 169–211.

Jung, Hwa Yol. "The Hermeneutics of Political Ideology and Cultural Change: Maoism as the Sinicization of Marxism." *CH* 3 (1975): 165–88.
———. "The Life-World, Historicity, and Truth: Reflection on Leo Strauss's Encounter with Heidegger and Husserl." *JBSP* 9 (1978): 11–25.
———. "Two Critics of Scientism: Leo Strauss and Edmund Husserl." *Independent Journal of Philosophy* 2 (1978): 81–88.

Kaelin, Eugene. "The Visibility of Things Seen: A Phenomenological View of Painting." In *INVITATION*, pp. 30–50.

Kalinowski, Georges. "La logique des normes d'Edmund Husserl." *Archives de Philosophie du Droit* 10 (1965): 111–22.
———. "La logique des valeurs d'Edmund Husserl." *Archives de Philosophie du Droit* 13 (1968): 267–82.

Kalsi, Marie-Louise S. *Alexius Meinong on Objects of Higher Order and Husserl's Phenomenology.* The Hague: Nijhoff, 1979.

Kates, Carol A. "Perception and Temporality in Husserl's Phenomenology." *PT* 14 (1970): 89–100.

Kattsoff, Louis Osgood. "The Relation of Science to Philosophy in the Light of Husserl's Thought." In *PHIL ESSAYS*, pp. 203–18.

Kaufman, J. N. "Husserl et le project d'une sémiotique phénoménologique." *D* 17 (1978): 24–34.

Kaufmann, E. "Bei Husserl in Göttingen." In *EH*, pp. 40–47.

Kaufmann, Fritz. "Art and Phenomenology." In *PHIL ESSAYS*, pp. 187–202.
———. "In Memoriam Edmund Husserl." *SR* 7 (1940): 61–91.
———. "Phenomenology and Logical Empiricism." In *PHIL ESSAYS*, pp. 124–42.
———. "The Phenomenological Approach to History." *PPR* 2 (1941): 159–72.
———. "Cassirer, Neo-Kantianism, and Phenomenology." In *The Philosophy of Ernst Cassirer*, edited by Paul Schilpp, pp. 801–54. New York: Tudor, 1949.
———. "Phenomenology of the Historical Present." *Proceedings of the 10th International Congress of Philosophy* 1 (1949): 967–70.
———. "Edmund Husserl." In *EH*, 40–47.

Kegley, Jacquelyn Ann. "Royce and Husserl: Some Parallels and Food for Thought." *TPS* 14 (1978): 184–99.

Kelkel, Lothar. "Le problème de l'autre dans la phénoménologie transcendentale de Husserl." *RMM* 61 (1956): 40–52.
———. "A propos d'un centenaire: E. Husserl (1859–1938)." *EP* 14 (1959): 435–48.
——— and Schérer, René. *Husserl. Sa vie, son oeuvre, avec un exposé de sa philosophie.* Paris: Presses Universitaires de France, 1964.
———. "Husserl et Kant: Reflexions à propos d'une thèse récente." *RMM* 71 (1966): 154–98.
———. *Husserl: Textes Choisis.* Paris: Presses Universitaires de France, 1971.
———. "History as Teleology and Eschatology: Husserl and Heidegger." In *TELEOLOGIES*, pp. 381–411.

Kelly, Derek. "Metaphysical Directives in Husserl's Phenomenology." *MS* 48 (1970): 1–18.

Kelly, Francis J. "The Structural and the Developmental Aspects of the Formulation of Categorical Judgments in the Philosophy of Edmund Husserl." Ph.D. dissertation, Georgetown University, 1978.

Kern, Iso. "Die drei Wege zur transzendental-phänomenologischen Reduktion Edmund Husserls." *TF* 24 (1962): 303–49.

―――. *Husserl und Kant: Eine Untersuchung über Husserls Verhältnis zu Kant und zum Neukantianismus.* The Hague: Nijhoff, 1964.

―――. "The Three Ways to the Transcendental Phenomenological Reduction in the Philosophy of Edmund Husserl." In *HEA*, pp. 126–49.

Kersten, Frederick I. "Husserl's Investigations toward a Phenomenology of Space." Ph.D. dissertation, New School for Social Research, 1964.

―――. "The Life-World Revisited." *RP* 1 (1971): 33–62.

―――. "On Understanding Idea and Essence in Husserl and Ingarden." *ANALH* 2 (1972): 55–63.

―――. "Husserl's Doctrine of Noesis-Noema." In *PHCC*, pp. 114–44.

―――― and Zaner, Richard M., eds. *Phenomenology: Continuation and Criticism: Essays in Memory of Dorion Cairns.* The Hague: Nijhoff, 1973.

―――. "Universals." *RIP* 4 (1974): 29–33.

―――. "The Occasion and Novelty of Husserl's Phenomenology of Essence." In *PP*, pp. 61–92.

―――. "The Originality of Gurwitsch's Theory of Intentionality." *RIP* 5 (1975): 12–27.

―――. "Zur transzendentalen Phänomenologie der Vernunft." *PSP* 1 (1975): 57–84.

Kim, Chin Tai. "Husserl and the Egocentric Predicament." *JP* 67 (1970): 821–22; *IS* 2 (1972): 116–32.

Kim, Hong-Woo. "Phenomenology and Political Philosophy: A Study of the Political Implications of Husserl's Account of the Life-World." Ph.D. dissertation, University of Georgia, 1975.

Kim, Sang-Ki. "The Problem of Contingency of the World in Husserl's Phenomenology." Ph.D. dissertation, State University of New York at Buffalo, 1973.

―――. *The Problem of the Contingency of the World in Husserl's Phenomenology.* Atlantic Highlands, N.J.: Humanities Press, 1977.

Kim, Y.-H. "Husserl and Natorp: Zur Problematik der Letzgründung der Philosophie bei Husserls Phänomenologie und Natorps neukantianischer Theorie." Ph.D. dissertation, Heidelberg University, 1974.

Kisiel, Theodore. "Husserl on the History of Science." In *PHNS*, pp. 68–90.

―――. "Ideology Critique and Phenomenology." *PT* 14 (1970): 151–60.

―――. "Repetition in Gadamer's Hermeneutics." *ANALH* 2 (1972): 196–203.

―――. "On the Dimension of a Phenomenology of Science in Husserl and the Young Dr. Heidegger." *JBSP* 4 (1973): 217–34.

―――. "Scientific Discovery: Logical, Psychological or Hermeneutical?" In *EXPLORATIONS*, pp. 263–84.

Klein, Jacob. "Phenomenology and the History of Science." In *PHIL ESSAYS*, pp. 143–63.

Klein, Theodore E., Jr. "The World as Horizon: Husserl's Constitutional Theory of the Objective World." Ph.D. dissertation, Rice University, 1967.

―――. "Husserl, Kant and the Idea of Transcendental Philosophy." *SWJP* 5 (1974).

―――. "Husserl's Kantian Meditations." *SWJP* 5 (1974): 69–82.

Knight, Everett W. "Husserl." In his *Literature Considered as Philosophy*, pp. 3–33. New York: Macmillan, 1950.

Kochler, Hans. "The A Priori Moment of the Subject-Object Dialectic in Transcendental Phenomenology." *ANALH* 3 (1974).

Kockelmans, J.J. "Realisme-idealisme en Husserls phénomènologie." *TF* 20 (1958): 395–441.

―――. *Phenomenology and Physical Science.* Pittsburgh: Duquesne University Press, 1966.

―――. *Edmund Husserl's Phenomenological Psychology.* Pittsburgh: Duquesne University Press, 1967.

―――. *A First Introduction to Husserl's Phenomenology.* Pittsburgh: Duquesne University Press, 1967.

————. "Husserl's Phenomenological Philosophy in the Light of Contemporary Criticism." In *PPEH*, pp. 221–36.

————. "Husserl's Transcendental Idealism." In *PPEH*, pp. 183–93.

————. "Intentional and Constitutive Analysis." In *PPEH*, pp. 137–46.

————, ed. *Phenomenology: The Philosophy of Edmund Husserl and Its Interpretation.* Garden City, N.Y.: Doubleday, 1967.

————. "What Is Phenomenology? Some Fundamental Themes of Husserl's Phenomenology." In *PPEH*, pp. 5–36.

————. "The Mathematization of Nature in Husserl's Last Publication, *Krisis*." In *PHNS*, pp. 45–67; *JBSP* 2 (1971): 45–67.

————and Kisiel, Theodore, eds. *Phenomenology and the Natural Sciences.* Evanston: Northwestern University Press, 1970.

————. "World-Constitution: Reflections on Husserl's Transcendental Idealism." *ANALH* 1 (1971): 11–35.

————. "Gestalt Psychology and Phenomenology in Gurwitsch's Conception of Thematics." In *LIFE-WORLD*, pp. 263–86.

————. "Phenomenologico-Psychological and Transcendental Reductions in Husserl's *Crisis*." *ANALH* 2 (1972): 78–89.

————. "On the Meaning and Function of Experience in Husserl's Phenomenology." In *ID*, pp. 297–317.

————. "Husserl and Kant on the Pure Ego." In *HEA*, pp. 269–85.

Kohák, Erazim. "Existence and the Phenomenological Epoché." *JE* 8 (1967): 19–47.

————. *Idea and Experience: Edmund Husserl's Project of Phenomenology in Ideas I.* Chicago: University of Chicago Press, 1978.

Kojima, H. "Zur philosophischen Erschliesung der religiösen Dimension: Überlegungen im Anschluss an Descartes, Husserl und den Zen-Buddhismus." *PJ* 85 (1978): 56–70.

————. "The Potential Plurality of the Transcendental Ego of Husserl and Its Relevance to the Theory of Space." *ANALH* 8 (1979): 55–61.

Kolakowski, Lezek. *Husserl and the Search for Certitude.* New Haven and London: Yale University Press, 1975.

Köppel, M. "Zur Analyse von Husserls Welt-Begriff." Ph.D. dissertation, Zurich, 1977.

Kouropoulos, Pétros. *Remarques sur le temps de l'homme selon Heidegger et Husserl.* Paris: Centre d'Etudes et de Recherches Marxistes, 1967.

Kraft, J. *Von Husserl zu Heidegger: Kritik der Phänomenologischen Philosophie.* 2nd ed. Frankfort, 1957.

Krämer, Ernst. "Bruno Erdmanns Wahreitsauffassung und ihre Kritik durch Husserl." Ph.D. dissertation, Munich, 1930.

Kuderowicz, Zbigniew. "Husserl as a Critic of Historicism." Translated by R. Legutko. *Rep Phil* (1978): 19–29.

Kuhn, Helmut. "The Phenomenological Concept of 'Horizon'." In *PHIL ESSAYS*, pp. 106–23.

————. "Rezension von: Edmund Husserl, *Méditations cartésiennes*. Introduction à la phénoménologie" (1931). In *NOACK*, pp. 174–87.

————; Are-Lallemant, Eberhard; and Gladiator, Reinhold, eds. *Die Münchner Phänomenologie.* The Hague: Nijhoff, 1975.

Kühndel, Jan. "Edmund Husserls Heimat und Herkunft." *AGP* 51 (1969): 286–90.

Kullman, Michael, and Taylor, Charles. "The Pre-Objective World." *RM* 12 (1958–59): 108–32.

Kumar, F.L. "Husserlian Notion of Intentionality." *MJP* 4 (1976): 35–42.

————. "The Concept of Person in Husserl's Phenomenology." *MJP* 6 (1978): 21–33.

Kumar, Jitendra. "Consciousness and Its Correlatives: Eliot and Husserl." *PPR* 28 (1968): 332–67.

Küng, Guido. "Language Analysis and Phenomenological Analysis." In *Akten des XIV Internationalen Kongress für Philosophie*, II, pp. 247–53. Vienna, 1968.

————. "The Role of Language in Phenomenological Analysis." *APQ* 6 (1969): 330–34.

————. "Ingarden on Language and Ontology (A Comparison with Some Trends in Analytic Philosophy)." *ANALH* 2 (1972): 204–17.

————. "The World as Noema and as Referent." *JBSP* 3 (1972): 15–26.

————. "Noema and Gegenstand." In *Jenseits von Sein und Nichtsein,* edited by R. Haller. Graz: Akademische Druck- und Verlaganstalt, 1972.

————. "Husserl on Pictures and Intentional Objects." *RM* 26 (1973): 670–80.

————. "The Phenomenological Reduction as *Epoché* and as Explication." *MO* 59 (1975): 63–80; *HEA,* pp. 338–49.

————. "Experience spontanée et théorie rationnelle." *SPS* 3 (1976): 90–106.

Kuntz, P.G. "Order in Language, Phenomena and Reality." *M* 49 (1965): 107–36.

Kunz, Hans. "Die Verfehlung der Phänomene bei Edmund Husserl." In *MÜN PHÄN,* pp. 53–77.

Kuroda, S.Y. "Edmund Husserl: *Grammaire générale et raisonnée,* and Anton Marty." *Foundations of Language* 10 (1973): 169–95.

Kuroda, Wataru. "Phenomenology and Grammar: A Consideration of the Relation between Husserl's *Logical Investigations* and Wittgenstein's Later Philosophy." *ANALH* 8 (1979): 89–107.

Kuspit, Donald. "Epoché and Fable in Descartes." *PPR* 25 (1964–65): 30–51.

————. "Parmenidean Tendencies in the Epoché." *RM* 18 (1965): 739–70.

————. "Fiction and Phenomenology." *PPR* 29 (1968–69): 16–33.

————. "The Continuity between Husserl and Kant." In *Proceedings of VIIth Inter-American Congress of Philosophy,* II (1968), pp. 282–87.

————. "Hegel and Husserl on the Problem of the Difficulty of Beginning Philosophy." *JBSP* 2 (1971): 52–57.

————. "The A Priori of Taste." *ANALH* 3 (1974).

Kuypers, K. "La conception de la philosophie comme science rigoureuse et les fondements des sciences chez Husserl." *ANTW* 51 (1958): 225–33; *HUSSERL,* pp. 72–82; in *Verspreide Geschriffen,* II, pp. 240–50. Assen: Van Gorcum, 1968.

————. "Die Wissenschaften von Menschen und Husserls Theorie von zwei Einstellungen." *ANALH* 1 (1971): 186–96.

————. "The Sciences of Man and the Theory of Husserl's Two Attitudes." *ANALH* 2 (1972): 186–95.

————. "Hermeneutik und die Interpretation der 'Logos' Idee." *RIP* 29 (1975): 52–77.

Kwakman, S. "The Beginning of Philosophy: On the Apodictic Way to the Object of Transcendental Experience in the Philosophy of Edmund Husserl." *TF* 36 (1974): 521–64.

Kwant, Remy C. "Merleau-Ponty's Criticism of Husserl's Eidetic Reduction." In *PPEH,* pp. 393–412.

Ladrière, J.P. "Hegel, Husserl, and Reason Today." *MS* 37 (1959): 171–95.

Lafont, Ghislain. "Genèse de la métaphysique." *Témoignages* 29 (1951): 214–23.

Lambert, F. "Husserl's Constitution of the Other in the Fifth Cartesian Meditation." *DJ* 17 (1974–75): 44–51.

Landgrebe, Ludwig. "Die Methode der Phänomenologie E. Husserls." *Neue Jahrbücher für Wissenschaft und Jugendbildung,* 1933.

————, and Patočka, Jean. *Edmund Husserl zum Gedächtnis: Schriften des Prager philosophischen Cercles.* Prague: Academic Verlagsbuchhandlung, 1938.

————. "Husserls Phänomenologie und die Motive zu ihrer Umbildung." *RIP* (1939): 227–316; in his *Phänomenologie und Metaphysik.* Hamburg: Marion von Schröder, 1949.

————. "The World as a Phenomenological Problem." *PPR* 1 (1940–41): 38–58.

————. "Phenomenology and Metaphysics." *PPR* 10 (1949–50): 197–205.

————. "Lettre sur un article de M. Jean Wahl concernant *Erfahrung und Urteil* de Husserl." *RMM* 57 (1952): 282–83.

————. "La phénoménologie de Husserl est-elle une philosophie transcendental?" *EP* 9 (1954): 315–23. Translated: "Ist Husserls Phänomenologie eine Transzendentalphilosophie?" In *HUSSERL,* pp. 316–24; *NOACK,* pp. 316–24.

————. *Philosophie der Gegenwart.* Bonn: Athenäum-Verlag, 1952, and Frankfort: Ullstein-Taschenbücher-Verlag, 1957. English translation: *Major Problems in Contemporary European Philosophy.* Translated by Kurt F. Reinhardt. New York: Ungar, 1966.

————. "Prinzipien der Lehre vom Empfinden." *ZPF* 8 (1954): 193–209.

————. "Seinsregionen und regionale Ontologien in Husserls Phänomenologie." *SG* 9 (1956): 313–24.

————. "Die Bedeutung der Phänomenologie Husserls für die Selbstbesinnung der Gegenwart." In *HPM*, pp. 216–23. Translated: "La signification de la phénoménologie de Husserl sur la réflexion de notre époque." Translated by J. Taminiaux. In *HPM*, pp. 223–29.

————. "Das Methodenproblem der transzendentalen Wissenschaft vom lebensweltlichen Apriori." In *EHS*, pp. 25–49.

————. "Husserls Abschied vom Cartesianismus." *PR* 9 (1961–62): 133–77.

————. *Der Weg der Phänomenologie: Das Problem einer ursprünglichen Erfahrung.* Gütersloh: Mohn, 1963.

————. "Husserl, Heidegger, Sartre: Trois aspects de la phénoménologie." *RMM* 69 (1964): 365–80.

————. *Phänomenologie und Geschichte.* Darmstadt: Mohr, 1967.

————. "Das Problem der Phänomenologischen Psychologie bei Husserl." In *Akten des XIV Internationalen Kongress für Philosophie*, II, pp. 151–63. Vienna, 1968. English translation: "The Problem of Phenomenological Psychology in Husserl." In International Congress of Philosophy, vol. 2, pp. 151–63. Vienna: Herder, 1968.

————. "Husserl's Departure from Cartesianism." In *ELV*, pp. 259–306.

————. "The Problem of the Beginning of Philosophy in Husserl's Phenomenology." In *LIFE-WORLD*, pp. 33–54.

————. "The Phenomenological Concept of Experience." *PPR* 34 (1973): 1–13.

————. "A Meditation on Husserl's Statement: 'History Is the Grand Fact of Absolute Being'." *SWJP* 5 (1974): 111–25.

————. "Reflexionen zu Husserls Konstitutionslehre." *TF* 36 (1974): 466–82.

————. "Meditationen über Husserls Wort 'Die Geschichte ist das grosse Faktum des absoluten Seins'." *TF* 36 (1974): 107–26.

————. "Geschichtsphilosophie Perspektiven bei Scheler und Husserl." In *Max Scheler im Gegenwartsgeschehen der Philosophie.* Edited by Paul Good, pp. 79–90. Bern and Munich: A. Francke A. G. Verlag, 1975.

————. "Die Phänomenologie als transzendental Theorie des Geschichte." In *Phänomenologie und Praxis*, pp. 17–47. Frieburg-Munich: Alber, 1976.

————. "Lebenswelt und Geschichtlichkeit des menschlichen Daseins." In *Phänomenologie und Marxismus*, edited by B. Waldenfels et al., pp. 13–58. Frankfort: Suhrkamp, 1977.

————. "Phenomenology as Transcendental Theory of History." In *HEA*, pp. 101–13.

————. "The Problem of Passive Constitution." Translated by Donn Wellan. *ANALH* 7 (1978): 23–36.

————. "The Problem Posed by the Transcendental Science of the A Priori of the Life World." In *APRIORI*, pp. 152–71.

————. "Regions of Being and Regional Ontologies in Husserl's Phenomenology." In *APRIORI*, pp. 132–51.

Landsberg, Paul-L. "Husserl et l'idée de la philosophie." *RIP* 1 (1938–39): 317–25.

Langan, Thomas. "The Future of Phenomenology." In *PERSPECTIVE*, pp. 1–15.

Langdorf, Lenore. "Husserl on Judging: A Critique of the Theory of Ideal Objects." Ph.D. dissertation, State University of New York at Stony Brook, 1977.

Langlois, Jean. "Observations sur Husserl et la phénoménologie." In *FEN*, pp. 148–50.

Lanteri-Laura, Georges. "L'usage de l'exemple dans la phénoménologie." *EP* 9 (1954): 57–72.

————. *La psychiatrie phénoménologique: Fondements philosoques.* Paris: Presses Universitaires de France, 1963.

Lanz, H. "The New Phenomenology." *M* 34 (1924): 511–27.

Laporte, Jean Marc. "Husserl's Critique of Descartes." *PPR* 23 (1962–63): 335–52.

Lapp, Adolf. *Versuch über den Wahrheitsbegriff mit besonder Berücksichtigung von Rickert, Husserl und Vaihinger.* Erlangen, 1912.

Larrabee, M.J. "Husserl on Sensation: Notes on the Theory of Hyle." *NS* 47 (1973): 179–203.

————. "Static and Genetic Phenomenology: A Study of Two Methods in Husserl's Philosophy." Ph.D. dissertation, University of Toronto, 1974.

————. "Husserl's Static and Genetic Phenomenology." *MW* 9 (1976): 163–74.

Laskey, Dallas. "Embodied Consciousness and the Human Spirit." *ANALH* 1 (1971): 197–207.

————. "Ingarden's Criticism of Husserl." *ANALH* 2 (1972): 48–54.

Lauer, J. Quentin. *Phénoménologie de Husserl: Essai sur la genèse de l'intentionnalité.* Paris: Presses Universitaires de France, 1955.
_____. *The Triumph of Subjectivity: An Introduction to Transcendental Phenomenology.* New York: Fordham University Press, 1958; reprinted as: *Phenomenology: Its Genesis and Prospect.* New York: Harper and Row, 1965.
_____. "The Subjectivity of Objectivity." In *EH*, pp. 167–74.
_____. Introduction to Edmund Husserl, *Phenomenology and the Crisis of Philosophy.* Translated by Quentin Lauer, pp. 1–68. New York: Harper Torchbooks, 1965.
_____. "Phenomenology: Hegel and Husserl." In *Beyond Epistemology: New Studies in the Philosophy of Hegel.* Edited by Frederick G. Weiss, pp. 174–96. The Hague: Nijhoff, 1974.

Lawrence, Nathaniel, and O'Connor, Daniel, eds. *Readings in Existential Phenomenology.* Englewood Cliffs: Prentice-Hall, 1967.

Lazlo, Ervin. *Beyond Scepticism and Realism. A Constructive Exploration of Husserlian and Whiteheadian Methods of Inquiry.* The Hague: Nijhoff, 1966.

Leavy, John P. "Undecidables and Old Names: Derrida's Deconstruction and 'Introduction' to Husserl's *The Origin of Geometry.*" Ph.D. dissertation, Emory University, 1976.

Ledrut, Raymond. "Phénoménologie et rationalisme." *CR* 117 (1957): 151–223.
_____. "La philosophie comme science rigoureuse." *Critique* 117 (1957): 123–51.

Lee, Edward, and Mandelbaum, Maurice, eds. *Phenomenology and Existentialism.* Baltimore: Johns Hopkins University Press, 1967.

Lehmann, Gerhard. "Edmund Husserl." In *Geschichte der Philosophie,* pp. 24–36. Berlin: De Gruyter, 1960.

Leiss, William. "Husserl and the Mastery of Nature." *T* 5 (1970): 82–97.
_____. "Husserl's *Crisis.*" *T* 8 (1971): 109–20.

Lejewski, Czeslaw, "Syntax and Semantics of Ordinary Language: Part 1." *AS* 49 (1975): 127–46.

Leland, Dorothy. "Edmund Husserl, Phenomenology and Crisis of Language." *PT* 23 (1979): 226–37.

Lenkowski, William Jan. "What Is Husserl's *Epoché:* The Problem of Beginning Philosophy in a Husserlian Context." *MW* 11 (1978): 299–323.

Lenzen, Wilhelm. "Die Intentionsgedanke in der Phänomenologie und die erkenntnistheoretische Repräsentation." Ph.D. dissertation, Bonn, 1929.

Leroux, Henri. "Sur la publication complète des *Ideen* de Husserl." *EP* 7 (1952): 261–77.

Levin, David M. "A Critique of Edmund Husserl's Theory of Adequate and Apodictic Evidence." Ph.D. dissertation, Columbia University, 1967.
_____. "Induction and Husserl's Method of Eidetic Variation." *PPR* 29 (1968–69): 1–15.
_____. "Husserlian Essences Reconsidered." In *EXPLORATIONS,* pp. 169–83.
_____. *Reason and Evidence in Husserl's Phenomenology.* Evanston: Northwestern University Press, 1970.
_____. "Husserl's Notion of Self-Evidence." In *PPU,* pp. 53–77.

Levinas, Emmanuel. "Sur les *Ideen* de Husserl." *RP* 107 (1929): 230–65. Translation: "Über die *Ideen* Edmund Husserls." Translated by Herbert Backes from the French. In *NOACK,* pp. 87–128.
_____. "L'oeuvre d'Edmond Husserl." *RPF* 65 (1940): 33–85.
_____. *De l'existence a l'existant.* Paris: Fontaine, 1947.
_____. "Intentionalité et métaphysique." *RPF* 84 (1959): 471–79.
_____. "Réflexions sur la *technique* phénoménologique." In *HUSSERL,* pp. 95–107.
_____. "La ruine de la représentation." In *EH,* pp. 73–85.
_____. "Le permanent et l'humain chez Husserl." *Age nouveau* 110 (1960): 51–56.
_____. *Théorie de l'intuition dans la phénoménologie de Husserl.* Paris: J. Vrin, 1963. English translation: *The Theory of Intuition in Husserl's Phenomenology.* Translated by André Orianne. Evanston: Northwestern University Press, 1973.
_____. "La signification et le sens." *RMM* 69 (1964): 125–56.
_____. "Intentionnalité et sensation." *RIP* 71 (1965): 34–54.
_____. *En découvrant l'existence avec Husserl et Heidegger suivi d'essais nouveaux.* 2nd edition. Paris: J. Vrin, 1967; 3rd edition. Paris: J. Vrin, 1974.

———. "Intuition of Essences." In *PPEH,* pp. 83–104.

———. *Autrement qu'être, ou au-delà de l'essense.* The Hague: Nijhoff, 1974.

———. "De la conscience à la veille. A partir de Husserl." *Bijdragen* 34 (1974): 235–49.

———. "La philosophie et l'eveil." *EP* 3 (1977): 307–17.

Libertson, J. "Levinas and Husserl: Sensation and Intentionality." *TF* 41 (1979): 485–502.

Lingis, Alphonso. "Intentionality and Corporeity." *ANALH* 1 (1971): 75–90.

———. "Hyletic Data." *ANALH* 2 (1972): 96–101.

———. "The Perception of Others." *RP* 2 (1972): 47–62; *PF* 5 (1974): 460–74.

———. "The Origin of Infinity." *RPH* 6 (1976): 22–45.

———. "On Phenomenological Explanation." *JBSP* 11 (1980): 54–68.

Linke, Paul Ferdinand. *Niedergangserscheinungen in der Philosophie der Gegenwart. Wege zu ihrer Überwindung.* Munich: Ernst Reinhardt-Verlag, 1961.

Linschoten, Johannes. *Auf dem Wege zu einer phänomenologischen Psychologie: Die Psychologie von William James.* Berlin: De Gruyter, 1961.

Lippitz, Wilfried. "Der Phänomenologische Begriff der 'Lebenswelt': Seine Relevanz für die Sozial-wissenschaften." *ZPF* 32 (1978): 416–35.

Lowit, Alexandre. "Pourquoi Husserl n'est pas platonicien." *EP* 9 (1954): 324–36.

———. "*L'épochè* de Husserl et le doute de Descartes." *RMM* 62 (1957): 399–415.

———. "D'où vient l'ambiguité de la phénoménologie?" *BSFP* 65 (1971): 3–68.

———. "Sur les *Cinq Lecons* de Husserl." *RMM* 76 (1971): 223–36.

Löwith, Karl. "Eine Erinnerung an E. Husserl." In *EH* pp. 48–55.

Lowry, Atherton C. "Merleau-Ponty and Fundamental Ontology." *IPQ* 15 (1975): 397–409.

Lozinski, Jerzg. "Some Remarks concerning David Rasmussen's *The Marxist Critique of Phenomenology.*" *DH* 2 (1975): 71–75.

———. "On the Problems of the Relation between Marxism and Phenomenology: Truth and Revolution—Husserl and Lenin." *DH* 3 (1976): 121–33.

Lübbe, Hermann. "Das Ende des phänomenologischen Platonismus: Eine kritische Betrachtung aus Anlass eines neuen Buches." *TF* 16 (1954): 639–66.

———. "Husserl und die europäische Krise." *K* 48 (1957): 225–37.

———. "Die geschichtliche Bedeutung der Subjektivitätstheorie Edmund Husserls." *Neue Zeitschrift für systematische Theologie* 2 (1960): 300–19.

———. "Positivismus und Phänomenologie (Mach und Husserl)." *Beiträge zu Philosophie und Wissenschaft. Wilhelm Szilasi zum 70. Geburtstag,* pp. 161–84. Munich: Francke, 1960.

———. *Bewusstsein in Geschichten: Studien zur Phänomenologie der Subjektivität: Mach, Husserl, Schapp, Wittgenstein.* Freiburg: Rombach, 1972.

Luijpen, William A. *Existential Phenomenology.* Translated by Henry J. Koren. Pittsburgh: Duquesne University Press, 1960.

Lynch, Timothy. "Husserl: From Logic to Philosophy." *PST* 26 (1979): 26–40.

Lyons, Joseph. "Edmund Husserl." In *The International Encyclopedia of the Social Sciences,* edited by David L. Suls, pp. 27–31. New York: Macmillan, 1968.

Lyotard, Jean-F. *La phénoménologie.* Paris: Presses Universitaires de France, 1954.

Macann, Christopher. "Genetic Production and the Transcendental Reduction in Husserl." *JBSP* 2 (1971): 28–34.

Mackie, J.L. "Problems of Intentionality." In *PPU,* pp. 37–52.

MacLeod, R.B. "Phenomenology: A Challenge to Experimental Psychology." In *WANN,* pp. 47–79.

Madden, Robert E. "Husserl and the Problem of Hidden Reason: Intentionality as Accomplished Life." Ph.D. dissertation, Duquesne University, 1973.

———. "Phenomenology in Its Beginnings." *RPH* 8 (1978): 203–15.

Madison, Gary B. "Phenomenology and Existentialism: Husserl and the End of Idealism." In *HEA,* pp. 247–68.

Mahnke, D. "Von Hilbert zu Husserl." *Unterrichsblätter Für Mathematik und Naturwissenschaften* 29: 34–37.

_____. "Eine neue Monadologie." *K* 39 (1917).

_____. "From Hilbert to Husserl: First Introduction to Phenomenology, Especially That of Formal Mathematics." Translated by David I. Boyer. *Studies in History and Philosophy of Science* 8 (1977): 71–84.

Malhotra, M.K. "Die indische Philosophie und die Phänomenologie Husserls: Der Begriff der 'Wahrnehmung' in den beiden Denkrichtungen." *ZPF* 13 (1959): 339–46.

Mall, Rom Adhar. "Husserl's Criticism of Kant's Theory of Knowledge." *Journal of the Indian Academy of Philosophy* 6 (1976): 21–31,

_____. "Phenomenology of Reason." In *PTPF*, pp. 129–43.

_____. *Experience and Reason: The Phenomenology of Husserl and Its Relation to Hume's Philosophy*. The Hague: Nijhoff, 1972.

_____. "Der Induktionsbegriff. Hume und Husserl." *ZPF* 29 (1975): 34–62.

Malmgren, H. "Internal Relations in the Analysis of Consciousness." *TH* 41 (1975): 61–83.

Marbach, Eduard. "Ichlose Phänomenologie bei Husserl." *TF* 35 (1973): 518–59.

_____. *Das Problem des Ich in der Phänomenologie Husserls*. The Hague: Nijhoff, 1974.

_____. "Husserl's reine Phänomenologie und Piagets genetische Psychologie." *TF* 39 (1977): 81–103.

Marcus, John T. "East and West: Phenomenologies of the Self and the Existential Bases of Knowledge." *IPQ* 11 (1971): 5–48.

Marcuse, H. "On Science and Phenomenology." In *Boston Studies in the Philosophy of Science*. vol. 2, edited by R.S. Cohen and M.W. Wartofsky, pp. 279÷90. New York: Humanities Press, 1965. In *Positivism and Sociology*, edited by Anthony Giddens, pp. 225–36. London-New York: Heinemann, 1974.

Margeneau, Henry. "Phenomenology and Physics." *PPR* 5 (1944–45): 269–80.

Margolin, Julius. "Grundphänomene des intentionalen Bewusstseins." Ph.D. dissertation, Berlin, 1929.

Marsh, James L. "An Inconsistency in Husserl's *Cartesian Meditations*." *NS* 53 (1979): 460–74.

Martin, Gottfried. "Neuzeit und Gegenwart in der Entwicklung des mathematischen Denkens." *K* 45 (1953): 155–65; in *Gesammelte Abhandlungen*, vol. 1, pp. 138–50. Cologne: Kölner Universitäts-Verlag, 1961.

Martineau, E. "Mimesis dans la poetique: Pour une solution phénoménologique (A propos d'un livre recent)." *RMM* 18 (1976): 438–66.

Marx, Werner. "Vernunft und Leberswelt: Bemerkungen zu Husserls 'Wissenschaft von der Lebenswelt'." In his *Vernunft und Welt: Zwischen Traditions und anderem Anfang*, pp. 45–62. The Hague: Nijhoff, 1970. English translation: *Reason and World: Between Tradition and Another Beginning*, pp. 46–61. The Hague: Nijhoff, 1971.

_____. "The Life-World and Its Particular Sub-Worlds." In his *Reason and World: Between Tradition and Another Beginning*, pp. 62–76. The Hague: Nijhoff, 1971.

_____. "The Life-World and Gurwitsch's Orders of Existence." In *LIFE-WORLD*, pp. 445–60.

Mathur, D.C. *Naturalistic Philosophies of Experience: W. James, J. Dewey, M. Farber against the Background of Husserl's Phenomenology*. St. Louis: W.H. Green, 1971.

Maund, J.B. "Awareness of Sensory Experience." *M* 85 (1976): 412–16.

Maxsein, Agnes. *Die Entwicklung des Begriffs a priori von Bolzano über Lotze zu Husserl und den von ihm beeinflussten Phänomenologie*. Fulda, 1933.

Mayer-Hillebrand, Franziska. "Franz Brentanos ursprüngliche und spätere Seinslebre und ihre Beziehungen zu Husserls Phänomenologie." *ZPF* 13 (1959): 316–39.

Mays, Wolfe. "Husserl on Ryle's Review of *Sein und Zeit*." *JBSP* 1 (1970): 14–15.

_____. "Husserl and Phenomenology." *PY* 46 (1971): 262–68.

_____, and Brown, S.C., eds. *Linguistic Analysis and Phenomenology*. Lewisburg, Pa.: Bucknell University Press, 1972.

_____. "The Later Husserl." *INQ* 17 (1974): 113–25.

_____. "Genetic Analysis and Experience: Husserl and Piaget." *JBSP* 8 (1977): 51–55.

McCarthy, Thomas Anthony. "Logic, Mathematics and Ontology in Husserl." *JBSP* 3 (1972): 158–64.
———. *Husserl's Phenomenology and the Theory of Logic* (1968). Ann Arbor: University Microfilms International, 1976.

McCluskey, Frank B. "The Perceptual Basis of Phenomenology in Husserl and Hegel." Ph.D. dissertation, New Scool for Social Research, 1978.

McCormick, Peter. "Husserl's *Formal and Transcendental Logic* and *Bachelard's Study*." *JBSP* 2 (1971): 88–92.
———. "Husserl and the Intersubjectivity Materials." *RPH* 6 (1976): 134–51.
———. "Phenomenology and Metaphilosophy." In *HEA*, pp. 350–64.

McGaughey, D.R. "Husserl and Heidegger on Plato's Cave Allegory: A Study of Philosophical Influence." *IPQ* 16 (1976): 331–48.

McGill, V.J. "A Materialist's Approach to Husserl's Philosophy." In *PHIL ESSAYS*, pp. 231–50.
———. "The Bearing of Phenomenology on Psychiatry." *PPR* 7 (1946): 357–63.
———. "Evidence in Husserl's Phenomenology." In *PHCC*, pp. 145–66.

McGinn, Colin. "Mach and Husserl." *JBSP* 3 (1972): 146–57.

McIntyre, Ronald T. "Husserl and Referentiality: The Role of the Noema as an Intensional Entity." Ph.D. dissertation, Stanford University, 1970.
———, and Smith, David Woodruff. "Husserl's Identification of Meaning and Noema." *MO* 59 (1975): 115–32.
———, and Smith, David Woodruff. *Intentionality via Intensions: Husserl's Phenomenology and the Semantics of Modalities*. Dordrecht: D. Reidel, 1978.

McKenna, William. *Husserl's 'Introduction to Phenomenology'*. Forthcoming.
———; Harlan, Robert M.; and Winters, Lawrence E., eds. *Apriori and World: European Contributions to Husserlian Phenomenology*. The Hague: Nijhoff, 1981.

Medina, Angel. "Husserl on the Nature of the Subject." *NS* 45 (1971): 547–72.

Meiland, Jack W. "Psychologism in Logic: Husserl's Critique." *INQ* 19 (1976): 325–39.

Meinong, Alexius. *Philosophenbriefe: Aus den wissenschaftlichen Korrespondenz von Alexius Meinong*. Edited by R. Kindinger. Graz, 1965.
———. *On Emotional Presentation*. Translated by M.L.S. Kalsi. Evanston: Northwestern University Press, 1972.

Mende, Georg. "Die Geschichte der Philosophie nach den Auffassungen Edmund Husserls." *Wissenschaftliche Zeitschrift der Friedrich-Schiller-Universität Jena* 13 (1964): 243–48.
———. "L'histoire de la philosophie selon Husserl." *RTP* 98 (1965): 65–77.

Menges, Karl. "Robert Musil und Edmund Husserl: Über phänomenologischen Strukturen im *Mann ohne Eigenschaften*." *Modern Austrian Literature* 9 (1976): 131–54.

Mensch, James R. "The Quest of Being in Husserl's *Logical Investigations*." Ph.D. dissertation, University of Toronto, 1978.

Merlan, Philip. "Time Consciousness in Husserl and Heidegger." *PPR* 8 (1947): 23–54.
———. "Idéalisme, réalisme, phénoménologie." In *HUSSERL*, pp. 382–410.

Merleau-Ponty, Maurice. "Sur la phénoménologie du langage." In *PROBLÈMES*, pp. 89–109.
———. *Les sciences de l'homme et la phénoménologie*. Paris: Tournier et Constans, 1953.
———. "What Is Phenomenology?" Translated by J. Banna. *Cross Currents* 4 (1956): 59–70.
———. "Le philosophe et son ombre." In *EH*, pp. 195–220.
———. "Sur la phénoménologie du langage." In *Signes*, pp. 105–22. Paris: Gallimard, 1960.
———. "Phenomenology and the Sciences of Man." In his *The Primacy of Perception*, translated by John Wild, pp. 43–95. Evanston: Northwestern University Press, 1964.
———. "Husserl et la notion de nature." *RMM* 70 (1965): 257–69.

Messer, A. "Husserls Phänomenologie in ihrem Verhältnis zur Psychologie." *AGP* 22 (1912).

Messerich, Valerius. "An Apodictic Approach to Reality." *FS* 13 (1953): 1–36.

Metraux, Alexandre. "Edmund Husserl und Moritz Geiger." In *MÜN PHÄN*, pp. 139–57.

Metzger, Arnold. *Phänomenologie und Metaphysik*. Pfullingen: Neske, 1933; 1966.

———. "Die Frage nach dem Menschen in der Philosophie unserer Zeit von Husserl bis Heidegger und Sartre." *Universitas* 27 (1972): 65–77.

Meyer, Rudolf. "Descartes, Valéry, Husserl." *HAR* (1950): 753–69.

Meyn, Henning L. "Husserl's Transcendental Logic and the Problem of Its Justification." Ph.D. dissertation, Brown University, 1971.

———. "The Life-World and the A Priori—Opposites or Complementaries?" *ANALH* 3 (1974).

———. "Non-Empirical Investigations in Husserl and Ordinary Language Philosophy." *SWJP* 5 (1974): 245–59.

Miéville, Henri-Louis. "Le cogito de la phénoménologie de Husserl et le cogito de Descartes." *Jahrbuch Schweizer Philosophische Gesselschaft* 1 (1941).

———. "Du 'cogito' au transcendental et au métaphysique." *RTP* 92 (1964): 265–87.

Miguelez, J. *Sujet et historie.* Ottawa: Presses de l'Université d'Ottawa, 1975.

Mihalich, Joseph C. "Husserl and the Rise of Continental Existentialism." In his *Existentialism and Thomism,* pp. 51–62. New York: Philosophical Library, 1960.

Mijuskovic, Ben. "The Simplicity Argument and Absolute Morality." *TT* 10 (1975): 123–35.

Miller, Izchak. "The Phenomenology of Perception: Husserl's Account of Our Temporal Consciousness." Ph.D. dissertation, University of California at Los Angeles, 1979.

Miller, James P. "The Presence and Absence of Number in Husserl's Philosophy of Mathematics." Ph.D. dissertation, The Catholic University of America, 1980.

Minkowski, Eugene. *Lived Time.* Evanston: Northwestern University Press, 1970.

Misch, Georg. *Lebensphilosophie und Phänomenologie: Eine Auseinandersetzung d. Diltheyschen Richtung mit Heidegger und Husserl.* Stuttgart: Teubner, 1967.

Mohanty, Jitendranath. "Husserl's Phenomenology and Indian Idealism." *PQA* 24 (1951): 147–56.

———. "Fichte's *Science of Knowledge* and Husserl's Phenomenology." *PQA* 25 (1952): 113–21.

———. "The 'Object' in Husserl's Phenomenology." *PPR* 14 (1953–54): 343–53.

———. "Individual Fact and Essence in Edmund Husserl's Philosophy." *PPR* 20 (1959–60): 222–30.

———. *Edmund Husserl's Theory of Meaning.* The Hague: Nijhoff, 1964.

———. *Phenomenology and Ontology.* The Hague: Nijhoff, 1970.

———. "Husserl's Concept of Intentionality." *ANALH* 1 (1971): 100–32.

———. *The Concept of Intentionality.* St. Louis: W.H. Green, 1972.

———. "A Note on the Doctrine of Noetic-Noematic Correlation." *ANALH* 2 (1972): 317–21.

———. "Towards a Phenomenology of Self-Evidence." In *EXPLORATIONS,* pp. 208–29.

———. "The Frege-Husserl Correspondence." *SWJP* 5 (1974): 83–95.

———. "Life-World and A Priori in Husserl's Later Thought." *ANALH* 3 (1974): 46–65.

———. "On Husserl's Theory of Meaning." *SWJP* 5 (1974): 229–44; *HEA,* pp. 18–37.

———. "The Task and the Significance of the *Logical Investigations.*" In *MOHANTY,* pp. 197–215.

———. "Husserl and Frege. A New Look at Their Relationship." *RIP* 4 (1974): 51–62; in *MOHANTY,* pp. 22–32.

———. "Husserl's Thesis of the Ideality of Meanings." In *MOHANTY,* pp. 76–82.

———, ed. *Readings on E. Husserl's "Logical Investigations."* The Hague: Nijhoff, 1977.

———. "Consciousness and Existence: Remarks on the Relation between Husserl and Heidegger." *MW* 11 (1978): 324–35.

———. "Husserl's Transcendental Phenomenology and Existentialism." *RM* 32 (1978): 299–321.

———. "On the Roots of Reference: Quine, Piaget, and Husserl." *SWJP* 9 (1978): 21–34.

———. "Understanding Husserl's Transcendental Phenomenology." In *APRIORI,* pp. 1–20.

Molina, F. "The Husserlian Ideal of a Pure Phenomenology." In *INVITATION,* pp. 161–82.

Monasterio, X. "Paradoxes et mythes de la phénoménologie." *RMM* (1969): 268–80.

Moneta, Giuseppina Chiara. "The Foundation of Predicative Experience and the Spontaneity of Consciousness." In *LIFE-WORLD,* pp. 171–90.

———. "Identity in Manifolds: Commentary on Sokolowski's Interpretation." *RP* 4 (1974).

———. "The Refinement of the Concept of Constitution." *RP* 4 (1974).

Montague, W.P. "Concerning Husserl's Phenomenology." *JP* 36 (1939): 232–33.

Montpellier, Gerard de. "La psychologie est-elle la science du comportement?" *RPL* 68 (1970): 174–92.

Moreau, J. "The Problem of Intentionality and Classical Thought." *IPQ* 1 (1961): 215–34.

Morin, Serge. "Sense-Experience: A Stereoscopic View." *ANALH* 3 (1974): 229–51.

Morrison, James C. "Proust and Phenomenology." *MW* 1 (1968): 604–17.

———. "Husserl and Brentano on Intentionality." *PPR* 31 (1970–71): 27–46.

———. "Husserl's *Crisis:* Reflections on the Relationship of Philosophy and History." *PPR* 37 (1977): 312–30.

———. "Husserl and Heidegger: The Parting of the Ways." In *Heidegger's Existential Analytic,* edited by Frederick C. Elliston, pp. 47–59. The Hague: Mouton, 1978.

Morrison, Ronald P. "Kant, Husserl, and Heidegger on Time and the Unity of 'Consciousness'." *PPR* 39 (1978): 182–98.

Morriston, Barbara W. "Husserl and Other Minds." Ph.D. dissertation, Northwestern University, 1974.

Morriston, Wesley. "Intentionality and the Phenomenological Method: A Critique of Husserl's Transcendental Idealism." *JBSP* 7 (1976): 33–43.

Mortan, Günter. "Einige Bemerkungen zur Überwindung des Psychologismus durch Gottlob Frege und Edmund Husserl." In *Atti XII Congr. intern. Filos. XII,* pp. 327–34. Florence: Sansoni, 1961.

Mortoshilova, N. V. "The Problem of the Cognitive Subject as Viewed by Husserl and Ingarden." *DH* 2 (1975): 17–31.

Müller, Gustav E. "Experiential and Existential Time." *PPR* 6 (1945–46): 424–35.

———. "On the Historical Significance of Husserl's Phenomenology." *Sophia* 21 (1953): 54–62.

Müller, Max. "Phänomenologie, Ontologie und Scholastik." *TF* 14 (1952): 63–86; and in *Existenzphilosophie im geistigen Leben der Gegenwart,* 2nd edition, pp. 107–34. Heidelberg: Kerle, 1958.

Müller, Severin. "System und Erfahrung: Metaphysische Aspekte am Problem des Gegebenen bei Edmund Husserl." Ph.D. dissertation, University of Munich, 1971.

———. *Vernunft und Technik: d. Dialektik d. Erscheinung bei Edmund Husserl.* Alber-Broschur Philosophie. Freiburg i. Br.: Alber, 1976.

———. "Aspekte neurer Husserl-Forschung." *PJ* 84 (1977): 394–419.

Muller, W.H. *Die Philosophie Edmund Husserls nach den Grundzügen ihrer Entstehung und ihrem systematischen Gehalt.* Bonn: Bouvier, 1956.

Munson, Thomas. "Phenomenology and History." *PT* 13 (1969): 296–301.

Muralt, A. de. "La notion d'acte fondé dans les rapports de la raison et de la volonté selon les *Logische Untersuchungen* de Husserl." *RM* 82 (1977): 511–27.

Murphy, Richard T. "Phenomenology and the Dialectic of Pre-Reflexive Consciousness in the Phenomenological Theories of Husserl, Sartre, and Merleau-Ponty." Ph.D. dissertation, Fordham University, 1963.

———. "Husserl and Pre-Reflexive Constitution." *PPR* 26 (1965–66): 100–105.

———. "A Metaphysical Critique of Method: Husserl and Merleau-Ponty." *BC* 1 (1966): 175–207.

———. "Consciousness in Brentano and Husserl." *MS* 45 (1968): 227–41.

———. "The Transcendental A Priori in Husserl and Kant." *ANALH* 3 (1974): 66–79.

Muth, Frans. "Edmund Husserl und Martin Heidegger in ihrer Phänomenologie und Weltanschauung." Ph.D. dissertation, University of Munich, 1931.

Naess, Arne. "Husserl on the Apodictic Evidence of Ideal Laws." *TH* 20 (1954): 53–63; *MOHANTY,* pp. 67–75.

Natanson, Maurice. "Phenomenology from the Natural Standpoint: A Reply to Van Meter Ames." *PPR* 17 (1956–57): 241–45.

———. "The Empirical and Transcendental Ego." In *INGARDEN,* pp. 44–54.

———. "Phenomenology: A Viewing." *Methods* 10 (1959): 295–318.

———. "Phenomenology and Existentialism: Husserl and Sartre on Intentionality." *MS* 37 (1959–60): 1–10.

———. *Literature, Philosophy, and the Social Sciences.* The Hague: Nijhoff, 1962.

———, ed. *Essays in Phenomenology.* The Hague: Nijhoff, 1966.

———. "Phenomenology as a Rigorous Science." *IPG* 7 (1967): 5–44.

———. *Phenomenology and Social Reality: Essays in Memory of Alfred Schutz.* The Hague: Nijhoff, 1970.

———. "The 'Lebenswelt'." In *PHPA*, pp. 75–93.

———. *Edmund Husserl: Philosopher of Infinite Tasks.* Evanston: Northwestern University Press, 1973.

———. "Phenomenology and the Social Sciences." In *Phenomenology and the Social Sciences,* edited by M. Natanson, pp. 3–44. Evanston: Northwestern University Press, 1973.

Natorp, Paul. "Husserls *Ideen zu einer reinen Phänomenologie.*" In *NOACK,* pp. 36–60.

———. "On the Question of Logical Method in Relation to Edmund Husserl's *Prolegomena to Pure Logic.*" In *MOHANTY,* pp. 55–66.

———. "Zur Frage der logischen Methode. Mit Beziehung auf Edmund Husserls *Prolegomena zur reinen Logik.*" In *NOACK,* pp. 1–15.

Naville, Pierre. "Marx et Husserl." *RIP* (1946): 227–43 and 445–54.

Neeman, U. "Husserl und Bolzano." *Allegemeine Zeitschrift für Philosophie* 2 (1977): 52–66.

Neisser, Hans P. "The Phenomenological Approach in Social Science." *PPR* 20 (1959): 198–212.

———. "The Phenomenological Basis of Descartes' Doubt." *PPR* 25 (1964–65): 572–74.

Nemeth, T. "Husserl and Soviet Marxism." *SST* 15 (1975): 183–96.

———. "Husserl and Gramsci: The Life-World and Common Sense." *Independent Journal of Philosophy* 1 (1977): 165–68.

Nielson, H. A. "Is Phenomenology Based on an Oversight?" *NS* 52 (1978): 72–79.

Nink, C. "Vom Anfang der Philosophie." *Scholastik* 26 (1951): 177–90.

Nissim-Sabat, Marilyn. "Husserl's Theory of Motivation." Ph.D. dissertation, De Paul University, 1977.

Nitta, Y. "Husserl's Manuscript 'A Nocturnal Conversation': His Phenomenology of Intersubjectivity." Translated by Barbara Haupt Mohr. *ANALH* 8 (1979): 21–36.

Noack, Hermann, ed. *Husserl.* Darmstadt: Wissenschaftliche Buchgesellschaft, 1973.

Nordquest, David A. "Husserl and Mill's 'Psychologism'." *Mill News* 14 (1979): 2–9.

Null, Gilbert T. "*Experience and Judgment.*" Translated by J.S. Churchill. *MW* 7 (1974): 182–92.

———. "The Role of the Perceptual World in the Husserlian Theory of the Sciences." *JBSP* 7 (1976): 56–59.

———. "Generalizing Abstraction and the Judgment of Subsumption in Aron Gurwitsch's Version of Husserl's Theory of Intentionality." *PPR* 38 (1978): 469–88.

———. "On Connoting: The Relational Theory of the Concept in Husserlian Phenomenology." *JBSP* 11 (1980): 69–76.

Ny Airi, J.C. "Beim Sternenlicht der Nichtexistierenden: Zur ideologiekritischen Interpretation des Platonisierenden Antipsychologismus." *INQ* 17 (1974): 399–443.

Oberlander, George E. "Reflection and Husserl's Transcendental Phenomenological Epoché." Ph.D. dissertation, University of Texas at Austin, 1972.

———. "The Transcendental Self in Husserl's Phenomenology. Some Suggested Revisions." *RPH* 3 (1973): 45–62.

O'Connor, Robert. "Ortega's Reformulation of Husserlian Phenomenology." *PPR* 40 (1979): 53–63.

Odagawa, Masako. "Reflexion und Welt: Bericht über die Husserl-Interpretation bei einem japanischen Philosophen." *PSP* 3 (1977): 331–41.

Ogawa, Tadishi. "The Kyoto School of Philosophy and Phenomenology (K. Nishida and E. Husserl)." Translated by Barbara Haupt Mohr. *ANALH* 8 (1979): 207–21.

Oisermann, T.I. "E. Husserl's Philosophy of Philosophy." *DH* 2 (1975): 55–64.

Olafson, Frederick A. "Consciousness and Intentionality in Heidegger's Thought." *APQ* 12 (1975): 91–103.

———. "Husserl's Theory of Intentionality in Contemporary Perspective." *NO* 9 (1975): 73–83; *HEA,* pp. 160–67.

Oosthuizen, D.C.S. "The Pre-Objective Reconsidered." *RM* 12 (1958–59): 58–59.

———. "The Role of Imagination in Judgments of Fact." *PPR* 29 (1968): 34–58.

———. "Phenomenological Psychology." *M* 79 (1970): 477–501.

Orianne, André P. "Husserl's Theory of Meaning: A Commentary on the First *Logical Investigation.*" Ph.D. dissertation, University of California at Berkeley, 1971.

Ortega Y Gasset. *Man and People.* Translated by Willard R. Trask. New York: Norton, 1957.

Orth, Ernst Wolfgang. *Bedeutung, Sinn, Gegenstand: Studien zur Sprachphilosophie Edmund Husserls und Richard Hänigswalds.* Bonn: Bouvier, 1967.

———. "Husserls Begriff der cogitativen Typen und seine methodologische Reichweite." In *PHÄNH,* pp. 138–67.

———, ed. *Phänomenologische Heute.* Freiburg: Verlag Karl Alber, 1975.

———. "Husserl und Hegel: Ein Beitrag zum Problem des Verhaltresses historischer und systematischer Forschung in der Philosophie." In *WELT MEN,* pp. 213–50.

———. "Anthropologie und Intersubjektivität: Zur Frage von Transzendentalität oder Phänomenalität der Kommunikation." In *Mensch, Welt Verständigung,* edited by Helmut Rombach, pp. 103–29. Freiburg-Munich, Alber, 1977.

———. "Husserl, Scheler, Heidegger: Eine Einführing in das Problem der philosophischen Komparatistik." In *Husserl, Scheler, Heidegger in der Sicht neuer Quelen,* pp. 7–27. Freiburg: Alber, 1978.

Osborn, Andrew D. "The Philosophy of Edmund Husserl in Its Development from His Mathematical Interests to His First Conception of Phenomenology in *Logical Investigations.*" Ph.D. dissertation, Columbia University, 1934.

———. *The Philosophy of Edmund Husserl.* New York: International Press, 1934.

———. "A Philosopher's Philosopher." *JP* 36 (1939): 234–36.

———. *Edmund Husserl and His Logical Investigations.* 2nd ed. Cambridge: Harvard University Press, 1949.

Overhold, Gary E. "Husserl and the Science of Philosophy." PhD. dissertation, Claremont Graduate School and University Center, 1966.

Owens, Thomas J. *Phenomenology and Intersubjectivity.* The Hague: Nijhoff, 1970.

Oxenhandler, Neal. "The Quest for Pure Consciousness in Husserl and Mallarmé." In *The Quest for Imagination,* edited by O.B. Hardison, pp. 149–66. Cleveland: Press of Case Western Reserve University, 1971.

Paci, Enzo. "Über einige Verwandtschaften zwischen der Philosophie Whiteheads und der Phänomenologie Husserls." *RIP* 15 (1961): 237–59.

———. "Die Lebensweltwissenschaft." In *Symposium sobre la nocion husserliana de la "Lebenswelt,"* pp. 51–57.

———. "The Phenomenological Encyclopedia and the *Telos* of Humanity." *T* 1 (Fall 1968): 5–19.

———. "The *Lebenswelt* as Ground and as *Leib* in Husserl: Somatology, Psychology, Sociology." In *PATTERNS,* pp. 123–38.

———. "Towards a New Phenomenology." *T* 5 (1970): 58–81.

———. "Life-World, Time and Liberty in Husserl." In *LIFE-WORLD,* pp. 461–68.

———. *The Function of the Sciences and the Meaning of Man.* Translated by P. Piccore and J.E. Hansen. Evanston: Northwestern University Press, 1972.

———. "Husserl: From Naturalism to the Phenomenological Encyclopedia." In *PHNE,* pp. 131–42.

———. "Vérification empirique et transcendence de la vérité." In *VV,* pp. 59–70.

Pajano, Rosalba. "Italian Phen. Aesthetics." *T* (Fall 1969): 151–68.

Palermo, James. "Direct Experience in the Open Classroom: A Phenomenological Description." *PPE* 30 (1974): 241–54.

———. "Apodictic Truth: Husserl's Eidetic Reduction versus Induction." *NDJ* 19 (1978): 69–80.

Palmer, R. "Phenomenology as Foundation for Post-Modern Philosophy of Literature." *CH* 2 (1973): 207–22.

Parret, Herman. "Husserl and the Neo-Humboldtians on Language." *IPQ* 12 (1972): 43–68.
_____. "Expression et articulation." *RPL* 71 (1973): 72–113.
_____. "Le débat de la psychologie et de la logique concernant le langage: Marty et Husserl." In *History of Linguistic Thought,* edited by Herman Parret, pp. 732–71. Berlin and New York: Walter de Gruyter, 1976.

Passmore, J. *A Hundred Years of Philosophy,* pp. 185–99. Baltimore: Penguin, 1957.

Passweg, Salcia. *Phänomenologie und Ontologie: Husserl, Scheler, Heidegger.* Zurich: Heitz, 1939.

Patočka, Jean. "La doctrine husserlienne de l'intuition eidetique et ses critiques récents." *RIP* 71–72 (1965): 17–33. English translation: "The Husserlian Doctrine of Eidetic Intuition and Its Recent Critics." Translated by F. Elliston and P. McCormick. In *HEA,* pp. 150–59.
_____. "Der Subjektivismus des Husserlschen und die Möglichkeit einer 'a subjektiven' Phänomenologie." *PSP* 2 (1970): 317–34.
_____. "La philosophie de la crise des sciences d'après Edmund Husserl et sa conception d'une phénoménologie du 'monde de la vie'." *Archiwum historii filozofii i mysli spolecznej* (Warsaw) 18 (1972): 3–18.
_____. "Erinnerungen an Husserl." In *WELT MEN,* pp. vii–xix.

Patzig, Günther. "Kritische Bemerkungen zu Husserls Thesen über das Verhältnis von Wahrheit und Evidenz." *NH* 1 (1971) 12–32.
_____. "Husserl on Truth and Evidence." In *MOHANTY,* pp. 179–96.

Pazanin, Ante. "Das Problem der Philosophie als strenger Wissenschaft in der Phänomenologie Edmund Husserls." Ph.D. dissertation, University of Cologne, 1962.
_____. *Geschichte und Wissenschaft in der Phänomenologie Edmund Husserls.* The Hague: Nijhoff, 1972.
_____. "Das Problem der Geschichte bei Husserl, Hegel und Marx." In *Phänomenologie Heute,* pp. 173–201. The Hague: Nijhoff, 1972.
_____. "Wahrheit und Lebenswelt beim späten Husserl." In *VV,* pp. 71–116.
_____. "Überwindung der Gegensatz von Idealimus und Materialismus bei Husserl und Marx." In *Phänomenologie und Marxismus: I: Konzepte und Methoden,* edited by B. Waldenfles, J.M. Brockman, and A. Pazanin, pp. 105–27. Frankfort: Suhrkamp, 1977.

Pegis, Anton C. "Medalist's Address." *PC* 49 (1975): 228–37.

Pentzopoulou-Valalas, Thérèse. "Réflexions sur le fondement du rapport entre l'a priori et l'eidos dans la phénoménologie de Husserl." *K* 65 (1974): 135–51. English translation: "Reflections on the Foundation of the Relation between the A Priori and the Eidos in the Phenomenology of Husserl." In *APRIORI,* pp. 114–31.

Percy, Walker. "Symbol, Consciousness and Intersubjectivity." *JP* 55 (1958): 631–41.

Petrement, S. "Remarques sur Lagneau, Alain, et la philosophie allemande contemporaine." *RMM* 75 (1970): 292–300.

Pettit, Philip. *On the Idea of Phenomenology.* Chicago: Sceptre Books, 1969.
_____. "Is the Reduction Necessary for Phenomenology?: Husserl and Pfander's Replies. A Reply to Herbert Spiegelberg." *JBSP* 5 (1974): 16–19.
_____. "The Life-World and Role Theory." In *Phenomenology and Philosophical Understanding,* edited by Edo Pivčevíc, pp. 251–70. Cambridge: Cambridge University Press, 1975.

Piana, Giovanni. "History and Existence in Husserl's Manuscripts." *T* 13 (Fall 1972): 86–124.

Picard, Yvonne. "Le temps chex Husserl et chez Heidegger." *Deucalion* 1 (1946): 93–124.

Piccone, Paul. "Reading the *Crisis.*" *T* 8 (1971): 121–29.
_____. "Phenomenological Marxism." *T* 9 (1971): 3–31.

Picker, Bernold. "Die Bedeutung der Mathematik für die Philosophie Edmund Husserls." *PN* 7 (1961): 266–355.

Pietersma, Henry. "Edmund Husserl's Concept of Philosophical Clarification: Its Development from 1887 to 1913." Ph.D. dissertation, University of Toronto, 1962.
_____. "Husserl's Concept of Philosophy." *D* 5 (1966): 425–42.
_____. "Husserl and Frege." *AGP* 49 (1967): 298–323.

———. "Intuition and Horizon in the Philosophy of Edmund Husserl." *JP* 67 (1970): 822–23; *PPR* 34 (1973): 95–101.

———. "The Concept of Horizon." *ANALH* 2 (1972): 278–82.

———. "Husserl's Views on the Evident and the True." In *HEA*, pp. 38–53.

———. "Husserl and Heidegger." *PPR* 40 (1979): 194–211.

Pinkard, Terry P. "The Foundations of Transcendental Idealism: Kant, Hegel, Husserl." Ph.D. dissertation, State University of New York at Stony Brook, 1975.

Piorkowski, Henry, O.F.M. "The Path of Phenomenology: Husserl, Heidegger, Sartre, Merleau-Ponty." *Duns Scotus Philosophical Association* 30 (1966): 177–221.

Pivčević, Edo. "Husserl versus Frege." *M* 76 (1967): 155–65.

———. *Husserl and Phenomenology.* New York: Hutchinson University Library, 1970.

———. "*Logical Investigations.*" *M* 80 (1971): 462–72.

———. *Von Husserl zu Sartre.* Munich: List, 1972.

———, ed. *Phenomenology and Philosophical Understanding.* New York: Cambridge University Press, 1975.

Piwocki, K. "Husserl and Picasso." In *Aesthetics in Twentieth Century Poland,* edited by J.G. Harrell and A. Wierzbianka, pp. 143–63. Lewisburg, Pa.: Bucknell University Press, 1973.

Plessner, Helmut. "Ad memoriam Ed. Husserl." *Gemeenschap* 14 (1938): 310.

———. "Phänomenologie: Das Werk Edmund Husserls (1859–1938)." In *Zwischen Philosophie und Gesellschaft,* pp. 39ff. Bern: Francke, 1953.

———. "Bei Husserl in Göttingen." In *EH*, pp. 29–39.

———. *Husserl in Göttingen: Rede zur Feier d. 100. Geburtstages Edmund Husserls.* Göttingen: Vandenhoeck und Ruprecht, 1959.

Polinov, Hans. "Edmund Husserl." *Zeitschrift Freie Deutsche Forschung* 1 (1939): 105–8.

Pöll, M. *Wesen und Wesenerkenntnis: Untersuchen mit besonderer Berücksichtigung der Phänomenologie Husserls und Schelers.* Munich, 1936.

Poltawski, Andrej. "Ingarden's Way to Realism and His Idea of Man." *DH* 2 (1975): 65–76.

Ponsetto, Antonio. "Die Tradition in der Phänomenologie Husserls." Ph.D. dissertation, Cologne, 1974.

Port, K. "Betrachtungen zu Husserls Einteilung der Denkakte und ihrer erkenntnistheoretischen Bedeutung." *AGP* 63: 369–412.

Pos, H.J. "Valeur et limites de la phénoménologie." In *PROBLÈMES*, pp. 31–52.

Postow, B.C. "Husserl's Failure to Establish a Presuppositionless Science." *SJP* 14 (1976): 179–87.

Pótawski, Andrzej. "Constitutive Phenomenology and Intentional Objects." *ANALH* 2 (1972): 90–95.

———. "Consciousness and Action in Ingarden's Thought." *ANALH* 3 (1974).

Prauss, Gerald. "Zum Verhältnis innerer und äusserer Erfahrung bei Husserl." *ZPF* 31 (1977): 79–84.

Prendergast, Christopher. "Phenomenology and the Problem of Foundations: A Critique of Edmund Husserl's Theory of Science." Ph.D. dissertation, Southern Illinois University at Carbondale, 1979.

Presas, Mario A. "Leiblichkeit und Geschichte bei Husserl." *TF* 40 (1978): 111–28. English translation: "Bodilyness and History in Husserl." Translated by Kenneth L. Hieges. *ANALH* 7 (1978): 37–42.

Prufer, Thomas. "Reduction and Constitution." In *Ancients and Moderns,* edited by John K. Ryan, pp. 341–43. Washington, D.C.: The Catholic University of America Press, 1970.

———. "An Outline of Some Husserlian Distinctions and Strategies, Especially in *The Crisis.*" In *PHÄN H*, pp. 89–103.

Przywara, Erich. "Husserl et Heidegger." *EP* 16 (1961): 55–62.

Pucci, Raffaele. "Edmund Husserl." In *Les grands courants de la pensée mondiale contemporaine.* Portraits, vol. I, pp. 771–802. Paris-Milan: Fischbacher-Marzorati, 1964.

Puhakka, Kaisa, and Puligandla, R. "Methods and Problems in Husserl's Transcendental Logic." *ILR* 4 (1971): 202–18.

Puligandla, Ramakrishna. "Similarities between the Phenomenologies of Hegel and Husserl." *PQA* 18 (1965): 127–43.

Quintin, Paul-André. "Le monde du vécu chez Husserl." *D* 13 (1974): 543–59.

Rabeau, Gaston. "La logique d'Edmond Husserl." *RS* 26 (1932): 5–24.

Rang, Bernhard. *Kausalität und Motivation: Untersuchungen zum Verhältnis von Perspektivität und Objektivität in der Phänomenologie Edmund Husserls.* The Hague: Nijhoff, 1973.
_____. "Repräsentation und Selbstgegebenheit. Die Aporie der Phänomenologie der Wahrnehmung in den Frühschriften Husserls." In *PHÄN H*, pp. 105–37; *ID*, pp. 378–97.

Rauch, Leo. "Intentionality and Its Development in the Phenomenological Psychology of Edmund Husserl." Ph.D. dissertation, New York University, 1968.
_____. "Sartre, Merleau-Ponty and the Hole in Being." *PST* 18 (1969): 119–32.
_____. "Edmund Husserl: *Experience and Judgment.*" *PST* 25 (1978): 244–53.

Raval, R.K. "An Essay on Phenomenology." *PPR* 22 (1972): 216–26.

Rawlinson, Mary C. "Identify and Differing: Husserl's Doctrine of Self-Constitution." Ph.D. dissertation, Northwestern University, 1978.

Reboul, Jean. "Husserl et le Vedanta." *RMM* 64 (1959): 320–36.

Rechtenwald, Friederike. *Die Phänomenologische Reduktion bie Edmund Husserl.* Munich, 1929.

Reeder, Harry P. "Public and Private Aspects of Language in Husserl and Wittgenstein." Ph.D. dissertation, University of Waterloo (Canada), 1977.
_____. "Language and the Phenomenological Reduction: A Reply to a Wittgensteinian Objection." *MW* 12 (1979): 35–46.
_____. "Husserl and Wittgenstein on the Mental Picture Theory of Meaning." *HS* 3 (1980): 157–67.

Reempaa, Irjö. *Über die Lehre vom Wissen.* Helsinki: Academia Scientiarum Fennica, 1966.

Reiman, Jeffrey H. "Time and the Epoché of Husserl." Ph.D. dissertation, Pennsylvania State University, 1968.

Reinach, Adolph. *Was ist Phänomenologie?* Munich, 1951.
_____. "What Is Phenomenology?" Translated by Derek Kelly. *PFB* 1 (1968): 231–56.

Reiner, Hans. "Freiheit, Wollen und Aktivität: Phänomenologische Untersuchungen in der Richtung auf das Problem der Willensfreiheit." Ph.D. dissertation, Freiburg, 1927.
_____. "Sinn und Recht der Phänomenologischen Methode." In *EH*, pp. 134–47.

Reinhardt, Kurt. "Husserl's Phenomenology and Thomist Philosophy." *NS* 11 (1937): 320–31.

Reyer, W. "Untersuchmengen zur Phänomenologie des begrifflichen Gestaltens: Beitrage zur Grundlegung einer eidetischen Intentionalpsychologie." Ph.D. dissertation, Hamburg, 1924.

Ricci, Louis M. "Independent Existence in Royce, Perry and Husserl." Ph.D. dissertation, State University of New York at Buffalo, 1970.

Richir, Marc. "Husserl: une pensée sans mesure." *CR* 25 (1969): 778–808.

Ricoeur, Paul. "Analyses et problèmes dans *Ideen II* de Husserl." *RMM* 56 (1951): 257–394; 57 (1952): 1–16; *PHEX*, pp. 23–76.
_____. "Méthode et tâches d'une phénoménologie de la volonté." In *PROBLÈMES*, pp. 111–40.
_____. "Etude sur les *Méditations cartésiennes* de Husserl." *RPL* 52 (1954): 75–109.
_____. "Kant et Husserl." *K* 46 (1954–1955): 44–67; *PT* 10 (1966): 145–68.
_____. *Freedom and Nature: The Voluntary and the Involuntary.* Translated by E.V. Kohák. Evanston: Northwestern University Press, 1966.
_____. "Husserl." In *Histoire de la philosophie allemande*, pp. 183–96. Paris: Vrin, 1967.
_____. *Husserl: An Analysis of His Philosophy.* Translated by E.G. Ballard and L.E. Embree. Evanston: Northwestern University Press, 1967.
_____. "Husserl and Wittgenstein on Language." In *LEE*, pp. 207–18.
_____. "New Developments in Phenomenology in France: The Phenomenology of Language." *SR* 34 (1967).

————. "Analogie et intersubjectivité chez Husserl d'après les inedits de le période 1905–20" (Edition Iso Kern, *Husserliana*, tome XIII [Nijhoff, 1973]).

————. "Husserl und der Sinn der Geschichte. Aus dem Französischen übersetz von Klaus Stichweh." In *NOACK*, pp. 231–76.

————. "Phenomenology." Translated by Dan Herman and Don Morano. *SWJP* 5 (1974): 149–68.

————. "Phénoménologie et hermeneutique." *MW* 7 (1974): 223–53. English translation: "Phenomenology and Hermeneutics." *NO* 9 (1975): 85–102.

————. "Gabriel Marcel et la phénoménologie." In *Entretiens antour de Gabriel Marcel*, pp. 53–74. Colloque organise par le centre culturel international de Cerisy-la-Salle, 24–31 aout 1973. Neuchatel: Editions de la Baconniere; Paris: Diffusion Payot, 1976.

————. "Hegel and Husserl on Intersubjectivity." In *Reason, Action and Experience: Essays in Honor of Raymond Klibanski*, edited by Helmut Kohlenberger. Hamburg: Meiner, 1979.

Riepe, Dale, ed. *Phenomenology and Natural Existence: Essays in Honor of Marvin Farber*. Albany: State University of New York Press, 1973.

Rieser, Max. "The Philosophy of Roman Ingarden in a Critical Light." *DH* 2 (1975): 89–94.

Rioux, Bertrand. "Ontologie du signifier." *MW* 4 (1971): 243–58.

Riska, Augustin. "The A Priori in Ingarden's Theory of Meaning Discussion." *ANALH* 3 (1974): 149–68.

Rizzacasa, Aurelio. "The Epistemology of the Sciences of Nature in Relation to the Teleology of Research in the Thought of the Later Husserl." In *TELEOLOGIES*, pp. 73–84.

Robberechts, Ludovic. "Réflexion phénoménologique et réflexion éthique." *EP* 17 (1962): 403–420.
————. *Husserl*. Paris: Editions Universitaires, 1964.
————. *Edmund Husserl: Ein Einführung in seine Phänomenologie*. Translated by Klaus and Margaret Held. Hamburg: Claassen, 1967.

Robert, Jean-Dominique. "Le problème du fondement de la vérité chez Husserl, dans les *Logische Untersuchungen* et la *Formale und transzendentale Logik*." *AP* 23 (1960): 608–32.
————. "Voix et phénomène: A propos d'un ouvrage récent." *RPL* 30 (1968): 159–63.
————. "Approche rétrospective de la phénoménologie husserlienne." *LTP* 28 (1972): 27–62.
————. "La phénoménologie comme 'referentiel' commun des sciences de l'homme." *LTP* 32 (1976): 277–82.

Roberts, Carl. "Husserlian Phenomenology and Parsonian Functionalism in Juxtaposition." *D* 18 (1976): 60–65.

Rockmore, Thomas. "Fichte, Husserl, and Philosophical Science." *IPQ* 19 (1979): 15–27.

Rollin, France. *La phénoménologie au départ: Husserl, Heidegger, Gaboriau*. Paris: P. Lethielleux, 1967.

Romani, Romano. "'Erlebnis' and 'Logos' in Husserl's *Crisis of the European Sciences*." In *TELEOLOGIES*, pp. 105–14.

Rosen, Klaus. *Evidenz in Husserls deskriptiver Transzendentalphilosophie*. Meisenheim a. Glan: Hain, 1977.

Rossi, Mario M. "Die Entwicklung der Lehre von Husserl: Phänomenologie und Phänomenologismus." *GM* 15 (1960): 492–500.

Rota, Gian-Carlo. "Edmund Husserl and the Reform of Logic." In *EXPLORATIONS*, pp. 299–305.

Rotenstreich, Nathan. "The Forms of Sensibility and Transcendental Phenomenology." In *LIFE-WORLD*, pp. 389–406.
————. "Ambiguities of Husserl's Notion of Constitution." In *PHNE*, pp. 151–70.
————. "Reflection and Philosophy." *RA* 17 (1975): 1–17.
————. "Evidence and the Aim of Cognitive Activity." *ANALH* 7 (1978): 245–58.
————. "Exposition of Intuition and Phenomenology [Kant and Husserl]." *Studi Internazionali di Filosofia* 9 (1979): 43–84.

Roth, Aloss. *Edmund Husserls ethische Untersuchungen: Dargestellt anhand seiner Vorlesungsmanuskripte*. The Hague: Nijhoff, 1960.

Röttges, Heinz. *Evidenz und Solipsismus in Husserls Cartesianischen Meditationen*. Frankfort: Heiderhoff, 1970.

Routila, Lauri. "Wahrnehmung und Interpretation." *AJ* 36 (1974): 125–41.

Rovatti, P.A. "A Phenomenological Analysis of Marxism." *T* (Spring 1970): 160–74.

Runzo, Joseph. "The Propositional Structure of Perception." *APQ* 14 (1977): 211–20.

Ryan, W. "Intentionality in Edmund Husserl and Bernard Lonergan." *IPQ* 13 (1973): 173–90.

———. "Passive and Active Elements in Husserl's Notion of Intentionality." *MS* 55 (1977): 37–55.

Ryle, G. "Phenomenology." *AS* 30 (1932): 68–115.

Salemi, Roselina. "Bibliography of Husserlian Studies in Italy with an Introduction by Angela Ales Bello." In *TELEOLOGIES*, pp. 461–84.

Sallis, John. "On the Ideal of Phenomenology." In *LIFE-WORLD*, pp. 125–34.

———. "Phenomenology and Language." *PE* 48 (1967): 490–508.

———. "The Problem of Judgment in Husserl's Later Thought." *TSP* 16 (1967): 129–52.

———. "On the Limitation of Transcendental Reflection or Is Intersubjectivity Transcendental?" *MO* 55 (1971): 312–33.

———. "Time, Subjectivity, and the Phenomenology of Perception." *MS* 48 (1971): 343–58.

———. *Phenomenology and the Return to Beginnings*. Pittsburgh: Duquesne University Press; New York: Humanities Press, 1974.

———. "Image and Phenomenon." *RIP* 5 (1975): 61–75.

Salmon, C.V. *The Central Problem of David Hume's Philosophy: An Essay towards a Phenomenological Interpretation of the First Book of the 'Treatise of Human Nature'*. Halle: Niemeyer, 1929. Originally published in *Jahrbuch für Philosophie und phänomenologische Forschung*, vol. X.

———. "The Starting Point of Husserl's Phenomenology." *AS* 39 (1929–30): 55–78.

———. "La phénoménologie après Husserl." *RS* 31 (1947): 237–40.

Sancipriano, Mario. "The Activity of Consciousness: Husserl and Bergson." *ANALH* 3 (1974): 161–67.

Saraiva, Maria Manuela. *L'imagination selon Husserl*. The Hague: Nijhoff, 1970.

Sartre, Jean-Paul. "Une idée fondamentale de la philosophie de Husserl: l'intentionalité." *Nouvelle Revue Française* 17 (1939): 129–32.

———. *Being and Nothingness: An Essay on Phenomenological Ontology*. Translated by Hazel E. Barnes. New York: Philosophical Library, 1956.

———. *The Transcendence of the Ego: An Existentialist Theory of Consciousness*. Translated by Forest Williams and Robert Kirkpatrick. New York: Noonday, 1957.

———. "Intentionality: A Fundamental Idea of Husserl's Phenomenology." Translated by Joseph P. Fell, *JBSP* 1 (1970): 4–5.

Sauer, Friedrich. "Über das Verhältnis der Husserlschen Phänomenologie zu David Hume." *K* 35 (1931): 151–82.

Scanlon, John D. "Husserl's Conception of Philosophy as a Rigorous Science." Ph.D. dissertation, Tulane University, 1968.

———. "Intolerable Human Responsibility." *RP* 1 (1971): 75–90.

———. "Consciousness, the Streetcar, and the Ego: Pro Husserl, contra Sartre." *PFB* 2 (1971): 332–54.

———. "The *Epoché* and Phenomenological Anthropology." *RP* 2 (1972): 95–110.

———. "Radical Geometry: *Review of Ding und Raum* by Edmund Husserl." *RP* 4 (1974): 129–36.

———. "Formal Logic and Formal Ontology." *RIP* 5 (1975): 95–107.

Schacht, Richard L. "Husserlian and Heideggerian Phenomenology." *PS* 23 (1972): 293–314.

———. "Husserl and Heidegger." In *Hegel and After: Studies in Contemporary Philosophy between Kant and Sartre*, pp. 207–28. Pittsburgh: University of Pittsburgh Press, 1975.

Schapp, Wilhelm. *In Geschichten verstrickt: Zum Sein von Mensch und Ding*. Hamburg: Meiner, 1953.

———. "Erinnerungen an Husserl." In *EH*, pp. 12–25.

Scheler, Max. *The Nature of Sympathy*. Translated by Peter Heath. London: Routledge & Kegan Paul, 1954.

———. *Ressentiment*. Translated by W.W. Holdheim. New Jersey: Free Press, 1961.

———. *Selected Philosophical Essays*. Translated by D. Lachterman. Evanston: Northwestern University Press, 1973.

Schérer, René. "Sur la philosophie transcendentale et l'objectivité de la connaissance scientifique." *RMM* 62 (1957): 436–64.

———. *La phénoménologie des 'Recherches Logiques' de Husserl*. Paris: Presses Universitaires de France, 1967.

———. "Clôture et faille dans la phénoménologie de Husserl." *RMM* 73 (1968): 344–60.

———. "Points de repère et points de vue sur le cheminement philosophique." *SPS* 30 (1970–71): 244–71.

———. "Edmund Husserl, la phénoménologie et ses développements." *Histoire de la philosophie: idées, doctrines,* edited by François Chatelet, chapter 9. Paris: Hachette, 1972–73.

———. "Husserl." In *Histoire de la philosophie,* III: Du XIXᵉ siècle a nos jours. Publié sous la direction d'Yvon Belaval. Encyclopedie de la Pleiade, 38. Paris: Gallimard, 1974.

Schermann, Hans. "Husserls II. *Logische Untersuchung* und Meinongs *Hume-Studien.*" In *Jenseits von Sein und Nichtsein,* pp. 103–15. Graz: Akademische Druck, 1972.

Schilpp, P.A. "Edmund Husserl: A Founder of a New School of Thought." In *Commemorative Essays,* pp. 31–37. Stockton, 1930.

Schmidt, Herman. "Der Horizontbegriff Husserls in Anwendung auf die ästhetische Erfahrung." *ZPF* 21 (1967): 499–511.

Schmitt, Richard. *Husserl's Phenomenology: Reconstruction in Empiricism.* New Haven: Yale University Press, 1956.

———. "Husserl's Transcendental-Phenomenological Reduction." *PPR* 20 (1959): 238–45; *PPEH,* pp. 58–67.

———. "Phenomenology and Analysis." *PPR* 23 (1962): 101–10.

———. "Phenomenology." In *Encyclopedia of Philosophy,* vol. 6, edited by Paul Edwards, pp. 135–151. New York: Macmillan and Free Press, 1967.

———. "On Knowing One's Own Body." *ANALH* 1 (1971): 152–69.

———. "Transcendental Phenomenology: Muddle or Mystery." *JBSP* 2 (1971): 19–27.

Schneider, Robert O. "Husserl and Heidegger: An Essay on the Question of Intentionality." *PT* 21 (1977): 306–26.

Schönrock, W. "Das Bewusstein: Ein psychologische-phänomenologischer Versuch." Ph.D. dissertation, Erlangen, 1924.

Schräder, H. "Die Theorie des Denkens bei Kulpe und bei Husserl." Ph.D. dissertation, Munster, 1924.

Schrag, Calvin O. "John Wild on Contemporary Phenomenology." *PPR* 21 (1961): 409–11.

———. *Experience and Being.* Evanston: Northwestern University Press, 1969.

———. "The Life-World and Its Historical Horizon." In *PATTERNS,* pp. 107–22.

Schroder, William R. "Others: An Examination of Sartre and His Predecessors: Vol. I: Husserl, Hegel, Heidegger. Vol. II: Sartre." Ph.D. dissertation, University of Michigan, 1979.

Schuhl, P.M. "Sur un problème d'édition husserlienne." *RPF* 91 (1966): 447–48.

Schuhmann, Karl. *Die Fundamentalbetrachtung der Phänomenologie: Zum Weltproblem in der Philosophie Edmund Husserls.* The Hague: Nijhoff, 1971.

———. "Forschungsnotizen über Husserls 'Entwurt einer, Verrede' zu den *Logischen Untersuchungen.*" *TF* 34 (1972): 513–24.

———. "Husserl and Hodgson: Some Historical Remarks." *JBSP* 3 (1972): 63–65.

———. *Die Dialektik der Phänomenologie.* 2 vols. The Hague: Nijhoff, 1973.

———. "Ein Brief Husserls und Theodor Lipps." *TF* 39 (1977): 141–50.

———. *Husserl-Chronik: Denk- und Lebensweg Edmund Husserls.* The Hague: Nijhoff, 1977.

———. "Zu Heideggers Spiegel-Gespräch über Husserl." *ZPF* 32 (1978): 591–612.

Schümmer, Heinz. *Die Wahrnehmungs und Erkenntnismetaphysik Max Schelers in den Stadien ihrer Entwicklung: Unter besonderer Berüksichtigung der Beziehungen Schelers zu Husserl.* Bonn: Bouvier, 1954.

Schuppe, Wilhelm. "Zum Psychologismus und zum Normcharakter der Logik. Eine Ergänzung zu Husserls *Logischen Untersuchungen.*" In *NOACK,* pp. 1–15.

Schütz, Alfred. "Edmund Husserl: Cartesianische Meditationen und Pariser Vorträge (review)." *PPR* 11 (1950): 421–23.

_____. "Edmund Husserl's *Ideas*, volume II." *PPR* 13 (1952): 394–413.
_____. "Edmund Husserl's *Ideas*, volume III." *PPR* 13 (1952): 506–14.
_____. "Das Problem der transzendentalen Intersubjektivität bei Husserl." *PR* 5 (1957): 82–107. Translation: "Le problème de l'intersubjectivité transcendentale chez Husserl." In *HUSSERL*, pp. 334–65.
_____. "Husserl's Importance for the Social Sciences." In *EH*, pp. 86–98.
_____. "Type and Eidos in Husserl's Late Philosophy." *PPR* 20 (1959): 147–65.
_____. *Collected Papers*. Vol. 1: *The Problem of Social Reality*. The Hague: Nijhoff, 1962.
_____. *Collected Papers*. Vol. 2. The Hague: Nijhoff, 1962.
_____. *Collected Papers*. Vol. 3. The Hague: Nijhoff, 1966.
_____. *The Phenomenology of the Social World*. Evanston: Northwestern University Press, 1967.
_____. "The Problem of Transcendental Intersubjectivity in Husserl." In his *Collected Papers, III: Studies in Phenomenological Psychology*, pp. 51–83. The Hague: Nijhoff, 1970.
_____. *Reflections on the Problem of Relevance*. New Haven: Yale University Press, 1970.
_____. "Husserl and His Influence on Me." In *Interdisciplinary Phenomenology*, edited by Don Ihde and Richard M. Zaner, pp. 124–29. The Hague: Nijhoff, 1977.

Schuwer, André. "Remarks on the Idea of Authentic Thinking in the *Logical Investigations*." *RP* 1 (1971): 17–32.

Scott, Charles E. "Existence and Consciousness." In *EXPLORATIONS*, pp. 434–44.

Seebohm, Thomas. *Die Bedingungen der Möglichkeit der Transzendental-Philosophie: Edmund Husserls transzendental-phänomenologischer Ansatz, dargestellt im Anschluss an seine Kant-Kritik*. Bonn: H. Bouvier, 1962.
_____. "Reflexion and Totality in the Philosophy of E. Husserl." *JBSP* 4 (1973): 20–30.

Seeburger, Francis F. "Heidegger and the Phenomenological Reduction." *PPR* 36 (1975): 212–21.

Seidler, Michael J. "Philosophy as a Rigorous Science: An Introduction to Husserlian Phenomenology." *PT* 21 (1977): 306–26.

Seifert, Josef. "Relativismus und Immanentismus in Edmund Husserls *Cartesianischen Meditationen*: Die Äquivokation im Ausdruk transzendentales Ego an der Basis jedes transzendentalen Idealismus." *SJ* 14 (1970): 85–109.
_____. "Über die Möglichkeit einer Metaphysik. Die Antwort der 'Münchener Phänomenologen' auf E. Husserls Transzendental Philosophie." In *MÜN PHÄN*, pp. 81–104.

Seltzer, Edward C. "The Problem of Objectivity: A Study of Objectivity Reflected in a Comparison of the Philosophies of Ernst Cassierer, Jean Piaget, and Edmund Husserl." Ph.D. dissertation, New School for Social Research, 1969.

Sen, H.B. *Science and Person*. New York: Humanities Press, 1973.

Senn, Silvio. "La question de la realité dans la phénoménologie de Husserl." *SPS* 36 (1976): 159–81.

Serrus, Charles. "L'oeuvre philosophique d'Edmond Husserl." *EP* 4 (1930): 42–46, 126–33; and ibid. 5 (1931): 18–23.
_____. "E. Husserl's *Nachwort* et *Méditations cartésiennes*." *EP* 5 (1931).

Shestov, Leon. "In Memory of a Great Philosopher: Edmund Husserl." *PPR* 22 (1961–62): 449–71.

Shin, Gui Hyin. *Die Struktur des inneren Zeitbewusstseins: Eine Studie über d. Begriff d. Protention in d. veröf. Schriften Edmund Husserls*. Bern: Lang, 1978.

Shiner, L.E. "Husserl and Historical Science." *SR* 37 (1970): 511–32.

Shmueli, Efraim. "Critical Reflections on Husserl's Philosophy of History." *JBSP* 2 (1971): 35–51.
_____. "Can Phenomenology Accommodate Marxism?" *T* (1973): 169–80.
_____. "Consciousness and Action: Husserl and Marx on Theory and Praxis." *ANALH* 5 (1976): 343–82.

Siegfried, Hans. "Descriptive Phenomenology and Constructivism." *PPR* 37 (1976): 248–61.

Silverman, Hugh J. "The Self in Husserl's *Crisis*." *JBSP* 7 (1976): 24–32.

Siméon, J.P. "Maurice Merleau-Ponty et l'idéalisme." *RMM* 82 (1977): 296–311.

Simoes Saraiva, Maria Manuela. "L'imagination selon Husserl." Ph.D. dissertation, Université Catholique de Louvain, 1963.

Sindoni, Paola Ricci. "Teleology and Philosophical Historiography: Husserl and Jaspers." In *TELEOLOGIES*, pp. 281–99.

Sinha, Debabrata. "The Phenomenology of Edmund Husserl." *The Calcutta Review* 1960: 241–50.
———. "Phenomenology and Positivism." *PPR* 23 (1962): 562–77.
———. "The Crisis of Science and Husserl's Phenomenology." *The Journal of the Indian Academy of Philosophy* 2 (1963): 29–38.
———. "Der Begriff der Person in der Phänomenologie Husserls." *ZPF* 18 (1964): 597–613.
———. "'Person' in Husserl's Phenomenology." *PQA* 1964: 121–29.
———. *Studies in Phenomenology*. The Hague: Nijhoff, 1969.
———. "Theory and Practice in Indian Thought: Husserl's Observations." *PEW* 21 (1971): 255–64.
———. "Phenomenology: A Break-Through to a New Intuitionism." In *PHÄN H*, pp. 27–48.

Sinn, Dieter. *Die transzendentale Intersubjektivität bei Edmund Husserl mit ihren Seinshorizonten.* Heidelberg, 1958.

Smillie, David. "A Psychological Contribution to the Phenomenology of the Other." *PPR* 22 (1971–72): 64–77.

Smith, Barry. "The Ontology of Reference: Studies in Logic and Phenomenology." Ph.D. dissertation, Manchester University, 1976.
———. "Frege and Husserl: The Ontology of Reference." *JBSP* 9 (1978): 111–25.

Smith, David Woodruff. "Intentionality, Noemata, and Individuation: The Role of Individuation in Husserl's Theory of Intentionality." Ph.D. dissertation, Stanford University, 1971.
———, and McIntyre, Ronald. "Intentionality via Intensions." *JP* 68 (1971): 541–61.

Smith, F. Joseph. "Being and Subjectivity: Heidegger and Husserl." In *PERSPECTIVE*, pp. 122–56.
———, ed. *Phenomenology in Perspective*. The Hague: Nijhoff, 1970.
———. "Musical Sound as a Model for Husserlian Intuition and Time Consciousness." *JPP* 4 (1973–74): 271–96.

Smith, Joseph. "Jacques Derrida's Husserl Interpretation." *PT* 2 (1967): 10–23.

Smith, Quentin. "Husserl and the Inner Structure of Feeling Acts." *RPH* 6 (1976): 84–104.
———. "On Husserl's Theory of Consciousness in the Fifth *Logical Investigation*." *PPR* 37 (1977): 482–97.
———. "A Phenomenological Examination of Husserl's Theory of Hyletic Data." *PT* 21 (1977): 356–67.
———. "The Phenomenology of Feeling: A Critical Development of the Theories of Feeling in Husserl, Scheler, and Sartre." Ph.D. dissertation, Boston College, 1977.
———. "Scheler's Critique of Husserl's Theory of the World of the Natural Standpoint." *MS* 55 (1978): 387–96.
———. "Husserl's Theory of the Phenomenological Reduction in the *Logical Investigations*." *PPR* 39 (1979): 433–37.

Sokolowski, Robert. "Immanent Constitution in Husserl's Lectures on Time." *PPR* 24 (1963): 530–51.
———. *The Formation of Husserl's Concept of Constitution*. The Hague: Nijhoff, 1964.
———. "The Husserl Archives and the Edition of Husserl's Works." *NS* 38 (1964): 473–82.
———. "Husserl's Interpretation of the History of Philosophy." *Franciscan Studies* 24 (1964): 261–80.
———. "The Logic of Parts and Wholes in Husserl's *Investigations*." *PPR* 28 (1967–68): 537–53; *MOHANTY*, pp. 94–111.
———. "Edmund Husserl and the Principles of Phenomenology." In *Twentieth Century Thinkers*, edited by J.K. Ryan, pp. 133–57. New York: Alba House, 1968.
———. "The Structure and Content of Husserl's *Logical Investigations*." *INQ* 14 (1971): 318–47.
———. "Husserl's Protreptic." In *LIFE-WORLD*, pp. 55–82.
———. "Logic and Mathematics in Husserl's *Formal and Transcendental Logic*." In *EXPLORATIONS*, pp. 306–30.
———. *Husserlian Meditations*. Evanston: Northwestern University Press, 1974.
———. "Identities in Manifolds: A Husserlian Pattern of Thought." *RP* 4 (1974): 63–79.
———. "Ontological Possibilities in Phenomenology: The Dyad and the One." *RM* 29 (1975–76): 451–71.
———. "The Work of Aron Gurwitsch." *RPH* 5 (1975): 7–10.

Solomon, Robert C. "Sense and Essence: Frege and Husserl." *IPQ* 10 (1970): 378–401.
———. "Edmund Husserl and Phenomenology: The New Way of Philosophy." In his *From Rational-*

ism to Existentialism: The Existentialists and Their Nineteenth Century Backgrounds, pp. 141–73. New York: Harper and Row, 1972.

———, ed. *Phenomenology and Existentialism*. New York: Harper and Row, 1972.

———. "Husserl's Private Language." *SWJP* 5 (1974): 203–28.

———. "Husserl's Concept of the Noema." In *HEA*, pp. 168–81.

Soloviov, E.Y. "Phenomenology and Ethics." *DH* 2 (1975): 51–58.

Son, B.H. *Science and Persons: A Study on the Idea of 'Philosophy as Rigorous Science' in Kant and Husserl*. Assen: Van Gorcum, 1972.

Souche-Dagues, D. *Le développement de l'intentionnalité dans la phénoménologie husserlienne*. The Hague: Nijhoff, 1972.

———. "Le platonisme de Husserl." *ANALH* 3 (1974): 335–60.

Spear, Otto. "Philosophie als Menschheitsaufgabe: der Philosoph Edmund Husserl in der Situation unserer Zeit." *Universitas* 24 (1969): 1315–24.

Specht, Ernst Konrad. *Sprache und Sein*. Berlin: de Gruyter, 1967.

Spencer, James C. "Husserl's Conception of the Transcendental: A Critical Analysis." Ph.D. dissertation, State University of New York at Buffalo, 1974.

Spicker, Stuart. "Shadsworth Hodgson's Reduction as an Anticipation of Husserl's Phenomenological Psychology." *JBSP* 2 (1971): 57–73.

———. "Inner-Time and Lived-Through Time: Husserl and Merleau-Ponty." *JBSP* 4 (1973): 235–47.

Spiegelberg, Herbert. "Der Begriff der Intentionalität in der Scholastik, bei Brentano und bei Husserl." *Philosophische Hefte* 5 (1936): 75–91.

———. "The *Reality Phenomenon* and Reality." In *PHIL ESSAYS*, pp. 84–105.

———. "Critical Phenomenological Realism." *PPR* 1 (1940–41): 154–76.

———. "Phenomenology of Direct Evidence." *PPR* 2 (1941–42): 427–56.

———. "Husserl's and Peirce's Phenomenologies: Coincidence or Interaction." *PPR* 17 (1956–57): 164–85.

———. "How Subjective Is Phenomenology?" *PC* 33 (1959): 28–36.

———. "Perspektivenwandel: Konstitution eines Husserlbildes." In *EH*, pp. 56–63.

———. "Husserl's Phenomenology and Existentialism." *JP* 57 (1960): 62–74.

———. *The Phenomenological Movement. A Historical Introduction*. Vol. I–II. The Hague: Nijhoff, 1960.

———. "Phenomenology through Vicarious Experience." In *PHPA*, pp. 105–26.

———. "Toward a Phenomenology of Experience." *APQ* 1 (1964): 325–32.

———. "A Phenomenological Analysis of Approval." In *INVITATION*, pp. 183–210.

———. "Husserl's Phenomenology and Sartre's Existentialism." In *PPEH*, pp. 252–66.

———. "Phenomenology." In *Encyclopedia Britannica* (1967) 18: 810–12.

———. "'Intention' und 'Intentionalität' in der Scholastik bei Brentano und Husserl." *SPS* 29 (1969): 189–216.

———. "Husserl in England: Facts and Lessons." *JBSP* 1 (1970): 4–15.

———. "Notes on the Text of Husserl's Syllabus." *JBSP* 1 (1970): 16–17.

———. "On Some Human Uses of Phenomenology." In *PERSPECTIVE*, pp. 16–31.

———. "From Husserl to Heidegger." *JBSP* 2 (1971): 58–62, 77–83.

———. "On the Misfortunes of Edmund Husserl's *Encyclopedia Britannica* Article *Phenomenology*." *JBSP* 2 (1971): 74–76.

———. "The Last Portrait of Edmund Husserl by Franz and Ida Brentano." In *Philomathes: Studies and Essays in the Humanities in Memory of Philip Merlan*, pp. 341–45. The Hague: Nijhoff, 1972.

———. *Psychology and Psychiatry*. Evanston: Northwestern University Press, 1972.

———. "Remarks on Findlay's Translation of Edmund Husserl's *Logical Investigations*." *JBSP* 3 (1972): 195–96.

———. "What William James Knew about Edmund Husserl." In *LIFE-WORLD*, pp. 407–22.

———. "Husserl's Way into Phenomenology for Americans: A Letter and Its Sequel." In *PHCC*, pp. 168–91.

———. "Is the Reduction Necessary for Phenomenology? Husserl's and Pfänder's Replies." *JBSP* 4 (1973): 3–15.

————. "*Epoché* without Reduction: Some Replies to My Critics." *JBSP* 5 (1974): 256–61.

————. "Neues Licht auf die Beziehung Zwischen Husserl und Pfänder: Bemerkungen und Erganzungen anlässlich von Karl Schuhmanns 'Husserl über Pfänder'." *TF* 36 (1974): 565–73.

————. "Husserl's Syllabus for His Paris Lectures on 'Introduction to Transcendental Phenomenology'." *JBSP* 7 (1976): 18–23.

————. "'Intention' and 'Intentionality' in the Scholastics, Brentano and Husserl." Translated from the German by Linda L. McAlister and Margarete Schattle. In *The Philosophy of Brentano*, edited with introduction by Linda L. McAlister, pp. 108–27. London: G. Duckworth & Co., 1976.

————. "On the Significance of the Correspondence between F. Brentano and E. Husserl." *Grazer Philosophischen Studien* 5 (1978): 95–116.

Stack, George J. "Husserl's Concept of the Human Sciences." *PT* 17 (1973): 52–60.

————. "Husserl's Concept of Person." *IS* 4 (1974): 267–75.

Stamps, Ann. "Shifting Focus from Sartre to Husserl." *JT* 8 (1973): 51–53.

Stapleton, Timothy J. "Husserl and Neo-Kantianism." *Auslegung* 4 (1977): 81–104.

————. "Husserl and Heidegger: The Question of a Phenomenological Beginning." Ph.D. dissertation, The Pennsylvania State University, 1978.

Stegmüller, Wolfgang. *Hauptströmungen der Gegenwarts-philosophie: Eine kritisch-historische Einführung.* Vienna-Stuttgart: Humboldt, 1952. English translation: *Main Currents in Contemporary German, British, and American Philosophy.* Dordrecht: Reidel, 1969.

Stein, Edith. *On the Problem of Empathy.* The Hague: Nijhoff, 1970.

————. "Husserls Phänomenologie und die Philosophie des Hl. Thomas v. Aquino. Versuch einer Gegenüberstellung." In *NOACK*, pp. 61–86.

Stephens, James W. "Phenomenology and Realism: An Essay on Husserl's *Logical Investigations.*" Ph.D. dissertation, Princeton University, 1978.

Stern, Alfred. "Husserl's Phenomenology and the Scope of Philosophy." *PE* 35 (1954): 267–84.

Sternfeld, Robert. "Contemporary Philosophies of Experience: Philosophic Method in Dewey, Bradley, and Husserl." Ph.D. dissertation, University of Chicago, 1948.

Stevens, Richard. *James and Husserl: The Foundations of Meaning.* The Hague: Nijhoff, 1974.

————. "Spatial and Temporal Models in Husserl's *Ideen II.*" *CH* 3 (1975): 105–16.

Stewart, David. "Paul Ricoeur and the Phenomenological Movement." *PT* 12 (1968): 227–35.

————, and Mickunas, Algis. *Exploring Phenomenology: A Guide to the Field and Literature.* Chicago: American Library Association, 1974.

Stewart, J. McKellar. "Husserl's Phenomenological Method." *Australasian Journal of Psychology and Philosophy* 11 (1933): 221–31; 12 (1934): 62–73.

Stewart, Roderick M. "The Problem of Logical Psychologism for Husserl and the Early Heidegger." *JBSP* 10 (1979): 184–93.

Stone, Robert V. "The Self as Agent-in-the-World: An Alternative to Husserl's and Sartre's Accounts of the Ego." Ph.D. dissertation, University of Texas at Austin, 1972.

————. "The Self Consciousness in Self Activity." In *EXPLORATIONS*, pp. 253–62.

Strasser, Stephan. "Die doppelte Ich-Spaltung in der transzendentalen Phänomenologie Edmund Husserls." In *Seele und Beseeltes: Phänomenologische Untersuchungen über das Problem der Seele in der metaphysischen und empirischen Psychologie*, pp. 45–54. Vienna: Deuticke, 1955.

————. "Phenomenological Trends in European Psychology." *PPR* 18 (1957–58): 18–34.

————. "Das Gottesproblem in der Spätphilosophie Edmund Husserls." *PJ* 69 (1958): 130–42.

————. "Intuition und Dialektik in der Philosophie Edmund Husserls." In *EH*, pp. 148–53.

————. "Misère et grandeur du 'fait': une méditation phénoménologique." In *HUSSERL*, pp. 170–84.

————. *Phenomenology and the Human Sciences.* Pittsburgh: Duquesne University Press, 1963.

————. "Phenomenologies and Psychologies." *REX* 5 (1965): 80–105.

————. *Phenomenological Psychology: Selected Papers.* New York: Basic Books, 1966.

————. *The Idea of Dialogal Phenomenology.* Pittsburgh: Duquesne University Press, 1969.

————. "Grundgedanken der Sozialontologie Edmund Husserls." *ZPF* 29 (1975): 3–33.

————. "Antiphénoménologie et phénoménologie dans la philosophie d'Emmanuel Levinas." *RPL* 75 (Fall 1977): 101–25.

_____. "Der Begriff der Welt in der phänomenologischen Philosophie." In *Phänomenologie und Praxis*, pp. 151–79. Freiburg-Munich: Alber, 1976.

_____. "Der Gott des Monadenalls: Gedanken zum Gottesproblem in der Spätphilosophie Husserls." *PSP* 4 (1978): 361–78.

_____. "History, Teleology, and God in the Philosophy of Husserl." In *TELEOLOGIES*, pp. 317–33.

Stratton, Melville J. "The Immanent and the Transcendent in Husserl's *Cartesian Meditations*." Ph.D. dissertation, State University of New York at Buffalo, 1970.

Straus, Erwin W., ed. *Phenomenology: Pure and Applied*. Pittsburgh: Duquesne University Press, 1964.

Ströker, Elisabeth. "Das Problem der *Epoché* in der Philosophie Edmund Husserls." *ANALH* 1 (1971): 170–85.

_____. "Edmund Husserl's Phenomenology as a Foundation of Natural Science." *ANALH* 2 (1972): 245–57.

_____. "Zur phänomenologischen Theorie der Wahrnehmung." *AJ* 36 (1974): 106–24.

_____. "Husserls Evidenzprinzip: Sinn und Grenzen einer methodischen Norm der Phänomenologie als Wissenschaft." *ZPF* 32 (1978): 3–30.

_____, ed. *Lebenswelt und Wissenschaft in der Philosophie Edmund Husserls*. Frankfort-am-Main, 1979.

Sweeney, R.D. "The Affective A Priori." *ANALH* 3 (1974): 80–97.

Swiecimski, Jerzy. "Scientific Information Function and Ingarden's Theory of Forms in the Constitution of the Real World." *ANALH* 3 (1974): 290–322.

Szilasi, Wilhelm. *Einführung in die Phänomenologie Edmund Husserls*. Tübingen: Max Niemeyer, 1959.

_____. "Werk und Wirkung Husserls." *Die Neue Rundschau* 70 (1950): 636–55.

Taminiaux, Jacques. "Phenomenology in Merleau-Ponty's Late Work." In *LIFE-WORLD*, pp. 307–22.

_____. "Heidegger and Husserl's *Logical Investigations*." *RPH* 7 (1977): 58–83.

_____. "Le regard et l'excedent: remarques sur Heidegger et les *Recherches logiques* de Husserl." *RPL* 75 (1977): 74–100.

_____. *Le regard et l'excedent*. The Hague: Nijhoff, 1977.

Tarnowski, Karol. "Roman Ingarden's Critique of Transcendental Constitution." *DH* 3 (1976): 111–19.

Tatarkiewicz, V. "Réflexions chronologiques sur l'époque où a vécu Husserl." In *HUSSERL*, pp. 16–36.

Taylor, C. "Phenomenology and Linguistic Analysis." *AS* 33 (1959): 93–110.

Taylor, Darrell D. "Husserl and Merleau-Ponty and the Problem of the Cultural Studies." Ph.D. dissertation, University of Southern California, 1966.

Taylor, Earl. "*Lebenswelt* and *Lebensformen*: Husserl and Wittgenstein on the Goal and Method of Philosophy." *HS* 1 (1978): 184–200.

Tehennepe, E. "The Life-World and the World of Ordinary Language." In *INVITATION*, pp. 133–46.

Temuralq, T. *Über die Granzen der Erkennbarkeit bei Husserl und Scheler*. Berlin, 1937.

Tertulian, Nicolas. "Genèse et structure." *RE* 25 (1972): 279–85.

Tevuzzi, Michael. "A Note on Husserl's Dependence on William James." *JBSP* 10 (1979): 194–96.

Theunissen, Michael. "Intentionaler Gegenstand und ontologische Differenz: Ansätze zur Fragestellung Heideggers in der Phänomenologie Husserls." *PJ* 70 (1963): 344–62.

_____. "Die destruierende Wiederholung der transzendentalen Intersubjektivitätstheorie Husserls in der Sozialontologie Sartres." In *Der Andere: Studien zur Sozialontologie der Gegenwart*, pp. 187–240. Berlin: de Gruyter, 1965.

Thévenaz, Pierre. "Qu'est-ce que la phénoménologie: I: La phénoménologie de Husserl." *RTP* (1952): 9–30.

_____. "La question du point de départ radical chez Descartes et Husserl." In *PROBLÈMES*, pp. 9–30.

_____. *What Is Phenomenology?* Chicago: Quadrangle, 1962.

————. *De Husserl à Merleau-Ponty: Qu'est-ce que la phénoménologie?* Neuchâtel: Editions de la Baconnière, 1966.

Thiele, Joachim. "Ein Brief Edmund Husserls an Ernst Mach." *ZPF* 19: 134–38.

Thyssen, Johannes. "Zur Neubegründung des Realismus in Auseinandersetzung mit Husserl." *ZPF* 7 (1953): 145–70; 368–85.

————. "Wege aus dem geschlossenen System von Husserls Monadologie." In *Actes du XIe Congrès International de Philosophie*, II, pp. 188–94.

————. "Husserls Lehre von den 'Bedeutungen' und das Begriffsproblem." *ZPF* 13 (1959): 163–86; 438–58.

————. "Die Husserlsche Faszination." *ZPF* 17 (1963): 553–85.

Tillman, F. "Phenomenology and Philosophical Analysis." *IPQ* 6 (1966): 465–82.

————. "Transcendental Phenomenology and Analytic Philosophy." *IPQ* 7 (1967): 31–40.

Tillman, Mary Catherine. "Dilthey and Husserl." *JBSP* 7 (1976): 123–30.

Tiryakian, Edward A. "Durkheim and Husserl: A Comparison of the Spirit of Positivism and the Spirit of Phenomenology." In *Phenomenology and the Social Sciences: A Dialogue*, edited by Joseph Bien, pp. 20–43. The Hague: Nijhoff, 1978.

Tischner, J. "Autour de la pensée d'Husserl." In *Archiwum historii filozofii i mysli spolecznej*, edited by Andrzej Walicki. Wroclaw Ossoliveum, 1978.

Todes, Samuel J., and Dreyfus, Hubert L. "The Existentialist Critique of Objectivity." In *PATTERNS*, pp. 346–88.

Toulemont, René. "La spécificité du social d'après Husserl." *CIS* 25 (1958): 135–51.

————. *L'essence de la société selon Husserl.* Paris: Presses Universitaires de France, 1962.

————. "The Specific Character of the Social according to Husserl." In *APRIORI*, pp. 226–42.

Tragesser, Robert. "On the Phenomenological Foundations of Mathematics." In *EXPLORATIONS*, pp. 285–98.

————. *Phenomenology and Logic.* Ithaca: Cornell University Press, 1977.

Tran-Duc-Thao. "Les origines de la réduction phénoménologique chez Husserl." *Deucalion* 3 (1950): 128–42.

————. *Phénoménologie et matérialisme dialectique.* Paris: Editions Minh-Tan, 1951.

Tremblay, Remi. "L'auto-méditation phénoménologique pour une communauté des philosophes." *Philosophiques* 7 (1980): 3–39.

Trepanier, Emmanuel. "Phénoménologie et ontologie: Husserl et Heidegger." *LTP* 28 (1972): 249–65.

Troller, Alois. *Die Begegnung von Philosophie, Rechtsphilosophie und Rechtswissenschaft.* Basel and Stuttgart: Schwabe, 1971.

Troutner, Leroy F. "Toward a Phenomenology of Education: An Exercise in the Foundations." *PPE* 30 (1974): 148–64.

Tugendhat, Ernst. *Der Wahrheitsbegriff bei Husserl und Heidegger.* 2nd ed. Berlin: De Gruyter, 1970.

————. "Phenomenology and Linguistic Analysis." In *HEA*, pp. 325–37.

Turnbull, R. "Linguistic Analysis, Phenomenology, and the Problems of Philosophy." *MO* 49 (1965): 44–69.

Tymieniecka, Anna-Teresa, ed. *For Roman Ingarden: Nine Essays in Phenomenology.* The Hague: Nijhoff, 1959.

————. *Phenomenology and Science in Contemporary European Thought.* New York: Farrar, Straus, 1962.

————. "Die phänomenologische Selbstbesinnung." *ANALH* 1 (1971): 1–10.

————. "Phenomenology Reflects upon Itself." *ANALH* 2 (1972): 3–17.

————, ed. *The Later Husserl and the Idea of Phenomenology: Idealism-Realism, Historicity and Nature.* Analecta Husserliana, vol. 2. Dordrecht: Reidel, 1972.

————. "Imaginatio Creatrix: The 'Creative' versus the 'Constitutive' Function of Man, and the 'Possible Worlds'." *ANALH* 3 (1974): 3–14.

————. "Beyond Ingarden's Idealism/Realism Controversy with Husserl—The New Contextual Phase of Phenomenology." *ANALH* 4 (1976): 241–418.

_____, ed. *The Teleologies in Husserlian Phenomenology.* Analecta Husserliana, vol. 9. Dordrecht: Reidel, 1979.

Uhler, Kathleen J. "A Clarification of Husserl's Distinction between Phenomenological Psychology and Transcendental Phenomenology." Ph.D. dissertation, Georgetown University, 1975.

Uygur, Nermi. "Die Phänomenologie Husserl und die 'Gemeinschaft'." *K* 59 (1958): 439–60.

Vajda, Mihaly. "Marxism, Existentialism, Phenomenology: A Dialogue." *T* 6 (1971): 3–29.
_____. "Truth or Truths." *CH* 3 (1975): 29–39.
_____. "Lukacs' and Husserl's Critique of Science." *T* 38 (1978–79): 104–18.

Valone, James J. "Conflicts in the Later Husserl's Ontology and Theory of Knowledge." *PC* 51 (1977): 212–19.

Valori, Paolo. "Inédits husserliens sur la théologie de l'histoire." In his *La philosophie et l'histoire de la philosophie*, pp. 121–23. Rome: Instituto di Studi filosofici; Paris: Vrin, 1956.

Van Breda, Herman Leo. "Husserl et le problème de Dieu." In *Proceedings of the Xth International Congress of Philosophy*, pp. 1210–12. Amsterdam, 1948.
_____. "Note sur E. Husserl." In *Philosophie de la religion*, edited by R.P. Ortegat, pp. 702–5. Louvain-Paris: Ed. de l'Institut Superieur de Philosophie, Vrin, 1948.
_____. "Husserl et le problème de la liberté." In *Actes du IVe Congrès des Sociétés de philosophie de langue française: Etre et Penser*, pp. 377–81. Neuchâtel: Editions de la Baconnière, 1949.
_____. "Note sur: réduction et authenticité d'après Husserl." *RMM* 56 (1951): 4–5; *PHEX*, pp. 7–9. English translation: "A Note on Reduction and Authenticity according to Husserl." In *HEA*, pp. 124–25.
_____, ed. *Problèmes actuels de la phénoménologie.* Paris: Desclée de Brouwer, 1952.
_____. "Notes sur les Archives Husserl à Louvain." In *PROBLÈMES*, pp. 155–159.
_____, and Boehm, R. "Aus dem Husserl-Archiv zu Löwen." *PJ* 62 (1953): 241–52.
_____. "La phénoménologie husserlienne comme philosophie de l'intentionalité." In *La Fenomenologia*, pp. 41–48. Brescia: Morcelliana, 1956.
_____. "La fécondité des grands thèmes husserliens pour le progrès de la recherche philosophique." *PJ* 66 (1957): 5–11. English translation: "Great Themes in Husserl's Thought: Their Fruitfulness and Influence." *PT* 3 (1959): 192–98.
_____. "La phénoménologie." In *La philosophie au milieu du vingtième siècle*, vol. 2, pp. 53–70. La Nuova Italia Editrice, 1958.
_____. "Geist und Bedeutung des Husserl-Archivs." In *EH*, pp. 166–22.
_____. "Great Themes in Husserl's Thought: Their Fruitfulness and Influence." *PT* 3 (1959): 192–98.
_____, and Taminiaux, Jacques, eds. *Husserl et la pensée moderne. Husserl und das Denken der Neuzeit.* The Hague: Nijhoff, 1959.
_____. "Husserl und das Problem der Freiheit. Aus dem Franzosischen übersetz von Katharina Arndt." In *HUSSERL*, pp. 277–81.
_____. "La réduction phénoménologique." In *HUSSERL*, pp. 307–18.
_____. "Le sauvetage de l'héritage husserlien et la fondation des Archives-Husserl." In *HPM*, pp. 1–42.
_____. "La phénoménologie." In *Les grands courants de la pensée mondiale contemporaine*, pp. 401–35 (mise à jour de Enzo Paci, pp. 435–40). Paris-Milan: Fischbacher-Marzorati, 1961.
_____. "Maurice Merleau-Ponty et les Archives-Husserl à Louvain." *RMM* 67 (1962): 410–30.
_____. "Leibniz' Einfluss auf das Denken Husserls." In *Akten des internationalen Leibniz-Kongresses*, pp. 124–45. Hannover, 1966.
_____. "The Actual State of the Work on Husserl's *Inedita*: Achievements and Projects." *ANALH* 2 (1972): 149–59.
_____, ed. *Vérité et vérification. Wahrheit und Verifikation.* The Hague: Nijhoff, 1974.
_____. "L'itinéraire husserlien de la phénoménologie pure a la phénoménologie transcendentale." In *WELT MEN*, pp. 301–18.

Vancourt, Raymond. "Deux conceptions de la philosophie: Husserl et Kierkegaard." *Mélanges de Sciences Religieuses* 1 (1944): 193–240.
_____. *La phénoménologie et la foi.* Tournai: Desclée de Brouwer, 1953.

Van De Pitte, Margaret M. "The Epistemological Function of an Affective Principle in the Phenomenology in Intersubjectivity." Ph.D. dissertation, University of Southern California, 1966.
———. "On Bracketing the *Epoché*." *D* 11 (1972): 535–45.
———. "Husserl Literatur 1965–71." *AGP* 57 (1975): 36–53.
———. "Husserl: The Idealist 'malgré lui'." *PPR* 37 (1976–77): 70–78.
———. "Husserl's Solipsism." *JBSP* 8 (1977): 123–25.
———. "Is There a Phenomenological Method?" *MT* 8 (1977): 21–35.

Van Peursen, Cornelius A. "Phénoménologie et ontologie." In *Rencontre: Contributions à une psychologie humaine dédiées au Professeur F.J.J. Buytendijk*, pp. 308–17. Utrecht-Antwerpen: Het Spectrum, 1975.
———. "Edmund Husserl and Ludwig Wittgenstein." *PPR* 20 (1959): 180–97.
———. "La notion du temps et de l'ego transcendental chez Husserl." In *HUSSERL*, pp. 196–207.
———. "Phenomenology and Ontology." *PT* 3 (1959): 35–42.
———. "Some Remarks on the Ego in the Phenomenology of Husserl." In *HUSSERL*, pp. 29–41.
———. "Die Phänomenologie Husserls und die Erneuerung der Ontologie." *ZPF* 16 (1962): 489–501.
———. "Life-World and Structures." In *PATTERNS*, pp. 139–53.
———. "The Concept of the Body in Transcendental Phenomenology and in Modern Biology." *ANALH* 1 (1971): 133–51.
———. "The Importance of Husserl's Phenomenology for Ontology." In his *Phenomenology and Reality*, pp. 92–112. Pittsburgh: Duquesne University Press, 1972.
———. *Phenomenology and Analytic Philosophy*. Pittsburgh: Duquesne University Press, 1972.
———. *Phenomenology and Reality*. Pittsburgh: Duquesne University Press, 1972.
———. "The Horizon." In *HEA*, pp. 182–201.

Van Riet, Georges. "Réalisme thomiste et phénoménologie husserlienne." *RPL* 55 (1957): 58–92.

Vasquex Hoyos, Guillermo. *Intentionalität als Verantwortung: Geschichtsteleologie und Teleologie der Intentionalität bei Husserl*. The Hague: Nijhoff, 1976.

Veatch, Henry B. "Why Be Uncritical about the Life-World?" In *PATTERNS*, pp. 19–39.

Verdenal, René. "La sémiotique de Husserl: La logique des signes (A propos de certin inédits)." *EP* 4 (1973): 553–64.

Ver Eecke, Wilfried. "Freedom, Self-Reflection and Intersubjectivity or Psychoanalysis and the Limits of the Phenomenological Method." *ANALH* 3 (1974): 252–70.

Vial, J. *Philosophes d'aujourd'hui en présence du droit: Sartre, Husserl, Gabriel Marcel, Teilhard de Chardin, Ernst Bloch, Reinach*. Paris: Sirey, 1965.

Vidal, Jacques. "Phénoménologie et conversions." *AP* 35 (1972): 209–43.

Vierwec, Theodor. "Husserl, Hauriou und die deutsche Rechtswissenschaft." *Archiv für Rechts- und Sozialphilosophie* (Bern) 31 (1937): 84–89.

Volkmann-Schluck, K.H. "Husserls Lehre von der Idealität der Bedeutung als metaphysisches Problem." In *HPM*, pp. 230–41. Translation: "La doctrine de Husserl au sujet de l'idealité de la signification en tant que problème métaphysique." Translated by J. Ladrière. In *HPM*.

Vuillemin, Jules. "Le problème phénoménologique: intentionnalité et réflexion." *RPF* 84 (1959): 463–70.

Vuorinen, R. "Edmund Husserl and the Quest for a Rigorous Science of Psychology." *AJ* 33 (1971): 64–105.

Wagner, Hans. "Kritische Betrachtungen zu Husserls Nachlass." *PR* 1 (1953–54): 1–22, 93–123. English translation: "Critical Observations concerning Husserl's Posthumous Writings." In *ELV*, pp. 204–58.
———. "An Examination of Husserl's Transcendental Explication of the Sense and the Constitution of the Modern Concept of Nature and of Modern Natural Science." *SWJP* 5 (1974).
———. "Husserl's Ambiguous Philosophy of Science." *SWJP* 5 (1974): 169–85.

Wagner, Helmut R. "Husserl and Historicism." *SR* 39: 4 (1972): 696–719.

Wahl, Jean. "Notes sur la première partie de *Erfahrung und Urteil* de Husserl." *RMM* 56 (1951): 6–34.
———. "Conclusions." In *PROBLÈMES*, pp. 141–51.

_____. "Notes sur quelques aspects empiristes de la pensée de Husserl." *RMM* 57 (1952): 17–45.

_____. *Les aspects qualitatifs du réel. I: Introduction, la philosophie de l'existence. II: Début d'une étude sur Husserl. III: La philosophie de la nature de Nicolaï Hartmann.* Paris: Centre de documentation universitaire, 1955.

_____. *Husserl, I.* Paris: Centre de documentation universitaire, 1958.

_____. *Husserl, II.* Paris: Centre de documentation universitaire, 1958.

_____. *L'ouvrage posthume de Husserl: la Krisis. La crise des sciences européennes et la phénoménologie transcendante.* Paris: Centre de documentation universitaire, 1958.

_____. "Au sujet des jugements de Husserl sur Descartes et sur Locke." In *HUSSERL,* pp. 119–31.

_____. "Clôture du colloque phénoménologique." In *HUSSERL,* pp. 428–32.

_____. *Husserl, la "Philosophie première," Erste Philosophie.* Paris: Centre de documentation universitaire, 1961.

_____. "A Note on Some Empiricist Aspects of the Thought of Husserl." In *APRIORI,* pp. 205–25.

_____. "Notes on the First Part of *Experience and Judgment.*" In *APRIORI,* pp. 172–97.

Waldenfels, Bernhard. "Weltliche und soziale Einzigkeit bei Husserl." *ZPF* 25 (1971): 157–71.

_____. *Das Zwischenreich des Dialogs: Sozialphilosophische Untersuchungen in Anschluss an Edmund Husserl.* The Hague: Nijhoff, 1971.

Walther, Gerda. "Bei Edmund Husserl in Freiburg i. Br." In *Zum anderen Ufer: Vom Marxismus und Atheismus zum Christentum,* pp. 196–220. Remagen: Reichl, 1960.

Wann, T.W., ed. *Behaviourism and Phenomenology.* Chicago: University of Chicago Press, 1964.

Warnke, Camillia. "Husserl's Transcendental Subject." *DH* 3 (1976): 103–9.

Wartofsky, Marx W. "Consciousness, Praxis and Reality: Marxism vs. Phenomenology." In *HEA,* pp. 304–13.

Wassmer, Thomas A. "Phenomenology: Its Method and Influence." *SE* 21 (1969): 149–60.

Watson, Lawrence. "A Study of the Origins of Formal Logic in Husserl's *Formal and Transcendental Logic.*" Ph.D. dissertation, De Paul University, 1973.

_____. "A Remark on Husserl's Theory of Multiplicities." *JBSP* 11 (1980): 180–84.

Weidaur, Friedrich. *Kritik der Transzendentalphänomenologie Husserls.* Leipzig, 1933.

Weier, Winifried. "Wege einer metaphysischen Phänomenologie." *FZ* 16 (1969): 388–427.

Weiher, Charles. "Three Notions of Number." *PM* 7 (1970): 25–56.

Weinzweig, Marjorie. "Phenomenology and Ordinary Language Philosophy." *MP* 8 (1977): 116–46.

Welch, E. Parl. *Edmund Husserl's Phenomenology.* Los Angeles: University of Southern California Press, 1939.

_____. *The Philosophy of Edmund Husserl: The Origin and Development of His Phenomenology.* New York: Columbia University Press, 1941; 2nd ed., 1948.

_____. "Edmund Husserl: An Appreciation." *The Personalist* (1940).

Wells, Donald A. "Phenomenology and Value Theory." *JP* 52 (1955): 64–70.

Welton, Donn. "Intentionality and Language in Husserl's Phenomenology." *RM* 27 (1973): 260–98.

_____. "Theory of Knowing in Husserl's Phenomenology." Ph.D. dissertation, Southern Illinois University, 1973.

_____. "Structure and Genesis in Husserl's Phenomenology." In *HEA,* pp. 54–69.

Werkmeister, William H. "Husserl und Hegel." In *Akten XIV International Congress of Philosophy,* vol. 6, pp. 553–58.

Wertz, S.K. "Brentano's Psycho-Intentional Criterion." *T* 1 (Spring 1968): 5–16.

Westphal, Merold. "Nietzsche and the Phenomenological Ideal." *M* 60 (1977): 278–88.

Wewel, Meinolf. *Die Konstitution der Transzendenten Etwas im Vollzug des Sehens.* Düsseldorf: Wewel, 1968.

Wheatley, John. "Phenomenology: English and Continental." In *EXPLORATIONS,* pp. 230–42.

White, David A. "Husserl and the Poetic Consciousness." *PE* 53 (1972): 408–24.

White, Morton G. "Phenomenology: Edmund Husserl." In his *Age of Analysis,* pp. 100–15. Boston: Houghton-Mifflin, 1955.

Widmer, Hans. "Ammerkungen zum zeitdiagnostischen Anspruch der Philosophie." *SPS* 36 (1976): 204–25.

Wild, J.W. "Husserl's Critique of Psychologism: Its Historical Roots and Contemporary Relevance." In *PHIL ESSAYS*, pp. 19–43.

————. "On the Nature and Aims of Phenomenology." *PPR* 3 (1942–43): 85–95.

————. "An Introduction to the Phenomenology of Signs." *PPR* 8 (1948): 217–33.

————. "Phenomenology and Metaphysics." In *WILD*, pp. 36–76.

————, ed. *The Return to Reason.* Chicago: Henry Regnery, 1953.

————. "L'anthropologie philosophique et la crise des sciences européennes." In *HUSSERL*, pp. 271–92.

————. "Contemporary Phenomenology and the Problem of Existence." *PPR* 20 (1959): 166–80.

————. "Man and His Life-World." In *INGARDEN*, pp. 90–109.

————. "The Exploration of the Life-World." In *Proceedings of the American Philosophical Association*, pp. 5–25. Antioch Press, 1961.

————. "Husserl's Life-World and the Lived-Body." In *Phenomeno-Symposium sobre la noción husserliana de la 'Lebenswelt'*, pp. 77–93. Mexico: UNAM, 1963. In *PHPA*, pp. 10–28.

Wilhelm, Frederick E. "Theory of Knowing in Husserl's Phenomenology." Ph.D. dissertation, University of California at Los Angeles, 1974.

Willard, Dallas A. "Meaning and Universals in Husserl's *Logische Untersuchungen.*" Ph.D. dissertation, University of Wisconsin, 1964.

————. "Husserl's Essay 'On the Concept of Number'." *PM* 9 (1972): 40–43.

————. "The Paradox of Logical Psychologism: Husserl's Way Out." APQ 9 (1972): 94–100; *HEA*, pp. 10–17; *MOHANTY*, pp. 43–54.

————. "A Comparison of Husserl's Analysis of the Concept with Frege's and Russell's." *SWJP* 5 (1974).

————. "Concerning Husserl's View of Number." *SWJP* 5 (1974): 97–109.

————. "Husserl's Critique of Extensionalist Logic: 'A Logic That Does Not Understand Itself'." *IS* 9 (1979): 143–64.

————. "Husserl on a Logic That Failed." *PRC* 89 (1980): 46–64.

Williams, Forest. "Doubt and Phenomenological Reduction." *PPR* 18 (1957): 379–81.

Williams, Robert. "*Ecclesial Man:* A Radical Approach to Theology through Husserl's Phenomenology." *PT* 19 (1975): 369–76.

Wilming, Josef. "Husserls Lehre von den intentionellen Erlebnissen." Ph.D. dissertation, Leipzig, 1925.

Wilshire, Bruce. *William James and Phenomenology.* Bloomington: Indiana University Press, 1968.

Wilson, Arnold. "Husserl and the Idealists." *T* 4 (1969): 83–94.

Winance, Eleuthere. "Logique, mathématique et ontologie comme 'mathesis universalis' chez Edmond Husserl." *RT* 66 (1966): 410–34.

Winter, Michael F. "Lived Time in Husserl and Whitehead: A Comparative Study." Ph.D. dissertation, Northwestern University, 1975.

Winthrop, H. "The Constitution of Error in the Phenomenological Reduction." *PPR* 9 (1948): 741–48.

Witschel, Günter. "Zwei Beiträge Husserls zum Problem der sekundären Qualitäten." *ZPF* 18 (1964): 30–49.

Wolf, Alan E. "Husserlian Phenomenology: Translated and Adapted as a Possible Analytic Technique for Communication Scholars." Ph.D. dissertation, Pennsylvania State University, 1972.

Xirau, Joaquin. "A Crisis: Husserl and Bergson." *The Personalist* (1946): 27–33 and 269–94.

Yee, Stevan T. "Husserl's Idea of Phenomenological Psychology and the Problem of Its Relation to Transcendental Phenomenological Philosophy." Ph.D. dissertation, Pennsylvania State University, 1976.

Zaner, Richard M. *The Problem of Embodiment*. The Hague: Nijhoff, 1964.

———. "Awakening towards a Phenomenology of the Self." In *PERSPECTIVE,* pp. 171–86.

———. *The Way of Phenomenology*. New York: Pegasus, 1970.

———. "Discussion of Jacques Derrida: *The Ends of Man.*" *PPR* 32 (1972): 384–89.

———. "Reflections on Evidence and Criticism in the Theory of Consciousness." In *LIFE-WORLD,* pp. 209–30.

———. "The Art of Free Phantasy in Rigorous Phenomenological Science." In *PHCC,* pp. 192–219.

———. "Examples and Possibles: A Criticism of Husserl's Theory of Free-Phantasy Variation." *RP* 3 (1973): 29–44.

———. "On Phenomenological Method: The Path of Dorion Cairns." *RP* 4 (1974).

———. "Passivity and Activity of Consciousness in Husserl." *ANALH* 3 (1974): 199–202.

———. "On the Sense of Method in Phenomenology." In *Phenomenology and Philosophical Understanding,* edited by Edo Pivčević, pp. 125–42. Cambridge: Cambridge University Press, 1975.

Zeltner, Hermann. "Das Ich und die Andern: Husserls Beitrag zur Grundlegung der Sozialphilosophie." *ZPF* 13 (1959): 288–315.

Zocher, R. *Husserls Phänomenologie und Schuppes Logik: Ein Beitrag zur Kritik des intuitionistischen Ontologismus in der Immandenzidee*. Munich, 1932.

Editors

PETER MCCORMICK, Professor of Philosophy and Literature at the University of Ottawa, received his D. Phil (1970) and his Doctorat d'État (1980) from the University of Paris. A former Fulbright Scholar in France and Humboldt Fellow in Germany, he has taught at the University of Maryland, University of Notre Dame, and Denison University. Besides articles and translations, he has written *Heidegger and the Language of the World*, edited *Roman Ingarden: Selected Papers in Aesthetics* (forthcoming), and coedited *Husserl: Expositions and Appraisals*. His most recent work, the subject of his d'État thesis, is on the nature of literary truths.

FREDERICK A. ELLISTON received his Ph.D. from the University of Toronto (1974) and has taught at Trinity College, York University, the University of Victoria, and Rennselaer Polytechnic Institute. He has published several books in philosophy: *Husserl: Expositions and Appraisals*; *Heidegger's Existential Analytic*; and *Sartre*. In addition he has edited two volumes on sexual morality: *Philosophy and Sex* and *Feminism and Philosophy*. His most recent work at the School of Criminal Justice in Albany deals with *Police Ethics* (forthcoming) and *Ethics, Public Policy and Criminal Justice* (forthcoming).

Contributors

JEFFNER MARIE ALLEN teaches philosophy at DePaul University, Chicago, and has contributed many articles to journals in the areas of her principal interests, including phenomenology, existentialism, and Husserl. She has translated Edmund Husserl's *First Philosophy (1923/24): First Part, Critical History of Ideas* (*Husserliana* 7).

KARL AMERIKS teaches philosophy at the University of Notre Dame. In addition to having published in philosophy journals, he was cotranslator of Edmund Husserl's *Experience and Judgment.*

WALTER BIEMEL, Professor of Philosophy at the University of Aachen, has edited several volumes of the *Husserliana,* and is now general editor of Heidegger's works. He has published numerous articles and books, including *Le Concept du monde chez Heidegger, Kants Begründung der Asthetik,* and *Analyzen zur Kunst der Gegenwart.*

JOHN B. BROUGH teaches philosophy at Georgetown University and has had published several papers on Husserl's theories of time.

DAVID CARR is Professor of Philosophy at the University of Ottawa. He received an Alexander von Humboldt Fellowship in 1975–76 and 1979. The author of *Phenomenology and the Problem of History,* he has published many articles on Husserl and phenomenology.

RICHARD HUDSON is a doctoral candidate in philosophy at the University of Ottawa. He is currently preparing a thesis on Heidegger's concept of a scientific philosophy in the 1920s.

ROBERT WELSH JORDAN teaches philosophy at Colorado State University at Fort Collins, Colorado. His journal publications include several on Husserl and phenomenology.

FRED KERSTEN is Professor of Philosophy at the University of Wisconsin-Green Bay. In addition to translation of Edmund Husserl, Aaron Gurwitsch, and Alfred Schutz, he has published studies in various fields of phenomenology, and has recently completed the forthcoming works on Husserl: *Space, Time and Other* and *Problems in Transcendental Phenomenology.*

ERAZIM KOHÁK is Professor of Philosophy at Boston University. He has published widely in the areas of phenomenology and social philosophy in both English and his native Czech. His recent publications include *Idea and Exerience* and *Národ v nás.*

RICHARD E. PALMER teaches philosophy at MacMurray College in Jacksonville, Illinois, and has contributed studies to philosophy journals.

JOHN D. SCANLON, Professor of Philosophy at Duquesne University, has, in addition to contributing to philosophy journals, translated Edmund Husserl's *Phenomenological Psychology.*

THOMAS SHEEHAN teaches philosophy at Loyola University of Chicago. Besides articles that have appeared in numerous journals, he is the editor of *Heidegger, the Man and the Thinker* and the translator of Martin Heidegger's *Logic: The Question of Truth.* His study *Karl Rahner: The Philosophical Foundations* is forthcoming.

HERBERT SPIEGELBERG teaches philosophy at Washington University in St. Louis. His extensive list of publications includes numerous articles in philosophy journals as well as the study *Psychology and Psychiatry.*

MARGARET VAN DE PITTE teaches philosophy at the University of Alberta, Edmonton. An Alexander von Humboldt Fellow in 1976–78, Professor Van de Pitte has published articles on Husserl's phenomenology.

DALLAS WILLARD teaches philosophy at the University of Southern California, Los Angeles. His articles on epistemology and logic have appeared in a variety of philosophy journals.

Index